THE COMPLETE
ST TERESA OF AVILA
Volume 2

LITTLE SISTERS OF THE POOR
ST JOSEPH'S HOME
56 COTHAM HILL
BRISTOL BS6 6JT

THE COMPLETE WORKS OF
ST TERESA OF JESUS

Volume 2

The Complete Works of St Teresa of Avila
Volume 2

Translated and edited by
E. Allison Peers

From the critical edition of
P. Silverio de Santa Teresa, C.D.

BURNS & OATES
A Continuum imprint
LONDON • NEW YORK

Complete Works Vol 2

Burns & Oates
A Continuum imprint
The Tower Building, 11 York Road, London SE1 7NX
370 Lexington Avenue, New York, NY 10017-6503

www.continuumbooks.com

First published by Sheed & Ward Ltd, 1946
This edition (twelfth impression) printed 1991 by Sheed & Ward Ltd
Reprinted 2002 by Burns & Oates

Copyright © 2002 by Burns & Oates

British Library Cataloguing-in-Publication Data
A catalogue record for this book is available from the British Library.

ISBN 0 8601 2329 4

All rights reserved. No part of this publication may be reproduced or transmitted in any form or by any means, electronic or mechanical, including photocopying, recording, or any information storage or retrieval system, without prior permission in writing from the publishers.

Nihil-obstat George Smith, Censor. *Imprimatur* E. Morrogh Bernard, V.G., Westminster, 6 February 1946.

Printed and bound in Great Britain by Bookcraft (Bath) Ltd, Midsomer Norton

CONTENTS OF VOLUME II

BOOK CALLED WAY OF PERFECTION

	PAGE
INTRODUCTION	xii
TRANSLATOR'S NOTE	xx
GENERAL ARGUMENT	xxv
PROTESTATION	xxvi
PROLOGUE	1

CHAPTER I.—Of the reason which moved me to found this convent in such strict observance 3

CHAPTER II.—Treats of how the necessities of the body should be disregarded and of the good that comes from poverty . . . 5

CHAPTER III.—Continues the subject begun in the first chapter and persuades the sisters to busy themselves constantly in beseeching God to help those who work for the Church. Ends with an exclamatory prayer . 10

CHAPTER IV.—Exhorts the nuns to keep their Rule and names three things which are important for the spiritual life. Describes the first of these three things, which is love of one's neighbour, and speaks of the harm which can be done by individual friendships 15

APPENDIX TO CHAPTER IV 21

CHAPTER V.—Continues speaking of confessors. Explains why it is important that they should be learned men 22

CHAPTER VI.—Returns to the subject of perfect love, already begun . 26

CHAPTER VII.—Treats of the same subject of spiritual love and gives certain counsels for gaining it 30

CHAPTER VIII.—Treats of the great benefit of self-detachment, both interior and exterior, from all things created 37

CHAPTER IX.—Treats of the great blessing that shunning their relatives brings to those who have left the world and shows how by doing so they will find truer friends 39

CHAPTER X.—Teaches that detachment from the things aforementioned is insufficient if we are not detached from our own selves and that this virtue and humility go together. 42

CHAPTER XI.—Continues to treat of mortification and describes how it may be attained in times of sickness 46

CONTENTS

CHAPTER XII.—Teaches that the true lover of God must care little for life and honour 49

CHAPTER XIII.—Continues to treat of mortification and explains how one must renounce the world's standards of wisdom, in order to attain to true wisdom. 53

CHAPTER XIV.—Treats of the great importance of not professing anyone whose spirit is contrary to the things aforementioned . . . 57

CHAPTER XV.—Treats of the great advantage which comes from our not excusing ourselves, even though we find we are unjustly condemned . 59

CHAPTER XVI.—Describes the difference between perfection in the lives of contemplatives and in the lives of those who are content with mental prayer. Explains how it is sometimes possible for God to raise a distracted soul to perfect contemplation and the reason for this. This chapter and that which comes next are to be noted carefully . . . 63

CHAPTER XVII.—How not all souls are fitted for contemplation and how some take long to attain it. True humility will walk happily along the road by which the Lord leads it 68

CHAPTER XVIII.—Continues the same subject and shows how much greater are the trials of contemplatives than those of actives. This chapter offers great consolation to actives 72

CHAPTER XIX.—Begins to treat of prayer. Addresses souls who cannot reason with the understanding 76

CHAPTER XX.—Describes how, in one way or another, we never lack consolation on the road of prayer. Counsels the sisters to include this subject continually in their conversation. 85

CHAPTER XXI.—Describes the great importance of setting out upon the practice of prayer with firm resolution and of heeding no difficulties put in the way by the devil. 88

CHAPTER XXII.—Explains the meaning of mental prayer . . 93

CHAPTER XXIII.—Describes the importance of not turning back when one has set out upon the way of prayer. Repeats how necessary it is to be resolute 97

CHAPTER XXIV.—Describes how vocal prayer may be practised with perfection and how closely allied it is to mental prayer . . 100

CHAPTER XXV.—Describes the great gain which comes to a soul when it practises vocal prayer perfectly. Shows how God may raise it thence to things supernatural 104

CHAPTER XXVI.—Continues the description of a method for recollecting the thoughts. Describes means of doing this. This chapter is very profitable for those who are beginning prayer 106

CHAPTER XXVII.—Describes the great love shown us by the Lord in the first words of the Paternoster and the great importance of our making no account of good birth if we truly desire to be the daughters of God. 110

CHAPTER XXVIII.—Describes the nature of the Prayer of Recollection and sets down some of the means by which we can make it a habit 113

CONTENTS

CHAPTER XXIX.—Continues to describe methods for achieving this Prayer of Recollection. Says what little account we should make of being favoured by our superiors 119

CHAPTER XXX.—Describes the importance of understanding what we ask for in prayer. Treats of these words in the Paternoster: "Sanctificetur nomen tuum, adveniat regnum tuum". Applies them to the Prayer of Quiet, and begins the explanation of them 123

CHAPTER XXXI.—Continues the same subject. Explains what is meant by the Prayer of Quiet. Gives several counsels to those who experience it. This chapter is very noteworthy. 126

CHAPTER XXXII.—Expounds these words of the Paternoster: "Fiat voluntas tua sicut in coelo et in terra." Describes how much is accomplished by those who repeat these words with full resolution and how well the Lord rewards them for it 134

CHAPTER XXXIII.—Treats of our great need that the Lord should give us what we ask in these words of the Paternoster: "Panem nostrum quotidianum da nobis hodie." 140

CHAPTER XXXIV.—Continues the same subject. This is very suitable for reading after the reception of the Most Holy Sacrament . . 143

CHAPTER XXXV.—Describes the recollection which should be practised after Communion. Concludes this subject with an exclamatory prayer to the Eternal Father 151

CHAPTER XXXVI.—Treats of these words in the Paternoster: "Dimitte nobis debita nostra" 154

CHAPTER XXXVII.—Describes the excellence of this prayer called the Paternoster, and the many ways in which we shall find consolation in it 160

CHAPTER XXXVIII.—Treats of the great need which we have to beseech the Eternal Father to grant us what we ask in these words: "Et ne nos inducas in tentationem, sed libera nos a malo." Explains certain temptations. This chapter is noteworthy 163

CHAPTER XXXIX.—Continues the same subject and gives counsels concerning different kinds of temptation. Suggests two remedies by which we may be freed from temptations. 169

CHAPTER XL.—Describes how, by striving always to walk in the love and fear of God, we shall travel safely amid all these temptations . 172

CHAPTER XLI.—Speaks of the fear of God and of how we must keep ourselves from venial sins 177

CHAPTER XLII.—Treats of these last words of the Paternoster: "Sed libera nos a malo. Amen." "But deliver us from evil. Amen." . 182

INTERIOR CASTLE

INTRODUCTION 187

[PROLOGUE] 199

CONTENTS

FIRST MANSIONS

CHAPTER I.—Treats of the beauty and dignity of our souls; makes a comparison by the help of which this may be understood; describes the benefit which comes from understanding it and being aware of the favours which we receive from God; and shows how the door of this castle is prayer.   PAGE 201

CHAPTER II.—Describes the hideousness of a soul in mortal sin, some part of which God was pleased to manifest to a certain person. Says something also of self-knowledge. This chapter is profitable, since it contains some noteworthy matters. Explains in what sense the Mansions are to be understood 205

SECOND MANSIONS

CHAPTER I.—Treats of the great importance of perseverance if we are to reach the final Mansions and of the fierce war which the devil wages against us. Tells how essential it is, if we are to attain our goal, not to miss our way at the beginning. Gives a method which has proved very efficacious 213

THIRD MANSIONS

CHAPTER I.—Treats of the insecurity from which we cannot escape in this life of exile, however lofty a state we may reach, and of how good it is for us to walk in fear. This chapter contains several good points . 219

CHAPTER II.—Continues the same subject and treats of aridities in prayer and of what the author thinks may result from them; and of how we must test ourselves; and of how the Lord proves those who are in these Mansions   223

FOURTH MANSIONS

CHAPTER I.—Treats of the difference between sweetness or tenderness in prayer and consolations, and tells of the happiness which the author gained from learning how different thought is from understanding. This chapter is very profitable for those who suffer greatly from distractions during prayer 230

CHAPTER II.—Continues the same subject and explains by a comparison what is meant by consolations and how we must obtain them without striving to do so 236

CHAPTER III.—Describes what is meant by the Prayer of Recollection, which the Lord generally grants before that already mentioned. Speaks of its effects and of the remaining effects of the former kind of prayer, which had to do with the consolations given by the Lord . . 240

FIFTH MANSIONS

CHAPTER I.—Begins to explain how in prayer the soul is united with God. Describes how we may know that we are not mistaken about this . 247

CHAPTER II.—Continues the same subject. Explains the Prayer of Union by a delicate comparison. Describes the effects which it produces in the soul. Should be studied with great care 253

CHAPTER III.—Continues the same matter. Describes another kind of union which, with the help of God, the soul can attain, and the important part played in it by the love of our neighbour. This chapter is of great profit 258

CONTENTS

CHAPTER IV.—Continues the same subject and gives a further explanation of this kind of prayer. Describes the great importance of proceeding carefully, since the devil is most careful to do all he can to turn souls back from the road they have begun to tread 264

SIXTH MANSIONS

CHAPTER I.—Shows how, when the Lord begins to grant the soul greater favours, it has also to endure greater trials. Enumerates some of these and describes how those who are in this Mansion must conduct themselves. This is a good chapter for any who suffer interior trials . . 269

CHAPTER II.—Treats of several ways in which Our Lord awakens the soul; there appears to be nothing in these to be feared, although the experience is most sublime and the favours are great ones. . . . 275

CHAPTER III.—Treats of the same subject and describes the way in which, when He is pleased to do so, God speaks to the soul. Gives instructions as to how we should behave in such a case: we must not be guided by our own opinions. Sets down a few signs by which we may know when this favour is, and when it is not, a deception. This chapter is very profitable 279

CHAPTER IV.—Treats of occasions when God suspends the soul in prayer by means of rapture, or ecstasy, or trance (for I think these are all the same), and of how great courage is necessary if we are to receive great favours from His Majesty 286

CHAPTER V.—Continues the same subject and gives an example of how God exalts the soul through flights of the spirit in a way different from that described. Gives some reasons why courage is necessary here. Says something of this favour which God grants in a way so delectable. This chapter is highly profitable 293

CHAPTER VI.—Describes one effect of the prayer referred to in the last chapter, by which it will be known that it is genuine and no deception. Treats of another favour which the Lord grants to the soul so that He may use it to sing His praises 297

CHAPTER VII.—Treats of the kind of grief felt for their sins by the souls to whom God grants the favours aforementioned. Says that, however spiritual people may be, it is a great mistake for them not to practise keeping in mind the Humanity of Our Lord and Saviour Jesus Christ, His most sacred Passion and life, and His glorious Mother and the Saints. This chapter is of great profit 302

CHAPTER VIII.—Treats of the way in which God communicates Himself to the soul through intellectual vision. Describes the effects which this produces when genuine. Charges that these favours be kept secret . 309

CHAPTER IX.—Treats of the way in which the Lord communicates Himself to the soul through imaginary visions and gives an emphatic warning that we should be careful not to desire to walk in this way. Gives reasons for the warning. This chapter is of great profit . . . 314

CHAPTER X.—Speaks of other favours which God grants to the soul in a different way from those already mentioned, and of the great profit that they bring 321

CHAPTER XI.—Treats of the desires to enjoy God which He gives the soul and which are so great and impetuous that they endanger its life. Treats also of the profit which comes from this favour granted by the Lord . 323

CONTENTS

SEVENTH MANSIONS

CHAPTER I.—Treats of great favours which God bestows on the souls that have attained entrance to the Seventh Mansions. Describes how in the author's opinion there is some difference between the soul and the spirit, although both are one. There are notable things in this chapter . . 329

CHAPTER II.—Continues the same subject. Describes the difference between spiritual union and spiritual marriage. Explains this by subtle comparisons 333

CHAPTER III.—Treats of the striking effects produced by this prayer aforementioned. It is necessary to observe and remember the effects it produces, for the difference between them and those already described is remarkable 338

CHAPTER IV.—Concludes by describing what appears to be Our Lord's aim in granting the soul such great favours and says how necessary it is for Martha and Mary to walk in each other's company. This chapter is very profitable 344

[EPILOGUE] 350

CONCEPTIONS OF THE LOVE OF GOD

INTRODUCTION 352

PROLOGUE 357

CHAPTER I.—Treats of the veneration with which the Sacred Scriptures must be read, and of the difficulty which women have in understanding them. This applies particularly to the *Song of Songs* . . 359

CHAPTER II.—Describes nine kinds of false peace offered to the soul by the world, the flesh and the devil. Explains the sanctity of the religious state which leads to the true peace desired by the Bride in the *Canticles* 364

CHAPTER III.—Treats of the true peace which God grants to the soul, of His union with it and of the examples of heroic charity given by certain of God's servants 377

CHAPTER IV.—Speaks of the Prayer of Quiet and of Union and of the sweetness and the consolations which these bring to the spirit, by comparison with which the delights of earth are nothing . . 383

CHAPTER V.—Continues to describe the Prayer of Union and speaks of the riches which the soul acquires therein through the mediation of the Holy Spirit and of its determination to suffer trials for the Beloved . 387

CHAPTER VI.—Describes how the benefits of this loving union surpass all the Bride's desires. Speaks of the suspension of the faculties and describes how some souls rise in a very short time to this sublime degree of prayer 390

CHAPTER VII.—Describes the great desires felt by the Bride to suffer much for God's sake and her neighbour's, and the abundant fruits borne in the Church by these souls that are favoured by Divine union and detached from self-interest. Quotes the Samaritan woman as an example of love for one's neighbour. Ends by recalling the aim proposed for this book 395

EXCLAMATIONS OF THE SOUL TO GOD

INTRODUCTION 400

I–VII. 402

BOOK CALLED WAY OF PERFECTION

INTRODUCTION

We owe this book, first and foremost, to the affectionate importunities of the Carmelite nuns of the Primitive Observance at Ávila, and, in the second place, to that outstanding Dominican who was also St. Teresa's confessor, Fray Domingo Báñez. The nuns of St. Joseph's knew something of their Mother Foundress' autobiography, and, though in all probability none of them had actually read it, they would have been aware that it contained valuable counsels to aspirants after religious perfection, of which, had the book been accessible to them, they would have been glad to avail themselves. Such intimate details did it contain, however, about St. Teresa's spiritual life that her superiors thought it should not be put into their hands; so the only way in which she could grant their persistent requests was to write another book dealing expressly with the life of prayer. This P. Báñez was very anxious that she should do.

Through the entire *Way of perfection* there runs the author's desire to teach her daughters to love prayer, the most effective means of attaining virtue. This principle is responsible for the book's construction. St. Teresa begins by describing the reason which led her to found the first Reformed Carmelite convent—viz., the desire to minimize the ravages being wrought, in France and elsewhere, by Protestantism, and, within the limits of her capacity, to check the passion for a so-called "freedom", which at that time was exceeding all measure. Knowing how effectively such inordinate desires can be restrained by a life of humility and poverty, St. Teresa extols the virtues of poverty and exhorts her daughters to practise it in their own lives. Even the buildings in which they live should be poor: on the Day of Judgment both majestic palaces and humble cottages will fall and she has no desire that the convents of her nuns should do so with a resounding clamour.

In this preamble to her book, which comprises Chapters I–III, the author also charges her daughters very earnestly to commend to God those who have to defend the Church of Christ—particularly theologians and preachers.

The next part of the book (Chaps. IV–XV) stresses the importance of a strict observance of the Rule and Constitutions, and before going on to its main subject—prayer—treats of three essentials of the prayer-filled life—mutual love, detachment from created things and true humility, the last of these being the most important and including all the rest. With the mutual love which nuns should have for one another she deals most minutely, giving what might be termed homely prescriptions for the domestic disorders of convents with the skill which we should expect of a writer with so perfect a knowledge of the psychology of the cloister. Her counsels are the fruit, not of lofty mental speculation, but of mature practical experience. No less aptly does she speak of the relations between nuns and their confessors, so frequently a source of danger.

Since excess is possible even in mutual love, she next turns to detachment. Her nuns must be detached from relatives and friends, from the world, from worldly honour, and—the last and hardest achievement—from themselves. To a large extent their efforts in this direction will involve humility, for, so long as we have an exaggerated opinion of our own merits, detachment is impossible. Humility, to St. Teresa, is nothing more nor less than truth, which will give us the precise estimate of our own worth that we need. Fraternal love, detachment and humility: these three virtues, if they are sought in the way these chapters direct, will make the soul mistress and sovereign over all created things—a "royal soul", in the Saint's happy phrase, the slave of none save of Him Who bought it with His blood.

The next section (Chaps. XVI–XXVI) develops these ideas, and leads the reader directly to the themes of prayer and contemplation. It begins with St. Teresa's famous extended simile of the game of chess, in which the soul gives check and mate to the King of love, Jesus. Many people are greatly attracted by the life of contemplation because they have acquired imperfect and misleading notions of the ineffable mystical joys which they believe almost synonymous with contemplation. The Saint protests against such ideas as these and lays it down clearly that, as a general rule, there is no way of attaining to union with the Beloved save by the practice of the "great virtues", which can be acquired only at the cost of continual self-sacrifice and self-conquest. The favours which God grants to contemplatives are only exceptional and of a transitory kind and they are intended to incline them more closely to virtue and to inspire their lives with greater fervour.

And here the Saint propounds a difficult question which has occasioned no little debate among writers on mystical theology. Can a soul in grave sin enjoy supernatural contemplation? At first sight, and judging from what the author says in Chapter XVI,

INTRODUCTION

the answer would seem to be that, though but rarely and for brief periods, it can. In the original (or Escorial) autograph, however, she expressly denies this, and states that contemplation is not possible for souls in mortal sin, though it may be experienced by those who are so lukewarm, or lacking in fervour, that they fall into venial sins with ease. It would seem that in this respect the Escorial manuscript reflects the Saint's ideas, as we know them, more clearly than the later one of Valladolid; if this be so, her opinions in no way differ from those of mystical theologians as a whole, who refuse to allow that souls in mortal sin can experience contemplation at all.

St. Teresa then examines a number of other questions, on which opinion has also been divided and even now is by no means unanimous. Can all souls attain to contemplation? Is it possible, without experiencing contemplation, to reach the summit of Christian perfection? Have all the servants of God who have been canonized by the Church necessarily been contemplatives? Does the Church ever grant non-contemplatives beatification? On these questions and others often discussed by the mystics much light is shed in the seventeenth and eighteenth chapters.

Then the author crosses swords once more with those who suppose that contemplatives know nothing of suffering and that their lives are one continuous series of favours. On the contrary, she asserts, they suffer more than actives: to imagine that God admits to this closest friendship people whose lives are all favours and no trials is ridiculous. Recalling the doctrine expounded in the nineteenth chapter of her *Life* she gives various counsels for the practice of prayer, using once more the figures of water which she had employed in her first description of the Mystic Way. She consoles those who cannot reason with the understanding, shows how vocal prayer may be combined with mental, and ends by advising those who suffer from aridity in prayer to picture Jesus as within their hearts and thus always beside them—one of her favourite themes.

This leads up to the subject which occupies her for the rest of the book (Chaps. XXVII-XLII)—the Lord's Prayer. These chapters, in fact, comprise a commentary on the Paternoster, taken petition by petition, touching incidentally upon the themes of Recollection, Quiet and Union. Though nowhere expounding them as fully as in the *Life* or the *Interior Castle*, she treats them with equal sublimity, profundity and fervour and in language of no less beauty. Consider, for example, the apt and striking simile of the mother and the child (Chap. XXXI), used to describe the state of the soul in the Prayer of Quiet, which forms one of the most beautiful and expressive expositions of this degree of contemplation to be found in any book on the interior life whatsoever.

In Chapter XXXVIII, towards the end of the commentary on the Paternoster, St. Teresa gives a striking synthetic description of the excellences of that Prayer and of its spiritual value. She enters at some length into the temptations to which spiritual people are exposed when they lack humility and discretion. Some of these are due to presumption: they believe they possess virtues which in fact they do not—or, at least, not in sufficient degree to enable them to resist the snares of the enemy. Others come from a mistaken scrupulousness and timidity inspired by a sense of the heinousness of their sins, and may lead them into doubt and despair. There are souls, too, which make overmuch account of spiritual favours: these she counsels to see to it that, however sublime their contemplation may be, they begin and end every period of prayer with self-examination. While others, whose mistrust of themselves makes them restless, are exhorted to trust in the Divine mercy, which never forsakes those who possess true humility.

Finally, St. Teresa writes of the love and fear of God—two mighty castles which the fiercest of the soul's enemies will storm in vain—and begs Him, in the last words of the Prayer, to preserve her daughters, and all other souls who practise the interior life, from the ills and perils which will ever surround them, until they reach the next world, where all will be peace and joy in Jesus Christ.

Such, in briefest outline, is the argument of this book. Of all St. Teresa's writings it is the most easily comprehensible and it can be read with profit by a greater number of people than any of the rest. It is also (if we use the word in its strictest and truest sense) the most ascetic of her treatises; only a few chapters and passages in it, here and there, can be called definitely mystical. It takes up numerous ideas already adumbrated in the *Life* and treats them in a practical and familiar way—objectively, too, with an eye not so much to herself as to her daughters of the Discalced Reform. This last fact necessitates her descending to details which may seem to us trivial but were not in the least so to the religious to whom they were addressed and with whose virtues and failings she was so familiar. Skilfully, then, and in a way profitable to all, she intermingles her teaching on the most rudimentary principles of the religious life, which has all the clarity of any classical treatise, with instruction on the most sublime and elusive tenets of mystical theology.

ESCORIAL AUTOGRAPH—The Way of perfection—or *Paternoster*, as its author calls it, from the latter part of its content—was written twice. Both autographs have been preserved in excellent condition, the older of them in the monastery of San Lorenzo el Real, El Escorial, and the other in the convent of the Discalced Carmelite nuns at Valladolid. We have already seen how Philip II acquired a number of Teresan autographs for his new Escorial library, among them that of the *Way of perfection*. The Escorial manuscript bears the title "Treatise of the Way of Perfection", but this is not in St. Teresa's hand. It plunges straight into the prologue: both the title and the brief account of the contents, which are found in most of the editions, are taken from the autograph of Valladolid, and the humble protestation of faith and submission to the Holy Roman Church was dictated by the Saint for the edition of the book made in Évora by Don Teutonio de Braganza—it is found in the Toledo codex, which will be referred to again shortly.

The text, divided into seventy-three short chapters, has no chapter-divisions in the ordinary sense of the phrase, though the author has left interlinear indications showing where each chapter should begin. The chapter-headings form a table of contents at the end of the manuscript and only two of them (LV and LVI) are in St. Teresa's own writing. As the remainder, however, are in a feminine hand of the sixteenth century, they may have been dictated by her to one of her nuns: they are almost identical with those which she herself wrote at a later date in the autograph of Valladolid.

There are a considerable number of emendations in this text, most of them made by the Saint herself, whose practice was to obliterate any unwanted word so completely as to make it almost illegible. None of such words or phrases was restored in the autograph of Valladolid—a sure indication that it was she who erased them, or at least that she approved of their having been erased. There are fewer annotations and additions in other hands than in the autographs of any of her remaining works, and those few are of little importance. This may be due to the fact that a later redaction of the work was made for the use of her convents and for publication: the Escorial manuscript would have circulated very little and would never have been subjected to a minute critical examination. Most of what annotations and corrections of this kind there are were made by the Saint's confessor, P. García de Toledo, whom, among others, she asked to examine the manuscript.

There is no direct indication in the manuscript of the date of its composition. We know that it was written at St. Joseph's,

Ávila, for the edification and instruction of the first nuns of the Reform, and the prologue tells us that only "a few days" had elapsed between the completion of the *Life* and the beginning of the *Way of perfection*.[1] If, therefore, the *Life* was finished at the end of 1565 [or in the early weeks of 1566][2] we can date the commencement of the *Way of perfection* with some precision. [But even then there is no indication as to how long the composition took and when it was completed.]

A complication occurs in the existence, at the end of a copy of the *Way of perfection* which belongs to the Discalced Carmelite nuns of Salamanca, and contains corrections in St. Teresa's hand, of a note, in the writing of the copyist, which says: "This book was written in the year sixty-two—I mean fifteen hundred and sixty-two." There follow some lines in the writing of St. Teresa, which make no allusion to this date; her silence might be taken as confirming it (though she displays no great interest in chronological exactness) were it not absolutely impossible to reconcile such a date with the early chapters of the book, which make it quite clear that the community of thirteen nuns was fully established when they were written (Chap. IV: p. 17, below). There could not possibly have been so many nuns at St. Joseph's before late in the year 1563, in which María de San Jerónimo and Isabel de Santo Domingo took the habit, and it is doubtful if St. Teresa could conceivably have begun the book before the end of that year. Even, therefore, if the reference in the preface to the *Way of perfection* were to the first draft of the *Life* (1562), and not to that book as we know it, there would still be the insuperable difficulty raised by this piece of internal evidence.[3] We are forced, then, to assume an error in the Salamanca copy and to assign to the beginning of the *Way of perfection* the date 1565-6.

VALLADOLID AUTOGRAPH. In writing for her Ávila nuns, St. Teresa used language much more simple, familiar and homely than in any of her other works. But when she began to establish more foundations and her circle of readers widened, this language must have seemed to her too affectionately intimate, and some of her figures and images may have struck her as too domestic and trivial, for a more general and scattered public. So she conceived the idea of rewriting the book in a more formal style;

---

[1] [It is in this way that P. Silverio interprets the phrase. For another interpretation of it see p. 2, n. 4, below.]
[2] Cf. Vol. I, pp. 2-5, above.
[3] See also the reference, in the "General Argument" of the Valladolid redaction, to her being Prioress of St. Joseph's when the book was written. Presumably the original draft is meant.

it is the autograph of this redaction which is in the possession of the Discalced Carmelite nuns of Valladolid.

The additions, omissions and modifications in this new autograph are more considerable than is generally realized. From the preface onwards, there is no chapter without its emendations and in many there are additions of whole paragraphs. The Valladolid autograph, therefore, is in no sense a copy, or even a recast, of the first draft, but a free and bold treatment of it. As a general rule, a second draft, though often more correctly written and logically arranged than its original, is less flexible, fluent and spontaneous. It is hard to say how far this is the case here. Undoubtedly some of the charm of the author's natural simplicity vanishes, but the corresponding gain in clarity and precision is generally considered greater than the loss. Nearly every change she makes is an improvement; and this not only in stylistic matters, for one of the greatest of her improvements is the lengthening of the chapters and their reduction in number from 73 to 42, to the great advantage of the book's symmetry and unity.

It is clear that St. Teresa intended the Valladolid redaction to be the definitive form of her book since she had so large a number of copies of it made for her friends and spiritual daughters: among these were the copy which she sent for publication to Don Teutonio de Braganza and that used for the first collected edition of her works by Fray Luis de León. For the same reason this redaction has always been given preference over its predecessor by the Discalced Carmelites.

TRANSLATOR'S NOTE

In the text of each of the chapters, of the Valladolid autograph there are omissions—some merely verbal, often illustrating the author's aim in making the new redaction, others more fundamental. If the Valladolid manuscript represents the *Way of perfection* as St. Teresa wrote it in the period of her fullest powers, the greater freshness and individuality of the Escorial manuscript are engaging qualities, and there are many passages in it, omitted from the later version, which one would be sorry to sacrifice.

In what form, then, should the book be presented to English readers? It is not surprising if this question is difficult to answer, since varying procedures have been adopted for the presentation of it in Spain. Most of them amount briefly to a re-editing of the Valladolid manuscript. The first edition of the book, published at Évora in the year 1583, follows this manuscript, apparently using a copy (the so-called "Toledo" copy) made by Ana de San Pedro and corrected by St. Teresa; it contains a considerable number of errors, however, and omits one entire chapter—the thirty-first, which deals with the Prayer of Quiet, a subject that was arousing some controversy at the time when the edition was being prepared. In 1585, a second edition, edited by Fray Jerónimo Gracián, was published at Salamanca: the text of this follows that of the Evora edition very closely, as apparently does the text of a rare edition published at Valencia in 1586. When Fray Luis de León used the Valladolid manuscript as the foundation of his text (1588) he inserted for the first time paragraphs and phrases from that of El Escorial, as well as admitting variants from the copies corrected by the author: he is not careful, however, to indicate how and where his edition differs from the manuscript.

Since 1588, most of the Spanish editions have followed Fray Luis de León with greater or less exactness. The principal exception is the well-known "Biblioteca de Autores Españoles" edition, in which La Fuente followed a copy of the then almost forgotten Escorial manuscript, indicating in footnotes some of the variant readings in the codex of Valladolid. In the edition of 1883, the work of a Canon of Valladolid Cathedral, Francisco Herrero Bayona, the texts of the two manuscripts are reproduced in parallel columns. P. Silverio de Santa Teresa gives the place of honour to the Valladolid codex, on which he bases his text, showing only the principal variants of the Escorial manuscript but printing the Escorial text in full in an appendix as well as the text of the Toledo copy referred to above.

The first translations of this book into English, by Woodhead (1675: reprinted 1901) and Dalton (1852), were based, very naturally, on the text of Luis de León, which in less critical ages than our own enjoyed great prestige and was considered quite authoritative. The edition published in 1911 by the Benedictines of Stanbrook, described on its title-page as "including all the variants" from both the Escorial and the Valladolid manuscript, uses Herrero Bayona and gives an eclectic text based on the two originals but with no indications as to which is which. The editors' original idea of using one text only, and showing variants in footnotes, was rejected in the belief that "such an arrangement would prove bewildering for the generality of readers" and that anyone who could claim the title of "student" would be able to read the original Spanish and would have access to the Herrero Bayona edition. Father Zimmerman, in his introduction, claimed that while the divergences between the manuscripts are sometimes "so great that the [Stanbrook] translation resembles a mosaic composed of a large number of small bits, skilfully combined", "the work has been done most conscientiously, and while nothing has been added to the text of the Saint, nothing has been omitted, except, of course, what would have been mere repetition".

This first edition of the Benedictines' translation furnished the general reader with an attractive version of what many consider St. Teresa's most attractive book, but soon after it was published a much more intelligent and scholarly interest began to be taken in the Spanish mystics and that not only by students with ready access to the Spanish original and ability to read it. So, when a new edition of the Stanbrook translation was called for, the editors decided to indicate the passages from the Escorial edition which had been embodied in the text by enclosing these in square brackets. In 1911, Father Zimmerman, suspecting that the procedure then adopted by the translators would not "meet with the approval of scholars", had justified it by their desire "to benefit the souls of the faithful rather than the intellect of the student"; but now, apparently, he thought it practicable to achieve both these aims at once. This resolution would certainly have had the support of St. Teresa, who in this very book describes intelligence as a useful staff to carry on the way of perfection. The careful comparison of two separate versions of such a work of genius may benefit the soul of an intelligent reader even more than the careful reading of a version compounded of both by someone else.

When I began to consider the preparation of the present translation it seemed to me that an attempt might be made to do a little more for the reader who combined intelligence with devoutness than had been done already. I had no hesitation about basing my version on the Valladolid MS., which is far the better of the two, whether we consider the aptness of its illustrations, the clarity of its expression, the logical development of its argument or its greater suitability for general reading. At the same time, no Teresan who has studied the Escorial text can fail to have an affection for it: its greater intimacy and spontaneity and its appeal to personal experience make it one of the most characteristic of all the Saint's writings—indeed, excepting the *Letters* and a few chapters of the *Foundations*, it reveals her better than any. Passages from the Escorial MS. must therefore be given: thus far I followed the reasoning of the Stanbrook nuns.

Where this translation diverges from theirs is in the method of presentation. On the one hand I desired, as St. Teresa must have desired, that it should be essentially her mature revision of the book that should be read. For this reason I have been extremely conservative as to the interpolations admitted into the text itself: I have rejected, for example, the innumerable phrases which St. Teresa seems to have cut out in making her new redaction because they were trivial or repetitive, because they weaken rather than reinforce her argument, because they say what is better said elsewhere, because they summarize needlessly[1] or because they are mere personal observations which interrupt the author's flow of thought, and sometimes, indeed, are irrelevant to it. I hope it is not impertinent to add that, in the close study which the adoption of this procedure has involved, I have acquired a respect and admiration for St. Teresa as a reviser, to whom, as far as I know, no one who has written upon her has done full justice. Her shrewdness, realism and complete lack of vanity make her an admirable editor of her own work, and, in debating whether or no to incorporate some phrase or passage in my text I have often asked myself: "Would St. Teresa have included or omitted this if she had been making a fresh revision for a world-wide public over a period of centuries?"

At the same time, though admitting only a minimum of interpolations into my text, I have given the reader all the other important variants in footnotes. I cannot think, as Father Zimmerman apparently thought, that anyone can find the presence of a few notes at the foot of each page "bewildering". Those for whom they have no interest may ignore them; others, in

[1] E.g., at places where a chapter ends in E. but not in V.

studying them, may rest assured that the only variants not included (and this applies to the variants from the Toledo copy as well as from the Escorial MS.) are such as have no significance in a translation. I have been rather less meticulous here than in my edition of St. John of the Cross, where textual problems assumed greater importance. Thus, except where there has been some special reason for doing so, I have not recorded alterations in the order of clauses or words; the almost regular use by E. of the second person of the plural where V. has the first; the frequent and often apparently purposeless changes of tense; such substitutions, in the Valladolid redaction, as those of "Dios" or "Señor mío" for "Señor"; or merely verbal paraphrases as (to take an example at random) "Todo esto que he dicho es para . . ." for "En todo esto que he dicho no trato . . .". Where I have given variants which may seem trivial (such as "hermanas" for "hijas", or the insertion of an explanatory word, like "digo") the reason is generally that there seems to me a possibility that some difference in tone is intended, or that the alternative phrase gives some slight turn to the thought which the phrase in the text does not.

The passages from the Escorial version which I have allowed into my text are printed in italics. Thus, without their being given undue prominence (and readers of the Authorized Version of the Bible will know how seldom they can recall what words are italicized even in the passages they know best) it is clear at a glance how much of the book was intended by its author to be read by a wider public than the nuns of St. Joseph's. The interpolations may be as brief as a single expressive word, or as long as a paragraph, or even a chapter: the original Chapter XVII of the Valladolid MS., for example, which contains the famous similitude of the Game of Chess, was torn out of the codex by its author (presumably with the idea that so secular an illustration was out of place) and has been restored from the Escorial MS. as part of Chapter XVI of this translation. No doubt the striking bull-fight metaphor at the end of Chapter XXXIX was suppressed in the Valladolid codex for the same reason. With these omissions may be classed a number of minor ones—of words or phrases which to the author may have seemed too intimate or colloquial but do not seem so to us. Other words and phrases have apparently been suppressed because St. Teresa thought them redundant, whereas a later reader finds that they make a definite contribution to the sense or give explicitness and detail to what would otherwise be vague, or even obscure.[1]

[1] One special case of this class is the suppression in V. of one out of two or three almost but not quite synonymous adjectives referring to the same noun.

A few suppressions seem to have been due to pure oversight. For the omission of other passages it is difficult to find any reason, so good are they: the conclusion of Chapter XXXVIII and the opening of Chapter XLI are cases in point.

The numbering of the chapters, it should be noted, follows neither of the two texts, but is that traditionally employed in the printed editions. The chapter headings are also drawn up on an eclectic basis, though here the Valladolid text is generally followed.

The system I have adopted not only assures the reader that he will be reading everything that St. Teresa wrote and nothing that she did not write, but that he can discern, almost at a glance, what she meant to be read by her little group of nuns at St. Joseph's and also how she intended her work to appear in its more definitive form. Thus we can see her both as the companion and Mother and as the writer and Foundress. In both rôles she is equally the Saint.

But it should be made clear that, while incorporating in my text all important passages from the Escorial draft omitted in that of Valladolid, I have thought it no part of my task to provide a complete translation of the Escorial draft alone, and that, therefore, in order to avoid the multiplication of footnotes, I have indicated only the principal places where some expression in the later draft is not to be found in the earlier. In other words, although, by omitting the italicized portions of my text, one will be able to have as exact a translation of the Valladolid version as it is possible to get, the translation of the Escorial draft will be only approximate. This is the sole concession I have made to the ordinary reader as opposed to the student, and it is hardly conceivable, I think, that any student to whom this could matter would be unable to read the original Spanish.

One final note is necessary on the important Toledo copy, the text of which P. Silverio also prints in full. This text I have collated with that of the Valladolid autograph, from which it derives. In it both St. Teresa herself and others have made corrections and additions—more, in fact, than in any of the other copies extant. No attempt has been made here either to show what the Toledo copy omits or to include those of its corrections and additions—by far the largest number of them—which are merely verbal and unimportant, and many of which, indeed, could not be embodied in a translation at all. But the few additions which are really worth noting have been incorporated in the text (in square brackets, so as to distinguish them from the Escorial additions) and all corrections which have seemed to me of any significance will be found in footnotes.

BOOK CALLED WAY OF PERFECTION[1]

Composed by TERESA OF JESUS, Nun of the Order of Our Lady of Carmel, addressed to the Discalced Nuns of Our Lady of Carmel of the First Rule.[2]

General Argument of this Book
J. H. S.

This book treats of maxims and counsels which Teresa of Jesus gives to her daughters and sisters in religion, belonging to the Convents which, with the favour of Our Lord and of the glorious Virgin, Mother of God, Our Lady, she has founded according to the First Rule of Our Lady of Carmel. In particular she addresses it to the sisters of the Convent of Saint Joseph of Ávila, which was the first Convent, and of which she was Prioress when she wrote it.[3]

---

[1] With few exceptions, the footnotes to the *Way of perfection* are the translator's, Square brackets are therefore not used to distinguish them from those of P. Silverio. as elsewhere. Ordinary brackets, in the footnote translations, are placed round words inserted to complete the sense.

[2] This title, in St. Teresa's hand, appears on the first page of the Valladolid autograph (V.) which, as we have said in the Introduction, is the basis of the text here used. The Escorial autograph (E.) has the words "Treatise of the Way of Perfection" in an unknown hand, followed by the Prologue, in St. Teresa's. The Toledo copy (T.) begins with the Protestation.

[3] These lines, also in St. Teresa's hand, follow the title in the Valladolid autograph. P. Báñez added, in his own writing, the words: "I have seen this book and my opinion of it is written at the end and signed with my name." Cf. p. 186, below.

PROTESTATION[1]

In all that I shall say in this Book, I submit to what is taught by Our Mother, the Holy Roman Church; if there is anything in it contrary to this, it will be without my knowledge. Therefore, for the love of Our Lord, I beg the learned men who are to revise it to look at it very carefully and to amend any faults of this nature which there may be in it and the many others which it will have of other kinds. If there is anything good in it, let this be to the glory and honour of God and in the service of His most sacred Mother, our Patroness and Lady, whose habit, though all unworthily, I wear.

[1] This Protestation, taken from T., was dictated by St. Teresa for the edition of the *Way of perfection* published at Évora in 1583 by D. Teutonio de Braganza.

BOOK CALLED WAY OF PERFECTION

PROLOGUE

J. H. S.

The sisters of this Convent of Saint Joseph, knowing that I had had leave from Father Presentado Fray Domingo Bañes,[1] of the Order of the glorious Saint Dominic, who at present is my confessor, to write certain things about prayer, which it seems I may be able to succeed in doing since I have had to do with many holy and spiritual persons, have, *out of their great love for me*, so earnestly begged me to say something to them about this[2] that I have resolved to obey them. I realize that the great love which they have for me may render the imperfection and the poverty of my style in what I shall say to them more acceptable than other books which are very ably written by those who[3] have known what they are writing about. I rely upon their prayers, by means of which the Lord may be pleased to enable me to say something concerning the way and method of life which it is fitting should be practised in this house. If I do not succeed in doing this, Father Presentado, who will first read what I have written, will either put it right or burn it,[4] so that I shall have lost nothing by obeying these servants of God, and they will see how useless I am when His Majesty does not help me.

My intent is to suggest a few remedies for a number of small temptations which come from the devil, and which, because they are so slight, are apt to pass unnoticed. I shall also

---

[1] The words "Fray Domingo Bañes" are crossed out, probably by P. Báñez himself. T. has: "from the Father Master Fray Domingo Báñez, Professor at Salamanca." Báñez was appointed to a Chair at Salamanca University in 1577.

[2] E. continues: "that, although there are many books which treat of this and persons with a good knowledge of what they write, good-will seems to make certain things which are imperfect and faulty more acceptable than others which are quite perfect; and, as I say, their wishes and their importunity have been such as to determine me to do it, for their prayers and their humility have made me believe that it is the Lord's will to enable me to say something profitable to them and to give me what I am to say. If I do not succeed, etc."

[3] The pronoun (*quien*) in the Spanish is singular, but in the sixteenth century it could have plural force and the context would favour this. A manuscript note in V., however (not by P. Báñez, as the Paris Carmelites—*Oeuvres*, V, 30—suggest), evidently takes the reference to be to St. Gregory, for it says: "And he wrote something on Job, and the *Morals*, importuned by servants of God, and trusting in their prayers, as he himself says."

[4] E.: "will burn it." T.: "the learned men who will first read what I have written will tear it up."

write[1] of other things, according as the Lord reveals them to me and as they come to my mind; since I do not know what I am going to say I cannot set it down in suitable order; and I think it is better for me not to do so, for it is quite unsuitable that I should be writing in this way at all. May the Lord lay His hand on all that I do so that it may be in accordance with His holy will;[2] this is always my desire, although my actions may be as imperfect as I myself am.

I know that I am[3] lacking neither in love nor in desire to do all I can to help the souls of my sisters to make great progress in the service of the Lord. It may be that this love, together with my years and the experience which I have of a number of convents, will make me more successful in writing about small matters than learned men can be. For these, being themselves strong and having other and more important occupations, do not always pay such heed to things which in themselves seem of no importance but which may do great harm to persons as weak as we women are. For the snares laid by the devil for strictly cloistered nuns are numerous and he finds that he needs new weapons if he is to do them harm. I, being a wicked woman, have defended myself but ill, and so I should like my sisters to take warning by me. I shall speak of nothing of which I have no experience, either in my own life or in the observation of others, *or which the Lord has not taught me in prayer.*

A few days ago I was commanded to write an account of my life in which I also dealt with certain matters concerning prayer.[4] It may be that my confessor will not wish you to see this,[5] for which reason I shall set down here some of the things which I said in that book and others which may also seem to me necessary.[6] May the Lord direct this, as I have begged Him to do, and order it for His greater glory. Amen.

---

[1] E.: "I am thinking of suggesting a few remedies for temptations which come to nuns and of describing my motives for the foundation of this house—I mean, in the perfection which is observed here, quite independently of our Constitution. I shall also write, etc."

[2] E. omits: "holy."

[3] T.: "'I hope in God that I shall be."

[4] E.: "A few days ago I wrote an account of my life." [This phrase is generally taken as indicating that the *Way of perfection* was written immediately after the *Life*. If "wrote", in E., means "completed", we can take "a few days" literally; otherwise it must be equivalent to "a short time", as it frequently is in St. Teresa—this will in any case, be its meaning in the context of V. Cf. pp. xvii–xviii, above.]

[5] T. adds: "so quickly", but these words are crossed out in the manuscript.

[6] E.: "As my confessor may not wish you to read this, I shall set down certain matters concerning prayer, which will be in agreement with the things I have said there, together with other things that may seem to me necessary."

CHAPTER I

Of the reason which moved me to found this convent in such strict observance.

When this convent[1] was originally founded, for the reasons set down in the book which, as I say, I have already written, and also because of certain wonderful revelations by which the Lord showed me how well He would be served in this house, it was not my intention that there should be so much austerity in external matters, nor that it should have no regular income: on the contrary, I should have liked there to be no possibility of want. I acted, in short, like the weak and wretched woman that I am, although I did so with good intentions and not out of consideration for my own comfort.

At about this time there came to my notice the harm and havoc that were being wrought in France by these Lutherans and the way in which their unhappy sect was increasing.[2] This troubled me very much,[3] and, as though I could do anything, or be of any help in the matter, I wept before the Lord and entreated Him to remedy this great evil. I felt that I would have laid down a thousand lives to save a single one of all the souls that were being lost there. And, seeing that I was a woman, and a sinner,[4] and incapable of doing all I should like in the Lord's service, and as my whole yearning was, and still is, that, as He has so many enemies and so few friends, these last should be trusty ones, I determined to do the little that was in me—namely, to follow the evangelical counsels as perfectly as I could, and to see that these few nuns who are here should do the same, confiding in the great goodness of God, Who never fails to help those who resolve to forsake everything for His sake. As they are all that I have ever painted them[5] as being in my desires, I hoped that their virtues would more than counteract my defects, and I should thus be able to give the Lord some pleasure, and all of us, by busying ourselves in prayer for those who are defenders of the Church, and for the preachers and learned men who defend her, should do everything we could to aid this Lord of mine Who is so much oppressed by those to whom He has shown

---

[1] "Of St. Joseph's, Ávila," adds T.
[2] French Protestantism, which had been repressed during the reigns of Francis I and Henry II, increased after the latter's death in 1559, and was still doing so at the time of the foundation of St. Joseph's.
[3] T. omits: "This . . . much."
[4] *Lit.*: "and bad"—which T. omits.
[5] T.: "imagined them."

so much good that it seems as though these traitors[1] would send Him to the Cross again and that He would have nowhere to lay His head.

Oh, my Redeemer, my heart cannot conceive this without being sorely distressed! What has become of Christians now? Must those who owe Thee most always be those who distress Thee?[2] Those to whom Thou doest the greatest kindnesses, whom Thou dost choose for Thy friends, among whom Thou dost move, communicating Thyself to them through the Sacraments? Do they not think, *Lord of my soul*, that they have made Thee endure more than sufficient torments?[3]

It is certain, my Lord, that in these days withdrawal from the world means no sacrifice at all. Since worldly people have so little respect for Thee, what can we expect them to have for us? Can it be that we deserve that they should treat us any better than they have treated Thee? Have we done more for them than Thou hast done that they[4] should be friendly to us? What then? What can we expect—we who, through the goodness of the Lord, are free from that pestilential infection, and do not, like those others, belong to the devil? They have won severe punishment at his hands[5] and their pleasures have richly earned them eternal fire. So to eternal fire they will have to go,[6] though none the less it breaks my heart to see so many souls travelling to perdition. I would the evil were not so great and I did not see[7] more being lost every day.

Oh, my sisters in Christ! Help me to entreat this of the Lord, Who has[8] brought you together here for that very purpose. This is your vocation; this must be your business; these must be your desires; these your tears; these your petitions. Let us not pray for worldly things, my sisters. It makes me laugh, and yet[9] it makes me sad, when I hear of the things which people come here to beg us to pray to God for; we are to ask His Majesty to give them money and to provide them with incomes—I wish that some of these people would entreat God[10] to enable them to trample all such things beneath their feet. Their intentions are

---

[1] T.: "as though they."
[2] E.: "Must it always be they who distress Thee most"?
[3] E. reads: "the Jews have" for "they have."
[4] E.: "that Christians."
[5] T. omits: "at his hands."
[6] *Allá se lo hayan.* "And serve them right!" would, in most contexts, be a more exact rendering of this colloquial phrase, but there is no suspicion of *Schadenfreude* here.
[7] T.: "I would I did not see."
[8] E.: "Help me to entreat this, for the Lord has."
[9] T. has "Certainly" for "It makes me laugh, and yet".
[10] E.: "which people come here to commend to us, until we pray God for their business affairs and for their lawsuits about money—I wish that they would entreat God." In T., the words "I wish . . . feet" are crossed out.

quite good, and I do as they ask because I see that they are really devout people, though I do not myself believe that God ever hears me when I pray for such things.[1] The world is on fire. Men try to condemn Christ once again, as it were,[2] for they bring a thousand false witnesses against Him. They would raze His Church to the ground[3]—and are we to waste our time upon things which, if God were to grant them, would perhaps bring one soul less to Heaven? No, my sisters, this is no time to treat with God for things of little importance.

Were it not necessary to consider human frailty, which finds satisfaction in every kind of help—and it is always a good thing if we can be of any help to people[4]—I should like it to be understood that it is not for things like these that God should be importuned with such anxiety.[5]

CHAPTER II

Treats of how the necessities of the body should be disregarded and of the good that comes from poverty.

Do not think, my sisters, that because you do not go about trying to please people in the world[6] you will lack food. You will not, I assure you: never try to sustain yourselves by human artifices, or you will die of hunger, and rightly so. Keep your eyes fixed upon your Spouse: it is for Him to sustain you; and, if He is pleased with you, even those who like you least will give you food, if unwillingly, as you have found by experience. If you should do as I say and yet die of hunger, then happy are the nuns of Saint Joseph's![7] For the love of the Lord, let us not forget this: you have forgone a regular income; forgo worry about food as well, or you will lose everything. Let those whom the Lord wishes to live on an income do so: if that is their vocation,[8] they are perfectly justified; but for us to do so, sisters, would be inconsistent.

Worrying about getting money from other people seems to me like thinking about what other people enjoy. However much

---

[1] E.: "and I commend it [*i.e.*, their affairs] to God, so that I may be telling the truth [*i.e.*, when I tell them I will], but I do not myself believe that He ever hears me."
[2] T.: "Men would like, if they could, to condemn Christ once again."
[3] In T., St. Teresa has substituted for this phrase: "His Church, with heresies."
[4] E. omits the words in parenthesis.
[5] E. reads: "importuned at Saint Joseph's."
[6] E.: "that for this reason."
[7] E. adds: "I tell you here that your prayers will be accepted and we shall do something of what we are trying to do."
[8] In T., "vocation" is altered to "office", but not in St. Teresa's hand.

you worry, you will not make them change their minds nor will they become desirous of giving you alms. Leave these anxieties to Him Who can move everyone,[1] Who is the Lord of all money and of all who possess money. It is by His command that we have come here and His words are true—they cannot fail: Heaven and earth will fail first.[2] Let us not fail Him, and let us have no fear that He will fail us; if He should ever do so it will be for our greater good, just as the saints failed to keep their lives[3] when they were slain for the Lord's sake, and their bliss was increased through their martyrdom. We should be making a good exchange if we could have done with this life quickly and enjoy everlasting satiety.

Remember, sisters, that this will be important when I am dead; and that is why I am leaving it to you in writing. For, *with God's help*, as long as I live, I will remind you of it myself, as I know by experience what a great help it will be to you. It is when I possess least that I have the fewest worries and the Lord knows that, as far as I can tell, I am more afflicted when there is excess of anything than when there is lack of it;[4] I am not sure if that is the Lord's doing, but I have noticed that He provides for us immediately. To act otherwise would be to deceive the world by pretending to be poor when we are not poor in spirit but only outwardly.[5] My conscience would give me a bad time. It seems to me it would be like stealing what was being given us, as one might say; for I should feel[6] as if we were rich people asking alms: please God this may never be so. Those who worry too much about the alms that they are likely to be given[7] will find that sooner or later this bad habit will lead them to go and ask for something which they do not need, and perhaps from someone who needs it more than they do. Such a person[8] would gain rather than lose by giving it us but we should certainly be the worse off for having it. God forbid this should ever happen, my daughters; if it were likely to do so, I should prefer you to have a regular income.

I beg you, for the love of God, just as if I were begging alms for you, never to allow this to occupy your thoughts. If the very least of you ever hears of such a thing happening in this house, cry out about it to His Majesty and speak to your Superior.

---

[1] T.: "can move us all."
[2] An apparent reference to St. Mark xiii, 31.
[3] E. ends the sentence: "and they cut off their heads, in order to give them more and to make them martyrs."
[4] E.: "when they give us more than when there is nothing."
[5] T. ends this sentence at "spirit".
[6] E.: "for it would be."
[7] E. adds, parenthetically: "I mean, if anyone did so."
[8] T.: "Those who give it."

Tell her humbly that she is doing wrong; this is so serious a matter that it may cause true poverty gradually to disappear. I hope in the Lord that this will not be so and that He will not forsake His servants; and for that reason, if for no other, what you have told me to write may be useful to you as a reminder.[1]

My daughters must believe that it is for their own good that the Lord has enabled me to realize in some small degree[2] what blessings are to be found in holy poverty.[3] Those of them who practise it will also realize this, though perhaps not as clearly as I do;[4] for, although I had professed poverty, I was not only without poverty of spirit, but my spirit was devoid of all restraint. Poverty is good and contains within itself all the good things in the world.[5] It is a great domain—I mean that he who cares nothing for the good things of the world has dominion over them all.[6] What do kings and lords matter to me if I have no desire to possess their money, or to please them, if by so doing I should cause the least displeasure to God? And what do their honours mean to me if I have realized that the chief honour of a poor man consists in his being truly poor?[7]

For my own part, I believe that honour and money nearly always go together, and that he who desires honour never hates money, while he who hates money cares little for honour. Understand this clearly, for I think this concern about honour always implies some *slight* regard for endowments or money:[8] seldom *or never* is a poor man honoured by the world; however worthy of honour he may be, he is apt rather to be despised by it. With true poverty there goes a different kind of honour to[9] which nobody can take objection. I mean that, if poverty is embraced for God's sake alone, no one has to be pleased save God. It is certain that a man who has no need of anyone has

---

[1] E. reads: "and for that reason, as I have been told to write this, the advice of this miserable sinner may be useful as a reminder." In T. all this paragraph, except the words "Never allow this to occupy your thoughts," is crossed out.

[2] T. omits: "in some small degree."

[3] E. has: "in poverty of spirit", and continues: "and you, if you give heed to it, will understand it, though not as clearly as I do."

[4] E. continues: "for my spirit had been devoid of all restraint, and not poor, though I had made the profession of being so." In T., St. Teresa has crossed out the words: "for although . . . restraint" and substituted: "for I have proved the contrary."

[5] E. adds: "and, I believe, much of what good there is in all the virtues. I do not affirm this, for I do not know the worth of each, and I shall not speak of what I think I do not properly understand: still, I am sure it embraces many virtues."

[6] E. adds: "and if I were to say that he has dominion over them all I should not be lying."

[7] E. omits this sentence, after varying the preceding one slightly, and continues: "We shall spoil everything; for I believe for my own part that, etc."

[8] T. omits: "for . . . money."

[9] T. reads *honra* (honour: cf. Vol. I, p. 14, n. 2 above) for *honraza*, translated above as "different kind of honour".

many friends: in my own experience I have found this to be very true.

A great deal has been written about this virtue which I cannot understand, still less express,[1] and I should only be making things worse if I were to eulogize it, so I will say no more about it now. I have only spoken of what I have myself experienced and I confess that I have been so much absorbed that until now I have hardly[2] realized what I have been writing. However, it has been said now. Our arms are holy poverty, which was so greatly esteemed and so strictly observed by our holy Fathers at the beginning of the foundation of[3] our Order. (Someone who knows[4] about this tells me that they never kept anything from one day to the next.) For the love of the Lord, then, [I beg you] now that the rule of poverty is less perfectly observed as regards outward things, let us strive to observe it inwardly. Our life lasts only for a couple of hours; our reward is boundless; and, if there were no reward but to follow the counsels given us by the Lord,[5] to imitate His Majesty in any degree would bring us a great recompense.

These arms must appear on our banners and at all costs we must keep this rule—as regards our house, our clothes, our speech, and (which is much more important) our thoughts. So long as this is done, there need be no fear, with the help of God, that[6] religious observances in this house will decline, for, as Saint Clare said, the walls of poverty are very strong. It was with these walls, she said, and with those of humility,[7] that she wished to surround her convents;[8] and assuredly, if the rule of poverty is truly kept, both chastity and all the other virtues are fortified much better than by the most sumptuous edifices. Have a care to this, for the love of God; and this I beg of you by His blood. If I may say what my conscience bids me, I should wish that, on the day when you build such edifices, they[9] may fall down *and kill you all*.[10]

---

[1] E. omits from "and I should . . ." to "experienced and". T. reads, after "this virtue": "and I do not know why I speak of it, for I cannot understand it" and omits following words down to "experienced and".

[2] E. continues: "realized how foolish I was being to speak of it: now that I have realized this, I shall be silent. But, as it has been said, let it remain said if it is said well. However, etc."

[3] E. omits: "the foundation of."

[4] E.: "who has read."

[5] E. ends this paragraph by adding: "it would be a great one."

[6] T. reads: "So long as we do this, I hope in God that."

[7] E. omits: "and with those of humility."

[8] E.: "her convent."

[9] In the Spanish the subject is in the singular: P. Báñez inserted "the house", but crossed this out later.

[10] E. further adds: " I say this with a good conscience and I shall entreat it of God." As will be observed, she softens the expression greatly in V.

It seems very wrong, my daughters, that great houses should be built with the money of the poor; may God forbid that this should be done; let our houses be small and poor in every way.[1] Let us to some extent resemble our King, Who had no house save the porch in Bethlehem where He was born and the Cross on which He died. These were houses where little comfort could be found.[2] Those who erect large houses will no doubt have good reasons for doing so. *I do not utterly condemn them*: they are moved by various holy[3] intentions. But any corner is sufficient for thirteen poor women.[4] If grounds should be thought necessary, on account of the strictness of the enclosure, and also as an aid to prayer and devotion, *and because our miserable nature needs such things*, well and good; and let there be a few hermitages[5] in them in which the sisters may go to pray.[6] But as for a large ornate convent, with a lot of buildings—God preserve us from that![7] Always remember that these things will all fall down on the Day of Judgment, and who knows how soon that will be?[8]

It would hardly look well if the house of thirteen[9] poor women made a great noise when it fell, for those who are really poor must make no noise:[10] unless they[11] live a noiseless life people will never take pity on them. And how happy my sisters will be if they see someone freed from hell by means of the alms which he has given them; and this is quite possible, since they are strictly bound to offer continual prayer for persons who[12] give them food. It is also God's will that, although the food comes from Him,[13] we should thank the persons by whose means He gives it to us:[14] let there be no neglect of this.

I do not remember what I had begun to say, for I have strayed from my subject. But I think this must have been the Lord's will, for I never intended to write what I have said here.[15] May His Majesty always keep us in His hand so that we may never fall. Amen.

---

[1] T.: "let us be poor in every way and let our house be small."
[2] E. omits: "and the Cross . . . found."
[3] E. omits: "holy."
[4] T.: "for one [*fem.*] who is truly poor."
[5] St. Teresa liked to have hermitages in the grounds of her convents to give the nuns opportunity for solitude.
[6] E. abbreviates verbally.
[7] T., less dramatically: "But God preserve us from a large, etc."
[8] T.: "and we do not know if that will be soon."
[9] E.: "of twelve."
[10] E.: "for the poor never make a noise."
[11] E.: "unless the really poor."
[12] The MS. has: "for they are strictly bound, continually, since they". This has been corrected by P. García de Toledo to read as translated above. E. reads as in the text above except that it has "for *the souls of* persons."
[13] E.: "although it is He Who gives it to us."
[14] E.: "we should pray for those who give it to us on His behalf."
[15] E.: "to write this."

CHAPTER III

Continues the subject begun in the first chapter and persuades the sisters to busy themselves constantly in beseeching God to help those who work for the Church. Ends with an exclamatory prayer.

Let us now return to the principal reason for which the Lord has brought us together in this house, for which reason I am most desirous that we may be able to please His Majesty. Seeing how great are the evils of the present day and how no human strength will suffice to quench the fire kindled by these heretics[1] (though attempts have been made to organize opposition to them, as though such a great and rapidly spreading evil could be remedied by force of arms),[2] it seems to me that it is like a war in which the enemy has overrun the whole country, and the Lord of the country, hard pressed, retires into a city, which he causes to be well fortified, and whence from time to time he is able to attack. Those who are in the city[3] are picked men who can do more by themselves than they could do with the aid of many soldiers if they were cowards. Often this method gains the victory; or, if the garrison does not conquer, it is at least not conquered; for, as it contains no traitors, *but picked men*, it can be reduced only by hunger.[4] In our own conflict, however, we cannot be forced to surrender by hunger; we can die but we cannot be conquered.

Now why have I said this? So that you may understand, my sisters, that what we have to ask of God is that, in this little castle of ours, inhabited as it is by good Christians,[5] none of us may go over to the enemy. We must ask God, too, to make the captains in this castle or city—that is, the preachers and theologians—highly proficient in the way of the Lord. And as most of these are religious, we must pray that they may advance in perfection,[6] and in the fulfilment of their vocation, for this is very needful. For, as I have already said, it is the ecclesiastical and not the secular arm which must defend us.

---

[1] E.: "to quench this fire."

[2] T. omits the parenthetical clause and continues: "which is spreading so much, it seems to me like a war, etc."

[3] E. has "in the castle" here, but "city" just above.

[4] T. adds: "This hunger may be sufficient to kill them, but it will not lead them to be conquered."

[5] E. continues, after "Christians": "no traitor may rise up, but God may have [us] all in His hands, and also that the captains in this castle or city—that is, the preachers and theologians—may be highly proficient, etc."

[6] T.: "in religion."

And as we can do nothing by either of these means to help our King, let us strive to live in such a way that our prayers may be of avail to help these servants of God, who, at the cost of so much toil, have fortified themselves with learning and virtuous living and have laboured to help the Lord.[1]

You may ask why I emphasize this[2] so much and why I say we must help people who are better than ourselves. I will tell you, for I am not sure if you properly understand as yet how much we owe to the Lord for bringing us to a place where we are so free from business matters, occasions of sin and the society of worldly people. This is a very great favour and one which is not granted to the persons of whom I have been speaking, nor is it fitting that it should be granted to them; it would be less so now, indeed, than at any other time, for it is they who must strengthen the weak[3] and give courage to God's little ones. A fine thing it would be for soldiers if they lost their captains! These preachers and theologians have to live among men and associate with men and stay in palaces and sometimes even behave as people in palaces do[4] in outward matters. Do you think, my daughters, that it is an easy matter to have to do business with the world, to live in the world, to engage in the affairs of the world, and, as I have said, to live as worldly men do, and yet inwardly to be strangers to the world, and enemies of the world, like persons who are in exile—to be, in short, not men but angels? Yet unless these persons act thus, they neither deserve to bear the title of captain nor to be allowed by the Lord to leave their cells, for they would do more harm than good. This is no time for imperfections in those whose duty it is to teach.

And if these teachers are not inwardly fortified by realizing the great[5] importance of spurning everything beneath their feet and by being detached from things which come to an end on earth, and attached to things eternal, they will betray this defect in themselves, however much they may try to hide it.[6] For with whom are they dealing but with the world?[7] They need not fear: the world will not pardon them or fail to observe their imperfections. Of the good things they do many will pass unnoticed, or will even not be considered good at all;[8] but they need not fear that any evil or imperfect thing they do will be overlooked.

---

[1] E.: "and labours."
[2] E.: "why I charge this."
[3] E.: "strengthen people."
[4] This is the reading of E. V.: "as they do."
[5] F. omits: "great."
[6] E.: "however much they do."
[7] T. continues: "which never fails to observe their imperfections."
[8] E.: "or will even be considered bad."

I am amazed when I wonder from whom they learned about perfection, when, instead of practising it themselves (for they think they have no obligation to do that and have done quite enough by a reasonable observance of the Commandments),[1] they condemn others, and at times mistake virtue for indulgence. Do not think, then, that they need but little Divine favour in this great battle upon which they have entered; on the contrary, they need a great deal.

I beg you to try to live in such a way as to be worthy to obtain two things from God. First, that there may be many of these very learned and religious men who have the qualifications for their task which I have described; and that the Lord may prepare those who are not completely prepared already *and who lack anything*, for a single one who is perfect will do more than many who are not.[2] Secondly, that after they have entered upon this struggle, which, as I say, is not light, *but a very heavy one*, the Lord may have them in His hand so that they may be delivered from all the dangers[3] that are in the world, and, while sailing on this perilous sea, may shut their ears to the song of the sirens. If we can prevail with God in the smallest degree about this, we shall be fighting His battle even while living a cloistered life and I shall consider as well spent all the trouble to which I have gone in founding this retreat,[4] where I have also tried to ensure that this Rule of Our Lady and Empress shall be kept in its original perfection.[5]

Do not think that offering this petition continually[6] is useless. Some people think it a hardship not to be praying all the time for their own souls. Yet what better prayer could there be than this?[7] You may be worried because you think it will do nothing to lessen your pains in Purgatory, but actually praying in this way will relieve you of some of them and anything else that is left—well, let it remain. After all, what does it matter if I am in Purgatory until the Day of Judgment provided a single soul should be saved[8] through my prayer? And how much less does it matter if many souls profit by it and the Lord is honoured! Make no account of any pain which has an end if by means of it any greater service can be rendered to Him Who bore such pains

---

[1] E. adds: "as if they had not the obligation to please God."
[2] E.: "than many imperfect."
[3] E.: "from the dangers."
[4] *Lit.*: "making this corner." The reference is to St. Joseph's, Ávila.
[5] E.: "shall be kept as it began." "And Empress" is not found in E.
[6] E.: "always."
[7] E. continues: "If you think it is necessary for the lessening of the pains which you will have to suffer in Purgatory for your sins, praying so righteously does in fact lessen them, and what is left will have to remain."
[8] E.: "is saved."

for us. Always try to find out wherein lies the greatest perfection.[1] And for the love of the Lord I beg you to beseech His Majesty to hear us in this; I, miserable creature though I am, beseech this of His Majesty, since it is for His glory and the good of His Church, which are my only wishes.

It seems over-bold of me to think that I can do anything towards obtaining this. But I have confidence, my Lord, in these servants of Thine who are here, knowing that they neither desire nor strive after anything but to please Thee. For Thy sake they have left the little they possessed, wishing they had more so that they might serve Thee with it. Since Thou, my Creator, art not ungrateful, I do not think Thou wilt fail to do what they beseech of Thee,[2] for when Thou wert in the world, Lord,[3] Thou didst not despise women, but didst always help them and show them great compassion.[4] *Thou didst find more faith and no less love in them than in men, and one of them was Thy most sacred Mother, from whose merits we derive merit, and whose habit we wear, though our sins make us unworthy to do so.*[5] *We can do nothing in public that is of any use to Thee, nor dare we speak of some of the truths over which we weep in secret, lest Thou shouldst not hear this our just petition. Yet, Lord, I cannot believe this of Thy goodness and righteousness, for Thou art a righteous Judge, not like judges in the world, who, being, after all, men and sons of Adam, refuse to consider any woman's virtue as above suspicion. Yes, my King, but the day will come when all will be known. I am not speaking on my own account, for the whole world is already aware of my wickedness, and I am glad that it should become known; but, when I see what the times are like, I feel it is not right to repel spirits which are virtuous and brave, even though they be the spirits of women.*

Hear us not when we ask Thee for honours, endowments,[6] money, or anything that has to do with the world; but why shouldst Thou not hear us, Eternal Father, when we ask only for the honour of Thy Son, when we would forfeit a thousand honours and a thousand lives for Thy sake? Not for ourselves, Lord, for we do not deserve to be heard, but for the blood of Thy Son and for His merits.

---

[1] E. continues: "You must always treat [i.e., about spiritual matters] with learned men: I shall often ask you (to do this) and give you my reasons, for you must have reasons given you. What I now beg you to do is to beseech God (about this), and I, miserable creature, etc."
[2] E.: "Thou wilt give less than they beseech of Thee, but rather much more."
[3] E.: "Lord of my soul."
[4] The italicized lines which follow, and are in the nature of a digression, do not appear in V., and in E. they have been crossed out.
[5] Here follow two erased lines which are illegible but for the words "Thou didst honour the world". The exact sense of the following words ("We can . . . in secret") is affected by these illegible lines and must be considered uncertain.
[6] E. omits this word.

Oh, Eternal Father![1] Surely all these scourgings and insults and grievous tortures will not be forgotten. How, then, my Creator, can a heart so [merciful and] loving as Thine endure that an act which was performed by Thy Son in order to please Thee the more (for He loved Thee most deeply and Thou didst command Him to love us) should be treated as lightly as those heretics treat the Most Holy Sacrament to-day, in taking it from its resting-place when they destroy the churches? Could it be that [Thy Son and our Redeemer][2] had failed to do something to please Thee? No: He fulfilled everything. Was it not enough, Eternal Father, that while He lived He had no place to lay His head and had always to endure so many trials? Must they now deprive Him of the places[3] to which He can invite His friends,[4] seeing how weak we are and knowing[5] that those who have to labour need such food to sustain them? Had He not already more than sufficiently paid for the sin of Adam? Has this most loving Lamb to pay once more whenever we relapse into sin? Permit it not, my Emperor; let Thy Majesty be appeased; look not upon our sins but upon our redemption by Thy Most Sacred Son, upon His merits and upon those of His glorious Mother and of all the saints and martyrs who have died for Thee.

Alas, Lord, who is it that has dared to make this petition in the name of all? What a poor mediator am I, my daughters, to gain a hearing for you and to present your petition! When this Sovereign Judge sees how bold I am it may well move Him to anger, as would be both right and just. But behold, Lord, Thou art a God of mercy; have mercy upon this poor sinner, this miserable worm who is so bold with Thee. Behold my desires, my God, and the tears with which I beg this of Thee; forget my deeds, for Thy name's sake, and have pity upon all these souls who are being lost, and help Thy Church. Do not permit more harm to be wrought to Christendom, Lord; give light to this darkness.

For the love of the Lord, my sisters, I beg you[6] to commend this poor sinner[7] to His Majesty and to beseech Him to give her humility, as you are bound to do.[8] I do not charge you to

---

[1] T.: "Oh, our Lord!"
[2] V.: "that He." T. has "He left everything fulfilled" for "He fulfilled everything".
[3] *Lit.*: "of those." P. Báñez wrote in the margin "of the mansions" using the word which is thus translated in the titles of the seven main divisions of the *Interior Castle*. T. has: "of the houses."
[4] "And give them the precious food of His Body and Blood," adds T.
[5] T.: "which He wishes to give us because He sees how weak we are and knows."
[6] E.: "I beg all."
[7] *Lit.*: "poor little one." E.: "poor little daring one."
[8] E. omits the next two sentences and continues: "And if your prayers . . ."

pray particularly for kings and prelates of the Church, especially for our Bishop,[1] for I know that those of you now here are very careful about this and so I think it is needless for me to say more. Let those who are to come remember that, if they have a prelate who is holy, those under him will be holy too, and let them realize how important it is to bring him continually before the Lord. If your prayers and desires and disciplines and fasts are not performed for the intentions of which I have spoken, reflect [and believe] that you are not carrying out the work or fulfilling the object[2] for which the Lord has brought you here.

CHAPTER IV

Exhorts the nuns to keep their Rule and names three things which are important for the spiritual life. Describes the first of these three things, which is love of one's neighbour, and speaks of the harm which can be done by individual friendships.

Now, daughters, you have looked at the great enterprise which we are trying to carry out. What kind of persons shall we have to be if we are not to be considered over-bold in the eyes of God and of the world?[3] It is clear that we need to labour hard and it will be a great help to us if we have sublime thoughts so that we may strive to make our actions sublime also. If we endeavour to observe our Rule and Constitutions in the fullest sense, and with great care, I hope in the Lord that He will grant our requests.[4] I am not asking anything new of you, my daughters—only that we should hold to our profession, which, as it is our vocation, we are bound to do, although there are many ways of holding to it.

Our Primitive Rule[5] tells us to pray without ceasing. Provided we do this with all possible care (and it is the most important

---

[1] Don Álvaro de Mendoza, then Bishop of Ávila. T. adds: "and for this Order of the most sacred Virgin and the other (Orders)." But this interpolation breaks the sense.

[2] E. ends: ". . . the object for which you came together here, and may the Lord never allow this to depart from your memory, for His Majesty's own sake."

[3] E. begins: "Now you have looked at the great enterprise which you are going to carry out for the sake of your Superior and your Bishop (for he is your Superior), and for that of the Order, as is to be understood from what has been said, for all is for the good of the Church, and this is of obligation. Well, as I say, when a person has had the boldness to carry out such an enterprise, what kind of person will she have to be if she is not to be considered over-bold in the eyes of God and of the world?"

[4] T.: "our prayers."

[5] E.: "The beginning of our Rule."

thing of all) we shall not fail to observe the fasts, disciplines and periods of silence which the Order commands; for, as you know, if prayer is to be genuine it must be reinforced with these things—prayer cannot be accompanied by self-indulgence.

It is about prayer that you have asked me to say something to you. As an acknowledgment of what I shall say, I beg you to read frequently and with a good will what I have said about it thus far, and to put this into practice. Before speaking of the interior life—that is, of prayer—I shall speak of certain things which those who attempt to walk along the way of prayer[1] must of necessity practise. So necessary are these that, even though not greatly given to contemplation, people who have them can advance a long way in the Lord's service, while, unless they have them, they cannot possibly be great contemplatives, and, if they think they are, they are much mistaken. May the Lord help me in this task and teach me[2] what I must say, so that it may be to His glory. Amen.

Do not suppose, my friends and sisters,[3] that I am going to charge you to do a great many things; may it please the Lord that[4] we do the things which our holy Fathers ordained and practised and by doing which they merited that name.[5] It would be wrong of us to look for any other way or to learn from anyone else. There are only three things which I will explain at some length and which are taken from our Constitution itself. It is essential that we should understand how very important they are to us in helping us to preserve that peace, both inward and outward, which the Lord so earnestly recommended to us. One of these is love for each other; the second, detachment from all created things; the third, true humility, which, although I put it last, is the most important of the three and embraces all the rest.[6]

With regard to the first—namely, love for each other[7]—this is of very great importance; for there is nothing, however annoying, that cannot easily[8] be borne by those who love each other, and anything which causes annoyance must be quite exceptional.

---

[1] E.: "to practise prayer."
[2] E.: "and tell me."
[3] T.: "my sisters."
[4] In T. St. Teresa has substituted for this: "I only desire that."
[5] E.: "the things which our Fathers duly ordained in the Rule and Constitutions, through which virtue is altogether fulfilled." It omits the following sentence ("It would . . . else.")
[6] Here, in both E. and V., the chapter ends; but T. has a marginal note in St. Teresa's hand: "There should not be a new chapter here." All the editions have observed this injunction. The heading to this chapter given above comprises those prefixed in V to Chapters IV and V.
[7] E.: "namely, great love."
[8] E.: "quickly."

If this commandment were kept in the world, as it should be, I believe it would take us a long way towards the keeping of the rest; but, what with having too much love for each other or too little, we never manage to keep it perfectly. It may seem that for us to have too much love for each other cannot be wrong, but I do not think anyone who had not been an eye-witness of it[1] would believe how much evil and how many imperfections can result from this. The devil sets many snares here which the consciences of those who aim only in a rough-and-ready way at pleasing God seldom observe—indeed, they think they are acting virtuously —but those who are aiming at perfection understand what they are very well: little by little they deprive the will of the strength which it needs if it is to employ itself wholly in the love of God.

This is even more applicable to women than to men and the harm which it does to community life is very serious. One result of it is that all the nuns do not love each other equally: some injury done to a friend is resented; a nun desires to have something to give to her friend or tries to make time for talking to her, and often her object in doing this is to tell her how fond she is of her, and other irrelevant things,[2] rather than how much she loves God. These intimate friendships are seldom calculated[3] to make for the love of God; I am more inclined to believe that the devil initiates them so as to create factions within religious Orders.[4] When a friendship has for its object the service of His Majesty,[5] it at once becomes clear that the will is devoid of passion and indeed is helping to conquer other passions.

Where a convent is large I should like to see many friendships of that type; but in this house, where there are not, and can never be, more than thirteen nuns,[6] all must be friends with each other, love each other, be fond of each other and help each other. For the love of the Lord, refrain from making individual friendships, however holy, for even among brothers and sisters such things are apt to be poisonous and I can see no advantage in them;[7] when they are between other relatives,[8] they are much

---

[1] T. adds: "as I have elsewhere." But this reads awkwardly in the Spanish and it is not found in the Évora edition.

[2] E. omits: "and other irrelevant things."

[3] *Lit.*: "are seldom ordered in such a way as."

[4] E.: "These intimate friendships are never ordered by the devil for the greater service of the Lord, but for the creation of factions within religious Orders."

[5] E.: "its object to help us to serve Him."

[6] E.: "of that type. In Saint Joseph's, where there are not, and can never be, more than thirteen nuns, (there must be) none of them. All, etc." T.: "in this house, where there are few (of us), all, etc."

[7] "Consider the case of Joseph," adds E., parenthetically: the reference is presumably to the treatment of Joseph by his brothers, recorded in Genesis xxxvii.

[8] "Other" is not in the Spanish. "When they are only between", is the reading of T., which also omits: "and become a pest."

more dangerous and become a pest. Believe me, sisters, though I may seem to you extreme in this, great perfection and great peace come of doing what I say and many occasions of sin may be avoided by those who are not very strong. If our will becomes inclined more to one person than to another (this cannot be helped, because it is natural—it often leads us to love[1] the person who has the most faults if she is the most richly endowed by nature), we must exercise a firm restraint on ourselves and not allow ourselves to be conquered by our affection. Let us love the virtues and inward goodness, and let us always apply ourselves and take care to avoid attaching importance to externals.[2]

Let us not allow our will to be the slave of any, sisters, save of Him Who bought it with His blood. Otherwise, before we know where we are, we shall find ourselves trapped, and unable to move. God help me![3] The puerilities which result from this are innumerable. And, because they are so trivial that only those who see how bad they are will realize and believe it, there is no point in speaking of them here except to say that they are wrong in anyone, and, in a prioress, pestilential.

In checking these preferences[4] we must be strictly on the alert from the moment that such a friendship begins[5] and we must proceed diligently and lovingly rather than severely. One effective precaution against this is that the sisters should not be together except at the prescribed hours, and that they should follow our present custom in not talking with one another, or being alone together, as is laid down in the Rule:[6] each one should be alone in her cell. There must be no work-room at Saint Joseph's;[7] for, although it is a praiseworthy custom to have one, it is easier to keep silence if one is alone,[8] and getting

---

[1] T.: "because our nature often leads us to love."

[2] T. omits: "apply ourselves and" and ends: "to be successful in not attaching importance to externals."

[3] E. omits: "God help me!" and continues: "The puerilities which result from this are, I think, innumerable. Lest those who know nothing about women's weaknesses should learn about them and come to realize (how bad they are), I will not describe them in detail. But it used sometimes really to amaze me to see them; for, by the goodness of God, and perhaps because I was so much worse in other respects, I never had many attachments of this kind. But, as I say, I often observed them in others, and I am afraid they exist in the majority of religious houses, for I have seen them in some, and I know that, wherever they occur, they are the worst thing for strict religious observance and perfection, and in a prioress they would be pestilential. This has already been said."

[4] T.: "In putting from us these private (affections)."

[5] E.: "But in removing these preferences, we must be on the alert from the moment that we become aware of them."

[6] E.: "in our Constitution."

[7] E adds: "to bring them together."

[8] E. continues: "and solitude is a great thing when one has got used to it, and it is a great blessing for persons given to prayer to get used to it. Since prayer must be the foundation on which this house is built, and it is for this purpose that we have

used to solitude is a great help to prayer. Since prayer must be the foundation on which this house is built, it is necessary for us to learn to like whatever gives us the greatest help in it.

Returning to the question of our love for one another, it seems quite unnecessary to commend this to you, for where are there people so brutish as not to love one another when they live together, are continually in one another's company,[1] indulge in no conversation, association or recreation with any outside their house and believe that God loves us and that they themselves love God since they are leaving everything for His Majesty? More especially is this so as virtue always attracts love, and I hope in God that, with the help of His Majesty, there will always be love in the sisters of this house. It seems to me, therefore, that there is no reason for me to commend this to you any further.

With regard to the nature of this mutual love and what is meant by the virtuous love which I wish you to have here, and how we shall know when we have this virtue, which is a very great one, since Our Lord[2] has so strongly commended it to us and so straitly enjoined it upon His Apostles—about all this I should like to say a little now as well as my lack of skill will allow me; if you find this explained in great detail in other books, take no notice of what I am saying here, for it may be that I do not understand what I am talking about.[3]

There are two kinds of love which I am describing.[4] The one is *purely* spiritual, and apparently has nothing to do with sensuality or the tenderness of our nature, either of which might stain its purity.[5] The other is also spiritual, but mingled with it are our sensuality and weakness;[6] yet it is a worthy love, which, as between relatives and friends, seems lawful. Of this I have already said sufficient.

It is of the first kind of spiritual love that I would now speak. It is untainted by any sort of passion, for such a thing would completely spoil its harmony. If it leads us to treat virtuous people, especially confessors, with moderation and discretion, it is profitable; but, if the confessor is seen to be tending in any way towards vanity, he should be regarded with grave suspicion,

---

come together, we must learn, more than anything else, to like whatever gives us the greatest profit in it."

[1] T.: "for I think people will love one another if they are together in one company."
[2] E.: "this exceeding great virtue, for it is a very great one, since Christ, our Master and Lord, etc."
[3] E. adds: "unless the Lord gives me light."
[4] E.: "which I now want to describe."
[5] T. has "its charity." E. omits: "either of which might stain its purity."
[6] Here begins the passage reproduced in the Appendix to Chapter IV (pp. 21-2, below).

and, in such a case, conversation with him, however edifying, should be avoided, and the sister should make her confession briefly and say nothing more. It would be best for her, indeed, to tell the superior that she does not get on with him and go elsewhere; this is the safest way, providing it can be done without injuring his reputation.[1]

In such cases, and in other difficulties with which the devil might ensnare us, so that we have no idea where to turn, the safest thing will be for the sister to try to speak with some learned person; if necessary, permission to do this can be given her, and she can make her confession to him and act in the matter as he directs her. For he cannot fail to give her some good advice about it, without which she might go very far astray. How often people stray through not taking advice, especially when there is a risk of doing someone harm! The course that must on no account be followed is to do nothing at all; for, when the devil begins to make trouble in this way, he will do a great deal of harm if he is not stopped quickly; the plan I have suggested, then, of trying to consult another confessor is the safest one if it is practicable, and I hope in the Lord that it will be so.[2]

Reflect upon the great importance of this, for it is a dangerous matter, and can be a veritable hell, and a source of harm to everyone. I advise you not to wait until a great deal of harm has been done but to take every possible step that you can think of and stop the trouble at the outset;[3] this you may do with a good conscience. But I hope in the Lord that He will not allow persons who are to spend their lives in prayer[4] to have any attachment save to one who is a great servant of God;[5] and I am quite certain He will not, unless they have no love for prayer and for striving after perfection in the way we try to do here. For, unless they see that he understands their language and likes to speak to them of God,[6] they cannot possibly love him, as he is not like them. If he is such a person, he will have very few opportunities of doing any harm, and, unless he is very simple,[7] he will not seek to disturb his own peace of mind and that of the servants of God.[8]

As I have begun to speak about this, I will repeat that the

[1] *Honra.* Cf. Vol. I, p. 14, n. 2, above.
[2] "And . . . be so" is crossed out in T.
[3] E. is more emphatic: "at the very outset" (*muy al principio*).
[4] E.: "to spend so much time in prayer."
[5] E.: "who has a great attachment to God and is very virtuous."
[6] E.: "no love for prayer. For if they have such love and see that he does not understand their language or like to speak to them of God."
[7] E.: "exceedingly simple."
[8] E. adds: "(in a place) where their desires can have so little satisfaction, or even none at all."

devil can do a great deal of harm here,[1] which will long remain undiscovered, and thus the soul that is striving after perfection can be gradually ruined[2] without knowing how.[3] For, if a confessor gives occasion for vanity through being vain himself, he will be very tolerant with it in [the consciences of] others. May God, for His Majesty's own sake, deliver us from things of this kind. It would be enough to unsettle all the nuns[4] if their consciences and their confessor[5] should give them exactly opposite advice; and, if it is insisted that they must have one confessor only, they will not know what to do, nor how to pacify their minds, since the very person who should be calming them and helping them is the source of the harm. In some places there must be a great deal of trouble of this kind: I always feel very sorry about it and so you must not be surprised if I attach great importance to your understanding this danger.[6]

APPENDIX TO CHAPTER IV

The following variant reading of the Escorial Manuscript seems too important to be relegated to a footnote. It occurs at p. 19 (cf. n. 6), and deals, as will be seen, with the qualifications and character of the confessor. Many editors substitute it in their text for the corresponding passage in V. As will be seen, however, by comparing it with pp. 19–20, it is not a pure addition; we therefore reproduce it separately.

The important thing is that these two kinds of mutual love should be untainted by any sort of passion, for such a thing would completely spoil this harmony. If we exercise this love, of which I have spoken, with moderation and discretion, it is wholly meritorious, because what seems to us sensuality is turned into virtue. But the two may be so closely intertwined with one another that it is sometimes impossible to distinguish them, especially where a confessor is concerned. For if persons who are practising prayer find that their confessor is a holy man and understands the way they behave, they become greatly attached to him. And then forthwith the devil lets loose upon them a whole battery of scruples which produce a terrible disturbance within the soul, this being what he is aiming at. In particular, if the confessor is guiding such persons to greater perfection,

---

[1] E.: "can do the very greatest harm in convents so strictly enclosed."
[2] E.: "is gradually ruined."
[3] E.: "how or by what means."
[4] E.: "It is enough to unsettle all the sisters."
[5] T. omits: "and their confessor."
[6] The last sentence in E. is more definite and personal: "I have seen much trouble of this kind in religious houses, though not in my own, and these cases have moved me to great compassion." T. ends: "if I take great care about some of these things."

they become so depressed that they will go so far as to leave him for another and yet another, only to be tormented by the same temptation every time.

What you can do here is not to let your minds dwell upon whether you like your confessor or not, but just to like him if you feel so inclined. For, if we grow fond of people who are kind to our bodies, why should we not love those who are always striving and toiling to help our souls? Actually, if my confessor is a holy and spiritual man and I see that he is taking great pains for the benefit of my soul, I think it will be a real help to my progress for me to like him. For so weak are we that such affection sometimes helps us a great deal to undertake very great things in God's service.

But, if your confessor is not such a person as I have described, there is a possibility of danger, and for him to know that you like him may do the greatest harm, most of all in houses where the nuns are very strictly enclosed. And as it is a difficult thing to get to know which confessors are good, great care and caution are necessary. The best advice to give would be that you should see he has no idea of your affection for him and is not told about it. But the devil is so active that this is not practicable: you feel as if this is the only thing you have to confess and imagine you are obliged to confess it. For this reason I should like you to think that your affection for him is of no importance and to take no more notice of it.

Follow this advice if you find that everything your confessor says to you profits your soul; if you neither see nor hear him indulge in any vanity (and such things are always noticed except by one who is wilfully dull) and if you know him to be a God-fearing man, do not be distressed over any temptation about being too fond of him, and the devil will then grow tired and stop tempting you. But if you notice that the confessor is tending in any way towards vanity in what he says to you, you should regard him with grave suspicion; in such a case conversation with him, even about prayer and about God, should be avoided—the sister should make her confession briefly and say nothing more. It would be best for her to tell the Mother (Superior) that she does not get on with him and go elsewhere. This is the safest way if it is practicable, and I hope in God that it will be, and that you will do all you possibly can to have no relations with him, though this may be very painful for you.

Reflect upon the great importance of this, etc. (p. 20).

CHAPTER V

Continues speaking of confessors. Explains why it is important that they should be learned men.

May the Lord grant, for His Majesty's own sake, that no one in this house shall experience the trials that have been described, or find herself oppressed in this way in soul and body. I hope the superior will never be so intimate with the confessor that no one will dare to say anything about him to her or about her to him. For this will tempt *unfortunate* penitents to leave very grave sins unconfessed because they will feel uncomfortable about confessing them. God help me! What trouble the devil can make here[1] and how dearly people have to pay for their *miserable* worries and concern about honour! If they consult only one confessor, they think they are acting in the interests of their Order and for the *greater* honour of their convent: and that is the way the devil lays his snares for souls when he can find no other. If the *poor* sisters ask for another confessor, they are told that this would mean the *complete* end of all discipline in the convent; and, if he is not a priest of their Order, even though he be a saint,[2] they are led to believe that they would be disgracing their entire Order[3] by consulting him.

Give great praise to God, daughters, for this liberty that you have, for, though there are not a great many priests whom you can consult, there are a few, other than your ordinary confessors, who can give you light upon everything. I beg every superior,[4] for the love of the Lord, to allow a holy liberty here: let the Bishop[5] or Provincial be approached for leave for the sisters to go from time to time beyond their ordinary confessors and talk about their souls with persons of learning, especially if the confessors, though good men, have no learning; for learning is a great help in giving light upon everything. It should be possible to find a number of people who combine both learning and spirituality, and the more favours the Lord grants you in prayer, the more needful is it that your good works and your prayers should have a sure foundation.[6]

You already know that the first stone of this foundation must be a good conscience and that you must make every effort to free yourselves from even[7] venial sins and follow the greatest possible perfection. You might suppose that any confessor would

---

[1] E.: "How many souls the devil must catch in this way!"
[2] E.: "even if he were a Saint Jerome."
[3] So E. V. has, more vaguely, "disgracing them."
[4] *Lit.*: "I beg her who is in the position of a senior (*mayor*)" *Mayor* was the title given to the superior at the Incarnation, Ávila, and many other convents in Spain, at that time.
[5] In T. St. Teresa alters "Bishop" to "Prelate"—no doubt because St. Joseph's was, in August 1577, transferred from the jurisdiction of the Bishop to that of the Order.
[6] E.: "I beg every superior, for the love of God, to try always to consult persons of learning and to see that her nuns do so. God preserve them from being directed entirely by one person, if he be not a learned man, however spiritual they may think him, or he may in fact be; for, the more favours the Lord grants them in prayer, the more needful is it that their devotions, and their prayers, and all their good works, should have a sure foundation."
[7] E. omits: "even."

know this, but you would be wrong:[1] it happened that I had to go about matters of conscience[2] to a man who had taken a complete course in theology; and he did me a great deal of mischief by telling me[3] that certain things were of no importance.[4] I know that he had no intention of deceiving me, or any reason for doing so: it was simply that he knew no better. And in addition to this instance I have met with two or three similar ones.[5]

Everything depends on our having[6] true light to keep the law of God perfectly. This is a firm basis for prayer; but without this strong foundation the whole building will go awry.[7] In making their confessions, then, the nuns must be free to discuss spiritual matters with such persons as I have described. I will even go farther and say that they should sometimes do as I have said even if their confessor has all these good qualities, for he may quite easily make mistakes and it is a pity that he should be the cause of their going astray. They must try, however, never to act in any way against obedience, for they will find ways of getting all the help they need: it is of great importance to them that they should, and so they must make every possible effort to do so.[8]

All this that I have said has to do with the superior. Since there are no consolations but spiritual ones to be had here, I would beg her once again to see[9] that the sisters get these consolations,[10] for God leads [His handmaidens] by different ways and it is impossible that one confessor should be acquainted with them all.[11] I assure you that, if your souls are as they ought to be,

---

[1] E.: "be quite wrong." In the margin of V. P. García de Toledo has written: "This is well (said), for there are some spiritual masters who, in order not to err, condemn all the spirits there are as demons, and they err more in (doing) this, as they quench the spirits of the Lord, as the Apostle says." T. has: "It seems that every confessor knows this, but it is not so, because it happened, etc."

[2] E. omits: "about matters of conscience."

[3] E.: "by making me think."

[4] E.: "were not wrong."

[5] E. omits this sentence.

[6] In T. St. Teresa substituted for this: "It is a great thing to have."

[7] T. has "every building" for "the whole building". E. continues: "so it is necessary for the nuns to consult people of spirituality and learning. If they cannot find a confessor who has both, they may from time to time go to others; and, if by any chance they have been instructed to make their confessions only to one priest, let them talk about their souls to such persons as I have described without making their confessions to them. I will even go farther, etc."

[8] E.: "it is of great importance that every possible effort should be made to secure the good of a soul—much more the good of a great many."

[9] E. reads "let her see" for "I would beg her once again to see".

[10] E.: "the sisters are not without consolations."

[11] E. continues: "So (the superior) must see that they obtain consolations from such persons as these. She need not fear that there will be any lack of such persons if the nuns are what they ought to be, even though they are poor. As God maintains them and gives food to their bodies, which is less necessary, He will provide them with persons who will be most willing to give light to their souls, and thus this evil of which, as has been said, I am so much afraid, will be remedied."

there is no lack of holy persons who will be glad to advise and console you, even though you are poor. For He Who sustains our bodies will awaken and encourage someone to give light to our souls, and thus this evil of which I am so much afraid will be remedied. For if the devil should tempt the confessor, with the result that he leads you astray on any point of doctrine,[1] he will go slowly and be more careful about all he is doing when he knows that the penitent is also consulting others.[2]

If the devil is prevented from entering convents in this way, I hope in God that he will never get into this house at all; so, for love of the Lord, I beg whoever is Bishop[3] to allow the sisters this liberty and not to withdraw it so long as the confessors are persons both of learning and of good lives, a fact which will soon come to be known in a little place like this.[4]

In what I have said here, I am speaking from experience of things that I have seen and heard *in many convents* and gathered from conversation with learned and holy people[5] who have considered what is most fitting for this house, so that it may advance in perfection. Among the perils which exist everywhere, for as long as life lasts, we shall find that this is the least. No vicar should be free to go in and out of the convent, and no confessor should have this freedom either.[6] They are there to watch over the recollectedness and good living of the house and its progress in both interior and exterior matters,[7] so that they may report to the superior whenever needful, but they are never to be superiors themselves. *As I say, excellent reasons have been found why, everything considered, this is the best course, and why, if any priest hears confessions frequently, it should be the chaplain; but, if the nuns think it necessary, they can make their confessions to such persons as have been*

---

[1] E.: "tempt the confessor to any vanity."

[2] E.: "he will go slowly, and the devil will be prevented from entering convents in this way—I hope in God he will never get into this house at all."

[3] "Bishop or Provincial," says T.; and someone, probably the author, has crossed out "Bishop or", no doubt for the reason given on p. 23, n. 5 above.

[4] E. begins: "So, for love . . ." and, after "liberty", continues: "being sure that, with the help of God, he will have good subjects; and he must never withdraw it so long as the confessors are persons both of learning and of good lives, a fact which, in such a little place, will soon come to be known. He should not forbid them to make their confessions occasionally to such persons, and to discuss their method of prayer with them, even if they have their own confessors, for I know that for many reasons this is a good thing, and the harm it may cause is nothing by comparison with the grave, secret and almost irremediable harm which will result from the contrary procedure. For the life of a religious house is such that what is good soon disappears, unless it is most carefully preserved, whereas if once anything bad gets a foothold, it is most difficult to eradicate: in details of imperfection custom very soon becomes habit and second nature."

[5] E.: "with prudent and spiritual people."

[6] E.: "should have power to go in and out of the convent or to give orders, nor should a confessor give orders."

[7] E.: "over the good living of the house and its interior and exterior recollectedness."

described, provided the superior is informed of it, and the prioress is such that the Bishop can trust her discretion. As there are very few nuns here, this will not take up much time.

This is our present practice; and it is not followed merely on my advice.[1] Our present Bishop, Don Álvaro de Mendoza, under whose obedience we live (since for many reasons we have not been placed under the jurisdiction of the Order), is greatly attached to holiness and the religious life, and, besides being of most noble extraction, is a great servant of God. He is always very glad to help this house in every way, and to this very end he brought together persons of learning, spirituality and experience, and this decision was then come to. It will be only right that future superiors should conform to his opinion, since it has been decided on by such good men, and after so many prayers to the Lord that He would enlighten them in every possible way, which, so far as we can at present see, He has certainly done. May the Lord be pleased to promote the advancement of this to His greater glory. Amen.

CHAPTER VI

Returns to the subject of perfect love, already begun.

I have digressed a great deal but no one will blame me who understands the importance of what has been said.[2] Let us now return to the love which it is good[3] [and lawful] for us to feel. This I have described as purely[4] spiritual; I am not sure if I know what I am talking about, but it seems to me that there is no need to speak much of it, since so few, I fear, possess it; let any one of you to whom the Lord has given it praise Him fervently, for she

---

[1] T. goes on: "but on that of the prelate whom we now have", and omits the passage about Don Álvaro de Mendoza, which follows. E. continues and ends the chapter thus: "This decision was made after much prayer by many people, including myself, miserable though I am, and they were persons of great learning and understanding and prayer, so I hope in the Lord it is for the best.

"It seemed so to the Lord Bishop, who is now Don Álvaro de Mendoza, a person very glad to further the well-being of this house, both spiritual and temporal. He considered it very carefully, as he desires the house to make still further progress in what is good, and I believe God will not allow it to go astray since the Bishop is in His place and desires nothing but His greater glory. I think future superiors, with the help of God, will not wish to oppose a thing which has been so carefully considered and is for many reasons of such great importance."

[2] E.: "but what has been said is of the greatest importance if this is not lost through its having been said by me."

[3] E.: "is good and lawful, my sisters." V. also adds "and lawful", but the two words have been crossed out by the author. T. restores them.

[4] E.: "wholly."

must be a person of the greatest perfection. It is about this that I now wish to write.[1] Perhaps what I say may be of some profit, for if you look at a virtue you desire it and try to gain it, and so become attached to it.[2]

God grant that I may be able to understand this, and even more that I may be able to describe it, for I am not sure that I know when love is spiritual and when there is sensuality mingled with it, or how to begin speaking about it. I am like one who hears a person speaking in the distance and, *though he can hear that he is speaking,* cannot distinguish what he is saying. It is just like that with me: sometimes I cannot understand what I am saying, yet the Lord is pleased to enable me to say it well. If at other times what I say is [ridiculous and] nonsensical, it is only natural for me to go completely astray.

Now it seems to me that, when God has brought someone to a clear knowledge of the world, and of its nature, and of the fact that another world (*or, let us say, another kingdom*) exists, and that there is a great difference between the one and the other, the one being eternal and the other only a dream; and of what it is to love the Creator and what to love the creature (this must be discovered by experience, for it is a very different matter from merely thinking about it and believing it);[3] when one understands by sight and experience[4] what can be gained by the one practice and lost by the other, and what the Creator is and what the creature, and many other things which the Lord teaches to those who are willing to devote themselves to being taught by Him in prayer, or whom His Majesty wishes to teach[5]—then one loves[6] very differently from those of us who have not advanced thus far.

It may be, sisters, that you think it irrelevant for me to treat of this, and you may say that you already know everything that I have said.[7] God grant that this may be so, and that you may indeed know it in the only way which has any meaning,[8] and that it may be graven upon your inmost being, *and that you may never for a moment depart from it*; for, if you know it, you will see

---

[1] E. reads: "Let anyone who has it praise God", and adds: "and He will be well praised. (Such a person) must be of the greatest perfection. Perhaps we shall profit by it. Let us say something (about it)."
[2] E. renders this sentence as in the last note and then continues: "But it is this other (love) which we must most often feel, and, though I say there is something sensual about it, this may not be so, for I am not sure that I know when love is sensual, and when spiritual, or how to begin speaking about it."
[3] E. omits the parenthetical clause.
[4] T. omits: "and experience."
[5] E.: "teaches truly and clearly to those whom His Majesty wishes to teach."
[6] T.: "then these souls love each other."
[7] E.: "that you think this some nonsense of mine and say that you all know it."
[8] E.: "in the way it should be known."

that I am telling nothing but the truth when I say that he whom the Lord brings thus far possesses this love.[1] Those whom God brings to this state are, *I think*, generous and royal souls; they are not content with loving anything so miserable as these bodies, however beautiful they be[2] and however numerous the graces they possess. If the sight of the body gives them pleasure they praise the Creator, but as for dwelling upon it *for more than just a moment*—no! When I use that phrase "dwelling upon it", I refer to having love for such things. If they had such love, they would think they were loving something insubstantial and were conceiving fondness for a shadow; they would feel shame for themselves and would not have the effrontery to tell God that they love Him,[3] without feeling great confusion.

You will answer me that such persons cannot love or repay the affection shown to them by others.[4] Certainly they care little about having this affection. They may from time to time experience a natural and momentary pleasure at being loved; yet, as soon as they return to their normal condition, they realize that such pleasure is folly save when the persons concerned can benefit their souls, either by instruction or by prayer. Any other kind of affection wearies them, for they know it can bring them no profit and may well do them harm; none the less they are grateful for it and recompense it by commending those who love them to God. They take this affection as something for which those who love them lay the responsibility upon the Lord,[5] from Whom, since they can see nothing lovable in themselves, they suppose the love comes, and think that others love them because God loves them; and so they leave His Majesty to recompense them for this and beg Him to do so, thus freeing themselves and feeling they have no more responsibility. When I ponder it carefully, I sometimes think this desire for affection is sheer blindness, except when, as I say, it relates to persons who can lead us to do good so that we may gain blessings in perfection.

It should be noted here that, when we desire anyone's affection, we always seek it because of some interest, profit or pleasure of our own. Those who are perfect, however, have trodden all these things beneath their feet—[and have despised] the blessings which may come to them in this world, and its pleasures and

---

[1] T. adds: "which I shall describe."
[2] T. interpolates, parenthetically: "I mean love which subjects and binds."
[3] T. ends the sentence here.
[4] E. continues: "For by what are they attracted save by what they see? They (do) love much more, and with greater passion, with a more genuine love and with a love which brings more profit. This, in a word, is love, and those other base affections have robbed it of the name. They do love what they see, etc." (p. 29, below).
[5] T.: "Taking this affection as if those who loved them were laying the responsibility (for doing so) upon the Lord."

delights—in such a way that, even if they wanted to, so to say, they could not love anything outside God, or unless it had to do with God. What profit, then, can come to them from being loved themselves?[1]

When this truth is put to them, they laugh at the distress which had been assailing them in the past as to whether their affection was being returned or no. Of course, however pure our affection may be, it is quite natural for us to wish it to be returned. But, when we come to evaluate the return of affection, we realize that it is insubstantial, like a thing of straw, as light as air and easily carried away by the wind. For, however dearly we have been loved, what is there that remains to us? Such persons, then, except for the advantage that the affection may bring to their souls (because they realize that our nature is such that we soon tire of life without love), care nothing whether they are loved or not. Do you think that such persons will love none and delight in none save God? No; they will love others much[2] more than they did, with a more genuine love, with greater passion and with a love which brings more profit; that, in a word, is what love really is. And such souls are always much fonder of giving than of receiving, even in their relations with the Creator Himself. This [holy affection], I say, merits the name of love, which name has been usurped from it by those other base affections.

Do you ask, again, by what they are attracted if they do not love things they see? They do love what they see[3] and they are greatly attracted by what they hear; but the things which they see are everlasting. If they love anyone[4] they immediately look right beyond the body (*on which, as I say, they cannot dwell*), fix their eyes on the soul[5] and see what there is to be loved in that. If there is nothing, but they see any suggestion or inclination which shows them that, if they dig deep, they will find gold within this mine, they think nothing of the labour of digging, since they have love. There is nothing that suggests itself to them which they will not willingly do for the good of that soul since they desire their love for it to be lasting,[6] and they know quite well that that is impossible unless the loved one has certain good qualities and a great love for God. I really mean that it is impossible, however great their obligations and even if that soul were to die for love of them[7] and do them all the kind actions

---

[1] "By lovers of the world," adds T.
[2] T. omits: "much."
[3] E. picks up the thread here (cf. p. 28, n. 4, above).
[4] E.: "If they love a friend."
[5] E.: "pass to the soul."
[6] E.: "they desire to love it."
[7] E.: "I really mean that it is impossible, even if that soul were to die for them."

in its power; even had it all the natural graces joined in one, their wills would not have strength enough to love it nor would they remain fixed upon it. They know and have learned and experienced the worth of all this; no false dice can deceive them.[1] They see that they are not in unison with that soul and that their love for it cannot possibly last; for, unless that soul keeps the law of God, their love will end with life[2]—they know that unless it loves Him they will go to different places.

Those into whose souls the Lord has already infused true wisdom do not esteem this love, which lasts only on earth, at more than its true worth—if, indeed, at so much. Those who like to take pleasure in[3] worldly things, delights, honours and riches, will account it of some worth if their friend is rich and able to afford them pastime *and pleasure* and recreation; but those who already hate all this[4] will care little or nothing[5] for such things. If they have any love for such a person, then, it will be a passion[6] that he may love God so as to be loved by Him;[7] for, as I say, they know that no other kind of affection but this can last,[8] and that this kind will cost them dear, for which reason they do all they possibly can for their friend's profit;[9] they would lose a thousand lives to bring him a small blessing. Oh, precious love, forever imitating the Captain of Love, Jesus, our Good!

CHAPTER VII

Treats of the same subject of spiritual love and gives certain counsels for gaining it.

It is strange to see how impassioned this love is; how many tears, penances and prayers it costs; how careful is the loving soul to commend the object of its affection to all who it thinks may prevail with God and to ask them to intercede with Him for it; and how constant is its longing, so that it cannot be happy

---

[1] E.: "yet their wills would not have strength enough (to love it), for they are wise wills, which know by experience the worth of all this, and no false dice can deceive them."

[2] E.: "cannot possibly last, and they fear that their enjoyment will end with life."

[3] T.: "Those who seek pleasures (consisting) in."

[4] E.: "but those who have this already beneath their feet."

[5] E. omits: "or nothing."

[6] In T. the author has emended "passion" to "affection". T. also omits: "that he may love God".

[7] The words "that he may love God" are interlinear.

[8] E.: "for, as I say, they know that, if (their love) is not (like) this, they will have to forsake it."

[9] E. adds, for greater emphasis, the redundant phrase: "as far as in them lies."

unless it sees that its loved one is making progress.[1] If that soul seems to have advanced,[2] and is then seen to fall some way back, her friend seems to have no more pleasure in life: she neither eats nor sleeps, is never free from this fear and is always afraid[3] that the soul whom she loves so much may be lost, and that the two may be parted for ever. She cares nothing for[4] physical death, but she will not suffer herself to be attached to something which a puff of wind may carry away so that she is unable to retain her hold upon it. This, as I have said, is love without any degree whatsoever of self-interest;[5] all that this soul wishes and desires is to see[6] the soul [it loves] enriched with blessings from Heaven. This is love, quite unlike our ill-starred earthly affections[7]—to say nothing of illicit affections, from which may God keep us free.

These last affections are a very hell, and it is needless for us to weary ourselves by saying how evil they are, for the least of the evils which they bring are terrible beyond exaggeration. There is no need for us ever to take such things upon our lips, sisters, *or even to think of them,* or to remember that they exist anywhere in the world; you must never listen to anyone speaking of such affections, either in jest or in earnest, nor allow them to be mentioned or discussed in your presence. No good can come from our doing this and it might do us harm even to hear them mentioned.[8] But with regard to the lawful affections which, as I have said, we may have for each other, or for relatives and friends, it is different. Our whole desire is that they should not die:[9] if their heads ache, our souls seem to ache too; if we see them in distress, we are unable (as people say) to sit still under it;[10] and so on.

This is not so with spiritual affection. Although the weakness of our nature may at first allow us to feel something of all this,

---

[1] E. omits: "unless . . . progress."
[2] E.: "to be advancing."
[3] "It must not be understood that it is with interior disquiet," adds T., parenthetically.
[4] E.: "She cares not two farthings (*maravedis*) for."
[5] E. omits: "as I have said" and "self-". T. omits: "any degree whatsoever of."
[6] E.: "all its interest consists in seeing."
[7] E.: "This, in short, is love which grows ever more like the love which Christ had for us. It deserves the name of love and is quite different from our petty, ill-starred, frivolous earthly affections."
[8] E.: "There is no profit in this, nor is there any reason (for us to do it) and it might do us harm."
[9] T.: "Let our desire be such that it will not rob us of our peace and liberty, so that, if their heads ache, etc."
[10] *Lit.*: "There remains, as people say, no patience"; but, as the phrase "as people say" (which E. omits) suggests that this was a popular phrase, I have translated rather more freely and picturesquely. T. has (after "ache too"): "and it upsets us, and so on."

our reason soon begins to reflect whether our friend's trials are not good for her, and to wonder if they are making her richer in virtue and how she is bearing them, and then we shall ask God to give her patience so that they may win her merit. If we see that she is being patient, we feel[1] no distress—indeed, we are gladdened and consoled. If all the merit and gain which suffering is capable of producing[2] could be made over to her, we should still prefer suffering her trial ourselves to seeing her suffer it, but we are not worried or disquieted.[3]

I repeat once more that this love is a similitude and copy of that which was borne for us by the good Lover, Jesus. It is for that reason that it brings us such immense benefits, for it makes us embrace[4] every kind of suffering, so that others, without having to endure the suffering, may gain its advantages. The recipients of this friendship, then, profit greatly, but their friends should realize that either this intercourse—I mean, this exclusive friendship—must come to an end or that they must prevail upon Our Lord that their friend may walk in the same way as themselves, as Saint Monica prevailed with Him for Saint Augustine. Their heart does not allow them to practise duplicity: if they see their friend straying from the road, or committing any faults, they will speak to her about it; they cannot allow themselves to do anything else. And if after this the loved one does not amend, they will not flatter her or hide anything from her. Either, then, she will amend or their friendship will cease; for otherwise they would be unable to endure it, nor is it in fact endurable. It would mean continual war for both parties. A person may be indifferent to all other people in the world and not worry whether they are serving God or not, since the person she has to worry about is herself.[5] But she cannot take this attitude with her friends: nothing they do can be hidden from her; she sees the smallest mote in them. This, I repeat, is a very heavy cross for her to bear.[6]

---

[1] E.: "it causes us."
[2] E.: "if all the merit and the good which remain."
[3] E.: "killed" [i.e., "worried to death"].
[4] T.: "want to embrace."
[5] T. omits: "and not worry . . . herself."
[6] In E. this paragraph reads: "I repeat that this is love without (self-)interest, like that which Christ bore us. It is for that reason that it brings so much advantage to those who reach this state, for they would like to do nothing but undertake every kind of suffering so that others might profit and rejoice in its benefits. Those, then, who have this friendship profit greatly, for it is evident that they would like to teach by deeds rather than by words, although they may not actually do so. I say they may not do so, meaning that there may be things which they cannot do; in so far as they are able, they would like to be always working for those they love and bringing them profit. Their heart does not allow them to practise duplicity or to see their friends lack anything if they think such a thing will be for their good. Very often

Happy the souls that are loved by such as these! Happy the day on which they came to know them! O my Lord, wilt Thou not grant me the favour of giving me many who have such love for me? Truly, Lord, I would rather have this than be loved by all the kings and lords of the world—and rightly so, for such friends use every means in their power to make us lords of the whole world and to have all that is in it subject to us. When you make the acquaintance of any such persons, sisters, the Mother Prioress should employ every possible effort to keep you in touch with them. Love such persons as much as you like. There can be very few of them, but none the less it is the Lord's will that their goodness should be known. When one of you is striving after perfection, she will at once be told that she has no need to know such people—that it is enough for her to have God. But to get to know God's friends is a very good way of "having" Him; as I have discovered by experience, it is most helpful. For, under the Lord, I owe it to such persons that I am not in hell; I was always very fond of asking them to commend me to God, and so I prevailed upon them to do so.

Let us now return to what we were saying. It is this kind of love which I should like us to have; at first it may not be perfect but the Lord will make it increasingly so.[1] Let us begin with the methods of obtaining it. At first it may be mingled with emotion,[2] but this, as a rule, will do no harm. It is sometimes good and necessary[3] for us to show emotion in our love, and also to feel it,[4]

---

they do not even stop to think of this, so earnestly do they desire to see them very rich, though they do not tell them so. What roundabout paths they take to gain their end! They may be indifferent to everyone else in the world and not worry if they are serving God or not, for they have only to worry about themselves. But nothing that their friends do can be hidden from them: they see the smallest mote in them."

[1] E.: "us to have, but at first this will not be possible."
[2] *Ternura. Lit.*: "tenderness."
[3] E.: "It is quite good and in part necessary."
[4] E. continues: "and to be distressed by any of the weaknesses and trials of a sister, for sometimes people are troubled at mere nothings which others would laugh at. But we must not be dismayed, for the devil may well have worked at this with all his might, much more so than he did to make you distressed at great trials and griefs. To take your recreation with your sisters, when they are taking theirs, though you may not be enjoying it, is real charity, for all considerate treatment of them will grow into perfect love. I had been wanting to say something of love which is less perfect, but I find no reason for thinking that it will be good for us to have any of it among us in this house: if our love is real, as I say, it will all be referred to its source, which is the love that I have described.

"I had thought of saying a great deal about that other love, but, now that I come to the point, I do not think it can possibly exist here, with the kind of life that we lead. For that reason I will add nothing to what I have said, hoping in God that, although you may not always be quite perfect, there will be no suggestion in this house of your loving each other in any other way than the best. It is a very good thing for us to take compassion on one another's needs, though we must show no lack of discretion. I mean, lack of discretion in anything contrary to obedience—that is to say, against the prioress's orders. Though you may think these orders harsh ones, and say so to yourself privately, do not tell anyone about it, etc." (p. 34, below).

and to be distressed by some of our sisters' trials and weaknesses, however trivial they may be. For on one occasion as much distress may be caused by quite a small matter as would be caused on another by some great trial, and there are people whose nature it is to be very much cast down by small things. If you are not like this, do not neglect to have compassion on others; it may be that Our Lord wishes to spare us these sufferings and will give us sufferings of another kind which will seem heavy to us, though to the person already mentioned they may seem light. In these matters, then, we must not judge others by ourselves, nor think of ourselves as we have been at some time when, perhaps without any effort on our part, the Lord has made us stronger than they; let us think of what we were like at the times when we have been weakest.

Note the importance of this advice for those of us who would learn to sympathize with our neighbours' trials, however trivial these may be. It is especially important for such souls as have been described, for, desiring trials as they do, they make light of them all. They must therefore try hard to recall what they were like when they were weak, and reflect that, if they are no longer so, it is not due to themselves. For otherwise, little by little, the devil could easily cool our charity toward our neighbours and make us think that what is really a failing on our part is perfection. In every respect we must be careful and alert, for the devil never slumbers. And the nearer we are to perfection, the more careful we must be, since his temptations are then much more cunning because there are no others that he dare send us; and if, as I say, we are not cautious, the harm is done before we realize it. In short, we must always watch and pray, for there is no better way than prayer of revealing these hidden wiles of the devil and making him declare his presence.

Contrive always, even if you do not care for it, to take part in your sisters' necessary recreation and to do so for the whole of the allotted time, for all considerate treatment of them is a part of perfect love.[1] It is a very good thing for us to take compassion on each others' needs. See that you show no lack of discretion about things which are contrary to obedience. Though privately you may think the prioress' orders harsh ones, do not allow this to be noticed or tell anyone about it (except that you may speak of it, with all humility, to the prioress herself), for if you did so you would be doing a great deal of harm. Get to know what are the things in your sisters which you should be sorry to see and those about which you should sympathize with them; and always show your grief at any notorious fault which you may see in

[1] T. omits: "perfect."

one of them. It is a good proof and test of our love if we can bear with such faults[1] and not be shocked by them. Others, in their turn, will bear with your[2] faults, which, if you include those of which you are not aware, must be much more numerous. Often commend to God any sister who is at fault and strive for your own part to practise the virtue which is the opposite of her fault with great perfection. Make determined efforts to do this[3] so that you may teach your sister by your deeds what perhaps she could never learn by words nor gain by punishment.[4]

The habit of performing some conspicuously virtuous action through seeing it performed by another is one which very easily takes root. This is good advice: do not forget it.[5] Oh, how true and genuine will be the love of a sister who can bring profit to everyone by sacrificing her own profit to that of the rest! She will make a great advance in each of the virtues and keep her Rule with great perfection. This will be a much truer kind of friendship than one which uses every possible loving expression (such as are not used, and must not be used,[6] in this house): "My life!" "My love!" "My darling!"[7] and suchlike things, one or another of which people are always saying. Let such endearing words be kept for your Spouse,[8] for you will be so often and so much alone with Him[9] that you will want to make use of them all, and this His Majesty permits you. If you use them among yourselves they will not move the Lord so much; and, quite apart from that, there is no reason why you should do so. They are very effeminate; and I should not like you to be that, or even to appear to be that, in any way, my daughters;[10] I want you to be strong men. If you do all that is in you, the Lord will make you so manly that men themselves will be amazed at you. And how easy is this for His Majesty, Who made us out of nothing at all![11]

It is also a very clear sign of love to try[12] to spare others household

---

[1] E.. "the things which you should be sorry to see in your sisters, and always show your grief at any fault. This is love, when we can bear with such faults."
[2] E. has "my", and uses the first person to the end of the sentence.
[3] E. continues: "so that, through your being with her, (your sister) cannot fail to learn better than by suffering all the reproofs and punishments that might be inflicted upon her."
[4] Thus T. V. reads, more awkwardly: "nor gain, nor punishment."
[5] E. omits: "The habit . . . forget it."
[6] E. omits: "and must not be used."
[7] *Lit.*: "My life!" "My soul!" "My good!" E. omits the last of these phrases. T. ends the sentence at "suchlike things".
[8] E.: "for the Lord."
[9] E.: "for you will be with Him so many times a day, and sometimes so much alone."
[10] E.: "like my daughters to appear in any way to be that." T. reads: "I should not like you to be that, in any way, my daughters, but to appear to be men."
[11] *Nonada.* T. has simply *nada* ("nothing").
[12] T. omits: "to try."

work by taking it upon oneself and also to rejoice and give great praise to the Lord if you see[1] any increase in their virtues. All such things, quite apart from the intrinsic good they bring, add greatly to the peace and concord which we have among ourselves, as, through the goodness of God, we can now see by experience. May His Majesty be pleased ever to increase it, for it would be terrible if it did not exist, and very awkward if, when there are so few of us, we got on badly together. May God forbid that.[2]

If one of you should be cross with another because of some hasty word, the matter must at once be put right and you must betake yourselves to earnest prayer.[3] The same applies to the harbouring of any grudge, or to party strife, or to the desire to be greatest, or to any nice point concerning your honour. (My blood seems to run cold,[4] as I write[5] this, at the very idea that this can ever happen,[6] but I know it is the chief trouble in convents.) If it should happen to you, consider yourselves lost. Just reflect and realize that you have driven your Spouse from His home:[7] He will have to go and seek another abode, since you are driving Him from His own house. Cry aloud to His Majesty and try to put things right; and if frequent confessions and communions do not mend them, you may well fear that there is some Judas among you.

For the love of God, let the prioress be most careful not to allow this to occur. She must put a stop to it from the very outset,[8] *and, if love will not suffice, she must use heavy punishments,* for here we have the whole of the mischief and the remedy. If you gather that any of the nuns is making trouble, see that she is sent to some other

---

[1] T.: "if He gives."
[2] T. omits: "May God forbid that." E. reads: "It is also a sign of love, as has been said, to try to spare others work, and for each to take it herself, and to rejoice in the increase in another's virtues as though they were her own. In many other ways (the sisters) will know if they have this virtue, which is very great, for in it resides all mutual peace, which is so necessary in religious houses. I hope in the Lord we shall always have it in this convent, for, if we did not have it, it would be a terrible thing for there to be so few of us getting on badly together. May God forbid that. But all the good that has been begun here by the Lord's hand would have to be lost before so great an evil could happen."
[3] E.: "put right. If it is not, and you see that (the trouble) is getting worse, you must betake yourselves to earnest prayer."
[4] E. adds: "so to speak."
[5] T.: "as I say and write."
[6] E. omits: "at . . . happen."
[7] E. reads: "driven your Lord," and omits: "He will . . . own house." In T. a page is missing here which comprises the rest of the chapter. P. Silverio inserts the corresponding passage from the Evora edition, which differs considerably from both E. and V.
[8] E. reads: "careful to put a stop to this quickly", and later omits: "for here we have the whole of the mischief and the remedy." The sense of this phrase, which in the Spanish has "or" for "and," is not very clear.

convent and God will provide them with a dowry for her. Drive away this plague; cut off the branches as well as you can; and, if that is not sufficient, pull up the roots. If you cannot do this, shut up anyone who is guilty of such things and forbid her to leave her cell; far better this than that all the nuns should catch so incurable a plague. Oh, what a great evil is this! God deliver us from a convent into which it enters: I would rather our convent caught fire and we were all burned alive. As this is so important I think I shall say a little more about it elsewhere, so I will not write at greater length here,[1] *except to say that, provided they treat each other equally, I would rather that the nuns showed a tender and affectionate love and regard for each other, even though there is less perfection in this than in the love I have described, than that there were a single note of discord to be heard among them. May the Lord forbid this, for His own sake. Amen.*

CHAPTER VIII

Treats of the great benefit of self-detachment, both interior and exterior, from all things created.

Let us now come to the detachment which we must practise, for if this is carried out perfectly it includes everything else. I say "it includes everything else" because, if we care nothing for any created things, but embrace the Creator alone, His Majesty will infuse the virtues into us in such a way that, provided we labour to the best of our abilities day by day, we shall not have to wage war much longer, for the Lord will take our defence in hand against the devils and against the whole world. Do you suppose, daughters, that it is a small benefit to obtain for ourselves this blessing of giving ourselves wholly to Him,[2] and keeping nothing for ourselves? Since, as I say, all blessings are in Him, let us give Him hearty praise, sisters, for having brought us together here,[3] where we are occupied in this alone. I do not know why I am saying this, when all of you here are capable of teaching me, for I confess that, in this important respect, I am not as perfect as I should like to be and as I know I ought to be;[4] and I must say the same about all the virtues and about all that I am dealing with here, for it is easier to write of such things than to practise

---

[1] E.: "As I shall deal with this again elsewhere, I say no more here."
[2] *Lit.: de darnos todas a Él todo:* "giving ourselves wholly to Him wholly." But E. reads *al todo*, "to the All", which, though more like St. John of the Cross's phraseology than St. Teresa's, may represent more exactly the idea in her mind.
[3] E.: "let us give many thanks to the Lord, Who brought us together here."
[4] T. continues: "because it is easier, etc."

them. I may not even be able to write of them effectively, for sometimes ability to do this comes only from experience—[that is to say, if I have any success, it must be because] I explain the nature of these virtues by describing the contraries of the qualities I myself possess.[1]

As far as exterior matters are concerned, you know how completely cut off we are from everything.[2] *Oh, my Creator and Lord! When have I merited so great an honour? Thou seemest to have searched everywhere for means of drawing nearer to us. May it please Thy goodness that we lose not this through our own fault.* Oh, sisters, for the love of God, try to realize what a great favour the Lord has bestowed on those of us whom He has brought here.[3] Let each of you apply this to herself, since there are only twelve of us[4] and His Majesty has been pleased for you to be one. How many people—*what a multitude of people!*—do I know who are better than myself and would gladly take this place of mine, yet the Lord has granted it to me who so ill deserve it! Blessed be Thou, my God, and let *the angels and* all created things praise Thee, for I can no more repay this favour than all the others Thou hast shown me. It was a wonderful thing to give me the vocation to be a nun; but I have been so wicked, Lord, that Thou couldst not trust me. In a place where there were many good women living together my wickedness would not *perhaps* have been noticed right down to the end of my life: *I should have concealed it, as I did for so many years.* So Thou didst bring me[5] here, where, as there are so few of us that it would seem impossible for it to remain unnoticed, Thou dost remove occasions of sin from me so that I may walk the more carefully.[6] There is no excuse for me, then, O Lord, I confess it, and so I have need of Thy mercy, that Thou mayest pardon me.

Remember, my sisters, that if we are not good we are much more to blame than others.[7] What I earnestly beg of you is that anyone who knows she will be unable to follow our customs will say so [before she is professed]: there are other convents in which the Lord is

[1] E.: "I confess that, in this important respect, I am the most imperfect; but, as you order me to do so, I will touch upon a few things that occur to me."

[2] E.: "how completely cut off (we are): it seems as if in bringing (*traer*) us here it is the Lord's will to cut us off from everything, so that His Majesty should get us (*llegarnos*) here without hindrance." In all the editions this sentence closes the preceding paragraph but it seems more properly to belong to this.

[3] E.: "try to realize fully the greatness of this favour."

[4] The thirteenth was St. Teresa. See Vol. I, p. 260, above.

[5] E.: "So Thou bringest me."

[6] E.: "from me, so that on the Day of Judgment I may have no room for excuse if I should not do as I ought." E. also omits the last sentence of this paragraph.

[7] E. continues: "and so I earnestly charge anyone who, after making the attempt, finds that she has not sufficient spiritual strength to observe what is observed here, to say so; there are other convents, in which perhaps the Lord is served much better. She should not remain here, etc."

also well served and she should not remain here and disturb these few of us whom His Majesty has brought together *for His service.* In other convents nuns are free to have the pleasure of seeing their relatives, whereas here, if relatives are ever admitted, it is only for their own pleasure. A nun who [very much] wishes[1] to see her relatives in order to please herself, *and does not get tired of them after the second visit*, must, unless they are spiritual persons *and do her soul some good*, consider herself imperfect and realize that she is neither detached nor healthy, and will have no freedom of spirit or perfect peace. She needs a physician[2]—and I consider that if this desire does not leave her, and she is not cured, she is not intended for this house.[3]

The best remedy, I think, is that she should not see her relatives again until she feels free in spirit and has obtained this freedom from God by many prayers. When she looks upon such visits as crosses, let her receive them by all means, for then they will do the visitors good and herself no harm.[4] *But if she is fond of the visitors, if their troubles are a great distress to her and if she delights in listening to the stories which they tell her about the world, she may be sure that she will do herself harm and do them no good.*

CHAPTER IX

Treats of the great blessing that shunning their relatives brings to those who have left the world and shows how by doing so they will find truer friends.

Oh, if we religious understood what harm we get from having so much to do with our relatives,[5] how we should shun them! I do not see what pleasure they can give us, or how, quite apart from *the harm they do us as touching* our obligations to God, they can bring us any peace or tranquillity.[6] For we cannot take part in their recreations, as it is not lawful for us to do so;[7] and, though we can certainly share their troubles, we can never help weeping for them,[8] sometimes more than they do themselves. If they

---

[1] E.: "needs."
[2] E. continues: "and I know of no other better cure than never to see them again until she feels free in spirit and has gained (this) for herself. When she looks, etc."
[3] T. substitutes for this clause: "her spirituality will not grow very much."
[4] E.: "by all means, in order to do the visitors good, as she certainly will."
[5] E. has: "comes to us from this", but in the next sentence reads "the relatives" where the text has "they".
[6] T.: "what pleasure or tranquillity they can give us."
[7] E. omits: "as it . . . do so."
[8] E. abbreviates: "and we can never help weeping for their troubles."

bring us any bodily comforts, there is no doubt that our[1] spiritual life *and our poor souls* will pay for it. From this you are [quite] free here; for, as you have everything in common and none of you may accept any private gift, all the alms given us being held by the community, you are under no obligation to entertain your relatives in return for what they give you, since, as you know, the Lord will provide for us all in common.[2]

I am astounded at the harm which intercourse with our relatives does us: I do not think anyone who had not experience of it would believe it.[3] And how our religious Orders nowadays, *or most of them, at any rate,* seem to be forgetting about perfection, *though all, or most, of the saints wrote about it*![4] I do not know how much of the world we really leave when we say that we are leaving everything for God's sake, if we do not withdraw ourselves from[5] the chief thing of all—namely, our kinsfolk. The matter has reached such a pitch that some people think, when religious are not fond of their relatives and do not see much of them, it shows a want of virtue in them. And they not only assert this but allege reasons for it.

In this house, daughters,[6] we must be most careful to commend our relatives to God,[7] for that is only right. For the rest, we must keep them out of our minds as much as we can, as it is natural that our desires should be attached to them more than to other people.[8] My own relatives were very fond of me, or so they used to say, and I was so fond of them that I would not let them forget me.[9] But I have learned, by my own experience and by that of others, that it is God's servants who have helped me in trouble;[10] my relatives, apart from my parents, have helped me very little. Parents are different, for they very rarely fail to help their children, and it is right that when they need our comfort we should not refuse it them: if we find our main purpose[11] is not

---

[1] St. Teresa substitutes for this, in T.: "So that, if they bring us any physical pleasure, our, etc."
[2] E.: "and no one (of you) may have anything private, you have no need of gifts from relatives."
[3] E.: "I should not believe it if I had not experience (of it)."
[4] T. simplifies farther even than V.: "And how our religious Orders have forgotten about perfection!"
[5] E.: "do not leave."
[6] E.: "my daughter."
[7] E. adds the not very lucid phrase: "after what has been said touching His Church"—meaning, presumably, "after praying for the Church". In T. the sentence reads: "In this house, daughters, we must care about our relatives only in order to commend them to God."
[8] E. omits: "as . . . people."
[9] E. omits: "and I . . . forget me."
[10] T. omits: "it is God's . . . in trouble," reading: "that my relatives, etc."
[11] E.: "if we find our soul." In T., the clause "if . . . so doing" is crossed out.

harmed by our so doing we can give it them and yet be completely detached; and this also applies to brothers and sisters.[1]

Believe me, sisters,[2] if you serve God as you should, you will find no better relatives[3] than those [of His servants] whom His Majesty sends you. I know this is so,[4] and, if you keep on as you are doing *here*, and realize that by doing otherwise you will be failing[5] your true Friend and Spouse,[6] you may be sure that you will very soon gain this freedom. Then you will be able to trust those who love you for His sake alone more than all your relatives, and they will not fail you, so that you will find parents and brothers and sisters where you had never expected to find them. For these help us and look for their reward only from God; those who look for rewards from us soon grow tired of helping us when they see that we are poor and can do nothing for them. This cannot be taken as a generalization, but it is the most usual thing to happen in the world, for it is the world all over! If anyone tells you otherwise, and says it is a virtue to do such things,[7] do not believe him. I should have to write at great length, *in view of my lack of skill and my imperfection*, if I were to tell you of all the harm that comes from it;[8] as others have written about it who know what they are talking about better than I, what I have said will suffice. If, imperfect as I am, I have been able to grasp as much as this, how much better will those who are perfect do so!

All the advice which the saints give us about fleeing[9] from the world is, of course, good. Believe me, then, attachment to our relatives is, as I have said, the thing which sticks to us most closely and is hardest to get rid of. People are right, therefore, when they flee from their own part of the country[10]—if it helps them, I mean, for I do not think we are helped so much by fleeing from any place in a physical sense as by resolutely embracing the good Jesus, Our Lord, with the soul. Just as we find every-

---

[1] E. omits: "and this . . . sisters."
[2] E.: "friends" [*amigas*, fem.].
[3] E.: "friends" [*amigos*, masc. or com.].
[4] E. omits: "I know this is so."
[5] T.: "displeasing."
[6] E.: "Friend, Christ."
[7] E. omits: "Then you will . . . all over!" and continues: "If anyone tells you that the rest is virtue."
[8] E. continues, and ends the paragraph, thus: "How much more would (it be explained by) those who are different [i.e., more skilful than I]. In many places, as I have said, you will find it written: most books treat of nothing else but of how good it is to flee from the world." E. also omits: "All . . . good" from the next paragraph.
[9] T.: "about withdrawing."
[10] *De sus tierras*. The phrase will also bear the interpretation: "from their own countries."

thing in Him, so for His sake we forget everything.[1] Still, it is a great help, until we have learned this truth, to keep apart from our kinsfolk; later on, it may be that the Lord will wish us to see them again, so that what used to give us pleasure may be a cross to us.[2]

CHAPTER X

Teaches that detachment from the things aforementioned is insufficient if we are not detached from our own selves and that this virtue and humility go together.

Once we have detached ourselves from the world, and from our kinsfolk, and are cloistered here, in the conditions already described,[3] it must look as if we have done everything and there is nothing left with which we have to contend. But, oh, my sisters,[4] do not feel secure and fall asleep, or you will be like a man who goes to bed quite peacefully,[5] after bolting all his doors for fear of thieves, when the thieves are already in the house. And you know[6] there is no worse thief *than one who lives in the house.* We ourselves are always the same;[7] unless we take great care and each of us looks well to it that she renounces her self-will, which is the most important business of all,[8] there will be many things to deprive us of the holy freedom of spirit *which our souls seek in order to soar to their Maker unburdened by the leaden weight of the earth.*

It will be a great help towards this if we keep constantly in our thoughts[9] the vanity of all things and the rapidity with which they pass away, so that we may withdraw our affections from things which are so trivial[10] and fix them upon what will never come to an end.[11] This may seem a poor kind of help but it will

---

[1] T. adds: "that we [*lit.* "it"—i.e., the soul] had here [i.e., on earth]."
[2] E.: "see them again, so as to give us a cross."
[3] E.: "Once we have detached ourselves from this, and taken great pains to do so, in view of its great importance—you should consider how important it is—and are cloistered here, without possessing anything."
[4] E.: "my daughters."
[5] E.: "who remains (at home) quite peacefully."
[6] E.: "And have you not heard that . . . ?"
[7] The sense of this passage, especially without the phrase from E. which V. omits, is not very clear. T. remodels thus: "You know there is no worse thief for the perfection of the soul than the love of ourselves; for unless, etc."
[8] E.: "and each of us looks well to herself, which is the chief thing that she has to do."
[9] E.: "if we keep a very constant care concerning."
[10] E.: "from everything."
[11] E.: "what is to last for ever."

have the effect of greatly fortifying the soul. With regard to small things, we must be very careful, as soon as we begin to grow fond of them, to withdraw our thoughts from them and turn them to God.[1] His Majesty will help us to do this. He has granted us the great favour of providing that, in this house, most of it is done already; *but it remains for us to become detached from our own selves* and it is a hard thing to withdraw from ourselves and oppose ourselves, because we are very close to ourselves and love ourselves very dearly.[2]

It is here that true humility can enter,[3] for this virtue and that of detachment from self, I think, always[4] go together. They are two sisters, who are inseparable. These are not the kinsfolk whom I counsel[5] you to avoid: no, you must embrace them, and love them, and never be seen without them. Oh, how sovereign are these virtues, mistresses of all created things, empresses of the world, our deliverers from all the snares and entanglements laid by the devil, so dearly loved by our Teacher, Christ,[6] Who was never for a moment without them! He that possesses them can safely go out and fight all the united forces of hell and the whole world and its temptations.[7] Let him fear none, for his is the kingdom of the Heavens. There is none whom he need fear, for he cares nothing if he loses everything, nor does he count this as loss: his sole fear is that he may displease his God and he begs Him to nourish[8] these virtues within him lest he lose them through any fault of his own.

These virtues, it is true, have the property of hiding themselves from one who possesses them, in such a way that he never sees them nor can believe that he has any of them, even if he be told so. But he esteems them so much that he is for ever trying to obtain them, and thus he perfects them in himself more and more. And those who possess them soon make the fact clear, even against their will, to any with whom they have intercourse. But how inappropriate it is for a person like myself to begin to praise humility and mortification,[9] when these virtues are so highly praised by the King of Glory—a praise exemplified in

---

[1] E.: "to think no more of them, but turn our thoughts to God."

[2] E. continues, after the italicized phrase: "This retiring is hard, for we are very close to ourselves and are very fond of each other."

[3] Here, in the margin, is written: "Humility and mortification, very great virtues."

[4] T. omits "always."

[5] E.: "I tell."

[6] E. omits: "Christ." T. has: "our Lord Jesus Christ", and ends the sentence here.

[7] E. adds: "and against the flesh", but these words have been crossed out, probably by St. Teresa herself.

[8] E.: "There is none whom he need fear, but he must beg God to nourish." E. begins the next paragraph at: "But how inappropriate . . ."

[9] E. adds, redundantly: "or mortification and humility."

all the trials He suffered.[1] It is to possess these virtues, then, my daughters,[2] that you must labour if you would leave the land of Egypt, for, when you have obtained them, you will also obtain the manna; all things will taste well to you; and, however much the world may dislike their savour,[3] to you they will be sweet.

The first thing, then, that we have to do, *and that at once*, is to rid ourselves of love for this body of ours—and some of us pamper our natures so much that this will cause us no little labour, *while others* are so concerned about their health that the trouble these things give us (this is especially so of *poor* nuns, but it applies to others as well)[4] is amazing. Some of us, however, seem to think that we embraced the religious life for no other reason than to keep ourselves alive[5] and each nun does all she can to that end. In this house, as a matter of fact, there is very little chance for us to act on such a principle, but I should be sorry if we even wanted to. Resolve, sisters,[6] that it is to die for Christ, and not to practise self-indulgence for Christ, that you have come here. The devil tells us that self-indulgence is necessary if we are to carry out and keep the Rule of our Order, and so many of us, forsooth, try to keep our Rule by looking after our health[7] that we die without having kept it for as long as a month—perhaps even for a day. I really do not know what we are coming to.

No one need be afraid of our committing[8] excesses here, by any chance—for as soon as we do any penances our confessors begin to fear that we shall kill ourselves with them.[9] We are so horrified at our own possible excesses—if only we were as conscientious about everything else! Those who tend to the opposite extreme will, I know, not mind[10] my saying this, nor shall I mind if they say I am judging others by myself, for they will be quite right.[11] *I believe—indeed, I am sure—that more nuns are of my way of thinking than are offended by me because they do just the opposite.* My own belief is that it is for this reason that the Lord is pleased to make us such weakly creatures; at least He has shown me great

---

[1] T.: "in all His trials."
[2] E.: "my sisters."
[3] E.: "however bad they may be in the eyes of the world."
[4] E.: "the trouble these two things give us."
[5] *Lit.*: "to contrive not to die." But the reading of E. ("to think that we came to the convent for no other reason than to serve our bodies and look after them") suggests that this is what is meant.
[6] E.: "my daughters."
[7] E.: "try to keep [i.e., indulge] ourselves in order to keep it [i.e., our Rule]."
[8] E.: "that nuns will commit." In T. St. Teresa has substituted for the opening words of the paragraph: "It is certain that we shall not commit."
[9] E.: "nor must our confessors be afraid of this and at once start thinking that we shall kill ourselves with penances."
[10] E.: "must not mind."
[11] E. omits: "for they will be quite right."

mercy in making me so; for, as I was sure to be self-indulgent in any case, He was pleased to provide me with an excuse for this. It is really amusing to see how[1] some people torture themselves about it, when the real reason lies in themselves; sometimes they get a desire[2] to do penances, as one might say, without rhyme or reason; they go on doing them for a couple of days; and then the devil puts it into their heads that they have been doing themselves harm and so he makes them afraid of penances, after which they dare not do even those that the Order requires—they have tried them once![3] They[4] do not keep the smallest points in the Rule, such as silence, which is quite incapable of harming us. Hardly have we begun to imagine that our heads are aching[5] than we stay away from choir, though that would not kill us either. *One day we are absent because we had a headache some time ago; another day, because our head has just been aching again; and on the next three days in case it should ache once more.*[6] Then we want to invent penances of our own, with the result that we do neither the one thing nor the other. Sometimes there is very little the matter with us, yet we think that it should dispense us from all our obligations and that if we ask to be excused from them we are doing all we need.[7]

But why, you will say, does the Prioress excuse us?[8] Perhaps she would not if she knew what was going on inside us; but *she sees one of you wailing about a mere nothing as if your heart were breaking, and you come and ask her to excuse you from keeping the whole of your Rule, saying it is a matter of great necessity, and, when there is any substance in what you say,*[9] there is always a physician at hand to confirm it[10] *or some friend or relative weeping at your side. Sometimes the poor Prioress sees that your request is excessive, but* what can she do? She feels a scruple if she thinks she has been lacking in charity and she would rather the fault were yours than hers: *she thinks, too, that it would be unjust of her to judge you harshly.*

[1] T. alters *donosa* ["amusing"] to *dañosa* and reads: "It is harmful when."
[2] E.: "a frenzy."
[3] E.: "and so—no more penances, not even those that the Order requires: they have tried them once!"
[4] I follow E. here: V. has "We".
[5] So E. V. has: "Hardly have our heads ached."
[6] E. ends the paragraph here.
[7] T. had: "if we comply with (the demands of) obedience", for which St. Teresa substituted, in her own hand: "if we ask the superior (*fem.*) to excuse us from them."
[8] E. reads: "You will say, friends, that the superior (*mayor*: see p. 23, n. 4, above) should not allow it," and omits the following "perhaps".
[9] I follow E. here. V. omits the italicized phrase as far as "breaking" and then reads: "you tell her about it and say it is necessary, and there is always a physician at hand, etc." E. is more picturesque and trenchant throughout the latter part of this chapter: the Saint evidently wrote it with specific incidents in mind.
[10] E.: "to confirm the account you give."

Oh, God help me! That there should be complaining like this among nuns! May He forgive me for saying so, but I am afraid it has become quite a habit. I happened to observe this incident once myself: a nun began complaining about her headaches and she went on complaining to me for a long time. In the end I made enquiries and found she had no headache whatever, but was suffering from some pain or other elsewhere.

These are things which may sometimes happen and I put them down here so that you may guard against them; for if once the devil begins to frighten us about losing our health, we shall never get anywhere. The Lord give us light so that we may act rightly in everything! Amen.

CHAPTER XI

Continues to treat of mortification and describes how it may be attained in times of sickness.

These continual moanings which we make about trifling ailments, my sisters, seem to me a sign of imperfection:[1] if you can bear a thing, say nothing about it. When the ailment is serious, it proclaims itself; that is quite another kind of moaning, which draws attention to itself immediately. Remember, there are only a few of you, and if one of you gets into this habit she will worry all the rest—that is, assuming you love each other and there is charity among you. On the other hand, if one of you is really ill, she should say so and take the necessary remedies; and, if you have got rid of your self-love, you will so much regret having to indulge yourselves in any way that there will be no fear of your doing so unnecessarily or of your making[2] a moan without proper cause.[3] When such a reason exists, it would be much worse to say nothing about it than to allow[4] yourselves unnecessary indulgence, and it would be very wrong if everybody were not sorry for you.

However, I am quite sure that where there is *prayer and* charity among you, and your numbers are so small *that you will be aware of each other's needs*,[5] there will never be any lack of care in your

---

[1] E.: "This constant talking and moaning and whining as if we were ill, my sisters, seems to me a sign of great imperfection. Do not do this, for the love of God, if you can avoid it."

[2] T.: "that you will do so unnecessarily or make."

[3] E., which shows slight variations of detail from V. in the preceding sentence, continues: "When such a reason exists, it would be very bad to say nothing about it, and much worse if everybody were not sorry for you."

[4] T.: "it would be a very good thing to say so and much better than to allow."

[5] T.: "However, where there is charity and your numbers are so small."

being looked after.¹ Do not think of complaining about the weaknesses² and minor ailments from which women suffer, for the devil sometimes makes you imagine them. They come and go; and unless you get rid of³ the habit of talking about them and complaining of everything (except to God) you will never come to the end of them. *I lay great stress on this, for I believe myself it is important, and it is one of the reasons for the relaxation of discipline in religious houses.* For this body of ours has one fault: the more you indulge it, the more things it discovers to be essential to it. It is extraordinary how it likes being indulged; and, if there is any reasonable pretext for indulgence, however little necessity for it there may be, the poor soul is taken in and prevented from making progress. Think how many poor people there must be who are ill and have no one to complain to, for poverty and self-indulgence make bad company. Think, too, how many married women—people of position, as I know—have serious complaints and sore trials and yet dare not complain to their husbands about them for fear of annoying them. Sinner that I am! Surely we have not come here to indulge ourselves more than they! Oh, how free you are from the great trials of the world! Learn to suffer a little for the love of God without telling everyone about it. When a woman has made an unhappy marriage she does not talk about it or complain of it, lest it should come to her husband's knowledge; she has to endure a great deal of misery and yet has no one to whom she may relieve her mind.⁴ Cannot we, then, keep secret between God and ourselves some of the ailments which He sends us because of our sins? The more so since talking about them does nothing whatever to alleviate them.

In nothing that I have said am I referring to serious illnesses, accompanied by high fever, though as to these, too, I beg you to observe moderation and to have patience: I am thinking rather of those minor indispositions which you may have and still keep going⁵ *without worrying everybody else to death*

---

¹ E.: "lack of comfort."
² E.: "Forget the weaknesses." V. reads, literally: "Forget to complain about the weaknesses."
³ E. uses the imperative: "Get rid of, etc."
⁴ Both E. and V. read: "she talks about it and complains of it without her husband's knowledge; and she has to endure, etc."

If, out of respect for these manuscripts, which agree exactly here, except that E. has "she grows very unhappy and suffers great trials", one translator literally, the passage will make fair sense. T., however, inserts a negative before "talks", enabling us to read: "she does not talk about it or complain of it lest her husband should know"; and some unknown hand has also made this emendation in V. This reading, followed by many later editions and translations, is distinctly preferable as to sense and also agrees better with the sentences preceding and following. I therefore adopt it, though it lacks the authority of the reading of E. and V.

⁵ *Lit.*: "which can be suffered on foot."

over them. What would happen if these lines should be seen outside this house? What would all the nuns[1] say of me? And how willingly would I bear what they said if it helped anyone to live a better life! For when there is one person of this kind,[2] the thing generally comes to such a pass that *some suffer on account of others, and nobody who says she is ill will be believed, however serious her ailment.*[3] *As this book is meant only for my daughters, they will put up with everything I say.* Let us remember our holy Fathers of past days, the hermits[4] whose lives we attempt to imitate. What sufferings they bore, what solitude, cold, [thirst] and hunger, what burning sun and heat![5] And yet they had no one to complain to except God. Do you suppose they were made of iron? No: they were as frail as we are. Believe me, daughters, once we begin[6] to subdue these miserable bodies of ours, they give us much less trouble. There will be quite sufficient people to see to what you really need,[7] so take no thought for yourselves except when you know it to be necessary. Unless we resolve to put up with death and ill-health once and for all, we shall[8] never accomplish anything.

Try not to fear these and commit yourselves wholly to God, come what may. What does it matter if we die?[9] How many times have our bodies not mocked us? Should we not occasionally mock them in our turn?[10] And, believe me, *slight as it may seem by comparison with other things,* this resolution is much more important than we may think;[11] for, if we continually make it, day by day, by the grace of the Lord, we shall gain dominion over the body. To conquer such an enemy is a great achievement in the battle of life. May the Lord grant, as He is able, that we may do this. I am quite sure that no one who does not enjoy such a victory, which I believe is a great one, will understand what advantage it brings, and no one will regret having gone through trials in order to attain this tranquillity and self-mastery.

---

[1] E.: "the convents" (*monasterios*).

[2] E.: "In the end."

[3] E. (after "others, and"): "if anyone is suffering (from an illness), the very doctors will not believe her, as they have seen others having very little the matter with them and complaining so much about it."

[4] E.: "Remember our holy Fathers of past days, and the holy hermits."

[5] E.: "how many suns!"

[6] E.: "they were made of flesh as much as we are ourselves, and once we begin."

[7] *Lit.*: "to look at (*or* to) what is needful"—the phrase is ambiguous and might mean: "to worry about their own needs." The word translated "people" is feminine.

[8] E.: "Unless you . . . you will." The second person is also used for the first in the paragraph following.

[9] E. omits this sentence.

[10] E. uses the imperative, reading: "Mock them yourselves for just one day."

[11] E. continues and ends the chapter thus: "Put it into practice in such a way that it becomes a habit and you will see that I am not lying. May the Lord, Who will help us in all we do, grant (that we may do) this, and may His Majesty do it for His own sake."

CHAPTER XII

Teaches that the true lover of God must care little for life and honour.

We now come to some other *little* things which are also of very great importance, though they will appear[1] trifling. All this seems a great task,[2] and so it is, for it means warring against ourselves. But once we begin to work, God, too, works in our souls and bestows such favours on them that the most we can do in this life seems to us very little. And we nuns are doing everything we can,[3] by giving up our freedom for the love of God and entrusting it to another, and in putting up with so many trials—fasts, silence, enclosure, service in choir—that however much we may want to indulge[4] ourselves we can do so only occasionally: perhaps, in all the convents I have seen, I am the only nun guilty of self-indulgence. Why, then, do we shrink from interior mortification, since this is the means by which every other kind of mortification[5] may become much more meritorious and perfect,[6] so that it can then be practised with greater tranquillity and ease? This, as I have said, is acquired by gradual progress and by never indulging our own will and desire, even in small things, until we have succeeded in subduing the body to the spirit.[7]

I repeat that this consists mainly or entirely in our ceasing to care about ourselves and our own pleasures, for the least that anyone who is beginning to serve the Lord truly can offer Him is his life. Once he has surrendered his will to Him, what has he to fear?[8] It is evident that if he is a true religious and a real man of prayer and aspires to the enjoyment of Divine consolations, he must not [turn back or] shrink from desiring to die and suffer martyrdom for His sake. And do you not know,

---

[1] E.: "they are."

[2] E. ends the sentence here.

[3] E. continues: "giving God the chief thing, which is the will, and entrusting it to another. Why (then) do we shrink from interior (mortification) in what is nothing? We put up with so many trials—fasts, silence, constant service in choir—that, however much we may want to indulge ourselves, we can only do so at times, and not always, and perhaps, etc."

[4] T.: "to excuse." The word "indulge" is crossed out, as is the phrase "and perhaps . . . self-indulgence".

[5] T.: "by which everything—everything, even this other (kind of mortification)—"

[6] T. continues: "I mean everything, so that it can be." These words are St. Teresa's own interlinear substitution for "them", which she deletes.

[7] E. repeats: "Why, then, do we shrink from mortifying these bodies as to mere trifles (*naderías*)—that is, giving them pleasure in nothing, and carefully taking them where they have no wish to go, until we have subdued them to the spirit?"

[8] E. begins: "I think, when anyone begins to serve God truly, the least he can offer Him, after surrendering his will, is his life, (which is) a mere nothing (*nonada*)."

sisters, that the life of a good[1] religious, who wishes to be among the closest friends of God, is one long martyrdom? I say "long", for, by comparison with decapitation, which is over very quickly, it may well be termed so, though life itself is short and some lives are short in the extreme.[2] How do we know but that ours will be so short that it may end only one hour or one moment after the time of our resolving to render our entire service to God? This would be quite possible; and so we must not set store by anything that comes to an end, *least of all by life, since not a day of it is secure*. Who, if he thought that each hour[3] might be his last, would not spend it in labour?[4]

Believe me, it is safest to think that this is so;[5] by so doing we shall learn to subdue our wills in everything; for if, as I have said, you are very careful *about your prayer*, you will *soon* find yourselves gradually reaching the summit of the mountain without knowing how.[6] But how harsh it sounds to say that we must take pleasure in nothing, unless we also say what consolations and delights[7] this renunciation brings in its train, and what a great gain it is,[8] even in this life! What security it gives us![9] Here, as you all practise this, you have done the principal part; each of you encourages[10] and helps the rest; and each of you must try to outstrip her sisters.

Be very careful about your interior thoughts, especially if they have to do with precedence. May God, by His Passion, keep us from expressing, or dwelling upon, such thoughts as these:[11] "But I am her senior [in the Order]"; "But I am older"; "But I have worked harder"; "But that other sister is being better treated than I am". If these thoughts come, you must quickly check them;[12] if you allow yourselves to dwell on them, or introduce them into your conversation, they will spread like the plague and *in religious houses* they may give rise to great abuses. *Remember, I know a great deal about this*. If you have a prioress who allows such things, however trifling,[13] you must

[1] E.: "a true."
[2] E. continues: "Briefly, we must not set store, etc."
[3] E.: "each day".
[4] E. adds—redundantly, no doubt for emphasis—"if he thought he had no more than that (day) to live."
[5] E.: "Reflect, then, sisters: it is safest to believe that that is so."
[6] E., which has used the second person from the beginning of the paragraph, here adds words implied in the context: "although this may not happen quickly."
[7] E.: "what consolation and pleasure."
[8] E.: "and how many delights are gained by it."
[9] T. omits this sentence.
[10] *Lit.*: "awakens." E.: "reminds." T.: "awakens and enlivens."
[11] E.: "keep us from saying."
[12] E.: "You must quickly check these first movements."
[13] adds, redundantly: "whether little or much." T. has "superior" (*fem.*) for "prioress".

believe that God has permitted her to be given to you[1] because of your sins and that she will be the beginning of your ruin. *Cry to Him, and let your whole prayer be that He may come to your aid by sending you either a religious or a person given to prayer; for, if anyone prays with the resolve to enjoy the favours and consolations which God bestows in prayer, it is always well that he should have this detachment.*[2]

You may ask[3] why I lay such stress on this, and think that I am being too severe about it, and say that God grants consolations to persons less completely detached than that. I quite believe He does; for, in His infinite wisdom, He sees that this will enable Him to lead them to leave everything for His sake. I do not mean, by "leaving" everything, entering the religious life, for there may be obstacles to this, and the soul that is perfect can be detached and humble anywhere. It will find detachment harder in the world, however, for worldly trappings will be a great impediment to it.[4] Still, believe me in this: questions of honour and *desires for* property can arise within convents[5] as well as outside them, and the more temptations of this kind are removed from us, the more we are to blame if we yield to them. Though persons who do so may have spent years in prayer, or rather in meditation (for perfect prayer eventually destroys [all] these attachments), they will never make great progress or come to enjoy the real fruit of prayer.

Ask yourselves, sisters, if these things, *which seem so insignificant*, mean anything to you, for the only reason you are here is that you may detach yourselves from them. Nobody honours you any the more for having them and they lose you advantages which might have gained you more honour;[6] the result is that you get both dishonour and loss at the same time. Let each of you ask herself how much humility she has and she will see what progress she has made. If she is really humble, I do not think the devil will dare[7] to tempt her to take even the slightest interest in matters of precedence, for he is so shrewd that he is afraid of the blow she would strike him. If a humble soul is tempted in this way by the devil, that virtue cannot fail to bring her[8] more fortitude and greater profit.[9] For clearly the temptation will

---

[1] Thus E. V. reads: "has permitted you to have her."
[2] Thus E., the last clause reading literally: "this (matter) of detachment is fitting for all." V. condenses thus: "Pray fervently, so that He may grant you His help, for you are in great danger." T. follows V., but ends the sentence at "help".
[3] E., more briefly: "Do not tell me that God grants consolations, etc."
[4] E. omits this sentence.
[5] T.: "within religious Orders."
[6] E.: "and they lose you profit, as we say."
[7] E.: "I consider it certain that the devil will not dare."
[8] T.: "that virtue gains her."
[9] E.: "and most high degrees of profit."

cause her to look into her life,[1] to compare the services she has rendered the Lord with what she owes Him and with the marvellous way in which He abased Himself to give us an example of humility, and to think over her sins and remember where she deserves to be on account of them.[2] Exercises like this[3] bring the soul such profit that on the following day Satan will not dare to come back again lest he should get his head broken.

Take this advice from me and do not forget it: you should see to it that your sisters profit by your temptations, not only interiorly (where it would be very wrong if they did not), but exteriorly as well. If you want to avenge yourself on the devil and free yourselves more quickly[4] from temptation, ask the superior, as soon as a temptation comes to you, to give you some lowly office to do, or do some such thing, as best you can, on your own initiative, studying as you do it how to bend your will to perform tasks you dislike. The Lord will show you ways of doing so and this will soon rid you of the temptation.[5]

God deliver us from people who wish to serve Him yet who are mindful of their own honour.[6] Reflect how little they gain from this; for, as I have said, the very act of desiring honour robs us of it, especially in matters of precedence:[7] there is no poison in the world which is so fatal to perfection. You will say that these are little things which have to do with human nature and are not worth troubling about;[8] do not trifle with them, for *in religious houses* they spread like foam on water, and there is no small matter so extremely dangerous as are punctiliousness about honour and sensitiveness to insult.[9] Do you know one reason, apart from many others, why this is so?[10] It may have its root, perhaps, in some trivial slight—hardly anything, in fact—and the devil will then induce someone else to consider it important, so that she will think it a real charity to tell you about it

---

[1] E.: "For she will be bound to review [*lit.*: "to bring out"] her sins."
[2] E. omits: "and to think . . . of them."
[3] The Spanish of V. has "The soul profits so much." T. reads: "These considerations bring, etc."
[4] E. omits: "more quickly."
[5] E.: "from temptation, unburden yourself to the superior, as soon as a temptation comes to you, and ask and beg her to give you some very lowly office, or study as best you can how to bend your will in this matter, for the Lord will show you many things: (you can also make use) of public mortifications, which are used in this house. Flee from such temptations of the devil as from the plague, and see to it that he is with you but little."
[6] E. adds: "or fear dishonour."
[7] E.: "especially in religious Orders."
[8] E.: "little things which are nothing (*nada*)."
[9] E. omits: "as are . . . insult." T. has: "as are these cases and punctiliousness, etc."
[10] *Lit.*: "Do you know why, apart from many other things?" E. has simply: "Do you know why?"

and to ask how you can allow yourself to be insulted so; and she will pray that God may give you patience and that you may offer it to Him, for even a saint could not bear more. The devil is simply putting his deceitfulness into this other person's mouth;[1] and, though you yourself are quite ready to bear the slight, you are tempted to vainglory because you have not resisted something else as perfectly as you should.

This human nature of ours is so *wretchedly* weak that, even while we are telling ourselves that there is nothing for us to make a fuss about, we imagine we are doing something virtuous, and begin to feel sorry for ourselves,[2] particularly when we see that other people are sorry for us too.[3] In this way the soul begins to lose the occasions of merit which it had gained; it becomes weaker; and thus a door is opened to the devil by which he can enter on some other occasion with a temptation worse than the last. It may even happen that, when you yourself are prepared to suffer an insult, your sisters come and ask you if you are a beast of burden, and say you ought to be more sensitive about things. Oh, my sisters, for the love of God, never let charity move you to show pity for another in anything to do with these fancied insults, for that is like the pity shown to holy Job by his wife and friends.

CHAPTER XIII

Continues to treat of mortification and explains how one must renounce the world's standards of wisdom in order to attain to true wisdom.[4]

I often tell you, sisters, and now I want it to be set down in writing,[5] not to forget that we in this house, and for that matter anyone who would be perfect,[6] must flee a thousand leagues from such phrases as: "I had right on my side"; "They had no

---

[1] E. ends the paragraph: "you cannot help suffering, but you are tempted to vainglory and told it is a great deal (to bear)."
[2] E.: "that, even while minimizing the thing to ourselves and saying it is nothing, we are feeling sorry for ourselves."
[3] E. ends the chapter thus: "Thinking we are in the right makes the trouble grow and the soul loses all the occasions of merit which it had gained, and becomes weaker, so that on the next day the devil may come with a worse temptation than the last. Often, indeed, it may happen that, when you yourself are prepared not to feel aggrieved, your sisters come and ask you if you are a beast of burden, and say you ought to be more sensitive about things, Oh, what it is to have friends!"
[4] E. begins this chapter with the last sentence of the preceding chapter, minus the reference to Job (see previous note), and continues: "I often tell you, etc."
[5] E.: "and I now write it here."
[6] E.: "and every perfect person."

right to do this to me"; "The person who treated me like this was not right".[1] God deliver us from such a false idea of right as that! Do you think that it was right for our good Jesus[2] to have to suffer so many insults, and that those who heaped them on Him[3] were right, and that they had any right to do Him those wrongs? I do not know why anyone is in a convent who is willing to bear only the crosses that she has a perfect right to expect: such a person should return to the world, though even there such rights will not be safeguarded. Do you think you can ever possibly have to bear so much that you ought not to have to bear any more? How does right enter into the matter at all? I really do not know.

Before we begin talking about not having our rights, let us wait until we receive some honour or gratification, or are treated kindly,[4] for it is certainly not right that we should have anything[5] in this life like that. When, on the other hand, some offence is done to us (and we do not feel it an offence to us that it should be so described), I do not see what we can find to complain of. Either we are the brides of this great King or we are not. If we are, what wife is there with a sense of honour who does not accept her share in any dishonour done to her spouse, even though she may do so against her will?[6] Each partner, in fact, shares in the honour and dishonour of the other. To desire to share in the kingdom [of our Spouse Jesus Christ], and to enjoy it, and yet not to be willing to have[7] any part in His dishonours and trials, is ridiculous.

God keep us from being like that! Let the sister who thinks that she is accounted the least among all consider herself the [happiest and] most fortunate, as indeed she *really* is, if she lives her life as she should, for in that case she will, *as a rule*, have no lack of honour either in this life or in the next. Believe me when I say this[8]—what an absurdity, though, it is for me to say "Believe me" when the words come from Him Who is true Wisdom, *Who is Truth Itself, and from the Queen of the angels*! Let us, my daughters, in some *small* degree, imitate the great humility of the most sacred Virgin,[9] whose habit we wear and whose nuns

---

[1] E.: "The sister was not right."
[2] E.: "for Christ our Good."
[3] *Lit.*: "did them to Him." E. has "said" for "did".
[4] T. omits: "or are treated kindly."
[5] T.: "any kind treatment."
[6] E. prefaces this last clause to the following sentence.
[7] E.: "To desire to participate in the kingdom of our Spouse, and to be companions with Him in rejoicing, and yet not to have."
[8] E. adds: "for I have experienced it"; but these words were erased by St. Teresa and do not appear in V.
[9] E.: "imitate this most sacred Virgin."

we are ashamed to call ourselves. *Let us at least imitate this humility of hers in some degree—I say "in some degree"* because, however much we may seem to humble ourselves, we fall far short of being the daughters of such a Mother, and the brides of such a Spouse. If, then, the habits I have described are not sternly checked, what seems nothing to-day will perhaps be a venial sin to-morrow,[1] and that is so infectious a tendency that, if you leave it alone, the sin will not be the only one for long; and that is a very bad thing for communities.

We who live in a community should consider this very carefully, so as not to harm those who labour to benefit us and to set us a good example. If we realize what great harm is done by the formation of a bad habit *of over-punctiliousness about our honour*, we should rather die *a thousand deaths* than be the cause of such a thing. For only the body would die, whereas the loss of a soul is a great loss which is apparently without end; some of us will die, but others will take our places and perhaps they may all be harmed more by the one bad habit which we started than they are benefited by many virtues. For the devil does not allow a single bad habit to disappear and the very weakness of our mortal nature destroys the virtues in us.

Oh, what a real charity it would be, and what a service would be rendered to God, if any nun who sees that she cannot [endure and] conform to the customs of this house would recognize the fact and go away [before being professed, as I have said elsewhere], *and leave the other sisters in peace! And no convent (at least, if it follows my advice) will take her or allow her to make her profession until they have given her many years' probation to see if she improves. I am not referring to shortcomings affecting penances and fasts, for, although these are wrong, they are not things which do so much harm. I am thinking of nuns who are of such a temperament that they like to be esteemed and made much of; who see the faults of others but never recognize their own; and who are deficient in other ways like these, the true source of which is want of humility. If God does not help such a person by bestowing great spirituality upon her, until after many years she becomes greatly improved, may God preserve you from keeping her in your community. For you must realize that she will neither have peace there herself nor allow you to have any.*

As you do not take dowries, God is very gracious to you in this respect. It grieves me that religious houses should often harbour one who is a thief

---

[1] E.: "however much we may abase and humble ourselves, that is nothing for one like myself, who, for her sins, deserves to be abased and despised by the devils, though she might not wish to be, and, while others have not committed so many sins as I, it will be surprising if any of them has failed to commit enough to merit hell. I repeat, then, that you must not consider these things as trifles: unless you are diligent in uprooting them, what was nothing to-day will perhaps be a venial sin to-morrow."

and robs them of their treasure, either because they are unwilling to return a dowry of out of regard for the relatives. In this house you have risked losing worldly honour and forgone it (for no such honour is paid to those who are poor); do not desire, then, that others should be honoured at such a cost to yourselves. Our honour, sisters, must lie in the service of God, and, if anyone thinks to hinder you in this, she had better keep her honour and stay at home. It was with this in mind that our Fathers ordered a year's probation (which in our Order we are free to extend to four years): personally, I should like it to be prolonged to ten years. A humble nun will mind very little if she is not professed: for she knows that if she is good she will not be sent away, and if she is not, why should she wish to do harm to one of Christ's communities?[1]

By not being good, I do not mean being fond of vanities, which, I believe, with the help of God, will be a fault far removed from the nuns in this house. I am referring to a want of mortification and an attachment to worldly things and to self-interest in the matter which I have described. Let anyone who knows that she is not greatly mortified take my advice and not make her profession[2] if she does not wish to suffer a hell on earth, and God grant there may not be another hell awaiting such a nun in the world to come![3] There are many reasons why she should fear there may be[4] and possibly neither she nor her sisters may realize this as well as I do.

Believe what I say here;[5] if you will not, I must leave it to time to prove the truth of my words. For the *whole* manner of life we are trying to live is making us, not only nuns, but hermits [like the holy Fathers our predecessors] and leading us to detachment from all things created. I have observed that anyone whom the Lord has specially chosen[6] for this life is granted that favour. She may not have it in full perfection, but that she has it will be evident from the great joy and gladness that such detachment gives her, and she will never have any more to do with worldly things, for her delight will be in all the practices of the religious life.[7] I say once more that anyone who is inclined to things of the world should leave the convent[8] if she sees she is not making progress. If she still wishes to be a nun she should go to another convent; if she does not, she will see what happens

---

[1] *Lit.*: "to this college of Christ." Cf. p. 112, below.
[2] V. reads (after "and go away" p. 55): "Let her see that she carries out her obligations if she does not wish, etc."
[3] T. omits: "if she does not . . . to come."
[4] E.: "there are many reasons for it in her." T. reads similarly.
[5] In T. these words are rather unintelligently deleted.
[6] E.: "the Lord specially desires."
[7] E. omits: "for her . . . religious life."
[8] I.e., St. Joseph's, Ávila. T. reads here: ". . . of the world is not (meant) for these convents [i.e., of the Reform]. If she wishes to be a nun she can go to another; if she does not, etc."

to her. She must not complain of me as the foundress of this convent and say I have not warned her.

This house is another Heaven, if it be possible to have Heaven upon earth. Anyone whose sole pleasure lies in pleasing God and who cares nothing for her own pleasure will find our life a very good one;[1] if she wants anything more, she will lose everything, for there is nothing more that she can have. A discontented soul is like a person suffering from severe nausea, who rejects all food, however nice it may be; things which persons in good health delight in eating only cause her *the greater* loathing. Such a person will save her soul better elsewhere[2] than here; she may even gradually reach a degree of perfection which she could not have attained here because we expected too much of her all at once. For although we allow time for the attainment of complete detachment and mortification in interior matters, in externals this has to be practised immediately,[3] *because of the harm which may otherwise befall the rest*; and anyone who sees this being done, and spends all her time in such good company, and yet, at the end of *six months or* a year, has made no progress, will, I fear, make none over a great many years, and will even go backward. I do not say that such a nun must be as perfect as the rest, but she must be sure that her soul is gradually growing healthier—and it will soon become clear if her disease is mortal.

CHAPTER XIV

Treats of the great importance of not professing anyone whose spirit is contrary to the things aforementioned.

I feel sure that the Lord bestows great help on anyone who makes good resolutions, and for that reason it is necessary to enquire into the intention[4] of anyone who enters [the life of religion]. She must not come, as many nuns [now] do, simply to further her own interests, although the Lord can perfect even this intention if she is a person of intelligence. If not intelligent, a person of this kind should on no account be admitted; for she will not understand her own reasons for coming, nor will she understand others who attempt subsequently to improve her. For, in general, a person who has this fault always thinks she knows

---

[1] T. omits: "will... one", and, after "upon earth", reads: "for anyone whose, etc."
[2] E. adds: "in a convent which is not so strict."
[3] E.: "very soon."
[4] E. reads: "gives help to" and: "for that reason it is important to consider what is the talent".

better than the wisest what is good for her; and I believe this evil is incurable, for it is rarely unaccompanied by malice. In a convent where there are a great many *nuns* it may be tolerated, but it cannot be suffered among a few.

When an intelligent person begins to grow fond of what is good, she clings to it manfully, for she sees that it is the best thing for her; this course may not bring her great spirituality but it will help her to give profitable advice, and to make herself useful in many ways, without being a trouble to anybody.[1] But I do not see how a person lacking in intelligence can be of any use in community life, and she may do a great deal of harm. This defect, *like others*, will not become obvious immediately; for many[2] people are good at talking and bad at understanding, while others speak in a sharp and none too refined a tone,[3] and yet they have intelligence and can do a great deal of good. There are also simple, holy people who are *quite* unversed in business matters and worldly conventions but have great skill in converse with God. Many enquiries, therefore, must be made before novices are admitted, and the period of probation before profession should be a long one. The world must understand once and for all that you are free to send them away *again*, as it is often necessary to do in a convent where the life is one of austerity; and then if you use this right no one will take offence.

I say this[4] because these times are so unhappy, and our weakness is so great,[5] that we are not content to follow the instructions of our predecessors and disregard the current ideas about honour, lest we should give offence to the novices' relatives.[6] God grant that those of us who admit unsuitable persons may not pay for it in the world to come! Such persons are never without a pretext for persuading us to accept them, *though in a matter of such importance no pretext is valid. If the superior is unaffected by her personal likings and prejudices, and considers what is for the good of the house, I do not believe God will ever allow her to go astray. But if she considers other people's feelings and trivial points of detail, I feel sure she will be bound to err.*

This is something which everyone must think out for herself; she must commend it to God and encourage her superior *when her courage fails her*, of such great importance is it. So I beg God

---

[1] E. adds: "but rather a recreation" [i.e., a refreshing companion].
[2] E.: "a few."
[3] An untranslatable play upon words: *corto y no muy cortado*—as though "sharpened" could be used in the sense of "refined".
[4] E.: "I say (the world must) understand (this)."
[5] E.: "the weakness of nuns is so great—I say this from my own experience—."
[6] E.: "our predecessors, but, lest we should give some slight offence and in order to stop people from talking—which is of no importance—we allow virtuous habits to be forgotten."

to give you light about it. You do very well not to accept dowries;[1] for, if you were to accept them, it might happen that, in order not to have to give back money which you no longer possess, you would keep a thief in the house who was robbing you of your treasure; and that would be no small pity.[2] So you must not receive dowries from anyone, for to do so may be to harm the very person to whom you desire to bring profit.[3]

CHAPTER XV

Treats of the great advantage which comes from our not excusing ourselves, even though we find we are unjustly condemned.

But how disconnectedly I am writing! I am just like a person who does not know what she is doing. It is your fault, sisters, for I am doing this at your command. Read it as best you can, for I am writing it as best I can, and, if it is too bad, burn it. I really need leisure, and, as you see, I have so little opportunity for writing that a week passes without my putting down a word, and so I forget what I have said and what I am going to say next. Now what I have just been doing—namely, excusing myself—is very bad for me, and I beg you not to copy it, for to suffer without making excuses is a habit of great perfection, and very edifying and meritorious; and, though I often teach you this, and by God's goodness you practise it, His Majesty has never granted this favour to me. May He be pleased to bestow it on me before I die.[4]

I am greatly confused as I begin to urge this virtue upon you, for I ought myself to have practised at least something of what[5] I am recommending you with regard to it: but actually I must confess I have made very little progress. I never seem unable to find a reason for thinking I am being virtuous when I make excuses for myself. There are times when this is lawful, and when not to do it would be wrong, but I have not the discretion (or, better, the humility) to do it only when fitting. For, indeed, it takes

[1] T. adds: "so that you may be able to choose persons, for this would be to blind yourselves by self-interest." It varies slightly from V. in the remaining sentences of the paragraph.
[2] Here St. Teresa is developing an idea found (in E. only) in the preceding chapter (pp. 55–6, above). As the language, though similar, is not identical, the passage is allowed to stand.
[3] E. ends the chapter: "since it is a matter of very great importance to everyone; and so I beg God to give you light about it."
[4] E. opens with this passage and then continues: "I am never unable to find a reason for thinking I am being virtuous, etc." Before taking up the thread of the argument here, however, I give the opening passage from V., which is shorter and equally personal, and, though similar, not identical in thought.
[5] T.: "practised what."

great humility to find oneself unjustly condemned and be silent,[1] and to do this is to imitate the Lord Who set us free from all our sins. I beg you, then, to study[2] earnestly to do so, for it brings great gain; whereas I can see no gain in our trying to free ourselves from blame: none whatever—save, as I say, in a few cases where hiding the truth might cause offence or scandal. Anyone will understand this who has more discretion than I.

I think it is very important to accustom oneself to practise this virtue and to endeavour to obtain from the Lord the true humility which must result from it. The truly humble person will have a genuine desire to be thought little of, and persecuted, and condemned unjustly, even in serious matters.[3] For, if she desires to imitate the Lord, how can she do so better than in this? And no bodily strength is necessary here, nor the aid of anyone save God.

These are great virtues, my sisters, and I should like us to study them closely, and to make them our penance.[4] As you know, I deprecate [other severe and] excessive penances, which, if practised indiscreetly, may injure the health. Here, however, there is no cause for fear; for, however great the interior virtues may be, they do not weaken the body so that it cannot serve the Order, while at the same time they strengthen the soul;[5] and, furthermore, they can be applied to very little things, and thus, as I have said on other occasions, they accustom one to gain great victories in *very* important matters.[6] I have not, however, been able to test this particular thing myself, for I never heard anything bad said of me which I did not *clearly* realize fell short of the truth. If I had not *sometimes—often, indeed*—offended God in the ways they referred to, I had done so in many others, and I felt they had treated me far too indulgently in saying nothing about these: I much preferred people to blame me for what was not true than to tell the truth about me. *For I disliked hearing things that were true said about me, whereas these other things, however serious they were, I did not mind at all. In small matters I followed my own inclinations, and I still do so, without paying any attention to*

---

[1] E. omits: "and be silent."
[2] E.: "I should like strongly to urge upon you to study." T. reads: "to be careful to do so."
[3] T.: "and condemned, although he may have done nothing to justify this."
[4] E.: "and I should like them to be our study and penance." T.: "closely, for they are a good penance."
[5] E.: "As you know, I deprecate other austerities, even good ones, when they are excessive. Great interior virtues do not weaken the body or rob it of strength so that it cannot serve the Order, and at the same time they strengthen the soul."
[6] E. omits: "as I have said on other occasions" and after the end of the sentence goes on: "But how well this can be written down and how badly I put it into practice! In reality I have not been able to test this myself in important matters, for I never, etc."

what is most perfect. So I should like you to begin to realize this at an early stage, and I want each of you to ponder how much there is to be gained in every way by this virtue, and how, so far as I can see, there is nothing to be lost by it. The chief thing we gain is being able, in some degree, to follow the Lord.[1]

It is a great help to meditate upon the great gain which in any case this is bound to bring us, and to realize how, properly speaking, we can never be blamed unjustly, since we are always full of faults, and a just man falls seven times a day,[2] so that it would be a falsehood for us to say we have no sin. If, then, we are not to blame for the thing that we are accused of, we are never wholly without blame in the way that our good Jesus was.

Oh, my Lord! When I think in how many ways Thou didst suffer, and in all of them undeservedly, I know not what to say for myself, or what I can have been thinking about when I desired not to suffer, or what I am doing when I make excuses for myself. Thou knowest, my Good, that if there is anything good in me it comes from no other hands than Thine own. For what is it to Thee, Lord, to give much instead of little? True, I do not deserve it, but neither have I deserved the favours which Thou hast shown me already. Can it be that I should wish a thing so evil as myself to be thought well of by anyone, when they have said such wicked things of Thee, Who art good above all other good? It is intolerable, my God, it is intolerable; nor would I that Thou shouldst have to tolerate anything displeasing in Thine eyes being found in Thy handmaiden. For see, Lord, mine eyes are blind and very little pleases them. Do Thou give me light and make me truly to desire that all should hate me, since I have so often left Thee, Who hast loved me with such[3] faithfulness.

What is this, my God? What advantage do we think to gain from giving pleasure to creatures? What does it matter to us if we are blamed by them all, provided we are without blame in the sight of the Lord?[4] Oh, my sisters, we shall never succeed in understanding this truth and we shall never attain perfection[5] unless we think and meditate upon what is real and upon what is not. If there were no other gain than the confusion which will be felt by the person[6] who has blamed you when she sees

---

[1] E. continues: "I say 'in some degree' because, as I have said, we are never blamed when we have done nothing wrong at all, for we are always full of faults, since a just man falls seven times a day, etc."
[2] Proverbs xxiv, 16.
[3] E.: "complete."
[4] E.: "if I am without blame in the sight of my Creator."
[5] E.: "attain the summit of perfection."
[6] E.: "the sister."

that you have allowed yourselves to be condemned unjustly, that would be a very great thing. Such an experience uplifts the soul more than ten sermons. And we must all try to be preachers by our deeds,[1] since both the Apostle and our own lack of ability forbid us to be preachers in word.

Never suppose that either the evil or the good that you do will remain secret,[2] however strict may be your enclosure. Do you suppose, daughter,[3] that, if you do not make excuses for yourself, there will not be someone else who will defend you? Remember how the Lord took the Magdalen's part in the Pharisee's house and also when her sister blamed her.[4] He will not treat you as rigorously as He treated Himself: it was not until He was on the Cross that He had even a thief to defend Him. His Majesty, then, will put it into somebody's mind to defend you; if He does not, it will be because there is no need. This I have myself seen, and it is a fact, although I should not like[5] you to think too much of it, but rather to be glad when you are blamed, and in due time you will see what profit you experience in your souls.[6] For it is in this way that you will begin to gain freedom; soon you will not care if they speak ill or well of you; it will seem like someone else's business. It will be as if two persons are talking *in your presence* and you are quite uninterested in what they are saying because you are not actually being addressed by them. So here: it becomes such a habit with us not to reply that it seems as if they are not addressing us at all. This may seem impossible to those of us who are very sensitive and not capable of great mortification. It is indeed difficult at first, but I know that, with the Lord's help, the *gradual* attainment of this freedom, and of renunciation and self-detachment, is quite possible.

[1] E.: "you must . . . your deeds."

[2] E. adds, parenthetically: "I think I have already told you this once and I should like to say it many times more."

[3] E. uses the plural throughout this paragraph.

[4] E. reads: " . . . part when Saint Martha was blaming her," and omits the next sentence ("He will not . . . defend Him.")

[5] E.: "His Majesty will put it into somebody's mind to defend you when it is necessary. I have the fullest experience of this, although I should not like."

[6] E. adds, redundantly: "for a great deal results from this. One kind of profit is that you begin to gain freedom." From here to "at all", E. uses the second person where V. uses the first.

CHAPTER XVI

Describes the difference between perfection in the lives of contemplatives and in the lives of those who are content with mental prayer. Explains how it is sometimes possible for God to raise a distracted soul to perfect contemplation and the reason for this. This chapter and that which comes next are to be noted carefully.[1]

I hope you do not think I have written too much about this already; for I have only been placing the board, as they say. You have asked me to tell you about the first steps in prayer; although God did not lead me by them, my daughters, I know no others, and even now I can hardly have acquired these elementary virtues. But you may be sure that anyone who cannot set out the pieces in a game of chess will never be able to play well, and, if he does not know how to give check, he will not be able to bring about a checkmate.[2] Now you will reprove me for talking about games, as we do not play them in this house and are forbidden to do so. That will show you what kind of a mother God has given you—she even knows about vanities like this! However, they say that the game is sometimes legitimate. How legitimate it will be for us to play it in this way, and, if we play it frequently, how quickly we shall give checkmate to this Divine King! He will not be able to move out of our check nor will He desire to do so.

It is the queen which gives the king most trouble in this game and all the other pieces support her. There is no queen who can beat this King as well as humility can; for humility brought Him down from Heaven into the Virgin's womb and with humility we can draw Him into our souls by a single hair. Be sure that He will give most humility to him who has most already and least to him who has least. I cannot understand how humility exists, or can exist, without love, or love without humility, and it is impossible for these two virtues to exist save where there is great detachment from all created things.

You will ask, my daughters, why I am talking to you about virtues when you have more than enough books to teach you about them and when you want me to tell you only about contemplation. My reply is that, if

---

[1] The first four paragraphs of this chapter originally formed part of V., but, after writing them, St. Teresa tore them out of the manuscript, as though, on consideration, she had decided not to leave on record her knowledge of such a worldly game as chess. The allegory, however, is so expressive and beautiful that it has rightly become famous, and from the time of Fray Luis de León all the editions have included it. The text here followed is that of E.

[2] Chess was very much in vogue in the Spain of St. Teresa's day and it was only in 1561 that its great exponent Ruy López de Segura had published his celebrated treatise, in Spanish, entitled "Book of the liberal invention and art of the game of chess".

you had asked me about meditation, I could have talked to you about it, and advised you all to practise it, even if you do not possess the virtues. For this is the first step to be taken towards the acquisition of the virtues and the very life of all Christians depends upon their beginning it. No one, however lost a soul he may be, should neglect so great a blessing if God inspires him to make use of it. All this I have already written elsewhere, and so have many others who know what they are writing about, which I certainly do not: God knows that.

But contemplation, daughters, is another matter. This is an error which we all make: if a person gets so far as to spend a short time each day in thinking about his sins, as he is bound to do if he is a Christian in anything more than name, people at once call him a great contemplative; and then they expect him to have the rare virtues which a great contemplative is bound to possess; he may even think he has them himself, but he will be quite wrong. In his early stages he did not even know how to set out the chess-board, and thought that, in order to give checkmate, it would be enough to be able to recognize the pieces. But that is impossible, for this King does not allow Himself to be taken except by one who surrenders wholly to Him.

Therefore, daughters, if you want me to tell you the way to attain to contemplation, do allow me to speak at some length about these things, even if at the time they do not seem to you very important,[1] for I think myself that they are.[2] If you have no wish either to hear about them or to practise them, continue your mental prayer all your life;[3] but in that case I assure you, and all persons who desire this blessing,[4] that *in my opinion* you will not attain true contemplation. I may, of course, be wrong about this, as I am judging by my own experience, but I have been striving after contemplation for twenty years.

I will now explain what mental prayer is, as some of you will not understand this. God grant that we may practise it as we should! I am afraid, however, that, if we do not achieve the virtues, this can only be done with great labour, although the virtues are not necessary here in such a high degree as they are for contemplation.[5] I mean that the King of glory will not come to our souls—that is, so as to be united with them—unless we strive to gain the greatest virtues.[6] I will explain this, for if you once catch me out in something which is not

---

[1] E.: "about things which will not seem to you very important."
[2] E.: "for all the things I have said here are (important)."
[3] "All your life" is deleted in T.
[4] E.: "and everybody."
[5] E.: "for that other (exercise)."
[6] *Lit.*: "the great virtues." In V. St. Teresa originally began this sentence thus: "In the last chapter I said that the King of glory, etc.," and ended it: "to gain the virtues which I there described as great." Later she altered it to read as above.

the truth, you will believe nothing I say—and if I were to say something untrue intentionally, from which may God preserve me, you would be right;[1] but, if I did, it would be because I knew no better or did not understand what I said. I will tell you, then, that God is sometimes pleased to show great favour to persons who are in an evil state [and to raise them to perfect contemplation], so that by this means He may snatch them out of the hands of the devil.[2] *It must be understood, I think, that such persons will not be in mortal sin at the time. They may be in an evil state, and yet the Lord will allow them to see a vision, even a very good one, in order to draw them back to Himself. But I cannot believe that He would grant them contemplation. For that is a Divine union, in which the Lord takes His delight in the soul and the soul takes its delight in Him; and there is no way in which the Purity of the Heavens can take pleasure in a soul that is unclean, nor can the Delight of the angels have delight in that which is not His own. And we know that, by committing mortal sin, a soul becomes the property of the devil, and must take its delight in him, since it has given him pleasure; and, as we know, his delights, even in this life, are continuous torture. My Lord will have no lack of children of His own in whom He may rejoice without going and taking the children of others. Yet His Majesty will do what He often does—namely, snatch them out of the devil's hands.*[3]

Oh, my Lord! How often do we cause Thee to wrestle with the devil! Was it not enough that Thou shouldst have allowed him to bear Thee in his arms when he took Thee to the pinnacle of the Temple in order to teach us how to vanquish him? What a sight it would have been, daughters, to see this Sun by the side of the darkness, and what fear that wretched creature must have felt, though he would not have known why, since God did not allow Him to understand! Blessed be such great pity and mercy; we Christians ought to feel great shame at making Him wrestle daily, in the way I have described, with such an unclean beast. Indeed, Lord, Thine arms had need to be strong, but how was it that they were not weakened by the many [trials and] tortures

---

[1] After "that other (exercise)" E. continues: "For I must not forget that I said you must not be afraid of the King's coming: I will explain myself, for if you catch me out in a lie you will not belie e me about anything, and you would be right if I knowingly told a lie, from which may God preserve me."

[2] E. reads: "It often happens that the Lord takes a very wretched soul" and then continues "It must be understood . . ." as in the text above. The insertion of this italicized passage necessitates the repetition of the phrase "snatch them out of the devil's hands", in which, after its omissions, V. takes up the thread of E.

[3] *Lit.*: "out of his hands"; but the meaning, made more explicit in V., is evident. On the doctrinal question involved in this paragraph, see Introduction, p. xv, above. P. Silverio (III, 75-6), has a more extensive note on the subject than can be given here and cites a number of Spanish authorities, from P. Juan de Jesús María (*Theologia Mystica*, Chap. III) to P. Seisdedos Sanz (*Principios fundamentales de la mística*, Madrid, 1913, II, 61-77.)

which Thou didst endure upon the Cross? Oh, how quickly all that is borne for love's sake heals again! I really believe that, if Thou hadst lived longer, the very love which Thou hast for us would have healed Thy wounds again and Thou wouldst have needed no other medicine.[1] Oh, my God, who will give me such medicine for all the things which grieve and try me? How eagerly should I desire them if it were certain that I could be cured by such a health-giving ointment!

Returning to what I was saying, there are souls whom God knows He may gain for Himself by this means; seeing that they are completely lost, His Majesty wants to leave no stone unturned to help them; and therefore, though they are in a sad way and lacking in virtues, He gives them consolations, favours and emotions[2] which begin to move their desires, and occasionally even brings them to a state of contemplation, though rarely and not for long at a time.[3] And this, as I say, He does because He is testing them to see if that favour will not make them anxious to prepare themselves to enjoy it often; if it does not, may they be pardoned; pardon Thou us, Lord, for it is a dreadful thing that a soul whom Thou hast brought near to Thyself should approach any earthly thing and become attached to it.

For my own part I believe there are many souls whom God our Lord tests in this way, and few who prepare themselves to enjoy this favour.[4] When the Lord does this and we ourselves leave nothing undone either, I think it is certain that He never ceases from giving until He has brought us to a very high degree of prayer. If we do not give ourselves to His Majesty as resolutely as He gives Himself to us, He will be doing more than enough for us if He leaves us in mental prayer and from time to time visits us as He would visit servants in His vineyard. But these others are His beloved children, whom He would never want to banish from His side; and, as they have no desire to leave Him, He never does so. He seats them at His table, and feeds them with His own food,[5] almost taking the food from His mouth in order to give it them.

Oh, what blessed care of us is this, my daughters! How happy shall we be if by leaving these few, petty[6] things we can

---

[1] E. continues: "I seem to be talking nonsense; for I do not act in this way, and yet Divine love does greater things than these. But, lest I should seem over-fond of detail (*curiosa*), which I am, and set you a bad example, I am not setting any of them down here." [A new chapter begins here.] "So, when it is the Lord's will to draw the soul back to Himself, He occasionally brings it to a state of contemplation, even when it has not these virtues, though rarely and for but a short time, etc."

[2] *Lit.*: "and tenderness."

[3] T.: "and for a short space of time."

[4] E. adds: "always."

[5] In T. the rest of this sentence is deleted.

[6] *Lit.*: "low", contrasting with "high" at the end of the sentence. E. has: "vain".

arrive at so high an estate! Even if the whole world should blame you, *and deafen you with its cries*, what matter so long as you are in the arms of God? He is powerful enough to free you from everything; for only once did He command the world to be made and it was done;[1] with Him, to will is to do. Do not be afraid, then, if He is pleased to speak with you, for He does this for the greater good of those who love Him.[2] His love for those to whom He is dear is by no means so weak: *He shows it in every way possible.*[3] Why, then, my sisters, do we not show Him love in so far as we can? Consider what a wonderful exchange it is if we give Him our love and receive His. Consider that He can do all things, and we can do nothing here below save as He enables us. And what is it that we do for Thee, O Lord, our Maker? We do hardly anything [at all]—just make some poor weak resolution. And, if His Majesty is pleased that by doing a mere nothing we should win everything,[4] let us not be so foolish as to fail to do it.

O Lord! All our trouble comes to us from not having our eyes fixed upon Thee. If we only looked at the way along which we are walking, we should soon arrive; but we stumble and fall a thousand times and stray from the way because, as I say, we do not set our eyes on the true Way. One would think that no one had ever trodden it before, so new is it to us. It is indeed a pity that this should sometimes happen.[5] *I mean, it hardly seems that we are Christians at all or that we have ever in our lives read about the Passion. Lord help us—that we should be hurt about some small point of honour! And then, when someone tells us not to worry about it, we think he is no Christian. I used to laugh—or sometimes I used to be distressed—at the things I heard in the world, and sometimes, for my sins, in religious Orders.* We refuse to be thwarted over the very smallest matter of precedence:[6] apparently such a thing is quite intolerable. We cry out at once: "Well, I'm no saint"; *I used to say that myself.*

God deliver us, sisters, from saying "We are not angels", or "We are not saints", whenever we commit some imperfection. We may not be; but what a good thing it is for us to reflect that we can be if we will only try and if God gives us His hand![7] Do not be afraid that He will fail to do His part if we do not fail

---

[1] E. omits: "He ... everything" and continues: "For only once did the Lord command the world to be made, or think (of its being made), and it was done."

[2] E.: "for He does this for your greater good."

[3] The words italicized are struck out in E. but they seem to follow quite naturally on the preceding sentence.

[4] Or "merit the All", as P. Silverio's text has it. T. has: "should buy Him Who is the All." Each text ends the sentence, literally: "let us not be foolish."

[5] E. omits: "that this should sometimes happen."

[6] E. ends the sentence here."

[7] E.: "to reflect that God will give us His hand so that we may be." In both E. and V., as often in idiomatic Spanish, "hand" is used in the sense of "strength", "power".

to do ours. And since we come here for no other reason, let us put our hands to the plough, as they say. Let there be nothing we know of which it would be a service to the Lord for us to do, and which, with His help, we would not venture to take in hand. I should like that kind of venturesomeness to be found in this house, as it always[1] increases humility. We must have a holy boldness, for God helps the strong[2], being no respecter of persons;[3] *and He will give courage to you and to me.*

I have strayed far from the point. I want to return to what I was saying—that is,[4] to explain the nature of mental prayer and contemplation. It may seem irrelevant, but it is all done for your sakes; you may understand it better as expressed in my rough style than in other books which put it more elegantly.[5] May the Lord grant me His favour, so that this may be so. Amen.

CHAPTER XVII

How not all souls are fitted for contemplation and how some take long to attain it. True humility will walk happily along the road by which the Lord leads it.

I seem now to be beginning my treatment of prayer, but there still remains a little for me to say, which is of great importance because it has to do with humility, and in this house that is necessary. For humility is the principal virtue which must be practised by those who pray,[6] and, as I have said, it is very fitting that you should try to learn how to practise it often:[7] that is one of the chief things to remember about it and it is very necessary that it should be known by all who practise prayer. How can anyone who is truly humble think herself as good as those who become contemplatives?[8] God, it is true, by His goodness and mercy, can make her so;[9] but my advice is that she should always sit down in the lowest place, for that is what the Lord instructed us to do and taught us by His own example.[10]

---

[1] E. omits: "always."
[2] E. reads: "We must always have courage, which God gives to the strong."
[3] Acts x, 34.
[4] E.: "which, I believe, was."
[5] E. ends the chapter here.
[6] E.: "For you have all to engage, and do engage, in prayer."
[7] E.: "in every way."
[8] E.: "who reach this state."
[9] E.: "God, it is true, through the merits of Christ, can make her good enough to merit this."
[10] St. Luke xiv, 10. E. omits: "for . . . example."

Let such a one make herself ready for God to lead her by this road if He so wills; if He does not, the whole point of *true* humility is that she should consider herself happy in serving the servants of the Lord[1] and in praising Him. For she deserves to be a slave of the devils in hell;[2] yet His Majesty has brought her here to live among His servants.[3]

I do not say this without good reason, for, as I have said, it is very important for us to realize that God does not lead us all by the same road, and perhaps she who believes herself to be going along the lowest of roads is the highest in the Lord's eyes. So it does not follow that, because all of us in this house practise prayer,[4] we are all *perforce* to be contemplatives. That is impossible; and[5] those of us who are not would be greatly discouraged if we did not grasp the truth that contemplation is something given by God, and, as it is not necessary for salvation and God does not ask it of us before He gives us our reward,[6] we must not suppose that anyone else will require it of us. We shall not fail to attain perfection if we do what has been said here; we may, in fact, gain much more merit, because what we do will cost us more labour; the Lord will be treating us like those who are strong and will be laying up for us all that we cannot enjoy in this life. Let us not be discouraged, then, and give up prayer or cease doing what the rest do; for the Lord sometimes tarries long, and gives us as great rewards all at once as He has been giving to others over many years.[7]

I myself spent over[8] fourteen years without ever being able to meditate except while reading. There must be many people like this, and others who cannot meditate[9] even after reading, but can only recite vocal prayers, in which they chiefly occupy themselves *and take a certain pleasure*. Some find their thoughts wandering so much that they cannot concentrate upon the same thing, but are always restless, to such an extent that, if they try to fix their thoughts upon God, they are attacked by a thousand foolish ideas[10] and scruples and doubts *concerning the*

---

[1] E.: "in being the servant of the servants of the Lord." Both E. and V. use the feminine form, for servant(s), *sierva(s)*, which I sometimes translate "handmaidens".

[2] T. omits: "in hell."

[3] This is an amplification of E.: "and in praising Him for bringing her here to live among His servants when she deserved to be in hell."

[4] E.: "that because, in this house, is (observed) the custom and practice of prayer."

[5] In T.: "That is impossible; and" is deleted.

[6] T. deletes: "before . . . reward."

[7] In T.: "to others" is deleted.

[8] E. omits: "over."

[9] T.: "contemplate."

[10] E.: "a thousand vanities."

Faith. I know a very old woman,[1] leading a most excellent life —*I wish mine were like hers*—a penitent[2] and a great servant of God, who for many years has been spending hours and hours in vocal prayer, but from mental prayer can get no help at all; the most she can do is to dwell upon each of her vocal prayers as she says them.[3] There are a great many other people *just* like this; if they are humble, they will not, I think, be any the worse off in the end,[4] but very much in the same state as those who enjoy numerous consolations. In one way they may feel safer, for we cannot tell if[5] consolations come from God or are sent by the devil. If they are not of God, they are the more dangerous; for the chief object of the devil's work on earth is to fill us with pride. If they are of God, there is no reason for fear, for they bring humility with them, as I explained in my other book at great length.[6]

Others[7] walk in humility, and *always* suspect that if they fail to receive consolations the fault is theirs, and are always most anxious to make progress. They never see a person shedding a tear without thinking themselves very backward in God's service unless they are doing the same, whereas they may perhaps be much more advanced.[8] For tears, though good, are not invariably signs of perfection; there is always greater safety[9] in humility, mortification, detachment and other virtues. There is no reason for fear, and you must not be afraid[10] that you will fail to attain the perfection of the greatest contemplatives.

Saint Martha was holy, but we are not told that she was a contemplative. What more do you want than to be able to grow to be like that blessed woman, who was worthy to receive Christ our Lord so often in her house, and to prepare meals for Him, and to serve Him and *perhaps* to eat at table with Him?[11] If she[12] had been absorbed in devotion [all the time], as the Magdalen was, there would have been no one to prepare a meal for this Divine Guest.[13] Now remember that this *little* community is Saint

---

[1] E. has "nun", omits "leading a most excellent life" and inserts "holy woman and" before "penitent".

[2] E. continues: "—altogether a great nun, much and habitually given to vocal prayer, but from mental prayer unable to get any help at all."

[3] E.: "upon each of her Avemarias and Paternosters, as she says them, which is a very holy practice."

[4] E.: "at the end of the year."

[5] E.: "For how do we know if . . .?"

[6] E.: "there is no reason for fear, as I wrote in my other book." The reference is to the *Life*, Chapters XVII, XIX, XXVIII.

[7] *Lit.*: "These others." T. has: "These others who do not receive consolations."

[8] E. omits: "perhaps."

[9] E.: "they are always safe."

[10] In T. "and you must not be afraid" is deleted.

[11] E. adds: "and even from His plate."

[12] Both E. and V. have "they" here and E. adds "both". T. prefers the singular.

[13] E.: "for the Heavenly Guest."

Martha's house and that there must be people of all kinds here. Nuns who are called to the active life must not murmur at others who are very much absorbed in contemplation,[1] for contemplatives know that, though they themselves may be silent, the Lord will speak for them, and this, as a rule, makes them forget themselves and everything else.[2]

Remember that there must be someone to cook the meals and count yourselves happy in being able to serve like Martha.[3] Reflect that true humility[4] consists to a great extent in being ready for what the Lord desires to do with you and happy that He should do it, and in always considering yourselves unworthy to be called His servants. If contemplation and mental and vocal prayer and tending the sick and serving in the house and working at[5] even the lowliest tasks are of service to the Guest who comes to stay with us and to eat and take His recreation with us, what should it matter to us if we do one of these things rather than another?

I do not mean that it is for us to say what we shall do, but that we must do our best in everything, for the choice is not ours but the Lord's. If after many years He is pleased to give each of us her office, it will be a curious kind of humility for you to wish to choose; let the Lord of the house do that, for He is wise and powerful and knows what is fitting for you and for Himself as well. Be sure that, if you do what lies in your power and prepare yourself for *high* contemplation with the perfection aforementioned, then, if He does not grant it you (and I think He will not fail to do so if you have true detachment and humility),[6] it will be because He has laid up this joy for you so as to give it you in Heaven,[7] and because, as I have said elsewhere, He is pleased to treat you like people who are strong and give you a cross to bear on earth like that which His Majesty Himself always bore.

What better sign of friendship is there than for Him to give you what He gave Himself? It might well be that you would not have had so great a reward from contemplation. His judgments are His own; we must not meddle in them. It is indeed a good thing that the choice is not ours; for, if it were, we should think it the more restful life and all become great contemplatives.

---

[1] E.: "in prayer."
[2] E. is shorter: "for this, as a rule, makes them forget themselves and everything else."
[3] E.: "Remember that, if they are silent, the Lord will answer for them, and let them count themselves happy to be going and preparing His meal."
[4] E. adds: "I really believe."
[5] E. adds: "desiring"—perhaps a slip for "and desiring".
[6] The words "and humility" are not found in E.
[7] The words "so as . . . Heaven" are not found in E.

Oh, how much we gain if we have no desire to gain what seems to us best and so have no fear of losing, since God never permits a truly mortified person to lose anything except when such loss will bring him greater gain![1]

CHAPTER XVIII

Continues the same subject and shows how much greater are the trials of contemplatives than those of actives. This chapter offers great consolation to actives.

I tell you, then, daughters—those of you whom God is not leading by this road [of contemplation]—that, as I know from what I have seen and been told by those who are following this road, they are not bearing[2] a lighter cross than you; you would be amazed at all the ways and manners in which God sends them crosses. I know about both types of life and I am well aware that the trials given by God to contemplatives are intolerable; and they are of such a kind that, were He not to feed them with consolations, they could not be borne. It is clear that, since God leads those whom He most loves by the way of trials, the more He loves them, the greater will be their trials; and there is no reason to suppose that He hates contemplatives, since with His own mouth He praises them and calls them friends.[3]

To suppose that He would admit to His close friendship pleasure-loving people who are free from all trials is ridiculous. I feel quite sure that God gives them much greater trials; and that He leads them by a hard and rugged road, so that they sometimes think they are lost and will have to go back and begin again.[4] Then His Majesty is obliged to give them sustenance—not water, but wine, so that they may become inebriated by it and not realize what they are going through and what they are capable of bearing. Thus I find few true contemplatives who are not courageous and resolute in suffering;[5] for, if they are weak, the first thing the Lord does is to give them courage so that they may fear no trials *that may come to them*.

I think, when those who lead an active life occasionally see contemplatives receiving consolations, they suppose that they never experience anything else. But I can assure you that you

---

[1] E. omits this last sentence.
[2] E.: "that those who are following this road are not bearing."
[3] E.: "and they are also friends."
[4] E.: "will have to begin again from the place they started from."
[5] E. omits: "and resolute in suffering." T. omits: "true."

might not be able to endure their sufferings for as long as a day. The point is that the Lord knows everyone as he really is and gives each his work to do—according to what He sees to be most fitting for his soul, and for His own Self, and for the good of his neighbour. Unless you have omitted to prepare yourselves for your work you need have no fear that it will be lost. Note that I say we must all strive to do this, for we are here for no other purpose; and we must not strive merely for a year, or for two years or ten years,[1] or it will look as if we are abandoning our work like cowards. It is well that the Lord should see we are not leaving anything undone. We are like soldiers who, however long they have served, must always be ready for their captain to send them away on any duty which he wants to entrust to them, since it is he who is paying them.[2] And how much better is the payment given by our King than by people on this earth! *For the unfortunate soldiers die, and God knows who pays them after that!*

When their captain sees they are all present, and anxious for service,[3] he assigns duties to them according to their fitness, *though not so well as our Heavenly Captain.* But if they were not present, He would give them neither pay[4] nor service orders. So practise mental prayer, sisters; or, if any of you cannot do that, vocal prayer, reading and colloquies with God, as I shall explain to you later. Do not neglect the hours of prayer which are observed by all the nuns;[5] you never know when the Spouse will call you (do not let what happened to the foolish virgins happen to you)[6] and if He will give you fresh trials under the disguise of consolations. If He does not,[7] you may be sure that you are not fit for them and that what you are doing is suitable for you. That is where both merit and humility come in,[8] when you really think that you are not fit for what you are doing.

Go cheerfully about whatever services you are ordered to do, as I have said; if such a servant is truly humble she will be blessed

---

[1] E.: "not merely for one year, or for ten." In this sentence E. also has the second person plural when V. has the first. T. follows E. in the first respect but V. in the second.

[2] E. has some slight verbal variations in this sentence, which ends: "is giving them their wages very well paid." It continues thus: "And how much better paid is (our soldier) than are those who serve the King!"

[3] E.: "When none of them is absent, and their captain sees they are desirous of serving." V. has "he" for "their captain", which I supply from E. In T., "present and" is deleted.

[4] *Lit.*: "would give them nothing", but the reference seems to be to payment. T. has "anxious" for "present".

[5] In T., "which . . . nuns" is deleted.

[6] This parenthetical sentence is not found in E., which also reads "Captain" for "Spouse".

[7] E. adds "call you", but the following sentence seems rather to refer to "give you fresh trials".

[8] E.: "That is where true humility comes in."

in her active life and will never make any complaint save of herself. *I would much rather be like her than like some contemplatives.* Leave others to wage their own conflicts, which are not light ones.[1] The standard-bearer is not a combatant, yet none the less he is exposed to great danger, and, inwardly, must suffer more than anyone, for he cannot defend himself, as he is carrying the standard, which he must not allow to leave his hands, even if he is cut to pieces. Just so contemplatives have to bear aloft the standard of humility and must suffer all the blows which are aimed at them without striking any themselves. Their duty is to suffer as Christ did, to raise the Cross on high, not to allow it to leave their hands, whatever the perils in which they find themselves, and not to let themselves be found backward in suffering. It is for this reason that they are given such an honourable duty. Let the contemplative consider what he is doing; for, if he lets the standard fall, the battle will be lost. Great harm, I think, is done to those who are not so far advanced if those whom they consider as captains and friends of God let them see them acting in a way unbefitting to their office.

The other soldiers do as best they can; at times they will withdraw from some position of extreme danger, and, as no one observes them, they suffer no loss of honour. But these others have all eyes fixed on them and cannot move. Their office, then, is a noble one, and the King confers great honour and favour upon anyone to whom He gives it, and who, in receiving it, accepts no light obligation. So, sisters,[2] as we *do not understand ourselves and* know not what we ask, let us leave everything to the Lord, *Who knows us better than we know ourselves. True humility consists in our being satisfied with what is given us.* There are some people who seem to want to ask favours from God as a right. A pretty kind of humility that is! He Who knows us all does well in seldom[3] giving things to such persons; He sees clearly that they are unable to drink of His chalice.

If you want to know whether you have made progress or not, sisters, you may be sure that you have if each of you thinks herself the worst of all and shows that she thinks this by acting

---

[1] E. continues: "Do you not know that in battles the standard-bearers and captains have the greatest obligations to fight? A poor soldier plods on step by step; and, if he sometimes hides, so as not to get into a place where he sees the mêlée to be thickest, no one observes him, and he loses neither his honour nor his life. (But) the standard-bearer is carrying the standard, which he must not allow to leave his hands even if he is cut to pieces: the eyes of all are upon him. Do you think those to whom the King gives these duties are being given a light task? In exchange for a little more honour they bind themselves to endure much more suffering; and, if they betray the slightest weakness, all is lost. So, friends, etc."
[2] E. (see preceding note) continues here, beginning: "So, friends (*fem.*)."
[3] E. has: "rarely." V. adds: "I think."

for the profit and benefit of the rest. Progress has nothing to do with enjoying the greatest number of consolations in prayer, or with raptures, visions or favours [often] given by the Lord,[1] the value of which we cannot estimate until we reach the world to come. The other things I have been describing are current coin, an unfailing source of revenue and a perpetual inheritance—not payments liable at any time to cease, like those favours which are given us and then come to an end. I am referring to the great virtues of humility, mortification and an obedience so *extremely* strict that we never go an inch[2] beyond the superior's orders, knowing that these orders come from God since she is in His place.[3] It is to this duty of obedience that you must attach the greatest importance. It seems to me that anyone who does not have it is not a nun at all, and so I am saying no more about it, as I am speaking to nuns whom I believe to be good, or, at least, desirous of being so. So well known is the matter, and so important,[4] that a single word will suffice[5] to prevent you from forgetting it.

I mean that, if anyone is under a vow of obedience and goes astray through not taking the greatest care to observe these vows with the highest degree of perfection, I do not know why she is in the convent. I can assure her, in any case, that, for so long as she fails in this respect, she will never succeed in leading the contemplative life, or even in leading a good active life: of that I am absolutely certain.[6] And even a person who has not this obligation, but who wishes or tries to achieve contemplation, must, if she would walk safely, be fully resolved to surrender her will to a confessor who is himself a contemplative[7] *and will understand her*. It is a well-known fact that she will make more progress in this way in a year than in a great many years if she acts otherwise.[8] As this does not affect you, however, I will say no more about it.

I conclude, my daughters, [by saying] that these are the virtues which I desire you to possess and to strive to obtain, and of which you should cherish a holy envy.[9] Do not be troubled because

---

[1] E.: "or things of that kind"
[2] V. has, literally, "a point"; E.: "a tittle."
[3] T. interpolates a sentence here which is not found elsewhere: "(One who is obedient?) has the great and certain prize, the worth of which is clear." This looks like a reflection of the copyist.
[4] E.: "So important is the matter."
[5] T. ends the sentence here.
[6] *Lit.*: "very, very certain"—a typically Teresan repetition. T. has only one "very"; E. has both.
[7] *Lit.*: "who is such."
[8] In E. this sentence reads: "This is very well known and many have written about it."
[9] T. omits: "and of which . . . envy."

you have no experience of those other kinds of devotion:[1] they are very unreliable. It may be that to some people they come from God,[2] and yet that if they came to you it might be because His Majesty had permitted you to be deceived and deluded by the devil, as He has permitted others:[3] *there is danger in this for women.* Why do you want to serve the Lord in so doubtful a way when there are so many ways of [serving Him in] safety?[4] Who wants to plunge you into these perils? I have said a great deal about this, because I am sure it will be useful, for this nature of ours is weak, though His Majesty will strengthen those on whom He wishes to bestow contemplation.[5] With regard to the rest, I am glad to have given them this advice, which will teach contemplatives humility also. *If you say you have no need of it, daughters, some of you may perhaps find it pleasant reading.* May the Lord, for His own sake,[6] give us light to follow His will in all things and we shall have no cause for fear.

CHAPTER XIX

Begins to treat of prayer. Addresses souls who cannot reason with the understanding.

It is a long time[7] since I wrote the last chapter and I have had no chance of returning to my writing, so that, without reading through what I have written, I cannot remember what I said. However, I must not spend too much time at this, so it will be best if I go right on[8] without troubling about the connection.[9] For those with orderly minds, and for souls who practise prayer and can be a great deal in their own company, many books have been written, and these are so good and are the work of such competent people that you would be making a mistake if you paid heed to anything about prayer that you learned from me. There are books, as I say, in which the mysteries of the life

---

[1] E., more succinctly: "Those other kinds of devotion—not in the least."
[2] E. has, literally: "Perhaps in another (person) it will be God."
[3] E.: "many" (*fem.*).
[4] E.: "If you can serve the Lord so well in ways which are safe, who wants to plunge you into these perils?"
[5] T. deletes part of the next sentence and substitutes: "These counsels are also (meant) to teach contemplatives humility."
[6] T. omits: "for His own sake."
[7] *Lit.*: "so many days." But on St. Teresa's indefinite use of the word "days" see p. 2, n. 4, above.
[8] *Lit.*: "it will have to go as it comes out."
[9] "It is necessary to point out this," adds T.

of the Lord and of His *sacred* Passion[1] are described in short passages, one for each day of the week; there are also meditations on the Judgment, on hell, on our own nothingness and on all that we owe to God,[2] and these books are excellent both as to their teaching and as to the way in which they plan the beginning and the end of the time of prayer.[3] There is no need to tell anyone who is capable of practising prayer in this way, and has already formed the habit of doing so, that by this good road the Lord will bring her to the harbour of light. If she begins so well, her end will be good also; and all who can walk along this road will walk restfully and securely, for one always walks restfully when the understanding is kept in restraint.[4] It is something else that I wish to treat of and help you about if the Lord is pleased to enable me to do so; if not, you will at least realize that there are many souls who suffer this trial, and you will not be so much distressed at undergoing it yourselves at first, *but will find some comfort in it.*

There are some souls, and some minds, as unruly as horses not yet broken in. No one can stop them: now they go this way, now that way; they are never still. *Although a skilled rider mounted on such a horse may not always be in danger, he will be so sometimes; and, even if he is not concerned about his life, there will always be the risk of his stumbling,*[5] *so that he has to ride with great care.* Some people are either like this by nature or God permits them to become so. I am very sorry for them; they seem to me like people who are very thirsty and see water a long way off, yet, when they try to go to it, find someone who all the time is barring their path[6]— at the beginning of their journey, in the middle and at the end. And when, after all their labour—and the labour is tremendous— they have conquered the first of their enemies, they allow themselves to be conquered by the second, and they prefer to die of thirst rather than drink water which is going to cost them so much trouble. Their strength has come to an end; their courage has failed them; and, though some of them are strong enough to conquer their second enemies as well as their first, when they meet the third group their strength comes to an end, though perhaps they are only a couple of steps from the fountain of living water, of which the Lord said to the Samaritan woman that

---

[1] E.: "in which the scenes (*pasos*) of the sacred Passion."
[2] E.: "and on the favours of God."
[3] St. Teresa is probably referring to the treatises of Luis de Granada and St. Peter of Alcántara (*S.S.M.*, I, 40–52, II, 106–20). Cf. *Constitutions* (Vol. III, p. 236, below).
[4] "So I am not speaking to such now," adds T.
[5] *Lit.*: "of his doing something on (the horse) which is not graceful."
[6] In E. and T. this sentence is in the singular, as it was originally in V. But the correction to the plural in V. seems to be in the Saint's own hand.

whosoever drinks of it shall not thirst again.[1] How right and *how very* true is that which comes from the lips of Truth Himself! In this life the soul will never thirst for anything more,[2] although its thirst for things in the life to come will exceed any natural thirst that we can imagine here below. How the soul thirsts to experience this thirst! For it knows how very precious it is, and, grievous though it be and exhausting, it creates the very satisfaction by which this thirst is allayed. It is therefore a thirst which quenches nothing but desire for earthly things, and, when God slakes it, satisfies in such a way that one of the greatest favours[3] He can bestow on the soul is to leave it with this longing, so that it has an even greater desire to drink of[4] this water again.

Water has three properties—three relevant properties which I can remember, that is to say, for it must have many more. One of them is that of cooling things; however hot we are, water[5] tempers the heat, and it will even put out a large fire, except when there is tar in the fire, in which case, *they say*, it only burns the more. God help me! What a marvellous thing it is that, when this fire is strong and fierce and subject to none of the elements, water should make it grow fiercer, and, though its contrary element, should not quench it but only cause it to burn the more! It would be very useful to be able to discuss this with someone who understands philosophy; if I knew the properties of things I could explain it myself;[6] but, though I love thinking about it, I cannot explain it[7]—perhaps I do not even understand it.

You will be glad, sisters, if God grants you to drink of this water, as are those who drink of it now, and you will understand how a genuine love of God, if it is really strong, and completely free from earthly things, and able to rise above them, is master of all the elements and of the whole world.[8] And, as water proceeds from the earth, there is no fear of its quenching this fire, which is the love of God;[9] though the two elements are con-

---

[1] St. John iv, 13.
[2] "In such a way as to lose God," interpolates T, "that is to say, by His taking His hand away from it; and so it must always walk with fear." In the next sentence, T. omits the words "natural thirst".
[3] E.: "that the greatest favour." This was also the original reading of V. and T., but in each of these it has been corrected by the author to read as in the text.
[4] E.: "to ask for."
[5] E.: "however hot one is, entering a river."
[6] E.: "How useful it would be if I were a philosopher and knew the properties of things and could explain myself!"
[7] E.: "I cannot express what I understand."
[8] "And how," adds T., "there is no need to be afraid, (if we are) trusting in the mercy of God." T. continues: "that the water, which proceeds from the earth, will quench this fire, etc."
[9] E. omits: "which is the love of God."

traries, it has no power over it. The fire is absolute master, and subject to nothing. You will not be surprised, then, sisters, at the way I have insisted in this book that you should strive to obtain this freedom. Is it not a funny thing that a poor *little* nun of Saint Joseph's should attain mastery over the whole earth and all the elements? What wonder that the saints did as they pleased with them by the help of God? Fire and water obeyed Saint Martin; even birds and fishes[1] were obedient to Saint Francis; and similarly with many other saints.[2] *Helped as they were by God, and themselves doing all that was in their power, they could almost have claimed this as a right.*[3] It was clear that they were masters over everything in the world, because they had striven so hard to despise it and subjected themselves to the Lord of the world with all their might. So, as I say, the water, which springs from the earth, has no power over this fire.[4] Its flames rise high and its source is in nothing so base as the earth. There are other fires of love for God—small ones, which may be quenched by the least little thing. But this fire will most certainly not be so quenched.[5] Even should a whole sea of temptations assail it, they will not keep it from burning or prevent it from gaining the mastery over them.

Water which comes down as rain from Heaven will quench the flames even less,[6] for in that case the fire and the water are not contraries, but have the same origin. Do not fear that the one element may harm the other; each helps the other and they produce the same effect.[7] For the water of genuine tears—that is, tears which come from true prayer—is a good gift[8] from the King of Heaven; it fans the flames and keeps them alight, while the

---

[1] E. omits: "birds and", and ends the sentence at "Francis".
[2] T.: "with other saints, who were masters, etc."
[3] The following passage is inserted here in E. but is lightly crossed out in the manuscript, probably by St. Teresa herself, and, as it does not occur in V., it would seem that she intended to omit it. "What do you suppose the Psalmist (means when he) says that all things are subjected to man and placed under his feet [the reference is to Psalm viii, 8]. Do you suppose (that means the feet) of all men? No fear of that! What I see is men subjected to them [i.e., the things of the world] and under *their* feet. I knew a man who was killed while he was arguing about a half-*real* [a small coin]: think what a wretched price he was paid for so subjecting himself. There are many things which you will see daily and which will tell you that I am speaking the truth. Indeed, the Psalmist could not lie, for his words are those of the Holy Spirit. I believe (though I may not understand it or I may be mistaken about having read it) that the perfect are said to be rulers over all the things of earth." E. then continues: "If it is water from Heaven, etc." (see n. 6.)
[4] V. ends the sentence at "power" but "over it" is found in the margin. The reading in the text is from T.
[5] *Lit.*: "But this one—no, no."
[6] E.: "If it is water from Heaven, do not fear that it will quench this fire, any more than that that other (water) will revive it."
[7] Deletions are made here in T. and the following is substituted: "Thus the one will not harm the other, but they will help (each other)."
[8] T. (?by an error) reads *vienen* (come) for *bien* (well, good): "is (*lit.*, comes) given by."

fire helps to cool the water.[1] God bless me! What a beautiful and wonderful thing it is that fire should cool water! But it does; and it even freezes all worldly affections,[2] when it is combined with the living water which comes from Heaven, the source of the above-mentioned tears, which are given us, and not acquired by our diligence.[3] Certainly, then, nothing worldly has warmth enough left in it to induce us to cling to it unless it is something which increases this fire, the nature of which is not to be easily satisfied, but, if possible, to enkindle the entire world.

The second property of water is that it cleanses things that are not clean already. What would become of the world if there were no water for washing? Do you know what cleansing properties there are in this living water, this heavenly water, this clear water,[4] when it is unclouded, and free from mud, and comes down from Heaven?[5] Once the soul has drunk of it I am convinced[6] that it makes it pure and clean of all its sins; for, as I have written, God does not allow us to drink of this water *of perfect contemplation* whenever we like: the choice is not ours; this Divine union is something quite supernatural, given that it may cleanse the soul and leave it pure and free from the mud and misery in which it has been plunged because of its sins. Other consolations, excellent as they may be, which come through the intermediacy of the understanding, are like water running all over the ground. This cannot be drunk directly from the source; and its course is never free from clogging impurities, so that it is neither so pure nor so clean as the other.[7] I should not say that this prayer I have been describing, which comes from reasoning with the intellect, is living water—I mean so far as my understanding of it goes. For, despite our efforts, there is always something clinging to the soul, through the influence of the body and of the baseness of our nature, which we should prefer not to be there.

I will explain myself further. We are meditating on the nature of the world, and on the way in which everything will

---

[1] E.: "For the water keeps the fire alight and helps to feed it while the fire helps to cool the water."

[2] E. ends the paragraph with the words: "affections. When with it is combined the living water which comes from Heaven, have no fear that it will give the slightest heat to anyone."

[3] Another hand than St. Teresa's has deleted the words "and not acquired by our diligence" in T. and substituted, after "given us", "by the King of Heaven". "Thus" is also substituted for "Certainly, then", in the following sentence.

[4] T. ends the sentence here.

[5] E.: "and is taken from the same source?"

[6] T.: "I think."

[7] E. ends the paragraph: "I should not say that this was living water—I mean as far as my understanding of it goes," and omits the whole of the paragraph following.

come to an end, so that we may learn to despise it, when, almost without noticing it, we find ourselves ruminating on things in the world that we love. We try to banish these thoughts, but we cannot help being slightly distracted by thinking of things that have happened, or will happen, of things we have done and of things we are going to do. Then we begin to think of how we can get rid of these thoughts; and that sometimes plunges us once again into the same danger. It is not that we ought to omit such meditations; but we need to retain our misgivings about them and not to grow careless. In contemplation the Lord Himself relieves us of this care, for He will not trust us to look after ourselves. So dearly does He love our souls that He prevents them from rushing into things which may do them harm just at this time when He is anxious to help them. So He calls them to His side at once, and in a single moment reveals more truths to them and gives them a clearer insight into the nature of everything than they could otherwise gain in many years. For our sight is poor and the dust which we meet on the road blinds us; but in contemplation the Lord brings us to the end of the day's journey without our understanding how.

The third property of water is that it satisfies and quenches thirst. Thirst, I think, means the desire for something which is very necessary for us—so necessary that if we have none of it we shall die. It is a strange thing that if we have no water we die, and that we can also lose our lives through having too much of it, as happens to many people who get drowned. Oh, my Lord, if only one could be plunged so deeply into this living water that one's life would end! Can that be? Yes:[1] this love and desire for God[2] can increase so much that human nature is unable to bear it, and so there have been persons who have died of it. I knew one person[3] who had this living water in such great abundance that she would almost have been drawn out of herself by raptures if God had not quickly succoured her.[4] *She had such*

---

[1] T., here and elsewhere, has *Sé* (I know) for *Sí* (yes). As this substitution is probably a slip, it is not normally recorded, though it sometimes changes the sense considerably.

[2] E.: "Oh, my Lord, if only one could be drowned by being plunged into this living water! But that is impossible. Still, the desire for it, this love and desire for God."

[3] The author probably refers to herself: Cf. *Life*, Chapter XX, and *Relations, passim.*

[4] V. and T. (the latter substituting "a great suspension" for "raptures") read: "who, if God had not quickly succoured her with this living water, in such great abundance that she would almost have been drawn out of herself." This leaves "who" without a verb and makes incomplete sense. St. Teresa's first editor, by substituting *era* for *con*, restored the sense and is followed in the text above. E., by means of the sentence given in italics, which combines with the preceding sentence, makes the substitution unnecessary, but at the cost of an unnatural word-sequence which St. Teresa was presumably trying to eliminate when she recast the passage in V.

a thirst, and her desire grew so greatly, that she realized clearly that she might quite possibly die of thirst if something were not done for her.[1] I say that she would almost have been drawn out of herself because in this state the soul is in repose. So intolerable does such a soul find the world that it seems to be overwhelmed,[2] but it comes to life again in God; and in this way His Majesty enables it to enjoy experiences which, if it had remained within itself, would perforce have cost it its life.

Let it be understood from this that, as there can be nothing in our supreme Good which is not perfect, all that He gives is for our welfare; and, however abundant this water which He gives may be,[3] in nothing that He gives can there be superfluity. For, if His gift is abundant, He also bestows on the soul, as I have said, an abundant capacity for drinking; just as a glass-maker moulds his vessels to the size[4] he thinks necessary, so that there is room for what he wishes to pour into them. As our desires for this water come from ourselves, they are never free from fault; any good that there may be in them comes from the help of the Lord. But we are so indiscreet that, as the pain is sweet and pleasant, we think we can never[5] have too much of it. We have an immeasurable longing for it,[6] and, so far as is possible on earth, we stimulate this longing: sometimes this goes so far as to cause death. How happy is such a death! And yet by living one might perhaps have helped others to die of the desire for it. I believe the devil has something to do with this: knowing how much harm we can do him by living, he tempts us to be indiscreet in our penances and so to ruin our health, which is a matter of no small moment to him.

I advise anyone who attains to an experience of this fierce thirst to watch herself carefully, for I think she will have to contend with this temptation. She may not die of her thirst, but her health will be ruined,[7] and she will involuntarily give her feelings outward expression, which ought at all costs to be avoided. Sometimes, however, all our diligence in this respect is unavailing and we are unable to hide our emotions as much as we should like. Whenever we are assailed by these strong

---

[1] E. ends the paragraph: "Blessed be He Who invites us to come and drink in His Gospel!"

[2] *Lit.*: "drowned."

[3] E. begins the paragraph: "And, as in our Good and Lord there can be nothing which is not perfect, and He alone gives us this water which we need, however much of it there may be."

[4] T.: "in the way."

[5] T.: "we never allow ourselves to."

[6] *Lit.*: "We eat it without measure."

[7] The next few lines are not found in E., which continues: "And when this increase of desire is very great let her try not to add to them, but check them gently, etc."

impulses stimulating the increase of our desire, let us take great care not to add to them ourselves but to check them gently[1] by thinking of something else. For our *own* nature may be playing as great a part in producing these feelings as our love. There are some people *of this type* who have keen desires for all kinds of things, even for bad things,[2] but I do not think such people can have achieved great mortification, for mortification is always profitable. It seems foolish to check so good a thing[3] as this desire, but it is not. I am not saying that the desire should be uprooted—only checked; one may be able to do this by stimulating some other desire which is equally praiseworthy.

In order to explain myself better I will give an illustration. A man has a great desire to be with God, as Saint Paul had, and to be loosed from this prison.[4] This causes him pain which yet is in itself a great joy, and no small degree of mortification will be needed if he is to check it—in fact, he will not always be able to do so. But when he finds it oppressing him so much he may almost lose his reason. I saw this happen to someone not long ago; she was[5] of an impetuous nature, but so accustomed to curbing her own will that, from what I had seen at other times, I thought her will was completely annihilated; yet, when I saw her for a moment, the great stress and strain caused by her efforts to hide her feelings had all but destroyed her reason.[6] In such an extreme case, I think, even did the desire come from the Spirit of God, it would be true humility to be afraid; for we must not imagine that we have sufficient charity to bring us to such a state of oppression.

I shall not think it at all wrong[7] (if it be possible, I mean, for it may not always be so) for us to change our desire by reflecting that, if we live, we have more chance of serving God, and that we might do this by giving light to some soul which otherwise would be lost;[8] as well as that, if we serve Him more, we shall

---

[1] *Lit.*: "to cut the thread." E. adds: "of the impulse."
[2] E. ends the sentence here.
[3] E.: "such a thing."
[4] Presumably a reminiscence of Romans vii, 24 or Philippians i, 23. E. continues: "and impetuous persons, without being conscious of it, will come to show outward signs (of their desire), which, as far as possible, should be avoided. Let us modify our desire, etc."
[5] T. inserts "not", perhaps in error, as another "not" precedes it, and the context suggests the affirmative sense. T. continues: "but accustomed, etc.", and the phrase "that, from . . . annihilated" is deleted.
[6] This, too, is generally taken as referring to St. Teresa herself.
[7] T.: "And so it will not be considered wrong."
[8] E. ends the sentence here and continues: "This is a consolation appropriate to so great a trial, which will allay our pain, and we shall gain by acquiring such great charity that, in order to serve the Lord Himself, we shall be willing to suffer here below for one day. It is as if a person were suffering a great trial or a grievous affliction and we consoled him by telling him to have patience. And if the devil had

deserve to enjoy Him more, and grieve that we have served Him so little. These are consolations appropriate to such great trials: they will allay our pain and we shall gain a great deal by them if in order to serve the Lord Himself we are willing to spend a long time here below and to live with our grief. It is as if a person were suffering a great trial or a grievous affliction and we consoled him by telling him to have patience and leave himself in God's hands so that His will might be fulfilled in him: it is always best to leave ourselves in God's hands.

And what if the devil had anything to do with these strong desires? This might be possible, as I think is suggested in Cassian's story of a hermit, leading the austerest of lives, who was persuaded by the devil to throw himself down a well so that he might see God the sooner.[1] I do not think this hermit can have served God either humbly or efficiently, for the Lord is faithful and His Majesty would never allow a servant of His to be blinded in a matter in which the truth was so clear. But, of course, if the desire had come from God, it would have done the hermit no harm; for such desires bring with them illumination, moderation and discretion. This is fitting, but our enemy and adversary seeks to harm us wherever he can; and, as he is not unwatchful, we must not be so either. This is an important matter in many respects:[2] for example, we must shorten our time of prayer, however much joy it gives us, if we see our bodily strength waning or find that our head aches: discretion is most necessary in everything.

Why do you suppose, daughters, that I have tried, *as people say*, to describe the end of the battle before it has begun and to point to its reward by telling you about the blessing which comes from drinking of the heavenly source of[3] this living water? I have done this so that you may not be distressed at[4] the trials and annoyances of the road, and may tread it with courage and not grow weary; for, as I have said, it may be that, when you have arrived, and have only to stoop and drink of the spring,[5] you may fail to do so and lose this blessing, thinking that you have not the strength to attain it and that it is not for you.

---

anything to do with such a strong desire, as he must have had in the case of one whom he persuaded to throw himself down a well so that he might go and see God, it would be a sign that (the person concerned) was not far from obtaining the increase of that desire, for, if it were from the Lord, it would do him no harm: it is impossible (that it should), for such desires bring with them, etc."

[1] Cassian: *Conferences*, II. v.
[2] E. ends the paragraph: "and sometimes it is very necessary that we should not forget it."
[3] E.: "of this heavenly source and of."
[4] T.: "may not complain of."
[5] E. omits: "have arrived, and" and "of the spring".

Remember, the Lord invites us all; and, since He is Truth Itself, we cannot doubt Him. If His invitation were not a general one, He would not have said: "I will give you to drink." He might have said: "Come, all of you, for after all you will lose nothing by coming; and I will give drink to those whom I think fit for it." But, as He said we were all to come, without making this condition, I feel sure that none will fail to receive this living water unless they cannot keep to the path.[1] May the Lord, Who promises it, give us grace, for His Majesty's own sake, to seek it as it must be sought.

CHAPTER XX

Describes how, in one way or another, we never lack consolation on the road of prayer. Counsels the sisters to include this subject continually in their conversation.

In this last chapter I seem to have been contradicting what I had previously said,[2] as, in consoling those who had not reached the contemplative state, I told them that the Lord had different roads by which they might come to Him, just as He also had many mansions.[3] I now repeat this: His Majesty, being Who He is and understanding our weakness, has provided for us. But He did not say: "Some must come by this way and others by that." His mercy is so great that He has forbidden none to strive to come and drink of this fountain of life. Blessed be He for ever! What good reasons there would have been for His forbidding me!

But as He did not order me to cease from drinking when I had begun to do so,[4] but caused me to be plunged into the depths of the water, it is certain that He will forbid no one to come: indeed, He calls us publicly, and in a loud voice, to do so.[5] Yet, as He is so good, He does not force us to drink, but enables those who wish to follow Him to drink in many ways so that none may lack comfort or die of thirst. For from this rich spring flow many streams—some large, others small, and also little pools for children, which they find quite large enough, for the

---

[1] E. ends the chapter here. This final paragraph appears to be based upon St. John vii, 37.
[2] E.: "I seem to be contradicting myself."
[3] E.: "that God, our Good, had different roads, and that they might come to Him by different roads, and that thus He had [literally, both here and in the text above: "there were"] many mansions (*moradas*)." There is a reference here to St. John xiv, 2.
[4] E. continues: "and He did not plunge me"—perhaps a slip (*sino que* for *no* would give the same sense as in V.).
[5] St. John vii, 37.

sight of a great deal of water would frighten them: by children, I mean those who are in the early stages.[1] Therefore, sisters, have no fear that you will die of thirst on this road; you will never lack so much of the water of comfort that your thirst will be intolerable;[2] so take my advice and do not tarry on the way, but strive like strong men until you die in the attempt, for you are here for nothing else than to strive. If you always pursue this determination to die rather than fail to reach the end of the road,[3] the Lord may bring you through this life with a certain degree of thirst, but in the life which never ends He will give you great abundance to drink and you will have no fear of its failing you. May the Lord grant us never to fail Him. Amen.[4]

Now, in order to set out upon this aforementioned road so that we do not go astray at the very start, let us consider for a moment how the first stage of our journey is to be begun, for that is the most important thing—or rather, every part of the journey is of importance to the whole. I do not mean to say that no one who has not the resolution that I am going to describe should set out upon the road, for the Lord will gradually bring her nearer to perfection. And even if she did no more than take one step, this alone[5] has such virtue that there is no fear of her losing it or of failing to be very well rewarded.[6] We might compare her to someone who has a rosary with a bead specially indulgenced:[7] one prayer in itself will bring her something, and the more she uses the bead the more she will gain; but if she left it in a box and never took it out it would be better for her not to have it. So, although she may never go any farther along the same road, the short distance she has progressed will give her light and thus help her to go along other roads, and the farther she goes the more light she will gain. In fact, she may be sure that she will do herself no kind of harm through having started on the road, even if she leaves it, for good never leads to evil.[8] So, daughters, whenever you meet people and

---

[1] *Lit.*: "these are they who are, etc." E. is shorter: "which those who are in a very early stage of virtue find quite large enough."
[2] T.: "you will never lack the water of comfort."
[3] E.: "to reach this spring."
[4] E.: "the Lord may bring you through this life without reaching it, but in the next life He will give it you with great abundance, and you will drink without fear of its failing you through your own fault. May the Lord grant that His mercy may not fail us. Amen."
[5] E.: "the road alone."
[6] V.: "paid." E.: "guerdoned." E. adds: "It contains within itself many pardons (*perdones*), both great and small." Note, in the next sentence, that the Spanish phrase repeats *perdones*.
[7] *Cuenta de perdones*: a bead larger in size than the remainder in the rosary and carrying special indulgences for the souls in purgatory.
[8] T. deletes: "for good . . . evil."

find them well-disposed and even attracted to the life of prayer, try to remove from them all fear of beginning a course which may bring them such great blessings.[1] For the love of God, I beg you always to see to it that your conversation is benefiting those with whom you speak. For your prayers must be for the profit of their souls; and, since you must always pray to the Lord for them, sisters, you would seem to be doing ill if you did not strive to benefit them in every possible way.

If you would be a good kinswoman, this is true friendship; if you would be a good friend, you may be sure that this is the only possible way. Let the truth be in your hearts, as it will be if you practise meditation, and you will see clearly what love we are bound to have for our neighbours. This is no time for child's play, sisters, and these worldly friendships, good though they may be, seem no more than that. Neither with your relatives[2] nor with anyone else must you use such phrases as "If you love me", or "Don't you love me?" unless you have in view some noble end and the profit of the person to whom you are speaking. It may be necessary, in order to get a relative—a brother or some such person—to listen to the truth and accept it, to prepare him for it by using such phrases and showing him signs of love, which are always pleasing to sense. He may possibly be more affected, and influenced, by one kind word, as such phrases are called, than by a great deal which you might say about God,[3] and then there would be plenty of opportunities for you to talk to him about God afterwards. I do not forbid such phrases, therefore, provided you use them in order to bring someone profit. But for no other reason can there be any good in them and they may even do harm without your being aware of it. Everybody knows that you are nuns and that your business is prayer. Do not say to yourselves: "I have no wish to be considered good," for what people see in you is bound to bring them either profit or harm. People like nuns,[4] on whom is laid the obligation to speak of nothing save in the spirit of God,[5] act very wrongly if they dissemble in this way, except occasionally[6] for the purpose of doing greater good. Your intercourse and conversation must be like this: let any who wish to talk to you learn

---

[1] *Lit.*: "of beginning so great a good." T. amplifies: "of beginning to search for this hidden treasure."
[2] E.: "with a brother."
[3] T. omits: "and influenced" and goes on: "but he would get to know about this afterwards and it would give him pleasure", ending the sentence here.
[4] E. omits: "like nuns."
[5] *Lit.*: "save in God"—i.e., save as those whose life is centred in God: not necessarily, I think, only *of* God.
[6] E. omits: "occasionally."

your language; and, if they will not, be careful never to learn theirs: it might lead you to hell.

It matters little if you are considered ill-bred and still less if you are taken for hypocrites: indeed, you will gain by this, because only those who understand your language will come to see you. If one knows no Arabic, one has no desire to talk a great deal[1] with a person who knows no other language. So worldly people will neither weary you nor do you harm—and it would do you no small harm to have to begin to *learn and talk* a new language; you would spend all your time learning it. You cannot know as well as I do, for I have found it out by experience, how very bad this is for the soul;[2] no sooner does it learn one thing than it has to forget another and it never has any rest. This you must at all costs avoid; for peace and quiet in the soul are of great importance on the road which we are about to tread.

If those with whom you converse wish[3] to learn your language, it is not for you to teach it to them, but you can tell them[4] what wealth they will gain by learning it.[5] Never grow tired of this, but do it piously, lovingly and prayerfully, with a view to helping them; they will then realize what great gain *it brings*, and will go and seek a master to teach it them. Our Lord would be doing you no light favour if through your agency He were to arouse some soul to obtain this blessing. When once one begins to describe this road, what a large number of things there are to be said about it,[6] even by those who have trodden it as unsuccessfully as I have! *I only wish I could write with both hands, so as not to forget one thing while I am saying another.* May it please the Lord, sisters, that you may be enabled to speak of it better than I have done.

CHAPTER XXI

Describes the great importance of setting out upon the practice of prayer with firm resolution and of heeding no difficulties put in the way by the devil.

Do not be dismayed, daughters,[7] at the number of things which you have to consider before setting out on this Divine

---

[1] E.: "to have a great deal to do."
[2] E.: "what great labour this gives the soul."
[3] E.: "If those who come (to see you) wish."
[4] E.: "but it will be for you to tell them."
[5] E.: "by trying to learn it."
[6] E. ends the sentence here and ends the chapter with the italicized sentence ("I only wish . . . another!"), which follows directly upon it.
[7] T.: "Do not marvel, sisters."

journey, which is the royal road to Heaven.[1] By taking this road we gain such precious treasures that it is no wonder if the cost seems to us a high one. The time will come when we shall realize that all we have paid has been nothing at all by comparison with the greatness of our prize.

Let us now return to those who wish to travel on this road, and will not halt until they reach their goal, which is the place where they can drink of this water of life.[2] *Although in some book or other—in several, in fact—I have read what a good thing it is to begin in this way, I do not think anything will be lost if I speak of it here.* As I say, it is most important—all-important, indeed—that they should begin well by making an earnest and most determined resolve[3] not to halt until they reach their goal, whatever may come, whatever may happen to them, however hard they may have to labour, whoever may complain of them, whether they reach their goal or die on the road or have no heart[4] to confront the trials which they meet, whether the very world dissolves before them. Yet again and again people will say to us: "It is dangerous", "So-and-so was lost through doing this", "Someone else got into wrong ways",[5] "Some other person, who was always praying, fell just the same", "It is bad for virtue", "It is not meant for women; it may lead them into delusions",[6] "They would do better to stick to their spinning", "These subtleties are of no use to them", "It is quite enough for them to say their Paternoster and Ave Maria."

With this last remark, sisters, I quite agree. Of course it is enough! It is always a great thing to base your prayer on prayers which were uttered by the very lips of the Lord.[7] People are quite right to say this, and, were it not for our great weakness and the lukewarmness of our devotion, there would be no need for any other systems of prayer or for any other books at all.[8] I am speaking to souls who are unable to recollect themselves by meditating upon other mysteries, and who think they need special methods of prayer; some people have such ingenious minds[9] that nothing is good enough for them! So I think I will start to

---

[1] E.: "Do not be surprised, daughters, for this is the royal road (*camino real*) to Heaven." A more idiomatic translation of *camino real* would be "king's highway": cf. the use of the phrase on p. 90, below.
[2] E.: "Let us now return to those who wish to drink of this water of life and wish to journey till they arrive at the spring itself."
[3] *Lit.*: "determined determination": this doubling of words is not uncommon in St. Teresa. Cf. n. 9, below.
[4] T.: "have not the devotion."
[5] E. omits this sentence.
[6] E.: "for women, who get delusions."
[7] E.: "by such lips."
[8] E. adds: "nor would other (kinds of) prayer be necessary."
[9] *Lit.*: "are such ingenious geniuses."

lay down some rules for each part of our prayer—beginning, middle and end—although I shall not spend long on the higher stages.[1] They cannot take books from you,[2] and, if you are studious and humble, you need nothing more.

I have always been fond of the words of the Gospels[3] and have found more recollection in them than in the most carefully planned books—especially books of which the authors were not fully approved,[4] and which I never wanted to read. If I keep close to this Master of wisdom,[5] He may perhaps give me some thoughts[6] which will help you. I do not say that I will explain these Divine prayers, for that I should not presume to do, and there are a great many explanations of them already. Even were there none,[7] it would be ridiculous for me to attempt any. But I will write down a few thoughts on the words of the Paternoster;[8] for sometimes, when we are most anxious to nurture our devotion, consulting a great many books will kill it. When a master is himself giving a lesson, he treats his pupil kindly and likes him[9] to enjoy being taught and does his utmost to help him learn. Just so will this heavenly Master do with us.

Pay no heed, then,[10] to anyone who tries to frighten you or depicts to you the perils of the way. What a strange idea that one could ever expect to travel on a road infested by thieves, for the purpose of gaining some great treasure, without running into danger! Worldly people like to take life peaceably; but they will deny themselves sleep, *perhaps* for nights on end, in order to gain a farthing's profit, and they will leave you no peace either of body or of soul. If, when you are on the way to gaining this treasure, or to taking it by force (as the Lord says the violent do)[11] and are travelling by this royal road—this safe road trodden by our King[12] and by His elect and His saints—if even then they

---

[1] E.: "although I shall only touch on the higher stages, for, as I say, I have already written about them."

[2] E. adds: "so that such a good book does not remain to you."

[3] E. adds: "which came from those most sacred lips just as He spoke them."

[4] V.: *muy aprobado*. E. is stronger: *muy muy aprobado*.

[5] E.: "of all wisdom." T.: "to this Lord and Master of wisdom."

[6] V.: *alguna consideración*: the use of the singular form in a plural sense, with the shade of meaning which might be conveyed by "some occasional thoughts," is common in Spanish. E. uses one of St. Teresa's characteristic diminutives (see Vol. I, p. xxi) *alguna consideracioncita*—"some (occasional) trifling thoughts."

[7] E. omits: "Even were there none."

[8] E.: "on some of the words of them."

[9] T. has "and seeks for him"; but this (*busca* for *gusta*) might be an error, and the construction suggests to me that it is.

[10] E. begins a new chapter here with the words: "Returning to what I was saying, pay no heed."

[11] The original has *robar* (steal), which is perhaps nearer the A.V. of St. Matthew xi, 12 than the D.V. "bear it away".

[12] E.: "by Christ our Emperor."

tell you it is full of danger and make you so afraid, what will be the dangers encountered by those who think they will be able to gain this treasure and yet are not on the road to it?

Oh, my daughters, how incomparably greater must be the risks they run! And yet they have no idea of this until they fall headlong into some real danger. Having *perhaps* no one to help them, they lose this water altogether, and drink neither much nor little of it, either from a pool or from a stream. How do you suppose they can do without a drop of this water and yet travel along a road on which there are so many adversaries to fight? Of course, sooner or later, they will die of thirst; for we must all journey to this fountain, my daughters, whether we will or no, though we may not all do so in the same way. Take my advice, then, and let none mislead you by showing you any other road than that of prayer.

I am not now discussing whether or no everyone must practise mental or vocal prayer; but I do say that you yourselves require both.[1] For prayer is the duty of religious. If anyone tells you it is dangerous, look upon that person himself as your principal danger and flee from his company. Do not forget this, for it is advice that you may possibly need. It will be dangerous for you if you do not possess humility and the other virtues; but God forbid that the way of prayer should be a way of danger! This fear seems to have been invented by the devil, who has apparently been very clever in bringing about the fall of some who practise prayer.[2]

See how blind the world is![3] It never thinks of all the thousands who have fallen into heresies and other great evils through yielding to distractions and not practising prayer.[4] As against these multitudes there are a few[5] who did practise prayer and whom the devil has been successful enough at his own trade to cause to fall: in doing this he has also caused some to be very much afraid of virtuous practices. Let those who make use of this pretext[6] to absolve themselves from such practices take heed, for in order to save themselves from evil they are fleeing from good. I have never heard of such a wicked invention; it must indeed

---

[1] E. is more concise: "but I do say—for you, both."

[2] E. and T. omit: "apparently." E. ends: "of some who were following this road." T. adds, after "practise prayer": "and in frightening some with regard to matters of virtue."

[3] E. reads: "See what great blindness!" and, instead of "all the (*muchos*) thousands", uses a hyperbolical expression then current: "the world of thousands, as they say." T. omits: "See how . . . virtuous practices."

[4] E. reads: "evils, and not practising prayer, or knowing what it is—a condition very much to be feared."

[5] "A very small number," adds E.

[6] E. has "who have these remedies and take (them) in order to absolve themselves, etc.", and a different construction, though the same sense, in the clause following.

come from the devil. Oh, my Lord, defend Thyself. See how Thy words are being misunderstood. Permit no such weakness in Thy servants.[1]

There is one great blessing—you will always find a few people ready to help you. For it is a characteristic of the true servant of God, to whom His Majesty has given light to follow the true path, that, when beset by these fears, his desire not to stop only increases. He sees clearly[2] whence the devil's blows are coming, but he parries each blow and breaks his adversary's head. The anger which this arouses in the devil is greater than all the satisfaction which he receives from the pleasures[3] given him by others. When, in troublous times, he has sown his tares, and seems to be leading men everywhere in his train, half-blinded, and [deceiving them into] believing themselves to be zealous for the right,[4] God raises up someone to open their eyes and bid them look at the fog with which the devil has obscured their path. (How great God is! To think that just one man, or perhaps two,[5] can do more by telling the truth than can a great many men all together!) And then they gradually begin to see the path again and God gives them courage. If people say there is danger in prayer,[6] this servant of God, by his deeds if not by his words, tries to make them realize what a good thing it is. If they say that frequent communion is[7] inadvisable, he only practises it[8] the more. So, because just one or two are fearlessly following the better path, the Lord gradually regains what He had lost.[9]

Cease troubling about these fears, then, sisters; and never pay heed to such matters of popular opinion. This is no time for believing everyone; believe only those whom you see modelling their lives on the life[10] of Christ. Endeavour always to have a good conscience; practise humility; despise all worldly things; and believe firmly in the teaching of our Holy Mother [the Roman][11] Church. You may then be quite sure that you are on

---

[1] E. adds: "It is well, daughters: they will not take the Paternoster and the Ave Maria from you" (cf. p. 90, n. 2, above), but these words, which constitute a somewhat violent transition, have been crossed out in the manuscript, nor do they appear in V. E. then continues: "You will always find many people ready to help you."
[2] T. deletes: "clearly".
[3] E.: "than all the pleasures."
[4] E.: "to be great Christians."
[5] E.: "one man, or perhaps ten."
[6] E.: "there must be no prayer."
[7] E.: "that so many communions are."
[8] E.: "he approaches the Most Holy Sacrament."
[9] E.: "If there is just one with courage, another comes at once, and the Lord regains what He had lost."
[10] T.: "the law."
[11] The interpolation in T. is in St. Teresa's own hand.

a [very] good road. Cease, as I have said, to have fear where no fear is; if any one attempts to frighten you, point out the road[1] to him in all humility. Tell him that you have a Rule which commands you, as it does, to pray without ceasing, and that that rule you must keep. If they tell you that you should practise only vocal prayer, ask whether your mind and heart ought not to be in what you say. If they answer "Yes"—and they cannot do otherwise—you see they are admitting that you are bound to practise mental prayer, and even contemplation, if God should grant it you. [Blessed be He for ever.]

CHAPTER XXII

Explains the meaning of mental prayer.

You must know, daughters, that[2] whether or no you are practising mental prayer has nothing to do with keeping the lips closed. If, while I am speaking with God,[3] I have a clear realization and full consciousness that I am doing so, and if this is more real to me than the words I am uttering, then I am combining mental and vocal prayer. When people tell you that you are speaking with God by reciting the Paternoster[4] and thinking of worldly things—well, words fail me. When you speak, as it is right for you to do, with so great a Lord, it is well that you should think of Who it is that you are addressing, and what you yourself are, if only that you may speak to Him with proper respect. How can you address a king[5] with the deference due to him, or how can you know what ceremonies have to be used when speaking to a grandee, unless you are clearly conscious of the nature of his position and of yours? It is because of this, and because it is the custom to do so, that you must behave respectfully to him[6], and must learn *what the custom is, and not be careless about such things*, or you will be dismissed as a simpleton and obtain none of the things you desire. *And furthermore, unless you are quite conversant with it, you must get all necessary information, and have what you are going to say written down for you.* It once

---

[1] T. deletes "road" and substitutes "truth".
[2] E. begins the chapter: "Yes, whether or no, etc."
[3] T. adds: "and praying vocally."
[4] E. has: "reciting the Ave Maria." On revising her work the Saint evidently reflected that the recitation of the Paternoster would provide a more suitable illustration of "speaking with God".
[5] E.: "a prince."
[6] E. omits: "respectfully."

happened to me, when I was not accustomed to addressing aristocrats, that I had to go on a matter of urgent business to see a lady who had to be addressed as "Your Ladyship".[1] *I was shown that word in writing; but I am stupid, and had never used such a term before; so when I arrived I got it wrong. So I decided to tell her about it and she laughed heartily and told me to be good enough to use the ordinary form of polite address,*[2] *which I did.*

How is it, my Lord, how is it, my Emperor, that Thou canst suffer this, *Prince of all Creation?* For Thou, my God, art a King without end, and Thine is no borrowed Kingdom, *but Thine own, and it will never pass away.* When the Creed says "Whose Kingdom shall have no end" the phrase nearly always makes me feel particularly happy. I praise Thee, Lord, and bless Thee, *and all things praise Thee* for ever—for Thy Kingdom will endure for ever. Do Thou never allow it to be thought right, Lord, for those who *praise Thee and* come to speak with Thee to do so with their lips alone. What do you mean, Christians, when you say that mental prayer is unnecessary?[3] Do you understand what you are saying? I really do not think you can. And so you want us all to go wrong: you cannot know what mental prayer is,[4] or how vocal prayers should be said, or what is meant by contemplation. For, if you knew this, you would not condemn on the one hand what you praise on the other.

Whenever I remember to do so, I shall always speak of mental and vocal prayer together, daughters, so that you may not be alarmed. I know what such fears lead to,[5] for I have suffered a certain number of trials in this respect,[6] and so I should be sorry if anyone were to unsettle you, for it is very bad for you to have misgivings[7] while you are walking on this path. It is most important that you should realize you are making progress; for if a traveller is told[8] that he has taken the wrong road, and has lost his way, he begins to wander to and fro and the constant

---

[1] This is generally taken as referring to St. Teresa's visit to Doña Luisa de la Cerda in 1562 (Vol. I, pp. 232, ff., above).

[2] *Lit.*: "to call her 'Honour'." The point of this delightfully unaffected reminiscence, omitted in V. and inserted here rather for its attractiveness than for its artistic appropriateness, is that "Your Honour" (*Vuestra Merced*: now abbreviated to Vd. and used as the third personal pronoun of ordinary polite address) was an expression merely of respect and not of rank: the Saint often uses it, for example, in addressing her confessors. It was as though a peer of the realm were to say "Just call me 'Sir'."

[3] E.: "What do you mean, Christians? Though only what I am, I should like to cry aloud and dispute with those who say that mental prayer is unnecessary."

[4] E.: "I am sure you do not, nor can you, know what mental prayer is."

[5] For "fears" the original has "things"; but that seems to be the meaning.

[6] This clause is not in E., which continues: "and I should be sorry if anyone were to deceive you, for it is very bad, etc."

[7] In T. a hand, not the author's, has crossed out "have misgivings" and written "be unsettled".

[8] E.: "if one is told."

search for the right road tires him, wastes his time and delays his arrival. Who can say that it is wrong if, before we begin reciting the Hours or the Rosary, we think Whom we are going to address,[1] and who we are that are addressing Him, so that we may do so in the way we should? I assure you, sisters, that if you gave all due attention to a consideration of these two points before beginning the vocal prayers which you are about to say[2] you would be engaging in mental prayer for a very long time. For we cannot approach a prince and address him in the same careless way that we should adopt in speaking to a peasant[3] or to some poor woman like ourselves, whom we may address however we like.[4]

The reason we sometimes do so is to be found in the humility[5] of this King, Who, unskilled though I am in speaking with Him, does not refuse to hear me[6] or forbid me to approach Him, or command His guards to throw me out. For the angels in His presence know well that their King is such that He prefers the unskilled language of a humble peasant boy, knowing that he would say more if he had more to say, to the speech of the wisest and most learned men, however elegant may be their arguments, if these are not accompanied by humility.[7] But we must not be unmannerly because He is good. If only to show our gratitude to Him for enduring our foul odour and[8] allowing such a one as myself to come near Him, it is well that we should try to realize His purity and His nature.[9] It is true that we recognize this at once when we approach Him, just as we do when we visit the lords of the earth. Once we are told about their fathers' names and their incomes and dignities, there is no more for us to know about them; for on earth one makes account of persons, and honours them,[10] not because of their merits but because of their possessions.

O miserable world! Give hearty praise to God, daughters, that you have left so wretched a place,[11] where people are

---

[1] T.: "we are addressing."
[2] E.: "before beginning vocal prayer, which consists in the recitation of Hours and Rosary."
[3] E. has: "to a little peasant-boy" (*labradorcito*, the familiar diminutive: cf. p. 90, n. 6, above).
[4] E.: "whom it matters not if we call *tú* or *vos*." *Tú* was the familiar form; *vos*, the polite form, eventually superseded by Vd. (cf. p. 94, n. 2, above).
[5] T.: "benignity."
[6] E.: "does not think any the less of me."
[7] E.: "to that of the most systematic theologies (*sic*) if they are not accompanied by great humility."
[8] T. omits: "enduring our foul odour and".
[9] E.: "for enduring the foul odour when He endures us, it is well that we should see Who He is." There is deeper self-abasement, and also greater clarity, in V.
[10] "And honours them" does not occur in E.
[11] *Lit.*: "a thing".

honoured, not for their own selves, but for what they get from their tenants and vassals:[1] if these fail them, they have no honour left.[2] It is a curious thing, and when you go out to recreation together you should laugh about it, for it is a good way of spending your time to reflect how blindly people in the world spend theirs.

O Thou our Emperor! Supreme Power, Supreme Goodness, Wisdom Itself, without beginning, without end and without measure in Thy works:[3] infinite are these and incomprehensible, a fathomless ocean of wonders, O Beauty[4] containing within Thyself all beauties. O Very Strength! God help me! Would that I could command all the eloquence of mortals and all wisdom, so as to understand, as far as is possible here below, that to know nothing is everything, and thus to describe some of the many things on which we may meditate in order to learn something of the nature of this our Lord and Good.[5]

When you approach God, then, try[6] to think and realize Whom you are about to address and continue to do so while you are addressing Him. If we[7] had a thousand lives, we should never fully understand how this Lord merits that we behave toward Him, before Whom[8] even the angels tremble. He orders all things and He can do all things:[9] with Him to will is to perform. It will be right, then, daughters, for us to endeavour to rejoice in these wondrous qualities[10] of our Spouse and to know Whom we have wedded and what our lives should be. Why, God save us, when a woman in this world is about to marry, she knows beforehand whom she is to marry, what sort of a person he is and what property he possesses. Shall not we, then, who are already betrothed,[11] think about our Spouse,[12] before we are wedded to Him and He takes us home to be with Him? If these thoughts are not forbidden to those who are betrothed to men on earth, how can we be forbidden to discover Who this Man is, Who is His Father, what is the country to

---

[1] In E. the sentence ends here.
[2] T.: "The world ceases to do them honour."
[3] T. deletes "works" and writes "perfections."
[4] *Lit.*: "a Beauty . . . . itself", as though referring to *obras*: "works."
[5] V. has expanded this paragraph, which reads in E.: "O King of glory, Lord of lords, Emperor of emperors, Holy of the holy, Power above all powers, Knowledge above all knowledge, Wisdom Itself: Thou, Lord, art Truth Itself, Riches Itself, and Thou shalt reign without fail for ever."
[6] *Lit.*: "Yes, approach God, and, in approaching, try." T. begins: "There is nothing more, when you approach God, but to think, etc."
[7] E. continues in the second person.
[8] T.: "before Whose presence."
[9] E. omits: "and He can do all things."
[10] E.: "to endeavour to comprehend at least something of these wondrous qualities."
[11] E. adds: "and all souls, through baptism."
[12] The words "think about our Spouse" appear in no manuscript but were added by Luis de León.

which He[1] will take me, what are the riches with which He promises to endow me,[2] what is His rank, how I can best make Him happy, what I can do that will give Him pleasure, and how I can bring my rank into line with His. If a woman is to be happy in her marriage, it is just those things that she is advised to see about,[3] even though her husband be a man of very low station.

Shall less respect be paid to Thee, then, my Spouse, than to men? If they think it unfitting to do Thee honour, let them at least leave Thee Thy brides, who are to spend their lives with Thee. A woman is indeed fortunate in her life if her husband is so jealous that he will allow her to speak with no one but himself;[4] it would be a pretty pass if she could not resolve to give him this pleasure, for it is reasonable enough that she should put up with this and not wish to converse with anyone else, since in him she has all that she can desire. To understand these truths, my daughters, is to practise mental prayer. If you wish to learn to understand them, and at the same time to practise vocal prayer, well and good. But do not, I beg you, address God while you are thinking of other things, for to do that is the result of not understanding what mental prayer is. I think I have made this clear. May the Lord grant us to learn how to put it into practice.[5] Amen.

CHAPTER XXIII

Describes the importance of not turning back when one has set out upon the way of prayer. Repeats how necessary it is to be resolute.

Now,[6] as I have said, it is most important that from the first we should be very resolute, and for this there are so many reasons that if I were to give them all I should have to write at great

---

[1] T.: "they"
[2] This clause is not in E., which has some other, but quite slight, divergences in this sentence.
[3] E. "to study."
[4] E.: "that he will not allow his wife to leave home or to speak with anyone other than himself."
[5] E., instead of the last sentence, has: "I think it has been shown that no one should alarm you with these fears. Praise God, Who is more powerful than all men, and they cannot take Him from you. If any one of you cannot say her vocal prayers with this attentiveness, she should know that she is not fulfilling her obligation, and that, if she wishes to say them perfectly, the obligation is upon her to strive after this (mental prayer) with all her might, under pain of not doing her duty as the bride of so great a King. Beseech Him, daughters, to give me grace to do as I admonish you, which I am very far from doing. May His Majesty supply this, for His own sake."
[6] V. substitutes "now" for the exclamation with which the chapter begins in E.: "How I do let myself wander!"

length. *Some of them are given in other books.* I will tell you just two or three of them, sisters. One is that when we decide to give anything—such as this slight effort of recollection[1]—to Him Who has given us so much, and Who is continually giving, it would be wrong for us not to be entirely resolute in doing so and to act like a person who lends something and expects to get it back again. (Not that we do not receive interest: on the contrary, we gain a great deal.) I do not call this "giving". Anyone who has been lent something always feels slightly displeased when the lender wants it back again, especially if he is using it himself and has come to look upon it as his own. If the two are friends[2] and the lender is indebted to the recipient for many things of which he has made him free gifts, he will think it meanness and a great lack of affection[3] if he will leave not even the smallest thing[4] in his possession, merely as a sign of love.

What wife is there who, after receiving many valuable jewels from her husband, will not give him so much as a ring—which he wants, not because of its value, for all she has is his, but as *a sign of love and* a token that she will be his until she dies? Does the Lord deserve less than this that we should mock Him by taking away the worthless gift[5] which we have given Him? Since we have resolved to devote to Him this very brief period of time—only a small part of what we spend upon ourselves and upon people who are not particularly grateful to us for it—let us give it Him freely, with our minds unoccupied by other things[6] and entirely resolved never to take it back again, whatever we may suffer through trials, annoyances or aridities. Let me realize that this time is being lent me and is not my own, and feel that I can rightly be called to account for it if I am not prepared to devote it wholly to God.

I say "wholly", but we must not be considered as taking it back if we should fail to give it Him for a day, or for a few days, because of legitimate occupations[7] or through some indisposition. Provided the intention remains firm,[8] my God is not in the least meticulous;[9] He does not look at trivial details; and, if you

---

[1] *Este cuidadito*: *lit.*, "this little attentiveness"—another characteristic diminutive (not used in T., which has *cuidado*). In "to give anything", V. simplifies the reading in E.: "to serve (in any way) or to give anything."
[2] E. omits: "he is. . . . If" and begins a new sentence at: "He will think. . . ."
[3] E.: "of good-will."
[4] The diminutive *cosita*: T. has *cosa*.
[5] *Lit.*: "a nothing at all" (*una nonada*).
[6] T. omits: "by other things."
[7] E. ends this sentence here.
[8] T. joins this phrase to the preceding sentence and continues: "That is a gift. The other way, etc."
[9] *No es nada delicado mi Dios*. "Fastidious" might be nearer to the characteristically bold adjective of the original.

are trying to please Him in any way, He will assuredly accept that as your gift. The other way is suitable for ungenerous souls, so mean that they are not large-hearted enough to give but find it as much as they can do to lend. Still, let them make some effort, for this Lord of ours[1] will reckon everything we do to our credit and accept everything we want to give Him.[2] In drawing up our reckoning, He is not in the least exacting, but generous; however large the amount we may owe Him, it is a small thing for Him to forgive us.[3] And, as to paying us, He is so careful about this that you need have no fear He will leave us without our reward[4] if only we raise our eyes to Heaven and remember Him.

A second reason why we should be resolute is that this[5] will give the devil less opportunity to tempt us. He is very much afraid of resolute souls, knowing by experience that they inflict great injury upon him, and, when he plans to do them harm, he only profits them and others and is himself the loser. We must not become unwatchful, or count upon this, for we have to do with treacherous folk, who are great cowards and dare not attack the wary, but, if they see we are careless, will work us great harm. And if they know anyone to be changeable, and not resolute in *doing* what is good and firmly determined to persevere, they will not leave him alone either by night or by day and will suggest to him endless misgivings and difficulties. This I know very well by experience and so I have been able to tell you about it: I am sure that none of us realize its great importance.

Another reason, very much to the point, is that a resolute person fights more courageously.[6] He knows that, come what may, he must not retreat. He is like a soldier in battle who is aware that if he is vanquished his life will not be spared and that if he escapes death in battle he must die afterwards. *It has been proved, I think, that* such a man will fight more resolutely and will try, as they say, to sell his life dearly, fearing the enemy's blows[7] the less because he understands the importance of victory[8] and knows that his very life depends upon his gaining it. We must also be *firmly* convinced from the start that, if we *fight courageously and* do not allow ourselves to be beaten, we shall

---

[1] E.: "this Emperor."
[2] T. continues: "He is generous; however large, etc."
[3] T.: "for Him to forgive us in order to gain us: He is so grateful that, if we only raise our eyes to Heaven and remember Him, He will not leave (us) without a reward."
[4] E.: "without our payment."
[5] T. begins the paragraph: "And this."
[6] E.: "fights courageously." T. omits: "very much to the point."
[7] E.: "will fight much more courageously and will fear the enemy's blows." T. omits: "as they say."
[8] E. ends the sentence here.

get what we want,[1] and there is no doubt that, however small our gains may be, they will make us very rich. Do not be afraid that the Lord Who has called us to drink of this spring will allow you[2] to die of thirst. This I have already said and I should like to repeat it; for people are often timid when they have not learned by experience[3] of the Lord's goodness, even though they know of it[4] by faith. It is a great thing to have experienced what friendship and joy He gives to those who walk on this road[5] and how He takes almost the whole cost of it upon Himself.

I am not surprised that those who have never made this test should want to be sure that they will receive some interest on their outlay. But you already know that even in this life we shall receive a hundredfold, and that the Lord says: "Ask and it shall be given you."[6] If you do not believe His Majesty in those passages of His Gospel where He gives us this assurance, it will be of little help to you, sisters, for me to weary my brains by telling you of it. Still, I will say to anyone who is in doubt that she will lose little by putting the matter to the test;[7] for this journey has the advantage[8] of giving us *very much* more than we ask or shall even get so far as to desire.[9] This is a never-failing truth: I know it; *though, if you do not find it so, do not believe any of the things I tell you.* I can call as witnesses those of you who, by God's goodness, know it from experience.[10]

CHAPTER XXIV

Describes how vocal prayer may be practised with perfection and how closely allied it is to mental prayer.

Let us now return to speak of those souls I have mentioned who cannot[11] practise recollection or tie down their minds to

---

[1] E. continues: "and without fail. However small your gains may be, He calls you to drink of this spring."
[2] T.: "very rich. For the Lord . . . spring, will not allow you, etc."
[3] E.: "learned to know by experience."
[4] T.: "they confess it."
[5] E. ends the sentence here.
[6] St. Luke xi, 9. E.: "says we are to ask and He will give us."
[7] E.: "in doubt: 'Put it to the test. What is lost (by your doing so)?'"
[8] *Lit.*: "the good." E.: "the excellence."
[9] E.: "as to ask."
[10] In E. this sentence reads: "You, sisters, already know it by experience, and I can call you as witnesses, by God's goodness." E. then adds: "This which has been said is good for those who are coming (after us)."
[11] E.: "I have already said that I am dealing with souls who cannot."

mental prayer or make a meditation. We must not talk to them of either of those two things—they will not hear of them; as a matter of fact, there are a great many people who seem terrified at the very name[1] of contemplation or mental prayer.[2]

In case any such person should come to this house (for, as I have said, not all are led by the same path), I want to advise you, or, I might even say, to teach you (for, as your mother, and by the office of prioress which I hold, I have the right to do so)[3] how you must practise vocal prayer, for it is right that you should understand what you are saying. Anyone unable to think of God may find herself wearied by long prayers, and so I will not begin to discuss these, but will speak simply of prayers which, as[4] Christians, we must perforce recite—namely, the Paternoster and the Ave Maria[5]—and then no one will be able to say of us that we are repeating words without understanding what we are saying. We may, of course, consider it enough to say our prayers as a mere habit, repeating the words and thinking that this will suffice.[6] Whether it suffices or no I will not now discuss.[7] Learned men must decide:[8] *they will instruct people to whom God gives light to consult them, and I will not discuss the position of those who have not made a profession like our own.* But what I should like, daughters, is for us not to be satisfied with that alone: when I say the Creed, it seems to me right, *and indeed obligatory*, that I should understand and[9] know what it is that I believe; and, when I repeat the "Our Father", my love should make me want to understand Who this Father of ours is and Who the Master is that taught us this prayer.[10]

If you assert that you know Who He is already, and so there is no need for you to think about Him, you are not right; there is a great deal of difference[11] between one master and another,

---

[1] E. ends the sentence here.
[2] T.: "consideration" (i.e., meditation, and so translated in the text below).
[3] E.: "for, as your mother, I now have this duty."
[4] E.: "which, if we are."
[5] E. continues: "It is clear that we must consider what we are saying, as I have said. No one must be able to say of us, etc."
[6] E.: "You may, of course, say that this [i.e., understanding] is unnecessary, that you say your prayers as a habit, that it suffices to repeat the words." T.: "repeating the words, which I will not now discuss. Learned men will say if it suffices or no. But what I should like, etc."
[7] The word rendered "discuss", both here and below, is a strong one, *entrometerse*, to intermeddle.
[8] E.: "It is a matter for learned men."
[9] "Understand and" is not found in E.
[10] E.: "and when I say 'Father', it should, I think, be a matter of love for me to understand Who this Father is. It will be well, too, for us to see Who the Master is that teaches us this prayer."
[11] E.: "If we assert that it is sufficient to know once and for all Who the Master is, without thinking of Him again, you might equally well say that it is sufficient to recite the prayer once in a lifetime. Yes, but there is a great deal of difference."

and it would be very wrong of us not to think about those who teach us, even on earth; if they are holy men and[1] spiritual masters, and we are good pupils, it is impossible for us *not to have great love for them, and indeed to hold them in honour and often to talk about them.*[2] And when it comes to the Master Who taught us this prayer, and Who loves us so much and is so anxious for us to profit by it, may God forbid that we should fail to think[3] of Him often when we repeat it, although our own weakness may prevent us from doing so every time.

Now, in the first place, you know that His Majesty[4] teaches that this prayer must be made when we are alone, just as He was often alone when He prayed,[5] not because this was necessary for Him, but for our edification. It has already been said that it is impossible to speak to God and to the world at the same time; yet this is just what we are trying to do when we are saying our prayers and at the same time listening to the conversation of others or letting our thoughts wander on any matter that occurs to us,[6] without making an effort to control them.[7] There are occasions when one cannot help doing this: times of ill-health (especially in persons who suffer from melancholia); or times when our heads are tired, and, however hard we try, we cannot concentrate; or times when, for their own good, God allows His servants for days on end to go through great storms. And, although they are distressed and strive to calm themselves, they are unable to do so and incapable of attending to what they are saying, however hard they try, nor can they fix their understanding on anything: they seem to be in a frenzy, so distraught are they.

The very suffering of anyone in this state will show her that she is not to blame, and she must not worry, for that only makes matters worse, nor must she weary herself by trying to put sense into something—namely, her mind—which for the moment is without any. She should pray as best she can: indeed, she need not pray at all, but may try to rest her spirit as though she were ill and busy herself with some other virtuous action. These directions are meant for persons who keep careful guard

---

[1] E. omits: "holy men and."
[2] Thus E., which I prefer here: V. has: "it is impossible for us not to do so."
[3] T.: "fail to profit by thinking."
[4] E.: "that this heavenly Master."
[5] V. has "always" for "often". T. reads: "Now, in the first place, it is best to be alone, just as His Majesty was often alone" and omits: "when He prayed." The adverbial correction of T. is clearly justified.
[6] E.: "or thinking of anything we like."
[7] E. continues: "This, we know quite well, is not good: we must try to be alone—and please God we may realize in Whose presence we are, etc." Cf. p. 103, n. 1, below.

over themselves and know that they must not speak to God and to the world at the same time. What we can do ourselves is to try to be alone—and God grant that this may suffice, as I say, to make us realize in Whose presence we are[1] and how the Lord answers our petitions. Do you suppose[2] that, because we cannot hear Him, He is silent? He speaks clearly to the heart when we beg Him from our hearts to do so. It would be a good idea for us to imagine[3] that He has taught this prayer to each one of us individually, and that He is continually expounding it to us. The Master is never so far away that the disciple needs to raise his voice in order to be heard: He is always right at his side. I want you to understand that, if you are to recite the Paternoster well, one thing is needful: you must not leave the side of the Master Who has taught it you.

You will say *at once* that this is meditation, and that you are not capable of it, and do not even wish to practise it, but are content with vocal prayer.[4] For there are impatient people who dislike giving themselves trouble, and it is troublesome at first to practise recollection of the mind when one has not made it a habit. So, in order not to make themselves the least bit tired, they say they are incapable of anything but vocal prayer and do not know how to do anything further. You are right to say that what we have described is mental prayer; but I assure you that I cannot distinguish it from vocal prayer faithfully recited with a realization of Who it is that we are addressing. Further, we are under the obligation of trying to pray attentively: may God grant that, by using these means, we may learn to say the Paternoster well and not find ourselves thinking of something irrelevant. I have sometimes experienced this myself, and the best remedy I have found for it is to try to fix my mind on the Person by Whom the words were first spoken. Have patience, then, and try to make this necessary practice into a habit,[5] *for necessary it is, in my opinion, for those who would be nuns, and indeed for all who would pray like good Christians.*

[1] This phrase ends the interpolation in V. referred to in the last note.
[2] T. has: "Do not suppose . . ."
[3] More literally: "consider", "reflect". E. begins: "With this presupposition, that we must be alone, we shall do well, etc."
[4] E. continues: "and to some extent you are right. But I assure you, etc."
[5] The phrase "and try . . . habit" is not found in E.

CHAPTER XXV

Describes the great gain which comes to a soul when it practises vocal prayer perfectly. Shows how God may raise it thence to things supernatural.

In case you should think there is little gain to be derived from practising vocal prayer perfectly, I must tell you that, while you are repeating the Paternoster or some other vocal prayer, it is quite possible for the Lord to grant you perfect contemplation.[1] In this way His Majesty shows that He is listening to the person who is addressing Him, and that, in His greatness, He is addressing her,[2] by suspending the understanding, putting a stop to all thought, and, as we say, taking the words out of her mouth, so that even if she wishes to speak she cannot do so, or at any rate not without great difficulty.

Such a person understands that, without any sound of words,[3] she is being taught by this Divine Master, Who is suspending her faculties, which, if they were to work, would be causing her harm rather than profit. The faculties rejoice without knowing how they rejoice; the soul is enkindled in love without understanding how it loves; it knows that it is rejoicing in the object of its love,[4] yet it does not know how it is rejoicing in it. It is well aware that this is not a joy which can be attained by the understanding; the will embraces it, without understanding how; but, in so far as it can understand anything, it perceives that this is a blessing which could not be gained by the merits of all the trials suffered on earth put together. It is a gift of the Lord of earth and Heaven, Who gives it like the God He is. This, daughters, is perfect contemplation.

You will now understand how different it is from mental prayer, which I have already described, and which consists in thinking of what we are saying, understanding it, and realizing Whom we are addressing, and who we are that are daring to address so great a Lord. To think of this and other similar things, such as how little we have served Him and how great is our obligation to serve Him, is mental prayer. Do not think of

---

[1] E. begins "It will be possible that, while you are repeating the Paternoster, the Lord may grant you perfect contemplation, if you repeat it well."

[2] *Lit.*: "and that His greatness is addressing her." E. has "His Majesty": the change may not have quite the full significance implied in the English version.

[3] E. continues, and ends the paragraph, thus: "her Master is working in her soul, and that her own faculties are not working, so far as she understands. This is perfect contemplation."

[4] T. omits: "it knows . . . its love."

it as one more thing with an outlandish name[1] and do not let the name frighten you. To recite the Paternoster and the Ave Maria,[2] or any other petition you like, is vocal prayer. But think how harsh your music will be without what must come first; sometimes even the words will get into the wrong order. In these two kinds of prayer, with God's help, we may accomplish something ourselves. In the contemplation which I have just described we can do nothing.[3] It is His Majesty Who does everything; the work is His alone and far transcends human nature.

I described this as well as I was able in the relation which I made of it, as I have said,[4] so that my confessors should see it when they read the account of my life which they had ordered me to write. As I have explained all this about contemplation at such length, therefore, I shall not repeat myself here and I am doing no more than touch upon it. If those of you who have experienced the happiness of being called by the Lord to this state of contemplation can get this book, you will find in it points and counsels which the Lord was pleased to enable me to set down. These should bring you great comfort and profit—in my opinion, at least, and in the opinion of several people who have seen it[5] and who keep it at hand in order to make frequent use of it. I am ashamed to tell you that anything of mine is made such use of and the Lord knows with what confusion I write a great deal that I do. Blessed be He for thus bearing with me. Those of you who, as I say, have experience of supernatural prayer should procure the book after my death;[6] those who have not have no need to do so but they should try to carry out what has been said in this one.[7] Let them leave everything to the Lord, to Whom it belongs to grant this gift, and He will not deny it you if you do not tarry on the road but press forward so as to reach the end of your journey.

[1] *algarabía. Lit.*: "Arabic" (as in p. 88, l. 6, above: cf. p. 131, n. 8, below) and hence "gibberish," "jargon."
[2] E. omits: "and the Ave Maria." Cf. p. 93 n. 4, above.
[3] "Except," adds P. Báñez in the margin, "prepare ourselves with prayer."
[4] P. Silverio has "Relation" and takes the reference to be to the first six *Relations* as well as to the *Life*. But the context and the apparent allusion to the Prologue to this book (pp. 1-2, above) suggest that what the author has in mind is only the *Life*. I therefore read "relation".
[5] T. ends the sentence here.
[6] E. abbreviates: "As I have explained all the best part of this in the book which, as I say, I have written, there is no need for me to treat it in such great detail here, for I said all that I knew about it there. Any one of you who has reached such a point that God has brought her to this state of contemplation (and, as I said, some of you are in it) should procure it, for it will be of great importance to you when I die."
[7] "About profiting in as many ways as is possible," adds E., ending the chapter thus: "and to be diligent, for if they entreat the Lord and do what they can for themselves, He will grant them this gift. For the rest, it is for the Lord Himself to grant it, and He denies it to no one who fights on till he reaches the end of the road, as has been said."

CHAPTER XXVI

Continues the description of a method for recollecting the thoughts. Describes means of doing this. This chapter is very profitable for those who are beginning prayer.

Let us now return to our vocal prayer, so that we may learn to pray in such a way that, without our understanding how, God may give us everything at once:[1] if we do this, as I have said, we shall pray as we ought. As you know, the first things must be examination of conscience, confession of sin and the signing of yourself with the Cross. Then, daughter, as you are alone, you must look for a companion—and who could be a better Companion than the very Master Who taught you the prayer that you are about to say? Imagine that this Lord Himself is at your side and see how lovingly and how humbly He is teaching you—and, believe me, you should stay with so good a Friend for as long as you can before you leave Him. If you become accustomed to having Him at your side, and if He sees that you love Him to be there and are always trying to please Him, you will never be able, as we put it, to send Him away, nor will He ever fail you. He will help you in all your trials and you will have Him everywhere. Do you think it is a small thing to have[2] such a Friend as that beside you?

O sisters, those of you whose minds cannot[3] reason for long or whose thoughts cannot dwell *upon God* but are *constantly* wandering must at all costs form this habit.[4] I know quite well that you are capable of it—for many years I endured this trial of being unable to concentrate on one subject, and a very sore trial it is. But I know the Lord does not leave us so devoid of help that if we approach Him humbly and ask Him to be with us He will not grant our request. If a whole year passes without our obtaining what we ask, let us be prepared to try for longer.[5] Let us never grudge time so well spent. Who, after all, is hurrying us? I am sure we can form this habit and strive to walk at the side of this true Master.

---

[1] T. continues: "and, as you know, (if we are) to pray as we ought, the first things must be, etc."
[2] T.: "See what a great thing it is to have."
[3] E.: "O souls, whose minds cannot."
[4] The original (both in E. and in V.) has, after "wandering": "get used (to this)! get used (to this)!" The repetition is typically Teresan.
[5] E. ends the paragraph: "I mean that it is possible to form the habit of walking at the side of this true Master."

I am not asking you now to think of Him, or to form numerous conceptions of Him, or to make long and subtle meditations with your understanding. I am asking you only to look at Him. For who can prevent you from turning the eyes of your soul (just for a moment, if you can do no more) upon this Lord? You are capable of looking at very ugly *and loathsome* things: can you not, then, look at the most beautiful thing imaginable?[1] Your Spouse never takes His eyes off you, daughters. He has borne with thousands of foul and abominable sins which you have committed against Him, yet even they have not been enough to make Him cease looking upon you. Is it such a great matter, then, for you to avert the eyes *of your soul* from outward things and sometimes to look at Him? See, He is only waiting for us to look at Him, as He says to the Bride.[2] If you want Him[3] you will find Him. He longs so much for us to look at Him once more that it will not be for lack of effort on His part if we fail to do so.

A wife, they say, must be like this if she is to have a happy married life with her husband. If he is sad, she must show signs of sadness; if he is merry, even though she may not in fact be so, she must appear merry too. See what slavery you have escaped from, sisters![4] Yet this, without any pretence, is really how we are treated by the Lord. He becomes subject to us and is pleased to let you be the mistress and to conform to your will. If you are happy, look upon your risen Lord, and the very thought of how He rose from the sepulchre will gladden you. How bright and how beautiful was He then! How majestic![5] How victorious! How joyful! He was like one emerging from a battle in which He had gained a great kingdom, all of which He desires you to have[6]—and with it Himself. Is it such a great thing that you should turn your eyes but once and look upon Him Who has made you such great gifts?

If you are suffering trials, or are sad, look upon Him[7] on His way to the Garden. What sore distress He must have borne in His soul, to describe His own suffering as He did and to complain of it! Or look upon Him bound to the Column, full of pain, His flesh all torn to pieces by His great love for you. How much

---

[1] E. adds, parenthetically: "If you do not think Him so, I give you leave to stop looking at Him."
[2] A vague reminiscence of some phrase from Canticles: perhaps ii, 14, 16, v, 2, or vi, 12.
[3] Or "love Him". The verb in the Spanish can have either meaning.
[4] This sentence does not appear in E.; the idea evidently came to St. Teresa's mind as she was rewriting the chapter.
[5] *Lit.*: "With what majesty!" E. reads: "With what dominion!" In T., "How victorious!" comes between "How bright!" and "how beautiful!"
[6] T. ends the sentence here.
[7] This first picture does not appear in E., which continues: "at the Column, full of pain, etc."

He suffered, persecuted by some, spat upon by others, denied by His friends, and even deserted by them,[1] with none to take His part, frozen with the cold and left so completely alone that you may well comfort each other! Or look upon Him bending under the weight of the Cross[2] and not even allowed to take breath: He will look upon you with His lovely and compassionate eyes, full of tears, and in comforting your grief will forget His own because you are bearing Him company in order to comfort Him and turning your head to look upon Him.

"O Lord of the world, my true Spouse!" you may say to Him, if seeing Him in such a plight has filled your heart with such tenderness that you not only desire to look upon Him but love to speak to Him, not using forms of prayer, but words issuing from the compassion of your heart, which means so much to Him: "Art Thou so needy, my Lord and my Good, that Thou wilt accept poor companionship like mine? Do I read in Thy face that Thou hast found comfort, even in me?[3] How can it be possible, Lord, that the angels are leaving Thee alone and that Thy Father is not comforting Thee?

"If Thou, Lord, art willing to suffer all this for me, what am I suffering for Thee?[4] What have I to complain of? I am ashamed, Lord,[5] when I see Thee in such a plight, and if in any way I can imitate Thee[6] I will suffer all trials that come to me and count them as a great blessing. Let us go[7] both together, Lord: whither Thou goest,[8] I must go; through whatsoever Thou passest, I must pass." Take up this cross, sisters: never mind if the Jews trample upon you provided you can save Him some of His trials.[9] Take no heed of what they say to you; be deaf to all detraction; stumble and fall with your Spouse, but do not draw back from your cross or give it up.[10] Think often of the weariness of His journey and of how much harder His trials were than those which you have to suffer.[11] However hard you may imagine yours to be, and however much affliction they may cause you, they will be a source of comfort

---

[1] The phrases "How much He suffered", "and even deserted by them", are not found in E.
[2] E.: "Or look upon Him in the Garden, or on the Cross, or bending under its weight."
[3] E., omits "like mine" in the previous sentence, and, for "that . . . in me", reads: "that Thou hast forgotten Thy griefs for mine?" [*lit.*: "with me"].
[4] E. omits: "for Thee."
[5] E.: "my Good."
[6] E.: "can resemble Thee."
[7] E.: "We are going."
[8] E.: "whither Thou wentest."
[9] "Provided . . . trials" is not found in E.
[10] "Or give it up" is not found in E.
[11] E.: "than yours."

to you, for you will see that they are matters for scorn compared with the trials endured by the Lord.

You will ask me, sisters, how you can possibly do all this, and say that, if you had seen His Majesty with your bodily eyes at the time when He lived in the world, you would have done it willingly and gazed at Him for ever. Do not believe it: anyone who will not make the slight effort necessary for recollection in order to gaze upon this Lord present within her, which she can do without danger and with only the minimum of trouble, would have been far less likely to stand at the foot of the Cross with the Magdalen, who looked death (*as they say*) straight in the face.[1] What the glorious Virgin and this blessed saint must have suffered! What threats, what malicious words, what shocks,[2] what insults! For the people they were dealing with were not exactly polite to them. No, indeed; theirs was the kind of courtesy you might meet in hell, for they were the ministers of the devil himself. Yet, terrible as the sufferings of these women must have been, they would not have noticed them[3] in the presence of pain so much greater.

So do not suppose, sisters, that you would have been prepared to endure such great trials then, if you are not ready for such trifling ones now.[4] Practise enduring these and you may be given others which are greater. *Believe that I am telling the truth when I say that you can do this, for I am speaking from experience.* You will find it very helpful if you can get an image or a picture of this Lord—one that you like[5]—not to wear round your neck and never look at but to use regularly whenever you talk to Him, and He will tell you what to say. If words do not fail you when you talk to people *on earth*, why should they do so when you talk to God?[6] Do not imagine that they will—I shall certainly not believe that they have done so if you once form the habit.[7] For when you never have intercourse with a person he soon becomes a stranger to you, and you forget how to talk to him; and before long, even if he is a kinsman, you feel as if you do not know him, for both kinship and friendship lose their influence when communication ceases.

It is also a great help to have a good book, written in the vernacular, simply as an aid to recollection. With this aid you

---

[1] T. weakens this vivid phrase to "who saw death present".
[2] "What shocks" is not in E.
[3] T.: "they did not notice them."
[4] E.: "endure the one . . . ready for the other."
[5] This parenthesis, not in E., is a characteristic later addition.
[6] "More than to others", interpolates T., redundantly.
[7] "If you once form the habit" is not in E., which also ends the paragraph at "done so". The Spanish is exceedingly condensed here and other interpretations are possible.

will learn to say your vocal prayers well, *I mean, as they ought to be said*—and little by little, persuasively and methodically, you will get your soul used to this, so that it will no longer be afraid of it. Remember that many years have passed since it went away from[1] its Spouse, and it needs very careful handling before it will return home. We sinners are like that: we have accustomed our souls and minds to go after their own pleasures (or pains, it would be more correct to say) until the unfortunate soul no longer knows what it is doing. When that has happened, a good deal of skill is necessary before it can be inspired with enough love to make it stay at home; but unless we can gradually do that we shall accomplish nothing.[2] Once again I assure you that, if you are careful to form habits of the kind I have mentioned, you will derive[3] such great profit from them that I could not describe it even if I wished.[4] Keep at the side of this good Master,[5] then, and be most firmly resolved to learn what He teaches you; His Majesty will then ensure your not failing to be good disciples, and He will never leave you unless you leave Him. Consider the words uttered by those Divine lips: the very first of them will show you at once what love He has for you, and it is no small blessing and joy for the pupil to see that his Master loves Him.

CHAPTER XXVII

Describes the great love shown us by the Lord in the first words of the Paternoster and the great importance of our making no account of good birth if we truly desire to be the daughters of God.

"Our Father, which art in the Heavens." O my Lord, how Thou dost reveal Thyself as the Father of such a Son, while Thy Son reveals Himself as the Son of such a Father! Blessed be Thou for ever and ever. Ought not so great a favour as this, Lord, to have come at the end of the prayer? Here, at the very beginning, Thou dost fill our hands and grant us so great a favour that it would be a very great blessing if our understanding

---

[1] E.: "went away, having fled from."
[2] E.: "a good deal of skill is necessary to make it conceive fresh love for its Spouse [*lit.*: "Husband"] and become accustomed to staying at home: this has to be done gradually and by means of love—otherwise we shall accomplish nothing."
[3] E. begins the sentence: "And be quite sure that if you accustom yourselves carefully to the idea that you have this Lord with you, and speak to Him frequently, you will derive."
[4] E.: "that, even if I want to describe it to you, you will perhaps not believe me."
[5] E.: "of your Master."

could be filled with it so that the will would be occupied and we should be unable to say another word. Oh, how appropriate, daughters, would perfect contemplation be here! Oh, how right would the soul be to enter within itself, so as to be the better able to rise above itself, that this holy Son might show it the nature of the place where He says His Father dwells—namely, the Heavens! Let us leave earth, my daughters, for it is not right that a favour like this should be prized so little, and that, after we have realized how great this favour is, we should remain on earth any more.

O Son of God and my Lord! How is it that Thou canst give us so much with Thy first word? It is so wonderful that Thou shouldst descend to such a degree of humility as to join with us when we pray and make Thyself the Brother of creatures so miserable and lowly! How can it be that, in the name of Thy Father, Thou shouldst give us all that there is to be given, by willing Him to have us as His children—and Thy word cannot fail?[1] [It seems that] Thou dost oblige Him to fulfil Thy word, a charge by no means light, since, being our Father, He must bear with us, however great our offences.[2] If we return to Him, He must pardon us, as He pardoned the prodigal son,[3] must comfort us in our trials, and must sustain us,[4] as such a Father is bound to do, for He must needs be better than any earthly father, since nothing good can fail to have its perfection in Him. *He must cherish us; He must sustain us*;[5] and at the last He must make us participants and fellow-heirs with Thee.

Behold, my Lord, with the love that Thou hast for us and with Thy humility, nothing can be an obstacle to Thee. And then, Lord, Thou hast been upon earth and by taking our nature upon Thee hast clothed Thyself with humanity: Thou hast therefore some reason to care for our advantage.[6] But behold, Thy Father is in Heaven, as Thou hast told us, and it is right that Thou shouldst consider His honour. Since Thou hast offered Thyself to be dishonoured by us, leave Thy Father free. Oblige Him not to do so much for people as wicked as I, who will make Him such poor acknowledgment.[7]

[1] E. adds: "but must be fulfilled."
[2] T. deletes: "a charge by no means light" and has here: "He must bear with our offences, however great they be."
[3] E.: "If we return to Him, as did the prodigal son, He must pardon us."
[4] E. omits: "and must sustain us."
[5] E. adds: "for He has the wherewithal," which spoils the rhythm of the sentence and is not explicit enough to be a valuable addition.
[6] E.: "and the part Thou dost play seems to oblige Thee to do us good." Originally this read: "and after the part Thou playest with us I do not know how Thou canst have so much humility." The alteration is in St. Teresa's hand.
[7] E. adds: "and there are also others who do not make Him [good [acknowledgment]."

O good Jesus! How clearly hast Thou shown that Thou art One with Him and that Thy will is His and His is Thine! How open a confession is this, my Lord! What is this love that Thou hast for us? Thou didst deceive the devil, and conceal from him that Thou art the Son of God, but Thy great desire for our welfare overcomes all obstacles to Thy granting us this greatest of favours. Who but Thou could do this, Lord? I cannot think how the devil failed to understand from that word of Thine Who Thou wert, beyond any doubt.[1] I, at least, my Jesus, see clearly that Thou didst speak as a dearly beloved son both for Thyself and for us,[2] and Thou hast such power that what Thou sayest in Heaven shall be done on earth. Blessed be Thou for ever, my Lord, Who lovest so much to give[3] that no obstacle can stay Thee.

Do you not think, daughters, that this is a good Master, since He begins by granting us this great favour so as to make us love to learn what He teaches us? Do you think it would be right for us,[4] while we are repeating this prayer with our lips, to stop trying to think of what we are saying, lest picturing such love[5] should tear our hearts to pieces? No one who realized His greatness could possibly say it would be. What son is there in the world who would not try to learn who his father was if he had one as good, and of as great majesty[6] and dominion, as ours? Were God not all this, it would not surprise me if we had no desire to be known as His children;[7] for the world is such that, if the father is of lower rank than his son, the son feels no honour in recognizing him as his father.[8] This does not apply here: God forbid that such a thing should ever happen in this house—it would turn the place into hell. Let the sister who is of the highest birth speak of her father least; we must all be equals.

O College of Christ, in which the Lord was pleased that Saint Peter, who was a fisherman, should have more authority than Saint Bartholomew, who was the son of a king![9] His Majesty knew what a fuss would be made in the world[10] about who was

---

[1] T. omits this sentence.
[2] E.: "and for all."
[3] T. ends the sentence here, deleting the words which follow.
[4] E., more bluntly: "Would it be right for us . . . ?" T. deletes the reading in the text and substitutes: "It would be right for us."
[5] E. reads: "lest so great a favour."
[6] E.: "goodness, majesty."
[7] E.: "daughters."
[8] E.: "than his son, in two words he will not recognize him as his father." In the next sentence, T. has "affect us" for "apply".
[9] "I do not know where she found this," observes P. García de Toledo (not P. Báñez, as the Paris Carmelites say) in the margin of V. There seems, in fact, to be no foundation for the assertion in the text. T. inserts "they say".
[10] E. omits: "in the world."

fashioned from the finer clay—which is like discussing whether clay is better for bricks or for walls.[1] Dear Lord, what a trouble we make about it![2] God deliver you, sisters, from such contentions,[3] even if they be carried on only in jest; I hope that His Majesty will indeed deliver you. If anything like this should be going on among you, apply the remedy immediately, and let the sister concerned fear lest she be a Judas among the Apostles.[4] *Do what you can to get rid of such a bad companion. If you cannot,* give her penances *heavier than for anything else* until she realizes that she has not deserved to be even the basest clay. You have a good Father, given you by the good Jesus:[5] let no other father be known or referred to here.[6] Strive, my daughters, to be such that you deserve to find comfort in Him and to throw yourselves into His arms. You know that, if you are good children, He will never[7] send you away. And who would not do anything rather than lose such a Father?

Oh, thank God, what cause for comfort there is here! Rather than write more about it I will leave it for you to think about; for, however much your thoughts may wander, between such a Son and such a Father there must needs be the Holy Spirit.[8] May He enkindle[9] your will and bind you to Himself with the most fervent love, since even the great advantage you gain will not suffice to do so.[10]

CHAPTER XXVIII

Describes the nature of the Prayer of Recollection and sets down some of the means by which we can make it a habit.

Consider now what your Master says next: "Who art in the Heavens."[11] Do you suppose it matters little what Heaven is and

---

[1] E.: "for mud or for bricks."
[2] E.: "what great blindness!" T.: "what great nonsense!"
[3] E.: "from such conversations."
[4] E.: "among you, do not allow it in the house, for it is (like having a) Judas among the Apostles."
[5] E.: "The good Jesus gives you a good Father."
[6] E. continues, repeating what has just been said: "save Him Whom your Spouse gives you."
[7] E.: "He has the obligation never to." T. deletes much of this and the last sentence and substitutes: "deserve to imitate Him in something; for, if you are good children, He will never."
[8] In T. this reading is altered to the following: "for, your thoughts being between such a Son and such a Father, the Holy Spirit will come (to you)."
[9] E.: "May He work in."
[10] E.: "with the strongest love, supposing that the advantage you will gain does not bind you (to Him)."
[11] E.: "in Heaven."

where you must seek your most holy Father? I assure you that for minds which wander it is of great importance not only to have a right belief about this but to try to learn it by experience,[1] for it is one of the best ways of concentrating the mind[2] and effecting recollection in the soul.

You know[3] that God is everywhere; and *this is a great truth, for*, of course, wherever the king is, or so they say, the court is too: that is to say, wherever God is, there is Heaven. No doubt you can believe that, in any place where His Majesty is, there is fulness of glory.[4] Remember how Saint Augustine tells us[5] about his seeking God in many places and eventually finding Him within himself. Do you suppose[6] it is of little importance that a soul which is often distracted should come to understand this truth and to find that, in order to speak to its Eternal Father and to take its delight in Him, it has no need to go to Heaven or to speak[7] in a loud voice? However quietly we speak, He is so near that[8] He will hear us: we need no wings to go in search of Him but have only to find a place where we can be alone and look upon Him present within us. Nor need we feel strange in the presence of so kind a Guest; we must talk to Him very humbly, as we should to our father,[9] ask Him for things as we should ask a father, tell Him our troubles, beg Him to put them right, and yet realize that we are not worthy to be called His children.

Avoid being bashful with God, as some people are, in the belief that they are being humble. It would not be humility on your part if the King were to do you a favour and you refused to accept it; but you would be showing humility by taking it, and being pleased with it, yet realizing how far you are from deserving it. A fine humility it would be if I had the Emperor of Heaven and earth in my house, coming to it to do me a favour and to delight in my company, and I were so humble that I would not answer His questions, nor remain with Him, nor

---

[1] E.: "but to think about it a great deal."
[2] E.: "the very best ways of concentrating the thoughts."
[3] E.: "You will have heard."
[4] T. deletes "wherever the king. . . . God is" and substitutes: "You know that God is everywhere, for, of course, wherever His Majesty is, there is Heaven. No doubt you can believe that, and fulness of glory." The deletion of "in any . . . there is" is quite in keeping with St. Teresa's elliptical style.
[5] E. adds: "in the book of his Meditations, I believe." The actual reference is *Confessions*, Bk. X., Chap. XXVII.
[6] T. deletes: "Do you suppose" and turns the sentence into an affirmation with "Believe that it is of great importance, etc."
[7] E.: "to pray."
[8] E. and T. omit: "He is so near that."
[9] E. continues, and ends the paragraph thus: "seek comfort in Him as in a father, yet realize that we are not worthy for Him to be so."

accept what He gave me,[1] but left Him alone. Or if He were to speak to me and beg me[2] to ask for what I wanted, and I were so humble that I preferred to remain poor and even let Him go away, so that He would see I had not sufficient resolution.

Have nothing to do with that kind of humility, daughters, but speak with Him as with a Father, a Brother, a Lord and a Spouse—and, sometimes in one way and sometimes in another, He will teach you what you must do to please Him. Do not be foolish; ask Him to let you speak to Him, and, as He is your Spouse, to treat you as His brides. *Remember how important it is for you to have understood this truth—that the Lord is within us and that we should be there with Him.*

If one prays in this way, the prayer may be only vocal, but the mind will be recollected much sooner; and this is a prayer which brings with it many blessings.[3] It is called recollection because the soul collects together all the faculties and enters within itself to be with its God. Its Divine Master comes more speedily to teach it, and to grant it the Prayer of Quiet, than in any other way. For, hidden there within itself, it can think about[4] the Passion, and picture the Son, and offer Him to the Father, without wearying the mind by going to seek Him on Mount Calvary, or in the Garden, or at the Column.

Those who are able to shut themselves up in this way within this little Heaven of the soul, wherein dwells the Maker of Heaven and earth,[5] and who have formed the habit of looking at nothing and staying in no place which will distract these outward senses,[6] may be sure that they are walking on an excellent road, and will come without fail to drink of the water of the fountain, for they will journey a long way in a short time. They are like one who travels in a ship, and, if he has a little good wind, reaches the end of his voyage in a few days, while those who go by land take *much* longer.[7]

These souls have already, as we may say, put out to sea; though they have not sailed quite out of sight of land, they do what they can to get away from it, in the time at their disposal, by recol-

---

[1] "Nor accept what He gave me" is not found in E.
[2] E.: "Or if He were to tell me."
[3] E.: "a thousand blessings."
[4] E.: "about all."
[5] This is the reading of E. V. has: "the Maker of it, and of the earth."
[6] E.: "where it hears anything to destroy it." But "destroy" (*destruya*) looks like a slip of the pen for "distract" (*destraya*: mod. *distraiga*—the form used in V.).
T. omits: "looking at nothing and", and, just below, reads: "on a good road, and, with the favour of God, will come, etc."
[7] E. continues: "This is the road to Heaven. I say 'to Heaven' because there they are hidden in the King's palace, and are not on earth, and are more secure from many occasions of sin." (cf. p. 117, l. 6).

lecting their senses. If their recollection is genuine, the fact becomes very evident, for it produces certain effects which I do not know how to explain but which anyone will recognize who has experience of them. It is as if the soul were rising from play, for it sees that worldly things are nothing but toys;[1] so in due course it rises above them, like a person entering a strong castle, in order that it may have nothing more to fear from its enemies. It withdraws the senses from all outward things and spurns them so completely that, without its understanding how, its eyes close and it cannot see them and the soul's spiritual sight becomes clear. Those who walk along this path almost invariably close their eyes when they say their prayers; this, for many reasons, is an admirable custom, since it means that they are making an effort not to look at things of the world. The effort has to be made only at the beginning; later it becomes unnecessary: eventually, in fact, it would cost a greater effort to open the eyes during prayer than to close them. The soul seems to gather up its strength and to master itself at the expense of the body, which it leaves weakened and alone: in this way it becomes stronger for the fight against it.

This may not be evident at first, if the recollection is not very profound—for at this stage it is sometimes more so and sometimes less. At first it may cause a good deal of trouble, for the body insists on its rights, not understanding that if it refuses to admit defeat it is, as it were, cutting off its own head. But if we cultivate the habit, make the necessary effort and practise the exercises for several days,[2] the benefits will reveal themselves, and when we begin to pray we shall realize that the bees are coming to the hive and entering it to make the honey, and all without any effort of ours. For it is the Lord's will that, in return for the time which their efforts have cost them, the soul and the will should be given this power over the senses. They will only have to make a sign to show that they wish to enter into recollection and the senses will obey and allow themselves to be recollected. Later they may come out again, but it is a great thing that they should ever have surrendered, for if they come out it is as captives and slaves and they do none of the harm that they might have done before. When the will calls them afresh they respond more quickly, until, after they have entered the soul many times, the Lord is pleased that they should remain there altogether in perfect contemplation.

What has been said should be noted with great care, for,

---

[1] T. deletes part of this and substitutes: "rising from worldly things with the fire that it feels within itself."

[2] T. omits: "if we . . . several days."

though it seems obscure, it will be understood by anyone desirous of putting it into practice. The sea-voyage, then, can be made; and, as it is very important that we should not travel too slowly, let us just consider how we can get accustomed to these good habits. Souls who do so are more secure from many occasions of sin,[1] and the fire of Divine love is the more readily enkindled in them; for they are so near that fire that, however little the blaze has been fanned with the understanding, any small spark that flies out at them will cause them to burst into flame. When no hindrance comes to it from outside, the soul remains alone with its God and is thoroughly prepared to become enkindled.[2]

And now let us imagine that we have within us a palace of priceless worth,[3] built entirely of gold and precious stones— a palace, in short, fit for so great a Lord. Imagine that it is partly your doing that this palace should be what it is[4]—and this is really true, for there is no building so beautiful as a soul that is pure and full of virtues, and, the greater these virtues are, the more brilliantly do the stones shine. Imagine that within the palace dwells this great King, Who has vouchsafed to become your Father, and Who is seated upon a throne of supreme price— namely, your heart.

At first you will think this irrelevant—I mean the use of this figure to explain my point—but it may prove very useful, especially to persons like yourselves. For, as we women are not learned *or fine-witted*, we need all these things to help us realize that we actually have something within us incomparably more precious than anything we see outside. Do not let us suppose that the interior of the soul is empty;[5] God grant that only women may be so thoughtless as to suppose that. If we took care always to remember what a Guest we have within us, I think it would be impossible for us to abandon ourselves to *vanities and* things of the world, for we should see how worthless they are by comparison with those which we have within us. What does an animal do beyond satisfying his hunger by seizing whatever attracts him when he sees it? There should surely be a great difference between the brute beasts and ourselves, *as we have such a Father*.

---

[1] Everything between p. 115, l. 32 and this point is an interpolation of V. E. takes up the argument here.
[2] E. reads: "to understand itself (*entenderse*)." But I feel sure that the author intended to write *encenderse* ("become enkindled") as she does in V. E. rounds off the paragraph with the somewhat redundant sentence: "I should like you to have a very good grasp of (*que entendiésedes muy bien*) this method of prayer, which, as I have said, is called recollection," and with the metaphor of the palace begins a new chapter.
[3] E.: "Imagine that you have within you a palace."
[4] E.: "should be so precious."
[5] E. adds: "which is very important."

Perhaps you will laugh at me and say that this is obvious enough; and you will be right, though it was some time before I came to see it. I knew perfectly well that I had a soul, but I did not understand what that soul merited, or Who dwelt within it, until[1] I closed my eyes to the vanities of this world in order to see it. I think, if I had understood then,[2] as I do now, how this great King *really* dwells within this little palace of my soul, I should not have left Him alone so often, but should have stayed with Him and never have allowed His dwelling-place to get so dirty. How wonderful it is that He Whose greatness could fill a thousand worlds, and very many more,[3] should confine Himself within so small a space, *just as He was pleased to dwell within the womb of His most holy Mother!* Being the Lord, He has, of course, perfect freedom, and, as He loves us, He fashions Himself to our measure.

When a soul sets out upon this path, He does not reveal Himself to it, lest it should feel dismayed at seeing that its littleness can contain such greatness; but gradually He enlarges it to the extent requisite for what He has to set within it. It is for this reason that I say He has perfect freedom, since He has power to make the whole of this palace great.[4] The important point is that we should be absolutely resolved to give it to Him for His own and should empty it so that He may take out and put in just what He likes, as He would with something of His own. His Majesty is right in demanding this; let us not deny it to Him.[5] And, as He refuses to force our will, He takes what we give Him but does not give Himself wholly until *He sees that we are giving ourselves wholly to Him.* This is certain, and, as it is of such importance,[6] I often remind you of it. Nor does He work within the soul as He does when it is wholly His and keeps nothing back. I do not see how He can do so, since He likes everything to be done in order. If we fill the palace with vulgar people and all kinds of junk, how can the Lord and His Court occupy it? When such a crowd is there it would be a great thing if He were to remain for even a short time.

[1] In T., the copyist, apparently misunderstanding the sense, altered "until" to "because".
[2] The words "I had understood then" were added to the text by Luis de León in order to complete the sense.
[3] "And very many more" is not in E.
[4] The passage in the text from "How wonderful" (in the preceding paragraph) down to this point was crossed out by St. Teresa in V., and does not appear in T. nor in the Évora edition. Luis de León, however, published it, and it is also found in E.
[5] E. adds here a charmingly natural phrase which, however, somewhat interrupts the trend of thought: "Even in this world, it worries us to have visitors in the house when we cannot tell them to go."
[6] E.: "and for that reason."

Do you suppose, daughters, that He is alone when He comes to us? Do you not see[1] that His *most holy* Son says: "Who art in the Heavens"? Surely such a King would not be abandoned by His courtiers. They stay with Him and pray to Him on our behalf and for our welfare, for they are full of charity. Do not imagine that Heaven is like this earth, where, if a lord or prelate shows anyone favours, whether for some particular reason or simply because he likes him, people at once become envious, and, though the poor man has done nothing to them, he is maliciously treated, *so that his favours cost him dear*.

CHAPTER XXIX

Continues to describe methods for achieving this Prayer of Recollection. Says what little account we should make of being favoured by our superiors.

For the love of God, daughters, avoid making any account of these favours.[2] You should each do your duty; and, if this is not appreciated by your superior, you may be sure that it will be appreciated and rewarded by the Lord. We did not come here to seek rewards in this life, *but only in the life to come*. Let our thoughts always be fixed upon what[3] endures, and not trouble themselves with earthly things which do not endure even for a lifetime. For to-day some other sister will be in your superior's good books; whereas to-morrow, if she sees you exhibiting some additional virtue, it is with you that she will be better pleased—and if she is not it is of little consequence. Never give way to these thoughts, which sometimes begin in a small way but may cost you a great deal of unrest.[4] Check them by remembering that your kingdom is not of this world, and that everything comes quickly to an end, *and that there is nothing in this life that goes on unchangingly*.

But even that is a poor remedy and anything but a perfect one; it is best that this state of things should continue, and that you should be humbled and out of favour, and should wish to be so for the sake of the Lord Who dwells in you.[5] Turn your

[1] T.: "know."
[2] E.: "avoid such things." That is, such partiality shown to one by persons in authority, as is described at the end of the last chapter. E. does better than V. here by not beginning a new chapter till after the end of this paragraph. T. attempts to clarify the sense by adding, after "favours", "of superiors".
[3] T.: "upon the little, which".
[4] E.: "Never give way to these first movements."
[5] E.: "of Him Who dwells in you." *Lit.*, in both E. and V., "with you."

eyes upon yourself and look at yourself inwardly, as I have said. You will find your Master;[1] He will not fail you: indeed, the less outward comfort you have, the [much] greater the joy He will give you. He is full of compassion and never fails those who are afflicted and out of favour[2] if they trust in Him alone. Thus David tells us that *he never saw the just forsaken*[3], and again, *that the Lord is with the afflicted*.[4] Either you believe this or you do not: if you do, *as you should*, why do you wear yourselves to death with worry?[5]

O my Lord, if we had a real knowledge of Thee, we should make not the slightest account of anything,[6] since Thou givest so much to those who will set their whole trust on Thee.[7] Believe me, friends, it is a great thing to realize the truth of this so that we may see how deceptive are earthly *things and favours when they deflect the soul in any way from its course and hinder it from entering within itself*.[8] God help me! If only someone could make you[9] realize this! I myself, *Lord*, certainly cannot; I know that [in truth] I owe *Thee* more than anyone else but I cannot realize this myself as well as I should.

Returning to what I was saying, I should like to be able to explain[10] the nature of this holy companionship with our great Companion,[11] the Holiest of the holy, in which there is nothing to hinder the soul and her Spouse from remaining alone together, when the soul desires to enter within herself, to shut the door behind her so as to keep out all that is worldly and to dwell in that Paradise with her God.[12] I say "desires", because you must understand[13] that this is not a supernatural state but depends upon our volition, and that, by God's favour, we can enter it of our own accord: *this condition must be understood of everything that we say in this book can be done*,[14] for without it nothing can be accomplished and we have not the power to think a single good

---

[1] E. omits "as I have said" and has "your Spouse" for "your Master".
[2] "And out of favour" is not found in E.
[3] Psalm xxxvi (A.V., xxxvii), 25.
[4] Psalm xxxiii, 20-1 (A.V., xxxiv, 19-20).
[5] The original, both in E. and V., has: "With what do you kill yourselves?"
[6] E.: "of anyone."
[7] E.: "will truly give themselves to Thee."
[8] *Lit.*: "when they deflect the soul in any way from going within itself." E.: "deflect in any way from this truth."
[9] E.: "make mortals."
[10] E. begins: "Oh, if only one could explain."
[11] E.: "with the Companion of souls."
[12] T. omits: "with her God."
[13] E. begins the sentence with the imperative: "Understand . . ." and omits: "but depends upon our volition."
[14] E. ends the sentence by adding: "and without it absolutely nothing [*nada, nada*] can be done."

thought. For this is not a silence of the faculties: it is a shutting-up of the faculties within itself by the soul.[1]

There are many ways in which we can gradually acquire this habit, as various books[2] tell us. We must cast aside everything else, they say, in order to approach God inwardly and we must retire within ourselves even during our ordinary occupations. If I can recall the companionship which I have within my soul for as much as a moment, that is of great utility.[3] *But as I am speaking only about the way to recite vocal prayers well, there is no need for me to say as much as this. All I want is that we should know*[4] *and abide with the Person with Whom we are speaking, and not turn our backs upon Him; for that, it seems to me, is what we are doing when we talk to God and yet think of all kinds of vanity. The whole mischief comes from our not really grasping the fact that He is near us, and imagining Him far away—so far, that we shall have to go to Heaven in order to find Him. How is it, Lord, that we do not look at Thy face, when it is so near us? We do not think people are listening to us when we are speaking to them unless we see them looking at us. And do we close our eyes so as not to see that Thou art looking at us? How can we know if Thou hast heard what we say to Thee?*

The great thing I should like to teach you is that, in order to accustom ourselves gradually to giving our minds confidence, so that we may readily understand what we are saying, and with Whom we are speaking, we must recollect our outward senses, take charge of them ourselves and give them something which will occupy them. It is in this way that we have Heaven within ourselves since the Lord of Heaven is there. If once we accustom ourselves to being glad[5] that there is no need to raise our voices in order to speak to Him, since His Majesty will make us conscious that He is there, we shall be able to say the Paternoster and whatever other prayers we like with great peace of mind, and the Lord Himself will help us not to grow tired.[6] Soon after we have begun to force ourselves to remain near the Lord, He will give us indications by which we may understand that, though we have had to say the Paternoster

---

[1] In T., St. Teresa corrects this to: "of the faculties within themselves."
[2] E. substitutes the ordinary for the continuous form of the present tense of "acquire", which is rendered in our text by the adverb "gradually", and adds: "(by) those who write on mental prayer."
[3] "And we must . . . utility" is not found in E.
[4] *Lit.*: "see."
[5] *Lit.*: "once we begin to be glad."
[6] This sentence is from E., which in the context gives the better reading. V. has: "In brief, we must gradually accustom ourselves to being glad that there is no need to raise our voices in order to speak to Him, since His Majesty will make us conscious that He is there. We shall then be able to say our vocal prayers with great peace of mind, and this will save us much worry."

many times, He heard us the first time.[1] For He loves to save us worry; and, even though we may take a whole hour over saying it once, if we can realize that we are with Him, and what it is we are asking Him, and how willing He is, *like any father*, to grant it to us, and how He loves to be with us, *and comfort us*, He has no wish for us to tire our brains by a great deal of talking.[2]

For love of the Lord, then, sisters, accustom yourselves to saying the Paternoster in this recollected way, and before long you will see how you gain by doing so. It is a method of prayer which establishes habits that prevent the soul from going astray and the faculties from becoming restless. This you will find out in time: I only beg you to test it, even at the cost of a little trouble, which always results when we try to form a new habit. I assure you, however, that before long you will have the great comfort of finding it unnecessary to tire yourselves with seeking this holy Father to Whom you pray, for you will discover Him within you.

May the Lord teach this to those of you who do not know it: for my own part I must confess that, until the Lord taught me this method, I never knew what it was to get satisfaction and comfort out of prayer, and it is because I have always gained such great benefits from this custom of interior recollection[3] that I have written about it at such length. *Perhaps you all know this, but some sister may come to you who will not know it, so you must not be vexed at my having spoken about it here.*[4]

I conclude by advising anyone who wishes to acquire it (since, as I say, it is in our power to do so) not to grow weary of trying to get used to the method which has been described, for it is equivalent to a gradual gaining of the mastery over herself and is not vain labour. To conquer oneself for one's own good is to make use of the senses in the service of the interior life. If she is speaking she must try to remember that there is One within her to Whom she can speak; if she is listening, let her remember that she can listen to Him Who is nearer to her than anyone else. Briefly, let her realize that, if she likes, she need never[5] withdraw from this good companionship, and let her grieve when she has left her Father alone for so long though her need of Him is so sore.

If she can, let her practise recollection many times daily; if not, let her do so occasionally. As she grows accustomed to it, she will feel its benefits, either sooner or later. Once the Lord has granted it to her, she would not exchange it for any treasure.

---

[1] T. deletes: "He will . . . first time" and substitutes: "it will (come to) be very easy for us." In the next sentence T. has "the Paternoster" for "it".
[2] E. ends the sentence at "brains".
[3] *Lit.*: "of recollection within me." T. omits: "within me."
[4] E. continues: "We must now come, etc." (Cf. p. 123, n. 2.)
[5] T.: "need not."

Nothing, sisters, can be learned without a little trouble, so do, for the love of God, look upon any care which you take about this as well spent. I know that, with God's help, if you practise it for a year, or perhaps for only six months, you will be successful in attaining it. Think what a short time that is for acquiring so great a benefit, for you will be laying a good foundation, so that, if the Lord desires to raise you up to achieve great things, He will find you ready, because you will be close to Himself. May His Majesty never allow us to withdraw ourselves from His presence. Amen.

CHAPTER XXX

Describes the importance of understanding what we ask for in prayer. Treats of these words in the Paternoster: "Sanctificetur nomen tuum, adveniat regnum tuum."[1] Applies them to the Prayer of Quiet, and begins the explanation of them.

We must now come to consider the next petition in our good Master's prayer, in which He begins to entreat His holy Father on our behalf, and see what it is that He entreats, as it is well that we should know this.[2]

What person, however careless, who had to address someone of importance, would not spend time in thinking how to approach him so as to please him and not be considered tedious? He would also think what he was going to ask for and what use he would make of it, especially if his petition were for some particular thing, as our good Jesus tells us our petitions must be. This point seems to me *very* important. Couldst Thou not, my Lord, have ended this prayer in a single sentence, by saying: "Give us, Father, whatever is good for us"? For, in addressing One Who knows everything, there would seem to be no need to say any more.

This would have sufficed, O Eternal Wisdom,[3] as between Thee and Thy Father. It was thus that Thou didst address Him in the Garden, telling Him of Thy will and Thy fear, but leaving Thyself in His hands.[4] But Thou knowest us, my Lord, and Thou knowest that we are not as resigned as wert Thou to the will of Thy Father; we needed, therefore, to[5] be taught to ask for particular things so that we should stop *for a moment* to think

---

[1] "Hallowed be Thy name. Thy kingdom come."
[2] In E. this paragraph comes at the end of the preceding chapter. The context seems to place it more naturally here, or as a sub-title to Chapter XXX.
[3] E.: "O Wisdom of the angels!"
[4] T. deletes this sentence.
[5] T. deletes "we . . . to" and writes "we would rather".

if what we ask of Thee is good for us, and if it is not, should not ask for it. For, being what we are and having our free will, if we do not receive what we ask for, we shall not accept what the Lord gives us. The gift might be the best one possible—but we never think we are rich unless we actually see money in our hands.

Oh, God help me! What is it that sends our faith to sleep, so that we cannot realize how certain we are, on the one hand, to be punished, and, on the other, to be rewarded? It is for this reason, daughters, that it is good for you to know what you are asking for in the Paternoster, so that, if the Eternal Father gives it you, you shall not cast it back in His face. You must think carefully if what you are about to ask for will be good for you; if it will not, do not ask for it, but[1] ask His Majesty to give you light. For we are blind[2] and often we have such a loathing for life-giving food that we cannot eat it but prefer what will cause us death—and what a death: so terrible and eternal!

Now the good Jesus bids us say these words, in which we pray that this Kingdom may come in us:[3] "Hallowed be Thy Name, Thy Kingdom come in us." Consider now, daughters, how great is our Master's[4] wisdom. I am thinking here of what we are asking in praying for this kingdom, and it is well that we should realize this. His Majesty, knowing of how little we are capable, saw that, unless He provided for us by giving us His Kingdom here on earth, we could neither hallow nor praise nor magnify nor glorify *nor exalt* this holy name of the Eternal Father in a way befitting it. The good Jesus, therefore, places these two petitions next to each other. Let us understand this thing that we are asking for, daughters, and how important it is that we should pray for it without ceasing[5] and do all we can to please Him Who will give it us: it is for that reason that I want to tell you what I know about the matter now. If you do not like the subject, think out some other meditations for yourselves, for our Master will allow us to do this, provided we submit in all things to the teaching of the [Holy Roman] Church, as I do here.[6] *In any case I shall not give you this book to read until persons who understand these matters have seen it: so, if there is anything wrong with it, the reason will be, not wickedness, but my imperfect knowledge.*

To me, then, it seems that, of the many joys[7] to be found in the kingdom of Heaven, the chief is that we shall have no more

---

[1] T. interpolates: "remembering that (your) prayer) must be in conformity with the will of God, as we say in this prayer, ask, etc."
[2] T.: "For you (*fem.*) are blind."
[3] E.: "Now the good Jesus says."
[4] E.: "our Spouse's."
[5] E.: "that we should ask for it."
[6] E.: "as I always do."
[7] E. begins: "Of the many joys."

to do with the things of earth; for in Heaven we shall have an intrinsic tranquillity and glory, a joy in the rejoicings of all, a perpetual peace, and a great interior satisfaction which will come to us when we see that all are hallowing and praising the Lord, and are blessing His name, and that none is offending Him. For all love Him there and the soul's one concern is loving Him, nor can it cease from loving Him because it knows Him. And this is how we should love Him on earth, though we cannot do so[1] with the same perfection nor yet all the time; still, if we knew Him, we should love Him very differently from the way we do now.

It looks as though I were going to say that we must be angels to make this petition and to say our vocal prayers well. This would indeed be our Divine Master's wish, since He bids us make so sublime a petition. You may be quite sure[2] that He never tells us to ask for impossibilities, so it must be possible, with God's help, for a soul living in that state of exile to reach such a point, though not as perfectly as those who have been freed from this prison, for we are making a sea-voyage and are still on the journey. But there are times when we are wearied with travelling and the Lord grants our faculties tranquillity and our soul quiet, and while they are in that state He gives us a clear[3] understanding of the nature of the gifts He bestows upon those whom He brings to His Kingdom. Those to whom, while they are still on earth, He grants what we are asking Him for receive pledges which will give them a great hope of eventually attaining to a perpetual enjoyment of what on earth He only allows them to taste.

If it were not that you would tell me I am treating of contemplation, it would be appropriate, in writing of this petition, to say a little about the beginning of pure contemplation, which those who experience it call the Prayer of Quiet; but, as I have said, I am discussing vocal prayer here, and anyone ignorant of[4] the subject might think that the two had nothing to do with one another, though I know this is *certainly* not true. Forgive my wanting to speak of it, for I know there are many people who practise vocal prayer in the manner already described and are raised[5] by God to the higher kind of contemplation without *having had any hand in this themselves or even* knowing how it has happened. *For this reason, daughters, I attach great importance to your saying your vocal prayers well.* I know a nun[6] who could never

---

[1] T. interpolates: "in the same way and."
[2] T.: "It is clear."
[3] T.: "gives us an."
[4] T.: "anyone who did not like."
[5] E.: "prayer and are raised."
[6] So E. V. has "a person".

practise anything but vocal prayer[1] but who kept to this and found she had everything else; yet if she omitted saying her prayers her mind wandered so much that she could not endure it. May we all practise such mental prayer as that.[2] She would say a number of paternosters, corresponding to the number of times Our Lord shed His blood, and on nothing more than these and a few other prayers she would spend two or three[3] hours. She came to me once in great distress, saying that she did not know how to practise mental prayer,[4] and that she could not contemplate but could only say vocal prayers. *She was quite an old woman and had lived an extremely good and religious life.* I asked her what prayers she said, and *from her reply* I saw that, though keeping to the Paternoster, she was experiencing pure contemplation, and the Lord was raising her to be with Him in union.[5] She spent her life so well, too, that her actions made it clear she was receiving great favours.[6] So I praised the Lord and envied her her vocal prayer. If this story is true—and it is—none[7] of you who have had a bad opinion of contemplatives can suppose that you will be free from the risk of becoming like them if you say your vocal prayers as they should be said and keep a pure conscience.[8] *I shall have to say still more about this. Anyone not wishing to hear it may pass it over.*

CHAPTER XXXI

Continues the same subject. Explains what is meant by the Prayer of Quiet. Gives several counsels to those who experience it. This chapter is very noteworthy.[9]

Now, daughters, I still want to describe this Prayer of Quiet to you, in the way I have heard it talked about, and as the Lord has been pleased to teach it to me, perhaps in order that I might describe it to you. It is in this kind of prayer, as I have said, that the Lord seems to me to begin to show us that He is hearing our petition: He begins to give us His[10] Kingdom on earth so

---

[1] T.: "practise mental prayer."
[2] T.: "such as that."
[3] So E. V. has "several".
[4] E. makes the anecdote still more striking by omitting "mental".
[5] E.: "I saw that, while she was keeping to the Paternoster, the Lord was raising her to experience union."
[6] E. omits this sentence. T. ends it at "clear".
[7] E. begins the sentence: "So none."
[8] T. turns this sentence into a question (". . . can any of you suppose . . . ?") and closes the chapter with the words: "You (*pl.*) are mistaken."
[9] In the Évora edition, the whole of this chapter is omitted.
[10] T. has *declarar* ("declare", "show forth") for *dar* ("give").

that we may truly praise Him and hallow His name and strive to make others do so likewise.[1]

This is a supernatural state, and, however hard we try, we cannot reach it for ourselves;[2] for it is a state in which the soul enters into peace, or rather in which the Lord gives it peace through His presence, as He did to that just man Simeon.[3] In this state all the faculties are stilled. The soul, in a way which has nothing to do with the outward senses, realizes that it is now very close to its God, and that, if it were but a little closer, it would become one with Him through union. This is not because it sees Him either with its bodily or with its spiritual eyes. The just man Simeon saw no more than the glorious Infant—a poor little Child, Who, to judge from the swaddling-clothes in which He was wrapped and from the small number of the people whom He had *as a retinue* to take Him up to the Temple, might well have been[4] the son of these poor people rather than the Son of his Heavenly Father. But the Child Himself revealed to him Who He was. Just so, though less clearly, does the soul know Who He is. It cannot understand how it knows Him, yet it sees that it is in the Kingdom[5] (or at least is near to the King Who will give it the Kingdom), and it feels such reverence that it dares to ask nothing. It is, as it were, in a swoon, both inwardly and outwardly, so that the outward man (let me call it the "body", and then you will understand me better)[6] does not wish to move, but rests, like one who has almost reached the end of his journey,[7] so that it may the better start again upon its way, with redoubled strength for its task.

The body experiences the greatest delight and the soul is conscious of a deep satisfaction. So glad is it merely to find itself near the fountain that, even before it has begun to drink, it has had its fill.[8] There seems nothing left for it to desire.

---

[1] E. begins: "This Prayer of Quiet (is that) in which, as I have said, I believe the Lord begins to show us that He is hearing our petition, and begins to give us His Kingdom here, so that we may truly praise His name and strive that others may praise it. Though, having written of this elsewhere, as I have said, I shall not describe it at great length, I shall say something about it." T. has "praise and hallow Him".

[2] "By our ability," adds P. Báñez, in the margin.

[3] The allusion is, of course, to St. Luke ii, 25 ("just and devout"), 29.

[4] E. interpolates here, in apposition with "son", the word *romerito*: "a little pilgrim."

[5] E.: "it can only understand that it is in the Kingdom."

[6] "And then you will understand me better" is a softened (some might say a regrettably emasculated) version of the reading in E.: "or some little simpleton [*simplecita*] will come along not knowing what 'inward' and 'outward' mean." But as the revised version is the more suitable for the Saint's wider audience, my text respects her amendment.

[7] E. continues: "and experiences the greatest delight in the body and deep satisfaction." The word translated "deep" in both text and note is *grande*, "great".

[8] T. omits: "even . . . fill" and reads: "near the fountain that there seems, etc."

The faculties are stilled and have no wish to move, for any movement they may make appears to hinder the soul from loving God.[1] They are not completely lost, however, since, two of them being free, they can realize in Whose Presence they are.[2] It is the will that is in captivity now; and, if while in this state it is capable of experiencing any pain, the pain comes when it realizes that it will have to resume its liberty. The mind[3] tries to occupy itself with only one thing, and the memory has no desire to busy itself with more: they both see that this is the one thing needful and that anything else will unsettle them. Persons in this state prefer the body to remain motionless, for otherwise their peace would be destroyed: for this reason they dare not stir. Speaking is a distress to them: they will spend a whole hour on a single repetition of the Paternoster. They are so close to God that they know they can make themselves understood by signs.[4] They are in the palace, near to their King,[5] and they see that He is already beginning to give them His Kingdom on earth. *Sometimes tears come to their eyes, but they weep very gently and quite without distress: their whole desire is the hallowing of this name.* They seem not to be in the world, and have no wish to see or hear anything but their God; nothing distresses them, nor does it seem that anything can possibly do so.[6] In short, for as long as this state lasts, they are so overwhelmed and absorbed by the joy and delight which they experience that they can think of nothing else to wish for, and will gladly say with Saint Peter: "Lord, let us make here three mansions."[7]

Occasionally, during this Prayer of Quiet, God grants the soul another favour which is hard to understand if one has not had long experience of it. But any of you who have had this will at once recognize it and it will give you great comfort to know what it is. I believe God often grants this favour together with the other. When this quiet is felt in a high degree and lasts for a long time, I do not think that, if the will were not made fast to

---

[1] The phrase "for any . . . loving God" does not appear in E.
[2] E. omits: "two of them being free", and adds, rather confusedly: "and (?what they) can (?do): it is a restful thought." The following sentences in V. are an enlargement of E., which continues: "(Persons in this state) prefer the body to remain motionless, lest it should cause them unrest. They think of one thing and not of many. Speaking is distress to them: they will spend a whole hour on a single repetition of the Paternoster, etc."
[3] "As before," adds P. Báñez, marginally.
[4] T. omits: "by signs."
[5] E. continues: "they are in His Kingdom, which the Lord is already beginning to give them on earth."
[6] E. ends the paragraph here. The next four paragraphs in the text above are omitted (cf. however, P. Silverio, III, 313, n. 1) and E. continues: "With respect to the Prayer of Quiet, I omitted to say this. It may come about, etc." (p. 130, n. 1)
[7] *Moradas.* Cf. p. 85, n. 3, above. The "three tabernacles" of St. Matthew xvii, 4.

something, the peace could be of such long duration. Sometimes it goes on for a day, or for two days, and we find ourselves—I mean those who experience this state—full of this joy without understanding the reason. They see clearly that their whole self is not in what they are doing, but that the most important faculty is absent—namely, the will, which I think is united with its God—and that the other faculties are left free to busy themselves with His service. For this they have much more capacity at such a time, though when attending to worldly affairs they are dull and sometimes[1] stupid.

It is a great favour which the Lord grants to these souls, for it unites the active life with the contemplative. At such times they serve the Lord in both these ways at once; the will, while in contemplation, is working without knowing how it does so; the other two faculties are serving Him as Martha did. Thus Martha and Mary work together. I know someone to whom the Lord often granted this favour; she could not understand it and asked a great contemplative[2] about it; he told her that what she described was quite possible and had happened to himself. I think, therefore, that as the soul experiences such satisfaction in this Prayer of Quiet the will must be almost continuously united with Him Who alone can give it happiness.

I think it will be well, sisters, if I give some advice here to any of you whom the Lord, out of His goodness alone, has brought to this state, as I know that this has happened to some of you. First of all, when such persons experience this joy, without knowing whence it has come to them, but knowing at least that they could not have achieved it of themselves, they are tempted to imagine that they can prolong it and they may even try not to breathe. This is ridiculous: we can no more control this prayer than we can make the day break, or stop night from falling; it is supernatural and something we cannot acquire. The most we can do to prolong this favour is to realize that we can neither diminish nor add to it, but, being most unworthy and undeserving of it, can only receive it with thanksgiving. And we can best give thanks, not with many words, but by lifting up our eyes, like the publican.[3]

---

[1] T. omits: "sometimes."

[2] In the margin of T. the author adds, in her own hand, that this contemplative was St. Francis Borgia, Duke of Gandía (Cf. *Life*, Chapter XXIV: Vol. I, p. 154, above). No doubt, then, the other person referred to was St. Teresa herself. The addition reads: "who was a religious of the Company of Jesus, who had been Duke of Gandía," and to this are added some words, also in St. Teresa's hand, but partially scored out and partially cut by the binder, which seem to be: "who knew it well by experience."

[3] St. Luke xviii, 13. St. Teresa apparently forgot that the publican " would not so much as lift his eyes towards heaven".

It is well to seek greater solitude so as to make room for the Lord and allow His Majesty to do His own work in us. The most we should do is occasionally, and quite gently, to utter a single word, like a person giving a little puff to a candle, when he sees it has almost gone out, so as to make it burn again; though, if it were fully alight, I suppose the only result of blowing it would be to put it out. I think the puff should be a gentle one because, if we begin to tax our brains by making up long speeches, the will may become active again.

Note carefully, friends, this piece of advice which I want to give you now. You will often find that these other two faculties are of no help to you. It may come about that the soul[1] is enjoying the highest degree of quiet, and that the understanding[2] has soared so far aloft that what is happening to it seems not to be going on in its own house at all; it *really* seems to be a guest in somebody else's house, looking for other lodgings, since its own lodging no longer satisfies it and it cannot remain there for long together. Perhaps this is only my own experience and other people[3] do not find it so. But, speaking for myself, I sometimes long to die because I cannot cure this wandering of the mind.[4] At other times the mind seems to be settled in its own abode and to be remaining there with the will as its companion. When all three faculties work together[5] it is wonderful. The harmony is like that between husband and wife: if they are happy and love each other, both desire the same thing; but if the husband is unhappy in his marriage he soon begins to make the wife restless. Just so, when the will finds itself in this state of quiet,[6] it must take no more notice of the understanding[7] than it would of a madman, for, if it tries to draw the understanding along with it, it is bound to grow preoccupied and restless, with the result that this state of prayer will be all effort and no gain and the soul will lose what God has been giving it without any effort of its own.

Pay great attention to the following comparison, which *the Lord suggested to me when I was in this state of prayer, and which* seems to me very appropriate.[8] The soul is like an infant still at its mother's breast: such is the mother's care for it that she gives

---

[1] E. here picks up the argument again, continuing: "is often enjoying true quiet."
[2] "Or thought," adds T. As will be seen, the author or the copyist seems to have been rather afraid of using the word "understanding" in this context, and to have tried to explain it.
[3] E.: "Perhaps other people."
[4] E. omits: "wandering of the mind."
[5] E.: "If both work together."
[6] "And this counsel should be carefully noted," adds E., "for it is important."
[7] "Or thought, or imagination, for I do not know what it is," adds T.
[8] "And explains it," adds T., which does not include the italicized phrase from E.

it its milk without its having to ask for it so much as by moving its lips. That is what happens here. The will simply loves, and[1] no effort needs to be made by the understanding, for it is the Lord's pleasure that, without exercising its thought, the soul should realize that it is in His company, and should merely drink the milk which His Majesty puts into its mouth and enjoy its sweetness. The Lord desires it to know that it is He Who is granting it that favour and that in its enjoyment of it He too rejoices. But it is not His will that the soul should try to understand how it is enjoying it, or what it is enjoying; it should lose all thought of itself, and He Who is at its side will not fail to see what is best for it. If it begins to strive with its mind so that the mind may be apprised of what is happening and thus induced to share in it,[2] it will be quite unable to do so, and the soul will perforce lose the milk[3] and forgo that Divine sustenance.

This state of prayer is different from that in which the soul is wholly united with God,[4] for in the latter state it does not even swallow its nourishment:[5] the Lord places this within it, and it has no idea how. But in this state it *even* seems to be His will that the soul should work a little, though so quietly that it is hardly conscious of doing so.[6] What disturbs it is the understanding,[7] and this is not the case when there is union of all the three faculties, since He Who created them suspends them: He keeps them occupied with the enjoyment that He has given them, without their knowing, or being able to understand, the reason. *Anyone who has had experience of this kind of prayer will understand quite well what I am saying if, after reading this, she considers it carefully, and thinks out its meaning: otherwise it will be Greek*[8] *to her.*

Well, as I say, the soul is conscious of having reached this state of prayer, which is a quiet, deep *and peaceful* happiness of the will, without being able to decide precisely what it is, although it can clearly see how it differs from the happiness of the world. To have dominion over the whole world, with all its happiness, would not suffice to bring the soul such inward satisfaction as it enjoys now in the depths of its will. For other kinds of happiness

---

[1] E. omits: "the will simply loves, and". After "understanding", E. continues: "for the Lord puts it into the soul, and His will is that it should realize He is there, and should swallow the milk that He gives it, and should realize all the time (*y esté entendiendo*) that He is giving it, and should love (*y [esté] amando*). If it begins to strive, so that the mind may be apprised, etc."

[2] *Lit.*: "and drawn along with it"; the same phrase is found at the end of the preceding paragraph.

[3] *Lit.*: "let the milk fall out of its mouth."

[4] E.: "is different, in this and in other ways, from union."

[5] E. omits: "its nourishment" and substitutes that phrase for the following "this".

[6] E. continues: "Anyone who has, etc."

[7] "Or imagination," adds T.

[8] *Algarabía.* Cf. p. 105, n. 1 above.

in life, it seems to me, touch only the outward part of the will, which we might describe as its rind.

When[1] one of you finds herself in this sublime state of prayer, which, as I have already said, is most markedly[2] supernatural, and the understanding (or, to put it more clearly, the thought)[3] wanders off after the most ridiculous things in the world, she should laugh at it and treat it as the silly thing it is, and remain in her state of quiet. For thoughts will come and go, but the will is mistress and all-powerful, and will recall them without your having to trouble about it.[4] But if you try to drag the understanding back by force, you lose your power over it, which comes from your taking and receiving that Divine sustenance, and neither will nor understanding will gain[5], but both will be losers. There is a saying that, if we try very hard to grasp all, we lose all;[6] and so I think it is here. Experience will show you the truth of this;[7] and I shall not be surprised if those of you who have none think this very obscure and unnecessary. But, as I have said, if you have only a little experience of it you will understand it and be able to profit by it, and you will praise the Lord for being pleased to enable me to explain it.

Let us now conclude by saying that, when the soul is brought to this state of prayer, it would seem that the Eternal Father has already granted its petition that He will give it His Kingdom on earth.[8] O blessed request, in which we ask for so great a good without knowing what we do! Blessed manner of asking! It is for this reason, sisters, that I want us to be careful how we say this prayer, the Paternoster, and all other vocal prayers,[9] *and what we ask for in them.* For *clearly*, when God has shown us this favour, we shall have to forget worldly things,[10] all of which the Lord of the world has come and cast out. I do not mean that everyone who experiences[11] the Prayer of Quiet must perforce

---

[1] E.: "I mean that, when."
[2] T. omits: "most markedly."
[3] This parenthesis is not found in E.
[4] E.: "without your doing anything."
[5] *Lit.*: "neither the one nor the other will gain." E. continues: "But we might say that, if we try very hard, etc."
[6] E. ends the sentence here.
[7] E. ends the paragraph thus: "for we need much experience to understand it without having it explained to us, though we need little to practise it and to understand it after we have read about it."
[8] E. begins the paragraph thus: "Finally, in view of the permanence of the satisfaction and delight that the soul experiences, it may rightly be said that it is in its kingdom, and that the Eternal Father has heard its petition for (the kingdom) to come to it."
[9] E.: "this heavenly prayer", with "it" for "them" to end the sentence.
[10] E.: "affairs." The author added "even against our will", but afterwards crossed these words out.
[11] E.: "who prays for."

be detached from everything in the world; but at least I should like all such persons to know what they lack and to humble themselves *and not to make so great a petition as though they were asking for nothing, and, if the Lord gives them what they ask for, to throw it back in His face.*[1] They must try to become more and more detached from everything, for otherwise they will only remain where they are. If God gives a soul such pledges, it is a sign that He has great things in store for it. It will be its own fault if it does not make great progress. But if He sees that, after He has brought the Kingdom of Heaven into its abode, it returns to earth, not only will He refrain from showing it the secrets of His Kingdom but He will grant it this other favour only for short periods and rarely.

I may be mistaken about this, but I have seen it and know that it happens, and, for my own part, I believe this is why spiritual people are not much more numerous. They do not respond to so great a favour in a practical way: instead of preparing themselves to receive this favour again, they[2] take back from the Lord's hands the will which He considered His own and centre it upon base things. So He seeks out others who love Him in order to grant them His greater gifts, although He will not take away all that He has given from those who live in purity of conscience. But there are persons—and I have been one of them—to whom the Lord gives tenderness of devotion and holy inspirations and light on everything. He bestows this Kingdom on them and brings them to this Prayer of Quiet, and yet they deafen their ears to His voice. For they are so fond of talking and of repeating a large number of vocal prayers in a great hurry, as though they were anxious to finish their task[3] of repeating them daily, that when the Lord, as I say, puts His Kingdom into their very hands, *by giving them this Prayer of Quiet and this inward peace*, they do not accept it, but think that they will do better to go on reciting their prayers, which only distract them from their purpose.

Do not be like that, sisters, but be watchful[4] when the Lord grants you this favour. Think what a great treasure you may be losing and realize that you are doing much more by occasionally repeating a single petition of the Paternoster than by repeating the whole of it many times in a hurry *and not thinking what you are saying*. He to Whom you are praying is very near to you and

---

[1] E. omits the rest of this paragraph and part of the next, continuing: "There are many—and I have been one of these—to whom the Lord gives tenderness, etc."
[2] T. adds: "rather."
[3] E.: "in order to finish their task."
[4] "But be watchful" is not found in E. The rest of this paragraph in T. is on a page which is missing from the copy.

will not[1] fail to hear you; and you may be sure that you are truly praising Him and hallowing His name, since you are glorifying the Lord as a member of His household and praising Him with increasing affection and desire so that it seems you can never forsake His service. *So I advise you to be very cautious about this, for it is of the greatest importance.*

CHAPTER XXXII

Expounds these words of the Paternoster: "Fiat voluntas tua sicut in coelo et in terra."[2] *Describes how much is accomplished by those who repeat these words with full resolution and how well the Lord rewards them for it.*[3]

Now that our good Master has asked on our behalf, and has taught us ourselves to ask, for a thing so precious that it includes all we can desire on earth, and has granted us the great favour of making us His brethren, let us see what He desires us to give to His Father, and what He offers Him on our behalf, and what He asks of us, for it is right that we should render Him some service in return for such great favours. O good Jesus! Since Thou givest so little (little, that is to say, on our behalf)[4] how canst Thou ask [so much] for us? What we give is in itself nothing at all by comparison with all that has been given us and with the greatness of Our Lord.[5] But in truth, my Lord, Thou dost not leave us with nothing to give and we give all that we can—I mean if we give in the spirit of these words: "Thy will be done; as in Heaven, so on earth."

Thou didst well, O our good Master,[6] to make this last petition, so that we may be able to accomplish what Thou dost promise in our name. For truly, Lord, hadst Thou not done this, I do not think it would have been possible *for us to accomplish it*. But, since Thy Father does what Thou askest Him in granting us His Kingdom on earth, I know that we can truly fulfil Thy word by giving what Thou dost promise in our name. For since my earth has now become Heaven, it will be possible for Thy will to be done

---

[1] E.: "and cannot."
[2] "Thy will be done: as in Heaven, so on earth."
[3] The title of this chapter, the first two paragraphs and part of the third paragraph are not found in T. P. Silverio supplies the corresponding text of the Évora edition.
[4] Évora adds: "because of our weakness", but there is no means of telling if this is an addition made by St. Teresa or no.
[5] E.: "of (our) King."
[6] E.: "O good Master and Lord."

in me. Otherwise, on an earth so wretched as mine, and so barren of fruit, I know not, Lord, how it could be possible. It is a great thing that Thou dost offer.[1]

When I think of this, it amuses me that there should be people who dare not ask the Lord for trials,[2] thinking that His sending them to them depends upon their asking for them! I am not referring to those who omit to ask for them out of humility because they think themselves to be incapable of bearing them, though for my own part I believe that He who gives them love enough to ask for such a stern method of proving it will give them love enough to endure it. I should like to ask those who are afraid to pray for trials lest they should at once be given them what they mean when they beg the Lord to fulfil His will in them. Do they say this because everyone else says it and not because they want it to be done? That would not be right,[3] sisters. Remember that the good Jesus is our Ambassador here, and that His desire has been to mediate between us and His Father at no small cost to Himself: it would not be right for us to refuse to give what He *promises and* offers on our behalf[4] or to say nothing about it. Let me put it in another way. Consider, daughters, that, whether we wish it or no, God's will must be done,[5] and must be done both in Heaven and on earth. Believe me, then, do as I suggest and make[6] a virtue of necessity.

O my Lord, what a great comfort it is to me that Thou didst not entrust the fulfilment of Thy will to one so wretched as I! Blessed be Thou for ever and let all things praise Thee. May Thy name be for ever glorified. I should indeed have had to be good, Lord, if the fulfilment or non-fulfilment of Thy will [in Heaven and on earth] were in my hands. But as it is, though my will is not yet free from self-interest, I give it to Thee freely.[7] For I have proved, by long experience, how much I gain by leaving it freely in Thy hands. O friends,[8] what a great gain is this—and how much we lose through not fulfilling our promises to the Lord in the Paternoster, and giving Him what we offer Him!

---

[1] "For that reason, daughters," adds E., "I should like you to understand this."
[2] E. reads: "who say that it is not well to ask the Lord for trials", and continues: "(saying) that this shows little humility. And I have found some persons so pusillanimous that, even without making this pretext of humility, they have not the courage to pray for trials, because they think that these would be given them at once. I should like to ask them what they understand this will to mean which they ask His Majesty to fulfil in them. Do they say, etc."
[3] E.: "That would be very wrong, daughters."
[4] T. ends the sentence here.
[5] E.: "See, sisters, and do as I suggest: it will have to be, whether you wish it or no."
[6] E.: "Believe me, then, and make."
[7] T. adds: "with Thy help."
[8] E.: "O daughters."

Before I tell you in what this gain consists, I will explain to you how much you are offering, lest later you should exclaim that you had been deceived and had not understood what you were saying. Do not behave like some religious among us,[1] who do nothing but promise, and then excuse ourselves for not fulfilling our promises by saying that we had not understood what we were promising.[2] That may well be true,[3] *for it is easy to say things and hard to put them into practice, and anyone who thought that there was no more in the one than in the other certainly did not understand.*[4] It seems very easy to say that we will surrender our will to someone, until we try it and realize that it is the hardest thing we can do if we carry it out as we should. Our superiors do not always treat us strictly when they see we are weak; and sometimes they treat both weak and strong in the same way. That is not so with the Lord; He knows what each of us can bear, and, when He sees that one of us is strong, He does not hesitate to fulfil His will in him.

So I want you to realize with Whom (as they say) you are dealing and what the good Jesus offers on your behalf to the Father, and what you are giving Him when you pray that His will may be done in you: it is nothing else than this that you are praying for.[5] Do not fear that He will give you riches or pleasures or *great* honours or any such earthly things; His love for you is not so poor as that. And He sets a very high value on what you give Him and desires to recompense you for it since He gives you His Kingdom while you are still alive. Would you like to see how He treats those who make this prayer from their hearts? Ask His glorious Son, Who made it thus in the Garden. Think with what resolution[6] and fullness of desire He prayed; and consider if the will of God was not perfectly fulfilled in Him through the trials, sufferings, insults and persecutions which He gave Him, until at last His life ended with death on a Cross.

So you see, daughters, what God gave to His best Beloved, and from that you can understand what His will is.[7] These, then, are His gifts in this world. He gives them in proportion to

---

[1] E. reads "like some nuns" and continues in the third, not, like V., in the first person.

[2] E.: "and, when they fulfil nothing, say that, when they made their profession, they did not understand what they were promising."

[3] E.: "I quite believe it."

[4] E. continues: "Make those who profess here understand, by means of a long probation, that they must not only talk but act as well. So I want you to realize, etc."

[5] V. abridges this passage to read: "I want to counsel you and remind you what His will is."

[6] E.: "with what truth."

[7] E. continues: "Consider what you are doing: try not to let the prayers, etc."

the love which He bears us. He gives more to those whom He loves most, and less to those He loves least; and He gives in accordance with the courage which He sees that each of us has and the love we bear to His Majesty. When He sees a soul who loves Him greatly, He knows that soul can suffer much for Him, whereas one who loves Him little will suffer little. For my own part, I believe that love is the measure of our ability to bear crosses, whether great or small. So if you have this love, sisters, try not to let the prayers you make to so great a Lord be words of mere politeness but brace yourselves to suffer what His Majesty desires. For if you give Him your will in any other way, you are just showing Him a jewel,[1] making as if to give it to Him and begging Him to take it, and then, when He puts out His hand to do so, taking it back and holding on to it tightly.

Such mockery is no fit treatment for One who endured so much for us. If for no other reason than this, it would not be right to mock Him so often—and it is by no means seldom that we say these words to Him in the Paternoster. Let us give Him once and for all the jewel which we have so often undertaken to give Him. For the truth is that He gives it to us first[2] so that we may give it back to Him. *Ah, my God! How well Jesus knows us and how much He thinks of our good! He did not say we must surrender our wills to the Lord until we had been well paid for this small service. It will be realized from this how much the Lord intends us to gain by rendering it to Him: even in this life He begins to reward us for this, as I shall presently explain.* Worldly people will do a great deal if they sincerely resolve to fulfil the will of God. But you, daughters, must both say and act, and give Him both words and deeds, as I really think we religious do. Yet sometimes not only do we undertake to give God the jewel but we even put it into His hand[3] and then take it back again. We are so generous all of a sudden, and then we become so mean, that it would have been better if we had stopped to think before giving.

The aim of all my advice to you in this book is that we should surrender ourselves wholly to the Creator, place our will in His hands and detach ourselves from the creatures. As you will already have understood how important this is, I will say no more about it, but I will tell you why our good Master puts these words here. He knows how much we shall gain by rendering this

---

[1] E. continues: "and telling Him to take it, and then, etc."

[2] E. ends the sentence here. Both E. and V. have: "He does not give to us first", a reading which may be thought to find some support in the following sentences of E., but in the context of V. would be inexplicable. It seems to me likely that the negative was inserted in error.

[3] E.: "Yet sometimes we put the jewel into the Lord's hand."

service to His Eternal Father. We are preparing ourselves for the time, which will come very soon, when we shall find ourselves at the end of our journey[1] and shall be drinking of living water from the fountain I have described. Unless we make a total surrender of our will[2] to the Lord, *and put ourselves in His hands so that He may do in all things what is best for us in accordance with His will*, He will never allow us to drink of it. This is the perfect contemplation of which you asked me to write to you.

In this matter, as I have already said, we can do nothing of ourselves, either by working hard or by making plans,[3] nor is it needful that we should. For everything else[4] hinders and prevents[5] us from saying [with real resolution], "Fiat voluntas tua": that is, may the Lord fulfil His will in me, in every way and manner which Thou, my Lord, desirest. If Thou wilt do this by means of trials, give me strength and let them come. If by means of persecutions and sickness and dishonour and need, here I am, my Father, I will not turn my face away from Thee nor have I the right to turn my back upon them. For Thy Son gave Thee this will of mine[6] in the name of us all and it is not right that I for my part should fail. Do Thou grant me the grace of bestowing on me Thy Kingdom so that I may do Thy will, since He has asked this of me. Dispose of me as of that which is Thine own, in accordance with Thy will.

Oh, my sisters, what power this gift has! If it be made with due resolution, it cannot fail to draw the Almighty to become one with our lowliness and to transform us into Himself[7] and to effect a union between the Creator[8] and the creature. Ask yourselves if that will not be a rich reward for you, and if you have not a good Master. For, knowing how the good will of His Father is to be gained, He teaches us how and by what means we must serve Him.

The more *resolute we are in soul and the more* we show Him by our actions that the words we use to Him are not words of mere politeness, the more and more does Our Lord draw us to Himself and raise us above all *petty* earthly things, and above ourselves, in order to prepare us to receive great favours *from Him*, for His

---

[1] T. adds: "as can be seen here on earth."
[2] E.: "of ourselves."
[3] T. ends the sentence here.
[4] "If by our own industry and skill we try to attain to Quiet," adds P. Báñez.
[5] T. has a semi-colon after "hinders" and continues: "it suffices to say, with real, etc."
[6] T.: "gave Thee my will."
[7] T.: "to draw our lowliness to become one with the Almighty and to transform it into God."
[8] E.: "the Maker." T.: "the creature and the Creator." Neither this emendation nor that of the last note is by St. Teresa.

rewards for our service will not end with this life. So much does He value this service of ours that we do not know for what more we can ask, while His Majesty never wearies of giving. Not content with having made this soul one with Himself, through uniting it to Himself,[1] He begins to cherish it, to reveal secrets to it, to rejoice in its understanding of what it has gained and in the knowledge which it has of all He has yet to give it. He causes it gradually to lose its exterior senses so that nothing may occupy it. This we call rapture. He begins to make such a friend of the soul that not only does He restore its will to it but He gives it His own also. For, now that He is making a friend of it, He is glad to allow it to rule with Him, as we say, turn and turn about. So He does what the soul asks of Him, just as the soul does what He commands, only in a much better way, since He is all-powerful and can do whatever He desires, and His desire never comes to an end.

But the poor soul, despite its desires, is *often* unable[2] to do all it would like, nor can it do anything at all unless it is given the power.[3] And so it grows richer and richer; and the more it serves, the greater becomes its debt; and often, growing weary of finding itself subjected to all the inconveniences and impediments and bonds[4] which it has to endure while it is in the prison of this body, it would gladly pay something of what it owes, for it is quite worn out. But even if we do all that is in us, how can we repay God, since, as I say, we have nothing to give save what we have first received? We can only learn to know ourselves and do what we can[5]—namely, surrender our will and fulfil God's will in us.[6] Anything else must be a hindrance to the soul which the Lord has brought to this state. It causes it, not profit, but harm, for nothing but humility is of any use here, and this is not acquired by the understanding but by a clear perception of the truth, which comprehends in one moment what could not be attained over a long period by the labour of the imagination—namely, that we are nothing and that God is infinitely great.

---

[1] E. reads: "through converting it to Himself", but the word "converting" was crossed through and "uniting" substituted by P. García de Toledo and the author incorporated the correction in the text of V.
[2] T.: "is unable always."
[3] *Lit.*: "given it." E. continues: "Its debt becomes greater all the time; and often, etc."
[4] E. omits: "and impediments and bonds."
[5] T. adds: "with the favour of God."
[6] The rest of this paragraph is not found in E., which ends it on a more personal note: "Since, as I have said, the nature of this prayer has already been described elsewhere, together with the way in which the soul should behave at such a time, and since a great deal has been said about what the soul feels and how it knows this to be the work of God, I do no more here than touch on these details of (the life of) prayer so as to show you how to repeat this prayer, the Paternoster."

I will give you one piece of advice: do not suppose that you can reach this state by your own effort or diligence; that would be too much to expect. On the contrary, you would turn what devotion you had quite cold. You must practise simplicity and humility, for those are the virtues which achieve everything. You must say: "Fiat voluntas tua."

CHAPTER XXXIII

Treats of our great need that the Lord should give us what we ask in these words of the Paternoster: "Panem nostrum quotidianum da nobis hodie."[1]

The good Jesus understands, as I have said, how difficult a thing He is offering on our behalf, for He knows our weakness,[2] and how often we show that we do not understand what the will of the Lord is, since we are weak[3] while He is so merciful. He knows that some means must be found[4] by which we shall not omit to give what He has given on our behalf, for if we did that it would be anything but good for us, since everything we gain comes from what we give. Yet He knows that it will be difficult for us to carry this out; for if anyone were to tell some wealthy, pampered person[5] that it is God's will for him to moderate his eating so that others, who are dying of hunger, shall have at least bread to eat, he will discover a thousand reasons for not understanding this but interpreting it in his own way. If one tells a person who speaks ill of others that it is God's will that he should love his neighbour as himself,[6] he will lose patience and no amount of reasoning will convince him.[7] If one tells a religious[8] who is accustomed to liberty and indulgence that he must be careful to set a good example and to remember that when he makes this petition it is his duty to keep what he has sworn and promised, and that not in word alone; that it is the will of God that he should fulfil his vows and see

---

[1] "Give us this day our daily bread."
[2] T.: "misery."
[3] T. ends the sentence here.
[4] In T. St. Teresa has deleted the following words and substituted: "for its fulfilment, so He begs the Eternal Father a remedy as sovereign as that of the Most Holy Sacrament, which gives strength and fortitude. For if anyone, etc."
[5] E. omits "pampered".
[6] *Lit.*: "should want as much *for himself as for his neighbour, and* for his neighbour as for himself." The italicized phrase is found in E. only.
[7] T.: "will make him want to do it even though he be convinced."
[8] V. has *relisioso* (masc.); E., *relisioso . . . u relisiosa.*

that he gives no occasion for scandal by acting contrarily to them, even though he may not actually break them; that he has taken the vow of poverty and must keep it without evasions, because that is the Lord's will—it would be impossible, in spite of all this, that some religious should not still want their own way. What would be the case, then, if the Lord had not done most of what was necessary by means of the remedy He has given us? There would have been very few who could have fulfilled this petition, which the Lord made to the Father on our behalf:[1] " Fiat voluntas tua."[2] Seeing our need, therefore, the good Jesus has sought[3] the admirable means whereby He has shown us the extreme love which He has for us, and in His own name and in that of His brethren He has made this petition: "Give us, Lord, this day our daily bread."

For the love of God, sisters, let us realize the meaning of our good Master's petition,[4] for our very life depends on our not disregarding it. Set very little store by what you have given, since there is so much that you will receive. It seems to me, in the absence of a better opinion, that the good Jesus knew what He had given for us and how important it was for us to give this to God, and yet how difficult it would be for us to do so, as has been said, because of our natural inclination to base things and our want of love and courage. He saw that, before we could be aroused, we needed His aid, not once but every day, and it must have been for this reason that He resolved to remain with us. As this was so weighty and important a matter, He wished it to come from the hand of the Eternal Father. Though both Father and Son are one and the same, and He knew that whatever He did on earth God would do in Heaven, and would consider it good, since His will and the Father's will were one,[5] yet the humility of the good Jesus was such that He wanted, as it were, to ask leave of His Father, for He knew that He was His beloved Son and that He was well pleased with Him. He knew quite well that in this petition He was asking for more than He had asked for[6] in the others, but He already knew what death He was to suffer and what dishonours and affronts He would have to bear.

What father could there be, Lord, who, after giving us his

---

[1] E.: "fulfilled His petition [*lit.*: "word," as also in V.], and what He offered to the Father."
[2] E. adds the reflection: "and may it please His Majesty that, as it is, there may be a great many."
[3] E.: "the Lord has thought of."
[4] E.: "of the good Jesus' petition."
[5] E.: "on earth would be done in Heaven, and that His will and His Father's will were one for so great a thing."
[6] E.: "than He asks for."

son, and such a Son, would allow Him to remain among us[1] day by day to suffer as He had done already? None, Lord, in truth, but Thine: well dost Thou know of Whom Thou art asking this. God help me! What a great love is that of the Son and what a great love is that of the Father! I am not so much amazed at the good Jesus, because, as He had already said "Fiat voluntas tua", He was bound, being Who He is, to put what He had said into practice. Yes, for He is not like us; knowing that He was carrying out His words by loving us as He loves Himself, He went about seeking how He could carry out this commandment more perfectly, even at His own cost. But how, Eternal Father, couldst Thou[2] consent to this? How canst Thou see Thy Son every day in such wicked hands? Since first Thou didst permit it and consent to it, Thou seest how He has been treated. How can Thy Mercy, day by day and every day,[3] see Him affronted? And how many affronts are being offered to-day to this Most Holy Sacrament? How often must the Father see Him in the hands of His enemies? What desecrations these heretics commit!

O Eternal Lord! How canst Thou grant such a petition? How canst Thou consent to it? Consider not His love,[4] which, for the sake of fulfilling Thy will and of helping us, would allow Him to submit day by day to being cut to pieces. It is for Thee to see to this, my Lord, since Thy Son allows no obstacle to stand in His way. Why must all the blessings that we receive be at His cost? How is it that He is silent in face of all, and cannot speak for Himself, but only for us? Is there none who will speak for this most loving[5] Lamb? *Give me permission to speak for Him, Lord, since Thou hast been pleased to leave Him in our power, and let me beseech Thee on His behalf, since He gave Thee such full obedience and surrendered Himself to us with such great love.*

I have been reflecting how in this petition alone the same words are repeated: first of all the Lord speaks of "our daily bread" and asks Thee to give it,[6] and then He says: "Give it us to-day, Lord."[7] He lays the matter before His Father in this

---

[1] T. ends the sentence here.
[2] E,T.: "canst Thou."
[3] *Lit.*: "each day, each day."
[4] P. Báñez altered "His love" to "the love of your Spouse"; and, just below, "Thy will" to "the will of the Father". He also made the following sentence begin: "It was for Thee to care for Thy son, O Eternal Father; He allows, etc." These adulterations of the text are not found in T., nor were they adopted by Luis de León.
[5] E.: "most meek."
[6] T. deletes "and asks Thee to give it," and, for "He lays . . . this way," has "As much as to say:"
[7] This, as will be observed from the title to this chapter, is the order of the words in the Latin.

way: the Father gave us His Son once and for all to die for us, and thus He is our own;[1] yet He does not want the gift to be taken from us[2] until the end of the world but would have it left to be a help to us every day. Let this melt your hearts, my daughters, and make you love your Spouse, for there is no slave who would willingly call himself by that name, yet the good Jesus seems to think it an honour.

O Eternal Father, how great is the merit of this humility! With what a treasure are we purchasing Thy Son! How to sell Him we already know, for He was sold for thirty pieces of silver; but, if we would purchase Him, no price is sufficient.[3] Being made one with us through the portion of our nature which is His, and being Lord of His own will, He reminds His Father that, as our nature is His, He is able to give it to us, and thus He says "our bread".[4] He makes no difference between Himself and us, though we make one between ourselves and Him through not giving ourselves daily for His Majesty's sake.[5]

CHAPTER XXXIV

Continues the same subject. This is very suitable for reading after the reception of the Most Holy Sacrament.

We have now reached the conclusion that the good Jesus, being ours, asks His Father to let us have Him daily—which appears[6] to mean "for ever". *While writing this I have been wondering*[7] *why, after saying "our 'daily' bread", the Lord repeated the idea in the words "Give us this day, Lord."*[8] *I will tell you my own foolish idea: if it really is foolish, well and good—in any case, it is quite bad enough that I should interfere in such a matter at all. Still, as we are trying to understand what we are praying for, let us think carefully what this means, so that we may pray rightly, and thank Him Who is taking such care about teaching us. This bread, then, is*[9] *ours*

---

[1] T. omits: "to die for us, and thus He is our own."
[2] E. ends the sentence here and continues: "See, then, my sisters, and let this melt your hearts, and make you, etc."
[3] E.: "what price is sufficient?"
[4] E.: "and thus He calls Himself 'ours'."
[5] E.: "though we make one through not giving ourselves daily for His sake." T.: "so let us not make one: uniting our prayer with His, it will have merit before God and thus what we ask in it will be granted."
[6] So E. V. begins: "In this petition the word 'daily' appears, etc."
[7] E.: "I have had the desire to know."
[8] E.: "in the word 'to-day'." T. has "Our Lord" and continues: "I think myself that He said 'daily' because we have Him here on earth, etc."
[9] V.: "It is."

daily, it seems to me, because we have Him here on earth, *since He has remained with us here and we receive Him*; and, if we profit by His company, we shall also have Him in Heaven, for the only reason He remains with us is to help and encourage and sustain us so that we shall do that will, which, as we have said, is to be fulfilled in us.

In using the words "this day" He seems to me to be *thinking of a day of the length of this life*.[1] And a day indeed it is! As for the unfortunate souls who *will* bring damnation upon themselves and will not have fruition of Him in the world to come, *they are His own creatures, and He did everything to help them on, and was with them, to strengthen them, throughout the "to-day" of this life, so* it is not His fault if they are vanquished.[2] They will have no excuse to make nor will they be able to complain of the Father for taking this bread from them at the time when they most needed it.[3] Therefore the Son prays the Father that,[4] since this life[5] lasts no more than a day, He will allow Him to spend it in our service.[6] As His Majesty has already given His Son to us, by sending Him, of His will alone,[7] into the world, so now, of that same will,[8] He is pleased not to abandon us, but to remain here with us for the greater glory of His friends and the discomfiture of His enemies.[9] He prays for nothing more than this "to-day" since He has given us this most holy Bread.[10] He has given it to us for ever, as I have said, as the sustenance and manna of humanity. We can have it[11] whenever we please and we shall not die of hunger save through our own fault, for, in whatever way the soul desires to partake of food, it will find

---

[1] Thus E., which seems preferable here. V. has: "to be indicating a period of time equivalent to the duration of the world."

[2] V. adds a shortened version of the passage it has omitted: "for He never fails to encourage them down to the very end of the battle."

[3] E. omits this sentence, though working the phrase "at . . . needed it" into the argument below.

[4] E.: "And, so that the Father may grant Him (His petition, the Son) puts it to Him that."

[5] E.: "the world"; V.: "it." But E. obviously means by "world" "life in the world."

[6] *Lit.*: "in service"—*en servidumbre*, a strong word, better rendered, perhaps, "servitude," and not far removed from "slavery." Luis de León softened the phrase to "spend it among His own."

[7] T. has "of His goodness alone," but these words are deleted.

[8] T. omits "of that same will."

[9] E.: "As (His Majesty) has given Him to us, it is unlikely that He will take Him when we most need Him, for all this evil treatment which He is being offered undeservingly will last only for a day. Let Him consider how He is bound to help us in every possible way, since for our sakes He has made so great an offer (on our behalf) as the resignation of our wills to the will of God."

[10] E. continues: "It is certain that we have it for ever, this sustenance, etc." St. Teresa also interpolated, after "ever," and subsequently crossed out, the words: "and He gave it us without our asking for it."

[11] E. adds: "it seems." "Have it whenever" is, literally, "find it however".

joy and comfort in the Most Holy Sacrament.[1] There is no need or trial or persecution that cannot be easily borne if we begin to *partake and* taste of[2] *those which He Himself bore, and to make them the subject of our meditations.*

With regard to other bread[3]—*the bread of bodily necessaries and sustenance—I neither like to think that the Lord is always being reminded of it nor would I have you remember it yourselves. Keep on the level of the highest contemplation, for anyone who dwells there no more remembers that he is in the world than if he had already left it—still less does he think about food. Would the Lord ever have insisted upon our asking for food, or taught us to do so by His own example? Not in my opinion. He teaches us to fix our desires upon heavenly things and to pray that we may begin to enjoy these things while here on earth: would He, then, have us trouble about so petty a matter as praying for food? As if He did not know that, once we begin to worry about the needs of the body, we shall forget the needs of the soul! Besides, are we such moderately minded people that we shall be satisfied with just a little and pray only for a little? No: the more food we are given, the less we shall get of the water from Heaven. Let those of you, daughters, who want more of the necessaries of life pray for this.*

Join with the Lord, then, daughters, in begging the Father to let you have[4] your Spouse to-day, so that, *as long as you live,* you may never find yourself in this world without Him. Let it suffice to temper your great joy[5] that He should remain disguised beneath these accidents of bread and wine,[6] which is a real torture to those who have nothing else to love[7] and no other consolation. Entreat Him not to fail you but to prepare you to receive Him worthily.

As for that other bread, have no anxiety about it if you have truly resigned yourselves to God's will. I mean that at these hours of prayer you are dealing with more important matters and there is time enough for you to labour and earn your daily bread.[8] Try never at any time to let your thoughts dwell on this; work with your body, for it is good for you to try to support yourselves, but let your soul be at rest. Leave anxiety about this to your Spouse, as has been said at length already, and He will always bear it for you.[9] *Do not fear that He will fail you if*

---

[1] E.: "it will find in it joy and comfort and sustenance."
[2] E.: "and masticate."
[3] The whole of this paragraph is lightly crossed out in the manuscript.
[4] E. begins: "Beg Him to let you have."
[5] E. omits: "to temper your great joy."
[6] E. omits: "and wine."
[7] E.: "who have no other love."
[8] E.: "and there are other times when the person whose office it is to do so will see about what you have to eat—I mean, will give you what she has."
[9] T.: "but let your soul be at rest, as has been said at length already. He is your Spouse and He will be with you."

you do not fail to do what you have promised and to resign yourselves to God's will. I assure you, daughters, that, if I myself were to fail in this, because of my wickedness, as I have often done in the past, I would not beg Him to give me that bread, or anything else to eat. Let Him leave me to die of hunger. Of what use is life to me if it leads me daily nearer to eternal death?

If, then, you are really surrendering yourselves to God, as you say, cease to be anxious for yourselves, for He bears your anxiety, and will bear it always. It is as though a servant had gone into service and were anxious to please his master in everything. The master is bound to give him food for so long as he remains in his house, and in his service, unless he is so poor that he has food neither for his servant nor for himself. Here, however, the comparison breaks down, for God is, and will always be, rich and powerful. It would not be[1] right for the servant to go to his master *every day* and ask him for food when he knew that his master would see that it was given him and so he would be sure to receive it. *To do this would be a waste of words.* His master would quite properly tell him that he should look after his own business of serving and pleasing him, for, if he worried himself unnecessarily, he would not do his work as well as he should.[2] So, sisters, those who will may worry about asking for[3] earthly bread; let our own task be to beg the Eternal Father that we may merit our heavenly bread, so that,[4] although our bodily eyes cannot feast themselves on the sight of Him since He is thus hidden from us, He may reveal Himself to the eyes of the soul and may make Himself known to us as another kind of food, full of delight and joy, which sustains our life.[5]

Do you suppose that this most holy food[6] is not *ample* sustenance even for the body and a potent medicine for bodily ills? I am sure that it is. I know a person who was subject to serious illnesses and often suffered great pain; and this pain was taken away from her in a flash[7] and she became quite well again.

---

[1] E. omits "rich and", and makes the next sentence interrogative: "Now would it be . . . ?"

[2] This sentence is an expansion from E.

[3] E.: "those who will may ask for."

[4] E.: "let us beg Him Whose business it is and beseech the Father to give us grace to prepare ourselves to receive so great a gift and such heavenly sustenance, so that."

[5] E. interrupts the thread of thought thus: "We shall quite unconsciously come and desire or ask Him (for earthly bread) more often than we wish. There is no need to arouse ourselves to do this, for our miserable inclination toward base things will arouse us, as I say, more often than we wish. But let us not purposely take any trouble except about entreating the Lord for what I have described. If we have that, we shall have everything."

[6] E.: "this Most Holy Sacrament."

[7] *Lit.*: "as if by (someone's) hand." St. Teresa is thought here to be referring to herself.

This often occurs, I believe; and cures are recorded from quite definite illnesses which could not be counterfeited. As the wondrous effects produced by this most holy bread in those who worthily receive it are very well known, I will not describe all the things that could be related about this person I mentioned,[1] though I have been enabled to learn about them and I know that they are not fabrications. The Lord had given this person[2] such a lively faith that, when she heard people[3] say they wished they had lived when Christ[4] walked on this earth, she would smile to herself, for she knew that we have Him as truly with us in the Most Holy Sacrament as people had Him then, and wonder what more they could possibly want.

I know, too, that for many years this person, though by no means perfect, always tried to strengthen her faith, when she communicated, by thinking that it was exactly as if she saw the Lord entering her house, with her own bodily eyes,[5] for she believed in very truth that this Lord was entering her poor abode, and she ceased, as far as she could, to think of outward things, and went into her abode with Him. She tried to recollect her senses so that they might all become aware of this great blessing, or rather, so that they should not hinder the soul from becoming conscious of it. She imagined herself at His feet and wept with the Magdalen exactly as if she had seen Him with her bodily eyes in the Pharisee's house. Even if she felt no devotion, faith told her that it was good for her to be there.[6]

For, unless we want to be foolish and to close our minds to facts, we cannot suppose that this is the work of the imagination, as it is when we think of the Lord on the Cross, or of other incidents of the Passion, and picture within ourselves[7] how these things happened. This is something which is happening now; it is absolutely true; and we have no need to go and seek Him somewhere a long way off.[8] For we know that, until the accidents of bread have been consumed by our natural heat, the

---

[1] E.: "As for the many other effects produced in this soul, there is no need to speak of them."
[2] E.: "This person had so much devotion and."
[3] E. adds: "at certain festivals."
[4] So E. V. adds: "our Good."
[5] E. continues: "for this made her believe that it was the same thing, and that she had Him in a house as poor as her own, and she ceased to think of outward things, and went into a corner, trying to recollect her senses so that she might be alone with her Lord, and imagined herself at His feet, and remained there, even if she felt no devotion, speaking with Him."
[6] T.: "faith told her that her Good was there."
[7] T. omits: "within ourselves."
[8] E.: "For, unless we want to be blind and foolish, and if we have faith, it is clear that He is within us. Why, then, do we need to go and seek Him a long way off, as has been said?"

good Jesus is with us and we should [not lose so good an opportunity but should] come to Him.[1] If, while He went about in the world, the sick were healed merely by touching His clothes, how can we doubt that He will work miracles when He is within us, if we have faith, or that He will give us what we ask of Him since He is in our house? His Majesty is not wont to offer us too little payment for His lodging if we treat Him well.[2]

If you grieve[3] at not seeing Him with the eyes of the body, remember that that would not be good for us,[4] for it is one thing to see Him glorified and quite another to see Him as He was when He lived in the world. So weak is our nature that nobody could endure the sight—in fact, there would be no one left to endure it, for no one would wish to remain in the world any longer. Once having seen this Eternal Truth, people would realize that all the things we prize here are mockery and falsehood.[5] And if such great Majesty could be seen, how could a miserable sinner like myself, after having so greatly offended Him, remain so near to Him? Beneath those accidents of bread,[6] we can approach Him; for, if the King disguises Himself, it would seem that we need not mind coming to Him without so much circumspection and ceremony: by disguising Himself, He has, as it were, obliged Himself to submit to this. Who, otherwise, would dare to approach Him so unworthily, with so many imperfections and with such lukewarm zeal?

Oh, we know not what we ask! How much better does His Wisdom know what we need! He reveals Himself to those who He knows will profit by His presence;[7] though unseen by bodily eyes, He has many ways of revealing Himself to the soul through deep inward emotions and by various other means. Delight to remain with Him; do not lose such an excellent time for talking with Him as the hour after Communion.[8] *Remember that this is a very profitable hour for the soul; if you spend it in the company of the*

---

[1] "And we should . . . come to Him" is not found in E. In the following sentence the singular of the first person is used, not the plural, as in the text. V. begins in the singular and continues in the plural.

[2] E. omits this sentence.

[3] E. is even stronger: "If it causes you anguish" (*os congojáis*).

[4] E.: "that it is good for us (that it should be so)."

[5] E. omits: "and falsehood", and continues: "Have no fear that, because He is not seen with these bodily eyes, He is quite hidden from His friends. Delight to remain with Him, etc."

[6] Luis de León's emendation of St. Teresa's "Beneath that bread," also found in T. Cf. pp. 145, 147, above, where St. Teresa herself uses that phrase.

[7] T. omits: "by His presence."

[8] E. omits: "Do not . . . Communion". The word translated "time" is *sazón*, rendered more conveniently as "opportunity" in a similar phrase in l. 1, above. T. uses a much stronger word, *coyuntura*, which might be freely translated here as "Heaven-sent chance".

good Jesus, you are doing Him a great service. Be very careful, then, daughters, not to lose it. If you are compelled by obedience to do something else, try to leave your soul with the Lord. *For He is your Master, and, though it be in a way you may not understand, He will not fail to teach you.* But if you take your thoughts elsewhere, and pay no *more* attention to Him[1] *than if you had not received Him*, and care nothing for His being within you,[2] how can He make Himself known to you? *You must complain, not of Him, but of yourself.* This, then, is a good time for our Master to teach us and for us to listen to Him.[3] *I do not tell you to say no prayers at all, for if I did you would take hold of my words and say I was talking about contemplation, which you need practise only if the Lord brings you to it. No: you should say the Paternoster, realize that you are verily and indeed in the company of Him Who taught it you* and kiss His feet in gratitude to Him for having desired to teach you and beg Him *to show you how to pray and* never to leave you.

You may be in the habit of praying while looking at a picture of Christ,[4] but *at a time like this* it seems foolish to me[5] to turn away from *the living image*—the Person Himself—to look at His picture. Would it not be foolish if we had a portrait of someone whom we dearly loved and, when the person himself came to see us, we refused to talk with him and carried on our entire conversation with the portrait? Do you know when I find the use of a picture an excellent thing,[6] and take great pleasure in it? When the person is absent and we are made to feel his loss by our great aridity,[7] it is then that we find it a great comfort to look at the picture of Him Whom we have such reason to love.[8] *This is a great inspiration*, and *makes us* wish that, in whichever direction we turn our eyes, we could see the picture. What can we look upon that is better or more attractive to the sight[9] than upon Him Who so dearly loves us and contains within Himself all good things? Unhappy are those heretics, who through their own fault have lost this comfort, as well as others.[10]

---

[1] E. has here: "to His being within you," which V. alters to "and . . . within you" as in the text.
[2] T. ends the sentence: "you will not perceive the favours that He works."
[3] E. omits this sentence and in a few other minor respects differs from V. in this paragraph.
[4] So T. "Which we are looking at," adds V., redundantly and ungrammatically. E. reads: "If you are in the habit of praying to a picture of Christ, in Whose presence you are, do you not see, etc." (v. next note).
[5] E. makes this a question: "do you not see that it is foolish . . . ?"
[6] E.: "a good and very holy thing."
[7] "And . . . aridity" is not found in E.
[8] E.: "It is a great comfort to look at a picture of Our Lady, or of some saint to whom we have devotion—and how much more at a picture of Christ!"
[9] E. omits the rest of this sentence.
[10] E.: "who lack this comfort and blessing among others."

When you have received the Lord, and are in His very presence, try to shut the bodily eyes and to open the eyes of the soul and to look into your own hearts. I tell you, and tell you again, for I should like to repeat[1] it often, that if you practise this habit *of staying with Him, not just once or twice, but* whenever you communicate, and strive to keep your conscience clear so that you can often rejoice in this your Good, He will not, as I have said, come so much disguised as to be unable to make His presence known to you in many ways, according to the desire which you have of seeing Him. So great, indeed, may be your longing for Him that He will reveal Himself to you wholly.

But if we pay no heed to Him save when we have received Him, and go away from Him in search of other and baser things, what can He do?[2] Will He have to drag us by force to look at Him *and be with Him* because He desires to reveal Himself to us? No; for when He revealed Himself to all men plainly,[3] and told them clearly who He was, they did not treat Him at all well— very few of them, indeed, even believed Him. So He grants us an exceeding great favour when He is pleased to show us that it is He Who is in the Most Holy Sacrament. But He will not reveal Himself openly and communicate His glories and bestow His treasures save on those who He knows greatly desire Him, for these are His true friends. I assure you that anyone who is not a true friend[4] and does not come to receive Him as such, after doing all in his power to prepare for Him, must never importune Him to reveal Himself to him. Hardly is the hour over which such a person has spent in fulfilling the Church's commandment than he goes home[5] and tries to drive Christ out of the house. What with all his other business and occupations and worldly[6] hindrances, he seems to be making all possible haste to prevent the Lord from taking possession of the house which is His own.[7]

---

[1] E.: "I shall repeat."
[2] T.: "away from Him to other, etc." E.: "But if you pay no heed to Him when you receive Him, though He is so near you, and go and look for Him elsewhere, or for other and base (*sic*) things, what do you expect Him to do?"
[3] E. omits: "plainly."
[4] E.: "who offends Him."
[5] So E. V. has: "than he leaves his home and tries to drive Christ [*lit.*: "Him", both here and in E.] out of himself." The thought underlying each phrase is quite distinct; E. seems to me preferable.
[6] "Bodily," is the reading of T.
[7] In E. the final sentence reads: "So, if he enters within himself, it is to think of vanities in His very presence."

CHAPTER XXXV

Describes the recollection which should be practised after Communion. Concludes this subject with an exclamatory prayer to the Eternal Father.

I have written at length about this, although, when writing of the Prayer of Recollection, I spoke of the great importance of our entering into solitude with God.[1] When you hear Mass without communicating, daughters, you may communicate spiritually, which is extremely profitable, and afterwards you may practise inward recollection in exactly the same way,[2] for this impresses upon us a deep love of the Lord. If we prepare to receive Him, He never fails to give, and He gives in many ways that we cannot understand. It is as if we were to approach a fire: it might be a very large one, but, if we remained a long way from it and covered our hands,[3] we should get little warmth from it,[4] although we should be warmer than if we were in a place where there was no fire at all. But when we try to approach the Lord there is this difference: if the soul is properly disposed, and comes with the intention of driving out the cold, and stays for some time where it is, it will retain its warmth for several hours,[5] *and if any little spark flies out, it will set it on fire.*

It is of such importance, daughters, for us to prepare ourselves in this way that you must not be surprised if I often repeat this counsel. If at first[6] you do not get on[7] with this practice (which may happen, for the devil will try to oppress and distress your heart, knowing what great harm he can do in this way),[8] the devil will make you think that you can find more devotion in other things and less in this.[9] But [trust me and] do not give up this method, for the Lord will use it to prove your love for Him. Remember

---

[1] "Since it is a very important thing indeed," adds T., which also has "being in" for "entering into" in the same sentence.
[2] V. is more explicit than E., which says merely: "and do the same."
[3] E.: "if we covered our hands." In both E. and V. the person changes abruptly from first to second in the course of the sentence. In the text above, the first person is kept throughout.
[4] E. continues: "You will remain cold, although that is better than not seeing the fire: one gets warmth by being near it. But when we try, etc."
[5] E. omits: "and comes with . . . several hours."
[6] So E. V. begins: "Remember, sisters, that if at first." T. has: "Do not trouble, sisters, if at first" and recasts this and the following sentence.
[7] E. reads: "If at first He does not reveal Himself to you, and you do not get on," and omits "which may happen."
[8] E. continues: "and if you find more devotion in other things and less in this do not give up, etc."
[9] T. omits: "and less in this."

that there are few souls who stay with Him and follow Him in His trials; let us endure something for Him and His Majesty will repay us. Remember, too, that there are actually people who not only have no wish to be[1] with Him but who insult Him and *with great irreverence* drive Him away *from their homes.*[2] We must endure something, therefore, to show Him that we have the desire to see Him. *In many places He is neglected and ill-treated, but* He suffers everything, and will continue to do so, if He finds but one single soul which will receive Him and love to have Him as its Guest.[3] Let this soul be yours, then, for, if there were none, the Eternal Father would rightly refuse to allow Him to remain with us. Yet the Lord is so good a Friend to those who are His friends, and so good a Master to those who are His servants, that, when He knows it to be the will of His Beloved Son, He will not hinder Him in so excellent a work, in which His Son so fully reveals the love which He has for His Father,[4] *as this wonderful way which He seeks of showing how much He loves us and of helping us to bear our trials.*

Since, then, Holy Father, Who art in the Heavens, Thou dost will and accept this (and it is clear[5] that Thou couldst not deny us a thing which is so good for us) there must be someone, as I said at the beginning, who will speak for Thy Son, for He has never defended[6] Himself.[7] Let this be the task for us, daughters, though, having regard to what we are, it is presumptuous of us to undertake it. Let us rely, however, on Our Lord's command to us to pray to Him, and, in fulfilment of our obedience to Him, let us beseech His Majesty, in the name of the good Jesus, that, as He has left nothing undone that He could do for us in granting sinners so great a favour, He may be pleased of His mercy[8] to prevent Him from being so ill-treated. Since His Holy Son has given us this excellent way in which we can offer Him up frequently as a sacrifice, let us make use of this precious gift so that it may stay the advance of such terrible evil and irreverence as in many places is paid to this Most Holy Sacrament.[9] For these Lutherans[10] *seem to want to drive Him out*

---

[1] So E. V. reads: "who not only wish not to be."
[2] V.: "from themselves," as in p. 150, n. 5, above.
[3] *Lit.*: "and have Him within itself [cf. last note] with love." E. reads: "which will love to admit Him and keep Him company."
[4] T. omits: "which He has for His Father."
[5] T.: "certain."
[6] E.: "never been able to defend."
[7] E. continues: "and so I ask you, daughters, to help me beg our Holy Father, in His name, that, as He has left nothing undone, etc."
[8] E.: "of His majesty."
[9] E.: "as is committed in places where this Most Holy Sacrament is (found)."
[10] E. is less explicit: "For they."

of the world again: they destroy churches, cause the loss of many priests and abolish the sacraments.[1] *And there is something of this even among Christians, who sometimes go to church meaning to offend Him rather than to worship Him.*

Why is this, my Lord and my God? Do Thou bring the world to an end or give us a remedy for such grievous wrongs, which even our wicked hearts cannot endure. I beseech Thee, Eternal Father, endure it no longer: quench this fire, Lord,[2] for Thou canst do so if Thou wilt. Remember that Thy Son is still in the world; may these dreadful things be stopped out of respect for Him, horrible and abominable and foul[3] as they are. With His beauty and purity He does not deserve to be in a house where such things happen.[4] Do this, Lord, not for our sake, for we do not deserve it, but for the sake of Thy Son. We dare not entreat Thee that He should no longer stay with us,[5] *for Thou hast granted His prayer to Thee to leave Him with us for to-day—that is, until the end of the world.*[6] If He were to go, what would become of us?[7] *It would be the end of everything.* If anything can placate Thee it is to have on earth such a pledge as this. Since some remedy must be found for this, then, my Lord, I beg Thy Majesty to apply it. *For if Thou wilt, Thou art able.*

O my God, if only I could indeed importune Thee! If only I had served Thee well so that I might be able to beg of Thee this great favour as a reward for my services, for Thou leavest no service unrewarded! But I have not served Thee, Lord; indeed, it may perhaps be for my sins, and because I have so greatly offended Thee, that so many evils come. What, then, can I do, my Creator, but present to Thee this most holy Bread,[8] which, though Thou gavest it to us, I return to Thee, beseeching Thee, by the merits of Thy Son,[9] to grant me this favour, which on so many counts He has merited? Do Thou, Lord,[10] calm this sea, and no longer allow this ship, which is Thy Church, to endure so great a tempest. Save us, my Lord, for we perish.[11]

---

[1] The sense of the verb here rendered "cause the loss of" is vague. Literally the phrase reads: "so many priests are lost." E. has: "They take Him out of the temples, cause the loss of so many priests and profane so many churches."
[2] E. ends the sentence here: the words which immediately follow in V. are found at the very end of the paragraph.
[3] E.: "horrible and foul."
[4] V. softens the phrase in E.: "where there are such evil stenches."
[5] E.: "We dare not ask Thee not to leave Him with us here."
[6] On this interpretation of "to-day", see p. 144, n. 1, above.
[7] This sentence is not found in E.
[8] E.: "this blessed Bread."
[9] E.: "by Its (or "His") merits."
[10] T. repeats "Do Thou, Lord."
[11] St. Matthew viii, 25.

CHAPTER XXXVI

Treats of these words in the Paternoster: " Dimitte nobis debita nostra."[1]

Our good[2] Master sees that, if we have this heavenly food,[3] everything is easy for us, except when we are ourselves to blame, and that we are well able to fulfil our undertaking to the Father that His will shall be done in us. So He now asks Him to forgive us our debts, as we ourselves forgive others.[4] Thus, continuing the prayer which He is teaching us, He says these words:[5] "And forgive us, Lord, our debts, even as we forgive them to our debtors."

Notice, sisters, that He does not say: "as we shall forgive." We are to understand that anyone who asks for so great a gift as that just mentioned, and has already yielded his own will to the will of God, must have done this already. And so He says: "as we forgive our debtors." Anyone, then, who sincerely repeats this petition, "Fiat voluntas tua", must, at least in intention, have done this already. You see now why the saints rejoiced in insults and persecutions: it was because these gave them something to present to the Lord when they prayed to Him. What can a poor creature like myself do, who has had so little to forgive others and has so much to be forgiven herself?[6] This, sisters, is something which we should consider carefully; it is such a serious and important matter that God should pardon us our sins, which have merited eternal fire, that we must pardon all trifling things which have been done to us *and which are not wrongs at all, or anything else. For how is it possible, either in word or in deed, to wrong one who, like myself, has deserved to be plagued*[7] *by devils for ever? Is it not only right that I should be plagued in this world too?* As I have so few, Lord, even of these trifling things, to offer Thee,[8] Thy pardoning of me must be a free gift: there is abundant scope here for Thy mercy. *Thy Son must pardon me, for no one has done me any injustice, and so there has been nothing that*

---

[1] "Forgive us our debts."
[2] E.: "precious."
[3] E.: "this sustenance."
[4] E.: "to forgive us as we forgive."
[5] The sentence "Thus . . . words" is not in E.
[6] E.: "What will sinners like myself do, who have so much to be forgiven?" In both E. and V. the rest of this paragraph is lightly crossed out and some editors omit it. It does not appear in T.
[7] *Lit.*: "ill-treated." The same verb is used in the following sentence.
[8] E. reads: "For this reason, then, my Lord, I have nothing to give Thee in begging Thee to forgive my debts," and begins a fresh sentence with "Thy Son must pardon me, etc."

I can pardon for Thy sake. But take my desire to do so, Lord, for I believe I would forgive any wrong if Thou wouldst forgive me and I might unconditionally do Thy will. True, if the occasion were to arise, and I were condemned without cause, I do not know what I should do. But at this moment I see that I am so guilty in Thy sight that everything I might have to suffer would fall short of my deserts, though anyone not knowing, as Thou knowest, what I am, would think I was being wronged. Blessed be Thou, Who endurest one that is so poor: when Thy *most holy* Son makes this petition in the name of all mankind, I cannot be included, being such as I am and having nothing to give.[1]

And supposing, my Lord, that there are others who are like myself but have not realized that this is so? If there are any such, I beg them, in Thy name, to remember this truth, and to pay no heed to little things about which they think they are being slighted,[2] for, if they insist on these nice points of honour, they become like children building houses of straw. Oh, God help me, sisters! If we only knew what honour really is and what is meant by losing it! I am not speaking now about ourselves, for it would indeed be a bad business if we did not understand this; I am speaking of myself as I was when I prided myself on my honour without knowing what honour meant; I just followed the example of others.[3] Oh, how easily I used to feel slighted! I am ashamed to think of it now; and I was not one of those who worried most about such things either. But I never grasped the essence of the matter,[4] because I neither thought nor troubled about true honour, which it is good for us to have because it profits the soul. How truly has someone said: "Honour and profit cannot go together." I do not know if this was what that person was thinking of when he said it; but it is literally true, for the soul's profit and what the world calls honour can never be reconciled. Really, the topsy-turviness of the world is terrible.[5] Blessed be the Lord for taking us out of it! *May His Majesty grant that this house shall always be as far from it as it is now! God preserve us from religious houses where they worry about points of honour! Such places never do much honour to God.*

God help us, how absurd it is for religious to connect their honour with things so trifling that they amaze me! You know nothing about this, sisters, but I will tell you about it so that you may be wary. You

---

[1] E. omits: "and having nothing to give", which, in V., reads literally: "and so (completely) without treasure."
[2] E.: "to tiny slights."
[3] E. adds: "(going) by what I heard (them say)." On "honour", see Vol. I, p. 14, n. 2, above.
[4] E.: "But I went astray, like everyone, about the essence of the matter."
[5] E.: "Oh, God help me, how topsy-turvy the world is!"

see, sisters, the devil has not forgotten us.[1] He has invented honours of his own for religious houses and has made laws by which we go up and down in rank, as people do in the world. Learned men have to observe this with regard to their studies (a matter of which I know nothing): anyone, for example, who has got as far as reading theology must not descend and read philosophy—that is their kind of honour, according to which you must always be going up and never going down. Even if someone were commanded by obedience to take a step down, he would *in his own mind* consider himself slighted; and then someone[2] would take his part [and say] it was an insult; next, the devil would discover reasons for this—and he seems to be an authority even in God's own law. Why, among ourselves,[3] anyone who has been a prioress is thereby incapacitated from holding any lower office[4] *for the rest of her life*. We must defer to the senior among us, and we are not allowed to forget it either: sometimes it would appear to be a positive merit for us to do this, because it is a rule of the Order.[5]

The thing is enough[6] to make one laugh—or, it would be more proper to say,[7] to make one weep. After all, the Order does not command us not to be humble: it commands us to do everything in due form. And in matters which concern my own esteem I ought not to be so formal as to insist that this detail of our Rule shall be kept[8] as strictly as the rest, which we may in fact be observing very imperfectly. We must not put all our effort into observing just this one detail: let my interests be looked after by others—I will forget about myself altogether. The fact is, although we shall never rise as far as Heaven in this way, we are attracted by the thought of rising higher, and we dislike climbing down. O, Lord, Lord, art Thou our Example and our Master? Yes, indeed. And wherein did Thy honour consist,[9] O Lord, Who hast honoured us?[10] Didst Thou perchance[11] lose it when Thou

---

[1] In E. this sentence is omitted and the following sentence reads: "Know that in religious houses there are also laws about honour: and the religious go up in rank, as in the world."

[2] E.: "many." V. continues: ".... would take his part, for it is an insult."

[3] E.: "among nuns."

[4] E.: "any other kind of office than that."

[5] E.: "We must give precedence to seniority, and you need have no fear that that will be forgotten: apparently it is a merit, because it is a rule of the Order."

[6] E.: "is funnier than can be imagined, and enough."

[7] E.: "or, to put it better, and very properly."

[8] E. omits the rest of the sentence and reads: "It may be that I observe all the rest imperfectly, whereas about this I never budge an inch: let my interests, etc."

[9] E. completes the sentence with the words: "my King?"

[10] *Lit.*: "our Honourer"—*Honrador nuestro*: a rather unusual phrase which T. changes into the quite conventional *honrado Maestro*—"honoured Master."

[11] Thus E. V. has: "Certainly Thou didst not,"

wert humbled even to death? No, Lord, rather didst Thou gain it for all.[1]

For the love of God, sisters! We have lost our way; we have taken the wrong path from the very beginning.[2] God grant that no soul be lost through its attention to these wretched niceties about honour, when it has no idea wherein honour consists. We shall get to the point of thinking that we have done something wonderful because we have forgiven a person for some trifling thing,[3] which was neither a slight nor an insult nor anything else.[4] Then we shall ask the Lord to forgive us as people who have done something important, just because we have forgiven someone. Grant us, my God, to understand how little we understand ourselves[5] and how empty our hands are when we come to Thee that Thou, of Thy mercy, mayest forgive us.[6] For in truth, Lord, since all things have an end and punishment is eternal, I can see nothing meritorious which I may present to Thee that Thou mayest grant us so great a favour. Do it, then, for the sake of Him Who asks it of Thee, *and Who may well do so, for He is always being wronged and offended.*

How greatly the Lord must esteem this mutual love of ours one for another! *For, having given Him our wills, we have given Him complete rights over us, and we cannot do that without love. See, then, sisters, how important it is for us to love one another and to be at peace.*[7] The good Jesus might have put everything else before our love for one another, and said: "Forgive us, Lord, because we are doing a great deal of penance, or because we are praying often, and fasting, and because we have left all for Thy sake and love Thee greatly." But He has never said:[8] "Because we would lose our lives for Thy sake"; or any of these [numerous] other things which He might have said. He simply says: "Because we forgive." Perhaps *the reason He said* this *rather than anything else*

---

[1] E.: "gain it, and profit for all."

[2] In T. St. Teresa has made a long marginal addition to this sentence, but it has unfortunately been mutilated by the binder. As P. Silverio (III, 466) has reconstructed it from the Évora edition, it is a rambling digression which hardly merits reproduction.

[3] E.: "some mere nothing."

[4] E.: "nor had anything to do with a slight."

[5] E.: "Grant them, Lord, to understand that they know not what they say."

[6] E.: "and how empty their hands are when they come to beg of Thee, as I do. Do this of Thy mercy, and for Thine own sake." The rest of this paragraph is scored through by St. Teresa in V. It does not appear in T. nor in other early copies and editions.

[7] E. continues: "For of the many things that we have given—or He has given in our name—to the Father, the Lord put in the first place none other than this. He might have said: 'Because we love Thee, and suffer trials, and desire to suffer them for Thee, or because of fasts and other good works, which are done by a soul that loves God and has given Him its will.' And yet He spoke only of this."

[8] T. omits this sentence and unites the two quotations with "and."

was because He knew that our fondness for this dreadful honour made mutual love the hardest virtue for us to attain,[1] though it is the virtue dearest to His Father. *Because of its very difficulty He put it where He did, and after having asked for so many great gifts for us*, He offers it on our behalf to God.

Note particularly, sisters, that He says: "As we forgive." As I have said, He takes this for granted. And observe especially[2] with regard to it that unless, after experiencing the favours granted by God in the prayer that I have called perfect contemplation, a person is very resolute, and makes a point, if the occasion arises, of forgiving, not [only] these mere nothings which people call wrongs, but any wrong, however grave, you need not think much of that person's prayer[3]. For wrongs have no effect upon a soul whom God draws to Himself in such sublime prayer as this,[4] nor does it care if it is highly esteemed or no.[5] That is not quite correct: it does care, for honour distresses much more than dishonour and it prefers trials to a great deal of rest and ease. For anyone to whom the Lord has really given His Kingdom no longer wants a kingdom in this world, knowing that he is going the right way to reign in a much more exalted manner, and having already discovered by experience what great benefits the soul gains and what progress it makes[6] when it suffers for God's sake. For only very rarely does His Majesty grant it such great consolations, and then only to those who have willingly borne many trials for His sake. For contemplatives, as I have said elsewhere in this book, have to bear heavy trials, and therefore the Lord seeks out for Himself souls of great experience.

Understand, then, sisters, that as these persons have already learned to rate everything at its proper valuation, they pay little attention to things which pass away. A great wrong, or a

---

[1] The clause which follows was crossed out by the author and both T. and some of the editions omit it.

[2] E.: "And understand."

[3] St. Teresa left this sentence uncompleted. Luis de León added: "You need not . . . prayer" in his edition, since when it has always been included. It figures as an anonymous correction in T.

[4] E.: "brings to that (point)." The word "brings" (*llega*) is that translated "draws" in the text above.

[5] T. condenses, after "For a soul whom God . . . as this," and reads: "is distressed much more by honour than by dishonour, etc." E. continues: "it regrets honour, indeed, much more than dishonour. So you may be sure that, unless they produce these effects, the favours are not of God, but of the devil: a kind of indulgence and illusion which he makes you think to be good, hoping that you will then attach more importance to your honour. And as the good Jesus well knows that He produces these effects wherever He goes, He gives the Father a definite assurance that we are forgiving our debtors." This takes us to the end of the present chapter.

[6] T.: "discovered by experience the good which comes to it and the progress it makes."

great trial, may cause them some momentary distress, but they will hardly have felt it when reason will intervene, and will seem to raise its standard aloft, and drive away their distress by giving them the joy of seeing how God has entrusted them with the opportunity of gaining, in a single day, more lasting favours and graces in His Majesty's sight[1] than they could gain in ten years by means of trials which they sought on their own account. This, as I understand (and I have talked about it with many contemplatives), is quite usual, and I know for a fact that it happens[2]. Just as other people prize gold and jewels, so these persons prize and desire trials, for they know quite well that trials will make them rich.

Such persons would never on any account esteem themselves:[3] they want their sins to be known and like to speak about them to people who they see have any esteem for them. The same is true of their descent, which they know quite well will be of no advantage to them in the kingdom which has no end. If being of good birth were any satisfaction to them, it would be because this would enable them to serve God better. If they are not well born, it distresses them when people think them better than they are, and it causes them no distress to disabuse them, but only pleasure. The reason for this is that those to whom God grants the favour of possessing such humility and great love for Him forget themselves when there is a possibility of rendering Him greater services, and simply cannot believe that others are troubled by things which they themselves do not consider as wrongs at all.

These last effects which I have mentioned are produced in persons who have reached a high degree of perfection and to whom the Lord commonly grants the favour of uniting them to Himself by perfect contemplation. But the first of these effects—namely, the determination to suffer wrongs even though such suffering brings distress—is very quickly seen in anyone to whom the Lord has granted this grace of prayer as far as the stage of union.[4] If these effects are not produced in a soul and it is not strengthened by prayer, you may take it that this was not Divine favour but indulgence and illusion coming from the devil, *which he makes us think to be good*, so that we may attach more importance to our honour.

It may be that, when the Lord first grants these favours, the soul will not immediately attain this fortitude. But, if He continues to grant them, He will soon give it fortitude—certainly, at least,

---

[1] T. omits: "in His Majesty's sight."
[2] T. omits: "and I know for a fact that it happens."
[3] T. varies here, but I think through a misapprehension, so I do not give its reading.
[4] T.: "this grace of attaining union."

as regards forgiveness, if not in the other virtues as well. I cannot believe that a soul which has approached so nearly to Mercy Itself, and has learned to know itself and the greatness of God's pardon, will not immediately and readily forgive, and be mollified and remain on good terms with a person who has done it wrong. For such a soul remembers the consolation and grace which He has shown it, in which it has recognized the signs of great love, and it is glad that the occasion presents itself for showing Him some love in return.

I repeat that I know many persons to whom Our Lord has granted the grace of raising them to supernatural experiences and of giving them this prayer, or contemplation, which has been described; and although I may notice other faults and imperfections in them, I have never seen such a person who had this particular fault, nor do I believe such a person exists, if the favours he has received are of God. If any one of you receives high favours, let her look within herself and see if they are producing these effects, and, if they are not, let her be very fearful,[1] and believe that these consolations are not of God, Who, as I have said, when He visits the soul, always enriches it. That is certain; for, although the grace and the consolations may pass quickly, it can be recognized in due course through the benefits which it bestows on the soul. And, as the good Jesus knows this well, He gives a definite assurance to His Holy Father that we are forgiving our debtors.

CHAPTER XXXVII

Describes the excellence of this prayer called the Paternoster, and the many ways in which we shall find consolation in it.

The sublimity of the perfection of this evangelical prayer is something for which we should give great praise to the Lord.[2] So well composed by the good Master was it, daughters, that each of us may[3] use it in her own way. I am astounded when I consider that in its few words are enshrined all contemplation and perfection,[4] so that if we study it no other book seems neces-

[1] T. omits: "If any one . . . fearful," and continues: "Otherwise, believe that these consolations, etc."
[2] E.: "is an amazing thing."
[3] E.: "It is (perfect), indeed, like the Master Who teaches it to us; so it is right, daughters, that each of us should."
[4] E.: "I was astounded to-day when I found all contemplation and perfection hidden in its few words."

sary. For thus far in the Paternoster the Lord has taught us the whole method of prayer and of high contemplation,[1] from the very beginnings of mental prayer, to Quiet and Union.[2] With so true a foundation to build upon, I could write a great book on prayer if only I knew how to express myself.[3] As you have seen, Our Lord is beginning here to explain to us the effects which it produces, when the favours come from Him.

I have wondered why His Majesty did not expound such obscure and sublime subjects in greater detail so that we might all[4] have understood them. It has occurred to me that, as this prayer[5] was meant to be a general one for the use of all, so that everyone could interpret it as he thought right, ask for what he wanted and find comfort in doing so, He left the matter in doubt;[6] and thus contemplatives, who no longer desire earthly things, and persons greatly devoted to God, can ask for the heavenly favours which, through the great goodness of God, may be given to us on earth. Those who still live on earth, and must conform to the customs of their state, may also ask for the bread which they need for their own maintenance and for that of their households, as is perfectly just and right, and they may also ask for other things according as they need them.

(*Blessed be His name for ever and ever. Amen. For His sake I entreat the Eternal Father to forgive my debts and grievous sins: though no one has wronged me, and I have therefore no one to forgive,[7] I have myself need for forgiveness every day. May He give me grace so that every day I may have some petition to lay before Him.*)

The good Jesus, then, has taught us a sublime method of prayer, and begged that, in this our life of exile, we may be like the angels, if we endeavour, with our whole might, to make our actions conform to our words—in short, to be like the children of such a Father, and the brethren of such a Brother. His Majesty knows that if, as I say, our actions and our words are one, the Lord will unfailingly fulfil our petitions, give us His kingdom and help us by means of supernatural gifts, such as the Prayer of Quiet, perfect contemplation and all the other favours which

---

[1] E.: "the whole of the highest method of contemplation."
[2] E.: "to the greatest heights of perfect contemplation." The change in V. is significant.
[3] E. reads: "if I had not written about it elsewhere, and also because I dare not enlarge upon it, for if I did it would be wearisome," and completes the paragraph with the sentence: "The Lord, too, is gradually showing us here the effects produced by prayer and contemplation, when they are of God."
[4] E. omits: "obscure and" and "all."
[5] T.: "this doctrine and prayer."
[6] *Lit.*: "He left it thus confused." Here follows in E., in place of the rest of this paragraph, a passage which interrupts the trend of the thought, and therefore, in the text above, is printed in italics and in brackets at the end of this paragraph.
[7] The words "though . . . forgive" are crossed out in the manuscript, as is the following sentence "May He . . . before Him."

the Lord bestows on our trifling efforts—and everything is trifling which we can achieve and gain by ourselves alone.

It must be realized, however, that these two things—surrendering our will to God and forgiving others[1]—apply to all. True, some practise them more and some less, as has been said: those who are perfect will surrender their wills like the perfect souls they are and will forgive others with the perfection that has been described.[2] For our own part, sisters, we will do what we can, and the Lord will accept it all. It is as if He were to make a kind of agreement on our behalf with His Eternal Father, and to say: "Do this, Lord, and My brethren shall do that." It is certain that He for His own part will not fail us. Oh, how well He pays us and how limitless are His rewards!

We may say[3] this prayer only once, and yet in such a way that He will know that there is no duplicity about us and that we shall do what we say; and so He will leave us rich. We must never be insincere with Him, for He loves us, in all our dealings with Him, to be honest,[4] and to treat Him frankly and openly, never saying one thing and meaning another; and then He will always give us more than we ask for. Our good Master knows that those who attain real perfection in their petitions will reach this high degree through the favours which the Father will grant them, and is aware that those who are already perfect, or who are on the way to perfection,[5] do not and cannot fear, for they say they have trampled the world beneath their feet, and the Lord of the world is pleased with them. They will derive the greatest hope of His Majesty's pleasure[6] from the effects which He produces in their souls; absorbed in these joys, they wish they were unable to remember that there is any other world at all, and that they have enemies.

O Eternal Wisdom! O good Teacher! What a wonderful thing it is, daughters, to have a wise and prudent Master who foresees our perils! This is the greatest blessing that the spiritual soul *still on earth* can desire, because it brings complete[7] security. No words could ever exaggerate the importance of this. The

---

[1] T. omits "and forgiving others"—presumably by an oversight, as it is essential to the sense.

[2] E. omits the foregoing part of this paragraph and reads: "by ourselves alone. But, if we do what we can, it is very certain that the Lord will help us, since His Son begs this (favour) for us, and it is as if, etc."

[3] E.: "You, daughters, may say." Throughout the first half of this paragraph, the second person plural is used in E.

[4] F.: "for He loves us not to try to bargain with Him, and if we do so we cannot succeed, as He knows everything." The simplified version of V. has greater unity of thought and seems distinctly preferable to E.

[5] E., more vaguely: "that those who are here."

[6] T.: "derive hope of His pleasure." "Majesty's" is scored through in the text.

[7] Thus E. V.: "great."

Lord, then, saw it was necessary to awaken such souls and to remind them that they have enemies, and how much greater danger they are in if they are unprepared,[1] and, since if they fall it will be from a greater height, how much more help they need from the Eternal Father. So, lest they should fail to realize their danger and suffer deception, He offers these petitions so necessary to us all while we live in this exile: "And lead us not, Lord, into temptation, but deliver us from evil."

CHAPTER XXXVIII

Treats of the great need which we have to beseech the Eternal Father to grant us what we ask in these words: "Et ne nos inducas in tentationem, sed libera nos a malo."[2] Explains certain temptations. This chapter is noteworthy.

There are great things here for us to meditate upon,[3] sisters, and to learn to understand as we pray. Remember I consider it quite certain that those who attain perfection[4] do not ask the Lord to deliver them from trials, temptations, persecutions and conflicts[5]—and that is another sure and striking sign that these favours and this contemplation which His Majesty gives them[6] are coming from the Spirit of the Lord and are not illusions. For, as I said a little way back,[7] perfect souls *are in no way repelled by trials, but rather* desire them and pray for them and love them. They are like soldiers: the more wars there are, the better they are pleased, because they hope to emerge from them with the greater riches.[8] If there are no wars, they serve for their pay,[9] but they know they will not get very far on that.

Believe me, sisters, the soldiers of Christ—namely, those who experience contemplation and practise prayer[10]—are always ready

---

[1] E. ends the chapter thus: "and how much more help they need from the eternal Father if they are not to fall, or walk without finding themselves deceived. So He makes these petitions." In E., the petition "And lead . . . evil" stands at the beginning of the following chapter.
[2] "And lead us not into temptation, but deliver us from evil."
[3] T.: "to note."
[4] E.: "attain this point of prayer."
[5] T. omits "persecutions."
[6] E.: "that these (things)."
[7] E. omits: "as . . . back."
[8] *Lit.*: "gains", as also in the next paragraph. E. has: "because they have hopes of becoming rich." The reference in both manuscripts is, of course, to the spoils and booty of war.
[9] E.: "they remain (content) with their pay."
[10] E.: "who practise prayer." T.: "who experience contemplation."

for the hour of conflict. They are never very much[1] afraid of their open enemies, for they know who they are and are sure that their strength can never prevail against the strength which they themselves have been given by the Lord: they will always be victorious and gain great riches,[2] so they will never turn their backs on the battle. Those whom they fear, and fear rightly, and from whom they always beg the Lord to deliver them, are enemies who are treacherous, devils who[3] transform themselves and come and visit them in the disguise of angels of light. The soul fails to recognize them until they have done it a great deal of harm; they suck our life-blood and put an end to our virtues[4] and we go on yielding to temptation without knowing it. From these enemies let us pray the Lord often, in the Paternoster, to deliver us: may He not allow us to run into temptations which deceive us; may their poison be detected; and may light and truth[5] not be hidden from us. How rightly does our good Master teach us to pray for this and pray for it in our name!

Consider, daughters, in how many-ways these enemies do us harm. Do not suppose that the sole danger lies in their making us believe that the consolations and the favours which they can counterfeit to us come from God.[6] This, I think, in a way, is the least harmful thing they can do;[7] it may even help some whom this sensible devotion entices to spend more time in prayer and thus to make greater progress.[8] Being ignorant that these consolations come from the devil, and knowing themselves to be unworthy of such favours, they will never cease to give thanks to God and will feel the greater obligation to serve Him; further, they will strive to prepare themselves for more favours which the Lord may grant them, since they believe them to come from His hand.[9]

Always strive after humility, sisters, and try to realize that you are not worthy of these graces, and do not seek them. It is because many souls do this, I feel sure, that the devil loses them: he thinks that he has caused their ruin, but out of the

[1] "Very much" is not in E.
[2] T. has "emerge" for "be." E.: "and with gains, and rich." V.: "and with great gains." Cf. p. 163, n., 8 above.
[3] E.: "are devils who are treacherous and."
[4] E.: "to our lives."
[5] E.: "and may truth." Throughout this paragraph E. prefers the second person plural to the first.
[6] E.: "believe, when they give us consolations, that these come from God."
[7] E.: "This is the least harmful thing."
[8] E. reads: "often, indeed, they will lead you to make greater progress and to spend more time in prayer," and continues: "Where they can do great harm to ourselves and to others is in making us believe, etc." (See next footnote but one).
[9] "This is doctrine of St. Augustine," adds P. Báñez in the margin.

evil which he has been trying to do the Lord brings good. For His Majesty regards our intention, which is to please Him and serve Him and keep near to Him in prayer, and the Lord is faithful. We shall do well to be cautious, and not to let our humility break down or to become in any way vainglorious. Entreat the Lord to deliver you from this, daughters, and you need then have no fear that His Majesty will allow you to be comforted much by anyone but Himself.

Where the devil can do great harm without our realizing it is in making us believe[1] that we possess virtues which we do not: that is pestilential. For, when consolations and favours come to us, we feel that we are doing nothing but receive, and have the greater obligation to serve; but when we suffer from this other delusion we think that we are giving and serving, and that the Lord will be obliged to reward us; and this, little by little, does us a great deal of harm. On the one hand, our humility is weakened, while, on the other, we neglect to cultivate that virtue, believing we have already acquired it. *We think we are walking safely, when, without realizing it, we stumble, and fall into a pit from which we cannot escape. Though we may not consciously have committed any mortal sin which would have sent us infallibly to hell, we have sprained our ankles and cannot continue on that road which I began to speak about and which I have not forgotten. You can imagine how much progress will be made by anyone who is at the bottom of a huge pit: it will be the end of him altogether and he will be lucky if he escapes falling right down to hell: at best, he will never get on with his journey. This being so, he will be unable to help either himself or others. It will be a bad thing for others, too, for, once the pit has been dug, a great many passers-by may fall into it. Only if the person who has fallen in gets out of it and fills it up with earth will further harm to himself and others be prevented. But I warn you that this temptation is full of peril. I know a great deal about it from experience, so I can describe it to you, though not as well as I should like.* What can we do about it, sisters? To me the best thing seems to be what our Master teaches us: to pray, and to beseech the Eternal Father not to allow us to fall into temptation.[2]

There is something else, too, which I want to tell you. If we think the Lord has given us a certain grace, we must understand that it is a blessing which we have received but which He may take away from us again, as indeed, in the great providence of God, often happens. Have you never observed this yourselves,

---

[1] E. takes up the thread here.

[2] No more of what follows in the V. text of this chapter is found in E. The paragraphs in italics at the end of the chapter, however, represent the continuation in E.: they were inserted in the text by Luis de León, who omitted the paragraph beginning: "The devil has yet another temptation."

sisters? I certainly have: sometimes I think I am extremely detached, and, in fact, when it comes to the test, I am; yet at other times I find I have such attachment to things which the day before I should perhaps have scoffed at that I hardly know myself. At some other time I seem to have so much courage that I should not quail at anything I was asked to do in order to serve God, and, when I am tested, I find that I really can do these things. And then on the next day I discover that I should not have the courage to kill an ant for God's sake if I were to meet with any opposition about it. Sometimes it seems not to matter in the least if people complain or speak ill of me, and, when the test comes, I still feel like this—indeed, I even get pleasure from it. And then there come days when a single word distresses me and I long to leave the world altogether, for everything in it seems to weary me. And I am not the only person to be like this, for I have noticed the same thing in many people better than myself, so I know it can happen.

That being so, who can say that he possesses any virtue, or that he is rich, if at the time when he most needs this virtue he finds himself devoid of it? No, sisters: let us rather think of ourselves as lacking it and not run into debt without having the means of repayment. Our treasure must come from elsewhere and we never know when God will leave us in this prison of our misery without giving us any. If others, thinking we are good, bestow favours and honours upon us, both they and we shall look foolish when, as I say, it becomes clear that our virtues are only lent us. The truth is that, if we serve the Lord with humility, He will sooner or later succour us in our needs. But, if we are not strong in this virtue, the Lord will leave us to ourselves, as they say, at every step. This is a great favour on His part, for it helps us to realize fully that we have nothing which has not been given us.

And now you must take note of this other piece of advice. The devil makes us believe that we have some virtue—patience, let us say—because we have determination and make continual resolutions to suffer a great deal for God's sake. We really and truly believe that we would suffer all this, and the devil encourages us in the belief, and so we are very pleased. I advise you to place no reliance on these virtues: we ought not to think that we know anything about them beyond their names, or to imagine that the Lord has given them to us, until we come to the test. For it may be that at the first annoying word which people say to you your patience will fall to the ground. Whenever you have frequently to suffer, praise God for beginning to teach you this virtue, and force yourself to suffer patiently, for this is a sign that He wants you to repay Him for the virtue which He is giving you, and you must think of it only as a deposit, as has already been said.

The devil has yet another temptation, which is to make us appear very poor in spirit: we are in the habit of saying that we want nothing and care nothing about anything: but as soon as the chance comes of our being given something, even though we do not in the least need it, all our poverty of spirit disappears. Accustoming ourselves to saying this goes far towards making us think it true. It is very important always to be on the watch and to realize that this is a temptation, both in the things I have referred to and in many others. For when the Lord really gives one of these solid virtues, it seems to bring all the rest in its train: that is a very well known fact. But I advise you once more, even if you think you possess it, to suspect that you may be mistaken;[1] for the person who is truly humble is always doubtful about his own virtues; very often they seem more genuine and of greater worth when he sees them in his neighbours.

The devil makes you think you are poor,[2] and he has some reason for doing so, because you have made (with the lips, of course) a vow of poverty, as have some other people who practise prayer. I say "with the lips" because, if before making the vow we really meant in our hearts what we were going to say, the devil could not possibly lead us into that temptation—not even in twenty years, or in our entire lifetime—for we should see that we were deceiving the whole world, and ourselves into the bargain. Well, we make our vow of poverty, and then one of us, believing herself all the time to be keeping it, says: "I do not want anything, but I am having this because I cannot do without it: after all, if I am to serve God, I must live, and He wants us to keep these bodies of ours alive." So the devil, in his angelic disguise, suggests to her that there are a thousand different things which she needs and that they are all good for her. And all the time he is persuading her to believe that she is still being true to her vow and possesses the virtue of poverty and that what she has done is no more than her duty.

And now let us take a test case, for we can only get to the truth of this by keeping a continual watch on ourselves: then, if there is any cause for anxiety on our part, we shall at once recognize the symptoms. Here is someone who has a larger income than he needs—I mean, needs for the necessaries of life—and, though he could do with a single manservant, he keeps three. Yet, when he is sued in the courts in connection with a part of his property, or some poor peasant omits to pay him his dues, he gets as upset and excited about it as if his life were at stake. He says he must

---

[1] T.: "deceived."   [2] Cf. p. 165, n. 2, above.

look after his property or he will lose it, and considers that that justifies him. I do not suggest that he ought to neglect his property: whether or no things go well with him, he should look after it. But a person whose profession of poverty is a genuine one makes so little account of these things that, although for various reasons he attends to his own interests, he never worries about them, because he never supposes he will lose everything he has; and, even if he should do so, he would consider it of no great moment, for the matter is one of secondary importance to him and not his principal concern. His thoughts rise high above it and he has to make an effort to occupy himself with it at all.

Now monks and nuns are demonstrably poor—they must be so, for they possess nothing: sometimes because there is nothing for them to possess. But if a religious of the type just mentioned is given anything, it is most unlikely that he will think it superfluous. He always likes to have something laid by; if he can get a habit of good cloth, he will not ask for one of coarse material. He likes to have some trifle, if only books, which he can pawn or sell, for if he falls ill he will need extra comforts. Sinner that I am! Is this the vow of poverty that you took? Stop worrying about yourself and leave God to provide for you, come what may. If you are going about trying to provide for your own future, it would be less trouble for you to have a fixed income. This may not involve any sin, but it is as well that we should learn to recognize our imperfections, so that we can see how far we are from possessing the virtue of poverty, which we must beg and obtain from God. If we think we already possess it, we shall grow careless, and, what is worse, we shall be deceiving ourselves.

The same thing happens with regard to humility.[1] We think that we have no desire for honour and that we care nothing about anything; but as soon as our honour comes to be slighted in some detail our feelings and actions at once show that we are not humble at all. If an opportunity occurs for us to gain more honour, we do not reject it; even those who are poor, and to whom I have just referred, are anxious to have as much profit as possible—God grant we may not go so far as actually to seek it! We always have phrases on our lips about wanting nothing, and caring nothing about anything, and we honestly think them to be true, and get so used to repeating them that we come to believe them more and more firmly. But when, as I say, we keep on the watch, we realize that this is a temptation, as regards both the virtue I have spoken of and all the rest; for when we really have one of these solid virtues, it brings all the rest in its train: that is a very well known fact.

[1] It will be noticed that this paragraph is similar to the last paragraph in the text of V. (p. 167, above). The differences, however, are so wide that each of the two is given as it stands.

CHAPTER XXXIX

Continues the same subject and gives counsels concerning different kinds of temptation. Suggests two remedies by which we may be freed from temptations.[1]

Beware also, daughters, of certain kinds of humility which the devil inculcates in us and which make us very uneasy about the gravity of our *past* sins.[2] There are many ways in which he is accustomed to depress us so that in time we withdraw from Communion and give up our private prayer, because the devil suggests to us that we are not worthy to engage in it. When we come to the Most Holy Sacrament, we spend the time during which we ought to be receiving grace in wondering whether we are properly prepared or no. The thing gets to such a pass that a soul can be made to believe that, through being what it is, it has been forsaken by God, and thus it almost doubts His mercy. Everything such a person does appears to her to be dangerous, and all the service she renders, however good it may be, seems to her fruitless. She loses confidence and sits with her hands in her lap because she thinks she can do nothing well and that what is good in others is wrong in herself.

Pay great attention, daughters, to this point which I shall now make, because sometimes thinking yourselves so wicked may be humility and virtue and at other times a very great temptation. I have had experience of this, so I know it is true. Humility, however deep it be, neither disquiets nor troubles nor disturbs the soul; it is accompanied by peace, joy and tranquillity. Although, on realizing how wicked we are, we can see clearly[3] that we deserve to be in hell, and are distressed by our sinfulness, and rightly think that everyone should hate us, yet, if our humility is true,[4] this distress is accompanied by an interior peace and joy

---

[1] A marginal addition made, in the autograph, to the title by another hand reads: "This chapter is very noteworthy, both for those tempted by false kinds of humility and for confessors." This is found in T. and in most of the editions.

[2] E. puts the suggestions, vividly but bluntly and briefly, in *oratio recta*, and abbreviates what follows, continuing thus: ". . . past sins. 'Am I worthy to approach the Sacrament?' 'Am I in a good disposition?' 'I am not fit to live among good people.' Things like these, when they come with tranquillity, joy and pleasure, and are suggested by our own knowledge of ourselves, are to be highly esteemed. But if they are accompanied by turmoil, unrest and depression of soul, and you cannot quiet your thoughts, you may be sure it is a temptation, and you must not count yourselves humble, for it does not come from humility at all. This is what happens, etc. (p. 170)"

[3] T. omits: "clearly."

[4] T.: "if this distress is true humility."

of which we should not like to be deprived. Far from disturbing or depressing the soul, it enlarges it and makes it fit to serve God better. The other kind of distress only disturbs and upsets the mind and troubles the soul, so grievous is it. I think the devil is anxious for us to believe that we are humble, and, if he can, to lead us to distrust God.

When you find yourselves in this state, cease thinking, so far as you can, of your own wretchedness, and think of the mercy of God and of His love and His sufferings for us. If your state of mind is the result of temptation, you will be unable to do even this, for it will not allow you to quiet your thoughts or to fix them on anything but will only weary you the more: it will be a great thing if you can recognize it as a temptation. This is what happens[1] when we perform excessive penances in order to make ourselves believe[2] that, because of what we are doing, we are more penitent than others. If we conceal our penances from our confessor or superior, or if we are told to give them up and do not obey, that is a clear case of temptation.[3] Always try to obey, however much it may hurt you to do so, for that is the greatest possible perfection.[4]

There is another very dangerous kind of temptation: a feeling of security caused by the belief that we shall never again return to our past faults and to the pleasures of the world. "I know all about these things now," we say, "and I realize that they all come to an end and I get more pleasure from the things of God." If this temptation comes to beginners it is very serious; for, having this sense of security, they think nothing of running once more into occasions of sin. They soon come up against these—and then God preserve them from falling back farther than before![5] The devil, seeing that here are souls which may do him harm and be of great help to others, does all in his power to prevent them from rising again.[6] However many consolations

---

[1] Here E. continues (see p. 169, n. 2, above). T. reads: "Thus, if (it is a question of) performing excessive penances, he [the devil?] will contrive to make us believe, etc."

[2] E.: "to put it into our minds."

[3] E.: "If, when your confessor or superior tells you not to do a thing, (his advice) hurts you and you do it again, that is a clear case of temptation. This, as I say, is so in everything: but be specially careful not to forget this particular thing." V., as well as E., has the second person in this passage, but as V. has the first person earlier in the paragraph, this is continued in the translation for the sake of uniformity.

[4] This sentence is not found in E.

[5] E. begins this paragraph: "There is also a feeling of security [caused by] the belief that I shall never again return to the past, that I know now what the world is. This temptation is the worst of all, especially if it comes to beginners, for it makes you run into occasions of sin, and thus you come up against them, and then God grant that you rise after this fall!"

[6] T., after omitting "and be of great help to others" has "does all in his power to deceive them". E. continues: "Now as to consolations, if the Lord brings you to

and pledges of love the Lord may give you, therefore, you must never be so sure of yourselves that you cease to be afraid of falling back again, and you must keep yourselves from occasions of sin.

Do all you can to discuss these graces and favours with someone who can give you light and have no secrets from him. However sublime your contemplation may be, take great care both to begin and to end every period of prayer with self-examination. If these favours come from God, you will do this more frequently, without either taking or needing any advice from me, for such favours bring humility with them and always leave us with more light by which we may see our own unworthiness. I will say no more here, for you will find many books which give this kind of advice. I have said all this because I have had experience of the matter and have sometimes found myself in difficulties of this nature. Nothing that can be said about it, however, will give us complete security.

What, then, Eternal Father, can we do but flee to Thee and beg Thee not to allow these enemies of ours to lead us into temptation?[1] If attacks are made upon us publicly, we shall easily surmount them, with Thy help.[2] But how can we be ready for these treacherous assaults,[3] my God? We need constantly to pray for Thy help. Show us, Lord, some way of recognizing them and guarding against them.[4] Thou knowest that there are not many who walk along this road, and if so many fears are to beset them, there will be far fewer.

What a strange thing it is! You might suppose that the devil never tempted those who do not walk along the road of prayer![5] People get a greater shock when deception overtakes a single one of the many persons who are striving to be perfect[6] than when a hundred thousand others are deceived and fall into open sin, whom there is no need to look at in order to see if they are good or evil, for Satan can be seen at their side a thousand leagues

---

contemplation, and gives you a special share in Himself, and pledges of His love for you, take care to begin and end with self-examination, to walk warily and to discuss everything with someone who understands you; for here he [the devil] is wont to launch his attacks in different ways. There are many books full of such advice as this, but all of them together cannot give complete security, for we cannot understand ourselves." This passage stands for the remainder of the paragraph and the whole of the next.

[1] E.: "Then, Eternal Father, lead us not into this temptation."
[2] E.: "Let attacks be made on us publicly if we have Thy help."
[3] *Lit*: "these treasons." T.: "these temptations."
[4] E.: "some sign, so that we may be able to walk without always being surprised."
[5] E.: "who do not practise prayer."
[6] E.: "a single one on this road."

away.[1] But as a matter of fact people are right about this, for very few who say the Paternoster in the way that has been described[2] are deceived by the devil, so that, if the deception of one of them causes surprise, that is because it is a new and an unusual thing. For human nature is such that we scarcely notice what we see frequently[3] but are astounded at what we see seldom or hardly at all.[4] And the devils themselves encourage this astonishment, for if a single soul attains perfection it robs them of many others.

It is so strange, I repeat, that I am not surprised if people are amazed at it; for, unless they are altogether at fault, they are much safer on this road than on any other, just as people who watch a bull-fight from the grand-stand are safer than the men who expose themselves to a thrust from the bull's horns. This comparison, which I heard somewhere, seems to me very exact. Do not be afraid to walk on these roads, sisters, for there are many of them in the life of prayer—and some people get most help by using one of them and others by using another, as I have said. This road is a safe one and you will the more readily escape from temptation if you are near the Lord than if you are far away from Him. Beseech and entreat this of Him, as you do so many times each day in the Paternoster.[5]

CHAPTER XL

Describes how, by striving always to walk in the love and fear of God, we shall travel safely amid all these temptations.

Show us, then, O our good Master, some way in which we may live through this most dangerous warfare without frequent surprise. The best way that we can do this, daughters, is to use the love and fear given us by His Majesty. For love will make us quicken our steps, while fear will make us look where we are setting our feet so that we shall not fall on a road where there are so many obstacles. Along that road all living creatures must pass, and if we have these two things we shall certainly not be deceived.[6]

[1] E.: "than when a hundred thousand are seen to be making, by other roads, straight for hell."
[2] E.: "who say the Paternoster with this attentiveness."
[3] E.: "what we see daily."
[4] E.: "at what has never happened."
[5] This paragraph, from E., was included by Luis de León in his edition.
[6] E. begins the chapter: "And take this advice, which comes, not from me, but from your Master. Strive to walk with love and fear, and I guarantee your safety:

You will ask me how you can tell if you *really* have these two very, very great virtues.[1] You are right to ask, for we can never be quite definite and certain about it; if we were sure that we possessed love, we should be sure that we were in a state of grace.[2] But you know, sisters, there are some indications which are in no way secret but so evident that even a blind man, as people say, could see them.[3] You may not wish to heed them, but they cry so loud for notice that they make quite an uproar, for there are not many who possess them to the point of perfection[4] and thus they are the more readily noticed. Love and fear of God! These are two strong castles whence we can wage war on the world and on the devils.

Those who really love God love all good, seek all good, help forward all good, praise all good, and invariably join forces with good men and help and defend them.[5] They love only truth and things worthy of love. Do you think it possible that anyone who really and truly loves God can love vanities, riches, worldly pleasures[6] or honours? Can he engage in strife or feel envy? No; for his only desire is to please the Beloved. Such persons die with longing for Him to love them and so they will give their lives to learn how they may please Him better.[7] Will they hide their love? No: if their love for God is genuine love they cannot.[8] Why, think of Saint Paul or the Magdalen. One of these—Saint Paul—found in three days that he was sick with love. The Magdalen discovered this on the very first day.[9] And how certain of it they were! For there are degrees of love for God, which shows itself in proportion to its strength. If there is little of it, it shows itself but little; if there is much, it shows itself a great

---

love will make you quicken your steps; fear will make you look where you are setting your feet so that you may not fall. With these two things, it is quite certain that you will not be deceived."

[1] *Lit.*: "these two virtues, so great, so great." This repetition does not occur in T., which reads "these very great virtues," nor in E., which continues: "It becomes evident at once: even a blind man, as people say, could see them: they are not things which are in any way secret. You may not wish, etc."

[2] "Which is not possible save by special privilege," adds P. Báñez, marginally. He also adds words in several places in this chapter to complete the sense of its rather numerous ellipses. These are not noted except where they affect the translation.

[3] V. has: "which even blind men seem to see." The reading in the text is based on E.

[4] "To the point of [*lit.*: "With"] perfection" is not found in E.

[5] E.: "and join forces with good men and invariably defend them."

[6] E.: "worldly things." In the next sentence T. omits "or feel envy."

[7] T. continues: "For their love for God, if it is genuine love, cannot possibly be very much concealed. Why, etc."

[8] E.: "No, it is impossible."

[9] E.: "in one [day]."

deal.¹ But it always shows itself, whether little or much, provided it is real love for God.

But to come to what we are chiefly treating of now²—the deceptions and illusions practised against contemplatives by the devil³—such souls have no little love; for had they not a great deal they would not be contemplatives,⁴ and so their love shows itself plainly and in many ways. Being a great fire, it cannot fail to give out a very bright light. If they have not much love, they should proceed with many misgivings and realize that they have great cause for fear; and they should try to find out what is wrong with them, say their prayers, walk in humility and beseech the Lord not to lead them into temptation, into which, I fear, they will certainly fall⁵ unless they bear this sign. But if they walk humbly and strive to discover the truth and do as their confessor bids them and tell him the plain truth, then *the Lord is faithful, and*, as has been said, by using the very means with which he had thought to give them death, the devil will give them life, with however many fantasies and illusions he tries to deceive them.⁶ *If they submit to the teaching of the Church, they need not fear; whatever fantasies and illusions the devil may invent, he will at once betray his presence.*

But if you feel this love for God which I have spoken of, and the fear which I shall now describe, you may go on your way with happiness and tranquillity. In order to disturb the soul and keep it from enjoying these great blessings, the devil will suggest to it a thousand false fears and will persuade other people to do the same; for if he cannot win souls he will at least⁷ try to make them lose something, and among the losers will be those who might have gained greatly had they believed that such great favours, bestowed upon so miserable a creature, come from God,⁸ and that it is possible for them to be thus bestowed, for sometimes we seem to forget His past mercies.

Do you suppose that it is of little use to the devil to suggest these fears?⁹ No, it is most useful to him,¹⁰ for there are two

---

¹ E. ends the paragraph here.
² E.: "to what we are speaking of now." T.: "to what we are treating of now."
³ E.: "against those who rise to perfect contemplation and to high things."
⁴ "For . . . contemplatives" is not found in E.
⁵ The verb, in both E. and V., is in the present tense. E. is more downright than V., omitting "I fear". T. has "see" for "bear."
⁶ E.: "and do as their confessor bids them, the Lord is faithful: be sure that, if you walk without malice and feel no pride, the devil will give you life by using the very means with which he had thought to give you death." T. has "things" (*cosas*) for "fantasies" (*cocos*).
⁷ T. has "does not try to" for "cannot" and omits "at least."
⁸ E. ends the paragraph here.
⁹ E.: "to throw doubt on this."
¹⁰ E. begins this sentence: "He gains a very great deal."

well-known ways in which he can make use of this means to harm us, *to say nothing of others*. First, he can make those who listen to him[1] fearful of engaging in prayer, because they think that they will be deceived. Secondly, he can dissuade many from approaching God who, as I have said, see that He is so good that He will hold intimate converse with sinners.[2] Many such souls think that He will treat them in the same way, and they are right:[3] I myself know certain persons inspired in this way who began the habit of prayer and in a short time became truly devout and received[4] great favours from the Lord.

Therefore, sisters, when you see someone to whom the Lord is granting these favours, praise Him fervently,[5] yet do not imagine that she is safe, but aid her with more prayer, for no one can be safe in this life amid the engulfing dangers of this stormy sea.[6] Wherever this love is, then, you will not fail to recognize it; I do not know how it could be concealed. For they say that it is impossible for us to hide our love even for creatures, and that, the more we try to conceal it, the more clearly is it revealed. And yet this is so worthless that it hardly deserves the name of love, for it is founded upon nothing at all:[7] *it is loathsome, indeed, to make this comparison.* How, then, could a love *like God's*[8] be concealed—so strong, so righteous, continually increasing, never seeing cause for ceasing to manifest itself, and resting upon the firm foundation of the love which is its reward? As to the reality of this reward there can be no doubt, for it is manifest in Our Lord's great sorrows, His trials, the shedding of His blood and even the loss of His life.[9] Certainly, then, there is no doubt as to this love.[10] *It is indeed love, and deserves that name, of which worldly vanities have robbed it.* God help me! How different must the one love be from the other to those who have experience of both!

May His Majesty be pleased to grant us *to experience* this before He takes us from this life, for it will be a great thing at the hour

---

[1] "And fear him," adds P. Báñez, marginally.
[2] E.: "that He can hold such close converse with a wicked person."
[3] So E. V. is much less explicit: "He makes them covetous, and they are right [to be so], etc."
[4] E.: "persons who became truly devout and in a short time received."
[5] E.: "when you recognize this love in one of yourselves, praise God for it and give Him thanks." T.: "give fervent praise."
[6] E.: "of this sea on which she is sailing."
[7] E. is more detailed, but hardly, I think, so effective: "For it is impossible for the love of a mere man or woman to be hidden; the more they try to hide it, the clearer does it seem to become. And yet love for which there is no object but a worm does not deserve the name, for it is founded upon nothing at all."
[8] So E., and there is nothing in V. to suggest that this sense was later rejected. But the context in both E. and V. would favour a reading "love like that *for* God."
[9] P. Báñez adds: "for our sakes."
[10] E.: "so strong, resting upon such a foundation, having so much to love, and so many causes for loving?"

of death, *when we are going we know not whither,* to realize that we shall be judged by One Whom we have loved above all things,[1] *and with a passion that makes us entirely forget ourselves.* Once our debts have been paid we shall be able to walk in safety. We shall not be going into a foreign land, but into our own country, for it belongs to Him Whom we have loved so truly[2] and Who Himself loves us. *For this love of His, besides its other properties, is better than all earthly affection in that, if we love Him, we are quite sure that He loves us too.* Remember, my daughters, the greatness of the gain which comes from this love, and of our loss if we do not possess it, for in that case we shall be delivered into the hands of the tempter, hands so cruel and so hostile to all that is good, and so friendly to all that is evil.

What will become of the poor soul when it falls into these hands after emerging from all the pains and trials of death? How little rest it will have![3] How it will be torn as it goes down to hell! What swarms and varieties of serpents it will meet! How dreadful is that place! How miserable that lodging! Why, a pampered person (and most of those who go to hell are that) can hardly bear to spend a single night in a bad inn: what, then, will be the feelings of that wretched soul when it is condemned to such an inn as this and has to spend eternity there?[4] Let us not try to pamper ourselves, daughters. We are quite well off here: there is only a single night for us to spend in this bad inn. Let us praise God[5] and strive to do penance in this life. How sweet will be the death of those who have done penance for all their sins and have not to go to purgatory! It may be that they will begin to enjoy glory even in this world, and will know no fear, but only peace.

Even if we do not attain to this, sisters, let us beseech God that, if in due course we must suffer these pains,[6] it may be with a hope of emerging from them. Then we shall suffer them willingly and lose neither the friendship nor the grace of God. May He grant us these in this life so that we may not unwittingly fall into temptation.

---

[1] E.: "to have loved . . . the Lord Who is to judge us."

[2] E. ends the sentence here.

[3] E. is more forcible, with its characteristically Teresan repetition: "Miserable (*negro*) the rest it will have—miserable!"

[4] *Lit.*: "to an inn for ever, *ever*, for eternity." The repetition of "ever" (*siempre*) reminds one of the famous reminiscence of St. Teresa's childhood, to be found in her *Life*, Chap. I (Vol. I, p. 11, above).

[5] E. ends the chapter thus: "Let us praise God and ever be careful to beseech Him to keep us, and all sinners, in His hand, and not to lead us into these hidden temptations."

[6] T.: "And if it is possible to attain to this, sisters, it will be very cowardly (of us) not to do so. Let us beseech God that, if we must go and suffer (these) pains."

CHAPTER XLI

Speaks of the fear of God and of how we must keep ourselves from venial sins.

How I have enlarged on this subject! Yet I have not said as much about it as I should like; for it is a delightful thing to talk about this love *of God*. What, then, must it be to possess it? May the Lord, for His own sake, give it me![1] *May I not depart from this life till there is nothing in it that I desire, till I have forgotten what it is to love anything but Thee and till I deny the name of love to any other kind of affection—for all love is false but love of Thee, and, unless the foundations of a building are true, the building itself will not endure. I do not know why it surprises us to hear people say:* "*So-and-so has made me a poor return for something.*" "*Someone else does not like me.*" *I laugh to myself when I hear that. What other sort of return do you expect him to make you? And why do you expect anyone to like you? These things will show you what the world is; your love itself becomes your punishment, and the reason why you are so upset about it is that your will strongly resents your involving it in such childish pastimes.*[2]

Let us now come to the fear of God—though I am sorry not to be able to say a little about this worldly love, which, for my sins, I know well and should like to acquaint you with, so that you may free yourself from it for ever. But I am straying from my subject and shall have to pass on.

This fear of God is another thing with which those who possess it and those who have to do with them[3] are very familiar. But I should like you to realize that at first it is not very deep, save in a few people, to whom, as I have said, the Lord grants such great favours as to make them rich in virtues *and to raise them, in a very short time, to great heights of prayer.*[4] It is not recognizable, therefore, at first, in everyone.[5] As it increases, it grows stronger each day, and then, of course, it can be recognized, for those who possess it forsake sin, and occasions of sin, and bad company, and other signs of it are visible in them.[6] When at last the soul

---

[1] E.: "O my Lord, do Thou give it me."
[2] Though not occurring in V., this graphic and effective passage is found in all the printed editions in the *Way of perfection*.
[3] E.: "those who are around them."
[4] E. differs considerably in the wording of this sentence, but the thought is almost identical with that of V.
[5] E.: "[In these persons], of course, it is easily recognizable."
[6] E.: "But where favours do not increase in the way I have described, where after one visit [from God] the soul is left rich in all the virtues, they increase little by little. But the love and fear of God always reveal themselves the more as they become more excellent, for those who possess them forsake sin, and occasions of sin, and bad company, and other signs of it are visible in them."

attains to contemplation, of which we are chiefly treating at the moment, its fear of God is plainly revealed, and its love is not dissembled even outwardly. However narrowly we watch such persons, we shall not find them growing careless; for, close as our watch on them may be, the Lord so preserves them that they would not[1] knowingly commit one venial sin even to further their own interests, and, as for mortal sin, they fear it like fire. These are the illusions, sisters, which I should like you always to fear; let us always beseech God that temptation may not be strong enough for us to offend Him[2] but that He may send it to us in proportion to the strength which He gives us to conquer it. *If we keep a pure conscience, we can suffer little or no harm.*[3] That is the important point; and that is the fear which I hope will never be taken from us, for it is that fear which will stand us in good stead.

Oh, what a great thing it is not to have offended the Lord, so that the servants and slaves of hell[4] may be kept under control! In the end, whether willingly or no, we shall all serve Him—they by compulsion and we with our whole heart. So that, if we please Him, they will be kept at bay and will do nothing that can harm us, however much they lead us into temptation and lay secret snares for us.[5]

Keep this in mind, for it is very important advice, so do not neglect it[6] until you find you have such a fixed determination not to offend the Lord that you would rather lose a thousand lives, *and be persecuted by the whole world*, than commit one mortal sin,[7] and until you are most careful not to commit venial sins. I am referring now to sins committed knowingly:[8] as far as those of the other kind are concerned, who can fail to commit them frequently? But it is one thing to commit a sin knowingly and after long deliberation, and quite another to do it so suddenly that the knowledge of its being a venial sin and its commission

---

[1] E.: "But when the soul has attained the growth in prayer of which we are now speaking, its fear of God is not dissembled, but becomes very evident, and it will not be found to be growing careless in outward things, however narrowly it may be watched, but God so preserves it that its great anxiety not to offend Him is clearly evident. For they would not."

[2] E. ends the sentence here.

[3] E. adds: "Everything will be a source of fresh loss to him." By "him" must be meant the devil, who has not, however, been previously mentioned in this paragraph.

[4] *Lit.* "the infernal slaves." In E. and in V. the sentence ends here. The five words which follow appear only in T. and were adopted by Luis de León to complete the sense. T. has "vassals the devils" for "slaves of hell", which it substitutes for a deleted phrase "animal slaves," probably an error of the copyist for "infernal slaves."

[5] E.: "nothing that will not bring us greater advantage."

[6] E.: "Keep this in mind as to interior matters and do not neglect it." The words "and [so] do not neglect it" are not found in the Spanish but were added by Luis de León.

[7] E. reads "venial" for "mortal" and ends the sentence at "sin".

[8] E.: "[committed] after definite consideration—I mean knowingly."

are one and the same thing, and we hardly realize[1] what we have done, *although we do to some extent realize it.* From any sin, however small, committed with full knowledge, may God deliver us,[2] especially since we are sinning against so great a Sovereign and realizing that He is watching us! That seems to me to be a sin committed of malice aforethought; it is as though one were to say: "Lord, although this displeases Thee, I shall do it. I know that Thou seest it and I know that Thou wouldst not have me do it; but, though I understand this, I would rather follow my own whim and desire[3] than Thy will." If we commit a sin in this way, however slight,[4] it seems to me that our offence is not small but very, very great.

For the love of God, sisters, *never be careless about this—and, glory be to the Lord, you are not so at present.* If you would gain this fear of God, *remember the importance of habit and of starting to realize what a serious thing it is to offend Him. Do your utmost to learn this and to turn it over in your minds*;[5] for our life, and much more than our life, depends upon this virtue being firmly planted in our souls. Until you are conscious within your soul of possessing it,[6] you need always to exercise very great care and to avoid all occasions of sin and any kind of company which will not help you to get nearer to God. Be most careful, in all that you do, to bend your will to it; see that all you say tends to edification; flee from all places where there is conversation which is not pleasing to God. Much care is needed if this fear *of God* is to be thoroughly impressed upon[7] the soul; though, if one has true love, it is quickly acquired.[8] Even when the soul has that firm inward determination which I have described, not to offend God[9] for the sake of any creature, *or from fear of a thousand deaths,* it may subsequently fall from time to time,[10] for we are weak and cannot trust ourselves, and, the more determined we are, the less self-confidence we should have, for confidence must come from God.[11]

---

[1] E.: "that until some little fault has been committed—until it is done—we seem not to have realized."

[2] E. ends the sentence here and continues: "I do not know how we are bold enough to sin against so great a Lord, even in the smallest thing—though nothing is small when it is committed against so great a Sovereign, and we realize, etc."

[3] E. omits: "and desire."

[4] E. omits: "however slight."

[5] V. reads: "If you would gain this fear of God, think how serious a thing it is to offend God, and turn it over often in your minds." E. ends the sentence: "so that you may keep planting in your hearts a very wholesome fear of God."

[6] So E. V. has: "Until you (are really conscious that you) possess it. The bracketed words were deleted by the author.

[7] E.: "is to be planted in."

[8] E.: "His Majesty quickly bestows it."

[9] E.: "not to commit a venial sin."

[10] E.: "it may subsequently do so."

[11] "Do not be discouraged," interpolates T. here, "for perhaps He permits it so that we may know ourselves better; but try to [i.e., see that you] beg forgiveness immediately."

But, when we find ourselves in this state, we need not feel constrained or depressed, for the Lord will help us and the habits we have formed will be of assistance to us so that we shall not offend Him;[1] we shall be able to walk in holy freedom, and associate with anyone, as seems right to us, even with dissolute people.[2] *These will do you no harm, if you hate sin.*[3] Before we had this true fear of God worldly people would have been poisonous to us and would have helped to ruin our souls; but now they will often help us[4] to love God more and to praise Him for having delivered us from what we see to be a notorious danger. And whereas we for our part may previously have helped to foster their weaknesses, we shall now be helping to repress them, because they will restrain themselves in our presence, and this is a compliment which they will pay us without our desiring it.

I often praise the Lord (though I also wonder why it should be so) that merely by his presence, and without saying a word, a servant of God should frequently prevent people from speaking against Him. It may be as it is in worldly intercourse: a person is always spoken of with respect, even in his absence, before those who are known to be his friends, lest they should be offended. Since this servant of God is in a state of grace, this grace must cause him to be respected, however lowly his station, for people will not distress him in a matter about which they know him to feel so strongly as giving offence to God. I really do not know the reason for this but I do know that it very commonly happens. Do not be too strict with yourselves, then, for, if your spirit begins to quail,[5] it will do great harm to what is good in you and may sometimes lead to scrupulosity, which is a hindrance to progress both in yourselves and in others. Even if things are not as bad as this, a person, however good in herself, will not lead many souls to God if they see that she is so strict and timorous. Human nature is such that these characteristics will frighten and oppress it[6] and lead people to avoid the road you are taking, even if they are quite clear it is the best one.

Another source of harm is this: we may judge others unfavour-

---

[1] E.: "for the Lord, and the habit [we have formed] will help us not to offend Him."
[2] E. is even more liberal: "and associate with anyone we meet, more particularly (*mejor*) with dissolute people."
[3] E. then continues: "Rather they will help you to further your good resolutions, for they will show you the difference between the one and the other. And if your spirit begins to quail, etc."
[4] T.: "give us an opportunity."
[5] Here E. takes up the argument again. See n. 3., above.
[6] E. reads: "will at once oppress it," and completes the paragraph thus: "and, lest they should find themselves similarly trammelled, people will no longer have the desire to draw near to the path of virtue."

ably, though they may be holier than ourselves, because they do not walk as we do, but, in order to profit their neighbours, talk freely and without restraint.[1] You think such people are imperfect; and if they are good and yet at the same time of a lively disposition, you think them dissolute. This is especially true of those of us who are unlearned and are not sure what we can speak about without committing sin. It is a very dangerous state of mind, leading to great uneasiness and to continual temptation, because it is unfair to our neighbour. It is very wrong to think that everyone who does not follow in your own timorous footsteps has something the matter with her. Another danger is that, when it is your duty to speak, and right that you should speak, you may not dare to do so lest you say too much and may perhaps speak well[2] of things that you ought to hate.[3]

Try, then, sisters, to be as pleasant as you can, without offending God, and to get on as well as you can with those you have to deal with, so that they may like talking to you and want to follow your way of life and conversation, and not be frightened and put off by virtue. This is very important for nuns: the holier they are, the more sociable they should be with their sisters.[4] Although you may be very sorry if all your sisters' conversation is not just as you would like it to be, never keep aloof from them if you wish to help them and to have their love. We must try hard to be pleasant, and to humour the people we deal with and make them like us, especially our sisters.[5]

So try, my daughters, to bear in mind that God does not pay great attention to all the trifling matters which occupy you, and do not allow these things to make your spirit quail and your courage fade, for if you do that you may lose many blessings. As I have said, let your intention be upright and your will determined not to offend God. But do not let your soul dwell in seclusion, or, instead of acquiring holiness, you will develop many imperfections, which the devil will implant in you in other ways, in which case, as I have said, you will not do the good that you might, either to yourselves or to others.[6]

You see that, with these two things—love and fear of God—we can travel along this road in peace and quietness,[7] *and not think at every step that we can see some pitfall, and that we shall never*

---

[1] E.: "talk without restraint." *Lit.* (as in V.): "without those restraints"—i.e., those just referred to.
[2] E.: "lest you offend God and (you) may speak well."
[3] The paragraph which follows is not found in E.
[4] This sentence was originally written with the nouns in the masculine and corrected by the author to read as in the text.
[5] T. omits: "especially our sisters."
[6] E.: "in which case, as I say, you will do good neither to yourselves nor to others."
[7] E.: "along this road quietly."

reach our goal.[1] *Yet we cannot be sure of reaching it,*[2] *so* fear will always lead the way, and then we shall not grow careless, for, as long as we live, we must never feel completely safe or we shall be in great danger. And that was our Teacher's meaning when at the end of this prayer He said these words to His Father,[3] knowing how necessary they were: "*But deliver us from evil. Amen.*"

CHAPTER XLII

Treats of these last words of the Paternoster: "Sed libera nos a malo. Amen." "But deliver us from evil. Amen."[4]

I think the good Jesus was right to ask this for Himself, for we know[5] how weary of this life He was when at the Supper He said to His Apostles: "With desire I have desired to sup with you"[6]—and that was the last supper of His life. From this it can be seen how weary He must have been of living;[7] yet nowadays people are not weary even at a hundred years old, but always want to live longer. It is true, however, that we do not live so difficult a life or suffer such trials or such poverty as His Majesty had to bear.[8] What was His whole life but a continuous death, with the picture of the cruel death that He was to suffer always before His eyes? And this was the least important thing, with so many offences being[9] committed against His Father and such a multitude of souls being lost.[10] If to any human being full of charity this is a great torment, what must it have been to the boundless and measureless charity[11] of the Lord? And how right He was to beseech the Father to deliver Him from so many evils and trials and to give Him rest for ever[12] in His kingdom, of which He was the true heir.

[1] Or "for [if we do this] we shall never reach our goal."
[2] E. continues: "[though] it is true that we have these two things, which are very necessary. As the Lord has pity on us because we live a life of such uncertainty, and [are] among so many temptations and dangers, His Majesty does well to teach us to ask for ourselves what He asks for Himself: 'But deliver us from evil. Amen.'"
[3] T. ends the sentence here.
[4] T. begins this chapter: "As our good Master knows the perils and trials of this life, He makes this petition for us. He had indeed proved by experience how distressing it is, for we can see how weary of it He was when at the Supper, etc."
[5] E.: "I say that He asks this for Himself, because it is quite evident."
[6] St. Luke xxii, 15.
[7] T.: "how delectable death would be to Him."
[8] E.: "that we do not live a life so full of trials and poverty as did the good Jesu."
[9] T.: "offences which He saw being."
[10] E.: "but a cross, with our ingratitude always before His eyes, and the sight of so many offences being committed against His Father and so many souls being lost."
[11] E.: "to the charity."
[12] E. ends the paragraph here.

By the word "Amen," as it comes at the end of every prayer,[1] I understand that the Lord is begging that we may be delivered from all evil for ever. *It is useless, sisters, for us to think that, for so long as we live, we can be free from numerous temptations and imperfections and even sins; for it is said that whosoever thinks himself to be without sin deceives himself, and that is true. But if we try to banish bodily ills and trials—and who is without very many and various trials of such kinds?—is it not right that we should ask to be delivered from sin?*

Still, let us realize that what we are asking here—this deliverance from all evil—seems an impossibility, whether we are thinking of bodily ills, as I have said, or of imperfections and faults in God's service. I am referring not to the saints, who, as Saint Paul said, can do all things in Christ,[2] *but to sinners like myself. When I find myself trammelled by weakness, lukewarmness, lack of mortification and many other things, I realize that I must beg for help from the Lord.*

You, daughters, must ask as you think best. Personally, I shall find no redress in this life, so I ask the Lord to deliver me from all evil "for ever." What good thing shall we find in this life, sisters, in which we are deprived of our great Good and are absent from Him? Deliver me, Lord, from this shadow of death; deliver me from all these trials; deliver me from all these pains; deliver me from all these changes, from all the formalities with which we are forced to comply for as long as we live, from all the many, many, many things which weary and depress me, and the enumeration of all of which would weary the reader if I were to repeat them. This life is unendurable. The source of my own depression must be my own wicked life and the realization that even now I am not living as I should, so great are my obligations.

I beseech the Lord,[3] then, to deliver me from all evil for ever, since I cannot[4] pay what I owe, and may perhaps run farther into debt each day. And the hardest thing to bear, Lord, is that I cannot know with any certainty if I love Thee and if my desires are acceptable in Thy sight. O my God and Lord, deliver me[5] from all evil and be pleased to lead me to that place where all good things are to be found. What can be looked for on earth by those to whom Thou hast given[6] some knowledge of what the world is and those who have a living faith[7] in what the

---

[1] V., T. have "of all things", though the reference is probably to prayers. E.: "of all things and arguments."

[2] Philippians iv, 13.

[3] T.: "I beseech His Majesty."

[4] T.: "I do not believe I can." The addition, deleted and then rewritten, is in St. Teresa's hand.

[5] E. begins the paragraph here, with: "O my Lord, deliver me, etc."

[6] E.: "by those of us who have."

[7] E.: "have some faith."

Eternal Father has laid up for them *because His Son asks it of Him and teaches us to ask Him for it too?*[1]

When contemplatives ask for this with fervent desire and full determination it is a *very* clear sign that *their contemplation is genuine and that* the favours which they receive in prayer are from God.[2] Let those who have these favours,[3] then, prize them highly. But if I myself make this request it is not for that reason (I mean, it must not be taken as being for that reason); it is because I am wearied by so many trials and because my life has been so wicked that I am afraid of living any longer. It is not surprising if those who share in the favours of God should wish to pass to a life where they no longer enjoy mere sips at them: *being already partakers in some knowledge of His greatness, they would fain see it in its entirety.* They have no desire to remain where[4] there are so many hindrances to the enjoyment of so many blessings; nor that they should desire to be where the Sun of justice never sets. Henceforward all the things they see on earth seem dim to them and I wonder that they can live *for even an hour.* No one[5] can be content to do so who has begun to enjoy such things, and has been given the Kingdom of God on earth, and must live to do, not his own will, but the will of the King.

Oh, far other must be that life in which we no longer desire death! How differently shall we then incline our wills towards the will of God![6] His will is for us to desire[7] truth, whereas we desire falsehood; His will is for us to desire the eternal, whereas we prefer that which passes away; His will is for us to desire great and sublime things, whereas we desire the base things of earth; He would have us desire only what is certain, whereas here on earth we love what is doubtful.[8] What a mockery it all is, my daughters, unless we beseech God to deliver us from these perils for ever and to keep us from all evil![9] And although

---

[1] E. begins the next paragraph with the words: "Believe that it is not good for us to live unless we desire to be free of all evil." These words, however, are crossed out in the MS. and do not appear in V.

[2] E. substitutes an impersonal subject for "contemplatives" and ends the sentence "and that it is God Who draws the soul to Himself." It then continues: "Being already partakers, etc." T. continues: "(their aim) being not to flee from trials, but only to enjoy Him. Let those to whom Our Lord gives (these favours), then, etc."

[3] *Lit.*: "Let those who are so."

[4] V. reads: "mere sips at them, and where."

[5] E. begins: "They cannot be content to do so," and continues: "A fine world is this to please one who has begun to enjoy God, and has been given, etc."

[6] E.: "How differently will the will of God incline towards our own!"

[7] Throughout this sentence E. has "His will desires" and not "His will is for us to desire".

[8] The words which follow, "What a mockery . . . our will", are lightly crossed out by St. Teresa in V. They do not appear in T., but were included by Luis de León in his edition.

[9] E.: "to deliver us for ever from all evil."

our desire for this may not be perfect, let us strive to make the petition. What does it cost us to ask it, since we ask it of One Who is so powerful? *It would be insulting a great emperor to ask him for a farthing.* Since we have already given Him our will, let us leave the giving to His will, so that we may be the more surely heard; and may His name be for ever hallowed in the Heavens and on the earth and may His will be ever done in me. Amen.

You see now, friends, what is meant by perfection in vocal prayer, in which we consider and know to Whom the prayer is being made, Who is making it and what is its object. When you are told that it is not good for you to practise any but vocal prayer, do not be discouraged, but read this with great care and beg God to explain to you anything about prayer which you cannot understand. For no one can deprive you of vocal prayer or make you say the Paternoster hurriedly, without understanding it. If anyone tries to do so, or advises you to give up your prayer, take no notice of him. You may be sure he is a false prophet; and in these days, remember, you must not believe everyone, for, though you may be told now that you have nothing to fear, you do not know what is in store for you. I had intended, as well as saying this, to talk to you a little about how you should say the Ave Maria, but I have written at such length that that will have to be left over. If you have learned how to say the Paternoster well, you will know enough to enable you to say all the other vocal prayers you may have to recite.

Now let us go back and finish the journey which I have been describing, for the Lord seems to have been saving me labour[1] by teaching both you and me the Way which I began to outline to you and by showing me how much we ask for when we repeat this evangelical prayer.[2] May He be for ever blessed, for it had certainly never entered my mind that there were such great secrets in it. You have now seen that it comprises the whole spiritual road,[3] right from the beginning, until God absorbs the soul and gives it to drink abundantly of the fountain of living water which I told you was at the end of the road.[4] It seems, sisters, that the Lord's will has been to teach us what great consolation is comprised in it, and this is a great advantage to those who cannot read. If they understood this prayer, they could derive a great deal of sound instruction from it and would find it a real comfort.[5] *Our books may be taken from us, but this is a book which no*

---

[1] Thus E. V. begins the paragraph: "See, now, sisters, what labour the Lord has saved me."
[2] E.: "both you and me what we have to ask for in this prayer."
[3] E.: "that there was such a great secret in this evangelical prayer that it comprises the whole spiritual road."
[4] E. reads: "water of which we spoke," and continues, parenthetically: "And so, having finished this prayer, I cannot go any farther."
[5] V. continues: "Let us learn, then, sisters, from the humility with which it is taught us by this our good Master. Beseech Him to forgive me, etc."

one can take away, and it comes from the lips of the Truth Himself, Who cannot err.

As we repeat the Paternoster so many times daily, then, as I have said, let us delight in it and strive to learn from so excellent a Master the humility with which He prays, and all the other things that have been described. May His Majesty forgive me for having dared to speak of such high matters. Well does His Majesty know that *I should not have ventured to do so, and that* my understanding would not have been capable of it, had He not taught me what I have said.[1] Give thanks to Him for this, sisters, for He must have done it because of the humility with which you asked me to write it for you in your desire to be instructed by one so unworthy.[2]

Well, sisters, Our Lord seems not to want me to write any more, for, although I had intended to go on, I can think of nothing to say. The Lord has shown you the road and has taught me what I wrote in the book which, as I say, I have already written.[3] *This tells you how to conduct yourselves on reaching this fount of living water and what the soul experiences when there, and how God satiates it and takes away its thirst for earthly things, and makes it grow in things pertaining to God's service. This will be very helpful to those who have reached the fount, and will give them a great deal of light.*

Before you see this book I shall give it to my confessor, Father Presentado Domingo Báñez[4] *of the Order of Saint Dominic.* If he thinks you will benefit by it, and gives it you to read, and if you find it of any comfort, I, too, shall be comforted. *If he gives you this book, he will give you the other*[5] *as well.* Should it be found unsuitable for anyone to read, you must take[6] the will for the deed, as I have obeyed your command by writing it.[7] I consider myself well repaid for my labour in writing, though it has certainly been no labour to me to think about what I have been going to say, *as the Lord has taught me the secrets of this evangelical prayer, which has been a great comfort to me.* Blessed and praised be the Lord, from Whom comes all the good that we speak and think and do. Amen.[8]

[1] E.: "had He not put it before me."
[2] This sentence is not found in E.
[3] The *Life.*
[4] P. Báñez deletes his own name in V. T. has "Master" for "Presentado" and adds "of the Order of Saint Dominic."
[5] The *Life*. I do not know what reason St. Teresa had to suppose this, but the Spanish of E. ("también os dará el otro") is quite definite. The sentence does not appear in either V. or T. Cf. the last paragraph of the Prologue (p. 2, above).
[6] E. begins the sentence: "If he does not, take."
[7] *Lit.*: "you will take my will, as I have obeyed your command with the work" [i.e. in deed]. T. has: "with the happiness [? blessing] of my confessor" for "with the work."
[8] E.: "Blessed and praised be He for ever. Amen. Jesus."

INTERIOR CASTLE
(THE MANSIONS)[1]

INTRODUCTION

Towards the end of her life, probably near the end of the year 1579, St. Teresa was travelling with three of her nuns from Medina del Campo, across the bleak Castilian plateau, on her way to St. Joseph's, Ávila. Accidentally (or, as it would be more accurate to say, providentially) she fell in with an old friend, a Hieronymite, Fray Diego de Yepes. Their meeting took place at an inn in the town of Arévalo, where he had arrived some time previously, and, as was fitting, he had been given the most comfortable room. When the little party of nuns, half frozen but still cheerful, reached the inn, there was mutual delight at the encounter; and Fray Diego not only gave up his room to them but appointed himself their personal servant for the period of their stay. They spent, so he tells us, "a very great part of the night" in conversation about their Divine Master. On the next day it was snowing so hard that no one could leave. So Fray Diego said Mass for the four nuns and gave them Communion, after which they spent the day "as recollectedly as if they had been in their own convent". In the evening, however, St. Teresa had a long conversation with her former confessor, who later was to become her biographer, and in the course of this she recounted to him the story of how she came to write the *Interior Castle*. The report of this narrative may suitably be given in the words of Fray Diego himself, taken from a letter which he wrote to Fray Luis de León about nine years later.[2]

"This holy Mother," he writes, "had been desirous of obtaining some insight into the beauty of a soul in grace. Just at that time she was commanded to write a treatise on prayer, about which she knew a great deal from experience. On the eve of the festival of the Most Holy Trinity she was thinking what subject she should choose for this treatise, when God, Who disposes all things in due form and order, granted this desire of hers, and

---

[1] [As has been said above, it is as *Las Moradas* ("The Mansions") that this book is known in Spain.]
[2] The letter [printed, in Spanish, by P. Silverio, II, 490–505] is dated September 4, 1588. The anecdote is told more briefly in Yepes' biography of St. Teresa, Bk. II, Chap. XX.

gave her a subject. He showed her a most beautiful crystal globe, made in the shape of a castle, and containing seven mansions, in the seventh and innermost of which was the King of Glory, in the greatest splendour, illumining and beautifying them all. The nearer one got to the centre, the stronger was the light; outside the palace limits everything was foul, dark and infested with toads, vipers and other venomous creatures.

"While she was wondering at this beauty, which by God's grace can dwell in the human soul, the light suddenly vanished. Although the King of Glory did not leave the mansions, the crystal globe was plunged into darkness, became as black as coal and emitted an insufferable odour, and the venomous creatures outside the palace boundaries were permitted to enter the castle.

"This was a vision which the holy Mother wished that everyone might see, for it seemed to her that no mortal seeing the beauty and splendour of grace, which sin destroys and changes into such hideousness and misery, could possibly have the temerity to offend God. It was about this vision that she told me on that day, and she spoke so freely both of this and of other things that she realized herself that she had done so and on the next morning remarked to me: 'How I forgot myself last night! I cannot think how it happened. These desires and this love of mine made me lose all sense of proportion. Please God they may have done me some good!' I promised her not to repeat what she had said to anyone during her lifetime."

Some days before she was granted this marvellous vision, St. Teresa had had a very intimate conversation on spiritual matters with P. Jerónimo Gracián; the upshot of this was that she undertook to write another book in which she would expound afresh the teaching on perfection to be found in her *Life*, at that time in the hands of the Inquisitors.[1] This we learn from a manuscript note, in Gracián's hand, to the sixth chapter of the fourth book of Ribera's biography of St. Teresa:

> What happened with regard to the *Book of the Mansions* is this. Once, when I was her superior, I was talking to her about spiritual matters at Toledo, and she said to me: "Oh, how well that point is put in the book of my life, which is at the Inquisition!" "Well," I said to her, "as we cannot get at that, why not recall what you can of it, and of other things, and write a fresh book and expound the teaching in a general way, without saying to whom the things that you describe have happened." It was in this way that I told her to write

[1] Cf. Vol. I, p. 7, above.

this *Book of the Mansions*, telling her (so as to persuade her the better) to discuss the matter with Dr. Velázquez, who used sometimes to hear her confessions; and he told her to do so too.[1]

Although she did as she was instructed, however, P. Gracián tells us that she made various objections, all of them dictated by her humility. "Why do they want me to write things?" she would ask. "Let learned men, who have studied, do the writing; I am a stupid creature and don't know what I am saying. There are more than enough books written on prayer already. For the love of God, let me get on with my spinning and go to choir and do my religious duties like the other sisters. I am not meant for writing; I have neither the health nor the wits for it."[2]

Such was the origin of the *Interior Castle*, one of the most celebrated books on mystical theology in existence. It is the most carefully planned and arranged of all that St. Teresa wrote. The mystical figure of the Mansions gives it a certain unity which some of her other books lack. The lines of the fortress of the soul are clearly traced and the distribution of its several parts is admirable in proportion and harmony. Where the book sometimes fails to maintain its precision of method, and falls into that "sweet disorder" which in St. Teresa's other works makes such an appeal to us, is in the secondary themes which it treats—in the furnishing of the Mansions, as we might say, rather than in their construction. A scholastic writer, or, for that matter, anyone with a scientific mind, would have carried the logical arrangement of the general plan into every chapter. Such a procedure, however, would have left no outlet for St. Teresa's natural spontaneity: it is difficult, indeed, to say how far experiential mysticism can ever lend itself to inflexible scientific rule without endangering its own spirit. Since God is free to establish an ineffable communion with the questing soul, the soul must be free to set down its experiences as they occur to it.

In its language and style, the *Interior Castle* is more correct, and yet at the same time more natural and flexible, than the *Way of perfection*. Its conception, like that of so many works of genius, is extremely simple. After a brief preface, the author comes at once to her subject:

I began to think of the soul as if it were a castle made of a single diamond or of very clear crystal, in which there are many rooms, just as in Heaven there are many mansions.

[1] Cf. *Relations*, VI (Vol. I, p. 334, above).
[2] *Dilucidario del verdadero espíritu*, Chap. V.

These mansions are not "arranged in a row one behind another" but variously—"some above, others below, others at each side; and in the centre and midst of them all is the chiefest mansion, where the most secret things pass between God and the soul."

The figure is used to describe the whole course of the mystical life—the soul's progress from the First Mansions to the Seventh and its transformation from an imperfect and sinful creature into the Bride of the Spiritual Marriage. The door by which it first enters the castle is prayer and meditation. Once inside, "it must be allowed to roam through these mansions" and "not be compelled to remain for a long time in one single room". But it must also cultivate self-knowledge and "begin by entering the room where humility is acquired rather than by flying off to the other rooms. For that is the way to progress".

How St. Teresa applies the figure of the castle to the life of prayer (which is also the life of virtue—with her these two things go together) may best be shown by describing each of the seven stages in turn.[1]

FIRST MANSIONS. This chapter begins with a meditation on the excellence and dignity of the human soul, made as it is in the image and likeness of God: the author laments that more pains are not taken to perfect it. The souls in the First Mansions are in a state of grace, but are still very much in love with the venomous creatures outside the castle—that is, with occasions of sin—and need a long and searching discipline before they can make any progress. So they stay for a long time in the Mansions of Humility, in which, since the heat and light from within reach them only in a faint and diffused form, all is cold and dim.

SECOND MANSIONS. But all the time the soul is anxious to penetrate farther into the castle, so it seeks every opportunity of advancement—sermons, edifying conversations, good company and so on. It is doing its utmost to put its desires into practice: these are the Mansions of the Practice of Prayer. It is not yet completely secure from the attacks of the poisonous reptiles which infest the courtyard of the castle, but its powers of resistance are increasing. There is more warmth and light here than in the First Mansions.

THIRD MANSIONS. The description of these Mansions of Exemplary Life begins with stern exhortations on the dangers of trusting to one's own strength and to the virtues one has already acquired, which must still of necessity be very weak. Yet, although the soul which reaches the Third Mansions may still

[1] [A fuller exposition, in English, will be found in *S.S.M.*, I, 162-91.]

INTRODUCTION

fall back, it has attained a high standard of virtue. Controlled by discipline and penance and disposed to performing acts of charity toward others, it has acquired prudence and discretion and orders its life well. Its limitations are those of vision: it has not yet experienced to the full the inspiring force of love. It has not made a full self-oblation, a total self-surrender. Its love is still governed by reason, and so its progress is slow. It suffers from aridity, and is given only occasional glimpses into the Mansions beyond.

FOURTH MANSIONS. Here the supernatural element of the mystical life first enters: that is to say, it is no longer by its own efforts that the soul is acquiring what it gains. Henceforward the soul's part will become increasingly less and God's part increasingly greater. The graces of the Fourth Mansions, referred to as "spiritual consolations", are identified with the Prayer of Quiet, or the Second Water, in the *Life*. The soul is like a fountain built near its source and the water of life flows into it, not through an aqueduct, but directly from the spring. Its love is now free from servile fear: it has broken all the bonds which previously hindered its progress; it shrinks from no trials and attaches no importance to anything to do with the world. It can pass rapidly from ordinary to infused prayer and back again. It has not yet, however, received the highest gifts of the Spirit and relapses are still possible.

FIFTH MANSIONS. This is the state described elsewhere as the Third Water, the Spiritual Betrothal, and the Prayer of Union—that is, incipient Union. It marks a new degree of infused contemplation and a very high one. By means of the most celebrated of all her metaphors, that of the silkworm, St. Teresa explains how far the soul can prepare itself to receive what is essentially a gift from God. She also describes the psychological conditions of this state, in which, for the first time, the faculties of the soul are "asleep". It is of short duration, but, while it lasts, the soul is completely possessed by God.

SIXTH MANSIONS. In the Fifth Mansions the soul is, as it were, betrothed to its future Spouse; in the Sixth, Lover and Beloved see each other for long periods at a time, and as they grow in intimacy the soul receives increasing favours, together with increasing afflictions. The afflictions which give the description of these Mansions its characteristic colour are dealt with in some detail. They may be purely exterior—bodily sickness; misrepresentation, backbiting and persecution; undeserved praise; inexperienced, timid or over-scrupulous spiritual direction. Or they may come partly or wholly from within—and the depression which can afflict the soul in the Sixth Mansions, says St. Teresa, is comparable only with the tortures of hell. Yet it has no desire to be freed from them except by entering the innermost Mansions of all.

SEVENTH MANSIONS. Here at last the soul reaches the Spiritual Marriage. Here dwells the King—"it may be called another Heaven": the two lighted candles join and become one; the falling rain becomes merged in the river. There is complete transformation, ineffable and perfect peace; no higher state is conceivable, save that of the Beatific Vision in the life to come.

While each of these seven Mansions is described with the greatest possible clarity, St. Teresa makes it quite plain that she does not regard her description as excluding others. Each of the series of *moradas* (the use of the plural throughout, especially in the title of each chapter, is noteworthy) may contain as many as a million rooms; all matters connected with spiritual progress are susceptible of numerous interpretations, for the grace of God knows no limit or measure. Her description is based largely on her own experience; and, though this has been found to correspond very nearly with that of most other great mystics, there are various divergences on points of detail. She never for a moment intended her path to be followed undeviatingly and step by step, and of this she is careful frequently to remind us.

At the end of this last, most mystical and most mature of her books, St. Teresa invites all her daughters to enter the Interior Castle, drawing a picturesque contrast between the material poverty of the convents of the Reform and the spiritual luxuriance and beauty of the Mansions—where, as she delightfully puts it, they can go as often as they please without needing to ask the permission of their superiors. There is no doubt whatever that she considered mystical experience to be within the reach of all her daughters: we find this conviction enunciated in the nineteenth chapter of the *Way of perfection* and repeated so frequently in the *Interior Castle* that it is needless to give references. She does not, of course, mean that every one of her nuns who prepares herself as far as she can to receive mystical favours does in fact receive them: she could not presume to pronounce upon the secret judgments of God. But she evidently believes that, generally speaking, infused contemplation is accessible to any Christian who has the resolution to do all that in him lies towards obtaining it.

It must not be forgotten that, notwithstanding the mystical character of the greater part of the *Interior Castle*, it is also a treasury of unforgettable maxims on such ascetic themes as self-

INTRODUCTION

knowledge, humility, detachment and suffering. The finest of these maxims alone would fill a book, and it would be as invidious as self-indulgent to quote any of them here. Yet many have supposed the Interior Castle to be concerned solely with raptures, ecstasies and visions, with Illumination and Union; or to be a work created by the imagination, instead of the record of a life. There is no life more real than the interior life of the soul; there is no writer who has a firmer hold on reality than St. Teresa.

Sublime as is the *Interior Castle*, it would be difficult for any conscientious student who practised what it taught to lose his way in it. St. Teresa did not write it in any sense as a spiritual autobiography or an account of the wonders which God's Spirit had wrought in her soul—still less as a literary work, a storehouse of spiritual maxims or a treatise on psychology. She intended it for the instruction of her own daughters and of all other souls who, either in her own day or later, might have the ambition to penetrate either the outer or the inner Mansions. At all times in the history of Christian perfection there has been a dearth of persons qualified to guide souls to the highest states of prayer: the *Interior Castle* will both serve as an aid to those there are and to a great extent supply the need for more.

The autograph of the *Interior Castle* is to be found in the convent of the Discalced Carmelite nuns of Seville. When the book was first written its author's intention was to divide it only into seven main sections, or "Mansions", and not to make any sub-division of these into chapters. But by the time the manuscript was completed she had changed her mind, and, utilizing her margins, she was able to subdivide each of the seven parts of the book as she thought best. The titles of these sub-divisions she wrote on a separate sheet and they have unfortunately been lost. During her own lifetime, however, the nuns of her Toledo convent made a copy of the book, including these titles, which are so Teresan in style that their authenticity cannot for a moment be doubted.[1]

From the note already referred to written by Gracián in Ribera's biography of St. Teresa we learn that the *Interior Castle*, on its completion, was submitted to the closest scrutiny by himself and a Dominican theologian, P. Yanguas, in the presence of the author. The picture which he draws of these sessions is a memorable one.

---

[1] The titles are here given in the form in which they appear in the *editio princeps*, which is practically identical with that of the Toledo copy.

I would take up numerous phrases in the book, saying that they did not sound well to me, and Fray Diego would reply, while she (St. Teresa) would tell us to expunge them. And we did expunge a few, not because there was any erroneous teaching in them, but because many would find them too advanced and too difficult to understand; for such was the zeal of my affection for her that I tried to make certain that there should be nothing in her writings which could cause anyone to stumble.

These meetings took place in the parlour of the Discalced Carmelite convent at Segovia during June and July 1580. It is regrettable that Gracián should not have described them in greater detail, for, as she knew both her critics well enough to be quite frank with them, and as her command of mystical theology was stronger than theirs on the experiential side and weaker only on the theoretical, many of her comments must have been well worthy of preservation.

Few corrections, in actual fact, were made in the autograph and none of them has any great doctrinal significance. It is a striking thing that, at a time when such care had perforce to be taken by writers on mystical theology, when false mystics of all kinds were springing up continually and when the Inquisition was therefore maintaining a greatly increased vigilance, so important and so ambitious a work as this should need modifying only here and there, merely to avoid the risk of misinterpretation by the ill-informed or the hypercritical.

A few of the corrections, together with some erasures and marginal additions, are in the hand of St. Teresa herself; the remainder, including a few which have been incorrectly attributed to P. Yanguas, were made by P. Gracián. It would seem that Gracián, besides being the critic at these Segovian sessions, was also the committee's secretary: that is to say, when the three had come to an agreement about some alteration that had to be made, it was he who would actually make it.

Some years later, the work of this committee was examined by another critic, who took objection to many of the corrections, including all those made by Gracián, and restored the original readings, adding to the first page of St. Teresa's manuscript a short note which will be found on the corresponding page of this edition.[1] Both early and recent editors, without exception, have believed this critic to have been Fray Luis de León: its style and content could not be more like that of St. Teresa's first editor as we have it, for example, in the famous letter to the

[1] See p. 199, n. 1, below.

INTRODUCTION

Carmelite nuns of Madrid which he prefixed to his edition, but the handwriting is certainly not that of Fray Luis. The note and the additions are in fact the work of St. Teresa's biographer P. Francisco de Ribera, whose concern for the fidelity with which her writings should be reproduced we learn from the letter which he wrote to M. María de Cristo, Vicaress of the Carmelite nuns at Valladolid. As we have already said, Ribera had himself projected a collected edition of St. Teresa's works, for which purpose he borrowed the autographs of the *Way of perfection* and the *Interior Castle*. There would therefore be no improbability in the assumption of his having made these corrections; and a comparison of them with manuscripts known to be his at the University of Salamanca, the Royal Academy of History and elsewhere seems to put the matter beyond doubt.

St. Teresa began the *Interior Castle*, as she herself tells us, on Trinity Sunday (June 2), 1577. She was then in Toledo, where she had been staying for nearly a year, but in July she left for St. Joseph's, Ávila, and it was there that she completed the book on November 29 of the same year. When we remember the difficult times through which the Reform was passing, the preoccupations of a practical kind with which the Mother Foundress was continually being assailed, and the large amount of time taken up by other activities, and by the daily observance of her Rule, we may well marvel at the serenity of mind which in so short a period could produce a work of this length, containing some of the very finest pages she ever wrote.

During the space of less than six months which elapsed between the beginning of the book and its completion took place that change of Nuncios which was so disastrous for the Reform, the transference of St. Joseph's, Ávila, from the jurisdiction of the Ordinary to that of the Order and that stormy scene at the Incarnation when the nuns endeavoured vainly to elect St. Teresa as their Prioress. So it is not surprising that, as we learn from the fourth chapter of the Fifth Mansions, "almost five months"[1] out of the six had gone by before she reached that chapter. As a Toledo nun copied the book while the Saint wrote it, and had reached the second chapter of the Fifth Mansions before she left for Ávila, she would seem to have worked hard at the book for the month or six weeks which she spent at Toledo after beginning it and then to have done nothing further until late in October. This means that the time actually spent in writing was not six months, but less than three.

---

[1] Cf. p.264, below. Some critics write as if there were an *interruption* of five months during the composition of the book, but that is not what the passage says. Were it so, it would mean that the book was written in about four weeks.

There is ample evidence as to the intensity with which St. Teresa worked at the *Interior Castle*. It will suffice to quote one witness. "At the time when our holy Mother was writing the book of the *Mansions* at Toledo," deposed M. María del Nacimiento, "I often saw her as she wrote, which was generally after Communion. She was very radiant and wrote with great rapidity, and as a rule she was so absorbed in her work that even if we made a noise she would never stop, or so much as say that we were disturbing her."[1] The same nun, according to M. Mariana de los Ángeles, once saw St. Teresa caught in a rapture while she was writing the book and is reported as asserting that she wrote a portion of it while in this condition.[2] This, however, is second-hand evidence, though it tends to confirm the direct evidence. Not that even this can always be trusted. Ana de la Encarnación, for example, declares that she saw St. Teresa writing the *Interior Castle* at Segovia, which is next to impossible, for we know a great deal about the Saint's movements during these years and there is no record of her having been at Segovia in 1577.

When the book was written, St. Teresa entrusted it to the keeping of P. Gracián, who in his turn gave it for a time to M. María de San José, Prioress of the Sevilian convent and a close friend of the writer. In November 1581, we find her authorizing M. María to read the chapters on the Seventh Mansions, under the seal of confession, to a former confessor of her own, P. Rodrigo Álvarez. "Read him the last Mansion," the letter runs, "and tell him that that person (i.e., herself) has reached that point and has the peace which goes with it".[3] As we shall see, P. Álvarez left a note on the manuscript attesting that the chapters in question had been duly read to him and declaring that they were entirely orthodox and in conformity with the teaching of the Saints.

Eventually P. Gracián took back the manuscript, and, except for short periods when it was lent to V. Ana de Jesús for the preparation of Luis de León's edition, and, as already related, to P. Ribera, he retained it for long after St. Teresa's death, presenting it finally to a Sevilian gentleman who had been a great benefactor of the Reform, Don Pedro Cerezo Pardo. When, in 1617, this gentleman's daughter Catalina took the habit in the Sevilian convent of the Reform, she brought the highly-prized manuscript as part of her dowry. Thus by a strange concatenation of events the autograph returned to the Sevilian house, where it has remained ever since.

[1] [Cit. P. Silverio, IV, xxxvi.]
[2] *Op. cit.*, IV, xxxvii.
[3] *Op. cit.*, IV, xxxviii.

A few words may be added on the copies and editions of the *Interior Castle*. The Toledo copy seems to be the oldest. It bears the date 1577—which may refer to the year of the book's composition but is generally supposed to indicate the year in which the copy was made. The copyists were four nuns, one of whom, as has been said, went as far as the second chapter of the Fifth Mansions, the remainder of the work being shared by the other three. The title given to the book by St. Teresa is placed at the end of the fourth chapter and the copy ends with the table of chapters and the summary of the contents of each chapter of which the original is now lost. It is noteworthy that the first amanuensis made no chapter-divisions, presumably because at that time the autograph had none. Some of St. Teresa's additions are not included and none of the corrections and glosses made by P. Gracián—again, it must be supposed, because they were not then in the autographs. All these facts point to the conclusion that this copy was made as St. Teresa wrote, and that, when she left Toledo for Ávila, taking the unfinished autograph with her, she left behind her an unfinished copy which was completed only at a later date. As the corrections in Gracián's hand were made in 1580 (p. 194, above), this date may be taken as falling between 1578 and 1580. Some critics believe that among the corrections in this copy are a number made by St. Teresa herself. [P. Silverio, however, does not share their opinion.]

An interesting copy, which belongs to the Discalced nuns of Córdoba, is that which was made by P. Gracián before he disposed of the autograph. The work is beautifully done in red and black ink and nowhere is Gracián's exquisite hand seen to better advantage: indeed, the calligraphy rivals that of any professional monastic copyist of the Middle Ages. The prologue and the epilogue are omitted, the former possibly because of its allusive reference to Gracián himself. The titles given to the chapters by St. Teresa are included. The copy makes a good many alterations, mainly verbal, in the text, due probably to the repeated requests of St. Teresa that, if it should ever be decided to print her writings, he would polish and revise them.

The copy now in the University of Salamanca was made in 1588 by P. Ribera and a Brother Antonio Arias at the College of the Society of Jesus in that city. The date suggests that the autograph was passed on to him after Luis de León had finished with it. Of the numerous other copies to be found in Carmelite houses the most noteworthy are two which were made from the autograph by a Discalced Carmelite, P. Tomás de Aquino, in the eighteenth century. One of these, used by La Fuente for his edition of 1861, in the "Biblioteca de Autores Españoles", contains a critical study from which the editor quotes.

Two editions—one early and one comparatively recent—merit remark.

The earliest of all the editions, Luis de León's (1588), rejects Gracián's emendations and respects only those in the handwriting of St. Teresa. It makes, however, a great many changes of its own, mainly of a verbal kind, though such an omission as the reference in Mansions V, iv to St. Ignatius of Loyola and the Society of Jesus is a striking exception to this rule. The majority of Luis de León's modifications have not been adopted in this edition; a few are referred to in the notes. Until La Fuente went to P. Tomás de Aquino's copy, the text of 1588 was followed by later editors with but few modifications.

In commemoration of the third centenary of St. Teresa's death, the Cardinal-Archbishop of Seville, a Carmelite of the Observance, Fray Joaquín Lluch, published a photo-lithographic edition of the autograph which did a good deal to restore the respect due to it. [P. Silverio's edition, however, is based on the autograph itself, which he was able to study at Seville, so that past neglect of it is now fully atoned for.]

INTERIOR CASTLE[1]
JHS.

Few tasks which I have been commanded to undertake by obedience have been so difficult as this present one of writing about matters relating to prayer: for one reason, because I do not feel that the Lord has given me either the spirituality or the desire for it; for another, because for the last three months I have been suffering from such noises and weakness in the head that I find it troublesome to write even about necessary business. But, as I know that strength arising from obedience has a way of simplifying things which seem impossible, my will very gladly resolves to attempt this task although the prospect seems to cause my physical nature great distress; for the Lord has not given me strength enough to enable me to wrestle continually both with sickness and with occupations of many kinds without feeling a great physical strain. May He Who has helped me by doing other and more difficult things for me help also in this: in His mercy I put my trust.

I really think I have little to say that I have not already said in other books which I have been commanded to write; indeed, I am afraid that I shall do little but repeat myself, for I write as mechanically[2] as birds taught to speak, which, knowing nothing but what is taught them and what they hear, repeat the same things again and again. If the Lord wishes me to say anything new, His Majesty will teach it me or be pleased to recall to my memory what I have said on former occasions; and I should be quite satisfied with this, for my memory is so bad that I should be delighted if I could manage to write down a few of the things which people have considered well said, so that they should not be lost. If the Lord should not grant me as much as this, I shall still be the better for having tried, even if this writing under

---

[1] As a kind of sub-title St. Teresa wrote on the back of the first page of the autograph: "This treatise, called 'Interior Castle', was written by Teresa of Jesus, nun of Our Lady of Carmel, to her sisters and daughters the Discalced Carmelite nuns." Below this is a note by P. Ribera (formerly attributed to Fray Luis de León) which asserts [somewhat verbosely, for which reason the full text is not here translated] that the marginal emendations in the autograph are often inconsistent with other parts of the text and in any case are inferior to the author's own words, and begs readers to respect "the words and letters written by that most holy hand". [It is noteworthy that the word "mansions" (*moradas*: cf. p. 201, n. 2, below), by which the book is generally known in Spain, does not appear in the title or sub-title of the autograph, though it occurs in the title of each of the seven sections of the book.]

[2] *Lit.*: "literally."

obedience tires me and makes my head worse, and if no one finds what I say of any profit.

And so I begin to fulfil my obligation on this Day of the Holy Trinity, in the year MDLXXVII,[1] in this convent of St. Joseph of Carmel in Toledo, where I am at this present, submitting myself as regards all that I say to the judgment of those who have commanded me to write, and who are persons of great learning. If I should say anything that is not in conformity with what is held by the Holy Roman Catholic Church,[2] it will be through ignorance and not through malice. This may be taken as certain, and also that, through God's goodness, I am, and shall always be, as I always have been, subject to her. May He be for ever blessed and glorified. Amen.

I was told by the person who commanded me to write that, as the nuns of these convents of Our Lady of Carmel need someone to solve their difficulties concerning prayer, and as (or so it seemed to him) women best understand each other's language, and also in view of their love for me, anything I might say would be particularly useful to them. For this reason he thought that it would be rather important if I could explain things clearly to them and for this reason it is they whom I shall be addressing in what I write—and also because it seems ridiculous to think that I can be of any use to anyone else. Our Lord will be granting me a great favour if a single one of these nuns should find that my words help her to praise Him ever so little better. His Majesty well knows that I have no hope of doing more, and, if I am successful in anything that I may say, they will of course understand that it does not come from me. Their only excuse for crediting me with it could be their having as little understanding as I have ability in these matters if the Lord of His mercy does not grant it me.

[1] June 2, 1577.
[2] The words "Roman Catholic" are inserted by the author interlineally.

FIRST MANSIONS

In which there are Two Chapters.

CHAPTER I

Treats of the beauty and dignity of our souls; makes a comparison by the help of which this may be understood; describes the benefit which comes from understanding it and being aware of the favours which we receive from God; and shows how the door of this castle is prayer.

While I was beseeching Our Lord to-day that He would speak through me, since I could find nothing to say and had no idea how to begin to carry out the obligation laid upon me by obedience, a thought occurred to me which I will now set down, in order to have some foundation on which to build. I began to think of the soul as if it were a castle made of a single diamond or of very clear crystal, in which there are many rooms,[1] just as in Heaven there are many mansions.[2] Now if we think carefully over this, sisters, the soul of the righteous man is nothing but a paradise, in which, as God tells us, He takes His delight.[3] For what do you think a room will be like which is the delight of a King so mighty, so wise, so pure and so full of all that is good? I can find nothing with which to compare the great beauty of a soul and its great capacity. In fact, however acute our intellects may be, they will no more be able to attain to a comprehension of this than to an understanding of God; for, as He Himself says, He created us in His image and likeness.[4] Now if this is so—and it is—there is no point in our fatiguing ourselves by attempting to comprehend the beauty of this castle; for, though it is His creature, and there is therefore as much difference between it and God as between creature and Creator, the very fact that His Majesty says it is made in His image means that we can hardly form any conception of the soul's great dignity and beauty.[5]

It is no small pity, and should cause us no little shame, that, through our own fault, we do not understand ourselves, or know who we are. Would it not be a sign of great ignorance, my daugh-

---

[1] [*Aposentos*—a rather more pretentious word than the English "room": dwelling-place, abode, apartment.]
[2] [*Moradas*: derived from *morar*, to dwell, and not, therefore, absolutely identical in sense with "mansions". The reference, however, is to St. John xiv, 2.]
[3] Proverbs viii, 31.
[4] Genesis i, 26.
[5] Here the Saint erased several words and inserted others, leaving the phrase as it is in the text.

ters, if a person were asked who he was, and could not say, and had no idea who his father or his mother was, or from what country he came? Though that is great stupidity, our own is incomparably greater if we make no attempt to discover what we are, and only know that we are living in these bodies, and have a vague idea, because we have heard it and because our Faith tells us so, that we possess souls. As to what good qualities there may be in our souls, or Who dwells within them, or how precious they are—those are things which we seldom consider and so we trouble little about carefully preserving the soul's beauty. All our interest is centred in the rough setting of the diamond, and in the outer wall of the castle—that is to say, in these bodies of ours.

Let us now imagine that this castle, as I have said, contains many mansions,[1] some above, others below, others at each side; and in the centre and midst of them all is the chiefest mansion where the most secret things pass between God and the soul. You must think over this comparison very carefully; perhaps God will be pleased to use it to show you something of the favours which He is pleased to grant to souls, and of the differences between them, so far as I have understood this to be possible, for there are so many of them that nobody can possibly understand them all, much less anyone as stupid as I. If the Lord grants you these favours, it will be a great consolation to you to know that such things are possible; and, if you never receive any, you can still praise His great goodness. For, as it does us no harm to think of the things laid up for us in Heaven, and of the joys of the blessed, but rather makes us rejoice and strive to attain those joys ourselves, just so it will do us no harm to find that it is possible in this our exile for so great a God to commune with such malodorous worms, and to love Him for His great goodness and boundless mercy. I am sure that anyone who finds it harmful to realize that it is possible for God to grant such favours during this our exile must be greatly lacking in humility and in love of his neighbour; for otherwise how could we help rejoicing that God should grant these favours to one of our brethren when this in no way hinders Him from granting them to ourselves, and that His Majesty should bestow an understanding of His greatness upon anyone soever? Sometimes He will do this only to manifest His power, as He said of the blind man to whom He gave his sight, when the Apostles asked Him if he were suffering for his own sins or for the sins of his parents.[2] He grants these favours, then, not because those who receive them are holier than those

---

[1] [*Moradas* (see p. 201, n. 2, above).]
[2] St. John ix, 2.

who do not, but in order that His greatness may be made known, as we see in the case of Saint Paul and the Magdalen, and in order that we may praise Him in His creatures.

It may be said that these things seem impossible and that it is better not to scandalize the weak. But less harm is done by their disbelieving us than by our failing to edify those to whom God grants these favours, and who will rejoice and will awaken others to a fresh love of Him Who grants such mercies, according to the greatness of His power and majesty. In any case I know that none to whom I am speaking will run into this danger, because they all know and believe that God grants still greater proofs of His love. I am sure that, if any one of you does not believe this, she will never learn it by experience. For God's will is that no bounds should be set to His works. Never do such a thing, then, sisters, if the Lord does not lead you by this road.

Now let us return to our beautiful and delightful castle and see how we can enter it. I seem rather to be talking nonsense; for, if this castle is the soul, there can clearly be no question of our entering it. For we ourselves are the castle: and it would be absurd to tell someone to enter a room when he was in it already! But you must understand that there are many ways of "being" in a place. Many souls remain in the outer court of the castle, which is the place occupied by the guards; they are not interested in entering it, and have no idea what there is in that wonderful place, or who dwells in it, or even how many rooms it has. You will have read certain books on prayer which advise the soul to enter within itself: and that is exactly what this means.

A short time ago I was told by a very learned man that souls without prayer are like people whose bodies or limbs are paralysed: they possess feet and hands but they cannot control them. In the same way, there are souls so infirm and so accustomed to busying themselves with outside affairs that nothing can be done for them, and it seems as though they are incapable of entering within themselves at all. So accustomed have they grown to living all the time with the reptiles and other creatures to be found in the outer court of the castle that they have almost become like them; and although by nature they are so richly endowed as to have the power of holding converse with none other than God Himself, there is nothing that can be done for them. Unless they strive to realize their miserable condition and to remedy it, they will be turned into pillars of salt for not looking within themselves, just as Lot's wife was because she looked back.[1]

As far as I can understand, the door of entry into this castle is prayer and meditation: I do not say mental prayer rather

[1] Genesis xix, 26.

than vocal, for, if it is prayer at all, it must be accompanied by meditation. If a person does not think Whom he is addressing, and what he is asking for, and who it is that is asking and of Whom he is asking it, I do not consider that he is praying at all even though he be constantly moving his lips. True, it is sometimes possible to pray without paying heed to these things, but that is only because they have been thought about previously; if a man is in the habit of speaking to God's Majesty as he would speak to his slave, and never wonders if he is expressing himself properly, but merely utters the words that come to his lips because he has learned them by heart through constant repetition, I do not call that prayer at all—and God grant no Christian may ever speak to Him so! At any rate, sisters, I hope in God that none of you will, for we are accustomed here to talk about interior matters. and that is a good way of keeping oneself from falling into such animal-like habits.[1]

Let us say no more, then, of these paralysed souls, who, unless the Lord Himself comes and commands them to rise, are like the man who had lain beside the pool for thirty years:[2] they are unfortunate creatures and live in great peril. Let us rather think of certain other souls, who do eventually enter the castle. These are very much absorbed in worldly affairs; but their desires are good; sometimes, though infrequently, they commend themselves to Our Lord; and they think about the state of their souls, though not very carefully. Full of a thousand preoccupations as they are, they pray only a few times a month, and as a rule they are thinking all the time of their preoccupations, for they are very much attached to them, and, where their treasure is, there is their heart also.[3] From time to time, however, they shake their minds free of them and it is a great thing that they should know themselves well enough to realize that they are not going the right way to reach the castle door. Eventually they enter the first rooms on the lowest floor, but so many reptiles get in with them that they are unable to appreciate the beauty of the castle or to find any peace within it. Still, they have done a good deal by entering at all.

You will think this is beside the point, daughters, since by the goodness of the Lord you are not one of these. But you must be patient, for there is no other way in which I can explain to you

---

[1] [*Lit.*, "into such bestiality".] P. Gracián deletes "bestiality" and substitutes "abomination." [I think the translation in the text, however, is a more successful way of expressing what was in St. Teresa's mind: cf. St. John of the Cross's observations on "animal penances"—*penitencias de bestias*—in his *Dark Night*, I, vi (*Complete Works*, I, 365–6).]

[2] P. Gracián corrects this to "thirty-eight years." St. John v, 5.

[3] St. Matthew vi, 21.

some ideas I have had about certain interior matters concerning prayer. May it please the Lord to enable me to say something about them; for to explain to you what I should like is very difficult unless you have had personal experience; and anyone with such experience, as you will see, cannot help touching upon subjects which, please God, shall, by His mercy, never concern us.

CHAPTER II

Describes the hideousness of a soul in mortal sin, some part of which God was pleased to manifest to a certain person. Says something also of self-knowledge. This chapter is profitable, since it contains some noteworthy matters. Explains in what sense the Mansions are to be understood.

Before passing on, I want you to consider what will be the state of this castle, so beautiful and resplendent, this Orient pearl, this tree of life, planted in the living waters of life[1]—namely, in God—when the soul falls into a mortal sin. No thicker darkness exists, and there is nothing dark and black which is not much less so than this. You need know only one thing about it—that, although the Sun Himself, Who has given it all its splendour and beauty, is still there in the centre of the soul, it is as if He were not there for any participation which the soul has in Him, though it is as capable of enjoying Him as is the crystal of reflecting the sun. While in a state like this the soul will find profit in nothing; and hence, being as it is in mortal sin, none of the good works it may do will be of any avail[2] to win it glory; for they will not have their origin in that First Principle, which is God, through Whom alone our virtue is true virtue. And, since this soul has separated itself from Him, it cannot be pleasing in His eyes; for, after all, the intention of a person who commits a mortal sin is not to please Him but to give pleasure to the devil; and, as the devil is darkness itself, the poor soul becomes darkness itself likewise.

I know of a person[3] to whom Our Lord wished to show what a soul was like when it committed mortal sin. That person says that, if people could understand this, she thinks they would find it impossible to sin at all, and, rather than meet occasions of sin, would put themselves to the greatest trouble imaginable. So she was very anxious that everyone should realize this. May

---

[1] Psalm i, 3.
[2] *Lit.*: "fruit", for which P. Gracián substitues "merit".
[3] St. Teresa herself. See Relation XXIV (Vol. I, p. 345, above).

you be no less anxious, daughters, to pray earnestly to God for those who are in this state and who, with all their works, have become sheer darkness. For, just as all the streamlets that flow from a clear spring are as clear as the spring itself, so the works of a soul in grace are pleasing in the eyes both of God and of men, since they proceed from this spring of life, in which the soul is as a tree planted. It would give no shade and yield no fruit if it proceeded not thence, for the spring sustains it and prevents it from drying up and causes it to produce good fruit. When the soul, on the other hand, through its own fault, leaves this spring and becomes rooted in a pool of pitch-black, evil-smelling water, it produces nothing but misery and filth.

It should be noted here that it is not the spring, or the brilliant sun which is in the centre of the soul, that loses its splendour and beauty, for they are always within it and nothing can take away their beauty. If a thick black cloth be placed over a crystal in the sunshine, however, it is clear that, although the sun may be shining upon it, its brightness will have no effect upon the crystal.

O souls redeemed by the blood of Jesus Christ! Learn to understand yourselves and take pity on yourselves! Surely, if you understand your own natures, it is impossible that you will not strive to remove the pitch which blackens the crystal? Remember, if your life were to end now, you would never enjoy this light again. O Jesus! How sad it is to see a soul deprived of it! What a state the poor rooms of the castle are in! How distracted are the senses which inhabit them! And the faculties, which are their governors and butlers and stewards—how blind they are and how ill-controlled! And yet, after all, what kind of fruit can one expect to be borne by a tree rooted in the devil?

I once heard a spiritual man say that he was not so much astonished at the things done by a soul in mortal sin as at the things not done by it. May God, in His mercy, deliver us from such great evil, for there is nothing in the whole of our lives that so thoroughly deserves to be called evil as this, since it brings endless and eternal evils in its train. It is of this, daughters, that we should walk in fear, and this from which in our prayers we must beg God to deliver us; for, if He keep not the city, we shall labour in vain,[1] since we are vanity itself. That person to whom I referred just now said that the favour which God had granted her had taught her two things: first, she had learned to have the greatest fear of offending Him, for which reason she continually begged Him not to allow her to fall, when she saw what terrible consequences a fall could bring; secondly, she had found it a

[1] Psalm cxxvi, 2 [AV., cxxvii, 1].

mirror of humility, for it had made her realize that any good thing we do has its source, not in ourselves but rather in that spring where this tree, which is the soul, is planted, and in that sun which sheds its radiance on our works. She says that she saw this so clearly that, whenever she did any good thing, or saw such a thing done, she betook herself straightway to its Source, realizing that without His help we are powerless. She then went on at once to praise God; and, as a rule, when she did any good action, she never gave a thought to herself at all.

If we can remember these two things, sisters, the time you have spent in reading all this, and the time I have spent in writing it, will not have been lost. Wise and learned men know them quite well, but we women are slow and need instruction in everything. So perhaps it may be the Lord's will that these comparisons shall be brought to our notice. May He be pleased of His goodness to give us grace to understand them.

These interior matters are so obscure to the mind that anyone with as little learning as I will be sure to have to say many superfluous and even irrelevant things in order to say a single one that is to the point. The reader must have patience with me, as I have with myself when writing about things of which I know nothing; for really I sometimes take up my paper, like a perfect fool, with no idea of what to say or of how to begin. I fully realize how important it is for you that I should explain certain interior matters to the best of my ability; for we continually hear what a good thing prayer is, and our Constitutions oblige us to engage in it for so many hours daily, yet they tell us nothing beyond what we ourselves have to do and say very little about the work done by the Lord in the soul—I mean, supernatural work. As I describe the things He does, and give various explanations of them, it will be very helpful for us to think of this celestial building which is within us and is so little understood by mortals, although many of them frequent it. And although the Lord has thrown some light upon many matters of which I have written, I do not think I have understood some of them, especially the most difficult, as well as I do now. The trouble, as I have said, is that, before I can get to them, I shall have to explain many things that are well known—it is bound to be so when a person is as stupid as I.

Let us now turn to our castle with its many mansions. You must not imagine these mansions as arranged in a row, one behind another, but fix your attention on the centre, the room or palace occupied by the King. Think of a palmito,[1] which has many

---

[1] The palmito is a shrub, common in the south and east of Spain, with thick layers of leaves enclosing a succulent edible kernel.

outer rinds surrounding the savoury part within, all of which must be taken away before the centre can be eaten. Just so around this central room are many more, as there also are above it. In speaking of the soul we must always think of it as spacious, ample and lofty; and this can be done without the least exaggeration, for the soul's capacity is much greater than we can realize, and this Sun, Which is in the palace, reaches every part of it. It is very important that no soul which practises prayer, whether little or much, should be subjected to undue constraint or limitation. Since God has given it such dignity, it must be allowed to roam through these mansions—through those above, those below and those on either side. It must not be compelled to remain for a long time in one single room—not, at least, unless it is in the room of self-knowledge.[1] How necessary that is (and be sure you understand me here) even to those whom the Lord keeps in the same mansion in which He Himself is! However high a state the soul may have attained, self-knowledge is incumbent upon it, and this it will never be able to neglect even should it so desire. Humility must always be doing its work like a bee making its honey in the hive: without humility all will be lost. Still, we should remember that the bee is constantly flying about from flower to flower, and in the same way, believe me, the soul must sometimes emerge from self-knowledge and soar aloft in meditation upon the greatness and the majesty of its God. Doing this will help it to realize its own baseness better than thinking of its own nature, and it will be freer from the reptiles which enter the first rooms—that is, the rooms of self-knowledge. For although, as I say, it is through the abundant mercy of God that the soul studies to know itself, yet one can have too much of a good thing, as the saying goes,[2] and believe me, we shall reach much greater heights of virtue by thinking upon the virtue of God than if we stay in our own little plot of ground and tie ourselves down to it completely.

I do not know if I have explained this clearly: self-knowledge is so important that, even if you were raised right up to the heavens, I should like you never to relax your cultivation of it; so long as we are on this earth, nothing matters more to us than humility. And so I repeat that it is a very good thing—excellent, indeed—to begin by entering the room where humility is acquired rather than by flying off to the other rooms. For that

[1] [The autograph has, after the word "room", "Oh, but if it is (*Uh, que si es*) in (the room of) self-knowledge!" Previous editors have altered this difficult Spanish phrase to *aunque sea*, "not even if it is." St. Teresa's meaning, however, seems to me quite clearly the opposite of this, though it is impossible to translate her exclamation literally.]

[2] [*Lit.*: "excess is as bad as defect."]

is the way to make progress, and, if we have a safe, level road to walk along, why should we desire wings to fly? Let us rather try to get the greatest possible profit out of walking. As I see it, we shall never succeed in knowing ourselves unless we seek to know God: let us think of His greatness and then come back to our own baseness; by looking at His purity we shall see our foulness; by meditating upon His humility, we shall see how far we are from being humble.

There are two advantages in this. First, it is clear that anything white looks very much whiter against something black, just as the black looks blacker against the white. Secondly, if we turn from self towards God, our understanding and our will become nobler and readier to embrace all that is good: if we never rise above the slough of our own miseries we do ourselves a great disservice. We were saying just now how black and noisome are the streams that flow from souls in mortal sin. Similarly, although this is not the same thing—God forbid! It is only a comparison—so long as we are buried in the wretchedness of our earthly nature these streams of ours will never disengage themselves from the slough of cowardice, pusillanimity and fear. We shall always be glancing round and saying: "Are people looking at me or not?" "If I take a certain path shall I come to any harm?" "Dare I begin such and such a task?" "Is it pride that is impelling me to do so?" "Can anyone as wretched as I engage in so lofty an exercise as prayer?" "Will people think better of me if I refrain from following the crowd?" "For extremes are not good," they say, "even in virtue; and I am such a sinner that if I were to fail I should only have farther to fall; perhaps I shall make no progress and in that case I shall only be doing good people harm; anyway, a person like myself has no need to make herself singular."

Oh, God help me, daughters, how many souls the devil must have ruined in this way! They think that all these misgivings, and many more that I could describe, arise from humility, whereas they really come from our lack of self-knowledge. We get a distorted idea of our own nature, and, if we never stop thinking about ourselves, I am not surprised if we experience these fears and others which are still worse. It is for this reason, daughters, that I say we must set our eyes upon Christ our Good, from Whom we shall learn true humility, and also upon His saints. Our understanding, as I have said, will then be ennobled, and self-knowledge will not make us timorous[1] and fearful; for, although this is only the first Mansion, it contains riches of great price, and any who can elude the reptiles which are to be found

---

[1] [*Ratero*: creeping, flying low, content with a low standard.]

in it will not fail to go farther. Terrible are the crafts and wiles which the devil uses to prevent souls from learning to know themselves and understanding his ways.

With regard to these first Mansions I can give some very useful information out of my own experience. I must tell you, for example, to think of them as comprising not just a few rooms, but a very large number.[1] There are many ways in which souls enter them, always with good intentions; but as the devil's intentions are always very bad, he has many legions of evil spirits in each room to prevent souls from passing from one to another, and as we, poor souls, fail to realize this, we are tricked by all kinds of deceptions. The devil is less successful with those who are nearer the King's dwelling-place; but at this early stage, as the soul is still absorbed in worldly affairs, engulfed in worldly pleasure and puffed up with worldly honours and ambitions, its vassals, which are the senses and the faculties given to it by God as part of its nature, have not the same power, and such a soul is easily vanquished, although it may desire not to offend God and may perform good works. Those who find themselves in this state need to take every opportunity of repairing to His Majesty, and to make His blessed Mother their intercessor, and also His saints, so that these may do battle for them, since their own servants have little strength for defending themselves. In reality it is necessary in every state of life for our help to come from God. May His Majesty grant us this through His mercy. Amen.

How miserable is this life which we live! As I have said a great deal elsewhere, daughters, about the harm which comes to us through our not properly understanding this matter of humility and self-knowledge, I am not saying more to you here, though it is a matter of the greatest importance to us. May the Lord grant that something I have said will be of use to you.

You must note that the light which comes from the palace occupied by the King hardly reaches these first Mansions at all; for, although they are not dark and black, as when the soul is in a state of sin, they are to some extent darkened, so that they cannot be seen (I mean by anyone who is in them); and this not because of anything that is wrong with the room, but rather (I hardly know how to explain myself) because there are so many bad things—snakes and vipers and poisonous creatures—which have come in with the soul that they prevent it from seeing the light. It is as if one were to enter a place flooded by sunlight with his eyes so full of dust[2] that he could hardly open them. The room itself is light enough, but he cannot enjoy the light

---

[1] *Lit.*: "a million."   [2] *Lit.*: "and had earth on his eyes."

because he is prevented from doing so by these wild beasts and animals, which force him to close his eyes to everything but themselves. This seems to me to be the condition of a soul which, though not in a bad state, is so completely absorbed in things of the world and so deeply immersed, as I have said, in possessions or honours or business, that, although as a matter of fact it would like to gaze at the castle and enjoy its beauty, it is prevented from doing so, and seems quite unable to free itself from all these impediments. Everyone, however, who wishes to enter the second Mansions, will be well advised, as far as his state of life permits, to try to put aside all unnecessary affairs and business. For those who hope to reach the principal Mansion, this is so important that unless they begin in this way I do not believe they will ever be able to get there. Nor, indeed, even though it has entered the castle, is the soul free from great peril in the Mansion which it actually inhabits; for, being among such poisonous things, it cannot, at some time or another, escape being bitten by them.

What would happen, then, daughters, if those who, like ourselves, are free from these obstacles, and have already entered much farther into other secret mansions of the castle, should, through their own fault, go out again into this hurly-burly? Our sins must have led many people whom God has granted favours to relapse through their faults into this wretched state. We here, so far as outward things are concerned, are free; may it please the Lord to make us free as regards inward things as well and to deliver us from evil. Beware, my daughters, of cares which have nothing to do with you. Remember that in few of the mansions of this castle are we free from struggles with devils. It is true that in some of them, the wardens, who, as I think I said, are the faculties, have strength for the fight; but it is most important that we should not cease to be watchful against the devil's wiles, lest he deceive us in the guise of an angel of light. For there are a multitude of ways in which he can deceive us, and gradually make his way into the castle, and until he is actually there we do not realize it.

As I told you before, he works like a noiseless file, and we must be on the look-out for him from the beginning. In order to explain this better I want to give you several illustrations. He inspires a sister with yearnings to do penance, so that she seems to have no peace save when she is torturing herself. This, in itself, is good; but, if the prioress has ordered that no penance is to be done without leave, and yet the sister thinks that she can venture to persist in so beneficial a practice, and secretly orders her life in such a way that in the end she ruins her health and is unable to do what her Rule demands, you see what this apparently good thing has led to. Another sister is inspired with zeal for the greatest possible perfection. This, again, is a very good thing; but the result of it might be that she would think any little fault on the part of the sisters a serious failure, and would always be looking out for such things and running to the prioress about them; sometimes she might even be so zealous about religious observances as to be unable to see her own faults; and this the others, observing only her zeal about their misdeeds and not understanding the excellence of her intentions, might well take none too kindly.

The devil's aim here must not be made light of, for he is trying to bring about a cooling of charity and love among the sisters, and if he could do this he would be working a great deal of harm. Let us realize, my daughters, that true perfection consists in the love of God and of our neighbour, and the more nearly perfect is our observance of these two commandments, the nearer to perfection we shall be. Our entire Rule and Constitutions are nothing but means which enable us to do this the more perfectly. Let us refrain from indiscreet zeal, which may do us great harm: let each one of you look to herself. As I have said a great deal to you about this elsewhere[1] I will not enlarge on it further.

This mutual love is so important for us that I should like you never to forget it; for if the soul goes about looking for trifling faults in others (which sometimes may not be imperfections at all, though perhaps our ignorance may lead us to make the worst of them) it may lose its own peace of mind and perhaps disturb that of others. See, then, how dearly perfection can be bought. The devil might also use this temptation in the case of a prioress, and then it would be more dangerous still. Much discretion is necessary here; for, if it were a question of her contravening the Rule and Constitutions, it would not always do to take a lenient view of the matter—she would have to be spoken to about it; and, if she did not then amend, the prelate would have to be told: to do this would be a charity. This would also apply to the sisters, where the fault was a grave one: to say nothing through fear that taking the matter up would be yielding to temptation would itself be to yield to temptation. However, to prevent deception by the devil, it should be strongly stressed that no sister must discuss such things with any other, for from this practice the devil can pluck great advantage and start habits of slander; these matters must be discussed, as I have said, only with the person whose concern they are. Here, glory be to God, we keep almost continuous silence, so that the opportunity does not arise; none the less, it is well that we should be on our guard.

[1] See *Life*, Chapter XIII and *Method for the visitation of convents*.

SECOND MANSIONS

In which there is One Chapter only.[1]

Treats of the great importance of perseverance if we are to reach the final Mansions and of the fierce war which the devil wages against us. Tells how essential it is, if we are to attain our goal, not to miss our way at the beginning. Gives a method which has proved very efficacious.

Let us now come to consider who the souls are that enter the second Mansions and what they do there. I want to say very little to you about this, because elsewhere I have written of it at length,[2] and it will be impossible for me to avoid repeating a great deal of this, because I cannot remember anything of what I said. If it could be arranged[3] in a different form, I am quite sure you would not mind, as we are never tired of books that treat of this, numerous though they are.

This chapter has to do with those who have already begun to practise prayer and who realize the importance of not remaining in the first Mansions, but who often are not yet resolute enough to leave those Mansions, and will not avoid occasions of sin, which is a very perilous condition. But it is a very great mercy that they should contrive to escape from the snakes and other poisonous creatures, if only for short periods, and should realize that it is good to flee from them. In some ways, these souls have a much harder time than those in the first Mansions; but they are in less peril, for they seem now to understand their position and there is great hope that they will get farther into the castle still. I say they have a harder time because the souls in the first Mansions are, as it were, not only dumb, but can hear nothing, and so it is not such a trial to them to be unable to speak; the others, who can hear and not speak, would find the trial much harder to bear. But that is no reason for envying those who do not hear, for after all it is a great thing to be able to understand what is said to one.

These souls, then, can understand the Lord when He calls them; for, as they gradually get nearer to the place where His Majesty dwells, He becomes a very good Neighbour to them. And such are His mercy and goodness that, even when we are

---

[1] Below this line St. Teresa wrote "Chapter," to which Luis de León prefixed the word "Only."
[2] *Life*, Chaps. XI—XIII; *Way of perfection*, Chaps. XX—XXIX.
[3] [The word (*guisar*: "season", "dress") is a homely one: "dished up" would hardly be too colloquial a translation.]

engaged in our worldly pastimes and businesses and pleasures and hagglings, when we are falling into sins and rising from them again (because these creatures are at once so venomous and so active and it is so dangerous for us to be among them that it will be a miracle if we escape stumbling over them and falling)—in spite of all that, this Lord of ours is so anxious that we should desire Him and strive after His companionship that He calls us ceaselessly, time after time, to approach Him; and this voice of His is so sweet that the poor soul is consumed with grief at being unable to do His bidding immediately; and thus, as I say, it suffers more than if it could not hear Him.

I do not mean by this that He speaks to us and calls us in the precise way which I shall describe later; His appeals come through the conversations of good people, or from sermons, or through the reading of good books; and there are many other ways, of which you have heard, in which God calls us. Or they come through sicknesses and trials, or by means of truths which God teaches us at times when we are engaged in prayer; however feeble such prayers may be, God values them highly. You must not despise this first favour, sisters, nor be disconsolate, even though you have not responded immediately to the Lord's call; for His Majesty is quite prepared to wait for many days, and even years, especially when He sees we are persevering and have good desires. This is the most necessary thing here; if we have this we cannot fail to gain greatly. Nevertheless, the assault which the devils now make upon the soul, in all kinds of ways, is terrible; and the soul suffers more than in the preceding Mansions; for there it was deaf and dumb, or at least it could hear very little, and so it offered less resistance, like one who to a great extent has lost hope of gaining the victory. Here the understanding is keener and the faculties are more alert, while the clash of arms and the noise of cannon are so loud that the soul cannot help hearing them. For here the devils once more show the soul these vipers—that is, the things of the world—and they pretend that earthly pleasures are almost eternal: they remind the soul of the esteem in which it is held in the world, of its friends and relatives, of the way in which its health will be endangered by penances (which the soul always wants to do when it first enters this Mansion) and of impediments of a thousand other kinds.

Oh, Jesus! What confusion the devils bring about in the poor soul, and how distressed it is, not knowing if it ought to proceed farther or return to the room where it was before! On the other hand, reason tells the soul how mistaken it is in thinking that all these earthly things are of the slightest value by comparison with what it is seeking; faith instructs it in what it must do to find satisfaction; memory shows it how all these things come to an end, and reminds it that those who have derived so much enjoyment from the things which it has seen have died. Sometimes they have died suddenly and been quickly forgotten by all: people whom we once knew to be very prosperous are now beneath the ground, and we trample upon their graves, and often, as we pass them, we reflect that their bodies are seething with worms—of these and many other things the soul is reminded by memory. The will inclines to love One in Whom it has seen so many acts and signs of love, some of which it would like to return. In particular, the will shows the soul how this true Lover never leaves it, but goes with it everywhere and gives it life and being. Then the understanding comes forward and makes the soul realize that, for however many years it may live, it can never hope to have a better friend, for the world is full of falsehood and these pleasures which the devil pictures to it are accompanied by trials and cares and annoyances; and tells it to be certain that outside this castle it will find neither security nor peace: let it refrain from visiting one house after another when its own house is full of good things, if it will only enjoy them. How fortunate it is to be able to find all that it needs, as it were, at home, especially when it has a Host Who will put all good things into its possession, unless, like the Prodigal Son, it desires to go astray and eat the food of the swine![1]

It is reflections of this kind which vanquish devils. But, oh, my God and Lord, how everything is ruined by the vain habits we fall into and the way everyone else follows them! So dead is our faith that we desire what we see more than what faith tells us about—though what we actually see is that people who pursue these visible things meet with nothing but ill fortune. All this is the work of these poisonous creatures which we have been describing. For, if a man is bitten by a viper, his whole body is poisoned and swells up; and so it is in this case, and yet we take no care of ourselves. Obviously a great deal of attention will be necessary if we are to be cured and only the great mercy of God will preserve us from death. The soul will certainly suffer great trials at this time, especially if the devil sees that its character and habits are such that it is ready to make further progress: all the powers of hell will combine to drive it back again.

Ah, my Lord! It is here that we have need of Thine aid, without which we can do nothing. Of Thy mercy, allow not this soul to be deluded and led astray when its journey is but begun. Give it light so that it may see how all its welfare consists in this and may flee from evil companionship. It is a very great thing for a person to associate with others who are walking

[1][St. Luke xv, 15–16].

in the right way: to mix, not only with those whom he sees in the rooms where he himself is, but with those whom he knows to have entered the rooms nearer the centre, for they will be of great help to him and he can get into such close touch with them that they will take him with them. Let him have a fixed determination not to allow himself to be beaten, for, if the devil sees that he has firmly resolved to lose his life and his peace and everything that he can offer him rather than to return to the first room, he will very soon cease troubling him. Let him play the man and not be like those who went down on their knees in order to drink when they went to battle—I forget with whom[1]—but let him be resolute, for he is going forth to fight with all the devils and there are no better weapons than the Cross.

There is one thing so important that, although I have said it on other occasions,[2] I will repeat it once more here: it is that at the beginning one must not think of such things as spiritual favours, for that is a very poor way of starting to build such a large and beautiful edifice. If it is begun upon sand, it will all collapse:[3] souls which build like that will never be free from annoyances and temptations. For it is not in these Mansions, but in those which are farther on, that it rains manna; once there, the soul has all that it desires, because it desires only what is the will of God. It is a curious thing: here we are, meeting with hindrances and suffering from imperfections by the thousand, with our virtues so young that they have not yet learned how to walk—in fact, they have only just been born: God grant that they have even been born at all!—and yet we are not ashamed to be wanting consolations in prayer and to be complaining about periods of aridity. This must not be true of you, sisters: embrace the Cross which your Spouse bore upon His shoulders and realize that this Cross is yours to carry too: let her who is capable of the greatest suffering suffer most for Him and she will have the most perfect freedom. All other things are of quite secondary importance: if the Lord should grant them to you, give Him heartfelt thanks.

You may think that you will be full of determination to resist outward trials if God will only grant you inward favours. His Majesty knows best what is suitable for us; it is not for us to advise Him what to give us, for He can rightly reply that we know not what we ask.[4] All that the beginner in prayer has to do—and you must not forget this, for it is very important—is to labour and be resolute and prepare himself with all possible diligence

---

[1] Judges vii, 5. "With Gedeon in the Judges," adds P. Gracián in the margin, crossing out the words "I forget with whom".
[2] *Life*, Chap. XI.
[3] [Probably a conscious reference to St. Matthew vii, 26-7.]
[4] St. Matthew xx, 22.

to bring his will into conformity with the will of God. As I shall say later, you may be quite sure that this comprises the very greatest perfection which can be attained on the spiritual road. The more perfectly a person practises it, the more he will receive of the Lord and the greater the progress he will make on this road; do not think we have to use strange jargon or dabble in things of which we have no knowledge or understanding; our entire welfare is to be found in what I have described. If we go astray at the very beginning and want the Lord to do our will and to lead us just as our fancy dictates, how can this building possibly have a firm foundation? Let us see that we do as much as in us lies and avoid these venomous reptiles, for often it is the Lord's will that we should be persecuted and afflicted by evil thoughts, which we cannot cast out, and also by aridities; and sometimes He even allows these reptiles to bite us, so that we may learn better how to be on our guard in the future and see if we are really grieved at having offended Him.

If, then, you sometimes fall, do not lose heart, or cease striving to make progress, for even out of your fall God will bring good, just as a man selling an antidote will drink poison before he takes it in order to prove its power. If nothing else could show us what wretched creatures we are and what harm we do to ourselves by dissipating our desires, this war which goes on within us would be sufficient to do so and to lead us back to recollection. Can any evil be greater than the evil which we find in our own house? What hope can we have of being able to rest in other people's homes[1] if we cannot rest in our own? For none of our friends and relatives are as near to us as our faculties, with which we have always to live, whether we like it or not, and yet our faculties seem to be making war upon us, as if they were resentful of the war made upon them by our vices. "Peace, peace," said the Lord, my sisters, and many a time He spoke words of peace to His Apostles.[2] Believe me, unless we have peace, and strive for peace in our own home, we shall not find it in the homes of others. Let this war now cease. By the blood which Christ shed for us, I beg this of those who have not begun to enter within themselves; and those who have begun to do so must not allow such warfare to turn them back. They must realize that to fall a second time is worse than to fall once. They can see that it will lead them to ruin: let them place their trust, not in themselves, but in the mercy of God, and they will see how His Majesty can lead them on from one group of Mansions to another and set

---

[1] The autograph has, not *casas* ("homes") but *cosas* ("things"). Luis de León, however, read *casas* and succeeding editors have followed him.
[2] St. John xx, 21.

them on safe ground where these beasts cannot harass or hurt them, for He will place the beasts in their power and laugh them to scorn; and then they themselves—even in this life, I mean—will enjoy many more good things than they could ever desire.

As I said first of all, I have already written to you about how you ought to behave when you have to suffer these disturbances with which the devil torments you;[1] and about how recollection cannot be begun by making strenuous efforts, but must come gently, after which you will be able to practise it for longer periods at a time. So I will say no more about this now, except that it is very important for you to consult people of experience; for otherwise you will imagine that you are doing yourselves great harm by pursuing your necessary occupations. But, provided we do not abandon our prayer, the Lord will turn everything we do to our profit, even though we may find no one to teach us. There is no remedy for this evil of which we have been speaking except to start again at the beginning; otherwise the soul will keep on losing a little more every day—please God that it may come to realize this.

Some of you might suppose that, if it is such a bad thing to turn back, it would have been better never to have begun, but to have remained outside the castle. I told you, however, at the outset, and the Lord Himself says this, that he who goes into danger shall perish in it,[2] and that the door by which we can enter this castle is prayer. It is absurd to think that we can enter Heaven without first entering our own souls—without getting to know ourselves, and reflecting upon the wretchedness of our nature and what we owe to God, and continually imploring His mercy. The Lord Himself says: "No one will ascend to My Father, but by Me"[3] (I am not sure if those are the exact words, but I think they are)[4] and "He that sees Me sees My Father."[5] Well, if we never look at Him or think of what we owe Him, and of the death which He suffered for our sakes, I do not see how we can get to know Him or do good works in His service. For what can be the value of faith without works, or of works which are not united with the merits of our Lord Jesus Christ? And what but such thoughts can arouse us to love this Lord? May it please His Majesty to grant us to understand how much we cost Him, that the servant is not greater than his Lord,[6] that we must needs work if we would enjoy His glory, and that for that reason we must perforce pray, lest we enter continually into temptation.[7]

---

[1] *Life*, Chaps. XI, XIX.   [2] Ecclesiasticus iii, 27.   [3] St. John xiv, 6.
[4] P. Gracián crossed through the bracketed words and wrote in the margin: "Both are said by St. John, Chapter xiv." [Actually the words are: "No man cometh . . . ."]
[5] St. John xiv, 9.   [6] St. Matthew x, 24.   [7] St. Matthew xxvi, 41.

THIRD MANSIONS

In which there are Two Chapters.

CHAPTER I

Treats of the insecurity from which we cannot escape in this life of exile, however lofty a state we may reach, and of how good it is for us to walk in fear. This chapter contains several good points.

To those who by the mercy of God have overcome in these combats, and by dint of perseverance have entered the third Mansions, what shall we say but "Blessed is the man that feareth the Lord"?[1] As I am so stupid in these matters, it has been no small thing that His Majesty should have enabled me to understand the meaning of this verse in the vernacular. We shall certainly be right in calling such a man blessed, for, unless he turns back, he is, so far as we can tell, on the straight road to salvation. Here, sisters, you will see the importance of having overcome in your past battles; for I am convinced that the Lord never fails to give a person who does this security of conscience, which is no small blessing. I say "security", but that is the wrong word, for there is no security in this life; so, whenever I use it, you must understand the words "unless he strays from the path on which he has set out".

It is really a perfect misery to be alive when we have always to be going about like men with enemies at their gates, who cannot lay aside their arms even when sleeping or eating, and are always afraid of being surprised by a breaching of their fortress in some weak spot. Oh, my Lord and my God! How canst Thou wish us to desire such a miserable life as that? It would be impossible to refrain from wishing and begging Thee to take us from it, were it not for our hope that we may lose it for Thy sake, or spend it wholly in Thy service—and, above all, for the realization that it is Thy will for us. If that is indeed so, my God, let us die with Thee, as Saint Thomas said,[2] for life without Thee is nothing but death many times over and constant dread at the possibility of losing Thee for ever. So I think, daughters, that the happiness we should pray for is to enjoy the complete security of the blessed;[3] for what pleasure can anyone have when beset by

---

[1] Psalm cxi, 1 (A.V. cxii, 1).
[2] St. John xi, 16. The last four words are a marginal addition of the author's.
[3] Gracián adds "in Heaven"; the addition is deleted by Ribera.

these fears if his only pleasure consists in pleasing God? Remember that all this, and much more, could be said of some of the saints, and yet they fell[1] into grave sins, and we cannot be certain that God will give us His hand and help us to renounce them[2] and do penance for them. (This refers to particular help.)[3]

Truly, my daughters, I am so fearful as I write this that, when it comes to my mind, as is very often the case, I hardly know how to get the words down, or how to go on living. Beseech His Majesty, my daughters, always to live within me, for otherwise what security can there be in a life as misspent as mine? And do not let it depress you to realize that I am like that—I have sometimes seen you depressed when I have told you so. The reason it affects you in that way is that you would like to think I had been very holy. That is quite right of you: I should like to think so myself. But what can I do about it when I have lost so much through my own fault? I shall not complain that God ceased giving me all the help I needed if your wishes were to be fulfilled: I cannot say this without tears and great confusion when I realize that I am writing for those who are themselves capable of teaching me. Rigorous has been the task that obedience has laid upon me![4] May it please the Lord that, as it is being done for His sake, you may gain some profit from it and may ask Him to pardon this wretched and foolhardy woman. But His Majesty well knows that I can count only upon His mercy, and, as I cannot help having been what I have, there is nothing for me to do but approach God and trust in the merits of His Son, and of the Virgin, His Mother, whose habit both you and I unworthily wear. Praise Him, my daughters, for you are really the daughters of Our Lady, and when you have as good a Mother as that there is no reason for you to be scandalized at my unworthiness. Imitate Our Lady and consider how great she must be and what a good thing it is that we have her for our Patroness; even my sins and my being what I am have not been sufficient to bring any kind of tarnish upon this sacred Order.

But of one thing I must warn you: although you are in this Order, and have such a Mother, do not be too sure of yourselves; for David was a very holy man, yet you know what Solomon[5]

---

[1] Gracián alters this to: "some who, although they are saints [*a more exact translation would be "are saintly"*], yet fell," but Ribera restores St. Teresa's reading.

[2] Gracián alters this to: "we have no certainty of abandoning them and of doing, etc."

[3] The bracketed words, which St. Teresa wrote in the margin of the autograph, are crossed out with two strokes. But Ribera has written underneath them: "This is not to be deleted."

[4] [A striking example of St. Teresa's untranslatably concise language. The original is: *Recia obediencia ha sido! Lit.*: "Rigorous obedience (it) has been!"]

[5] Gracián altered this word to "Absalom" but Ribera wrote in the margin: "This should read 'Solomon', as the holy Mother said."

became. Nor must you set store by the fact that you are cloistered and lead lives of penitence. Nor must you become confident because you are always talking about God, continually engaging in prayer, withdrawing yourselves completely from the things of this world and (to the best of your belief) abhorring them. All that is good, but, as I have said, it is not enough to justify us in laying aside our fears. So you must repeat this verse and often bear it in mind: *Beatus vir, qui timet Dominum.*[1]

And now I forget what I was saying—I have been indulging in a long digression. Whenever I think of myself I feel like a bird with a broken wing and I can say nothing of any value. So I will leave all this for now and return to what I had begun to explain concerning the souls that have entered the third Mansions. In enabling these souls to overcome their initial difficulties, the Lord has granted them no small favour, but a very great one. I believe that, through His goodness, there are many such souls in the world: they are most desirous not to offend His Majesty; they avoid committing even venial sins;[2] they love doing penance; they spend hours in recollection; they use their time well; they practise works of charity toward their neighbours; and they are very careful in their speech and dress and in the government of their household if they have one. This is certainly a desirable state and there seems no reason why they should be denied entrance to the very last of the Mansions; nor will the Lord deny them this if they desire it, for their disposition is such that He will grant them any favour.

Oh, Jesus! How could anyone ever say that he has no desire for such a wonderful thing, especially when he has got over the most troublesome stages leading to it? Surely no one could do so. We all say we desire it; but if the Lord is to take complete possession of the soul more than that is necessary. Words are not enough, any more than they were for the young man when the Lord told him what to do if he wished to be perfect.[3] Ever since I began to speak of these Mansions I have had that young man in mind, for we are exactly like him; and this as a rule is the origin of our long periods of aridity in prayer, although these have other sources as well. I am saying nothing here of interior trials, which vex many good souls to an intolerable degree, and through no fault of their own, but from which the Lord always rescues them, to their great profit, as He does also those who suffer from melancholy and other infirmities. In all things we must leave out of account the judgments of God.

---

[1] Psalm cxi, 1 (A.V., cxii, 1).
[2] The autograph makes this sentence negative, but partially deletes the negative particle. Luis de León, followed by later editors, omits it.
[3] St. Matthew xix, 16–22.

Personally, I think that what I have said is the most usual thing. These souls know that nothing would induce them to commit a sin—many of them would not intentionally commit even a venial sin—and they make good use of their lives and their possessions. So they cannot be patient when the door is closed to them and they are unable to enter the presence of the King, Whose vassals they consider themselves, and in fact are. Yet even on earth a king may have many vassals and they do not all get so far as to enter his chamber. Enter, then, enter within yourselves, my daughters; and get right away from your own trifling good works, for these you are bound, as Christians, to perform, and, indeed, many more. It will be enough for you that you are vassals of God; do not try to get so much that you achieve nothing. Look at the saints who have entered the King's chamber and you will see the difference between them and ourselves. Do not ask for what you have not deserved. For we have offended God, and, however faithfully we serve Him, it should never enter our heads that we can deserve anything.

Oh, humility, humility! I do not know why I have this temptation, but whenever I hear people making so much of their times of aridity, I cannot help thinking that they are somewhat lacking in it. I am not, of course, referring to the great interior trials of which I have spoken, for they amount to much more than a lack of devotion. Let us test ourselves, my sisters, or allow the Lord to test us; for He knows well how to do it, although often we refuse to understand Him. And now let us return to these carefully-ordered souls and consider what they do for God, and we shall then see how wrong we are to complain of His Majesty. For, if, when He tells us what we must do in order to be perfect, we turn our backs upon Him and go away sorrowfully, like the young man in the Gospel,[1] what do you expect His Majesty to do, for the reward which He is to give us must of necessity be proportionate with the love which we bear Him? And this love, daughters, must not be wrought in our imagination but must be proved by works. Yet do not suppose God has any need of our works; what He needs is the resoluteness of our will.

It may seem to us that we have done everything—we who wear the religious habit, having taken it of our own will and left all the things of the world and all that we had for His sake (for although, like Saint Peter, we may have left only our nets, yet He esteems a person who gives all that he has as one who gives

---

[1] The phrase "like . . . Gospel" was written by St. Teresa in the margin. [No doubt she recalled the reference to St. Matthew xix, 16–22, which she had made just above.]

in fullest measure).[1] This is a very good beginning; and, if we persevere in it, instead of going back, even if only in desire, to consort with the reptiles in the first rooms, there is no doubt that, by persevering in this detachment and abandonment of everything, we shall attain our object. But it must be on this condition —and note that I am warning you of this—that we consider ourselves unprofitable servants, as we are told, either by Saint Paul or by Christ,[2] and realize that we have in no way obliged Our Lord to grant us such favours; but rather that, the more we have received of Him, the more deeply do we remain in His debt. What can we do for so generous a God, Who died for us and created us and gives us being, without counting ourselves fortunate in being able to repay Him something of what we owe Him for the way He has served us[3] (I write this word reluctantly, but it is the truth,[4] for all the time He lived in the world He did nothing but serve) without asking Him once more for gifts and favours?

Consider carefully, daughters, these few things which have been set down here, though they are in rather a jumbled state, for I cannot explain them better; the Lord will make them clear to you, so that these periods of aridity may teach you to be humble, and not make you restless, which is the aim of the devil. Be sure that, where there is true humility, even if God never grants the soul favours, He will give it peace and resignation to His will, with which it may be more content than others are with favours. For often, as you have read, it is to the weakest that His Divine Majesty gives favours, which I believe they would not exchange for all the fortitude given to those who go forward in aridity. We are fonder of spiritual sweetness than of crosses. Test us, O Lord, Thou Who knowest all truth, that we may know ourselves.

CHAPTER II

Continues the same subject and treats of aridities in prayer and of what the author thinks may result from them; and of how we must test ourselves; and of how the Lord proves those who are in these Mansions.

I have known a few souls who have reached this state—I think I might even say a great many—and who, as far as we can see,

---

[1] [Or this clause might mean: "yet a person who gives all that he has thinks that he gives in fullest measure." But the interpretation in the text seems preferable.]
[2] [St. Luke xvii, 10.] Gracián, in a note, gives the correct authorship.
[3] "For what He has suffered for us" was substituted for the phrase by Gracián but the original text was restored by Ribera.
[4] Gracián deleted the words "I write . . . truth" but Ribera wrote in the margin: "Nothing is to be deleted, for what the Saint says is well said."

have for many years lived an upright and carefully ordered life, both in soul and in body; and then, after all these years, when it has seemed as if they must have gained the mastery over the world, or at least must be completely detached from it, His Majesty has sent them tests which have been by no means exacting and they have become so restless and depressed in spirit that they have exasperated me,[1] and have even made me thoroughly afraid for them. It is of no use offering them advice, for they have been practising virtue for so long that they think they are capable of teaching others and have ample justification for feeling as they do.

Well, I cannot find, and have never found, any way of comforting such people, except to express great sorrow at their trouble, which, when I see them so miserable, I really do feel. It is useless to argue with them, for they brood over their woes and make up their minds that they are suffering for God's sake, and thus never really understand that it is all due to their own imperfection. And in persons who have made so much progress this is a further mistake; one cannot be surprised if they suffer, though I think this kind of suffering ought to pass quickly. For often it is God's will that His elect should be conscious of their misery and so He withdraws His help from them a little—and no more than that is needed to make us recognize our limitations very quickly. They then realize that this is a way of testing them, for they gain a clear perception of their shortcomings, and sometimes they derive more pain from finding that, in spite of themselves, they are still grieving about earthly things, and not very important things either, than from the matter which is troubling them. This, I think, is a great mercy on the part of God, and even though they are at fault they gain a great deal in humility.

With those other persons of whom I am speaking it is different: they consider they have acted in a highly virtuous way, as I have said, and they wish others to think so too. I will tell you about some of them so that we may learn to understand and test ourselves before we are tested by the Lord—and it would be a very great advantage if we were prepared and had learned to know ourselves first.

A rich man, who is childless and has no one to leave his money to, loses part of his wealth; but not so much that he has not enough for himself and his household—he still has enough and to spare. If he begins to get restless and worried, as though he had not a crust of bread left to eat, how can Our Lord ask him to leave all for His sake? It may be, of course, that he is suffering

---

[1] [*Lit.*: "drove me silly"—"*me traían tonta*": a typically homely and forcible expression. Cf. p. 233, n. 5, below.]

because he wants to give the money to the poor. But I think God would rather I were resigned to what His Majesty does, and kept my tranquillity of soul, than that I should do such acts of charity as these. If this man cannot resign himself, because the Lord has not led him thus far, well and good; but he ought to realize that he lacks this freedom of spirit and in that case he will pray for it and prepare himself for the Lord to give it to him.

Another person, who has means enough to support himself, and indeed an excess of means, sees an opportunity of acquiring more property. Let him take such an opportunity, certainly, if it comes to him; but if he strives after it, and, on obtaining it, strives after more and more, however good his intention may be (and good it must be, because, as I have said, these are all virtuous people and given to prayer), he need not be afraid that he will ever ascend[1] to the Mansions which are nearest the King.

It is much the same thing if such people are despised in any way or lose some of their reputation. God often grants them grace to bear this well, for He loves to help people to be virtuous in the presence of others, so that the virtue itself which they possess may not be thought less of, or perhaps He will help them because they have served Him, for this our God is good indeed. And yet they become restless, for they cannot do as they would like to and control their feelings all at once. Yet oh, dear me! Are not these the same persons who some time ago were meditating upon how the Lord suffered, and upon what a good thing it is to suffer, and who were even desiring to suffer? They would like every one else to live as well-ordered a life as they do themselves; all we can hope is that they will not begin to imagine that the trouble they have is somebody else's fault and represent it to themselves as meritorious.

You will think, sisters, that I am wandering from the point, and am no longer addressing myself to you, and that these things have nothing to do with us, as we own no property and neither desire it nor strive after it and nobody ever slights us. It is true that these examples are not exactly applicable to us, but many others which are can be deduced from them, though it is unnecessary, and would be unseemly, for me to detail them. From these you will find out if you are really detached from the things you have abandoned, for trifling incidents arise, though not precisely of this kind, which give you the opportunity to test yourselves and discover if you have obtained the mastery over your passions. And believe me, what matters is not whether

---

[1] "Very easily," added Gracián, interlineally, but the addition is crossed out.

or no we wear a religious habit; it is whether we try to practise the virtues, and make a complete surrender of our wills to God and order our lives as His Majesty ordains: let us desire that not our wills, but His will, be done.[1] If we have not progressed as far as this, then, as I have said, let us practise humility, which is the ointment for our wounds; if we are truly humble, God, the Physician,[2] will come in due course, even though He tarry, to heal us.

The penances done by these persons are as carefully ordered as their lives. They have a great desire for penance, so that by means of it they may serve Our Lord—and there is nothing wrong in that—and for this reason they observe great discretion in their penances, lest they should injure their health. You need never fear that they will kill themselves: they are eminently reasonable folk! Their love is not yet ardent enough to overwhelm their reason. How I wish ours would make us dissatisfied with this habit of always serving God at a snail's pace! As long as we do that we shall never get to the end of the road. And as we seem to be walking along and getting fatigued all the time—for, believe me, it is an exhausting road—we shall be very lucky if we escape getting lost. Do you think, daughters, if we could get from one country to another in a week, it would be advisable, with all the winds and snow and floods and bad roads, to take a year over it? Would it not be better to get the journey over and done with? For there are all these obstacles for us to meet and there is also the danger of serpents. Oh, what a lot I could tell you about that! Please God I have got farther than this myself—though I often fear I have not!

When we proceed with all this caution, we find stumbling-blocks everywhere; for we are afraid of everything, and so dare not go farther, as if we could arrive at these Mansions by letting others make the journey for us! That is not possible, my sisters; so, for the love of the Lord, let us make a real effort: let us leave our reason and our fears in His hands and let us forget the weakness of our nature which is apt to cause us so much worry. Let our superiors see to the care of our bodies; that must be their concern: our own task is only to journey with good speed so that we may see the Lord. Although we get few or no comforts here, we shall be making a great mistake if we worry over our health, especially as it will not be improved by our anxiety about it—that I well know. I know, too, that our progress has nothing to do with the body, which is the thing that matters least. What the journey which I am referring to demands is great humility, and it is the lack of this, I think, if you see what I mean, which pre-

---

[1] St. Luke xxii, 42.   [2] [*Lit.*: "the Surgeon".]

vents us from making progress. We may think we have advanced only a few steps, and we should believe that this is so and that our sisters' progress is much more rapid; and further we should not only want them to consider us worse than anyone else, but we should contrive to make them do so.

If we act thus, this state is a most excellent one, but otherwise we shall spend our whole lives in it and suffer a thousand troubles and miseries. Without complete self-renunciation, the state is very arduous and oppressive, because, as we go along, we are labouring under the burden of our miserable nature, which is like a great load of earth and has not to be borne by those who reach the later Mansions. In these present Mansions the Lord does not fail to recompense us with just measure, and even generously, for He always gives us much more than we deserve by granting us a spiritual sweetness much greater than we can obtain from the pleasures and distractions of this life. But I do not think that He gives many consolations, except when He occasionally invites us to see what is happening in the remaining Mansions, so that we may prepare to enter them.

You will think that spiritual sweetness and consolations are one and the same thing: why, then, this difference of name? To me it seems that they differ a very great deal, though I may be wrong. I will tell you what I think about this when I write about the fourth Mansions, which will follow these, because, as I shall then have to say something about the consolations which the Lord gives in those Mansions, it will come more appropriately. The subject will seem an unprofitable one, yet none the less it may be of some use, for, once you understand the nature of each, you can strive to pursue the one which is better. This latter is a great solace to souls whom God has brought so far, while it will make those who think they have everything feel ashamed; and if they are humble they will be moved to give thanks. Should they fail to experience it, they will feel an inward discouragement—quite unnecessarily, however, for perfection consists not in consolations, but in the increase of love; on this, too, will depend our reward, as well as on the righteousness and truth which are in our actions.

If this is true—and it is—you will wonder what is the use of my discussing these interior favours, and explaining what they are. I do not know: you must ask the person who commanded me to write, for I am under an obligation not to dispute with my superiors, but to obey them, and it would not be right for me to dispute with them. What I can tell you truly is that, when I had had none of these favours, and knew nothing of them by experience, and indeed never expected to know about them all my life long (and rightly so, though it would have been the greatest joy for me to know, or even to conjecture, that I was in any way pleasing to God), none the less, when I read in books of these favours and consolations which the Lord grants to souls that serve Him, it would give me the greatest pleasure and lead my soul to offer fervent praises to God. Now if I, who am so worthless a person, did that, surely those who are good and humble will praise Him much more. If it only enables a single person to praise Him once, I think it is a good thing that all this should be said, and that we should realize what pleasure and what delights we lose through our own fault. All the more so because, if they come from God, they come laden with love and fortitude, by the help of which a soul can progress with less labour and grow continually in good works and virtues. Do not suppose that it matters little whether or no we do what we can to obtain them. But if the fault is not yours, the Lord is just, and what His Majesty denies you in this way He will give you in other ways—His Majesty knows how. His secrets are hidden deep; but all that He does will be best for us, without the slightest doubt.

What I think would be of the greatest profit to those of us who, by the goodness of the Lord, are in this state—and, as I have said, He shows them no little mercy in bringing them to it, for, when here, they are on the point of rising still higher—is that they should be most studious to render ready obedience. Even though they be not in a religious Order, it would be a great thing for them to have someone to whom they could go, as many people do, so that they might not be following their own will in anything, for it is in this way that we usually do ourselves harm. They should not look for anyone (as the saying has it) cast in the same mould as themselves[1] who always proceeds with great circumspection; they should select a man who is completely disillusioned with the things of the world. It is a great advantage for us to be able to consult someone who knows us, so that we may learn to know ourselves. And it is a great encouragement to see that things which we thought impossible are possible to others, and how easily these others do them. It makes us feel that we may emulate their flights and venture to fly ourselves, as the young birds do when their parents teach them; they are not yet ready for great flights but they gradually learn to imitate their parents. This is a great advantage, as I know. However determined such persons may be not to offend the Lord, they will do well not to run any risk of offending Him; for they are so near the

[1] [The Spanish phrase means, literally, "anyone of their humour", but there is no such "saying" as this in English.]

first Mansions that they might easily return to them, since their fortitude is not built upon solid ground like that of souls who are already practised in suffering. These last are familiar with the storms of the world, and realize how little need there is to fear them or to desire worldly pleasures. If those of whom I am speaking, however, had to suffer great persecutions, they might well return to such pleasures and the devil well knows how to contrive such persecutions in order to do us harm; they might be pressing onward with great zeal, and trying to preserve others from sin, and yet be unable to resist any temptations which came to them.

Let us look at our own shortcomings and leave other people's alone; for those who live carefully ordered lives are apt to be shocked at everything and we might well learn very important lessons from the persons who shock us. Our outward comportment and behaviour may be better than theirs, but this, though good, is not the most important thing: there is no reason why we should expect everyone else to travel by our own road, and we should not attempt to point them to the spiritual path when perhaps we do not know what it is. Even with these desires that God gives us to help others, sisters, we may make many mistakes, and thus it is better to attempt to do what our Rule tells us—to try to live ever in silence and in hope, and the Lord will take care of His own. If, when we beseech this of His Majesty, we do not become negligent ourselves, we shall be able, with His help, to be of great profit to them. May He be for ever blessed.

FOURTH MANSIONS
In which there are Three Chapters.

CHAPTER I

Treats of the difference between sweetness or tenderness in prayer and consolations, and tells of the happiness which the author gained from learning how different thought is from understanding. This chapter is very profitable for those who suffer greatly from distractions during prayer.

Before I begin to speak of the fourth Mansions, it is most necessary that I should do what I have already done—namely, commend myself to the Holy Spirit, and beg Him from this point onward to speak for me, so that you may understand what I shall say about the Mansions still to be treated. For we now begin to touch the supernatural[1] and this is most difficult to explain unless His Majesty takes it in hand, as He did when I described as much as I understood of the subject, about fourteen years ago.[2] Although I think I have now a little more light upon these favours which the Lord grants to some souls, it is a different thing to know how to explain them. May His Majesty undertake this if there is any advantage to be gained from its being done, but not otherwise.

As these Mansions are now getting near to the place where the King dwells, they are of great beauty and there are such exquisite things to be seen and appreciated in them that the understanding is incapable of describing them in any way accurately without being completely obscure to those devoid of experience. But any experienced person will understand quite well, especially if his experience has been considerable. It seems that, in order to reach these Mansions, one must have lived for a long time in the others; as a rule one must have been in those which we have just described, but there is no infallible rule about it, as you must often have heard, for the Lord gives when He wills and as He wills and to whom He wills, and, as the gifts are His own, this is doing no injustice to anyone.

---

[1] Cf. St. Teresa's definition of supernatural prayer in Relation V (Vol. I, p. 327, above).
[2] From the outline of St. Teresa's life given above (Vol. I, pp. xxvii–xxxvi), it will be seen that this computation is approximately correct. The reference is to *Life*, Chaps. XI–XXVII.

Into these Mansions poisonous creatures seldom enter, and, if they do, they prove quite harmless—in fact they do the soul good. I think in this state of prayer it is much better for them to enter and make war upon the soul, for, if it had no temptations, the devil might mislead it with regard to the consolations which God gives, and do much more harm than he can when it is being tempted. The soul, too, would not gain so much, for it would be deprived of all occasions of merit and be living in a state of permanent absorption. When a soul is continuously in a condition of this kind I do not consider it at all safe, nor do I think it possible for the Spirit of the Lord to remain in a soul continuously in this way during our life of exile.

Returning to what I was saying I would describe here—namely, the difference between sweetness in prayer and spiritual consolations—it seems to me that we may describe as sweetness what we get from our meditations and from petitions made to Our Lord. This proceeds from our own nature, though, of course, God plays a part in the process (and in everything I say you must understand this, for we can do nothing without Him). This spiritual sweetness arises from the actual virtuous work which we perform, and we think we have acquired it by our labours. We are quite right to feel satisfaction[1] at having worked in such a way. But, when we come to think of it, the same satisfaction[2] can be derived from numerous things that may happen to us here on earth. When, for example, a person suddenly acquires some valuable property; or equally suddenly meets a person whom he dearly loves; or brings some important piece of business or some other weighty matter to a successful conclusion, so that everyone speaks well of him; or when a woman has been told that her husband or brother or son is dead and he comes back to her alive. I have seen people shed tears over some great joy[3]; sometimes, in fact, I have done so myself.

It seems to me that the feelings[4] which come to us from Divine things are as purely natural as these, except that their source is nobler, although these worldly joys are in no way bad. To put it briefly, worldly joys have their source in our own nature and end in God, whereas spiritual consolations have their source in God, but we experience them in a natural way and enjoy them as much as we enjoy those I have already mentioned, and

---

[1] [The word is the same as is used above for "sweetness"—i.e., *contentos*, but in the singular. Such word-play, as we have seen, is common in St. Teresa: in the title of this very chapter we have an identical play on *contentos* ("sweetness") and *contento* ("happiness").]
[2] [*contentos*.]
[3] [*contento*.]
[4] [*contentos*.]

indeed much more. Oh, Jesus! How I wish I could make myself clear about this! For I think I can see a very marked difference between these two things and yet I am not clever enough to make my meaning plain: may the Lord explain it for me!

I have just remembered a verse which we say at the end of the last psalm at Prime. The last words of the verse are *Cum dilatasti cor meum*.[1] To anyone who has much experience, this will suffice to explain the difference between the two; though, to anyone who has not, further explanation is necessary. The spiritual sweetness which has been described does not enlarge the heart; as a rule, it seems to oppress it somewhat. The soul experiences a great happiness[2] when it realizes what it is doing for God's sake; but it sheds a few bitter tears which seem in some way to be the result of passion[3]. I know little about these passions of the soul; if I knew more, perhaps I could make the thing clear, and explain what proceeds from sensuality and what from our own nature. But I am very stupid; I could explain this state if only I could understand my own experience of it. Knowledge and learning are a great help in everything.

My own experience of this state—I mean of these favours and this sweetness in meditation—was that, if I began to weep over the Passion, I could not stop until I had a splitting headache; and the same thing happened when I wept for my sins. This was a great grace granted me by Our Lord, and I will not for the moment examine each of these favours and decide which is the better of the two; I wish, however, that I could explain the difference between them. In the state I am now describing, the tears and longings sometimes arise partly from our nature and from the state of preparedness we are in;[4] but nevertheless, as I have said, they eventually lead one to God. And this is an experience to be greatly prized, provided the soul be humble, and can understand that it does not make it any the more virtuous; for it is impossible to be sure that these feelings are effects of love, and, even so, they are a gift of God. Most of the souls which dwell in the Mansions already described are familiar with these feelings of devotion, for they labour with the understanding almost continuously, and make use of it in their meditations. They are right to do this, because nothing more has been given them; they would do well, however, to spend short periods in making various acts, and in praising God and rejoicing in His goodness

---

[1] [Psalm cxviii, 32: "(I have run the way of thy commandments,) when thou didst enlarge my heart". A.V. cxix, 32.]
[2] [*contento.*]
[3] The remainder of this paragraph was scored through in the autograph by Gracián and are omitted from the Córdoba copy. They are, however, quite legible.
[4] [*Lit.*: "from how the disposition is."]

and in His being Who He is, and in desiring His honour and glory. They should do this as well as they can, for it goes a long way towards awakening the will. But, when the Lord gives them this other grace, let them be very careful not to reject it for the sake of finishing their customary meditation.

As I have written about this at great length elsewhere,[1] I will not repeat it here. I only want you to be warned that, if you would progress a long way on this road and ascend to the Mansions of your desire, the important thing is not to think much, but to love much; do, then, whatever most arouses you to love. Perhaps we do not know what love is: it would not surprise me a great deal to learn this, for love consists, not in the extent of our happiness, but in the firmness of our determination to try to please God in everything, and to endeavour, in all possible ways, not to offend Him, and to pray Him ever to advance the honour and glory of His Son and the growth of the Catholic Church. Those are the signs of love; do not imagine that the important thing is never to be thinking of anything else and that if your mind becomes slightly distracted all is lost.

I have sometimes been terribly oppressed by this turmoil of thoughts and it is only just over four years ago that I came to understand by experience that thought (or, to put it more clearly, imagination[2]) is not the same thing as understanding. I asked a learned man about this and he said I was right, which gave me no small satisfaction. For, as the understanding is one of the faculties of the soul, I found it very hard to see why it was sometimes so timid[3]; whereas thoughts, as a rule, fly so fast that only God can restrain them; which He does by uniting us in such a way that we seem in some sense to be loosed from this body.[4] It exasperated me[5] to see the faculties of the soul, as I thought, occupied with God and recollected in Him, and the thought, on the other hand, confused and excited.

O Lord, do Thou remember how much we have to suffer on this road through lack of knowledge! The worst of it is that, as we do not realize we need to know more when we think about Thee, we cannot ask those who know; indeed we have not even any idea what there is for us to ask them. So we suffer terrible trials because we do not understand ourselves; and we

---

[1] *Life*, Chap. XII.
[2] The words in brackets were written in the margin by St. Teresa and lightly scored out. Ribera, however, adds: "Nothing to be deleted." Gracián has added, interlineally, after "imagination": "for so we women generally call it."
[3] [*tan tortolito*, an expressive phrase: "so like a little *tórtola* (turtle-dove)"—i.e. not only timid, but irresolute and apparently stupid, like an inexperienced fledgling.]
[4] [Here there is a play on words difficult to render in English: the word translated both "restrain" and "uniting" is *atar*—"tie", "bind."]
[5] [*Traíame tonta*. Cf. p. 224, n. 1, above.]

worry over what is not bad at all, but good, and think it very wrong. Hence proceed the afflictions of many people who practise prayer, and their complaints of interior trials—especially if they are unlearned people—so that they become melancholy, and their health declines, and they even abandon prayer altogether, because they fail to realize that there is an interior world close at hand. Just as we cannot stop the movement of the heavens, revolving as they do with such speed, so we cannot restrain our thought. And then we send all the faculties of the soul after it, thinking we are lost, and have misused the time that we are spending in the presence of God. Yet the soul may perhaps be wholly united with Him in the Mansions very near His presence, while thought remains in the outskirts of the castle, suffering the assaults of a thousand wild and venomous creatures and from this suffering winning merit. So this must not upset us, and we must not abandon the struggle, as the devil tries to make us do. Most of these trials and times of unrest come from the fact that we do not understand ourselves.

As I write this, the noises in my head are so loud that I am beginning to wonder what is going on in it.[1] As I said at the outset, they have been making it almost impossible for me to obey those who commanded me to write. My head sounds just as if it were full of brimming rivers, and then as if all the water in those rivers came suddenly rushing downward; and a host of little birds seem to be whistling, not in the ears, but in the upper part of the head, where the higher part of the soul is said to be; I have held this view for a long time, for the spirit seems to move upward with great velocity. Please God I may remember to explain the cause of this when I am writing of the later Mansions: here it does not fit in well. I should not be surprised to know that the Lord has been pleased to send me this trouble in my head so that I may understand it better, for all this physical turmoil is no hindrance either to my prayer or to what I am saying now, but the tranquillity and love in my soul are quite unaffected, and so are its desires and clearness of mind.

But if the higher part of the soul is in the upper part of the head, how is it that it experiences no disturbance? That I do not know, but I do know that what I say is true. I suffer when my prayer is not accompanied by suspension of the faculties, but, when the faculties are suspended, I feel no pain until the suspension is over; it would be a terrible thing if this obstacle forced me to give up praying altogether. It is not good for us to be disturbed by our thoughts or to worry about them in the slightest; for if we do not worry and if the devil is responsible

---

[1] Gracián scores out this sentence in the autograph.

for them they will cease, and if they proceed, as they do, from the weakness which we inherit from the sin of Adam, and from many other weaknesses, let us have patience and bear everything for the love of God. Similarly we are obliged to eat and sleep, and we cannot escape from these obligations, though they are a great burden to us.

Let us recognize our weakness in these respects and desire to go where nobody will despise us. I sometimes recall words I have heard, spoken by the Bride in the Canticles,[1] and really I believe there is no point in our lives at which they can more properly be used, for I do not think that all the scorn and all the trials which we may have to suffer in this life can equal these interior battles. Any unrest and any strife can be borne, as I have already said, if we find peace where we live; but if we would have rest from the thousand trials which afflict us in the world and the Lord is pleased to prepare such rest for us, and yet the cause of the trouble is in ourselves, the result cannot but be very painful, indeed almost unbearable. For this cause, Lord, do Thou take us to a place where these weaknesses, which sometimes seem to be making sport of the soul, do not cause us to be despised. Even in this life the Lord will free the soul from this, when it has reached the last Mansion, as, if it please God, we shall explain.

These weaknesses will not give everyone so much trouble, or assail everyone as violently, as for many years they troubled and assailed me. For I was a wicked person and it seemed as though I were trying to take vengeance on myself. As it has been such a troublesome thing for me, it may perhaps be so for you as well, so I am just going to describe it, first in one way and then in another, hoping that I may succeed in making you realize how necessary it is, so that you may not grow restless and distressed. The clacking old mill must keep on going round and we must grind our own flour: neither the will nor the understanding must cease working.

This trouble will sometimes be worse, and sometimes better, according to our health and according to the times and seasons. The poor soul may not be to blame for this, but it must suffer none the less, for, as we shall commit other faults, it is only right that we should have patience. And as we are so ignorant that what we read and are advised—namely, that we should take no account of these thoughts—is not sufficient to teach us, it does not seem to me a waste of time if I go into it farther and offer you some consolation about it; though this will be of little help to you until the Lord is pleased to give us light. But it is neces-

---

[1] Canticles viii, 1. Gracián has copied in the margin of the autograph the Spanish text of Canticles viii, 1-4.

sary (and His Majesty's will) that we should take proper measures and learn to understand ourselves, and not blame our souls for what is the work of our weak imagination and our nature and the devil.

CHAPTER II

Continues the same subject and explains by a comparison what is meant by consolations and how we must obtain them without striving to do so.

God help me in this task which I have embarked upon.[1] I had quite forgotten what I was writing about, for business matters and ill-health forced me to postpone continuing it until a more suitable time, and, as I have a poor memory, it will all be very much confused, for I cannot read it through again. It may even be that everything I say is confused; that, at least, is what I am afraid of. I think I was talking about spiritual consolations and explaining how they are sometimes bound up with our passions. They often cause fits of sobbing; I have heard, indeed, that some persons find they produce constrictions of the chest and even exterior movements, which cannot be controlled, and which are violent enough to make blood gush from the nose and produce similar disconcerting symptoms. About this I can say nothing, for I have not experienced it, but there must be some cause for comfort in it, for, as I say, it all leads to a desire to please God and to have fruition of His Majesty.

What I call consolations from God, and elsewhere have termed the Prayer of Quiet, is something of a very different kind, as those of you will know who by the mercy of God have experienced it. To understand it better, let us suppose that we are looking at two fountains, the basins of which can be filled with water. There are certain spiritual things which I can find no way of explaining more aptly than by this element of water; for, as I am very ignorant, and my wits give me no help, and I am so fond of this element, I have observed it more attentively than anything else. In all the things that have been created by so great and wise a God there must be many secrets by which we can profit, and those who understand them do profit by them, although I believe that in every little thing created by God there is more than we realize, even in so small a thing as a tiny ant.

These two large basins can be filled with water in different ways: the water in the one comes from a long distance, by

[1] [The original is quite colloquial: "in the mess I have got into" or "in what I have let myself in for" would be nearer its spirit.]

means of numerous conduits and through human skill; but the other has been constructed at the very source of the water and fills without making any noise. If the flow of water is abundant, as in the case we are speaking of, a great stream still runs from it after it has been filled; no skill is necessary here, and no conduits have to be made, for the water is flowing all the time. The difference between this and the carrying of the water by means of conduits is, I think, as follows. The latter corresponds to the spiritual sweetness which, as I say, is produced by meditation. It reaches us by way of the thoughts; we meditate upon created things and fatigue the understanding; and when at last, by means of our own efforts, it comes, the satisfaction which it brings to the soul fills the basin, but in doing so makes a noise, as I have said.

To the other fountain the water comes direct from its source, which is God, and, when it is His Majesty's will and He is pleased to grant us some supernatural favour, its coming is accompanied by the greatest peace and quietness and sweetness within ourselves—I cannot say where it arises or how. And that content and delight are not felt, as earthly delights are felt, in the heart—I mean not at the outset, for later the basin becomes completely filled, and then this water begins to overflow all the Mansions and faculties, until it reaches the body. It is for that reason that I said it has its source in God and ends in ourselves—for it is certain, and anyone will know this who has experienced it, that the whole of the outer man enjoys this consolation and sweetness.

I was thinking just now, as I wrote this, that a verse which I have already quoted, *Dilatasti cor meum*,[1] speaks of the heart's being enlarged. I do not think that this happiness has its source in the heart at all. It arises in a much more interior part, like something of which the springs are very deep; I think this must be the centre of the soul, as I have since realized and as I will explain hereafter. I certainly find secret things in ourselves which often amaze me—and how many more there must be! O my Lord and my God! How wondrous is Thy greatness! And we creatures go about like silly little shepherd-boys, thinking we are learning to know something of Thee when the very most we can know amounts to nothing at all, for even in ourselves there are deep secrets which we cannot fathom. When I say "amounts to nothing at all" I mean because Thou art so surpassingly great, not because the signs of greatness that we see in Thy works are not very wonderful, even considering how very little we can learn to know of them.

Returning to this verse, what it says about the enlargement of the heart may, I think, be of some help to us. For apparently,

[1] Psalm cxviii, 32 (A.V., cxix, 32). Cf. p. 232, above.

as this heavenly water begins to flow from this source of which I am speaking—that is, from our very depths—it proceeds to spread within us and cause an interior dilation and produce ineffable blessings, so that the soul itself cannot understand all that it receives there. The fragrance it experiences, we might say, is as if in those interior depths there were a brazier on which were cast sweet perfumes; the light cannot be seen, nor the place where it dwells, but the fragrant smoke and the heat penetrate the entire soul, and very often, as I have said, the effects extend even to the body. Observe—and understand me here—that no heat is felt, nor is any fragrance perceived: it is a more delicate thing than that; I only put it in that way so that you may understand it. People who have not experienced it must realize that it does in very truth happen; its occurrence is capable of being perceived, and the soul becomes aware of it more clearly than these words of mine can express it. For it is not a thing that we can fancy, nor, however hard we strive, can we acquire it, and from that very fact it is clear that it is a thing made, not of human metal, but of the purest gold of Divine wisdom. In this state the faculties are not, I think, in union, but they become absorbed and are amazed as they consider what is happening to them.

It may be that in writing of these interior things I am contradicting what I have myself said elsewhere. This is not surprising, for almost fifteen years have passed since then,[1] and perhaps the Lord has now given me a clearer realization of these matters than I had at first. Both then and now, of course, I may be mistaken in all this, but I cannot lie about it: by the mercy of God I would rather die a thousand deaths: I am speaking of it just as I understand it.

The will certainly seems to me to be united in some way with the will of God; but it is by the effects of this prayer and the actions which follow it that the genuineness of the experience must be tested and there is no better crucible for doing so than this. If the person who receives such a grace recognizes it for what it is, Our Lord is granting him a surpassingly great favour, and another very great one if he does not turn back. You will desire, then, my daughters, to strive to attain this way of prayer, and you will be right to do so, for, as I have said, the soul cannot fully understand the favours which the Lord grants it there or the love which draws it ever nearer to Himself; it is certainly desirable that we should know how to obtain this favour. I will tell you what I have found out about it.

We may leave out of account occasions when the Lord is pleased to grant these favours for no other reason than because

---

[1] Again, as above (p. 230, n. 2), the Saint's computation is exactly correct.

His Majesty so wills. He knows why He does it and it is not for us to interfere. As well as acting, then, as do those who have dwelt in the Mansions already described, have humility and again humility! It is by humility that the Lord allows Himself to be conquered so that He will do all we ask of Him, and the first way in which you will see if you have humility is that if you have it you will not think you merit these favours and consolations of the Lord or are likely to get them for as long as you live. "But how," you will ask, "are we to gain them if we do not strive after them?" I reply that there is no better way than this one which I have described. There are several reasons why they should not be striven for. The first is because the most essential thing is that we should love God without any motive of self-interest. The second is because there is some lack of humility in our thinking that in return for our miserable services we can obtain anything so great. The third is because the true preparation for receiving these gifts is a desire to suffer and to imitate the Lord, not to receive consolations; for, after all, we have often offended Him. The fourth reason is because His Majesty is not obliged to grant them to us, as He is obliged to grant us glory if we keep His commandments, without doing which we could not be saved, and He knows better than we what is good for us and which of us truly love Him. That is certain truth, as I know; and I also know people who walk along the road of love, solely, as they should, in order to serve Christ crucified, and not only do they neither ask for consolations nor desire them, but they beg Him not to give them to them in this life. The fifth reason is that we should be labouring in vain; for this water does not flow through conduits, as the other does, and so we gain nothing by fatiguing ourselves if it cannot be had at the source. I mean that, however much we may practise meditation, however much we do violence to ourselves,[1] and however many tears we shed, we cannot produce this water in those ways; it is given only to whom God wills to give it and often when the soul is not thinking of it at all.

We are His, sisters; may He do with us as He will and lead us along whatever way He pleases. I am sure that if any of us achieve true humility and detachment (I say "true" because it must not be in thought alone, for thoughts often deceive us; it must be total detachment) the Lord will not fail to grant us this favour, and many others which we shall not even know how to desire. May He be for ever praised and blessed. Amen.

[1] [A very strong word, *estrujarse*. In its non-reflexive form, the verb means to squeeze, crush or press hard, or to extract something by so doing. The sense is, therefore, that with all our efforts we cannot squeeze out a drop of this water.]

CHAPTER III

Describes what is meant by the Prayer of Recollection, which the Lord generally grants before that already mentioned. Speaks of its effects and of the remaining effects of the former kind of prayer, which had to do with the consolations given by the Lord.

The effects of this kind of prayer are numerous; some of them I shall explain. First of all, I will say something (though not much, as I have dealt with it elsewhere)[1] about another kind of prayer, which almost invariably begins before this one. It is a form of recollection which also seems to me supernatural, for it does not involve remaining in the dark, or closing the eyes, nor is it dependent upon anything exterior. A person involuntarily closes his eyes and desires solitude; and, without the display of any human skill there seems gradually to be built for him a temple in which he can make the prayer already described; the senses and all external things seem gradually to lose their hold on him, while the soul, on the other hand, regains its lost control.

It is sometimes said that the soul enters within itself and sometimes that it rises above itself;[2] but I cannot explain things in that kind of language, for I have no skill in it. However, I believe you will understand what I am able to tell you, though I may perhaps be intelligible only to myself. Let us suppose that these senses and faculties (the inhabitants, as I have said, of this castle, which is the figure that I have taken to explain my meaning) have gone out of the castle, and, for days and years, have been consorting with strangers, to whom all the good things in the castle are abhorrent. Then, realizing how much they have lost, they come back to it, though they do not actually re-enter it, because the habits they have formed are hard to conquer. But they are no longer traitors and they now walk about in the vicinity of the castle. The great King, Who dwells in the Mansion within this castle, perceives their good will, and in His great mercy desires to bring them back to Him. So, like a good Shepherd, with a call so gentle that even they can hardly recognize it, He teaches them to know His voice and not to go away and get lost but to return to their Mansion; and so powerful is this Shepherd's call that they give up the things outside the castle which had led them astray, and once again enter it.

---

[1] *Life*, Chap. XVI; *Way of perfection*, Chaps. XXVIII, XXIX; *Relations*, V.
[2] There is little doubt that St. Teresa is here using Bk. IX, Chap. VII of Francisco de Osuna's *Third Spiritual Alphabet*.

I do not think I have ever explained this before as clearly as here. When we are seeking God within ourselves (where He is found more effectively and more profitably than in the creatures, to quote Saint Augustine, who, after having sought Him in many places, found Him within)[1] it is a great help if God grants us this favour. Do not suppose that the understanding can attain to Him, merely by trying to think of Him as within the soul, or the imagination, by picturing Him as there. This is a good habit and an excellent kind of meditation, for it is founded upon a truth—namely, that God is within us. But it is not the kind of prayer that I have in mind, for anyone (with the help of the Lord, you understand) can practise it for himself. What I am describing is quite different. These people are sometimes in the castle before they have begun to think about God at all. I cannot say where they entered it or how they heard their Shepherd's call: it was certainly not with their ears, for outwardly such a call is not audible. They become markedly conscious that they are gradually retiring[2] within themselves; anyone who experiences this will discover what I mean: I cannot explain it better. I think I have read that they are like a hedgehog or a tortoise withdrawing into itself[3]; and whoever wrote that must have understood it well. These creatures, however, enter within themselves whenever they like; whereas with us it is not a question of our will—it happens only when God is pleased to grant us this favour. For my own part, I believe that, when His Majesty grants it, He does so to people who are already leaving the things of the world. I do not mean that people who are married must actually leave the world—they can do so only in desire: His call to them is a special one and aims at making them intent upon interior things. I believe, however, that if we wish to give His Majesty free course, He will grant more than this to those whom He is beginning to call still higher.

Anyone who is conscious that this is happening within himself should give God great praise, for he will be very right to recognize what a favour it is; and the thanksgiving which he makes for it will prepare him for greater favours. One preparation for listening to Him, as certain books tell us, is that we should contrive, not to use our reasoning powers, but to be intent upon discovering what the Lord is working in the soul;

---

[1] *Confessions*, Bk. X, Chap. XXVII [or *Soliloquies*, Chap. XXXI: cf. *St. John of the Cross*: II, 33, 196, n. 9.]

[2] [*Lit.*: "conscious of a gentle interior shrinking": *encogimiento*, the noun used, means "shrinkage", "contraction"; it should be distinguished from *recogimiento*, a word often used by St. Teresa and translated "recollection".]

[3] Osuna (*op. cit.*, Bk. VI, Chap. IV) uses this simile of the hedgehog in much the same way.

for, if His Majesty has not begun to grant us absorption, I cannot understand how we can cease thinking in any way which will not bring us more harm than profit, although this has been a matter of continual discussion among spiritual persons. For my own part, I confess my lack of humility, but their arguments have never seemed to me good enough to lead me to accept what they say. One person told me of a certain book by the saintly Fray Peter of Alcántara (for a saint I believe he is), which would certainly have convinced me, for I know how much he knew about such things; but we read it together, and found that he says exactly what I say, although not in the same words; it is quite clear from what he says that love must already be awake.[1] It is possible that I am mistaken, but I base my position on the following reasons.

First, in such spiritual activity as this, the person who does most is he who thinks least and desires to do least:[2] what we have to do is to beg like poor and needy persons coming before a great and rich Emperor and then cast down our eyes in humble expectation. When from the secret signs He gives us we seem to realize that He is hearing us, it is well for us to keep silence, since He has permitted us to be near Him and there will be no harm in our striving not to labour with the understanding—provided, I mean, that we are able to do so. But if we are not quite sure that the King has heard us, or sees us, we must not stay where we are like ninnies, for there still remains a great deal for the soul to do when it has stilled the understanding; if it did nothing more it would experience much greater aridity and the imagination would grow more restless because of the effort caused it by cessation from thought. The Lord wishes us rather to make requests of Him and to remember that we are in His presence, for He knows what is fitting for us. I cannot believe in the efficacy of human activity in matters where His Majesty appears to have set a limit to it and to have been pleased to reserve action to Himself. There are many other things in which He has not so reserved it, such as penances, works of charity and prayers; these, with His aid, we can practise for ourselves, as far as our miserable nature is capable of them.

The second reason is that all these interior activities are gentle and peaceful, and to do anything painful brings us harm rather than help. By "anything painful" I mean anything that we try to force ourselves to do; it would be painful, for example, to hold our breath. The soul must just leave itself in the hands

---

[1] The reference is presumably to the famous "Eighth Counsel" of the *Treatise of Prayer and Meditation* [Cf. *S.S.M.*, II, 113-14].
[2] "With his human skill", adds Gracián, interlineally.

of God, and do what He wills it to do, completely disregarding its own advantage and resigning itself as much as it possibly can to the will of God. The third reason is that the very effort which the soul makes in order to cease from thought will perhaps awaken thought and cause it to think a great deal. The fourth reason is that the most important and pleasing thing in God's eyes is our remembering His honour and glory and forgetting ourselves and our own profit and ease and pleasure. And how can a person be forgetful of himself when he is taking such great care about his actions that he dare not even stir, or allow his understanding and desires to stir, even for the purpose of desiring the greater glory of God or of rejoicing in the glory which is His? When His Majesty wishes the working of the understanding to cease, He employs it in another manner, and illumines the soul's knowledge to so much higher a degree than any we can ourselves attain that He leads it into a state of absorption, in which, without knowing how, it is much better instructed than it could ever be as a result of its own efforts, which would only spoil everything. God gave us our faculties to work with, and everything will have its due reward; there is no reason, then, for trying to cast a spell over them—they must be allowed to perform their office until God gives them a better one.

As I understand it, the soul whom the Lord has been pleased to lead into this Mansion will do best to act as I have said. Let it try, without forcing itself or causing any turmoil, to put a stop to all discursive reasoning, yet not to suspend the understanding, nor to cease from all thought, though it is well for it to remember that it is in God's presence and Who this God is. If feeling this should lead it into a state of absorption, well and good; but it should not try to understand what this state is, because that is a gift bestowed upon the will. The will, then, should be left to enjoy it, and should not labour except for uttering a few loving words, for although in such a case one may not be striving to cease from thought, such cessation often comes, though for a very short time.

I have explained elsewhere[1] the reason why this occurs in this kind of prayer (I am referring to the kind which I began to explain in this Mansion). With it I have included this Prayer of Recollection which ought to have been described first, for it comes far below the consolations of God already mentioned, and is indeed the first step towards attaining them. For in the Prayer of Recollection it is unnecessary to abandon meditation and the activities of the understanding. When, instead of coming through conduits, the water springs directly from its source, the understanding

[1] *Way of perfection*, Chap. XXXI.

checks its activity, or rather the activity is checked for it when it finds it cannot understand what it desires, and thus it roams about all over the place, like a demented creature, and can settle down to nothing. The will is fixed so firmly upon its God that this disturbed condition of the understanding causes it great distress; but it must not take any notice of this, for if it does so it will lose a great part of what it is enjoying; it must forget about it, and abandon itself into the arms of love, and His Majesty will teach it what to do next; almost its whole work is to realize its unworthiness to receive such great good and to occupy itself in thanksgiving.

In order to discuss[1] the Prayer of Recollection I passed over the effects or signs to be observed in souls to whom this prayer is granted by God Our Lord. It is clear that a dilation or enlargement of the soul takes place, as if the water proceeding from the spring had no means of running away, but the fountain had a device ensuring that, the more freely the water flowed, the larger became the basin. So it is in this kind of prayer; and God works many more wonders in the soul, thus fitting and gradually disposing it to retain all that He gives it. So this gentle movement and this interior dilation cause the soul to be less constrained in matters relating to the service of God than it was before and give it much more freedom. It is not oppressed, for example, by the fear of hell, for, though it desires more than ever not to offend God (of Whom, however, it has lost all servile fear), it has firm confidence that it is destined to have fruition of Him. A person who used to be afraid of doing penance lest he should ruin his health now believes that in God he can do everything, and has more desire to do such things than he had previously. The fear of trials that he was wont to have is now largely assuaged, because he has a more lively faith, and realizes that, if he endures these trials for God's sake, His Majesty will give him grace to bear them patiently, and sometimes even to desire them, because he also cherishes a great desire to do something for God. The better he gets to know the greatness of God, the better he comes to realize the misery of his own condition; having now tasted the consolations of God, he sees that earthly things are mere refuse; so, little by little, he withdraws from them and in this way becomes more and more his own master. In short, he finds himself strengthened in all the virtues and will infallibly continue to increase in them unless he turns back and commits offences against God—when that happens, everything is lost, however far a man may have climbed towards the crest of the mountain. It must not be understood, however, that all these things take place because once or twice God has granted

---

[1] St. Teresa had written "to discuss the effects of" but deleted the last three words.

a soul this favour; it must continue receiving them, for it is from their continuance that all our good proceeds.

There is one earnest warning which I must give those who find themselves in this state: namely, that they exert the very greatest care to keep themselves from occasions of offending God. For as yet the soul is not even weaned but is like a child beginning to suck the breast. If it be taken from its mother, what can it be expected to do but die? That, I am very much afraid, will be the lot of anyone to whom God has granted this favour if he gives up prayer; unless he does so for some very exceptional reason, or unless he returns to it quickly, he will go from bad to worse. I am aware how much ground there is for fear about this and I have been very much grieved by certain people I know, in whom I have seen what I am describing; they have left Him Who in His great love was yearning to give Himself to them as a Friend, and to prove His friendship by His works. I earnestly warn such people not to enter upon occasions of sin, because the devil sets much more store by one soul in this state than by a great number of souls to whom the Lord does not grant these favours. For those in this state attract others, and so they can do the devil great harm and may well bring great advantage to the Church of God. He may see nothing else in them except that His Majesty is showing them especial love, but this is quite sufficient to make him do his utmost to bring about their perdition. The conflict, then, is sterner for such souls than for others and if they are lost their fate is less remediable. You, sisters, so far as we know, are free from these perils. May God free you from pride and vainglory and grant that the devil may not counterfeit these favours. Such counterfeits, however, will be recognizable because they will not produce these effects, but quite contrary ones.

There is one peril of which I want to warn you, though I have spoken of it elsewhere; I have seen persons given to prayer fall into it, and especially women, for, as we are weaker than men, we run more risk of what I am going to describe. It is this: some women, because of prayers, vigils and severe penances, and also for other reasons, have poor health. When they experience any spiritual consolation, therefore, their physical nature is too much for them; and as soon as they feel any interior joy there comes over them a physical weakness and languor, and they fall into a sleep, which they call "spiritual", and which is a little more marked than the condition that has been described. Thinking the one state to be the same as the other, they abandon themselves to this absorption; and the more they relax, the more complete becomes this absorption, because their physical nature continues to grow weaker. So they get it into their heads that it is *arrobamiento*.

or rapture. But I call it *abobamiento*, foolishness;[1] for they are doing nothing but wasting their time at it and ruining their health.

One person was in this state for eight hours; she was not unconscious, nor was she conscious of anything concerning God. She was cured by being told to take more food and sleep and to do less penance; for, though she had misled both her confessor and other people and, quite involuntarily, deceived herself, there was one person who understood her. I believe the devil would go to any pains to gain such people as that and he was beginning to make good progress with this one.

It must be understood that although, when this state is something that really comes from God, there may be languor, both interior and exterior, there will be none in the soul, which, when it finds itself near God, is moved with great joy. The experience does not last long, but only for a little while. Although the soul may become absorbed again, yet this kind of prayer, as I have said, except in cases of physical weakness, does not go so far as to overcome the body or to produce in it any exterior sensation. Be advised, then, and, if you experience anything of this kind, tell your superior, and relax as much as you can. The superior should give such persons fewer hours of prayer—very few, indeed—and should see that they sleep and eat well, until their physical strength, if it has become exhausted, comes back again. If their constitution is so weak that this does not suffice, they can be certain that God is not calling them to anything beyond the active life. There is room in convents for people of all kinds; let anyone of this type, then, be kept busy with duties, and let care be taken that she is not left alone very much, or her health will be completely ruined. This sort of life will be a great mortification to her, but it is here that the Lord wishes to test her love for Him by seeing how she bears His absence and after a while He may well be pleased to restore her strength; if He is not, her vocal prayer and her obedience will bring her as much benefit and merit as she would have obtained in other ways, and perhaps more.

There may also be some who are so weak in intellect and imagination—I have known such—that they believe they actually see all they imagine. This is highly dangerous and perhaps we shall treat of it later, but no more shall be said here; for I have written at great length of this Mansion, as it is the one which the greatest number of souls enter. As the natural is united with the supernatural in it, it is here that the devil can do most harm; for in the Mansions of which I have not yet spoken the Lord gives him fewer opportunities. May He be for ever praised. Amen.

---

[1] [The two Spanish words, on which St. Teresa plays so trenchantly, are added to their English equivalents so as to make the phrase intelligible.]

FIFTH MANSIONS

In which there are Four Chapters.

CHAPTER I

Begins to explain how in prayer the soul is united with God. Describes how we may know that we are not mistaken about this.

Oh, sisters! How shall I ever be able to tell you of the riches and the treasures and the delights which are to be found in the fifth Mansions? I think it would be better if I were to say nothing of the Mansions I have not yet treated, for no one can describe them, the understanding is unable to comprehend them and no comparisons will avail to explain them, for earthly things are quite insufficient for this purpose. Send me light from Heaven, my Lord, that I may enlighten these Thy servants, to some of whom Thou art often pleased to grant fruition of these joys, lest, when the devil transfigures himself into an angel of light, he should deceive them, for all their desires are occupied in desiring to please Thee.

Although I said "to some", there are really very few who do not enter these Mansions that I am about to describe. Some get farther than others; but, as I say, the majority manage to get inside. Some of the things which are in this room, and which I will mention here, are, I am sure, attained by very few;[1] but, if they do no more than reach the door, God is showing them great mercy by granting them this; for, though many are called, few are chosen.[2] So I must say here that, though all of us who wear this sacred habit of Carmel are[3] called to prayer and contemplation—because that was the first principle of our Order and because we are descended from the line of those holy Fathers of ours from Mount Carmel who sought this treasure, this precious pearl of which we speak, in such great solitude and with such contempt for the world—few of us[4] prepare ourselves for the Lord to reveal it to us. As far as externals are concerned, we are on the right road to attaining the essential virtues; but we shall need to do a very great deal before we can attain to this higher state and we must on no account be careless. So let us pause here, my

---

[1] Gracián has scored through part of this sentence in the autograph.
[2] St. Matthew xx, 16.
[3] Gracián substitutes for "are": "follow the rule of being."
[4] Gracián inserts the word "perhaps".

sisters, and beg the Lord that, since to some extent it is possible for us to enjoy Heaven upon earth, He will grant us His help so that it will not be our fault if we miss anything; may He also show us the road and give strength to our souls so that we may dig until we find this hidden treasure, since it is quite true that we have it within ourselves. This I should like to explain if the Lord is pleased to give me the knowledge.

I said "strength to our souls", because you must understand that we do not need bodily strength if God our Lord does not give it us; there is no one for whom He makes it impossible to buy His riches; provided each gives what he has, He is content. Blessed be so great a God! But observe, daughters, that, if you are to gain this, He would have you keep back nothing; whether it be little or much, He will have it all for Himself, and according to what you know yourself to have given, the favours He will grant you will be small or great. There is no better test than this of whether or no our prayer attains to union. Do not think it is a state, like the last, in which we dream; I say "dream", because the soul seems to be, as it were, drowsy, so that it neither seems asleep nor feels awake. Here we are all asleep, and fast asleep, to the things of the world, and to ourselves (in fact, for the short time that the condition lasts, the soul is without consciousness and has no power to think, even though it may desire to do so). There is no need now for it to devise any method of suspending the thought. Even in loving, if it is able to love, it cannot understand how or what it is that it loves, nor what it would desire; in fact, it has completely died to the world so that it may live more fully in God. This is a delectable death, a snatching of the soul from all the activities which it can perform while it is in the body; a death full of delight, for, in order to come closer to God, the soul appears to have withdrawn so far from the body that I do not know if it has still life enough to be able to breathe.[1] I have just been thinking about this and I believe it has not; or at least, if it still breathes, it does so without realizing it. The mind would like to occupy itself wholly in understanding something of what it feels, and, as it has not the strength to do this, it becomes so dumbfounded that, even if any consciousness remains to it, neither hands nor feet can move; as we commonly say of a person who has fallen into a swoon, it might be taken for dead. Oh, the secrets of God! I should never weary of trying to describe them to you, if I

---

[1] Luis de León modifies this passage [which has been slightly paraphrased in translation, the construction in the Spanish being rather obscure], reading, after "delight": "for, although it [the soul] is in Him, according to the truth, it appears to have withdrawn so far from the body, in order to come closer to God, that I do not know, etc."

thought I could do so successfully. I do not mind if I write any amount of nonsense, provided that just once in a way I can write sense, so that we may give great praise to the Lord.

I said that there was no question here of dreaming, whereas in the Mansion that I have just described the soul is doubtful as to what has really happened until it has had a good deal of experience of it. It wonders if the whole thing was imagination, if it has been asleep, if the favour was a gift of God, or if the devil was transfigured into an angel of light. It retains a thousand suspicions, and it is well that it should, for, as I said, we can sometimes be deceived in this respect, even by our own nature. For, although there is less opportunity for the poisonous creatures to enter, a few little lizards, being very agile, can hide themselves all over the place; and, although they do no harm—especially, as I said, if we take no notice of them—they correspond to the little thoughts which proceed from the imagination and from what has been said it will be seen that they are often very troublesome. Agile though they are, however, the lizards cannot enter this Mansion, for neither imagination nor memory nor understanding can be an obstacle to the blessings that are bestowed in it. And I shall venture to affirm that, if this is indeed union with God,[1] the devil cannot enter or do any harm; for His Majesty is in such close contact and union with the essence of the soul[2] that he will not dare to approach, nor can he even understand this secret thing. That much is evident: for it is said that he does not understand our thoughts;[3] still less, therefore, will he understand a thing so secret that God will not even entrust our thoughts with it.[4] Oh, what a great blessing is this state in which that accursed one can do us no harm! Great are the gains which come to the soul with God working in it and neither we ourselves nor anyone else hindering Him. What will He not give Who so much loves giving and can give all that He will?

I fear I may be leaving you confused by saying "if this is indeed union with God" and suggesting that there are other kinds of union. But of course there are! If we are really very fond of vanities the devil will send us into transports over them; but these are not like the transports of God, nor is there the

[1] "Of the soul alone", inserts Gracián, interlineally.
[2] Gracián deletes "the essence of".
[3] Gracián substitutes "understanding" for "thoughts" and adds a marginal note: "This is (to be) understood of acts of the understanding and the will, for the thoughts of the imagination are clearly seen by the devil unless God blinds him in that respect." Luis de León included the marginal note in the text of his edition but Gracián did not reproduce it in either the text or the margin of the Córdoba copy, though he altered "thoughts" to "understanding".
[4] Gracián inserts the word "nature" here, interlineally.

same delight and satisfaction for the soul or the same peace and joy. That joy is greater than all the joys of earth, and greater than all its delights, and all its satisfactions, so that there is no evidence that these satisfactions and those of the earth have a common origin; and they are apprehended, too, very differently, as you will have learned by experience. I said once[1] that it is as if the one kind had to do with the grosser part of the body, and the other kind penetrated to the very marrow of the bones; that puts it well, and I know no better way of expressing it.

But I fancy that even now you will not be satisfied, for you will think that you may be mistaken, and that these interior matters are difficult to investigate. In reality, what has been said will be sufficient for anyone who has experienced this blessing, for there is a great difference between the false and the true. But I will give you a clear indication which will make it impossible for you to go wrong or to doubt if some favour has come from God; His Majesty has put it into my mind only to-day, and I think it is quite decisive. In difficult matters, even if I believe I understand what I am saying and am speaking the truth, I use this phrase "I think", because, if I am mistaken, I am very ready to give credence to those who have great learning. For even if they have not themselves experienced these things, men of great learning have a certain instinct[2] to prompt them. As God uses them to give light to His Church, He reveals to them anything which is true so that it shall be accepted; and if they do not squander their talents, but are true servants of God, they will never be surprised at His greatness, for they know quite well that He is capable of working more and still more. In any case, where matters are in question for which there is no explanation, there must be others about which they can read, and they can deduce from their reading that it is possible for these first-named to have happened.

Of this I have the fullest experience; and I have also experience of timid, half-learned men whose shortcomings have cost me very dear. At any rate, my own opinion is that anyone who does not believe that God can do much more than this, and that He has been pleased, and is sometimes still pleased, to grant His creatures such favours, has closed the door fast against receiving them. Therefore, sisters, let this never be true of you, but trust God more and more, and do not consider whether

---

[1] [P. Silverio refers here to *Way of perfection*, Chap. XXXI, but I hardly think this can be meant. Perhaps the author's allusion is to the first chapter of the Fourth Mansions (p. 232, above) or possibly to something she once said *viva voce*.]

[2] [*Lit.*: "a something": the Spanish is *un no sé qué*, an expression corresponding to the French *un je ne sais quoi*.]

those to whom He communicates His favours are bad or good. His Majesty knows all about this, as I have said; intervention on our part is quite unnecessary; rather must we serve His Majesty with humility and simplicity of heart, and praise Him for His works and wonders.

Turning now to the indication which I have described as[1] a decisive one: here is this soul which God has made, as it were, completely foolish in order the better to impress upon it true wisdom. For as long as such a soul is in this state, it can neither see nor hear nor understand: the period is always short and seems to the soul even shorter than it really is. God implants Himself in the interior of that soul in such a way that, when it returns to itself, it cannot[2] possibly doubt that God has been in it and it has been in God; so firmly does this truth remain within it that, although for years God may never grant it that favour again, it can neither forget it nor doubt that it has received it (and this quite apart from the effects which remain within it, and of which I will speak later). This certainty of the soul is very material.

But now you will say to me: How did the soul see it and understand it if it can neither see nor understand? I am not saying that it saw it at the time,[3] but that it sees it clearly afterwards, and not because it is a vision, but because of a certainty which remains in the soul, which can be put there only by God. I know of a person who had not learned that God was in all things by presence and power and essence; God granted her a favour of this kind, which convinced her of this so firmly[4] that, although one of those half-learned men whom I have been talking about, and whom she asked in what way God was in us (until God granted him an understanding of it he knew as little of it as she), told her that He was in us only by grace, she had the truth so firmly implanted within her that she did not believe him, and asked others, who told her the truth, which was a great consolation to her.[5]

Do not make the mistake of thinking that this certainty has anything to do with bodily form—with the presence of Our Lord Jesus Christ, for example, unseen by us, in the Most Holy Sacrament. It has nothing to do with this—only with His Divinity.

[1] Gracián alters "as" to "as being, I think".
[2] Gracián inserts: "it thinks."
[3] Gracián amends the following phrase to read: "but that there has since remained with it, as it thinks, a certainty, etc."
[4] Gracián alters this phrase to: "which made her understand this in such a way."
[5] St. Teresa refers to this experience of hers in *Life*, Chap. XVIII (Vol. I, p.111, above). Later, a favour which she received (*Relations*, LIV: Vol. I, p. 361, above) enlightened her further on this point. According to Yepes (II, xx) she asked him for theological guidance about it just before she began the *Interior Castle*.

How, you will ask, can we become so convinced of what we have not seen? That I do not know; it is the work of God. But I know I am speaking the truth; and if anyone has not that certainty, I should say that what he has experienced is not union of the whole soul with God but only union of one of the faculties or some one of the many other kinds of favour which God grants the soul. In all these matters we must stop looking for reasons why they happened; if our understanding cannot grasp them, why should we try to perplex it? It suffices us to know that He Who brings this to pass is all-powerful,[1] and as it is God Who does it and we, however hard we work, are quite incapable of achieving it, let us not try to become capable of understanding it either.

With regard to what I have just said about our incapability, I recall that, as you have heard, the Bride in the *Songs* says: "The King brought me" (or "put me", I think the words are) "into the cellar of wine."[2] It does not say that she *went*. It also says that she was wandering about in all directions seeking her Beloved.[3] This, as I understand it, is the cellar where the Lord is pleased to put us, when He wills and as He wills. But we cannot enter by any efforts of our own; His Majesty must put us right into the centre[4] of our soul, and must enter there Himself; and, in order that He may the better show us His wonders, it is His pleasure that our will, which has entirely surrendered itself to Him, should have no part in this. Nor does He desire the door of the faculties and senses, which are all asleep, to be opened to Him; He will come into the centre of the soul without using a door, as He did when He came in to His disciples, and said *Pax vobis*,[5] and when He left the sepulchre without removing the stone. Later on you will see how it is His Majesty's will that the soul should have fruition of Him in its very centre, but you will be able to realize that in the last Mansion much better than here.

Oh, daughters, what a lot we shall see if we desire to see no more than our own baseness and wretchedness and to understand that we are not worthy to be the handmaidens of so great a Lord, since we cannot comprehend His marvels. May He be for ever praised. Amen.

[1] The rest of this paragraph was omitted by Luis de León.
[2] Canticles i, 3; ii, 4. Gracián deletes the bracketed phrase but writes "put" above "brought".
[3] Canticles iii, 2.
[4] Here and just below Gracián has crossed out the word "centre".
[5] St. John xx, 19.

CHAPTER II

Continues the same subject. Explains the Prayer of Union by a delicate comparison. Describes the effects which it produces in the soul. Should be studied with great care.

You will suppose that all there is to be seen in this Mansion has been described already, but there is much more to come yet, for, as I said, some receive more and some less. With regard to the nature of union, I do not think I can say anything further; but when the soul to which God grants these favours prepares itself for them, there are many things to be said concerning what the Lord works in it. Some of these I shall say now, and I shall describe that soul's state. In order the better to explain this, I will make use of a comparison which is suitable for the purpose; and which will also show us how, although this work is performed by the Lord, and we can do nothing to make His Majesty grant us this favour, we can do a great deal to prepare ourselves for it.

You will have heard of the wonderful way in which silk is made—a way which no one could invent but God—and how it comes from a kind of seed which looks like tiny peppercorns[1] (I have never seen this, but only heard of it, so if it is incorrect in any way the fault is not mine). When the warm weather comes, and the mulberry-trees begin to show leaf, this seed starts to take life; until it has this sustenance, on which it feeds, it is as dead. The silkworms feed on the mulberry-leaves until they are full-grown, when people put down twigs, upon which, with their tiny mouths, they start spinning silk, making themselves very tight little cocoons, in which they bury themselves. Then, finally, the worm, which was large and ugly, comes right out of the cocoon a beautiful white butterfly.

Now if no one had ever seen this, and we were only told about it as a story of past ages, who would believe it? And what arguments could we find to support the belief that a thing as devoid of reason as a worm or a bee could be diligent enough to work so industriously for our advantage, and that in such an enterprise the poor little worm would lose its life? This alone, sisters, even if I tell you no more, is sufficient for a brief meditation, for it will enable you to reflect upon the wonders and the wisdom of our God. What, then, would it be if we knew the

---

[1] "Mustard-seeds," writes Gracián, interlineally, deleting the bracketed sentence which follows and adding the words: "It is so, for I have seen it."

properties of everything? It will be a great help to us if we occupy ourselves in thinking of these wonderful things and rejoice in being the brides of so wise and powerful a King.

But to return to what I was saying. The silkworm is like the soul which takes life when, through the heat which comes from the Holy Spirit, it begins to utilize the general help which God gives to us all, and to make use of the remedies which He left in His Church—such as frequent confessions, good books and sermons, for these are the remedies for a soul dead in negligences and sins and frequently plunged into temptation. The soul begins to live and nourishes itself on this food, and on good meditations, until it is full grown—and this is what concerns me now: the rest is of little importance.

When it is full-grown, then, as I wrote at the beginning, it starts to spin its silk and to build the house in which it is to die. This house may be understood here to mean Christ. I think I read or heard somewhere that our life is hid in Christ, or in God (for that is the same thing), or that our life is Christ.[1] (The exact form of this[2] is little to my purpose.)

Here, then, daughters, you see what we can do, with God's favour. May His Majesty Himself be our Mansion as He is in this Prayer of Union which, as it were, we ourselves spin. When I say He will be our Mansion, and we can construct it for ourselves and hide ourselves in it, I seem to be suggesting that we can subtract from God, or add to Him. But of course we cannot possibly do that! We can neither subtract from, nor add to, God, but we can subtract from, and add to, ourselves, just as these little silkworms do. And, before we have finished doing all that we can in that respect, God will take this tiny achievement of ours, which is nothing at all, unite it with His greatness and give it such worth that its reward will be the Lord Himself. And as it is He Whom it has cost the most, so His Majesty will unite our small trials with the great trials which He suffered, and make both of them into one.

On, then, my daughters! Let us hasten to perform this task and spin this cocoon. Let us renounce our self-love and self-will, and our attachment to earthly things. Let us practise penance, prayer, mortification, obedience, and all the other good works that you know of. Let us do what we have been taught; and we have been instructed about what our duty is. Let the silkworm die—let it die, as in fact it does when it has completed the work which it was created to do. Then we shall see God

---

[1] Colossians iii, 3. Gracián deletes "for that . . . my purpose" and supplies text and source in the margin.

[2] [*Lit.*: "Whether this be so or not." But the meaning is clear from the context.]

and shall ourselves be as completely hidden in His greatness as is this little worm in its cocoon. Note that, when I speak of seeing God, I am referring to the way in which, as I have said, He allows Himself to be apprehended in this kind of union.

And now let us see what becomes of this silkworm, for all that I have been saying about it is leading up to this. When it is in this state of prayer, and quite dead to the world, it comes out a little white butterfly. Oh, greatness of God, that a soul should come out like this after being hidden in the greatness of God, and closely united with Him, for so short a time—never, I think, for as long as half an hour! I tell you truly, the very soul does not know itself. For think of the difference between an ugly worm and a white butterfly; it is just the same here. The soul cannot think how it can have merited such a blessing —whence such a blessing could have come to it, I meant to say, for it knows quite well that it has not merited it at all.[1] It finds itself so anxious to praise the Lord that it would gladly be consumed and die a thousand deaths for His sake. Then it finds itself longing to suffer great trials and unable to do otherwise. It has the most vehement desires for penance, for solitude, and for all to know God. And hence, when it sees God being offended, it becomes greatly distressed. In the following Mansion we shall treat of these things further and in detail, for, although the experiences of this Mansion and of the next are almost identical, their effects come to have much greater power; for, as I have said, if after God comes to a soul here on earth it strives to progress still more, it will experience great things.

To see, then, the restlessness of this little butterfly—though it has never been quieter or more at rest in its life! Here is something to praise God for—namely, that it knows not where to settle and make its abode. By comparison with the abode it has had, everything it sees on earth leaves it dissatisfied, especially when God has again and again given it this wine which almost every time has brought it some new blessing. It sets no store by the things it did when it was a worm—that is, by its gradual weaving of the cocoon. It has wings now: how can it be content to crawl along slowly when it is able to fly? All that it can do for God seems to it slight by comparison with its desires. It even attaches little importance to what the saints endured, knowing by experience how the Lord helps and transforms a soul, so that it seems no longer to be itself, or even its own likeness. For the weakness which it used to think it had when it came to doing penance is now turned into strength. It is no longer bound by ties of relationship, friendship or property. Previously all its

[1] The words "I meant . . . at all" are omitted from the *editio princeps*.

acts of will and resolutions and desires were powerless to loosen these and seemed only to bind them the more firmly; now it is grieved at having even to fulfil its obligations in these respects lest these should cause it to sin against God. Everything wearies it, because it has proved that it can find no true rest in the creatures.

I seem to be enlarging on this subject and there is much more that I could say: anyone to whom God has granted this favour will realize that I have said very little. It is not surprising, then, that, as this little butterfly feels a stranger to things of the earth, it should be seeking a new resting-place. But where will the poor little creature go? It cannot return to the place it came from, for, as has been said, however hard we try, it is not in our power to do that until God is pleased once again to grant us this favour. Ah, Lord! What trials begin afresh for this soul! Who would think such a thing possible after it had received so signal a favour? But, after all,[1] we must bear crosses in one way or another for as long as we live. And if anyone told me that after reaching this state he had enjoyed continual rest and joy, I should say that he had not reached it at all, but that if he had got as far as the previous Mansion, he might possibly have experienced some kind of consolation the effect of which was enhanced by physical weakness, and perhaps even by the devil, who gives peace to the soul in order later to wage a far severer war upon it.

I do not mean that those who attain to this state have no peace: they do have it, and to a very high degree, for even their trials are of such sublimity and come from so noble a source that, severe though they are, they bring peace and contentment. The very discontent caused by the things of the world arouses a desire to leave it, so grievous that any alleviation it finds can only be in the thought that its life in this exile is God's will. And even this is insufficient to comfort it, for, despite all it has gained, the soul is not wholly resigned to the will of God, as we shall see later. It does not fail to act in conformity with God's will, but it does so with many tears and with great sorrow at being unable to do more because it has been given no more capacity. Whenever it engages in prayer, this is a grief to it. To some extent, perhaps, it is a result of the great grief caused by seeing how often God is offended, and how little esteemed, in this world, and by considering how many souls are lost, both of heretics and of Moors; although its greatest grief is over the loss of Christian souls, many of whom, it fears, are condemned, though so great is God's mercy that, however evil their lives have been, they can amend them and be saved.

[1] A characteristically emphatic phrase—*en fin, fin.*

Oh, the greatness of God! Only a few years since—perhaps only a few days—this soul was thinking of nothing but itself. Who has plunged it into such grievous anxieties? Even if we tried to meditate for years on end, we could not feel this as keenly as the soul does now. God help me! If I were able to spend many days and years in trying to realize how great a sin it is to offend God, and in reflecting that those who are damned are His children, and my brothers and sisters, and in meditating upon the dangers in which we live, and in thinking how good it would be for us to depart from this miserable life, would all that suffice? No, daughters; the grief I am referring to is not like that caused by these kinds of meditation. That grief we could easily achieve, with the Lord's help, by thinking a great deal about those things; but it does not reach to the depths of our being, as does this grief, which, without any effort on the soul's part, and sometimes against its will, seems to tear it to pieces and grind it to powder. What, then, is this grief? Whence does it come? I will tell you.

Have you not heard concerning the Bride (I said this a little while back,[1] though not with reference to the same matter) that God put her in the cellar of wine and ordained charity in her? Well, that is the position here. That soul has now delivered itself into His hands and His great love has so completely subdued it that it neither knows nor desires anything save that God shall do with it what He wills. Never, I think, will God grant this favour save to the soul which He takes for His very own. His will is that, without understanding how, the soul shall go thence sealed with His seal. In reality, the soul in that state does no more than the wax when a seal is impressed upon it— the wax does not impress itself; it is only prepared for the impress: that is, it is soft—and it does not even soften itself so as to be prepared; it merely remains quiet and consenting. Oh, goodness of God, that all this should be done at Thy cost! Thou dost require only our wills and dost ask that Thy wax may offer no impediment.

Here, then, sisters, you see what our God does to the soul in this state so that it may know itself to be His. He gives it something of His own, which is what His Son had in this life: He can grant us no favour greater than that. Who could have wanted to depart from this life more than His Son did? As, indeed, His Majesty said at the Last Supper: "With desire have I desired."[2] "Did not the painful death that Thou wert to die present itself to Thee, O Lord, as something grievous and terrible?" "No, because

---

[1] [Cf. p. 252, above. The reference here is clearly to Canticles ii, 4.]
[2] St. Luke xxii, 15.

My great love and My desire that souls shall be saved transcend these pains beyond all comparison and the very terrible things that I have suffered since I lived in the world, and still suffer, are such that by comparison with them these are nothing."

I have often thought about this: I know that the torment which a certain person of my acquaintance[1] has suffered, and suffers still, at seeing the Lord offended, is so intolerable that she would far sooner die than suffer it. And, I reflected, if a soul which has so very little charity by comparison with Christ's that it might be said to be almost nothing beside His felt this torment to be so intolerable, what must the feelings of Our Lord Jesus Christ have been, and what a life must He have lived, if He saw everything and was continually witnessing the great offences which were being committed against His Father? I think this must certainly have caused Him much greater grief than the pains of His most sacred Passion; for there He could see the end of His trials; and that sight, together with the satisfaction of seeing our redemption achieved through His death, and of proving what love He had for His Father by suffering so much for Him, would alleviate His pains, just as, when those who have great strength of love perform great penances, they hardly feel them, and would like to do more and more, and everything that they do seems very small to them. What, then, would His Majesty feel when He found Himself able to prove so amply to His Father how completely He was fulfilling the obligation of obedience to Him and showing His love for His neighbour? Oh, the great delight of suffering in doing the will of God! But the constant sight of so many offences committed against His Majesty and so many souls going to hell must, I think, have been so painful to Him that, had He not been more than man, one day of that grief would have sufficed to put an end to any number of lives that He might have had, let alone to one.

CHAPTER III

Continues the same matter. Describes another kind of union which, with the help of God, the soul can attain, and the important part played in it by the love of our neighbour. This chapter is of great profit.

Let us now return to our little dove, and see something of what God gives her in this state. It must always be understood that she will try to advance in the service of Our Lord and in self-

---

[1] St. Teresa herself.

knowledge. If she does no more than receive this favour, and, as though she enjoyed complete security, begins to lead a careless life and stray from the road to Heaven—that is, from the Commandments—there will happen to her what happens to the creature that comes out of the silkworm, which leaves seed for the production of more silkworms and then dies for ever. I say it leaves seed because for my own part I believe it is God's will that so great a favour should not be given in vain, and that if the soul that receives it does not profit by it others will do so. For, as the soul possesses these aforementioned desires and virtues, it will always profit other souls so long as it leads a good life, and from its own heat new heat will be transmitted to them. Even after losing this, it may still desire others to profit, and take pleasure in describing the favours given by God to those who love and serve Him.

I knew a person to whom this happened,[1] and who, though having herself gone far astray, was glad that others should profit by the favours God had shown her; she would describe the way of prayer to those who did not understand it, and she brought them very, very great profit.[2] Later, the Lord gave her new light. It is true that she had not yet experienced the effects which have been mentioned. But how many are called by the Lord to apostleship, as Judas was, and enjoy communion with Him, or are called to be made kings, as Saul was, and afterwards, through their own fault, are lost! From this, sisters, we may deduce that, if we are to acquire increasing merit, and not, like Saul and Judas, to be lost, our only possible safety consists in obedience and in never swerving from the law of God; I am referring to those to whom He grants these favours, and in fact to all.

Despite all I have said, this Mansion seems to me a little obscure. There is a great deal to be gained by entering it, and those from whom the Lord withholds such supernatural gifts will do well to feel that they are not without hope; for true union can quite well be achieved, with the favour of Our Lord, if we endeavour to attain it by not following our own will but submitting it to whatever is the will of God. Oh, how many of us there are who say we do this and think we want nothing else, and would die for this truth, as I believe I have said! For I tell you, and I shall often repeat this, that when you have obtained this favour from the Lord, you need not strive for that other delectable union which has been described, for the most

---

[1] St. Teresa herself. Cf. *Life*, Chap. VII (Vol. I, p. 46, above).
[2] [The phrase is very emphatic: *Harto provecho, harto*—"exceedingly great profit exceedingly."]

valuable thing about it is that it proceeds from this union which I am now describing; and we cannot attain to the heights I have spoken of if we are not sure that we have the union in which we resign our wills to the will of God.

Oh, how much to be desired is this union! Happy the soul that has attained to it, for it will live peacefully both in this life and in the next as well. Nothing that happens on earth will afflict it unless it finds itself in peril of losing God, or sees that He is offended—neither sickness nor poverty nor death, except when someone dies who was needed by the Church of God. For this soul sees clearly that He knows what He does better than it knows itself what it desires.

You must observe that there are many kinds of grief. Some of them come upon us suddenly, in natural ways, just as pleasures do; they may even arise from charity, which makes us pity our neighbours, as Our Lord did when He raised Lazarus;[1] and these do not prevent union with the will of God, nor do they cause a restless, unquiet passion which disturbs the soul and lasts for a long time. They are griefs which pass quickly; for, as I said of joys in prayer, they seem not to penetrate to the depth of the soul but only reach these senses and faculties. They characterize all the Mansions so far described but do not enter that which will be dealt with last of all, from which the suspension of the faculties already referred to is inseparable. The Lord can enrich souls in many ways and bring them to these Mansions by many other paths than the short cut which has been described.

But note very carefully, daughters, that the silkworm has of necessity to die; and it is this which will cost you most; for death comes more easily[2] when one can see oneself living a new life, whereas our duty now is to continue living this present life, and yet to die of our own free will.[3] I confess to you that we shall find this much harder, but it is of the greatest value and the reward will be greater too if you gain the victory. But you must not doubt the possibility of this true union with the will of God. This is the union which I have desired all my life; it is for this that I continually beseech Our Lord; it is this which is the most genuine and the safest.

But alas that so few of us are destined to attain it! A person who takes care not to offend the Lord and has entered the

---

[1] St. John xi, 35.

[2] St. Teresa added here the word *acullá*, "yonder", which Luis de León altered to *en lo susodicho*, "in what is (said) above". [This affects the sense: Luis de León's alteration suggests that the silkworm is referred to, which seems to me unlikely. I take *acullá* to refer to the end of one's life and *acá* to mean "here and now".]

[3] [*Lit.*: "to kill it ourselves." By "it", which in the Spanish can only stand for "life", is presumably meant the Pauline "old man".]

religious life may think he has done everything. But oh, there are always a few little worms which do not reveal themselves until, like the worm which gnawed through Jonas's ivy,[1] they have gnawed through our virtues. Such are self-love, self-esteem, censoriousness (even if only in small things) concerning our neighbours, lack of charity towards them, and failure to love them as we love ourselves. For, although late in the day we may fulfil our obligations and so commit no sin, we are far from attaining a point necessary to complete union with the will of God.

What do you suppose His will is, daughters? That we should be altogether perfect, and be one with Him and with the Father,[2] as in His Majesty's prayer. Consider what a long way we are from attaining this. I assure you that it causes me real distress to write in this way because I know how far I am from it myself, and entirely through my own fault. For we do not require great favours from the Lord before we can achieve this; He has given us all we need in giving us His Son to show us the way. Do not think that if, for example, my father or my brother dies, I ought to be in such close conformity with the will of God that I shall not grieve at his loss, or that, if I have trials or illnesses, I must enjoy bearing them. It is good if we can do this and sometimes it is a matter of common sense: being unable to help ourselves, we make a virtue of necessity. How often philosophers used to act thus in matters of this kind, or in similar matters—and they were very wise men! But here the Lord asks only two things of us: love for His Majesty and love for our neighbour. It is for these two virtues that we must strive, and if we attain them perfectly we are doing His will and so shall be united with Him. But, as I have said, how far we are from doing these two things in the way we ought for a God Who is so great! May His Majesty be pleased to give us grace so that we may deserve to reach this state, as it is in our power to do if we wish.

The surest sign that we are keeping these two commandments is, I think, that we should really be loving our neighbour; for we cannot be sure if we are loving God, although we may have good reasons for believing that we are, but we can know quite well if we are loving our neighbour. And be certain that, the farther advanced you find you are in this, the greater the love you will have for God; for so dearly does His Majesty love us that He will reward our love for our neighbour by increasing the love which we bear to Himself, and that in a thousand ways: this I cannot doubt.

It is most important that we should proceed in this matter very carefully, for, if we have attained great perfection here, we have

---

[1] Jonas iv, 6–7 [The "gourd" of A.V.]   [2] St. John xvii, 22.

done everything. Our nature being so evil, I do not believe we could ever attain perfect love for our neighbour unless it had its roots in the love of God. Since this is so important, sisters, let us strive to get to know ourselves better and better, even in the very smallest matters, and take no notice of all the fine plans which come crowding into our minds when we are at prayer, and which we think we will put into practice and carry out for the good of our neighbours in the hope of saving just one soul. If our later actions are not in harmony with those plans, we can have no reason for believing that we should ever have put them into practice. I say the same of humility and of all the virtues; the wiles of the devil are terrible; he will run a thousand times round hell if by so doing he can make us believe that we have a single virtue which we have not. And he is right, for such ideas are very harmful, and such imaginary virtues, when they come from this source, are never unaccompanied by vainglory; just as those which God gives are free both from this and from pride.

I like the way in which some souls, when they are at prayer, think that, for God's sake, they would be glad if they could be humbled and put to open shame—and then try to conceal quite a slight failure. Oh, and if they should be accused of anything that they have not done——! God save us from having to listen to them then! Let anyone who cannot bear trials like that be very careful to pay no heed to the resolutions he may have made when he was alone. For they could not in fact have been resolutions made by the will (a genuine act of the will is quite another matter); they must have been due to some freak of the imagination. The devil makes good use of the imagination in practising his surprises and deceptions, and there are many such which he can practise on women, or on unlettered persons, because we do not understand the difference between the faculties and the imagination, and thousands of other things belonging to the interior life. Oh, sisters, how clearly it can be seen what love of your neighbour really means to some of you, and what an imperfect stage it has reached in others! If you understood the importance of this virtue to us all you would strive after nothing but gaining it.

When I see people very diligently trying to discover what kind of prayer they are experiencing and so completely wrapt up[1] in their prayers that they seem afraid to stir, or to indulge in a moment's thought, lest they should lose the slightest degree

---

[1] [*Encapotadas*: lit., covering their faces with a cloak, muffled up. Metaphorically, the word can mean "frowning", "sullen". Here a less reprehensible meaning seems indicated.]

of the tenderness and devotion which they have been feeling, I realize how little they understand of the road to the attainment of union. They think that the whole thing consists in this. But no, sisters, no; what the Lord desires is works. If you see a sick woman to whom you can give some help, never be affected by the fear that your devotion will suffer, but take pity on her: if she is in pain, you should feel pain too; if necessary, fast so that she may have your food, not so much for her sake as because you know it to be your Lord's will. That is true union with His will. Again, if you hear someone being highly praised, be much more pleased than if they were praising you; this is really easy if you have humility, for in that case you will be sorry to hear yourself praised. To be glad when your sisters' virtues are praised is a great thing, and, when we see a fault in someone, we should be as sorry about it as if it were our own and try to conceal it from others.

I have said a great deal about this elsewhere,[1] sisters, because I know that, if we were to fail here, we should be lost. May the Lord grant us never to fail, and, if that is to be so, I tell you that you must not cease to beg His Majesty for the union which I have described. It may be that you have experienced devotion and consolations, so that you think you have reached this stage, and even enjoyed some brief period of suspension in the Prayer of Quiet, which some people always take to mean that everything is accomplished. But, believe me, if you find you are lacking in this virtue, you have not yet attained union. So ask Our Lord to grant you this perfect love for your neighbour, and allow His Majesty to work, and, if you use your best endeavours and strive after this in every way that you can, He will give you more even than you can desire. You must do violence to your own will, so that your sister's will is done in everything, even though this may cause you to forgo your own rights and forget your own good in your concern for theirs, and however much your physical powers may rebel. If the opportunity presents itself, too, try to shoulder some trial in order to relieve your neighbour of it. Do not suppose that it will cost you nothing or that you will find it all done for you. Think what the love which our Spouse had for us cost Him, when, in order to redeem us from death, He died such a grievous death as the death of the Cross.

[1] Cf. *Way of perfection*, Chap. VII.

CHAPTER IV

Continues the same subject and gives a further explanation of this kind of prayer. Describes the great importance of proceeding carefully, since the devil is most careful to do all he can to turn souls back from the road they have begun to tread.

I think you will be anxious now to learn what this little dove is doing, and where it is going to settle, for of course it cannot rest in spiritual consolations or in earthly pleasures. It is destined to fly higher than this and I cannot fully satisfy your anxiety until we come to the last Mansion. God grant I may remember it then and find an opportunity to write about it, for almost five months have passed since I began this book, and, as my head is not in a fit state for me to read it through again, it must all be very confused and I may possibly say a few things twice over. As it is for my sisters, however, that matters little.

I want to explain to you still further what I think this Prayer of Union is; and I will make a comparison as well as my wit will allow. Afterwards we will say more about this little butterfly, which never rests—though it is always fruitful in doing good to itself and to other souls—because it has not yet found true repose.[1] You will often have heard that God betrothes Himself to souls spiritually. Blessed be His mercy, which is pleased so to humble itself! I am only making a rough comparison, but I can find no other which will better explain what I am trying to say than the Sacrament of Matrimony. The two things work differently, for in this matter which we are treating there is nothing that is not spiritual: corporeal union is quite another thing and the spiritual joys and consolations given by the Lord are a thousand leagues removed from those experienced in marriage. It is all a union of love with love, and its operations are entirely pure, and so delicate and gentle that there is no way of describing them; but the Lord can make the soul very deeply conscious of them.

It seems to me that this union has not yet reached the point of spiritual betrothal, but is rather like what happens in our earthly life when two people are about to be betrothed. There is a discussion as to whether or no they are suited to each other and are both in love; and then they meet again so that they may learn to appreciate each other better. So it is here. The contract is already drawn up and the soul has been clearly given to under-

---

[1] The words "in . . . souls" were written by St. Teresa interlineally and "because . . . repose" were added by her in the margin.

stand the happiness of her lot and is determined to do all the will of her Spouse in every way in which she sees that she can give Him pleasure. His Majesty, Who will know quite well if this is the case, is pleased with the soul, so He grants her this mercy, desiring that she shall get to know Him better, and that, as we may say, they shall meet together,[1] and He shall unite her with Himself. We can compare this kind of union to a short meeting of that nature because it is over in the very shortest time. All giving and taking have now come to an end and in a secret way the soul sees Who this Spouse is that she is to take.[2] By means of the senses and faculties she could not understand in a thousand years what she understands in this way in the briefest space of time. But the Spouse, being Who He is, leaves her, after that one visit, worthier to join hands (as people say) with Him; and the soul becomes so fired with love that for her part she does her utmost not to thwart this Divine betrothal. If she is neglectful, however, and sets her affection on anything other than Himself, she loses everything, and that is a loss every bit as great as are the favours He has been granting her, which are far greater than it is possible to convey.

So, Christian souls, whom the Lord has brought to this point on your journey, I beseech you, for His sake, not to be negligent, but to withdraw from occasions of sin—for even in this state the soul is not strong enough to be able to run into them safely, as it is after the betrothal has been made—that is to say, in the Mansion which we shall describe after this one. For this communication has been no more than (as we might say) one single short meeting,[3] and the devil will take great pains about combating it and will try to hinder the betrothal. Afterwards, when he sees that the soul is completely surrendered to the Spouse, he dare not do this, for he is afraid of such a soul as that, and he knows by experience that if he attempts anything of the kind he will come out very much the loser and the soul will achieve a corresponding gain.

I tell you, daughters, I have known people of a very high degree of spirituality who have reached this state, and whom, notwithstanding, the devil, with great subtlety and craft, has won back to himself. For this purpose he will marshal all the powers of hell, for, as I have often said, if he wins a single soul in this way he will win a whole multitude. The devil has much experience in this matter. If we consider what a large number

---

[1] [*Vengan a vistas*: lit., "have sight of each other", "have an interview with each other"; and, in that sense, "come together" or "meet".]

[2] [This sounds contradictory, but the word "take" (*tomar* each time in the Spanish) is of course used in two different senses.]

[3] *No fué más de una vista.* [Cf. n. 1, above.]

of people God can draw to Himself through the agency of a single soul, the thought of the thousands converted by the martyrs gives us great cause for praising God. Think of a maiden like Saint Ursula. And of the souls whom the devil must have lost through Saint Dominic and Saint Francis and other founders of Orders, and is losing now through Father Ignatius, who founded the Company[1]—all of whom, of course, as we read, received such favours from God! What did they do but endeavour that this Divine betrothal should not be frustrated through their fault? Oh, my daughters, how ready this Lord still is to grant us favours, just as He was then! In some ways it is even more necessary that we should wish to receive them, for there are fewer than there used to be who think of the Lord's honour! We are so very fond of ourselves and so very careful not to lose any of our rights! Oh, what a great mistake we make! May the Lord in His mercy give us light lest we fall into such darkness.

There are two things about which you may ask me, or be in doubt. The first is this: If the soul is so completely at one with the will of God, as has been said, how can it be deceived, since it never desires to follow its own will? The second: By what avenues can the devil enter and lead you into such peril that your soul may be lost, when you are so completely withdrawn from the world and so often approach the Sacraments? For you are enjoying the companionship, as we might say, of angels, since, by the goodness of the Lord, you have none of you any other desires than to serve and please Him in everything. It would not be surprising, you might add, if this should happen to those who are immersed in the cares of the world. I agree that you are justified in asking this—God has been abundantly merciful to us. But when I read, as I have said, that Judas enjoyed the companionship of the Apostles, had continual intercourse with God Himself, and could listen to His own words, I realize that even this does not guarantee our safety.

To the first question, my reply would be that, if this soul invariably followed the will of God, it is clear that it would not be lost. But the devil comes with his artful wiles, and, under colour of doing good, sets about undermining it in trivial ways, and involving it in practices which, so he gives it to understand, are not wrong; little by little he darkens its understanding, and weakens its will, and causes its self-love to increase, until in one way and another he begins to withdraw it from the love of God and to persuade it to indulge its own wishes. And this is also

---

[1] Luis de León omitted the reference to St. Ignatius of Loyola and the Society of Jesus from his edition, reading: "and other founders of Orders, all of whom, as we read, etc."

an answer to the second question, for there is no enclosure so strictly guarded that he cannot enter it, and no desert so solitary that he cannot visit it. And I would make one further remark—namely, that the reason the Lord permits this may possibly be so that He may observe the behaviour of the soul which He wishes to set up as a light to others; for, if it is going to be a failure, it is better that it should be so at the outset than when it can do many souls harm.

What we should be most diligent about, I think, is this. First, we must continually ask God in our prayers to keep us in His hand, and bear constantly in mind that, if He leaves us, we shall at once be down in the depths, as indeed we shall. So we must never have any confidence in ourselves—that would simply be folly. But most of all we must walk with special care and attention, and watch what progress we make in the virtues, and discover if, in any way, we are either improving or going back, especially in our love for each other and in our desire to be thought least of, and in ordinary things; for if we look to this, and beg the Lord to give us light, we shall at once discern whether we have gained or lost. Do not suppose, then, that when God brings a soul to such a point He lets it go so quickly out of His hand that the devil can recapture it without much labour. His Majesty is so anxious for it not to be lost that He gives it a thousand interior warnings of many kinds, and thus it cannot fail to perceive the danger.

Let the conclusion of the whole matter be this. We must strive all the time to advance, and, if we are not advancing, we must cherish serious misgivings, as the devil is undoubtedly anxious to exercise his wiles upon us. For it is unthinkable that a soul which has arrived so far should cease to grow: love is never idle, so failure to advance would be a very bad sign. A soul which has once set out to be the bride of God Himself, and has already had converse with His Majesty and reached the point which has been described, must not lie down and go to sleep again. And so that you may see, daughters, how Our Lord treats those whom He makes His brides, let us begin to discuss the sixth Mansions, and you will see how slight is all the service we can render Him, all the suffering we can undergo for Him, and all the preparation we can make for such great favours. It may have been by Our Lord's ordinance that I was commanded to write this so that we shall forget our trivial earthly pleasures when we fix our eyes on the reward and see how boundless is the mercy which makes Him pleased to communicate and reveal Himself in this way to us worms. So, fired by love of Him, we shall run our race, with our eyes fixed upon His greatness.

May He be pleased to enable me to explain something of these difficult things, which I know will be impossible unless His Majesty and the Holy Spirit[1] guide my pen. Were it not to be for your profit I should beseech Him to prevent me from explaining any of it, for His Majesty knows that, so far as I myself can judge, my sole desire is that His name should be praised, and that we should make every effort to serve a Lord Who gives us such a reward here below, and thus conveys to us some idea of what He will give us in Heaven, without the delays and trials and perils incident to this sea of tempests. For, were it not that we might lose Him and offend Him, it would be a comfort if our life did not end until the end of the world, so that we could work for so great a God and Lord and Spouse. May it please His Majesty that we be worthy to do Him some service, unmarred by the many faults that we always commit, even in doing our good works! Amen.

[1] Gracián deletes, and León omits, the words "and the Holy Spirit".

SIXTH MANSIONS

In which there are Eleven Chapters

CHAPTER I

Shows how, when the Lord begins to grant the soul greater favours, it has also to endure greater trials. Enumerates some of these and describes how those who are in this Mansion must conduct themselves. This is a good chapter for any who suffer interior trials.

Let us now, with the help of the Holy Spirit, come to speak of the sixth Mansions, in which the soul has been wounded with love for the Spouse and seeks more opportunity of being alone, trying, so far as is possible to one in its state, to renounce everything which can disturb it in this its solitude. That sight of Him which it has had is so deeply impressed upon it that its whole desire is to enjoy it once more. Nothing, I must repeat, is seen in this state of prayer which can be said to be really seen, even by the imagination; I use the word "sight" because of the comparison I made.

The soul is now completely determined to take no other spouse; but the Spouse disregards its yearnings for the conclusion of the Betrothal, desiring that they should become still deeper and that this greatest of all blessings should be won by the soul at some cost to itself. And although everything is of but slight importance by comparison with the greatness of this gain, I assure you, daughters, that, if the soul is to bear its trials, it has no less need of the sign and token of this gain which it now holds. Oh, my God, how great are these trials, which the soul will suffer, both within and without, before it enters the seventh Mansion![1] Really, when I think of them, I am sometimes afraid that, if we realized their intensity beforehand, it would be most difficult for us, naturally weak as we are, to muster determination enough to enable us to suffer them or resolution enough for enduring them, however attractively the advantage of so doing might be presented to us, until we reached the seventh Mansion, where there is nothing more to be feared, and the soul will plunge deep into suffering for God's sake. The reason for this is that the soul is almost continuously near His Majesty

[1] [St. Teresa is not always consistent in her use of singular and plural in referring to each stage of the Mystic Way. The translation, throughout, follows her here exactly.]

and its nearness brings it fortitude. I think it will be well if I tell you about some of the things which I know are certain to happen here. Not all souls, perhaps, will be led along this path, though I doubt very much if souls which from time to time really taste the things of Heaven can live in freedom from earthly trials, in one way or in another.

Although I had not intended to treat of this, it has occurred to me that some soul finding itself in this state might be very much comforted if it knew what happens to those whom God grants such favours, at a time when everything really seems to be lost. I shall not take these experiences in the order in which they happen, but as each one presents itself to my memory. I will begin with the least of them. An outcry is made by people with whom such a person is acquainted, and even by those with whom she is not acquainted and who she never in her life supposed would think about her at all. "How holy she's getting!" they exclaim, or "She's only going to these extremes to deceive the world and to make other people look sinful, when really they are better Christians than she is without any of these goings-on!" (Notice, by the way, that she is not really indulging in any "goings-on" at all: she is only trying to live up to her profession.) Then people whom she had thought her friends abandon her and it is they who say the worst things of all and express the deepest regret that (as they put it) she is "going to perdition" and "obviously being deluded", that "this is the devil's work", that "she's going the way of So-and-so and So-and-so, who ruined their own lives and dragged good people down with them", and that "she takes in all her confessors". And they actually go to her confessors and tell them so, illustrating what they say by stories of some who ruined their lives in this way: and they scoff at the poor creature and talk about her like this times without number.

I know of a person[1] to whom these things were happening and who was terribly afraid that there would be nobody willing to hear her confession; but there is so much I could say about that that I will not stop to tell it here. The worst of it is, these things are not soon over—they last all one's life long. People warn each other to be careful not to have anything to do with persons like oneself. You will tell me that there are also those who speak well of one. But oh, daughters, how few there are who believe the good things they say by comparison with the many who dislike us! In any case, to be well spoken of is only one trial more and a worse one than those already mentioned. For the soul sees quite clearly that if there is any good in it this

[1] St. Teresa herself: cf. *Life*, Chap. XXVIII.

is a gift of God, and not in the least due to itself, for only a short time previously it saw itself in dire poverty and plunged deep into sin. So this praise is an intolerable torment to it, at least at the beginning: afterwards it is less so, and this for various reasons. The first of these is that experience shows it clearly how people will speak well of others as readily as ill, and so it takes no more notice of the former class than of the latter. The second, that the Lord has given it greater light and shown it that anything good it may have does not come from itself, but is His Majesty's gift; so it breaks into praises of God, but as though He were being gracious to a third person, and forgetting that it is itself concerned at all. The third reason is that, having seen others helped by observing the favours which God is granting it, the soul thinks that His Majesty has been pleased for them to think of it as good, though in fact it is not, so that they may be profited. The fourth is that, as the soul now prizes the honour and glory of God more than its own honour and glory, it no longer suffers from a temptation which beset it at first—namely, to think that these praises will do it harm, as it has seen them do to others. It cares little about being dishonoured itself, provided that it can be the cause of God's being even once praised—come afterwards what may.

These and other considerations mitigate the great distress caused by such praises, although some distress is nearly always felt, except when a soul takes no notice of such things whatsoever. But to find itself publicly and unmeritedly described as good is an incomparably greater trial than any of those already mentioned. Once the soul has learned to care little about this, it cares very much less about the other; which, indeed, makes it rejoice and sounds to it like sweetest music. This is absolutely true. The soul is fortified rather than daunted by censure, for experience has shown how great are the benefits it can bring; and it seems to the soul that its persecutors are not offending God, but that His Majesty is permitting this for its great advantage. Being quite clear about this, it conceives a special and most tender love for them and thinks of them as truer friends and greater benefactors than those who speak well of it.

The Lord is also in the habit of sending the most grievous infirmities. This is a much greater trial, especially if the pains are severe; in some ways, when they are very acute, I think they are the greatest earthly trial that exists—the greatest of exterior trials, I mean—however many a soul may suffer: I repeat that it is only to very acute pains that I am referring. For they affect the soul both outwardly and inwardly, till it becomes so much oppressed as not to know what to do with itself, and would much rather suffer any martyrdom than these pains. Still, at the very worst, they do not last so long—no longer, as a rule, than other bad illnesses do. For, after all, God gives us no more than we can bear, and He gives patience first.

I know a person of whom, since the Lord began to grant her this favour aforementioned, forty years ago,[1] it cannot be truly said that she has been a day without pains and other kinds of suffering; I mean because of her poor physical health, to say nothing of other great trials. It is true that she had been very wicked and it was all very slight by comparison with the hell that she had merited. Others, who have not so greatly offended Our Lord, will be led by Him along another way, but I should always choose the way of suffering, if only to imitate Our Lord Jesus Christ, and even were there no other special benefit to be obtained from it—and there are always a great many. But oh, when we come to interior sufferings! If these could be described they would make all physical sufferings seem very slight, but it is impossible to describe interior sufferings and how they happen.

Let us begin with the torture which it costs us to have to do with a confessor so scrupulous and inexperienced that he thinks nothing safe: he is afraid of everything, and doubtful about everything, as soon as he sees that he is dealing with anything out of the ordinary. This is particularly so if he sees any imperfection in the soul that is undergoing these experiences. He thinks that people to whom God grants these favours must be angels; and, as this is impossible while they are in the body, he attributes the whole thing to melancholy or to the devil. The world is so full of melancholy that this certainly does not surprise me; for there is so much abroad just now, and the devil makes so much use of it to work harm, that confessors have very good cause to be afraid of it and to watch for it very carefully. But, when the poor soul, harassed by the same fear, goes to the confessor as to a judge, and he condemns her, she cannot fail to be upset and tortured by what he says—and only a person who has passed through such a trial will know how great it is. For this is another of the great trials suffered by these souls, especially if they have been wicked—namely, to think that because of their sins God will permit them to be deceived—and although, when His Majesty grants them this favour, they feel secure and cannot believe that it comes from any other spirit than a spirit of God, yet, as it is a state which passes quickly, and the soul is ever mindful of its sins, and it sees faults in itself—for these are never

---

[1] The person referred to is no doubt the author. [It was almost exactly forty years since she had professed at the Incarnation.]

lacking—it then begins to suffer this torture. When the confessor reassures the soul, it becomes calm, though in due course it gets troubled again; but when all he can do is to make it still more fearful the thing grows almost intolerable, especially when on top of everything else come periods of aridity, during which the soul feels as if it has never known God and never will know Him, and as if to hear His Majesty spoken of is like hearing of a person from a great distance away.

All this would be nothing to the person concerned were it not followed immediately by the thought that she cannot be describing her case properly to her confessor and has been deceiving him; and, although when she thinks about it she feels sure she has not kept back even the first movement of her mind, it is of no use. For her understanding is so dim that it is incapable of seeing the truth, but believes what the imagination (now mistress of the understanding) presents to it and the nonsense which the devil attempts to present to it, when Our Lord gives him leave to test her soul, and even to make her think herself cast off by God. For there are many things which assault her soul with an interior oppression so keenly felt and so intolerable that I do not know to what it can be compared, save to the torment of those who suffer in hell, for in this spiritual tempest no consolation is possible.

If she decides to take up the matter with her confessor, it would look as if the devils have come to his aid so that he may torture her soul the more. A certain confessor, dealing with a person who had been in this state of torment, after it had passed away, thought that the oppression must have been of a dangerous type, since it had involved her in so many trials; so he told her, whenever she was in this state, to report to him; but this made her so much worse that he came to realize that he could no longer do anything with her. For, although she was quite able to read, she found that, if she took up a book written in the vernacular, she could understand no more of it than if she had not known her alphabet; her understanding was not capable of taking it in.

Briefly, in this tempest, there is no help for it but to wait upon the mercy of God, Who suddenly, at the most unlooked-for hour, with a single word, or on some chance occasion, lifts the whole of this burden from the soul, so that it seems as if it has never been clouded over, but is full of sunshine and far happier than it was before. Then, like one who has escaped from a perilous battle and gained the victory, the soul keeps praising Our Lord, for it is He Who has fought and enabled it to conquer. It knows very well that it did not itself do the fighting. For it saw that all the weapons with which it could defend itself were in the hands of its enemy, and was thus clearly aware of its misery and realized how little we can do of ourselves if the Lord should forsake us.

We have no need of reflection to enable us to understand this, for the soul's experience of enduring it, and of having found itself completely powerless, has made it realize that it is utterly helpless and that we are but miserable creatures. For, though it cannot be devoid of grace, since despite all this torment it does not offend God, and would not do so for anything upon earth, yet this grace is buried so deeply that the soul seems not to feel the smallest spark of any love for God, nor has it ever done so. If it has done anything good, or His Majesty has granted it any favour, the whole thing seems to it like a dream or a fancy: all it knows for certain is that it has sinned.

Oh, Jesus! How sad it is to see a soul thus forsaken, and how little, as I have said, can it gain from any earthly consolation! So do not suppose, sisters, if you ever find yourselves in this condition, that people who are wealthy, or free to do as they like, have any better remedy for such times. No, no; to offer them earthly consolations would be like telling criminals condemned to death about all the joys that there are in the world; not only would this fail to comfort them—it would but increase their torment; comfort must come to them from above, for earthly things are of no value to them any more. This great God desires us to know that He is a King and we are miserable creatures—a point of great importance for what follows.

Now what will a poor creature like that do if such a thing goes on for a very long time?[1] If she prays, she might as well not be doing so at all—I mean for all the comfort it will bring her, for interiorly she is incapable of receiving any comfort, nor, even when her prayer is vocal, can she understand what she is saying; while mental prayer at such a time is certainly impossible—her faculties are not capable of it. Solitude is still worse for her, though it is also torture for her to be in anyone's company or to be spoken to; and so, despite all her efforts to conceal the fact, she becomes outwardly upset and despondent, to a very noticeable extent. Is it credible that she will be able to say what is the matter with her? The thing is inexpressible, for this distress and oppression are spiritual troubles and cannot be given a name. The best medicine—I do not say for removing the trouble, for I know of none for that, but for enabling the soul to endure it—is to occupy oneself with external affairs and works of charity

---

[1] [*Lit.*: "for many days"; but, as we have already seen, St. Teresa often uses that phrase vaguely.]

and to hope in God's mercy, which never fails those who hope in Him. May He be blessed for ever. Amen.[1]

Other trials caused by devils, which are of an exterior kind, will not occur so commonly and thus there is no reason to speak of them nor are they anything like so grievous. For, whatever these devils do, they cannot, in my opinion, go so far as to inhibit the working of the faculties or to disturb the soul, in the way already described. After all, it thinks (and rightly), they cannot do more than the Lord permits, and, so long as it is not lost, nothing matters much by comparison with what has been described above.

We shall next deal with other interior troubles which occur in these Mansions, treating of the different kinds of prayer and favours of the Lord; for, although a few are still harder to bear than those referred to, as will be seen by the effects which they leave upon the body, they do not merit the name of trial, nor is it right that we should give them that name, since they are such great favours of the Lord and the soul understands them to be so, and far beyond its deservings. This severe distress comes just before the soul's entrance into the seventh Mansion, together with many more, only a few of which I shall describe, as it would be impossible to speak of them all, or even to explain their nature. For they are of another type than those already mentioned, and a much higher one; and if, in dealing with those of a lower kind, I have not been able to explain myself in greater detail, still less shall I be able to explain these others. The Lord give me His help in everything I do, through the merits of His Son. Amen.

CHAPTER II

Treats of several ways in which Our Lord awakens the soul; there appears to be nothing in these to be feared, although the experience is most sublime and the favours are great ones.

We seem to have left the little dove a long way behind, but we have not done so in reality, for these very trials enable it to make a higher flight. So let us now begin to treat of the way in which the Spouse deals with it, and see how, before it is wholly one with Him, He fills it with fervent desire, by means so delicate

---

[1] At this point in the autograph, St. Teresa wrote the word "Chapter", evidently intending to end the first chapter of the Sixth Mansions here, but deleted it again. Luis de León treated the insertion as valid and began the new chapter with the following paragraph: he was followed by other editors until the mid-nineteenth century. The autograph, however, does not support this procedure.

that the soul itself does not understand them, nor do I think I shall succeed in describing them in such a way as to be understood, except by those who have experienced it; for these are influences so delicate and subtle that they proceed from the very depth of the heart and I know no comparison that I can make which will fit the case.

All this is very different from what one can achieve in earthly matters, and even from the consolations which have been described. For often when a person is quite unprepared for such a thing, and is not even thinking of God, he is awakened by His Majesty, as though by a rushing comet or a thunderclap. Although no sound is heard,[1] the soul is very well aware that it has been called by God, so much so that sometimes, especially at first, it begins to tremble and complain, though it feels nothing that causes it affliction. It is conscious of having been most delectably wounded, but cannot say how or by whom; but it is certain that this is a precious experience and it would be glad if it were never to be healed of that wound. It complains to its Spouse with words of love, and even tries aloud, being unable to help itself, for it realizes that He is present but will not manifest Himself in such a way as to allow it to enjoy Him, and this is a great grief, though a sweet and delectable one; even if it should desire not to suffer it, it would have no choice—but in any case it never would so desire. It is much more satisfying to a soul than is the delectable absorption, devoid of distress, which occurs in the Prayer of Quiet.

I am straining every nerve,[2] sisters, to explain to you this operation of love, yet I do not know any way of doing so. For it seems a contradiction to say that the Beloved is making it very clear that He is with the soul and seems to be giving it such a clear sign that He is calling it that it cannot doubt the fact, and that the call is so penetrating that it cannot fail to hear Him. For the Spouse, Who is in the seventh Mansion, seems to be calling the soul in a way which involves no clear utterance of speech, and none of the inhabitants of the other Mansions—the senses, the imagination or the faculties—dares to stir. Oh, my powerful God, how great are Thy secrets, and how different are spiritual things from any that can be seen or understood here below. There is no way of describing this favour, small though it is by comparison with the signal favours which souls are granted by Thee.

So powerful is the effect of this upon the soul that it becomes consumed with desire, yet cannot think what to ask, so clearly

---

[1] The author had first written: "or a lightning-flash. Although no light is seen"; but she deleted this and substituted the phrase in the text.

[2] [The verb used is *deshacerse*, "to undo oneself", implying here the utmost effort.]

conscious is it of the presence of its God. Now, if this is so, you will ask me what it desires or what causes it distress. What greater blessing can it wish for? I cannot say; I know that this distress seems to penetrate to its very bowels; and that, when He that has wounded it draws out the arrow, the bowels seem to come with it, so deeply does it feel this love. I have just been wondering if my God could be described as the fire in a lighted brazier, from which some spark will fly out and touch the soul, in such a way that it will be able to feel the burning heat of the fire; but, as the fire is not hot enough to burn it up, and the experience is very delectable, the soul continues to feel that pain and the mere touch suffices to produce that effect in it. This seems the best comparison that I have been able to find, for this delectable pain, which is not really pain, is not continuous: sometimes it lasts for a long time, while sometimes it comes suddenly to an end, according to the way in which the Lord is pleased to bestow it, for it is a thing which no human means can procure. Although occasionally the experience lasts for a certain length of time, it goes and comes again; it is, in short, never permanent, and for that reason it never completely enkindles the soul; for, just as the soul is about to become enkindled, the spark dies, and leaves the soul yearning once again to suffer that loving pain of which it is the cause.

It cannot for a moment be supposed that this is a phenomenon which has its source in the physical nature, or that it is caused by melancholy, or that it is a deception of the devil, or a mere fancy. It is perfectly clear that it is a movement of which the source is the Lord, Who is unchangeable; and its effects are not like those of other devotions whose genuineness we doubt because of the intense absorption of the joy which we experience. Here all the senses and faculties are active, and there is no absorption; they are on the alert to discover what can be happening, and, so far as I can see, they cause no disturbance, and can neither increase this delectable pain nor remove it. Anyone to whom Our Lord has granted this favour will recognize the fact on reading this; he must give Him most heartfelt thanks and must not fear that it may be deception; let his chief fear be rather lest he show ingratitude for so great a favour, and let him endeavour to serve God and to grow better all his life long and he will see the result of this and find himself receiving more and more. One person who was granted this favour spent several years in the enjoyment of it and so completely did it satisfy her that, if she had served the Lord for very many years by suffering great trials, she would have felt well rewarded. May He be blessed for ever and ever. Amen.

It may be that you wonder why greater security can be felt

about this than about other things. For the following reasons, I think. First, because so delectable a pain can never be bestowed upon the soul by the devil: he can give pleasures and delights which seem to be spiritual, but it is beyond his power to unite pain—and such great pain!—with tranquillity and joy in the soul; for all his powers are in the external sphere, and, when he causes pain, it is never, to my mind, delectable or peaceful, but restless and combative. Secondly, this delectable tempest comes from another region than those over which he has authority. Thirdly, great advantages accrue to the soul, which, as a general rule, becomes filled with a determination to suffer for God's sake and to desire to have many trials to endure, and to be very much more resolute in withdrawing from the pleasures and intercourse of this world, and other things like them.

That this is no fancy is very evident; on other occasions the devil may create fancies of the kind, but he will never be able to counterfeit this. It is so wonderful a thing that it cannot possibly be created by the fancy (I mean, one cannot think it is there when it is not) nor can the soul doubt that it is there; if any doubt about it remains—I mean, if the soul doubts whether or no it has experienced it—it can be sure that the impulses are not genuine, for we perceive it as clearly as we hear a loud voice with our ears. Nor is there any possible way in which it can be due to melancholy, for the fancies created by melancholy exist only in the imagination, whereas this proceeds from the interior of the soul. I may conceivably be mistaken; but, until I hear arguments to the contrary from someone who understands the matter, I shall always be of this opinion; I know, for example, of a person who was terribly afraid of being deceived in this way, and yet who never had any fears about this kind of prayer.

Our Lord, too, has other methods of awakening the soul. Quite unexpectedly, when engaged in vocal prayer and not thinking of interior things, it seems, in some wonderful way, to catch fire. It is just as though there suddenly assailed it a fragrance so powerful that it diffused itself through all the senses or something of that kind (I do not say it is a fragrance; I merely make the comparison) in order to convey to it the consciousness that the Spouse is there. The soul is moved by a delectable desire to enjoy Him and this disposes it to make many acts and to sing praises to Our Lord. The source of this favour is that already referred to; but there is nothing here that causes pain, nor are the soul's desires to enjoy God in any way painful. This is what is most usually felt by the soul. For several of the reasons already alleged I do not think there is much reason here for fear; one must endeavour to receive this favour and give thanks for it.

CHAPTER III

Treats of the same subject and describes the way in which, when He is pleased to do so, God speaks to the soul. Gives instructions as to how we should behave in such a case: we must not be guided by our own opinions. Sets down a few signs by which we may know when this favour is, and when it is not, a deception. This chapter is very profitable.

There is another way in which God awakens the soul, and which, although in some respects it seems a greater favour than the others, may also be more perilous. For this reason I will spend a short time in describing it. This awakening of the soul is effected by means of locutions, which are of many kinds.[1] Some of them seem to come from without; others from the innermost depths of the soul; others from its higher part; while others, again, are so completely outside the soul that they can be heard with the ears, and seem to be uttered by a human voice. Sometimes—often, indeed—this may be a fancy, especially in persons who are melancholy—I mean, are affected by real melancholy—or have feeble imaginations.

Of persons of these two kinds no notice should be taken, in my view, even if they say they see or hear or are given to understand things, nor should one upset them by telling them that their experiences come from the devil. One should listen to them as one would to sick persons; and the prioress, or the confessor, or whatever person they confide in, should advise them to pay no heed to the matter, because the service of God does not consist in things like these, over which many have been deceived by the devil, although this may not be so with them. One should humour such people so as not to distress them further. If one tells them they are suffering from melancholy,

---

[1] P. Francisco de Santo Tomás, O.C.D., in his *Médula mystica* (Trat. VI, Cap. i), has a succinct description of the three types of locution referred to by St. Teresa, a classification applicable to visions also: "Some are corporeal, some imaginary and some spiritual or intellectual. Corporeal locutions are those actually heard by the physical powers of hearing.... Imaginary locutions are not heard in that way but the impression apprehended and received by the imaginative faculty is the same as though they had been.... In spiritual or intellectual locutions God imprints what He is about to say in the depth of the spirit: there is no sound, or voice, or either corporeal or imaginary representation of such, but an expression of (certain) concepts in the depth of the spirit and in the faculty of the understanding, and as this is not corporeal, but spiritual, the species, or similitudes, under which it is apprehended are not corporeal, but spiritual." Intellectual locutions, as explained by St. John of the Cross (*Ascent of Mount Carmel*, Book II, Chaps. XXVI–XXX), are of three kinds: successive, formal and substantial.

there will be no end to it. They will simply swear they see and hear things, and really believe that they do.

The real solution is to see that such people have less time for prayer, and also that, as far as is possible, they attach no importance to these fancies. For the devil is apt to take advantage of the infirmity of these souls, to the injury of others, if not to their own as well. Both with infirm and with healthy souls there is invariably cause for misgivings about these things until it becomes clear what kind of spirit is responsible. I believe, too, that it is always better for them to dispense with such things at first, for, if they are of God, dispensing with them will help us all the more to advance, since, when put to the proof in this way, they will tend to increase. Yet the soul should not be allowed to become depressed or disquieted, for it really cannot help itself.

Returning now to what I was saying about locutions, these may come from God, in any of the ways I have mentioned, or they may equally well come from the devil or from one's own imagination. I will describe, if I can, with the Lord's help, the signs by which these locutions differ from one another and when they are dangerous. For there are many people given to prayer who experience them, and I would not have you think you are doing wrong, sisters, whether or no you give them credence, when they are only for your own benefit, to comfort you or to warn you of your faults. In such cases it matters little from whom they proceed or if they are only fancies. But of one thing I will warn you: do not think that, even if your locutions come from God, you will for that reason be any the better. After all, He talked a great deal with the Pharisees: any good you may gain will depend upon how you profit by what you hear. Unless it agrees strictly with the Scriptures, take no more notice of it than you would if it came from the devil himself. The words may, in fact, come only from your weak imagination, but they must be taken as a temptation against things pertaining to the Faith and must therefore invariably be resisted so that they may gradually cease; and cease they will, because they will have little power of their own.

To return, then, to our first point: whether they come from within, from above or from without, has nothing to do with their coming from God. The surest signs that one can have of their doing this are, in my opinion, as follows. The first and truest is the sense of power and authority which they bear with them, both in themselves and in the actions which follow them. I will explain myself further. A soul is experiencing all the interior disturbances and tribulations which have been described, and all the aridity and darkness of the understanding. A single word of this kind—just a "Be not troubled"—is sufficient to calm it. No other word need be spoken; a great light comes to it; and all its trouble is lifted from it, although it had been thinking that, if the whole world, and all the learned men in the world, were to combine to give it reasons for not being troubled, they could not relieve it from its distress, however hard they might strive to do so. Or a soul is distressed because its confessor, and others, have told it that what it has is a spirit sent by the devil, and it is full of fear. Yet that single word which it hears: "It is I, fear not,"[1] takes all its fear from it, and it is most marvellously comforted, and believes that no one will ever be able to make it feel otherwise. Or it is greatly exercised because of some important piece of business and it has no idea how this will turn out. It is then given to understand that it must be calm and all will turn out well; and it acquires a new confidence and is no longer troubled. And so with many other things.

The second sign is that a great tranquillity dwells in the soul, which becomes peacefully and devoutly recollected, and ready to sing praises to God. Oh, Lord, if there is such power in a word sent by one of Thy messengers (for they say that, in this Mansion, at least, such words are uttered, not by the Lord Himself, but by some angel), what power wilt Thou not leave in the soul that is bound to Thee, as art Thou to it, by love.

The third sign is that these words do not vanish from the memory for a very long time: some, indeed, never vanish at all. Words which we hear on earth—I mean, from men, however weighty and learned they may be—we do not bear so deeply engraven upon our memory, nor, if they refer to the future, do we give credence to them as we do to these locutions. For these last impress us by their complete certainty, in such a way that, although sometimes they seem quite impossible of fulfilment, and we cannot help wondering if they will come true or not, and although our understanding may hesitate about it, yet within the soul itself there is a certainty which cannot be overcome. It may seem to the soul that everything is moving in the contrary direction to what it had been led to expect, and yet, even if many years go by, it never loses its belief that, though God may use other means incomprehensible to men, in the end what He has said will come true; as in fact it does. None the less, as I say, the soul is distressed when it sees things going badly astray. It may be some time since it heard the words; and both their working within it and the certainty which it had at the time that they came from God have passed away. So these doubts arise, and the soul wonders if the whole thing came from the

[1] [St. Luke xxiv, 36.]

devil, or can have been the work of the imagination. Yet at the time it had no such doubts and it would have died in defence of their veracity. But, as I say, all these imaginings must be put into our minds by the devil in order to distress us and make us fearful, especially if the matter is one in which obeying the locutions will bring others many blessings, or produce good works tending greatly to the honour and service of God but presenting considerable difficulties. What will the devil not do in this case by encouraging such misgivings? At the very least he will weaken the soul's faith, for it is most harmful not to believe that God is powerful and can do works which are incomprehensible to our understanding.

Despite all these conflicts, despite the assertions of some (I refer to confessors) that these locutions are pure nonsense, and despite all the unfortunate happenings which may persuade the soul that they cannot come true, there still remains within it such a living spark of conviction that they will come true (whence this arises I cannot tell) that, though all other hopes may be dead, this spark of certainty could not fail to remain alive, even if the soul wished it to die. And in the end, as I have said, the Lord's word is fulfilled, and the soul is so happy and glad that it would like to do nothing but praise His Majesty everlastingly—much more, however, because it has seen His assurances come true than because of the occurrence itself, even though this may be of very great consequence to it.

I do not know why it is, but the soul is so anxious for these assurances to be proved true that it would not, I think, feel it so much if it were itself caught in the act of lying—as though it could do anything more in the matter than repeat what is said to it! In this connection a certain person used continually to recall what happened to the prophet Jonas, when he feared that Ninive was not to be destroyed.[1] Of course, as the locutions come from the Spirit of God, it is right that we should have this trust in Him, and desire that He should never be thought false, since He is Supreme Truth. Great, therefore, is the joy of one who, after a thousand vicissitudes and in the most difficult circumstances, sees His word come true; such a person may himself have to suffer great trials on that account, but he would rather do this than that what he holds the Lord most certainly told him should not come to pass. Not everybody, perhaps, will have this weakness—if weakness it is, for I cannot myself condemn it as wrong.

If the locutions come from the imagination, none of these signs occur, nor is there any certainty or peace or interior consolation.

[1] Jonas iv.

It might, however, happen (and I even know of a few people to whom it has happened) that, when a person is deeply absorbed in the Prayer of Quiet and in spiritual sleep (for some, because of the weakness of their constitution, or of their imagination, or for some other reason, are so entirely carried out of themselves in this act of deep recollection, that they are unconscious of everything external, and all their senses are in such a state of slumber that they are like a person asleep—at times, indeed, they may even be asleep), he thinks that the locutions come to him in a kind of dream, and sees things and believes that these things are of God, and the effects of these locutions resemble those of a dream. It may also happen that, when such a person asks something of Our Lord with a great love, he thinks that the voices are telling him what he wants to be told; this does in fact sometimes happen. But anyone who has much experience of locutions coming from God will not, I think, be deceived in this way by the imagination.

The devil's locutions are more to be feared than those which come from the imagination; but, if the locutions are accompanied by the signs already described, one may be very confident that they are of God, although not to such an extent that, if what is said is of great importance and involves some action on the part of the hearer, or matters affecting a third person, one should do anything about it, or consider doing anything, without taking the advice of a learned confessor, a man of clear insight and a servant of God, even though one may understand the locutions better and better and it may become evident that they are of God. For this is His Majesty's will, so by carrying it out we are not failing to do what He commands: He has told us that we are to put our confessor in His place, even when it cannot be doubted that the words are His. If the matter is a difficult one, these words will help to give us courage, and Our Lord will speak to the confessor and if such is His pleasure will make him recognize the work of His spirit; if He does not, we have no further obligations. I consider it very dangerous for a person to do anything but what he has been told to do and to follow his own opinion in this matter; so I admonish you, sisters, in Our Lord's name, never to act thus.

There is another way in which the Lord speaks to the soul, which for my own part I hold to be very certainly genuine, and that is by a kind of intellectual vision, the nature of which I will explain later. So far down in the depths of the soul does this contact take place, so clearly do the words spoken by the Lord seem to be heard with the soul's own faculty of hearing, and so secretly are they uttered, that the very way in which the soul understands them, together with the effects produced by the vision itself, convinces it and makes it certain that no part in the matter is being played by the devil. The wonderful effects it produces are sufficient to make us believe this; at least one is sure that the locutions do not proceed from the imagination, and, if one reflects upon it, one can always be certain of this, for the following reasons.

The first reason is that some locutions are very much clearer than others. The genuine locution is so clear that, even if it consists of a long exhortation, the hearer notices the omission of a single syllable, as well as the phraseology which is used; but in locutions which are created fancifully by the imagination the voice will be less clear and the words less distinct; they will be like something heard in a half-dream.

The second reason is that often the soul has not been thinking of what it hears—I mean that the voice comes unexpectedly, sometimes even during a conversation, although it frequently has reference to something that was passing quickly through the mind or to what one was previously thinking of. But often it refers to things which one never thought would or could happen, so that the imagination cannot possibly have invented them, and the soul cannot be deceived about things it has not desired or wished for or that have never been brought to its notice.

The third reason is that in genuine locutions the soul seems to be hearing something, whereas in locutions invented by the imagination someone seems to be composing bit by bit what the soul wishes to hear.

The fourth reason is that there is a great difference in the words themselves: in a genuine locution one single word may contain a world of meaning such as the understanding alone could never put rapidly into human language.

The fifth reason is that frequently, not only can words be heard, but, in a way which I shall never be able to explain, much more can be understood than the words themselves convey and this without any further utterance. Of this way of understanding I shall say more elsewhere; it is a very subtle thing, for which Our Lord should be praised. Some people (especially one person with experience of these things, and no doubt others also) have been very dubious about this way of understanding locutions and about the differences between them, and have been quite unable to get the matter straight. I know that this person has thought it all over very carefully, because the Lord has granted her this favour very frequently indeed; her most serious doubt, which used to occur when she first experienced it, was whether she was not imagining the whole thing. When locutions come from the devil their source can be more quickly recognized, though his wiles are so numerous that he can readily counterfeit the spirit of light. He will do this, in my view, by pronouncing his words very clearly, so that there will be no more doubt about their being understood than if they were being spoken by the spirit of truth. But he will not be able to counterfeit the effects which have been described, or to leave in the soul this peace or light, but only restlessness and turmoil. He can do little or no harm if the soul is humble and does what I have said—that is, if it refrains from action, whatever the locutions may say.

If gifts and favours come to it from the Lord, the soul should consider carefully and see if they make it think any the better of itself; and if, as the words grow more and more precious, it does not suffer increasing confusion, it can be sure that the spirit is not of God; for it is quite certain that, when it is so, the greater the favour the soul receives, the less by far it esteems itself, the more keenly it remembers its sins, the more forgetful it is of its own interest, the more fervent are the efforts of its will and memory in seeking nothing but the honour of God rather than being mindful of its own profit, and the greater is its fear of departing in the least from the will of God and its certainty that it has never deserved these favours, but only hell. When these are the results of all the experiences and favours that come to the soul in prayer, it need not be afraid, but may rest confidently in the mercy of the Lord, Who is faithful, and will not allow the devil to deceive it, though it always does well to retain its misgivings.

It may be that those whom the Lord does not lead by this road think that such souls need not listen to these words which are addressed to them; that, if they are interior words, they should turn their attention elsewhere so as not to hear them; and that in this way they will run no risk of incurring these perils. My answer is that that is impossible—and I am not referring now to locutions invented by the fancy, a remedy for which is to be less anxious about certain things and to try to take no notice of one's own imaginings. When the locutions come from God there is no such remedy, for the Spirit Himself, as He speaks, inhibits all other thought and compels attention to what He says. So I really think (and I believe this to be true) that it would be easier for someone with excellent hearing not to hear a person who spoke in a very loud voice, because he might simply pay no heed and occupy his thought and understanding with something else. In the case of which we are speaking, however, that is impossible. We have no ears which we can stop nor have we the power to refrain from thought; we can only think of what is being said; for He who was able, at the request of Josue (I think it was), to make the sun stand still,[1] can still the faculties and all the interior part of a soul in such a way that the soul becomes fully aware that another Lord, greater than itself, is governing that Castle and renders Him the greatest devotion and humility. So it cannot do other than listen: it has no other choice. May His Divine Majesty grant us to fix our eyes only on pleasing Him and to forget ourselves, as I have said: Amen. May He grant that I have succeeded in explaining what I have attempted to explain and that I may have given some help to any who have experience of these locutions.

CHAPTER IV

Treats of occasions when God suspends the soul in prayer by means of rapture, or ecstasy, or trance (for I think these are all the same), and of how great courage is necessary if we are to receive great favours from His Majesty.

How much rest can this poor little butterfly have amid all these trials and other things that I have described? Its whole will is set on desiring to have ever-increasing fruition of its Spouse; and His Majesty, knowing our weakness, continues to grant it the things it wants, and many more, so that it may have the courage to achieve union with so great a Lord and to take Him for its Spouse.

You will laugh at my saying this and call it ridiculous, for you will all think courage is quite unnecessary and suppose there is no woman, however lowly, who would not be brave enough to betroth herself to the King. This would be so, I think, with an earthly king, but for betrothal with the King of Heaven I must warn you that there is more need of courage than you imagine, because our nature is very timid and lowly for so great an undertaking, and I am certain that, unless God granted us strength,[2] it would be impossible. And now you are going to see what His Majesty does to confirm this betrothal, for this, as I understand it, is what happens when He bestows raptures, which carry the

---

[1] Josue x, 12-13.

[2] [The original here interpolates two clauses, *con cuanto veis, u que nos está bien*, which, translated literally as "with all that you see or that it is acceptable to us", make no sense. I suspect that, if St. Teresa had re-read her work, the phrase would have been omitted or clarified. Freely it might be rendered: "wonderful as you see it to be and much as we appreciate it", or, "however many visions you see or however much we desire them", but I am not convinced that either of these translations represents the author's meaning and other paraphrases are admissible.]

soul out of its senses; for if, while still in possession of its senses, the soul saw that it was so near to such great majesty, it might perhaps be unable to remain alive. It must be understood that I am referring to genuine raptures, and not to women's weaknesses, which we all have in this life, so that we are apt to think everything is rapture and ecstasy. And, as I believe I have said, there are some people who have such poor constitutions that one experience of the Prayer of Quiet kills them. I want to enumerate here some different kinds of rapture which I have got to know about through conversations with spiritual people. I am not sure if I shall succeed in doing so, any more than when I wrote of this before.[1] For various reasons it has been thought immaterial if I should repeat myself in discussing this and other matters connected with it, if for no other object than that of setting down in one place all that there is to be said about each Mansion.

One kind of rapture is this. The soul, though not actually engaged in prayer, is struck by some word, which it either remembers or hears spoken by God. His Majesty is moved with compassion at having seen the soul suffering so long through its yearning for Him, and seems to be causing the spark of which we have already spoken to grow within it, so that, like the phoenix, it catches fire and springs into new life. One may piously believe that the sins of such a soul are pardoned, assuming that it is in the proper disposition and has used the means of grace, as the Church teaches.[2] When it is thus cleansed, God unites it with Himself, in a way which none can understand save it and He, and even the soul itself does not understand this in such a way as to be able to speak of it afterwards, though it is not deprived of its interior senses; for it is not like one who suffers a swoon or a paroxysm so that it can understand nothing either within itself or without.

The position, in this case, as I understand it, is that the soul has never before been so fully awake to the things of God or had such light or such knowledge of His Majesty. This may seem impossible; because, if the faculties are so completely absorbed that we might describe them as dead, and the senses are so as well, how can the soul be said to understand this secret? I cannot say, nor perhaps can any creature, but only the Creator Himself, nor can I speak of many other things that happen in this state—I mean in these two Mansions, for this and the last might be fused in one: there is no closed door to separate the one from the other. As, however, there are things in the latter Mansion which are not

[1] *Life*, Chap. XX; *Relations*, V.
[2] The phrase "assuming . . . teaches" was added by St. Teresa, in the autograph, as a marginal note.

shown to those who have not yet reached it, I have thought it best to separate them.

When the soul is in this state of suspension and the Lord sees fit to reveal to it certain mysteries, such as heavenly things and imaginary visions, it is able subsequently to describe these, for they are so deeply impressed upon the memory that they can never again be forgotten. But when they are intellectual visions they cannot be so described; for at these times come visions of so sublime a kind that it is not fitting for those who live on earth to understand them in such a way that they can describe them; although after regaining possession of their senses they can often describe many of these intellectual visions.

It may be that some of you do not understand what is meant by a vision, especially by an intellectual vision. I shall explain this in due course, as I have been commanded to do so by him who has authority over me; and although it may seem irrelevant there may possibly be souls who will find it helpful. "But," you will say to me, "if the soul is not going to remember these sublime favours which the Lord grants it in this state, how can they bring it any profit?" Oh, daughters, the profit is so great that it cannot be exaggerated, for, although one cannot describe these favours, they are clearly imprinted in the very depths of the soul and they are never forgotten. "But," you will say next, "if the soul retains no image of them and the faculties are unable to understand them, how can they be remembered?" This, too, is more than I can understand; but I know that certain truths concerning the greatness of God remain so firmly in the soul that even had it not faith which will tell it Who He is and that it is bound to believe Him to be God, the soul would adore Him as such from that very moment, just as Jacob adored Him when he saw the ladder.[1] He must, of course, have learned other secrets which he could not describe; for, if he had not had more interior light, he would not have understood such great mysteries merely from seeing a ladder on which angels were descending and ascending.

I do not know if I am right in what I am saying, for, although I have heard of the incident, I am not sure if I remember it correctly. Moses, again, could not describe all that he saw in the bush, but only as much as God willed him to;[2] yet, if God had not revealed secret things to his soul in such a way as to make him sure of their truth, so that he should know and believe Him to be God, he would not have taken upon himself so many and such arduous labours. Amid the thorns of that bush he must have learned marvellous things, for it was these things which gave him courage to do what he did for the people of Israel. Therefore,

[1] Genesis xxviii, 12. [2] Exodus iii, 2.

sisters, we must not seek out reasons for understanding the hidden things of God; rather, believing, as we do, in His great power, we must clearly realize that it is impossible for worms like ourselves, with our limited powers, to understand His greatness. Let us give Him hearty praise for being pleased to allow us to understand some part of it.

I am wishing I could find a suitable comparison which would give some sort of explanation of what I am saying. But I can think of none that will answer my purpose. Let us put it like this, however. You enter a private apartment in the palace of a king or a great lord (I think they call it a *camarín*), where they have an infinite variety of glassware, and earthenware, and all kinds of things, set out in such a way that you can see almost all of them as you enter. I was once taken into a room of this kind in the house of the Duchess of Alba, where I was commanded by obedience to stay,[1] in the course of a journey, at her pressing invitation. When I went in I was astounded and began to wonder what all this mass of things could be used for, and then I realized that the sight of so many different things might lead one to glorify the Lord. It occurs to me now how useful an experience it was for my present purpose. Although I was there for some time, there was so much to be seen that I could not remember it all, so that I could no more recall what was in those rooms than if I had never seen them, nor could I say what the things were made of; I can only remember having seen them as a whole.[2] It is just like that here. The soul becomes one with God. It is brought into this mansion of the empyrean Heaven which we must have in the depths of our souls; for it is clear that, since God dwells in them, He must have one[3] of these mansions. And although while the soul is in ecstasy the Lord will not always wish it to see these secrets (for it is so much absorbed in its fruition of Him that that great blessing suffices it), He is sometimes pleased that it should emerge from its absorption, and then it will at once see what there is in this room; in which case, after coming to itself, it will remember that revelation of the great things it has seen. It will not, however, be able to describe any of them, nor will its nature be able to apprehend more of the supernatural than God has been pleased to reveal to it.

Is this tantamount to an admission on my part that it has really seen something and that this is an imaginary vision? I do not

---

[1] "Two days", adds the *editio princeps*. The visit was made at the beginning of 1574: see "Outline, etc.", Vol. I, p. xxxi, above.
[2] The sentence "I can . . . whole" was written by St. Teresa in the margin of the autograph.
[3] [Or "some": the Spanish word, *alguna*, can have either a singular or a plural sense.]

mean that at all, for it is not of imaginary, but of intellectual visions that I am treating; only I have no learning and am too stupid to explain anything; and I am quite clear that, if what I have said so far about this kind of prayer is put correctly, it is not I who have said it. My own belief is that, if the soul to whom God has given these secrets in its raptures never understands any of them, they proceed, not from raptures at all, but from some natural weakness, which is apt to affect people of feeble constitution, such as women. In such cases the spirit, by making a certain effort, can overcome nature and remain in a state of absorption, as I believe I said when dealing with the Prayer of Quiet. Such experiences as these have nothing to do with raptures; for when a person is enraptured you can be sure that God is taking her entire soul to Himself, and that, as she is His own property and has now become His bride, He is showing her some little part of the kingdom which she has gained by becoming so. This part may be only a small one, but everything that is in this great God is very great. He will not allow her to be disturbed either by the faculties or by the senses; so He at once commands that all the doors of these Mansions shall be shut, and only the door of the Mansion in which He dwells remains open so that we may enter. Blessed be such great mercy! Rightly shall those who will not profit by it, and who thus forgo the presence of their Lord, be called accursed.

Oh, my sisters, what nothingness is all that we have given up, and all that we are doing, or can ever do, for a God Who is pleased to communicate Himself in this way to a worm! If we have the hope of enjoying this blessing while we are still in this life, what are we doing about it and why are we waiting? What sufficient reason is there for delaying even a short time instead of seeking this Lord, as the Bride did, through streets and squares?[1] Oh, what a mockery is everything in the world if it does not lead us and help us on the way towards this end,—and would be even though all the worldly delights and riches and joys that we can imagine were to last for ever! For everything is cloying and degrading by comparison with these treasures, which we shall enjoy eternally. And even these are nothing by comparison with having for our own the Lord of all treasures and of Heaven and earth.

Oh, human blindness! How long, how long shall it be before this dust is removed from our eyes? For although, as far as we ourselves are concerned, it seems not to be bad enough to blind us altogether, I can see some motes and particles which, if we allow them to become more numerous, will be sufficient to do us great harm. For the love of God, then, sisters, let us profit by these

[1] [The "streets and the broad ways" of Canticles iii, 2.]

faults and learn from them what wretched creatures we are, and may they give us clearer sight, as did the clay to the blind man who was healed by our Spouse;[1] and thus, realizing our own imperfections, we shall beseech Him more and more earnestly to bring good out of our wretchedness, so that we may please His Majesty in everything.

Without realizing it, I have strayed far from my theme. Forgive me, sisters; and believe me, now that I have come to these great things of God (come to write about them, I mean), I cannot help feeling the pity of it when I see how much we are losing, and all through our own fault. For, true though it is that these are things which the Lord gives to whom He will, He would give them to us all if we loved Him as He loves us. For He desires nothing else but to have those to whom He may give them, and His riches are not diminished by His readiness to give.

Returning now to what I was saying, the Spouse orders the doors of the Mansions to be shut, and even those of the Castle and its enclosure. For when He means to enrapture this soul, it loses its power of breathing, with the result that, although its other senses sometimes remain active a little longer, it cannot possibly speak. At other times it loses all its powers at once, and the hands and the body grow so cold that the body seems no longer to have a soul—sometimes it even seems doubtful if there is any breath in the body. This lasts only for a short time (I mean, only for a short period at any one time) because, when this profound suspension lifts a little, the body seems to come partly to itself again, and draws breath, though only to die once more, and, in doing so, to give fuller life to the soul. Complete ecstasy, therefore, does not last long.

But, although relief comes, the ecstasy has the effect of leaving the will so completely absorbed and the understanding so completely transported—for as long as a day, or even for several days—that the soul seems incapable of grasping anything that does not awaken the will to love; to this it is fully awake, while asleep as regards all that concerns attachment to any creature.

Oh, what confusion the soul feels when it comes to itself again and what ardent desires it has to be used for God in any and every way in which He may be pleased to employ it! If such effects as have been described result from the former kinds of prayer, what can be said of a favour as great as this? Such a soul would gladly have a thousand lives so as to use them all for God, and it would like everything on earth to be tongue so that it might praise Him. It has tremendous desires to do penance; and whatever penance it does it counts as very little, for its love is

[1] St. John ix, 6–7.

so strong that it feels everything it does to be of very small account and realizes clearly that it was not such a great matter for the martyrs to suffer all their tortures, for with the aid of Our Lord such a thing becomes easy. And thus these souls make complaint to Our Lord when He offers them no means of suffering.

When this favour is granted them secretly they esteem it very highly; for so great are the shame and the confusion caused them by having to suffer before others that to some extent they lessen the soul's absorption in what it was enjoying, because of the distress and the anxiety which arise from its thoughts of what others who have seen it will think. For, knowing the malice of the world, they realize that their suffering may perhaps not be attributed to its proper cause but may be made an occasion for criticism instead of for glorifying the Lord. This distress and shame are no longer within the soul's own power of control, yet they seem to me to denote a lack of humility; for if such a person really desires to be despitefully treated, how can she mind if she is? One who was distressed in this way heard Our Lord say: "Be not afflicted, for either they will praise Me or murmur at thee, and in either case thou wilt be the gainer."[1] I learned afterwards that that person had been greatly cheered and consoled by those words; and I set them down here for the sake of any who find themselves in this affliction. It seems that Our Lord wants everyone to realize that such a person's soul is now His and that no one must touch it. People are welcome to attack her body, her honour, and her possessions, for any of these attacks will be to His Majesty's honour. But her soul they may not attack, for unless, with most blameworthy presumption, it tears itself away from its Spouse, He will protect it from the whole world, and indeed from all hell.

I do not know if I have conveyed any impression of the nature of rapture: to give a full idea of it, as I have said, is impossible. Still, I think there has been no harm in my saying this, so that its nature may be understood, since the effects of feigned raptures are so different. (I do not use the word "feigned" because those who experience them wish to deceive, but because they are deceived themselves.)[2] As the signs and effects of these last do not harmonize with the reception of this great favour, the favour itself becomes discredited, so that those to whom the Lord grants it later on are not believed. May He be for ever blessed and praised. Amen. Amen.

[1] Cf. *Life*, Chap. XXXI [Vol. I, p. 209, above].
[2] This is Luis de León's emendation of the sentence in the autograph, which reads: "I do not use the word 'feigned', because those who experience them do not wish to deceive, but because [*sic*] they are deceived themselves." Gracián, in the Córdoba copy, emends similarly, though not identically. Both evidently express what St. Teresa meant but failed to put clearly.

CHAPTER V

Continues the same subject and gives an example of how God exalts the soul through flights of the spirit in a way different from that described. Gives some reasons why courage is necessary here. Says something of this favour which God grants in a way so delectable. This chapter is highly profitable.

There is another kind of rapture, or flight of the spirit, as I call it, which, though substantially the same, is felt within the soul[1] in a very different way. Sometimes the soul becomes conscious of such rapid motion that the spirit seems to be transported with a speed which, especially at first, fills it with fear, for which reason I told you that great courage is necessary for anyone in whom God is to work these favours, together with faith and confidence and great resignation, so that Our Lord may do with the soul as He wills. Do you suppose it causes but little perturbation to a person in complete possession of his senses when he experiences these transports of the soul? We have even read in some authors that the body is transported as well as the soul, without knowing whither it is going, or who is bearing it away, or how, for when this sudden motion begins the soul has no certainty that it is caused by God.

Can any means of resisting this be found? None whatever: on the contrary, resistance only makes matters worse. This I know from a certain person who said that God's will seems to be to show the soul that, since it has so often and so unconditionally placed itself in His hands, and has offered itself to Him with such complete willingness, it must realize that it is no longer its own mistress, and so the violence with which it is transported becomes markedly greater. This person, therefore, decided to offer no more resistance than a straw does when it is lifted up by amber (if you have ever observed this) and to commit herself into the hands of Him Who is so powerful, seeing that it is but to make a virtue of necessity. And, speaking of straw, it is a fact that a powerful man cannot bear away a straw more easily than this great and powerful Giant of ours can bear away the spirit.

I think that basin of water, of which we spoke in (I believe) the fourth Mansion (but I do not remember exactly where),[2]

---
[1] The mystics concur with St. Thomas in holding that ecstasy, rapture, transport, flight of the spirit, etc., are in substance one and the same, though there are accidental differences between them, as St. Teresa explains here, in *Life*, Chap. XX, and in *Relations*, V.
[2] IV, ii. [p. 236, above].

was being filled at that stage gently and quietly—I mean without any movement. But now this great God, Who controls the sources of the waters and forbids the sea to move beyond its bounds, has loosed the sources whence water has been coming into this basin; and with tremendous force there rises up so powerful a wave that this little ship—our soul—is lifted up on high. And if a ship can do nothing, and neither the pilot nor any of the crew has any power over it, when the waves make a furious assault upon it and toss it about at their will, even less able is the interior part of the soul to stop where it likes, while its senses and faculties can do no more than has been commanded them: the exterior senses, however, are quite unaffected by this.

Really, sisters, the mere writing of this makes me astounded when I reflect how the great power of this great King and Emperor manifests itself here. What, then, must be the feelings of anyone who experiences it? For my own part I believe that, if His Majesty were to reveal Himself to those who journey through the world to their perdition as He does to these souls, they would not dare—out of very fear, though not perhaps out of love—to offend Him. Oh, how great, then, are the obligations attending souls who have been warned in so sublime a way to strive with all their might so as not to offend this Lord! For His sake, sisters, I beseech you, to whom His Majesty has granted these favours or others like them, not merely to receive them and then grow careless, but to remember that anyone who owes much has much to pay.[1]

This is another reason why the soul needs great courage, for the thought is one which makes it very fearful, and, did Our Lord not give it courage, it would continually be in great affliction. When it reflects what His Majesty is doing with it, and then turns to reflect upon itself, it realizes what a little it is doing towards the fulfilment of its obligations and how feeble is that little which it does do and how full of faults and failures. If it does any good action, rather than remember how imperfect this action is, it thinks best to try to forget it, to keep nothing in mind but its sins, and to throw itself upon the mercy of God; and, since it has nothing with which to pay, it craves the compassion and mercy which He has always shown to sinners.

He may perhaps answer it as He answered someone who was very much distressed about this, and was looking at a crucifix and thinking that she had never had anything to offer God or to give up for His sake. The Crucified Himself comforted her by saying that He was giving her all the pains and trials which He

[1] St. Luke xii, 28.

had suffered in His Passion, so that she should have them for her own to offer to His Father.[1] That soul, as I have understood from her, was so much comforted and enriched by this experience that she cannot forget it, and, whenever she feels miserable, she remembers it and it comforts and encourages her. There are several other remarks on this subject which I might add; for, as I have had to do with many saintly and prayerful people, I know of a number of such cases, but I do not want you to think that it is to myself that I am referring, so I pass them over. This incident which I have described seems to me a very apt one for helping you to understand how glad Our Lord is when we get to know ourselves and keep trying all the time to realize our poverty and wretchedness, and to reflect that we possess nothing that we have not been given. Therefore, my sisters, courage is necessary for this and for many other things that happen to a soul which the Lord has brought to this state; and, to my thinking, if the soul is humble, more courage is necessary for this last state than for any other. May the Lord, of His own bounty, grant us humility.

Turning now to this sudden transport of the spirit, it may be said to be of such a kind that the soul really seems to have left the body; on the other hand, it is clear that the person is not dead, though for a few moments he cannot even himself be sure if the soul is in the body or no. He feels as if he has been in another world, very different from this in which we live, and has been shown a fresh light there, so much unlike any to be found in this life that, if he had been imagining it, and similar things, all his life long, it would have been impossible for him to obtain any idea of them. In a single instant he is taught so many things all at once that, if he were to labour for years on end in trying to fit them all into his imagination and thought, he could not succeed with a thousandth part of them. This is not an intellectual, but an imaginary vision, which is seen with the eyes of the soul very much more clearly than we can ordinarily see things with the eyes of the body; and some of the revelations are communicated to it without words. If, for example, he sees any of the saints, he knows them as well as if he had spent a long time in their company.

Sometimes, in addition to the things which he sees with the eyes of the soul, in intellectual vision, others are revealed to him—in particular, a host of angels, with their Lord; and, though he sees nothing with the eyes of the body or with the eyes of the soul, he is shown the things I am describing, and many others which

---

[1] St. Teresa received this favour at Seville about 1575-6. Cf. *Relations*, LI (Vol. I, p. 360, above).

are indescribable, by means of an admirable kind of knowledge. Anyone who has experience of this, and possesses more ability than I, will perhaps know how to express it; to me it seems extremely difficult. If the soul is in the body or not while all this is happening I cannot say; I would not myself swear that the soul is in the body, nor that the body is bereft of the soul.

I have often thought that if the sun can remain in the heavens and yet its rays are so strong that without its moving thence they can none the less reach us here, it must be possible for the soul and the spirit, which are as much the same thing as are the sun and its rays, to remain where they are, and yet, through the power of the heat that comes to them from the true Sun of Justice, for some higher part of them to rise above itself. Really, I hardly know what I am saying; but it is a fact that, as quickly as a bullet leaves a gun when the trigger is pulled, there begins within the soul a flight (I know no other name to give it) which, though no sound is made, is so clearly a movement that it cannot possibly be due to fancy. When the soul, as far as it can understand, is right outside itself, great things are revealed to it; and, when it returns to itself, it finds that it has reaped very great advantages and it has such contempt for earthly things that, in comparison with those it has seen, they seem like dirt to it. Thenceforward to live on earth is a great affliction to it, and, if it sees any of the things which used to give it pleasure, it no longer cares for them. Just as tokens of the nature of the Promised Land were brought back by those whom the Israelites sent on there,[1] so in this case the Lord's wish seems to have been to show the soul something of the country to which it is to travel, so that it may suffer the trials of this trying road,[2] knowing whither it must travel in order to obtain its rest. Although you may think that a thing which passes so quickly cannot be of great profit, the help which it gives the soul is so great that only the person familiar with it can understand its worth.

Clearly, then, this is no work of the devil; such an experience could not possibly proceed from the imagination, and the devil could never reveal things which produce such results in the soul and leave it with such peace and tranquillity and with so many benefits. There are three things in particular which it enjoys to a very high degree. The first is knowledge of the greatness of God: the more we see of this, the more deeply we are conscious of it. The second is self-knowledge and humility at realizing how a thing like the soul, so base by comparison with One Who is the Creator of such greatness, has dared to offend Him and

---

[1] Numbers xiii, 18-24.
[2] [*Los trabajos de este camino tan trabajoso*: the word-play is intentional.]

dares to raise its eyes to Him. The third is a supreme contempt for earthly things, save those which can be employed in the service of so great a God.

These are the jewels which the Spouse is beginning to give to His bride, and so precious are they that she will not fail to keep them with the greatest care. These meetings[1] with the Spouse remain so deeply engraven in the memory that I think it is impossible for the soul to forget them until it is enjoying them for ever; if it did so, it would suffer the greatest harm. But the Spouse Who gives them to the soul has power also to give it grace not to lose them.

Returning now to the soul's need of courage, I ask you: Does it seem to you such a trifling thing after all? For the soul really feels that it is leaving the body when it sees the senses leaving it and has no idea why they are going. So He Who gives everything else must needs give courage too. You will say that this fear of the soul's is well rewarded; so too say I. May He Who can give so much be for ever praised. And may it please His Majesty to grant us to be worthy to serve Him. Amen.

CHAPTER VI

Describes one effect of the prayer referred to in the last chapter, by which it will be known that it is genuine and no deception. Treats of another favour which the Lord grants to the soul so that He may use it to sing His praises.

Having won such great favours, the soul is so anxious to have complete fruition of their Giver that its life becomes sheer, though delectable, torture. It has the keenest longings for death, and so it frequently and tearfully begs God to take it out of this exile. Everything in this life that it sees wearies it; when it finds itself alone it experiences great relief, but immediately this distress returns till it hardly knows itself when it is without it. In short, this little butterfly can find no lasting repose; indeed, her love is so full of tenderness that any occasion whatever which serves to increase the strength of this fire causes the soul to take flight; and thus in this Mansion raptures occur continually and there is no way of avoiding them, even in public. Further, although the soul would fain be free from tears, these persecutions and murmurings never leave her; for these all kinds of persons are responsible, especially confessors.

[1] [*Vistas.* Cf. p. 265, above.]

Although on the one hand she seems to be feeling great interior security, especially when alone with God, on the other hand she is in great distress, for she is afraid that the devil may be going to deceive her so that she shall offend Him for Whom she has such love. She is not hurt by what people say about her except when her own confessor blames her, as though she could prevent these raptures. She does nothing but beg everyone to pray for her and beseech His Majesty to lead her by another road, as she is advised to do, since the road she is on is very dangerous. But she has gained so much from following it (for she cannot help seeing, and she reads and hears and learns from the commandments of God that it leads to Heaven) that, try as she may, she feels unable to desire any other; all she wants to do is to leave herself in His hands. And even this impotence of will distresses her, because she thinks she is not obeying her confessor, for she believes that her only remedy against deception consists in obeying and not offending Our Lord. So she feels that she would not intentionally commit so much as a venial sin, even were she to be cut in pieces; and thus she is greatly distressed to find that, without being aware of the fact, she cannot avoid committing a great many.

God gives these souls the keenest desire not to displease Him in any respect whatsoever, however trivial, or to commit so much as an imperfection if they can avoid doing so. For this reason alone, if for no other, the soul would like to flee from other people, and greatly envies those who live, or have lived, in deserts. On the other hand it would like to plunge right into the heart of the world, to see if by doing this it could help one soul to praise God more; a woman in this state will be distressed at being prevented from doing this by the obstacle of sex and very envious of those who are free to cry aloud and proclaim abroad Who is this great God of Hosts.

Oh, poor little butterfly, bound by so many fetters, which prevent you from flying whithersoever you will! Have pity on her, my God; and dispose things so that she may be able to do something towards fulfilling her desires to Thy honour and glory. Remember not the slightness of her merits and the baseness of her nature. Mighty art Thou, Lord, for Thou didst make the great sea to draw back, and the great Jordan, and didst allow the Children of Israel to pass over them.[1] And yet Thou needest not have pity on her, for, with the aid of Thy strength, she is capable of enduring many trials. And this she is determined to do: to suffer them is her desire. Stretch out Thy mighty arm, O Lord, and let not her life be spent in things so base. Let Thy

---

[1] Exodus xiv, 21-2; Josue iii, 13.

greatness appear in this creature, womanish and base though she is, so that men may realize that nothing she does comes from herself and may give Thee praise. Cost what it may, it is this that she desires, and she would give a thousand lives, if she had them, so that on her account one soul might praise Thee a little more. She would consider them all well spent, for she knows that in actual fact she deserves not to suffer the very smallest trial for Thy sake, still less to die for Thee.

I do not know why I have said this, sisters, nor to what purpose, for I have not understood it all myself. It should be realized that such, without any kind of doubt, are the effects which remain after these suspensions or ecstasies; the desires they inspire are not fleeting but permanent; and when any opportunity occurs of demonstrating the fact, it becomes evident that the experience was not feigned. You may ask why I use the word "permanent", since sometimes and in the most trifling matters the soul feels cowardly, and is so fearful and devoid of courage that it seems impossible it can be courageous enough to do anything whatsoever. But this, I take it, occurs at a time when the Lord leaves it to its own nature—an experience which is extremely good for it, making it realize that any usefulness it may have had has been a gift bestowed upon it by His Majesty. And this it realizes with a clearness which annihilates any self-interest in it and imbues it with a greater knowledge of the mercy of God and of His greatness, which He has been pleased to demonstrate to it in so small a matter. But more usually it is as we have already said.

Note one thing, sisters, concerning these great desires of the soul to see Our Lord: that they will sometimes oppress you so much that you must not encourage them but put them from you —if you can, I mean; because there are other desires, of which I shall write later, which cannot possibly be so treated, as you will see. These of which I am now speaking it is sometimes possible to put from you, since the reason is free to resign itself to the will of God, and you can echo the words of Saint Martin[1]; in such a case, where the desires are very oppressive, the thoughts may be deflected from them. For, as such desires are apparently found in souls which are very proficient, the devil might encourage them in us, so as to make us think ourselves proficient too; and it is always well to proceed with caution. But I do not myself believe he could ever fill the soul with the quietness and peace caused it by this distress; the feelings he arouses are apt to be passionate ones, like those which we experience when we are troubled about things of the world. Anyone without experience

---

[1] In the office of this Saint the Church recalls these words of his: "Lord, if I am still necessary to Thy people, I do not refuse toil: Thy will be done."

of each kind of distress will not understand that, and, thinking it a great thing to feel like this, will stimulate the feeling as much as possible. To do this, however, may be to injure the health, for the distress is continuous, or, at the least, occurs with great frequency.

Note also that distress of this kind is apt to be caused by weak health, especially in emotional people, who weep for the slightest thing; again and again they will think they are weeping for reasons which have to do with God but this will not be so in reality. It may even be the case (I mean when they shed floods of tears—and for some time they cannot refrain from doing so whenever they think of God or hear Him spoken of) that some humour has been oppressing the heart, and that it is this, rather than their love of God, which has excited their tears. It seems as if they will never make an end of weeping; having come to believe that tears are good, they make no attempt to control them. In fact, they would not do otherwise than weep even if they could, and they make every effort they can to induce tears. The devil does his best, in such cases, to weaken them, so that they may be unable either to practise prayer or to keep their Rule.

I seem to hear you asking whatever you are to do, as I am telling you there is danger in everything. If I think deception possible in anything as beneficial as shedding tears may I not be deceived myself? Yes, of course I may; but, believe me, I am not talking without having observed this in certain persons. I have never been like it myself, however, for I am not in the least emotional; on the contrary, my hardness of heart sometimes worries me; though, when the fire within my soul is strong, however hard my heart may be, it distils as if in an alembic. You will easily recognize when tears arise from this source, because they are comforting and tranquillizing rather than disturbing, and seldom do any harm. The great thing about this deception, when such it is, will be that, although it may harm the body, it cannot (if the soul is humble, I mean) hurt the soul. If it is not humble, it will do it no harm to keep its suspicions.

Do not let us suppose that if we weep a great deal we have done everything that matters; let us also set to and work hard, and practise the virtues, for these are what we most need. Let the tears come when God is pleased to send them: we ourselves should make no efforts to induce them. They will leave this dry ground of ours well watered and will be of great help in producing fruit; but the less notice we take of them, the more they will do, because they are the water which comes from Heaven.[1] When we ourselves draw water, we tire ourselves by digging for it, and the water we get is not the same; often we dig till we wear ourselves

[1] [Cf. *Life*, Chap. XVIII: Vol. I, p. 105, above.]

out without having discovered so much as a pool of water, still less a well-spring. For this reason, sisters, I think our best plan is to place ourselves in the Lord's presence, meditate upon His mercy and grace and upon our own lowliness, and leave Him to give us what He wills, whether it be water or aridity. He knows best what is good for us, and in this way we shall walk in tranquillity and the devil will have less opportunity to fool us.

Together with these things, which are at once distressing and delectable, Our Lord sometimes bestows upon the soul a jubilation and a strange kind of prayer, the nature of which it cannot ascertain. I set this down here, so that, if He grants you this favour, you may give Him hearty praise and know that such a thing really happens. I think the position is that the faculties are in close union, but that Our Lord leaves both faculties and senses free to enjoy this happiness, without understanding what it is that they are enjoying and how they are enjoying it. That sounds nonsense but it is certainly what happens. The joy of the soul is so exceedingly great that it would like, not to rejoice in God in solitude, but to tell its joy to all, so that they may help it to praise Our Lord, to which end it directs its whole activity. Oh, what high festival such a one would make to this end and how she would show forth her joy, if she could, so that all should understand it! For she seems to have found herself, and, like the father of the Prodigal Son,[1] she would like to invite everybody and have great festivities because she sees her soul in a place which she cannot doubt is a place of safety, at least for a time. And, for my own part, I believe she is right; for such interior joy in the depths of the soul's being, such peace and such happiness that it calls upon all to praise God cannot possibly have come from the devil.

Impelled as it is by this great joy, the soul cannot be expected to keep silence and dissemble: it would find this no light distress. That must have been the state of mind of Saint Francis, when robbers met him as he was going about the countryside crying aloud and he told them that he was the herald of the great King. Other saints retire to desert places, where they proclaim the same thing as Saint Francis—namely, the praises of their God. I knew one of these, called Fray Peter of Alcántara. Judging from the life he led, I think he is certainly a saint, yet those who heard him from time to time called him mad. Oh, what a blessed madness, sisters! If only God would give it to us all! And how good He has been to you in placing you where, if the Lord should grant you this grace and you show others that He has done so, you will not be spoken against as you would be in the world

[1] St. Luke xv, 11-32.

(where there are so few to proclaim God's praise that it is not surprising if they are spoken against), but will be encouraged to praise Him the more.

Oh, unhappy are the times and miserable is the life which we now live, and happy are those who have had the good fortune to escape from it! Sometimes it makes me specially glad when we are together and I see these sisters of mine so full of inward joy that each vies with the rest in praising Our Lord for bringing her to the convent; it is very evident that those praises come from the inmost depths of the soul. I should like you to praise Him often, sisters, for, when one of you begins to do so, she arouses the rest. How can your tongues be better employed, when you are together, than in the praises of God, which we have so many reasons for rendering Him?

May it please His Majesty often to bestow this prayer upon us since it brings us such security and such benefit. For, as it is an entirely supernatural thing, we cannot acquire it. It may last for a whole day, and the soul will then be like one who has drunk a great deal, but not like a person so far inebriated as to be deprived of his senses; nor will it be like a melancholiac, who, without being entirely out of his mind, cannot forget a thing that has been impressed upon his imagination, from which no one else can free him either. These are very unskilful comparisons to represent so precious a thing, but I am not clever enough to think out any more: the real truth is that this joy makes the soul so forgetful of itself, and of everything, that it is conscious of nothing, and able to speak of nothing, save of that which proceeds from its joy—namely, the praises of God. Let us join with this soul, my daughters all. Why should we want to be more sensible than she? What can give us greater pleasure than to do as she does? And may all the creatures join with us for ever and ever. Amen, amen, amen.

CHAPTER VII

Treats of the kind of grief felt for their sins by the souls to whom God grants the favours aforementioned. Says that, however spiritual people may be, it is a great mistake for them not to practise keeping in mind the Humanity of Our Lord and Saviour Jesus Christ, His most sacred Passion and life, and His glorious Mother and the Saints. This chapter is of great profit.

You will think, sisters, that these souls to whom the Lord communicates Himself in so special a way (I am speaking now particularly to those who have not attained these favours, for if they have been granted the enjoyment of such favours by God, they will know what I am about to say) will by now be so sure that they are to enjoy Him for ever that they will have no reason to fear or to weep for their sins. This will be a very great mistake, for, the more they receive from our God, the greater grows their sorrow for sin; I believe myself that this will never leave us until we reach that place where nothing can cause us affliction.

It is true that this sorrow can be more oppressive at one time than at another, and also that it is of different kinds; for the soul does not now think of the pain which it is bound to suffer on account of its sins, but only of how ungrateful it has been to Him Whom it owes so much, and Who so greatly merits our service. For through these manifestations of His greatness which He communicates to it the soul gains a much deeper knowledge of the greatness of God. It is aghast at having been so bold; it weeps for its lack of reverence; its foolish mistakes in the past seem to it to have been so gross that it cannot stop grieving, when it remembers that it forsook so great a Majesty for things so base. It thinks of this much more than of the favours it receives, great as they are like those which we have described and like those which remain to be described later. It is as if a mighty river were running through the soul and from time to time bringing these favours with it. But its sins are like the river's slimy bed; they are always fresh in its memory; and this is a heavy cross to it.

I know of a person who had ceased wishing she might die so as to see God, but was desiring death in order that she might not suffer such constant distress at the thought of her ingratitude to One to Whom her debts were so great. She thought nobody's evil deeds could equal hers, for she believed there was no one with whom God had borne for so long and to whom He had shown so many favours.

With regard to fear of hell, these souls have none; they are sometimes sorely oppressed by the thought that they may lose God, but this happens seldom. Their sole fear is that God may let them out of His hand and that they may then offend Him, and thus find themselves in as miserable a state as before. They have no anxiety about their own pain or glory. If they desire not to stay long in Purgatory, it is less for the pain which they will have to suffer than because while they are there they will not be with God.

However favoured by God a soul may be, I should not think it secure were it to forget the miserable state it was once in, for, distressing though the reflection is, it is often profitable.

Perhaps it is because I myself have been so wicked that I feel like this and for that reason always keep it in mind; those who have been good will have nothing to grieve for, although for as long as we live in this mortal body we shall always have failures. It affords us no relief from this distress to reflect that Our Lord has forgiven and forgotten our sins; in fact the thought of so much goodness and of favours granted to one who has merited only hell makes the distress greater. I think these reflections must have been a regular martyrdom for Saint Peter and for the Magdalen; because, as their love was so great and they had received so many favours and had learned to understand the greatness and majesty of God, they would find them terribly hard to bear, and must have been moved with the deepest emotion.

You will also think that anyone who enjoys such sublime favours will not engage in meditation on the most sacred Humanity of Our Lord Jesus Christ, because by that time he will be wholly proficient in love. This is a thing of which I have written at length elsewhere,[1] and, although I have been contradicted about it and told that I do not understand it, because these are paths along which Our Lord leads us, and that, when we have got over the first stages, we shall do better to occupy ourselves with matters concerning the Godhead and to flee from corporeal things, they will certainly not make me admit that this is a good way. I may be wrong and we may all be meaning the same thing; but it was clear to me that the devil was trying to deceive me in this way; and I have had to learn my lesson. So, although I have often spoken about this,[2] I propose to speak to you about it again, so that you may walk very warily. And observe that I am going so far as to advise you not to believe anyone who tells you otherwise. I will try to explain myself better than I did before. If by any chance a certain person has written about it, as he said he would, it is to be hoped that he has explained it more fully; to write about it in a general way to those of us who are not very intelligent may do a great deal of harm.

Some souls also imagine that they cannot dwell upon the Passion, in which case they will be able still less to meditate upon the most sacred Virgin and the lives of the saints, the remembrance of whom brings us such great profit and encouragement. I cannot conceive what they are thinking of; for, though angelic spirits, freed from everything corporeal, may remain permanently enkindled in love, this is not possible for those of us who live in this mortal body. We need to cultivate, and think upon, and seek the companionship of those who, though living

---
[1] *Life*, Chap. XXII.   [2] *Life*, Chaps. XXII–XXIV.

on earth like ourselves, have accomplished such great deeds for God; the last thing we should do is to withdraw of set purpose from our greatest help and blessing, which is the most sacred Humanity of Our Lord Jesus Christ. I cannot believe that people can really do this; it must be that they do not understand themselves and thus do harm to themselves and to others. At any rate, I can assure them that they will not enter these last two Mansions; for, if they lose their Guide, the good Jesus, they will be unable to find their way; they will do well if they are able to remain securely in the other Mansions. For the Lord Himself says that He is the Way;[1] the Lord also says that He is light[2] and that no one can come to the Father save by Him;[3] and "he that seeth Me seeth my Father."[4] It may be said that these words have another meaning. I do not know of any such meaning myself; I have got on very well with the meaning which my soul always feels to be the true one.

There are some people (and a great many of them have spoken to me about this) on whom Our Lord bestows perfect contemplation and who would like to remain in possession of it for ever. That is impossible; but they retain something of this Divine favour, with the result that they can no longer meditate upon the mysteries of the Passion and the life of Christ, as they could before. I do not know the reason for this, but it is quite a common experience in such cases for the understanding to be less apt for meditation. I think the reason must be that the whole aim of meditation is to seek God, and once He is found, and the soul grows accustomed to seeking Him again by means of the will, it has no desire to fatigue itself with intellectual labour. It also seems to me that, as the will is now enkindled, this generous faculty would have no desire to make use of that other faculty,[5] even if it could. There would be nothing wrong in its setting it aside, but it is impossible for it to do so, especially before the soul has reached these last Mansions, and it will only lose time by attempting it, for the aid of the understanding is often needed for the enkindling of the will.

Note this point, sisters, for it is important, so I will explain it further. The soul is desirous of employing itself wholly in love and it would be glad if it could meditate on nothing else. But this it cannot do even if it so desires; for, though the will is not dead, the fire which habitually kindles it is going out, and, if

---
[1] St. John xiv, 6.
[2] The words "the Lord . . . light" [which clearly interrupt the thought of the passage] are in the author's hand, but are marginal.
[3] St. John xiv, 6.
[4] St. John xiv, 9.
[5] [I.e., the understanding.]

it is to give off heat of itself, it needs someone to fan it into flame. Would it be a good thing for the soul to remain in that state of aridity, hoping for fire to come down from Heaven to burn up this sacrifice of itself which it is making to God as did our father Elias?[1] No, certainly not; nor is it a good thing to expect miracles: the Lord will perform them for this soul when He sees fit to do so, as has been said and as will be said again later. But His Majesty wants us to realize our wickedness, which makes us unworthy of their being wrought, and to do everything we possibly can to come to our own aid. And I believe myself that, however sublime our prayer may be, we shall have to do this until we die.

It is true that anyone whom Our Lord brings to the seventh Mansion very rarely, or never, needs to engage in this activity, for the reason that I shall set down, if I remember to do so, when I come to deal with that Mansion, where in a wonderful way the soul never ceases to walk with Christ our Lord but is ever in the company of both His Divine and His human nature. When, therefore, the aforementioned fire is not kindled in the will, and the presence of God is not felt, we must needs seek it, since this is His Majesty's desire, as the Bride sought it in the *Songs*.[2] Let us ask the creatures who made them, as Saint Augustine says that he did (in his *Meditations* or *Confessions*,[3] I think) and let us not be so foolish as to lose time by waiting to receive what has been given us once already. At first it may be that the Lord will not give it us, for as long as a year, or even for many years: His Majesty knows why; it is not our business to want to know, nor is there any reason why we should. Since we know the way we have to take to please God—namely, that of keeping His commandments and counsels—let us be very diligent in doing this, and in meditating upon His life and death, and upon all that we owe Him; and let the rest come when the Lord wills.

Such people will reply that they cannot stop to meditate upon these things, and here they may to some extent be right, for the reason already given. You know, of course, that it is one thing to reason with the understanding and quite another for the memory to represent truths to the understanding. You will say, perhaps, that you do not understand me, and it may very well be that I do not understand the matter myself sufficiently to be

---

[1] 3 Kings [A.V., 1 Kings] xviii, 30-9.
[2] Canticles iii, 3.
[3] "Or *Confessions*" is a marginal addition in St. Teresa's hand. The passage alluded to comes from Chapter XXXI of the *Soliloquies*, a work first published in Spanish at Venice in 1512 and often reprinted in Spain during the sixteenth century. A passage very similar to this will be found in the *Confessions*, Bk. X, Chap. VI.

able to explain it; but I will deal with it as well as I can. By meditation I mean prolonged reasoning with the understanding, in this way. We begin by thinking of the favour which God bestowed upon us by giving us His only Son; and we do not stop there but proceed to consider the mysteries of His whole glorious life. Or we begin with the prayer in the Garden and go on rehearsing the events that follow until we come to the Crucifixion. Or we take one episode of the Passion—Christ's arrest, let us say—and go over this mystery in our mind, meditating in detail upon the points in it which we need to think over and to try to realize, such as the treason of Judas, the flight of the Apostles, and so on. This is an admirable and a most meritorious kind of prayer.

This is the kind of prayer I was referring to which those whom God has raised to supernatural things and to perfect contemplation are right in saying they cannot practise. As I have said, I do not know why this should be the case; but as a rule they are in fact unable to do so. A man will not be right, however, to say that he cannot dwell upon these mysteries, for he often has them in his mind, especially when they are being celebrated by the Catholic Church; nor is it possible that a soul which has received so much from God should forget all these precious signs of His love, for they are living sparks which will enkindle the soul more and more in its love for Our Lord. But these mysteries will not be apprehended by the understanding: the soul will understand them in a more perfect way. First, the understanding will picture them to itself, and then they will be impressed upon the memory, so that the mere sight of the Lord on His knees, in the Garden, covered with that terrible sweat, will suffice us, not merely for an hour, but for many days. We consider, with a simple regard, Who He is and how ungrateful we have been to One Who has borne such pain for us. Then the will is aroused, not perhaps with deep emotion but with a desire to make some kind of return for this great favour, and to suffer something for One Who has suffered so much Himself. And so it is with other subjects, in which both memory and understanding will have a place. This, I think, is why the soul cannot reason properly about the Passion, and it is because of this that it believes itself unable to meditate upon it at all.

But if it does not already meditate in this way, it will be well advised to attempt to do so; for I know that the most sublime kind of prayer will be no obstacle to it and I believe omission to practise it often would be a great mistake. If while the soul is meditating the Lord should suspend it, well and good; for in that case He will make it cease meditation even against its own will. I consider it quite certain that this method of procedure is no hindrance to the soul but a great help to it in everything that is good; whereas, if it laboured hard at meditation in the way I have already described, this would indeed be a hindrance—in fact, I believe such labour is impossible for a person who has attained greater heights. This may not be so with everyone, since God leads souls by many ways, but those who are unable to take this road should not be condemned or judged incapable of enjoying the great blessings contained in the mysteries of Jesus Christ our Good. No one, however spiritual, will persuade me that to neglect these mysteries can be profitable for him.

Some souls, at the beginning of the spiritual life, or even when well advanced in it, get as far as the Prayer of Quiet, and are about to enjoy the favours and consolations given by the Lord in that state, and then think it would be a very great thing to be enjoying these gifts all the time. Let them take my advice, and become less absorbed in them, as I have said elsewhere.[1] For life is long and there are many trials in it and we have need to look at Christ our Pattern, and also at His Apostles and Saints, and to reflect how they bore these trials, so that we, too, may bear them perfectly. The good Jesus is too good company for us to forsake Him and His most sacred Mother. He is very glad when we grieve for His afflictions although sometimes we may be forsaking our own pleasures and consolations in order to do so—though for that matter, daughters, consolations in prayer are not so frequent that there is not time for everything. If anyone told me that she experienced them continuously (I mean so continuously that she could never meditate in the way I have described) I should consider it suspicious. Keep on with your meditation, then, and endeavour to be free from this error, and make every effort to avoid this absorption. If your efforts are not sufficient, tell the prioress, in order that she may give you some work which will keep you so busy that this danger will no longer exist. Any continuous exposure to it would be very bad for the brain and the head, if nothing worse.

I think I have explained what it is well for you to know—namely that, however spiritual you are, you must not flee so completely from corporeal things as to think that meditation on the most sacred Humanity can actually harm you. We are sometimes reminded that the Lord said to His disciples that it was expedient for them that He should go away:[2] I cannot, however, allow that as an argument. He did not say this to His most sacred Mother, because she was firm in the faith and knew

[1] *Foundations*, Chap. VI.   [2] St. John xvi, 7.

that He was God and Man; and, although she loved Him more than they, her love was so perfect that His being on earth was actually a help to her. The Apostles could not at that time have been as firm in the faith as they were later and as we have reason to be now. I assure you, daughters, that I consider this a perilous road and that if we took it the devil might end by causing us to lose our devotion to the Most Holy Sacrament.

The mistake, I think, which I used to make myself did not go as far as this; it was only that I would take less pleasure than previously in thinking of Our Lord Jesus Christ and would go about in that state of absorption, expecting to receive spiritual consolation. Then I saw clearly that I was going wrong; for, as it was impossible always to be having consolations, my thoughts would keep passing from one subject to another, until my soul, I think, got like a bird flying round and round in search of a resting-place and losing a great deal of time, without advancing in the virtues or making progress in prayer. I could not understand the cause—nor, I believe, should I ever have understood it, because I thought I was on the proper road, until one day, when I was telling a person who was a servant of God about my method of prayer, he gave me some counsel. This showed me clearly how far I had gone astray and I have never ceased regretting that there was once a time when I failed to realize that so great a loss could not possibly result in gain. Even if I could obtain it, I want no blessing save that which I acquire through Him by Whom all blessings come to us. May He be praised for ever. Amen.

CHAPTER VIII

Treats of the way in which God communicates Himself to the soul through intellectual vision.[1] *Describes the effects which this produces when genuine. Charges that these favours be kept secret.*

In order, sisters, that you may the better appreciate the accuracy of what I have been saying to you and see that the farther a soul progresses the closer becomes its companionship with this good Jesus, it will be well for us to consider how, when His Majesty so wills, we cannot do otherwise than walk with Him all the time, as is clear from the ways and methods whereby His Majesty communicates Himself to us, and reveals His love for us by means of such wonderful appearances and visions.

[1] For St. Teresa's treatment of intellectual vision, see *Life*, Chaps. XXVII, XXVIII.

Should the Lord grant you any of the favours which I shall describe (I mean, if He grants me ability to describe any of them), you must not be dismayed. Even though it be not to us that He grants them, we must give Him hearty praise that He should be pleased to commune with a creature—He Who is of such great majesty and power.

It may happen that, while the soul is not in the least expecting Him to be about to grant it this favour, which it has never thought it can possibly deserve, it is conscious that Jesus Christ Our Lord is near to it, though it cannot see Him either with the eyes of the body or with those of the soul. This (I do not know why) is called an intellectual vision. I saw a person to whom God had granted this favour, together with other favours which I shall describe later. At first that person was greatly perturbed, for she could not understand what the vision was, not having seen anything. She realized with such certainty that it was Jesus Christ Our Lord Who had revealed Himself to her in that way that she could not doubt it—I mean, could not doubt that that vision was there. But as to its being from God or no she had great misgivings, although the effects which it produced were so remarkable that they suggested it came from Him. She had never heard of an intellectual vision, or realized that there was any such thing, but she understood quite clearly that it was this Lord Who often spoke to her in the way I have described: until He granted her this favour to which I am referring she never knew Who was speaking to her, although she understood the words.

Being frightened about this vision (for it is not like an imaginary vision, which is quickly gone, but lasts for many days—sometimes for more than a year), she went off to her confessor in a state of great perturbation.[1] "If you see nothing," he asked her, "how do you know it is Our Lord?" Then he told her to tell him what His face was like. She replied that she did not know, that she had seen no face, and that she could not tell him more than she had done already: what she did know was that it was He Who was speaking to her and that it was no fancy. And, although people aroused grievous misgivings in her about it, she felt again and again that she could not doubt its genuineness, especially when He said to her: "Be not afraid: it is I." These words had such power that when she heard them she could not doubt, and she was greatly strengthened and gladdened by such good companionship. For she saw plainly that it was a great help to her to be habitually thinking of God wherever she went and to be taking such care to do nothing which would displease Him

[1] [Cf. *Life*, Chap. XXVII.]

because she felt that He was always looking at her. Whenever she wanted to draw near to His Majesty in prayer, and at other times as well, she felt He was so near that He could not fail to hear her; although she was unable to hear Him speaking to her whenever she wished, but did so at quite unexpected times, when it became necessary. She was conscious that He was walking at her right hand, but this consciousness arose, not from those senses which tell us that another person is near us, but in another and a subtler way which is indescribable. It is quite as unmistakable, however, and produces a feeling of equal certainty, or even greater. Other things of the kind might be attributable to fancy, but this thing is not, for it brings such great benefits and produces such effects upon the interior life as could not occur if it were the result of melancholy. The devil, again, could not do so much good: were it his work, the soul would not have such peace and such constant desires to please God and such scorn for everything that does not lead it to Him. Later, this person attained a clear realization that it was not the work of the devil, and came to understand it better and better.

None the less, I know she sometimes felt the gravest misgivings, and at other times the greatest confusion,[1] because she had no idea whence such a great blessing had come to her. She and I were so intimate that nothing happened in her soul of which I was ignorant and thus I can be a good witness and you may be sure that everything I say about it is true. This favour of the Lord brings with it the greatest confusion and humility. If it came from the devil, it would be just the reverse. As it is a thing which can be clearly recognized as the gift of God and such feelings could not possibly be produced by human effort, anyone who has it must know it does not in reality come from him, but is a gift from the hand of God. And although, as I believe, some of the other experiences that have been described are greater favours than this, yet this brings a special knowledge of God, and from this constant companionship is born a most tender love toward His Majesty, and yearnings, even deeper than those already described, to give oneself wholly up to His service, and a great purity of conscience; for the Presence Which the soul has at its side makes it sensitive to everything. For though we know quite well that God is present in all that we do, our nature is such that it makes us lose sight of the fact; but when this favour is granted it can no longer do so, for the Lord, Who is near at hand, awakens it. And even the favours aforementioned occur much more commonly, as the soul experiences a vivid and almost constant love for Him Whom it sees or knows to be at its side.

[1] Ibid.

In short, the greatness and the precious quality of this favour are best seen in what the soul gains from it. It thanks the Lord, Who bestows it on one that has not deserved it, and would exchange it for no earthly treasure or joy. When the Lord is pleased to withdraw it, the soul is left in great loneliness; yet all the possible efforts that it might make to regain His companionship are of little avail, for the Lord gives this when He wills and it cannot be acquired. Sometimes, again, the companionship is that of a saint and this is also a great help to us.

You will ask how, if this Presence cannot be seen, the soul knows that it is that of Christ, or when it is a saint, or His most glorious Mother. This is a question which the soul cannot answer, nor can it understand how it knows what it does; it is perfectly certain, however, that it is right. When it is the Lord, and He speaks, it is natural that He should be easily recognized; but even when it is a saint, and no words are spoken, the soul is able to feel that the Lord is sending him to be a help and a companion to it; and this is more remarkable. There are also other spiritual experiences which cannot be described, but they all help to show us how impotent our nature is, when it comes to understanding the great wonders of God, for we are not capable of understanding these but can only marvel and praise His Majesty for giving them to us. So let us give Him special thanks for them; for, as this is not a favour which is granted to all, it is one which should be highly esteemed and we must try to render the greatest services to God Who has so many ways of helping us. For this reason no one thus favoured has any better opinion of himself on that account. On the contrary, he feels that he is serving God less than anyone else on the earth, and yet that no one else has so great an obligation to serve Him. Any fault which he commits, therefore, pierces his very vitals and has every reason to do so.

These above-described effects which such visions cause in the soul may be observed by any one of you whom the Lord leads by this way, and you will then see that they are due neither to deception nor to fancy. For, as I have said, if they are of the devil, I do not think they can possibly last so long or do the soul such a great deal of good, or bring it such inward peace. It is not usual for one who is so evil to do so much good; he could not, in fact, even if he would. The soul would soon become clouded over by the mist of self-esteem and would begin to think itself better than others. But its continual occupation with God and its fixing of the thought on Him would make the devil so furious that, though he might attempt such a thing once, he would not do so often. God is so faithful that He will not allow the devil to have all this power over a soul whose one aim is to please Him and to devote its whole life to His honour and glory; He will see to it that the devil is speedily disillusioned.

My point is, and will continue to be, that, if the soul walks in the manner described above, and these favours of God are withdrawn from it, His Majesty will see that it is the gainer, and if He sometimes allows the devil to attack it, his efforts will be brought to confusion. Therefore, daughters, if any of you travel along this road, as I have said, do not be alarmed. It is well for us to have misgivings and walk the more warily; and you must not presume upon having received these favours and become careless, for if you do not find them producing in you the result already described it will be a sign that they are not of God. It will be well at first for you to communicate this, in confession, to some very learned man (for it is from such men that we must seek illumination) or to any highly spiritual person if you know one. Should your confessor not be a very spiritual man, someone with learning is better; or, if you know such a person, it is best to consult one both spiritual and learned. If he tells you that it is fancy, do not let that trouble you, for fancy can have little effect on your soul, either for good or for evil: commend yourself to the Divine Majesty and pray Him not to allow you to be deceived. If he tells you that it is the devil, this will be a greater trial to you, though no learned man would say such a thing if you have experienced the effects described; but, if he says it, I know that the Lord Himself, Who is walking at your side, will console you and reassure you, and will continue to give him light, so that he in his turn may give it to you.

If your director, though a man of prayer, has not been led in this way by the Lord, he will at once become alarmed and condemn it; that is why I advise you to go to a man who has both spirituality and great learning if such a one can be found. Your prioress should give you leave to do this; for although, seeing you are leading a good life, she may think your soul is safe, she will be bound to allow you to consult someone for your own safety and for hers as well. When you have finished these consultations, calm yourself and do not go on talking about the matter; for sometimes, when there is no reason for fear, the devil implants such excessive misgivings that they prevent the soul from being content with a single consultation, especially if the confessor has had little experience and treats the matter timorously and enjoins you to go and consult others. In such a case what should by rights be a close secret gets noised abroad and the penitent is persecuted and tormented; for she finds that what she thought was secret has become public, and this leads to many sore trials, which, as things are at present, might affect the Order. Great caution, then, is necessary here and such caution I strongly recommend to prioresses.

And let none of you imagine that, because a sister has had such experiences, she is any better than the rest; the Lord leads each of us as He sees we have need. Such experiences, if we use them aright, prepare us to be better servants of God; but sometimes it is the weakest whom God leads by this road; and so there is no ground here either for approval or for condemnation. We must base our judgments on the virtues. The saintliest will be she who serves Our Lord with the greatest mortification and humility and purity of conscience. Little, however, can be known with any certainty about this on earth, nor until the true Judge gives each his deserts. Then we shall be amazed to see how different His judgment is from the ideas which we have formed on earth. May He be for ever praised. Amen.

CHAPTER IX

Treats of the way in which the Lord communicates Himself to the soul through imaginary visions and gives an emphatic warning that we should be careful not to desire to walk in this way. Gives reasons for the warning. This chapter is of great profit.

Let us now come to imaginary visions, in which the devil is said to interfere more frequently than in those already described. This may well be the case; but when they come from Our Lord they seem to me in some ways more profitable because they are in closer conformity with our nature, except for those which the Lord bestows in the final Mansion, and with which no others can compare.

Let us now imagine, as I said in the last chapter, that this Lord is here. It is as if in a gold reliquary there were hidden a precious stone of the highest value and the choicest virtues: although we have never seen the stone, we know for certain that it is there and if we carry it about with us we can have the benefit of its virtues. We do not prize it any the less for not having seen it, because we have found by experience that it has cured us of certain illnesses for which it is a sovereign remedy. But we dare not look at it, or open the reliquary in which it is contained, nor are we able to do so; for only the owner of the jewel knows how to open it, and though he has lent it to us so that we may benefit by it, he has kept the key and so it is still his own. He will open it when he wants to show it to us and he will take it back when he sees fit to do so. And that is what God does, too.

And now let us suppose that on some occasion the owner of the reliquary suddenly wants to open it, for the benefit of the person to whom he has lent it. Obviously this person will get much greater pleasure from it if he can recall the wonderful brilliance of the stone, and it will remain the more deeply engraven upon his memory. This is what happens here. When Our Lord is pleased to bestow greater consolations upon this soul, He grants it, in whatever way He thinks best, a clear revelation of His sacred Humanity, either as He was when He lived in the world, or as He was after His resurrection; and although He does this so quickly that we might liken the action to a flash of lightning, this most glorious image is so deeply engraven upon the imagination that I do not believe it can possibly disappear until it is seen where it can be enjoyed to all eternity.

I speak of an "image", but it must not be supposed that one looks at it as at a painting; it is really alive, and sometimes even speaks to the soul and shows it things both great and secret. But you must realize that, although the soul sees this for a certain length of time, it can no more be gazing at it all the time than it could keep gazing at the sun. So the vision passes very quickly; though this is not because its brilliance hurts the interior sight— that is, the medium by which all such things are seen—as the brilliance of the sun hurts the eyes. When it is a question of exterior sight, I can say nothing about it, for the person I have mentioned, and of whom I can best speak, had not experienced this; and reason can testify only inadequately to things of which it has no experience. The brilliance of this vision is like that of infused light or of a sun covered with some material of the transparency of a diamond, if such a thing could be woven. This raiment looks like the finest cambric. Almost invariably the soul on which God bestows this favour remains in rapture, because its unworthiness cannot endure so terrible a sight.

I say "terrible", because, though the sight is the loveliest and most delightful imaginable, even by a person who lived and strove to imagine it for a thousand years, because it so far exceeds all that our imagination and understanding can compass, its presence is of such exceeding majesty that it fills the soul with a great terror. It is unnecessary to ask here how, without being told, the soul knows Who it is, for He reveals Himself quite clearly as the Lord of Heaven and earth. This the kings of the earth never do: indeed, they would be thought very little of for what they are, but that they are accompanied by their suites, or heralds proclaim them.

O, Lord, how little do we Christians know Thee! What will that day be like when Thou comest to judge us? If when Thou comest here in such a friendly way to hold converse with Thy bride the sight of Thee causes us such fear, what will it be, O daughters, when with that stern voice He says: "Depart, accursed of My Father"![1]

Let us keep that in mind when we remember this favour which God grants to the soul, and we shall find it of no small advantage to us. Even Saint Jerome, holy man though he was, did not banish it from his memory. If we do that we shall care nothing for all we have suffered through keeping strictly to the observances of our Order, for, however long this may take us, the time will be but short by comparison with eternity. I can tell you truly that, wicked as I am, I have never feared the torments of hell, for they seem nothing by comparison with the thought of the wrath which the damned will see in the Lord's eyes—those eyes so lovely and tender and benign. I do not think my heart could bear to see that; and I have felt like this all my life. How much more will anyone fear this to whom He has thus revealed Himself, and given such a consciousness of His presence as will produce unconsciousness![2] It must be for this reason that the soul remains in suspension; the Lord helps it in its weakness so that this may be united with His greatness in this sublime communion with God.

When the soul is able to remain for a long time looking upon the Lord, I do not think it can be a vision at all. It must rather be that some striking idea creates a picture in the imagination: but this will be a dead image by comparison with the other.

Some persons—and I know this is the truth, for they have discussed it with me; and not just three or four of them, but a great many—find that their imagination is so weak, or their understanding is so nimble, or for some other reason their imagination becomes so much absorbed, that they think they can actually see everything that is in their mind. If they had ever seen a true vision they would realize their error beyond the possibility of doubt. Little by little they build up the picture which they see with their imagination, but this produces no effect upon them and they remain cold—much more so than they are after seeing a sacred image. No attention, of course, should be paid to such a thing, which will be forgotten much more quickly than a dream.

[1] St. Matthew xxv, 41. [The abrupt change of pronoun is reproduced exactly from the Spanish.]
[2] [This characteristic example of St. Teresa's word-play is allowed to stand in translation, though to English ears it may sound artificial. See Introduction, Vol. I, p. xx, above.]

The experience we are discussing here is quite different. The soul is very far from expecting to see anything and the thought of such a thing has never even passed through its mind. All of a sudden the whole vision is revealed to it and all its faculties and senses are thrown into the direst fear and confusion, and then sink into that blessed state of peace. It is just as when Saint Paul was thrown to the ground and there came that storm and tumult in the sky; just so, in this interior world, there is a great commotion; and then all at once, as I have said, everything grows calm, and the soul, completely instructed in such great truths, has no need of another master. True wisdom, without any effort on its own part, has overcome its stupidity; and for a certain space of time it enjoys the complete certainty that this favour comes from God. However often it may be told that this is not so it cannot be induced to fear that it may have been mistaken. Later, when the confessor insinuates this fear, God allows the soul to begin to hesitate as to whether He could possibly grant this favour to such a sinner. But that is all; for, as I have said in these other cases, in speaking of temptations in matters of faith, the devil can disturb the soul, but he cannot shake the firmness of its belief. On the contrary, the more fiercely he attacks it, the more certain it becomes that he could never endow it with so many blessings—which is actually true, for over the interior of the soul he wields less power. He may be able to reveal something to it, but not with the same truth and majesty, nor can he produce the same results.

As confessors cannot see all this for themselves, and a soul to whom God has granted such a favour may be unable to describe it, they have misgivings about it, and quite justifiably. So they have to proceed cautiously, and even to wait for some time to see what results these apparitions produce, and to observe gradually how much humility they leave in the soul and to what extent it is strengthened in virtue; if they come from the devil there will soon be signs of the fact, for he will be caught out in a thousand lies. If the confessor is experienced, and has himself been granted such visions, it will not be long before he is able to form a judgment, for the account which the soul gives will at once show him whether they proceed from God or from the imagination or from the devil, especially if His Majesty has granted him the gift of discerning spirits. If he has this and is a learned man, he will be able to form an opinion perfectly well, even though he may be without experience.

The really essential thing, sisters, is that you should speak to your confessor very plainly and candidly—I do not mean here in confessing your sins, for of course you will do so then, but in describing your experiences in prayer. For unless you do this, I cannot assure you that you are proceeding as you should or that it is God Who is teaching you. God is very anxious for us to speak candidly and clearly to those who are in His place, and to desire them to be acquainted with all our thoughts, and still more with our actions, however trivial these may be. If you do this, you need not be disturbed, or worried, for, even if these things be not of God, they will do you no harm if you are humble and have a good conscience. His Majesty is able to bring good out of evil and you will gain by following the road by which the devil hoped to bring you to destruction. For, as you will suppose that it is God Who is granting you these great favours, you will strive to please Him better and keep His image ever in your mind. A very learned man used to say that the devil is a skilful painter, and that, if he were to show him an absolutely lifelike image of the Lord, it would not worry him, because it would quicken his devotion, and so he would be using the devil's own wicked weapons to make war on him. However evil the painter be, one cannot fail to reverence the picture that he paints, if it is of Him Who is our only Good.

This learned man thought that the counsel, given by some people, to treat any vision of this kind with scorn,[1] was very wrong: we must reverence a painting of our King, he said, wherever we see it. I think he is right; even on a worldly plane we should feel that. If a person who had a great friend knew that insulting things were being said about his portrait he would not be pleased. How much more incumbent upon us is it, then, always to be respectful when we see a crucifix or any kind of portrait of our Emperor!

Although I have written this elsewhere, I have been glad to set it down here, for I knew someone who was in great distress because she had been ordered to adopt this derisive remedy. I do not know who can have invented such advice, for, if it came from her confessor, it would have been a torture to her: she would be bound to obey him, and would have thought herself a lost soul unless she had done so. My own advice is that, if you are given such counsel, you should not accept it and should with all humility put forward this argument that I have given you. I was extremely struck by the good reasons against the practice alleged by the person who advised me in this case.

The soul derives great profit from this favour bestowed by the Lord, for thinking upon Him or upon His life and Passion recalls His most meek and lovely face, which is the greatest comfort,

---

[1] [*Dar higas.* Cf. note on this phrase, Vol. I, p. 165, n. 3, above. The theologian referred to was P. Báñez: cf. *Life*, Chap. XXIX, *Foundations*, Chap. VIII.]

just as in the earthly sphere we get much more comfort from seeing a person who is a great help to us than if we had never known him. I assure you that such a delectable remembrance gives the greatest help and comfort. It also brings many other blessings with it, but as so much has been said about the effects caused by these things, and there is more still to come, I will not fatigue myself or you by adding more just now. I will only warn you that, when you learn or hear that God is granting souls these graces, you must never beseech or desire Him to lead you along this road. Even if you think it a very good one, and to be greatly prized and reverenced, there are certain reasons why such a course is not wise.

The first reason is that it shows a lack of humility to ask to be given what you have never deserved, so I think anyone who asks for this cannot be very humble. A peasant of lowly birth would never dream of wishing to be a king; such a thing seems to him impossible because he does not merit it. Anyone who is humble feels just the same about these other things. I think they will never be bestowed on a person devoid of humility, because before the Lord grants a soul these favours He always gives it a high degree of self-knowledge. And how could one who has such ambitions realize that He is doing him a great favour in not casting him into hell?

The second reason is that such a person is quite certain to be deceived, or to be in great peril, because the devil has only to see a door left slightly ajar to enter and play a thousand tricks on us.

The third reason is to be found in the imagination. When a person has a great desire for something, he persuades himself that he is seeing or hearing what he desires, just as those who go about desiring something all day think so much about it that after a time they begin to dream of it.

The fourth reason is that it is very presumptuous in me to wish to choose my path, because I cannot tell which path is best for me. I must leave it to the Lord, Who knows me, to lead me by the path which is best for me, so that in all things His will may be done.

In the fifth place, do you suppose that the trials suffered by those to whom the Lord grants these favours are light ones? No, they are very heavy, and of many kinds. How do you know if you would be able to bear them?

In the sixth place, you may well find that the very thing from which you had expected gain will bring you loss, just as Saul only lost by becoming a king.

And besides these reasons, sisters, there are others. Believe me, the safest thing is to will only what God wills, for He knows us better than we know ourselves, and He loves us. Let us place ourselves in His hands so that His will may be done in us; if we cling firmly to this maxim and our wills are resolute we cannot possibly go astray. And you must note that you will merit no more glory for having received many of these favours; on the contrary, the fact that you are receiving more imposes on you greater obligations to serve. The Lord does not deprive us of anything which adds to our merit, for this remains in our own power. There are many saintly people who have never known what it is to receive a favour of this kind, and there are others who receive such favours, although they are not saintly. Do not suppose, again, that they occur continually. Each occasion on which the Lord grants them brings with it a great many trials; and thus the soul does not think about receiving more, but only about how to put those it receives to a good use.

It is true that to have these favours must be the greatest help towards attaining a high degree of perfection in the virtues; but anyone who has attained the virtues at the cost of his own toil has earned much more merit. I know of a person to whom the Lord had granted some of these favours—of two indeed; one was a man. Both were desirous of serving His Majesty, at their own cost, and without being given any of these great consolations; and they were so anxious to suffer that they complained to Our Lord because He bestowed favours on them, which, had it been possible, they would have excused themselves from receiving. I am speaking here, not of these visions, which bring us great gain, and are very much to be prized, but of consolations which the Lord gives in contemplation.

It is true that, in my opinion, these desires are supernatural, and come from souls fired with love, who would like the Lord to see that they are not serving Him for pay; for which reason, as I have said, they never spur themselves to greater efforts in God's service by thinking of the glory which they will receive for anything they do; rather do they serve Him for the satisfaction of their love, for the nature of love invariably finds expression in work of a thousand kinds. If it were able, the soul would invent methods by which to become consumed in Him, and if, for the greater honour of God, it were necessary that it should remain annihilated for ever, it would agree to this very willingly. May He be for ever praised Who is pleased to show forth His greatness by stooping to commune with such miserable creatures. Amen.

CHAPTER X

Speaks of other favours which God grants to the soul in a different way from those already mentioned, and of the great profit that they bring.

There are many ways in which the Lord communicates Himself to the soul by means of these apparitions. Some of them come when the soul is afflicted; others, when it is about to be visited by some heavy trial; others, so that His Majesty may take His delight in it and at the same time may comfort it. There is no need to particularize about each of these; my intention is only to explain in turn the different experiences which occur on this road, as far as I understand them, so that you, sisters, may understand their nature and the effects which they cause. And I am doing this so that you may not suppose everything you imagine to be a vision, and so that, when you do see a vision, you will know that such a thing is possible and will not be disturbed or distressed. For, when you are, it is a great gain for the devil; he is delighted to see a soul distressed and uneasy, because he knows that this will hinder it from employing itself in loving and praising God. His Majesty also communicates Himself in other ways, which are much more sublime, and are also less dangerous, because, I think, the devil cannot counterfeit them. But, being very secret things, they are difficult to describe, whereas imaginary visions can be explained more readily.

When the Lord so wills, it may happen that the soul will be at prayer, and in possession of all its senses, and that then there will suddenly come to it a suspension in which the Lord communicates most secret things to it, which it seems to see within God Himself. These are not visions of the most sacred Humanity; although I say that the soul "sees" Him, it really sees nothing, for this is not an imaginary, but a notably intellectual, vision, in which is revealed to the soul how all things are seen in God, and how within Himself He contains them all. Such a vision is highly profitable because, although it passes in a moment, it remains engraven upon the soul. It causes us the greatest confusion, by showing us clearly how wrongly we are acting when we offend God, since it is within God Himself—because we dwell within Him, I mean—that we are committing these great sins. I want, if I can, to draw a comparison to explain this, for, although it is a fact and we hear it stated frequently, we either pay no heed to it or refuse to understand it; if we really understood it, I do not think we could possibly be so presumptuous.

Let us imagine that God is like a very large and beautiful mansion or palace. This palace, then, as I say, is God Himself. Now can the sinner go away from it in order to commit his misdeeds? Certainly not; these abominations and dishonourable actions and evil deeds which we sinners commit are done within the palace itself—that is, within God. Oh, fearful thought, worthy of deep consideration and very profitable for us who are ignorant and unable to understand these truths—for if we could understand them we could not possibly be guilty of such foolish presumption! Let us consider, sisters, the great mercy and long-suffering of God in not casting us straight into the depths, and let us render Him the heartiest thanks and be ashamed of worrying over anything that is done or said against us. It is the most dreadful thing in the world that God our Creator should suffer so many misdeeds to be committed by His creatures within Himself, while we ourselves are sometimes worried about a single word uttered in our absence and perhaps not even with a wrong intention.

Oh, human misery! How long will it be, daughters, before we imitate this great God in any way? Oh, let us not deceive ourselves into thinking that we are doing anything whatever by merely putting up with insults! Let us endure everything, and be very glad to do so, and love those who do us wrong; for, greatly as we have offended this great God, He has not ceased loving us, and so He has very good reason for desiring us all to forgive those who have wronged us. I assure you, daughters, that, although this vision passes quickly, it is a great favour for the Lord to bestow it upon those to whom He grants it if they will try to profit by having it habitually present in their minds.

It may also happen that, very suddenly and in a way which cannot be described, God will reveal a truth that is in Himself and that makes any truth to be found in the creatures seem like thick darkness; He will also manifest very clearly that He alone is truth and cannot lie. This is a very good explanation of David's meaning in that Psalm where he says that every man is a liar.[1] One would never take those words in that sense of one's own accord, however many times one heard them, but they express a truth which is infallible. I remember that story about Pilate, who asked Our Lord so many questions, and at the time of His Passion said to Him: "What is truth?"[2] And then I reflect how little we understand of this Sovereign Truth here on earth.

I should like to be able to say more about this matter, but it is impossible. Let us learn from this, sisters, that if we are in any

---

[1] Psalm cxv, 11 [: "I said in my excess: 'Every man is a liar.'" Cf. A.V., Psalm cxvi, 11.]
[2] St. John xviii, 38.

way to grow like our God and Spouse, we shall do well always to study earnestly to walk in this truth. I do not mean simply that we must not tell falsehoods, for as far as that is concerned—glory be to God!—I know that in these convents of ours you take very great care never to lie about anything for any reason whatsoever. I mean that we must walk in truth, in the presence of God and man, in every way possible to us. In particular we must not desire to be reputed better than we are and in all we do we must attribute to God what is His, and to ourselves what is ours, and try to seek after truth in everything. If we do that, we shall make small account of this world, for it is all lying and falsehood and for that reason cannot endure.

I was wondering once why Our Lord so dearly loved this virtue of humility; and all of a sudden—without, I believe, my having previously thought of it—the following reason came into my mind: that it is because God is Sovereign Truth and to be humble is to walk in truth, for it is absolutely true to say that we have no good thing in ourselves, but only misery and nothingness; and anyone who fails to understand this is walking in falsehood. He who best understands it is most pleasing to Sovereign Truth because he is walking in truth. May it please God, sisters, to grant us grace never to fail to have this knowledge of ourselves. Amen.

Our Lord grants the soul favours like these because He is pleased to treat her like a true bride, who is determined to do His will in all things, and to give her some knowledge of the way in which she can do His will and of His greatness. I need say no more; I have said these two things because they seem to me so helpful; for there is no reason to be afraid of these favours, but only to praise the Lord, because He gives them. In my opinion, there is little scope here either for the devil or for the soul's own imagination, and when it knows this the soul experiences a great and lasting happiness.

CHAPTER XI

Treats of the desires to enjoy God which He gives the soul and which are so great and impetuous that they endanger its life. Treats also of the profit which comes from this favour granted by the Lord.

Have all these favours which the Spouse has granted the soul been sufficient to satisfy this little dove or butterfly (do not suppose that I have forgotten her) and to make her settle down in the place where she is to die? Certainly not; she is in a much worse state than before; for, although she may have been receiving these favours for many years, she is still sighing and weeping, and each of them causes her fresh pain. The reason for this is that, the more she learns about the greatness of her God, while finding herself so far from Him and unable to enjoy Him, the more her desire increases. For the more is revealed to her of how much this great God and Lord deserves to be loved, the more does her love for Him grow. And gradually, during these years, her desire increases, so that she comes to experience great distress, as I will now explain. I have spoken of years, because I am writing about the experiences of the particular person about whom I have been speaking here. But it must be clearly understood that no limitations can be set to God's acts, and that He can raise a soul to the highest point here mentioned in a single moment. His Majesty has the power to do all that He wishes and He is desirous of doing a great deal for us.

The soul, then, has these yearnings and tears and sighs, together with the strong impulses which have already been described. They all seem to arise from our love, and are accompanied by great emotion, but they are all as nothing by comparison with this other, for they are like a smouldering fire, the heat of which is quite bearable, though it causes pain. While the soul is in this condition, and interiorly burning, it often happens that a mere fleeting thought of some kind (there is no way of telling whence it comes, or how) or some remark which the soul hears about death's long tarrying, deals it, as it were, a blow, or, as one might say, wounds it with an arrow of fire. I do not mean that there actually is such an arrow; but, whatever it is, it obviously could not have come from our own nature. Nor is it actually a blow, though I have spoken of it as such; but it makes a deep wound, not, I think, in any region where physical pain can be felt, but in the soul's most intimate depths. It passes as quickly as a flash of lightning and leaves everything in our nature that is earthly reduced to powder. During the time that it lasts we cannot think of anything that has to do with our own existence: it instantaneously enchains the faculties in such a way that they have no freedom to do anything, except what will increase this pain.

I should not like this to sound exaggerated: in reality I am beginning to see, as I go on, that all I say falls short of the truth, which is indescribable. It is an enrapturing of the senses and faculties, except, as I have said, in ways which enhance this feeling of distress. The understanding is keenly on the alert to discover why this soul feels absent from God, and His Majesty now aids it with so lively a knowledge of Himself that it causes the distress to grow until the sufferer cries out aloud. However patient a sufferer she may be, and however accustomed to enduring great pain, she cannot help doing this, because this pain, as I have said, is not in the body, but deep within the soul. It was in this way that the person I have mentioned discovered how much more sensitive the soul is than the body, and it was revealed to her that this suffering resembles that of souls in purgatory; despite their being no longer in the body they suffer much more than do those who are still in the body and on earth.

I once saw a person in this state who I really believed was dying; and this was not at all surprising, because it does in fact involve great peril of death. Although it lasts only for a short time, it leaves the limbs quite disjointed, and, for as long as it continues, the pulse is as feeble as though the soul were about to render itself up to God. It really is quite as bad as this. For, while the natural heat of the body fails, the soul burns so fiercely within that, if the flame were only a little stronger, God would have fulfilled its desires. It is not that it feels any bodily pain whatsoever, notwithstanding such a dislocation of the limbs that for two or three days afterwards it is in great pain and has not the strength even to write; in fact the body seems to me never to be as strong as it was previously. The reason it feels no pain must be that it is suffering so keenly within that it takes no notice of the body. It is as when we have a very acute pain in one spot; we may have many other pains but we feel them less; this I have conclusively proved. In the present case, the soul feels nothing at all, and I do not believe it would feel anything if it were cut into little pieces.

You will tell me that this is imperfection and ask why such a person does not resign herself to the will of God, since she has surrendered herself to Him so completely. Down to this time she had been able to do so, and indeed had spent her life doing so; but now she no longer can because her reason is in such a state that she is not her own mistress, and can think of nothing but the cause of her suffering. Since she is absent from her Good, why should she wish to live? She is conscious of a strange solitude, since there is not a creature on the whole earth who can be a companion to her—in fact, I do not believe she would find any in Heaven, save Him Whom she loves: on the contrary, all earthly companionship is torment to her. She thinks of herself as of a person suspended aloft, unable either to come down and rest anywhere on earth or to ascend into Heaven. She is parched with thirst, yet cannot reach the water; and the thirst is not a tolerable one but of a kind that nothing can quench, nor does she desire it to be quenched, except with that water of which Our Lord spoke to the Samaritan woman,[1] and that is not given to her.

Ah, God help me! Lord, how Thou dost afflict Thy lovers! Yet all this is very little by comparison with what Thou bestowest upon them later. It is well that great things should cost a great deal, especially if the soul can be purified by suffering and enabled to enter the seventh Mansion, just as those who are to enter Heaven are cleansed in purgatory. If this is possible, its suffering is no more than a drop of water in the sea. So true is this that, despite all its torment and distress, which cannot, I believe, be surpassed by any such things on earth (many of which this person had endured, both bodily and spiritual, and they all seemed to her nothing by comparison), the soul feels this affliction to be so precious that it fully realizes it could never deserve it. But the anguish is of such a kind that nothing can relieve it; none the less the soul suffers it very gladly, and, if God so willed, would suffer it all its life long, although this would be not to die once, but to be always dying, for it is really quite as bad as that.

And now, sisters, let us consider the condition of those who are in hell. They are not resigned, as this soul is, nor have they this contentment and delight which God gives it. They cannot see that their suffering is doing them any good, yet they keep suffering more and more—I mean more and more in respect of accidental pains[2]—for the torment suffered by the soul is much more acute than that suffered by the body and the pains which such souls have to endure are beyond comparison greater than what we have here been describing. These unhappy souls know that they will have to suffer in this way for ever and ever: what, then, will become of them? And what is there that we can do—or even suffer—in so short a life as this which will matter in the slightest if it will free us from these terrible and eternal torments? I assure you it is impossible to explain to anyone who has not experienced it what a grievous thing is the soul's suffering and how different it is from the suffering of the body. The Lord will have us understand this so that we may be more conscious of how much we owe Him for bringing us to a state in which by His mercy we may hope that He will set us free and forgive us our sins.

Let us now return to what we were discussing when we left this soul in such affliction. It remains in this state only for a short

---

[1] St. John iv, 7-13.
[2] The words of the parenthesis were inserted by St. Teresa in the margin of the autograph.

time (three or four hours at most, I should say); for, if the pain lasted long, it would be impossible, save by a miracle, for natural weakness to suffer it. On one occasion it lasted only for a quarter of an hour and yet produced complete prostration. On that occasion, as a matter of fact, the sufferer entirely lost consciousness. The violent attack came on through her hearing some words about "life not ending".[1] She was engaged in conversation at the time—it was the last day of Eastertide, and all that Easter she had been afflicted with such aridity that she hardly knew it was Easter at all. So just imagine anyone thinking that these attacks can be resisted! It is no more possible to resist them than for a person thrown into a fire to make the flames lose their heat and not burn her. She cannot hide her anguish, so all who are present realize the great peril in which she lies, even though they cannot witness what is going on within her. It is true that they can bear her company, but they only seem to her like shadows —as all other earthly things do too.

And now I want you to see that, if at any time you should find yourselves in this condition, it is possible for your human nature, weak as it is, to be of help to you. So let me tell you this. It sometimes happens that, when a person is in this state that you have been considering, and has such yearnings to die,[2] because the pain is more than she can bear, that her soul seems to be on the very point of leaving the body, she is really afraid and would like her distress to be alleviated lest she should in fact die. It is quite evident that this fear comes from natural weakness, and yet, on the other hand, the desire does not leave her, nor can she possibly find any means of dispelling the distress until the Lord Himself dispels it for her. This He does, as a general rule, by granting her a deep rapture or some kind of vision, in which the true Comforter comforts and strengthens her so that she can wish to live for as long as He wills.

This is a distressing thing, but it produces the most wonderful effects and the soul at once loses its fear of any trials which may befall it; for by comparison with the feelings of deep anguish which its spirit has experienced these seem nothing. Having gained so much, the soul would be glad to suffer them all again

[1] Cf. *Relations*, XV. [Vol. I., p. 340, above. This incident took place at Salamanca in 1571. The singer was M. Isabel de Jesús. The song begins:
    Let mine eyes behold Thee,
    Sweetest Jesu, nigh;
    Let mine eyes behold Thee,
    And at once I'll die.

[It has no verbal reference, as our text suggests, to "life not ending", but this is its general theme, as it is also that of several poems by St. Teresa herself.]

[2] [*Lit.*: "and is dying in order to die"—a reference, no doubt, to the poem to be found in Vol. III, pp. 277-9, below.]

and again; but it has no means of doing so nor is there any method by which it can reach that state again until the Lord wills, just as there is no way of resisting or escaping it when it comes. The soul has far more contempt for the world than it had previously, for it sees that no worldly thing was of any avail to it in its torment; and it is very much more detached from the creatures, because it sees that it can be comforted and satisfied only by the Creator, and it has the greatest fear and anxiety not to offend Him, because it sees that He can torment as well as comfort.

There are two deadly perils, it seems to me, on this spiritual road. This is one of them—and it is indeed a peril, and no light one. The other is the peril of excessive rejoicing and delight, which can be carried to such an extreme that it really seems as if the soul is swooning, and as if the very slightest thing would be enough to drive it out of the body: this would really bring it no little happiness.

Now, sisters, you will see if I was not right in saying that courage is necessary for us here and that if you ask the Lord for these things He will be justified in answering you as He answered the sons of Zebedee: "Can you drink the chalice?"[1] I believe, sisters, that we should all reply: "We can"; and we should be quite right to do so, for His Majesty gives the strength to those who, He sees, have need of it, and He defends these souls in every way and stands up for them if they are persecuted and spoken ill of, as He did for the Magdalen[2]—by His actions if not in words. And in the end—ah, in the end, before they die, He repays them for everything at once, as you are now going to see. May He be for ever blessed and may all creatures praise Him. Amen.

---

[1] St. Matthew xx, 22: "'Can you drink the chalice that I shall drink?' They say to Him: 'We can.'"
[2] St. Luke vii, 44.

SEVENTH MANSIONS

In which there are Four Chapters

CHAPTER I

Treats of great favours which God bestows on the souls that have attained entrance to the Seventh Mansions. Describes how in the author's opinion there is some difference between the soul and the spirit although both are one. There are notable things in this chapter.

You will think, sisters, that so much has been said about this spiritual road that there cannot possibly be any more to say. It would be a great mistake to think that; just as the greatness of God is without limit, even so are His works. Who will ever come to an end of recounting His mercies and wonders? It is impossible that any should do so; do not be surprised, therefore, at what has been said and at what will be said now, for it is only a fraction of the things that still remain to be related about God. Great is the mercy that He shows us in communicating these things in such a way that we may come to learn of them; for the more we know of His communion with creatures, the more we shall praise His greatness, and we shall strive not to despise a soul in which the Lord takes such delight. Each of us possesses a soul, but we do not prize our souls as creatures made in God's image deserve and so we do not understand the great secrets which they contain. If it be His Majesty's will, may it please Him to guide my pen, and give me to understand how I may tell you some of the many things which there are to be said and which God reveals to every soul that He brings into this Mansion. Earnestly have I besought His Majesty, since He knows my intention is that His mercies be not hidden, to the greater praise and glory of His name.

I am hopeful, sisters, that, not for my sake but for your sakes, He will grant me this favour, so that you may understand how important it is that no fault of yours should hinder the celebration of His Spiritual Marriage with your souls, which, as you will see, brings with it so many blessings. O great God! Surely a creature as miserable as I must tremble to treat of anything so far beyond what I deserve to understand. And indeed I have been in a state of great confusion and have wondered if it will not be better for me in a few words to bring my account of this Mansion to an end. I am so much afraid it will be thought that my knowledge of it comes from experience, and this makes me very much ashamed; for, knowing myself as I do for what I am, such a thought is terrible. On the other hand, whatever your judgment about it may be, it has seemed to me that this shame is due to temptation and weakness. Let the whole world cry out upon me, so long as God is praised and understood a little better. At all events I may perhaps be dead when this comes to be seen. Blessed be He Who lives and shall live for ever. Amen.

When Our Lord is pleased to have pity upon this soul, which suffers and has suffered so much out of desire for Him, and which He has now taken spiritually to be His bride, He brings her into this Mansion of His, which is the seventh, before consummating the Spiritual Marriage. For He must needs have an abiding-place in the soul, just as He has one in Heaven, where His Majesty alone dwells: so let us call this a second Heaven. It is very important, sisters, that we should not think of the soul as of something dark. It must seem dark to most of us, as we cannot see it, for we forget that there is not only a light which we can see, but also an interior light, and so we think that within our soul there is some kind of darkness. Of the soul that is not in grace, I grant you, that is true—not, however, from any defect in the Sun of Justice, Who is within it and is giving it being, but because, as I think I said in describing the first Mansion, this soul is not capable[1] of receiving the light. A certain person came to see that these unhappy souls are, as it were, in a dark prison, with their feet and hands bound so that they can do no good thing which will help them to win merit;[2] they are both blind and dumb. We do well to take pity on them, realizing that there was a time when we were ourselves like them and that the Lord may have mercy on them also.

Let us take especial care, sisters, to pray to Him for them, and not be negligent. To pray for those who are in mortal sin is the best kind of almsgiving—a much better thing than it would be to loose a Christian whom we saw with his hands tied behind him, bound with a stout chain, made fast to a post and dying of hunger, not for lack of food, since he has beside him the most delicious things to eat, but because he cannot take them and put them into his mouth although he is weary to death and actually knows that he is on the point of dying, and not merely a death of the body, but one which is eternal. Would it not be extremely cruel to stand looking at such a man and not give him this food to eat? And supposing you could loose his chains by means of your prayers? You see now what I mean. For the love

---

[1] Gracián altered "capable" to "prepared".
[2] "To win merit" is the Saint's marginal addition.

of God, I beg you always to remember such souls when you pray.[1]

However, it is not of these that we are now speaking, but of those who, by God's mercy, have done penance for their sins and are in grace. We must not think of souls like theirs as mean and insignificant; for each is an interior world, wherein are the many and beauteous Mansions that you have seen; it is reasonable that this should be so, since within each soul there is a mansion for God. Now, when His Majesty is pleased to grant the soul the aforementioned favour of this Divine Marriage, He first of all brings it into His own Mansion. And His Majesty is pleased that it should not be as on other occasions, when He has granted it raptures, in which I certainly think it is united with Him, as it is in the above-mentioned Prayer of Union, although the soul does not feel called to enter into its own centre, as here in this Mansion, but is affected only in its higher part. Actually it matters little what happens: whatever it does, the Lord unites it with Himself, but He makes it blind and dumb, as He made Saint Paul at his conversion,[2] and so prevents it from having any sense of how or in what way that favour comes which it is enjoying; the great delight of which the soul is then conscious is the realization of its nearness to God. But when He unites it with Him, it understands nothing; the faculties are all lost.

But in this Mansion everything is different. Our good God now desires to remove the scales from the eyes of the soul,[3] so that it may see and understand something of the favour which He is granting it, although He is doing this in a strange manner. It is brought into this Mansion by means of an intellectual vision,[4] in which, by a representation of the truth in a particular way, the Most Holy Trinity reveals Itself, in all three Persons.[5] First of all the spirit becomes enkindled and is illumined, as it were, by a cloud of the greatest brightness. It sees these three Persons, individually, and yet, by a wonderful kind of knowledge which is given to it, the soul realizes that most certainly and truly all these three Persons are one Substance and one Power and one Knowledge and one God alone; so that what we hold by faith the soul

---

[1] This paragraph was considerably altered in the *editio princeps*.
[2] Acts ix, 8.
[3] [Acts ix, 18.]
[4] Gracián reads: "vision or knowledge, born of faith."
[5] Luis de León added the following note here: "Though man in this life, if so raised by God, may lose the use of his senses and have a fleeting glimpse of the Divine Essence, as was probably the case with St. Paul and Moses and certain others, the Mother is not speaking here of this kind of vision, which, though fleeting, is intuitive and clear, but of a knowledge of this mystery which God gives to certain souls, through a most powerful light which He infuses into them, not without created species. But, as this species is not corporeal, nor figured in the imagination, the Mother says that this vision is intellectual and not imaginary."

may be said here to grasp[1] by sight, although nothing is seen by the eyes, either of the body or of the soul,[2] for it is no imaginary vision. Here all three Persons communicate Themselves to the soul and speak to the soul and explain to it those words which the Gospel attributes to the Lord—namely, that He and the Father and the Holy Spirit will come to dwell with the soul which loves Him and keeps His commandments.[3]

Oh, God help me! What a difference there is between hearing and believing these words[4] and being led in this way to realize how true they are! Each day this soul wonders more, for she feels that they have never left her, and perceives quite clearly, in the way I have described, that They are in the interior of her heart—in the most interior place of all and in its greatest depths. So although, not being a learned person, she cannot say how this is, she feels within herself this Divine companionship.

This may lead you to think that such a person will not remain in possession of her senses but will be so completely absorbed that she will be able to fix her mind upon nothing. But no: in all that belongs to the service of God she is more alert than before; and, when not otherwise occupied, she rests in that happy companionship. Unless her soul fails God, He will never fail, I believe, to give her the most certain assurance of His Presence. She has great confidence that God will not leave her, and that, having granted her this favour, He will not allow her to lose it. For this belief the soul has good reason, though all the time she is walking more carefully than ever, so that she may displease Him in nothing.

This Presence is not of course always realized so fully—I mean so clearly—as it is when it first comes, or on certain other occasions when God grants the soul this consolation; if it were, it would be impossible for the soul to think of anything else, or even to live among men. But although the light which accompanies it may not be so clear, the soul is always aware that it is experiencing this companionship. We might compare the soul to a person who is with others in a very bright room; and then suppose that the shutters are closed so that the people are all in darkness. The light by which they can be seen has been taken away, and, until it comes back, we shall be unable to see them, yet we are none the less aware that they are there. It may be asked if, when the light returns, and this person looks for them again, she will be able to see them. To do this is not in her power; it depends on when Our Lord is pleased that the

---

[1] Gracián reads: "grasp better, it seems."
[2] Gracián reads: "either of the body (for God is Spirit) or of the imagination."
[3] St. John xiv, 23.
[4] Gracián adds: "as they are commonly believed and heard."

shutters of the understanding shall be opened. Great is the mercy which He grants the soul in never going away from her and in willing that she shall understand this so clearly.

It seems that the Divine Majesty, by means of this wonderful companionship, is desirous of preparing the soul for yet more. For clearly she will be greatly assisted to go onward in perfection and to lose the fear which previously she sometimes had of the other favours that were granted to her, as has been said above. The person already referred to found herself better in every way; however numerous were her trials and business worries, the essential part of her soul seemed never to move from that dwelling-place. So in a sense she felt that her soul was divided; and when she was going through great trials, shortly after God had granted her this favour, she complained of her soul, just as Martha complained of Mary.[1] Sometimes she would say that it was doing nothing but enjoy itself in that quietness, while she herself was left with all her trials and occupations so that she could not keep it company.

You will think this absurd, daughters, but it is what actually happens. Although of course the soul is not really divided, what I have said is not fancy, but a very common experience. As I was saying, it is possible to make observations concerning interior matters and in this way we know that there is some kind of difference, and a very definite one, between the soul and the spirit, although they are both one. So subtle is the division perceptible between them that sometimes the operation of the one seems as different from that of the other as are the respective joys that the Lord is pleased to give them. It seems to me, too, that the soul is a different thing from the faculties and that they are not all one and the same. There are so many and such subtle things in the interior life that it would be presumptuous for me to begin to expound them. But we shall see everything in the life to come if the Lord, of His mercy, grants us the favour of bringing us to the place where we shall understand these secrets.

CHAPTER II

Continues the same subject. Describes the difference between spiritual union and spiritual marriage. Explains this by subtle comparisons.

Let us now come to treat of the Divine and Spiritual Marriage, although this great favour cannot be fulfilled perfectly in us during our lifetime, for if we were to withdraw ourselves from

[1] St. Luke x, 40.

God this great blessing would be lost. When granting this favour for the first time, His Majesty is pleased to reveal Himself to the soul through an imaginary vision of His most sacred Humanity, so that it may clearly understand what is taking place and not be ignorant of the fact that it is receiving so sovereign a gift. To other people the experience will come in a different way. To the person of whom we have been speaking the Lord revealed Himself one day, when she had just received Communion, in great splendour and beauty and majesty, as He did after His resurrection, and told her that it was time she took upon her His affairs as if they were her own and that He would take her affairs upon Himself; and He added other words which are easier to understand than to repeat.[1]

This, you will think, was nothing new, since on other occasions the Lord had revealed Himself to that soul in this way. But it was so different that it left her quite confused and dismayed: for one reason, because this vision came with great force; for another, because of the words which He spoke to her; and also because, in the interior of her soul, where He revealed Himself to her, she had never seen any visions but this. For you must understand that there is the greatest difference between all the other visions we have mentioned and those belonging to this Mansion, and there is the same difference between the Spiritual Betrothal and the Spiritual Marriage as there is between two betrothed persons and two who are united so that they cannot be separated any more.

As I have already said, one makes these comparisons because there are no other appropriate ones, yet it must be realized that the Betrothal has no more to do with the body than if the soul were not in the body, and were nothing but spirit. Between the Spiritual Marriage and the body there is even less connection, for this secret union takes place in the deepest centre of the soul, which must be where God Himself dwells, and I do not think there is any need of a door by which to enter it. I say there is no need of a door because all that has so far been described seems to have come through the medium of the senses and faculties and this appearance of the Humanity of the Lord must do so too. But what passes in the union of the Spiritual Marriage is very different. The Lord appears in the centre of the soul, not through an imaginary, but through an intellectual vision (although this is a subtler one than that already mentioned),[2] just as He appeared to the Apostles, without entering through the

---

[1] Cf. *Relations*, XXXV (Vol. I, pp. 351–2, above).
[2] The words "but through an intellectual" and "although . . . mentioned" are substituted by St. Teresa for others which she has deleted.

door, when He said to them: "Pax vobis".[1] This instantaneous communication of God to the soul is so great a secret and so sublime a favour, and such delight is felt by the soul, that I do not know with what to compare it, beyond saying that the Lord is pleased to manifest to the soul at that moment the glory that is in Heaven, in a sublimer manner than is possible through any vision or spiritual consolation. It is impossible to say more than that, as far as one can understand, the soul (I mean the spirit of this soul) is made one with God, Who, being likewise a Spirit, has been pleased to reveal the love that He has for us by showing to certain persons the extent of that love, so that we may praise His greatness. For He has been pleased to unite Himself with His creature in such a way that they have become like two who cannot be separated from one another: even so He will not separate Himself from her.

The Spiritual Betrothal is different: here the two persons are frequently separated, as is the case with union, for, although by union is meant the joining of two things into one, each of the two, as is a matter of common observation, can be separated and remain a thing by itself. This favour of the Lord passes quickly and afterwards the soul is deprived of that companionship—I mean so far as it can understand. In this other favour of the Lord it is not so: the soul remains all the time in that centre with its God. We might say that union is as if the ends of two wax candles were joined so that the light they give is one: the wicks and the wax and the light are all one; yet afterwards the one candle can be perfectly well separated from the other and the candles become two again, or the wick may be withdrawn from the wax. But here it is like rain falling from the heavens into a river or a spring; there is nothing but water there and it is impossible to divide or separate the water belonging to the river from that which fell from the heavens. Or it is as if a tiny streamlet enters the sea, from which it will find no way of separating itself, or as if in a room there were two large windows through which the light streamed in: it enters in different places but it all becomes one.

Perhaps when St. Paul says: "He who is joined to God becomes one spirit with Him,"[2] he is referring to this sovereign Marriage, which presupposes the entrance of His Majesty into the soul by union. And he also says: *Mihi vivere Christus est, mori lucrum.*[3]

---

[1] St. John xx, 19, 21.

[2] 1 Corinthians vi, 17. [The Spanish has two verbs, *arrimarse* and *allegarse*, corresponding to "joined", and linked by the word "and". The Scriptural text reads: "He who is joined to the Lord is one spirit."] The whole of the passage "He who . . . by union" is St. Teresa's interlinear substitution for something deleted.

[3] Philippians i, 21: "For to me, to live is Christ; and to die is gain."

This, I think, the soul may say here, for it is here that the little butterfly to which we have referred dies, and with the greatest joy, because Christ is now its life.

This, with the passage of time, becomes more evident through its effects; for the soul clearly understands, by certain secret aspirations, that it is endowed with life by God. Very often these aspirations are so vehement that what they teach cannot[1] possibly be doubted: though they cannot be described, the soul experiences them very forcibly. One can only say that this feeling is produced at times by certain delectable words which, it seems, the soul cannot help uttering, such as: "O life of my life, and sustenance that sustaineth me!" and things of that kind. For from those Divine breasts, where it seems that God is ever sustaining the soul, flow streams of milk, which solace all who dwell in the Castle; it seems that it is the Lord's will for them to enjoy all that the soul enjoys, so that, from time to time, there should flow from this mighty river, in which this tiny little spring is swallowed up, a stream of this water, to sustain those who in bodily matters have to serve the Bridegroom and the bride. And just as a person suddenly plunged into such water would become aware of it, and, however unobservant he might be, could not fail to become so, the same thing may be said, with even greater confidence, of these operations to which I refer. For just as a great stream of water could never fall on us without having an origin somewhere, as I have said, just so it becomes evident that there is someone in the interior of the soul who sends forth these arrows and thus gives life to this life, and that there is a sun whence this great light proceeds, which is transmitted to the faculties in the interior part of the soul. The soul, as I have said, neither moves from that centre nor loses its peace, for He Who gave His peace to the Apostles when they were all together[2] can give peace to the soul.

It has occurred to me that this salutation of the Lord must mean much more than the mere words suggest, as must also His telling the glorious Magdalen to go in peace;[3] for the words of the Lord are like acts wrought in us, and so they must have produced some effect in those who were already prepared to put away from them everything corporeal and to leave the soul in a state of pure spirituality, so that it might be joined with Uncreated Spirit in this celestial union. For it is quite certain that, when we empty ourselves of all that is creature and rid

---

[1] [*Lit.*: "that they cannot."] The words "that what . . . doubted" are scored through in the original—we suspect by Gracián.
[2] St. John xx, 19, 21 [Cf. p. 335, n. 1 above].
[3] St. Luke vii, 50.

ourselves of it for the love of God, that same Lord will fill our souls with Himself. Thus, one day, when Jesus Christ was praying for His Apostles (I do not know where this occurs),[1] He asked that they might become one with the Father and with Him, even as Jesus Christ our Lord is in the Father and the Father is in Him. I do not know what greater love there can be than this. And we shall none of us fail to be included here, for His Majesty went on to say: "Not for them alone do I pray, but also for all who believe in Me"[2]; and again: "I am in them."[3]

Oh, God help me! How true are these words and how well the soul understands them, for in this state it can actually see their truth for itself. And how well we should all understand them were it not for our own fault! The words of Jesus Christ our King and Lord cannot fail; but, because we ourselves fail by not preparing ourselves and departing from all that can shut out this light, we do not see ourselves in this mirror into which we are gazing and in which our image is engraved.[4]

Let us now return to what we were saying. When Our Lord brings the soul into this Mansion of His, which is the centre of the soul itself (for they say that the empyrean heaven, where Our Lord is, does not move like the other heavens), it seems, on entering, to be subject to none of the usual movements of the faculties and the imagination, which injure it and take away its peace. I may seem to be giving the impression that, when the soul reaches the state in which God grants it this favour, it is sure of its salvation and free from the risk of backsliding. But that is not my meaning, and whenever I treat of this matter and say that the soul seems to be in safety I should be understood as meaning for so long as the Divine Majesty holds it thus by the hand and it does not offend Him. At all events, I know for certain that, even when it finds itself in this state, and even if the state has lasted for years, it does not consider itself safe, but goes on its way with much greater misgiving than before and refrains more carefully from committing the smallest offence against God. It is also strongly desirous of serving Him, as will be explained later on, and is habitually afflicted and confused when it sees how little it is able to do and how great is the extent of its obligations, which is no small cross to it and a very grievous penance; for the harder the penance which this soul performs, the greater is its delight. Its real penance comes when God takes away its health and strength so that it can no longer perform any.

---

[1] Gracián deletes the bracketed words and substitutes the Scriptural text, giving its source (St. John xvii, 21) in the margin.
[2] St. John xvii, 20.
[3] St. John xvii, 23.
[4] [Cf. St. Teresa's poem on this theme, Vol. III, pp. 287-8, below.]

I have described elsewhere the great distress which this brings, but it is much greater here. This must be due to the nature of the ground in which the soul is planted, for a tree planted by the streams of water is fresher and gives more fruit,[1] so how can we marvel at the desires of this soul, since its spirit is verily made one with the celestial water of which we have been speaking?

Returning to what I was saying, it must not be thought that the faculties and senses and passions are always in this state of peace, though the soul itself is. In the other Mansions there are always times of conflict and trial and weariness, but they are not of such a kind as to rob the soul of its peace and stability—at least, not as a rule. This "centre" of our soul, or "spirit," is something so difficult to describe, and indeed to believe, that I think, sisters, as I am so bad at explaining myself, I will not subject you to the temptation of disbelieving what I say, for it is difficult to understand how the soul can have trials and afflictions and yet be in peace. I want to put before you one or two comparisons: God grant they may be of some value, but, if they are not, I know that what I have said is the truth.

A king is living in His palace: many wars are waged in his kingdom and many other distressing things happen there, but he remains where he is despite them all. So it is here: although in the other Mansions there are many disturbances and poisonous creatures, and the noise of all this can be heard, nobody enters this Mansion and forces the soul to leave it; and, although the things which the soul hears cause it some distress, they are not of a kind to disturb it or to take away its peace, for the passions are already vanquished, and thus are afraid to enter there because to do so would only exhaust them further. Our whole body may be in pain, yet if our head is sound the fact that the body is in pain will not cause it to ache as well. These comparisons make me smile and I do not like them at all, but I know no others. Think what you will; what I have said is the truth.

CHAPTER III

Treats of the striking effects produced by this prayer aforementioned. It is necessary to observe and remember the effects it produces, for the difference between them and those already described is remarkable.

As we are saying, then, this little butterfly has now died, full of joy at having found rest, and within her lives Christ. Let us

[1] Psalm i, 3.

see what her new life is like, and how different it is from her earlier one, for it is by the effects which result from this prayer that we shall know if what has been said is true. As far as I can understand, the effects are these.

First, there is a self-forgetfulness which is so complete that it really seems as though the soul no longer existed, because it is such that she has neither knowledge nor remembrance that there is either heaven or life or honour for her, so entirely is she employed in seeking the honour of God. It appears that the words which His Majesty addressed to her have produced their effect—namely, that she must take care of His business and He will take care of hers.[1] And thus, happen what may, she does not mind in the least, but lives in so strange a state of forgetfulness that, as I say, she seems no longer to exist, and has no desire to exist—no, absolutely none—save when she realizes that she can do something to advance the glory and honour of God, for which she would gladly lay down her life.

Do not understand by this, daughters, that she neglects to eat and sleep (though having to do this is no little torment to her), or to do anything which is made incumbent upon her by her profession. We are talking of interior matters: as regards exterior ones there is little to be said. Her great grief is to see that all she can do of her own strength is as nothing. Anything that she is capable of doing and knows to be of service to Our Lord she would not fail to do for any reason upon earth.

The second effect produced is a great desire to suffer, but this is not of such a kind as to disturb the soul, as it did previously. So extreme is her longing for the will of God to be done in her that whatever His Majesty does she considers to be for the best: if He wills that she should suffer, well and good; if not, she does not worry herself to death as she did before.

When these souls are persecuted again, they have a great interior joy, and much more peace than in the state described above. They bear no enmity to those who ill-treat them, or desire to do so. Indeed they conceive a special love for them, so that, if they see them in some trouble, they are deeply grieved and would do anything possible to relieve them; they love to commend them to God, and they would rejoice at not being given some of the favours which His Majesty bestows upon them if their enemies might have them instead and thus be prevented from offending Our Lord.

What surprises me most is this. You have already seen what trials and afflictions these souls have suffered because of their desire to die and thus to enjoy Our Lord. They have now an

---

[1] [Cf. VII, ii: p. 334, above;] *Relations*, XXXV (Vol. I, p. 352, above).

equally strong desire to serve Him, and to sing His praise, and to help some soul if they can. So what they desire now is not merely not to die but to live for a great many years and to suffer the severest trials, if by so doing they can become the means whereby the Lord is praised, even in the smallest thing. If they knew for certain that, on leaving the body, they would have fruition of God, their attitude would not be affected, nor is it altered when they think of the glory which belongs to the saints, for they do not desire as yet to attain this. Their conception of glory is of being able in some way to help the Crucified, especially when they see how often people offend Him and how few there are who really care about His honour and are detached from everything else.

True, they sometimes forget this, turn with tender longing to the thought of enjoying God and desire to escape from this exile, especially when they see how little they are doing to serve Him. But then they turn back and look within themselves and remember that they have Him with them continually; and they are content with this and offer His Majesty their will to live as the most costly oblation they can give Him. They are no more afraid of death than they would be of a gentle rapture. The explanation of this is that it is He Who gave the soul those earlier desires, accompanied by such excessive torment, that now gives it these others. May He be blessed and praised for ever.

In short, the desires of these souls are no longer for consolations or favours, for they have with them the Lord Himself and it is His Majesty Who now lives in them. His life, of course, was nothing but a continual torment and so He is making our life the same, at least as far as our desires go. In other respects, He treats us as weaklings, though He has ample fortitude to give us when He sees that we need it. These souls have a marked detachment from everything and a desire to be always either alone or busy with something that is to some soul's advantage. They have no aridities or interior trials but a remembrance of Our Lord and a tender love for Him, so that they would like never to be doing anything but giving Him praise. When the soul is negligent, the Lord Himself awakens it in the way that has been described, so that it sees quite clearly that this impulse, or whatever it is called, proceeds from the interior of the soul, as we said when discussing these impulses. It is now felt very gently, but it proceeds neither from the thought nor from the memory, nor can it be supposed that the soul has had any part in it. This is so usual and occurs so frequently that it has been observed with special care: just as the flames of a fire, however great, never travel downwards, but always upwards, so here it is evident that this interior movement proceeds from the centre of the soul and awakens the faculties.

Really, were there nothing else to be gained from this way of prayer but our realization of God's special care for us in His communing with us and of the way He keeps begging us to dwell with Him (for He seems to be doing nothing less), I believe that all trials would be well endured if they led to the enjoyment of these gentle yet penetrating touches of His love. This, sisters, you will have experienced, for I think that, when the soul reaches the Prayer of Union, the Lord begins to exercise this care over us if we do not neglect the keeping of His commandments. When this experience comes to you, remember that it belongs to this innermost Mansion, where God dwells in our souls, and give Him fervent praise, for it is He who sends it to you, like a message, or a letter, written very lovingly and in such a way that He would have you alone be able to understand what He has written and what He is asking of you in it.[1] On no account must you fail to answer His Majesty, even if you are busy with exterior affairs and engaged in conversation. It may often happen that Our Lord will be pleased to bestow this secret favour upon you in public; as your reply must needs be an interior one, it will be very easy for you to do what I say and make an act of love or exclaim with Saint Paul: "Lord, what wilt Thou have me to do?"[2] Then He will show you many ways of pleasing Him. For now is the accepted time: He seems indeed to be listening to us and this delicate touch almost always prepares the soul to be able to do, with a resolute will, what He has commanded it.

The difference between this Mansion and the rest has already been explained. There are hardly any of the periods of aridity or interior disturbance in it which at one time or another have occurred in all the rest, but the soul is almost always in tranquillity. It is not afraid that this sublime favour may be counterfeited by the devil but retains the unwavering certainty that it comes from God. For, as has been said, the senses and faculties have no part in this: His Majesty has revealed Himself to the soul and taken it with Him into a place where, as I believe, the devil will not enter, because the Lord will not allow him to do so; and all the favours which the Lord grants the soul here, as I have said, come quite independently of the acts of the soul

---

[1] In the margin of the autograph St. Teresa wrote at this point: "Cuando dice aquí: *os pide*, léase luego este papel." ["When you get to the words *asking of you in it*, go straight on to this paper."] "This paper" is no longer extant, but Luis de León evidently had it, as the rest of this paragraph, though not in the autograph, figures in his edition. It is also found, with slight modifications, in early copies.

[2] Acts ix, 6.

itself, apart from that of its having committed itself wholly to God.

So tranquilly and noiselessly does the Lord teach the soul in this state and do it good that I am reminded of the building of Solomon's temple, during which no noise could be heard; just so, in this temple of God, in this Mansion of His, He and the soul alone have fruition of each other in the deepest silence. There is no reason now for the understanding to stir, or to seek out anything, for the Lord Who created the soul is now pleased to calm it and would have it look, as it were, through a little chink, at what is passing. Now and then it loses sight of it and is unable to see anything; but this is only for a very brief time. The faculties, I think, are not lost here; it is merely that they do not work but seem to be dazed.

And I am quite dazed myself when I observe that, on reaching this state, the soul has no more raptures (accompanied, that is to say, by the suspension of the senses),[1] save very occasionally, and even then it has not the same transports and flights of the spirit. These raptures, too, happen only rarely, and hardly ever in public as they very often did before.[2] Nor have they any connection, as they had before, with great occasions of devotion; if we see a devotional image or hear a sermon, it is almost as if we had heard nothing, and it is the same with music. Previously, the poor little butterfly was always so worried that everything frightened her and made her fly away. But it is not so now, whether because she has found her rest, or because the soul has seen so much in this Mansion that it can be frightened at nothing, or because it no longer has that solitude which it was wont to have, now that it is enjoying such companionship. Well, sisters, I do not know what the reason may be, but, when the Lord begins to reveal the contents of this Mansion and brings souls into it, they lose the great weakness which was such a trial to them and of which previously they could not rid themselves. Perhaps the reason is that the Lord has so greatly strengthened and dilated and equipped the soul, or it may be that, for reasons which His Majesty alone knows, He was anxious to make a public revelation of His secret dealings with such souls, for His judgments surpass all that we can imagine here on earth.

---

[1] The bracketed phrase is St. Teresa's marginal addition.
[2] Luis de León modifies this paragraph thus. After "save very occasionally" he adds, in parenthesis: "that is, as I say here, with respect to these exterior effects of the suspension of the senses and loss of heat; but they tell me that only the accidents disappear and that interiorly there is rather an increase." He then continues: "So the raptures, in the way I describe, cease, and it [the soul] has not these raptures and flights of the spirit; or, if it has them, only rarely, and hardly ever in public as it very often had before."

These effects God bestows, together with all those other good effects already described in the above-mentioned degrees of prayer, when the soul approaches Him, and He also gives the soul that kiss for which the Bride besought Him; for I understand it to be in this Mansion that that petition is fulfilled. Here to this wounded hart are given waters in abundance. Here the soul delights in the tabernacle of God.[1] Here the dove sent out by Noe to see if the storm is over finds the olive-branch[2] —the sign that it has discovered firm ground amidst the waters and storms of this world.

Oh, Jesus! If only one knew how many things there are in Scripture which describe this peace of the soul! My God, since Thou seest how needful it is for us, do Thou inspire Christians to desire to seek it; take it not, by Thy mercy, from those to whom Thou hast given it, and who, until Thou give them true peace and take them where peace will never end, must always live in fear. I say "true" peace, not because I think this peace is not true, but because in this life war might always begin again if we were to withdraw from God.

And what will be the feeling of these souls when they realize that they might lack so great a blessing? The thought makes them walk the more warily and endeavour to bring strength out of their weakness, so as not to be responsible for losing any opportunity which might offer itself to them of pleasing God better. The more they are favoured by God, the more timorous and fearful do they become concerning themselves, and as they have learned more about their own wretchedness by comparing it with His greatness and their sins are now so much more serious to them, they often go about, like the Publican, without daring to lift up their eyes.[3] At other times, they long to reach the end of their lives so as to be in safety, though they are soon anxious again to live longer so that they may serve Him because of the love which they bear Him, as has been said, and they trust all that concerns themselves to His mercy. Sometimes the many favours they receive leave them overwhelmed, and afraid lest they be like an overladen ship sinking to the bottom of the sea.

I assure you, sisters, that they have no lack of crosses, but these do not unsettle them or deprive them of their peace. The few storms pass quickly, like waves of the sea, and fair weather returns, and then the Presence of the Lord which they have within them makes them forget everything. May He be for ever blessed and praised by all His creatures. Amen.

[1] Apocalypse xxi, 3.   [2] Genesis viii, 8–9.   [3] St. Luke xviii, 13.

CHAPTER IV

Concludes by describing what appears to be Our Lord's aim in granting the soul such great favours and says how necessary it is for Martha and Mary to walk in each other's company. This chapter is very profitable.

You must not take it, sisters, that the effects which I have described as occurring in these souls are invariably present all the time; it is for this reason that, whenever I have remembered to do so, I have referred to them as being present "habitually". Sometimes Our Lord leaves such souls to their own nature, and when that happens, all the poisonous things in the environs and mansions of this castle seem to come together to avenge themselves on them for the time during which they have not been able to have them in their power.

It is true that this lasts only for a short time—for a single day, or a little longer, at the most—and in the course of the ensuing turmoil, which as a rule is the result of some chance happening, it becomes clear what the soul is gaining from the good Companion Who is with it. For the Lord gives it great determination, so that it will on no account turn aside from His service and from its own good resolutions. On the contrary, these resolutions seem to increase, and so the soul will not make the slightest move which may deflect it from its resolve. This, as I say, happens rarely, but Our Lord's will is for the soul not to forget what it is—for one reason, so that it may always be humble; for another, so that it may the better realize what it owes to His Majesty and what a great favour it is receiving, and may praise Him.

Do not, of course, for one moment imagine that, because these souls have such vehement desires and are so determined not to commit a single imperfection for anything in the world, they do not in fact commit many imperfections, and even sins. Not intentionally, it is true, for the Lord will give such persons very special aid as to this: I am referring to venial sins, for from mortal sins, as far as they know, they are free, though they are not completely proof against them; and the thought that they may commit some without knowing it will cause them no small agony. It also distresses them to see so many souls being lost; and, although on the one hand they have great hopes of not being among them, yet, when they remember some whom the Scriptures describe as having been favoured of the Lord—like

Solomon, who enjoyed such converse with His Majesty[1]—they cannot, as I have said, but be afraid. And let whichever of you feels surest of herself fear most, for, says David, "Blessed is the man that feareth God."[2] May His Majesty always protect us; let us beseech Him to do so, that we may not offend Him; this is the greatest security that we can have. May He be for ever praised. Amen.

It will be a good thing, sisters, if I tell you why it is that the Lord grants so many favours in this world. Although you will have learned this from the effects they produce, if you have observed them, I will speak about it further here, so that none of you shall think that He does it simply to give these souls pleasure. That would be to make a great error. For His Majesty can do nothing greater for us than grant us a life which is an imitation of that lived by His Beloved Son. I feel certain, therefore, that these favours are given us to strengthen our weakness, as I have sometimes said here, so that we may be able to imitate Him in His great sufferings.

We always find that those who walked closest to Christ Our Lord were those who had to bear the greatest trials. Consider the trials suffered by His glorious Mother and by the glorious Apostles. How do you suppose Saint Paul could endure such terrible trials? We can see in his life the effects of genuine visions and of contemplation coming from Our Lord and not from human imagination or from the deceit of the devil. Do you imagine that he shut himself up with his visions so as to enjoy those Divine favours and pursue no other occupation? You know very well that, so far as we can learn, he took not a day's rest, nor can he have rested by night, since it was then that he had to earn his living.[3] I am very fond of the story of how, when Saint Peter was fleeing from prison, Our Lord appeared to him and told him to go back to Rome and be crucified. We never recite the Office on his festival, in which this story is found, without my deriving a special consolation from it.[4] How did Saint Peter feel after receiving this favour from the Lord? And what did he do? He went straight to his death; and the Lord showed him no small mercy in providing someone to kill him.

---

[1] 3 Kings [A.V. 1 Kings] xi.
[2] Psalm cxi [A.V., cxii], 1.
[3] 1 Thessalonians ii, 9.
[4] In the old Carmelite Breviary, which St. Teresa would have used, the Antiphon of the Magnificat at First Vespers on June 29 runs: "The Blessed Apostle Peter saw Christ coming to meet him. Adoring Him, he said: 'Lord, whither goest Thou?' 'I am going to Rome to be crucified afresh.'" The story has it that St. Peter returned to Rome and was crucified.

Oh, my sisters, how little one should think about resting, and how little one should care about honours, and how far one ought to be from wishing to be esteemed in the very least if the Lord makes His special abode in the soul. For if the soul is much with Him, as it is right it should be, it will very seldom think of itself; its whole thought will be concentrated upon finding ways to please Him and upon showing Him how it loves Him. This, my daughters, is the aim of prayer: this is the purpose of the Spiritual Marriage, of which are born good works and good works alone.

Such works, as I have told you, are the sign of every genuine favour and of everything else that comes from God. It will profit me little if I am alone and deeply recollected, and make acts of love to Our Lord and plan and promise to work wonders in His service, and then, as soon as I leave my retreat and some occasion presents itself, I do just the opposite. I was wrong when I said it will profit me little, for anyone who is with God must profit greatly, and, although after making these resolutions we may be too weak to carry them out, His Majesty will sometimes grant us grace to do so, even at great cost to ourselves, as often happens. For, when He sees a very timorous soul, He sends it, much against its own will, some very sore trial the bearing of which does it a great deal of good; and later, when the soul becomes aware of this, it loses its fear and offers itself to Him the more readily. What I meant was that the profit is small by comparison with the far greater profit which comes from conformity between our deeds on the one hand and our resolutions and the words we use on the other. Anyone who cannot achieve everything at once must progress little by little. If she wishes to find help in prayer, she must learn to subdue her own will and in these little nooks of ours there will be very many occasions when you can do this.

Reflect carefully on this, for it is so important that I can hardly lay too much stress on it. Fix your eyes on the Crucified and nothing else will be of much importance to you. If His Majesty revealed His love to us by doing and suffering such amazing things, how can you expect to please Him by words alone? Do you know when people really become spiritual? It is when they become the slaves of God and are branded with His sign, which is the sign of the Cross, in token that they have given Him their freedom. Then He can sell them as slaves to the whole world, as He Himself was sold, and if He does this He will be doing them no wrong but showing them no slight favour. Unless they resolve to do this, they need not expect to make great progress. For the foundation of this whole edifice, as I have said, is humility, and, if you have not true humility, the Lord will not wish it to reach any great height: in fact, it is for your own good that it should not; if it did, it would fall to the ground. Therefore, sisters, if you wish to lay good foundations, each of you must try to be the least of all, and the slave of God, and must seek a way and means to please and serve all your companions. If you do that, it will be of more value to you than to them and your foundation will be so firmly laid that your Castle will not fall.

I repeat that if you have this in view you must not build upon foundations of prayer and contemplation alone, for, unless you strive after the virtues and practise them, you will never grow to be more than dwarfs. God grant that nothing worse than this may happen—for, as you know, anyone who fails to go forward begins to go back, and love, I believe, can never be content to stay for long where it is.

You may think that I am speaking about beginners, and that later on one may rest: but, as I have already told you, the only repose that these souls enjoy is of an interior kind; of outward repose they get less and less, and they have no wish to get more. What is the purpose, do you suppose, of these inspirations—or, more correctly, of these aspirations—which I have described, and of these messages which are sent by the soul from its innermost centre to the folk outside the Castle and to the Mansions which are outside that in which it is itself dwelling? Is it to send them to sleep? No, no, no. The soul, where it now is, is fighting harder to keep the faculties and senses and everything to do with the body from being idle than it did when it suffered with them. For it did not then understand what great gain can be derived from trials, which may indeed have been means whereby God has brought it to this state, nor did it realize how the companionship which it now enjoys would give it much greater strength than it ever had before. For if, as David says, with the holy we shall be holy,[1] it cannot be doubted that, if we are made one with the Strong, we shall gain strength through the most sovereign union of spirit with Spirit, and we shall appreciate the strength of the saints which enabled them to suffer and die.

It is quite certain that, with the strength it has gained, the soul comes to the help of all who are in the Castle, and, indeed, succours the body itself. Often the body appears to feel nothing, but the strength derived from the vigour gained by the soul after it has drunk of the wine from this cellar, where its Spouse has brought it and which He will not allow it to leave, overflows

---

[1] Psalm xvii (A.V. xviii), 26.

into the weak body, just as on the earthly plane the food which is introduced into the stomach gives strength to the head and to the whole body. In this life, then, the soul has a very bad time, for, however much it accomplishes, it is strong enough inwardly to attempt much more and this causes such strife within it that nothing it can do seems to it of any importance. This must be the reason for the great penances done by many saints, especially by the glorious Magdalen, who had been brought up in such luxury all her life long; there was also that hunger for the honour of his God suffered by our father Elias;[1] and the zeal of Saint Dominic and Saint Francis for bringing souls to God, so that He might be praised. I assure you that, forgetful as they were of themselves, they must have endured no little suffering.

This, my sisters, I should like us to strive to attain: we should desire and engage in prayer, not for our enjoyment, but for the sake of acquiring this strength which fits us for service. Let us not try to walk along an untrodden path, or at the best we shall waste our time: it would certainly be a novel idea to think of receiving these favours from God through any other means than those used by Him and by all His saints. Let us not even consider such a thing: believe me, Martha and Mary must work together when they offer the Lord lodging, and must have Him ever with them, and they must not entertain Him badly and give Him nothing to eat. And how can Mary give Him anything, seated as she is at His feet, unless her sister helps her? His food consists in our bringing Him souls, in every possible way, so that they may be saved and may praise Him for ever.

You will reply to me by making two observations. The first, that Mary was said to have chosen the better part[2]—and she had already done the work of Martha and shown her love for the Lord by washing His feet and wiping them with her hair.[3] And do you think it would be a trifling mortification to a woman in her position to go through those streets—perhaps alone, for her fervour was such that she cared nothing how she went—to enter a house that she had never entered before and then to have to put up with uncharitable talk from the Pharisee[4] and from very many other people, all of which she was forced to endure? What a sight it must have been in the town to see such a woman as she had been making this change in her life! Such wicked people as we know the Jews to have been would only need to see that she was friendly with the Lord, Whom they so bitterly hated, to call to mind the life which she had lived and to realize

---

[1] 3 Kings [A.V. 1 Kings] xix, 10.
[2] St. Luke x, 42.
[3] St. Luke vii, 37–8.
[4] St. Luke vii, 39.

that she now wanted to become holy, for she would of course at once have changed her style of dress and everything else. Think how we gossip about people far less notorious than she and then imagine what she must have suffered. I assure you, sisters, that that better part came to her only after sore trials and great mortification—even to see her Master so much hated must have been an intolerable trial to her. And how many such trials did she not endure later, after the Lord's death! I think myself that the reason she was not granted martyrdom was that she had already undergone it through witnessing the Lord's death.[1] The later years of her life, too, during which she was absent from Him, would have been years of terrible torment; so she was not always enjoying the delights of contemplation at the Lord's feet.

The other thing you may say is that you are unable to lead souls to God, and have no means of doing so; that you would gladly do this, but, being unable to teach and preach like the Apostles, you do not know how. That is an objection which I have often answered in writing, though I am not sure if I have done so in discussing this Castle. But, as it is a thing which I think must occur to you, in view of the desires which the Lord implants in you, I will not omit to speak of it here. I told you elsewhere that the devil sometimes puts ambitious desires into our hearts, so that, instead of setting our hand to the work which lies nearest to us, and thus serving Our Lord in ways within our power, we may rest content with having desired the impossible. Apart from praying for people, by which you can do a great deal for them, do not try to help everybody, but limit yourselves to your own companions; your work will then be all the more effective because you have the greater obligation to do it. Do you imagine it is a small advantage that you should have so much humility and mortification, and should be the servants of all and show such great charity towards all, and such fervent love for the Lord that it resembles a fire kindling all their souls, while you constantly awaken their zeal by your other virtues? This would indeed be a great service to the Lord and one very pleasing to Him. By your doing things which you really can do, His Majesty will know that you would like to do many more, and thus He will reward you exactly as if you had won many souls for Him.

"But we shall not be converting anyone," you will say, "for all our sisters are good already." What has that to do with it? If they become still better, their praises will be more pleasing to the Lord, and their prayers of greater value to their neighbours.

[1] This sentence is authentic but marginal.

In a word, my sisters, I will end by saying that we must not build towers without foundations, and that the Lord does not look so much at the magnitude of anything we do as at the love with which we do it. If we accomplish what we can, His Majesty will see to it that we become able to do more each day. We must not begin by growing weary; but during the whole of this short life, which for any one of you may be shorter than you think, we must offer the Lord whatever interior and exterior sacrifice we are able to give Him, and His Majesty will unite it with that which He offered to the Father for us upon the Cross, so that it may have the value won for it by our will, even though our actions in themselves may be trivial.

May it please His Majesty, my sisters and daughters, to bring us all to meet where we may praise Him and to give me grace to do some of the things of which I have told you, through the merits of His Son, Who liveth and reigneth for ever, Amen. As I say this to you I am full of shame and by the same Lord I beg you not to forget this poor miserable creature in your prayers.

JHS.

Although when I began to write what I have set down here it was with great reluctance, as I said at the beginning, I am very glad I did so now that it is finished, and I think my labour has been well spent, though I confess it has cost me very little. And considering how strictly you are cloistered, my sisters, how few opportunities you have of recreation and how insufficient in number are your houses, I think it will be a great consolation for you, in some of your convents, to take your delight in this Interior Castle, for you can enter it and walk about in it at any time without asking leave from your superiors.

It is true that, however strong you may think yourselves, you cannot enter all the Mansions by your own efforts: the Lord of the Castle Himself must admit you to them. So, if you meet with any resistance, I advise you not to make any effort to get in, for if you do you will displease Him so much that He will never admit you. He is a great Lover of humility. If you consider yourselves unworthy of entering even the third Mansions, He will more quickly give you the will to reach the fifth, and thenceforward you may serve Him by going to these Mansions again and again, till He brings you into the Mansion which He reserves as His own and which you will never leave, except when you are called away by the prioress, whose wishes this great

Lord is pleased that you should observe as if they were His own. And even if, at her command, you are often outside these Mansions, He will always keep the door open against your return. Once you have been shown how to enjoy this Castle, you will find rest in everything, even in the things which most try you, and you will cherish a hope of returning to it which nobody can take from you.

Although I have spoken here only of seven Mansions, yet in each there are comprised many more, both above and below and around, with lovely gardens and fountains[1] and things so delectable that you will want to lose yourselves in praise of the great God Who created it in His image and likeness. If you find anything good in this book which helps you to learn to know Him better, you can be quite sure that it is His Majesty Who has said it, and if you find anything bad, that it has been said by me.

By the earnest desire that I have to be of some use in helping you to serve this my God and Lord, I beg you, in my own name, whenever you read this, to give great praise to His Majesty and beg Him to multiply His Church and to give light to the Lutherans and to pardon my sins and set me free from Purgatory, where perhaps, by the mercy of God,[2] I shall be when this is given you to read, if, after being revised by learned men, it is ever published. And if there is any error in it, that is due to my lack of understanding, for in all things I submit to what is held by the Holy Roman Catholic Church, in which I live, and protest and promise that I will both live and die. Praised and blessed for ever be God our Lord. Amen, Amen.

The writing of this was finished in the convent of Saint Joseph of Ávila, in the year one thousand five hundred and seventy seven, on the vigil of Saint Andrew, to the glory of God, Who liveth and reigneth for ever and ever. Amen.

[1] "And mazes", adds Luis de León. The words also occur in several copies of the autograph, including that of Toledo, but not in the autograph itself. There is reason to suppose, however, that there may have been two autographs of this epilogue.
[2] "By the mercy of God" is the Saint's marginal addition.

CONCEPTIONS OF THE LOVE OF GOD

INTRODUCTION

The *Conceptions of the Love of God written . . . upon certain words of the "Songs" of Solomon* has a close affinity with the *Interior Castle* and with those chapters of the *Life* and the *Way of perfection* which deal with the contemplative life in its higher stages. So fervent a lover of God as St. Teresa could not fail to be inspired by the sublimity of the mystical conceptions which underlie the most ardent and luxuriant of love-songs in the world's literature. But here, as in her other works, she wrote chiefly for the edification of her spiritual daughters. She had often occasion, in the Divine Office, to read passages from the *Song of Songs*, and, dwelling upon these, as she did, with loving thought, she desired to make the results of her meditations known to others.[1]

Apart from a short preface, which has come down to us in a somewhat mutilated form, the work consists of seven chapters. The first of these emphasizes the veneration with which the Scriptures must be read and enlarges upon the difficulties which arise in the interpretation of them. The second enumerates "nine kinds of false peace offered to the soul by the world, the flesh and the devil", and contrasts with these the true peace desired by the Bride. The latter part of the description is continued into the third chapter, which is followed by three chapters dealing with the Prayer of Quiet and the Prayer of Union and with the benefits which come to the soul that goes through these experiences. The seventh chapter describes the Bride's desire to suffer, not only for God's sake but for her neighbour's, and, as elsewhere in her writings, stresses the intimacy of the connection between the contemplative's desire for union with God and his constant endeavour to serve his neighbour. Thus, although St. Teresa declares at the end of this opuscule that its aim was merely to expound a few texts ("to explain to you how to appreciate some of the texts in the *Canticles* when you hear them"), it will be seen to have a truer unity than would be suggested by this protestation.

The exact date of the composition of the *Conceptions* is unknown. Possibly it may not all have been written at one and the same time, but at long intervals, as other duties allowed. The prologue refers to "*these convents* which it has pleased His Majesty should

[1] The passages to which she devotes the greatest attention are Canticles, i, 1 and ii, 3-5.

INTRODUCTION

be founded according to the primitive Rule of Our Lady of Mount Carmel"; and, as it was not until August 1567 that the second of the Reformed convents was established—that of Medina del Campo—that phrase will serve as a *terminus ab quo* for our examination: it is probable, as a matter of fact, that considerably more than two houses are referred to. The *terminus ad quem*, supplied by an annotation in the hand of P. Báñez found in a copy of the book,[1] is May 1575. The seventh chapter refers to an incident which took place at Salamanca, in Eastertide of the year 1571, when St. Teresa went into a rapture on hearing a novice named Isabel de Jesús sing a simple song.[2] P. Jerónimo de San José observes that she refers to having written two books about prayer —the *Life* and the *Way of perfection*. Now the *Interior Castle*, as we have seen, was not begun until 1577, but the *Foundations* dates from August 1573, and the critic's inference is that the *Conceptions* must have been written before them, for otherwise, as St. Teresa writes about prayer in the *Foundations*, she would have made the number, not two, but three.[3]

These data suggest that the *Conceptions of the Love of God* was written between 1571 and 1573, probably at Ávila, Alba de Tormes or Salamanca. It is unlikely that, as the Carmelite nuns of Paris suppose,[4] the book was composed at Segovia, when St. Teresa went to make her foundation there in 1574. For her confessor at Segovia was P. Yanguas, who, as the Canonization documents make clear, would not have approved of her attempting to gloss so difficult a book as the *Song of Songs*, whereas she makes it clear that she took up her pen at her confessor's orders. It would seem more probable that, when she went to make her Segovian foundation, she took with her the completed manuscript; that, following her usual custom, she gave it to P. Yanguas, asking him for a frank opinion on it; and that subsequently he decided that it should be destroyed, not because it contained any erroneous doctrine, but because of the risk that, if it fell into indiscreet hands, it would involve the author in trouble with the Inquisition. After all, as recently as 1572, Fray Luis de León— no unlearned person but a theologian and a university professor— had been arrested and imprisoned by the Inquisition, one of the grounds given for his arrest being that he had translated the *Song of Songs* into the vernacular.

This theory would account for the fact that the original

[1] Cf. p. 399, n. 2, below.
[2] Cf. *Relations*, XV (Vol. I, p. 340, above).
[3] *Historia del Carmen Descalzo*, Vol. I, p. 871. [The inference seems to me rather a bold one, for the *Foundations* is only in a very incidental sense a book about prayer and the author can hardly have thought of it as such.]
[4] *Oeuvres complètes*, etc., Vol. V, p. 639.

manuscript of the *Conceptions* disappeared during St. Teresa's lifetime. Some critics believe that in its original form it was longer than the book which we have to-day; to others it gives the impression of being complete. The concluding lines of the seventh chapter have certainly the stamp of finality and none of the early copies of the book include any further chapters. The numerous divergences between these copies may quite well be explained by the postulation of a second autograph: indeed, this may even be thought an unescapable deduction from the evidence provided by the copies, since no amanuensis would be either careless enough or bold enough to make so many departures from the original.

In the course of the processes for the Beatification and Canonization of St. Teresa a good deal was said about the origins of this opuscule. Some of the nuns who were called as witnesses deposed that P. Yanguas had in fact burned the autograph and various copies of the work and that they knew this to be so from his own lips. María de San José, for example, the sister of P. Gracián, gave evidence as follows:

> I also heard the Father-Master Fray Diego de Yanguas say that, when he was [St. Teresa's] confessor, she showed him a book on the *Songs* that she had written, and that he had ordered it to be burned, because it did not seem suitable to him that a woman should write on the *Songs*. And she obeyed immediately, without questioning his decision. And afterwards the Father regretted what he had done, since there was nothing in the book contrary to our holy Faith.

Among other testimony to the same effect is a statement made in 1610 by Doña María Enríquez de Toledo y Colona, Duchess of Alba. "I have a copy," she deposed, "of what the said Mother wrote on the *Songs*, which was given me in the convent at Alba, at the time when P. Diego de Yanguas ordered her to have all the copies collected and burned, not because there was anything wrong in the book, but because he thought it unfitting that a woman should write on the *Songs*."

Apparently St. Teresa kept from her daughters the name of the confessor who ordered the book's destruction. Even her intimate confidant, P. Gracián, was ignorant of his identity, though he was aware of the fact itself, to which he refers thus in the preface to the first edition of the *Conceptions*, published by him in Brussels:

> Among the books which she wrote was one containing Divine conceptions and loftiest thoughts on the love of God, on prayer

and on other heroic virtues, in which were expounded many words from the *Songs of Solomon*. But one of her confessors, thinking it a new and dangerous thing that a woman should write on the *Songs*, ordered this book to be burned, moved with zeal for Saint Paul's instruction that "women should keep silence in the Church of God".[1] This he took to mean that they should not preach in churches, nor give lectures nor print books.

That little advance had been made in the intervening years may be deduced from the length at which Gracián himself defends his temerity in allowing the work to appear in print. He reminds his readers of the prevalence, in St. Teresa's day, of the "Lutheran heresy" which encouraged "women and idiots to read and expound the Divine writings", and attributes the confessor's zeal to the fact that her work was not really an exposition of the *Songs* at all but an account of certain thoughts, or "conceptions", with which God had inspired her.

Though the autograph, or autographs, of the *Conceptions* met with so premature a fate, a great many copies must have been made, and some of these, probably without St. Teresa's knowledge, were saved from the fire. The copy on which Gracián based his edition is no longer extant, and for this edition we have used that preserved by the Discalced Carmelite nuns of Alba de Tormes, which contains nine pages of critical observations, by P. Manuel de Santa María, and has the great recommendation of bearing two annotations, approving its contents, in the hand of P. Domingo Báñez. It has also the merit of being the most nearly complete copy known. It is the only one, for example, containing the prologue, for which reason it has been impossible to supply the lines wanting in the copy on account of the mutilation of the first page. The copyist, as his orthography shows, was familiar with both Latin and Italian, and did his work so conscientiously that occasionally he left a space where a word was indecipherable to him, no doubt with the intention (not always carried out) of filling it up later. The book is not divided into chapters.

Greatly inferior to the Alba copy, but the next best to it, is one which was long preserved at the Carmelite College in Baeza but was lost during the exclaustration of the religious Orders early in the nineteenth century: a transcript of it, made by P. Andrés de la Encarnación, is in the National Library of Spain (MS. 1400). The two other copies of importance are that of

---

[1] [1 Corinthians xiv, 34: "Let women keep silence in the churches."]

Consuegra, fragmentary and muddled in arrangement, the work of P. Gracián's cousin, M. Ana de San José and that of the Desierto de las Nieves, similar to it in detail, which again has disappeared and is available only in a transcript. [P. Silverio reproduces the text of these three copies as appendices but the Alba codex is so much superior to the rest that I have felt justified in translating and following it exclusively.]

Fray Luis de León, not unnaturally, seems to have shrunk from publishing the *Conceptions* in his edition of St. Teresa's collected writings, and it was not till 1611 that the work first appeared in printed form, with annotations by its editor, P. Gracián. His text is very similar to that of the Alba copy, though it is evident, from a comparison of it with those of the copies, that he must have made free and frequent use of the permission given him by the Saint long previously to modify everything that she wrote.

In a letter written to his sister Juliana de San José, a Sevilian Carmelite, P. Gracián describes his edition of this book, together with one of the *Foundations*, as having been "very fruitful". The *Conceptions* was, in fact, sold out within a year, and in 1612 was reprinted by the same publisher, with more of Gracián's annotations. The Inquisition made no difficulty about its free circulation and numerous editions appeared in Spain: only from 1623 to 1630 was any part of it forbidden, and that not the text but the editor's annotations. Until 1861, when La Fuente first used the Alba codex, Gracián's text alone was known. La Fuente, however, has numerous inaccuracies, and also intercalates occasional paragraphs from the Consuegra copy: where this is done in our text, the fact is always indicated in a footnote.

CONCEPTIONS OF THE LOVE OF GOD

Written by the Blessed Mother Teresa of Jesus upon certain words of the Songs of Solomon.[1]

PROLOGUE[2]

I have seen the mercies granted by Our Lord to the souls whom He has been bringing to these convents which it has pleased His Majesty should be founded according to the Primitive Rule of Our Lady of Mount Carmel. So great are the favours granted by Our Lord to some of these souls in particular that only those who realize how necessary it is that someone should explain to them certain of the things which pass between the soul and Our Lord can know what trials may have to be suffered by those who cannot understand them clearly. For several years past, the Lord has been giving me such great joy in the hearing or reading of some of the texts from the *Songs* of Solomon that, although I have not clearly understood the meaning of the Latin in the vernacular, they have caused me greater recollection and moved my soul more than the highly devotional books which I can understand. This is now almost habitual with me; even when they have told me the meaning of the texts in the vernacular, I have understood it no better . . . and without understanding it . . . withdraw my soul from itself.[3]

For about two years past, it has seemed to me that for a purpose of my own the Lord has been enabling me to understand something of the meaning of a few of these texts, which I think will bring comfort to those sisters whom Our Lord is leading along this road, as well as to myself. For sometimes the Lord enables me to understand a great deal that I should like not to forget though I have not dared to set any of it down in writing.

Now, having consulted the opinions of persons whom I am bound to obey, I shall write down some of the things which the Lord enables me to understand, enshrined in texts that gladden my soul on this way of prayer, to which, as I have said, the Lord

---

[1] Apparently St. Teresa gave her work no title. That used here is taken from Gracián's edition.

[2] The Alba codex has only "Jhs. Mᵃ" here. In the margin P. Báñez has written: "This is a meditation (*consideración*) by Teresa of Jesus. I have found nothing in it which offends me. Fr. Domingo Báñez."

[3] The Alba codex, which alone includes the prologue, is mutilated here, and the sense of these last lines cannot be established.

is leading the sisters in these convents, who are my own sisters. You must accept this poor little gift, if you happen to see it, from one who desires for you, as for herself, all the gifts of the Holy Spirit, in Whose name I begin it. If I should be in any way successful, it will not be due to myself. May it please His Divine Majesty to make me so. . . . [1]

[1] The mutilated state of the codex is responsible for the disappearance of several lines here.

CHAPTER I

Treats of the veneration with which the Sacred Scriptures must be read, and of the difficulty which women have in understanding them. This applies particularly to the Song of Songs.[1]

> Let the Lord kiss me with the kiss of his mouth, for thy breasts are better than wine. Canticles i. 1.

I have often noticed that, as far as we can understand, the soul appears here to be speaking with one person and asking for peace from another. For she says: "Let Him kiss me with the kiss of His mouth." And then she seems to be speaking to the person in whose presence she is—"Thy breasts are better."[2] I do not understand how this can be, and I am very glad not to do so. For really, daughters, the soul should not so much meditate upon or be taught to meditate upon or reverence her God in the things which with our lowly intelligence we can apparently comprehend in this life, as in the things which are quite incomprehensible. And so, when you read some book or hear a sermon or think upon the mysteries of our sacred Faith and find you cannot properly understand the subject, I strongly recommend you not to tire yourselves or strain your powers of thought by splitting hairs over it; it is something not meant for women— and many such things are not meant for men either!

When the Lord wishes to explain the matter to us, He does so without making us labour at it. I say this to women and also to such men as have not to defend the truth by their writings: those whom the Lord has chosen to expound such things to us must of course labour and they will gain greatly by so doing. But for us the task is simply to take what the Lord gives us; and not to tire ourselves out by worrying over what He does not give us, but to rejoice as we think what a great God and Lord we have, one of Whose words alone may contain within itself a thousand mysteries, so that we cannot even begin to understand it. If it were written in Latin or Hebrew or Greek, this would not be surprising; but even in our own vernacular, how many things there are in the Psalms of the glorious King David which, when explained to us in Spanish, are as obscure as if they were in Latin!

---

[1] As St. Teresa did not divide her work into chapters, we follow, except where otherwise stated, the division made by Gracián. We have, however, abbreviated the excessively long titles which he gave to the chapters.

[2] [The expression used here for "are better" (*mejores son*) is not the same as that of the epigraph—*más valen*, which means literally "are worth more."]

Always refrain, then, from tiring yourselves and straining your powers of thought with these things, for women need no more than what their intelligence is capable of. If they have that, God will grant them His grace; and, when His Majesty is pleased to teach us anything, we shall find that we have learned it without any trouble or labour of our own. For the rest, we must humble ourselves, and, as I have said, rejoice that we have such a Lord, Whose words, even when turned into our own vernacular, are beyond our understanding.

You may think that in these *Canticles*[1] there are some things which might have been said in a different way. We are so stupid that I should not be surprised if you did: I have heard some people say that they actually tried not to listen to them. O God, what miserable creatures we are! We are like poisonous things that turn all they eat into poison: the Lord grants us great favours by showing us the good things which come to the soul that loves Him and by encouraging it till it can hold converse with His Majesty and delight in Him; yet from these favours we derive only fears and we attribute meanings to them which sort well with the little love we feel for God.[2]

Oh, my Lord, how ill we profit from all the blessings which Thou hast granted us! Thy Majesty seeks methods and ways and inventions by which to show us what love Thou hast for us; yet we, inexperienced in loving Thee, set so little store by them that, unpractised as we are, our thoughts pursue their habitual path and cease pondering on the great mysteries hidden in this language used by the Holy Spirit. What more could be needed to enkindle our love for Him and to make us realize that He did not adopt this method of communication without good reason?

I remember, once upon a time, hearing a religious preach a most admirable sermon, the greater part of which was a description of the joys that result from the Bride's converse with God; and the people laughed so much and so completely misinterpreted what he said, for he was speaking of love (it was the *Mandatum* sermon,[3] where no other subject is possible), that I was astounded. It is quite clear to me that, as I have said, we have so little experience of the love of God that we think it impossible for a

---

[1] [*Cánticos*. St. Teresa sometimes uses this word, and sometimes the word *Cantares*, which I have rendered "Songs". The translation follows her usage exactly.]

[2] [There is a play here on the word *sentidos* ("meanings") and the verb *sentir* ("feel") used in the form of its substantival derivative *sentido*.]

[3] The *Mandatum* sermon [from the title of which is derived the English word "Maundy"] is preached during the ceremony of the washing of the feet of the poor, in memory of Christ's washing of His disciples' feet, on Maundy Thursday. The word is part of the antiphon—*Mandatum novum do vobis*.

soul to hold such converse with God as this. But although the people I was talking about gained little profit from what the preacher said, because they simply could not understand it, and I believe they really thought he was making it up out of his own head, I know certain others to whom it has brought such abundant blessings, such joy and such complete security from fear that they have often felt bound to give special praises to Our Lord for having left such a salutary help for souls who love Him with a fervent love. This has led them to see and understand that God can really so humble Himself; their experience alone would not have sufficed to remove their fears when the Lord granted them great favours, but in this they see a picture of their security.

I know someone who for many years had misgivings about this and nothing could reassure her until it pleased the Lord that she should hear some texts from the *Canticles* from which she realized that her soul was being well guided. For, as I have said, she knew that it is possible for a soul enamoured of her Spouse to experience all these joys and swoons and mortal agonies[1] and afflictions and delights and rejoicings in Him, when she has left all worldly joys for love of Him and has placed herself and left herself wholly in His hands. And this not only in word, as some do, but in very truth, with words confirmed by actions. Oh, my daughters, how well God recompenses us,[2] and what a Lord and Spouse you have—nothing happens to you without His seeing and knowing it! Even in the smallest things, then, do not fail to do what you can for love of Him. His Majesty will recompense us and He will look only at the love with which you do it.

I conclude by advising you, whenever there is anything that you do not understand, either in Holy Scripture or in the mysteries of our Faith, not to stop and think about it more than I have said, and not to be surprised at the tender words which you may read of in Scripture as passing between God and the soul. What amazes and bewilders me more, considering what we are, is the love which He had for us, and has still. Yet such love He has, and there can surely be no words with which He can express it as clearly as He has already expressed it by His actions. If you love me, I would beg you, when you reach this point, to pause a little and think of the love He has shown us, and of all He has done for us. Once we realize that His love was so strong and powerful that it made Him suffer so, how can we be amazed by any words which He may use to express it?

[1][*Lit.*: "and deaths". Various meanings are possible for this ambiguous phrase. It may be that "swoons and deaths" should be taken together, to indicate swoons that have the semblance of death.] St. Teresa appears to be referring to herself in this passage.
[2][*Lit.*: "What a very good Payer is God!"]

Returning now to what I had begun to say, there must be wonderful things and mysteries in these texts, for they are so precious that learned men, whom I have asked to explain what the Holy Spirit means by them, and their significance, tell me that the Doctors have written many expositions of them and have not yet fully explained them. As this is so, it would denote an excessive pride on my part if I tried to explain any part of them; and, deficient in humility as I may be, it is not my intention to suggest that I shall discover the truth. But, as I love learning what the Lord has to teach me when I hear any part of the *Canticles*, my hope is that, if I tell you something about it, you may perhaps be comforted by it, as I am. And, even if my words are irrelevant to the sense of the passage, I shall interpret these in my own way; for, providing I do not depart from what is held by the Church and the Saints (and very learned men will examine my book from this standpoint before you see it), the Lord, I think, allows this, as He allows us, when thinking upon His sacred Passion, to dwell in much greater detail than the Evangelists do upon the trials and the torments which He must have suffered. If, as I said at the beginning, we do not merely indulge our curiosity but accept what His Majesty allows us to understand, I feel sure He will not mind our finding comfort and delight in His words and works, just as the King would be glad and happy if he saw a little shepherd-boy who had won his affection and favour standing dumb with stupefaction at all the brocade on his robes and wondering what it was and how it was made. Just so, we women need not entirely refrain from enjoyment of the Lord's riches: what we must not do is to argue about them and expound them, thinking that we can do so successfully without having first submitted our opinions to learned men. So, as the Lord well knows, I do not suppose I shall be successful in writing about this; I am just like the little shepherd-boy I have alluded to. Although I may be saying a lot of stupid things, I like telling you about my meditations, as you are my daughters; and so, with the favour of this my Divine King and with the leave of my confessor, I will begin. May God, Who has been pleased to allow me to succeed in explaining other things to you (or perhaps it was His Majesty Who explained them through me, as they were intended for you), grant me equal success here. If He does not, I still think the time I shall have spent in writing this will have been well employed, since I have been thinking over such Divine matters which I had not deserved even to hear spoken of.

In these first words of the *Songs* it seems to me that the Bride is speaking to a third person, but that this is the same person whom she is speaking of. For there are two natures in Christ—the one Divine and the other human. I shall not dwell upon this because I want to say something about the way in which I think those of us who practise prayer may profit, though everything is profitable to a soul that loves the Lord with fervent desire, since it instils into it courage and wonder. His Majesty knows well that, although I have occasionally heard expositions of some of these words which have been made for me at my request, they have been few and I remember very little of them, for I have a very bad memory; and so I shall only be able to say what the Lord teaches me and what is to my purpose, and about these opening words I cannot remember ever having heard anything.

Let Him kiss me with a kiss of His mouth.[1] O my Lord and my God, what words are these for a worm to use to its Creator! Blessed be Thou, Lord, Who hast taught us in so many different ways! Who would dare to use these words, my King, save by Thy permission? It is an astounding thing—and it may well be thought astounding for me to say that they may be used by anyone whatsoever. It will be said that I am a stupid creature, that the Bride does not mean this at all, that these words have many meanings, that it is obvious we could not address them to God, and that for this reason it is well that such things should not be read by simple-minded people. I confess that the words may be taken in many senses, but the soul that is afire with love so that she hardly knows what she is saying is interested in none of them, but wishes only to repeat the words themselves. Yes, and the Lord does not forbid her to. Dear God! Why should we be astounded at this? Does not the reality give us greater cause for wonder? Do we not approach the Most Holy Sacrament? I have even wondered if the Bride was asking here for this favour which Christ afterwards gave us. I have also wondered if she was asking for a union as great as that of God being made man. For this was a friendship which He contracted with mankind, and of course the kiss is a sign of great friendship and peace between two persons. May the Lord help us to realize how many kinds of peace there are!

There is one thing which I want to say before I go any farther, and I think it is worth noting. It would come more naturally elsewhere, but I say it now so as not to forget it. I feel sure (God grant I be wrong!) that there must be many people who approach the Most Holy Sacrament while in grave mortal sin; and if they heard these words spoken by a soul that was dying for love of

---

[1] [St. Teresa sometimes writes *con el beso*, which I translate "with *the* kiss", and sometimes "con beso", of which "with *a* kiss" seems to be the nearest English equivalent to the elusive Spanish sense.]

God, they would be shocked and would think it great presumption. At least I am sure they would not themselves use these words, which, with others in the *Songs* like them, are spoken by love; as such persons have no love, they are quite capable of reading the *Songs* every day without making the words their own or even daring to take them upon their lips; for of a truth it causes one fear even to hear them, so great is the majesty which they enshrine.[1] And yet, my Lord, surpassing majesty is enshrined in the Most Holy Sacrament; but, as the faith of such souls is not living, but dead, Thou sayest nothing to them when they see Thee in Thy humility beneath the species of bread; and indeed they deserve not to hear Thee. It is for this reason that they dare to act with this presumption.

These words, then, if taken literally, would strike fear into anyone who was in a normal state of mind when he uttered them. But in anyone, Lord, whom love for Thee has drawn right out of himself Thou wilt pardon the use of them, and even of more words of the kind, notwithstanding their presumption. And if a kiss denotes peace and friendship, my Lord, why will not souls beg of Thee to give it to them? What better thing could we ask, O Lord, than that which I ask of Thee—that Thou wilt give me this peace, "with a kiss of Thy mouth"? This is the sublimest of petitions, daughters, as I shall explain to you later.

CHAPTER II

Describes nine kinds of false peace offered to the soul by the world, the flesh and the devil. Explains the sanctity of the religious state which leads to the true peace desired by the Bride in the Canticles.

God preserve you from many kinds of peace experienced by worldly people! God forbid that you should ever know these, for

[1] The Baeza MS. omits everything that precedes this phrase and begins the *Conceptions* with the following paragraph, after which it continues as in the text: "When I consider, my God and Lord, the loftiness of Thy Divine Majesty, and the greatness of Thy supreme bounty in Thy familiar communication of Thyself to vile creatures, I know not how it is that they can contain themselves with admiration and do not strive with all their might to obtain Thy grace and friendship. For they see that, besides gladdening the soul by giving Thyself to be its food and sustenance, Thou dost delight to be treated as its tender and beloved Spouse, for which reason it beseeches Thee to kiss it with the kiss of Thy sweet and Divine mouth. And, in order to communicate Thy gifts and favours to it, Thou dost speak to it and instruct it with great care so as to draw it to Thy Divine love. And the words which Thou art wont to address to souls interiorly in order that they may recognize their faults and miseries and strive to free themselves from earthly things are of such a kind that merely hearing them causes one to fear, so great is the majesty which they enshrine."

they bring perpetual war! When some worldly person, deeply involved though he is in grievous sin, leads a very placid life and rests so contentedly in his vices that he never feels the prick of conscience, this peace, as you will have read, is a sign that he is on good terms with the devil. For as long as such folk live, the devil will never wage war on them, because, if he did, they would return some part of the way to God out of their very wickedness—not because they love Him, that is to say, but to save themselves strife. Those who act thus, however, never serve Him for long. As soon as the devil sees this, he begins to amuse himself once more by gratifying them, and they become friendly with him again, until he has them in the place where he makes them realize how false his peace was. Of such as these we need say no more: they have what they want. I hope in the Lord that such wrong-doing will not be found in you, although the devil might begin by giving you another kind of peace, regarding little things, and we must be fearful about this, daughters, for as long as we live.

When a nun begins to grow slack in a few things, which in themselves seem unimportant, and persists in these bad habits and suffers no twinges of conscience, this is an evil peace, which the devil can use to lead her into a thousand kinds of sin. Such, for example, is some infringement of the Constitution, which is not in itself a sin, or inattention to some command of a Superior; this may not be attributable to malice—still, the Superior is in the place of God, and it is always well that we should realize this and pay continual attention to her wishes. All these are little things which occur from time to time, and in themselves do not seem to be sins—but we do commit faults, and we always shall, for we are miserable sinners. I do not deny this, but I say that when we commit them we must repent and realize how wrong we have been; for otherwise, as I say, the devil will be delighted with us and may gradually make our souls insensible to these little things. And I assure you, daughters, that when he has got thus far, he has won no small victory, and I am afraid he will go farther still. For the love of God, then, look to yourselves carefully; you cannot avoid war in this life, for with so many enemies it is impossible for us to sit with our hands in our laps; we must always be watchful and pay heed to both our outward and our inward behaviour.

I assure you that, although the Lord may grant you favours in prayer and bestow upon you what I will describe later, nevertheless, once you emerge from such favoured states, you will find a thousand little occasions of stumbling and a thousand little temptations. Now you will come to grief because of your unwatchfulness, now because of leaving something undone; and you will have interior disturbances and temptations. I do not say that such things will happen invariably, or even very commonly, but when they do they are the greatest of the Lord's favours, and the soul that receives them makes progress. We cannot be angels in this life—that is not our nature. So I am not perturbed when I see a soul beset by the greatest temptations: if she has love and fear for Our Lord, she will eventually be all the better for them—that I know. But if I see her always going placidly on her way, without any conflicts (I have met some souls like this), I invariably have misgivings, even though I may see that she is not offending the Lord; I can never be quite sure about her, and if I can I test her and try her, as the devil is not doing so, so that she may discover what sort of person she is. I have come across only a few such cases; but it is quite possible for them to occur, since the Lord can do great things for a soul through contemplation.

Individual cases differ, and yet such people can habitually enjoy interior happiness, although personally I think they do not understand their own state and it is not easy to explain it to them. Sometimes, though not very often, they have their minor conflicts. But I do not really envy these souls. I have considered the matter carefully and I find that those who experience the warfare I have described make much greater progress, though their prayer is not in itself so perfect, as far as we can humanly understand. We may disregard the case of souls which, after having suffered this warfare for many years, have become proficient and attained great mortification. As they are now dead to the world, Our Lord generally gives them peace, but not of such a kind as to make them unconscious of their faults, which cause them great distress.

There are many ways, then, daughters, by which the Lord leads us; but always be fearful, as I have said, when you feel no grief for any fault that you may have committed; for sin, even if venial, ought of course to wound you deeply, as, glory be to God, I believe and know it does. Note one thing—and for love of me remember this. If a person is alive, and is pricked by a pin or a tiny thorn, however small it be, does she not feel it? Well, then, if a soul is not dead, but has a living love for God, is it not a great favour on His part if she feels sad at every little thing that is contrary to her profession and obligations? Oh, does not His Majesty make a bed of roses and flowers for Himself in the soul to whom He gives this solicitude? It is impossible for Him to fail to come and cheer her, long though He may be in doing so, God help me! What are we nuns doing in our convent? What motive had we for leaving the world? For what purpose have we come here? In what can we better employ ourselves than in making a dwelling-place for our Spouse within the soul, and doing so in time to be able to ask Him for the kiss of His mouth? Happy will she be who makes such a petition; when the Lord comes she will not find that her lamp has gone out nor will she have to go away after having knocked repeatedly. Oh, my daughters, what a high calling is ours, since none save our own selves can forbid us to address these words to our Spouse, Whom we took as such when we were professed!

Let any souls who are scrupulous understand that I am not speaking of a single fault committed only once, or of faults which cannot always be recognized as such or always repented of. I am referring to one who habitually commits them, without paying any heed to them, and thinks they do not matter, and has no remorse for them, and never tries to make amends for them. To such a person, I repeat, peace is dangerous and you must beware of it. What will it not be, then, to those who can remain at peace and yet be very lax about keeping their Rule? God grant that there be none such here! There must be many ways in which the devil gives such peace, for God allows it because of our sins. There is no need to deal with this here: I merely wanted to give you this brief warning. Let us come to the friendship and peace which the Lord begins to bestow upon us in prayer and I will tell you whatever His Majesty may teach me.[1]

It has seemed well to me to say a little to you next about the peace given by the world and that given by our own sensual nature. For although in many places abler descriptions of this have been written than I can give, you may not, perhaps, as you are poor, have the wherewithal for buying these books and there may be no one who will make you a present of them; whereas what I am writing now will be kept in the house and you will be able to read the whole of it. There are many ways in which we might be misled about the peace which the world gives. From the few of them that I shall tell you about you can deduce the rest.[2]

Now, as to riches. Some people have everything they need and a good sum of money in their coffers as well, and if they keep free from grave sins they think they have done everything. They enjoy what they have, and from time to time give alms, but they never reflect that this property is not their own but

---

[1] The Baeza MS. adds: "as one who so much desires your spiritual profit."
[2] The nine following paragraphs are not found in Gracián's edition, nor in any later edition, until that of Rivadeneyra.

that the Lord has given it to them as to His stewards, so that they may distribute it among the poor, and that they will have to render a strict account for the time they have kept a surplus in their coffers, if the poor are suffering because of the way they have withheld it from them. This does not concern us except that you must ask the Lord to give people light so that they may not become engrossed in their wealth and suffer the fate of the rich miser,[1] and that you may praise His Majesty, Who made you poor, and count this as a special favour from Him.

Oh, my daughters! What a great relief it is not to have to endure these burdens! Even in this world it is a relief to us to be free from them: what it will mean on the Last Day you cannot imagine. Those burdened in this way are slaves, whereas you are your own mistresses. One single example will show you this. Who enjoys the greater ease—a gentleman, who has all his meals served at his own table and all his clothes laid out in readiness for him, or his steward, who has to account to him for every farthing he spends? The former enjoys his possessions without stint, for they are his own; it is the poor steward who has to suffer; and, the greater his master's wealth, the more he suffers; when account-day draws near, he has to pass sleepless nights, especially if the accounts have run on for a great many years and he has been rather careless and the total to be accounted for is a high one; I do not know in such a case how he can have any peace at all. Before you pass on from this, daughters, give fervent praise to Our Lord, and be more particular than ever about your present custom of possessing nothing of your own. We eat what the Lord sends us without worrying about it, and His Majesty sees to it that we lack nothing. Nor shall we have to render any account for the surplus, for His Majesty also sees to it that we have nothing which we are obliged to give away.

The essential thing, daughters, is that we should be satisfied with little: we must not desire as much as people possess who have to give a strict account of their possessions, as any rich man must, even though his wealth is not in his own hands but in those of his stewards. And how strict that account will be! If he realized it, he would not take his meals so contentedly, nor squander his wealth on vain, meaningless things. So, daughters, always try to be as poor as you can manage to be, both in dress and in food; for otherwise you will find yourselves cheated—God will give you no more and you will be dissatisfied. Always try to serve His Majesty, so that you never eat the food of the poor without earning it by serving Him, although you will find it difficult to earn all the peace and repose which the Lord is giving you by

[1] St. Luke xii, 20.

enabling you to live without having to render an account of any riches. I am quite sure you realize this, but from time to time you must give special thanks for it to His Majesty.

Against the peace which is given by the world in the shape of honours there is no need for me to warn you, as little honour is ever done to the poor. What may do you great harm, unless you are careful, is praise, which, once it begins, never ceases, but in the end only casts you down the more.[1] As a rule, this praise consists in your being told how holy you are, and in such attractive terms that you would think they had been learned from the devil. And so they sometimes are: if they were said in your absence, they would not matter; but, if you are there, what fruit can they bear, unless you walk very warily, but evil?

For the love of God, I beg you never to let such remarks lull you into a state of peace, for in that case they might gradually come to do you harm and you would think they were true and suppose that you had done all you had to do and finished all your work. You must never allow such things to be said of you without making a strong inward protest: and this you can easily do if you make a habit of it. Remember how ill the world treated Christ Our Lord, and yet how it had extolled Him on Palm Sunday. Reflect what esteem men lavished on Saint John Baptist, whom they were on the point of taking for the Messiah, and yet how afterwards they beheaded him, and why.

Never does the world extol any who are children of God, save to cast them down again. Of this I have ample experience. I used to be greatly distressed when I found people praising me so blindly, but now I laugh at them as if I were listening to a madman. Be mindful of your sins and remember that, if there is truth in any part of what they say to you, it does not proceed from yourself, and it obliges you to render God the greater service. Awaken fear in your soul lest it should be lulled to rest by that kiss of false peace which is given by the world. Realize that this is a Judas-kiss; it may not always be so intentionally, but the devil is on the watch and, unless you defend yourself, he may be enabled to add your soul to his booty. Realize that you must keep the sword of meditation in your hand; although you may think the praise does you no harm, do not place any trust in that. Remember how many are now in the depths who were once on the heights. There is no security in our life; so, for the love of God, sisters, always struggle with yourselves

---

[1] The Baeza MS. continues: "This is the general rule; and the way in which the world can harm you most is in telling you how holy you are, etc."

against these praises; in this way you will emerge with the great gain of humility, and both the devil, who is on the watch for you, and the world will be confounded.

A great deal could be said about the peace which our own flesh can bring us and the harm that comes from this. I will instruct you about it in several respects, from which, as I have said, you will deduce the rest. The body, as you know, is very fond of indulgence, and if we understood this, we should realize how highly dangerous it is for us to find peace in such things. I often think of this and I can never understand how people who indulge themselves so much have such peace and rest. Did the most sacred body of our Example and Light merit less indulgence than ours? Had He done anything to merit having to suffer so many trials? Have we read of any saints— and they, we know for certain, are in Heaven—who led a life of indulgence upon earth? Then how can we so calmly permit it to ourselves? Who has told us it is a good thing? How is it that people can spend their days so happily in feasting and sleeping and in pursuit of recreation and of all the ease they can get? I am astounded when I think of it. One would imagine that there was no other world but this, and that living in this way involved only the minimum of danger.

Oh, daughters, if you knew what great harm is concealed in it! The body grows robust, but the soul becomes so enfeebled that if we could see it we should think it was at the point of death. You will read in many places about the great harm which arises from our finding peace here. If only people realized it was wrong, we might have hope of their amendment, but I am afraid it never occurs to them. As the practice is so common, I am not surprised. I assure you that, though their bodies are at ease, they will have conflicts of a thousand kinds if they are to save their souls, and they would be better advised to understand this and to do the penance a little at a time which otherwise they will have to do all at once. I have said this, daughters, so that you may give great praise to God because you are in a place where your flesh cannot find peace in this way even if you desire that it should do so. But you might unwittingly suffer harm in this way, under cover of illness, and you need to be very careful about it. On a certain day it may be bad for you to take the discipline, but you need not necessarily postpone it for a full week. On another occasion it may harm you not to wear linen, but because you wear it for several days you need not make a regular practice of doing so. On another day it would disagree with you to eat fish, but, if you get used to taking it, your digestion accustoms itself and it does you no harm. It is so easy to think you are very delicate.[1] I have experience of all this and of much more; one does not realize how important it is to do these things even though in themselves they may not be really necessary. My point is that we must not allow ourselves to be persuaded into relaxations but test ourselves from time to time, for I know how treacherous this flesh of ours is and how we must learn to understand it. May the Lord, of His goodness, give us light for all our needs; it is a great thing to have discretion and to trust in our superiors and not in ourselves.

Let us return to our subject. When the Bride indicates what kind of peace she is asking for, she says: "Let Him kiss me with a kiss of His mouth", and this is a sign that the Lord has other ways of granting His peace and revealing His friendship. I want now to tell you about a few of these, so that you may see what this sublime petition means and what a difference there is between one kind of peace and another. Oh, our great God and Lord, what profound wisdom is this! The Bride might well say: "Let Him kiss me", but one would have expected her to have concluded her petition without saying more. Why does she add "with a kiss of His mouth"? For we may be quite sure that there is not a superfluous letter here. I do not understand why she does this but I will say something about it; as I have said, it matters little if this is not exactly relevant so long as we profit by it. Our King, as we see every day, confers peace and friendship on souls in many ways, both during prayer and apart from it, but in our own friendship with His Majesty we stand on ceremony, as they say. You must consider, daughters, what state you have reached so as to be able to utter the petition of the Bride, if the Lord should bring you near to Himself; if He does not, do not lose heart, for any kind of friendship that you have with God will make you very rich unless you yourselves fail Him. But it is a matter for deep grief and distress if through our own fault some of us do not attain to this most excellent friendship and are contented with very little.

O Lord, ought we not to remember that the reward is great and never-ending, and that, once we have attained such friendship, the Lord will give it to us here on earth? How many remain at the foot of the mountain who might climb to its summit! I have said this to you many times in other little things that I have written and now I repeat it to you once more and beg you always to think courageously, for that will lead the Lord to grant you

---

[1] [*Lit.*: "You will think yourselves so delicate."] This phrase is obviously incomplete: it is amplified, however, in the Baeza MS.: ". . . so delicate that you cannot do without eating meat, and that your weakness requires you never to do a day's fasting."

grace so that you may act courageously too. Be sure that this is most important; for there are many people who have attained to friendship with the Lord through making sincere confession of their sins and repenting of them, and yet, within a couple of days, return to them. This, most certainly, is not the friendship for which the Bride asks. Oh, daughters, try not to go to your confessor every time with the same fault.

It is true that we cannot be free from sin, but at least let our sins not be always the same, or they will strike root, and be the harder to eradicate, and it may even happen that many other sins will arise from them. If we plant a flower or a shrub and water it daily it will grow so tall that in time we shall need a spade and a hoe to uproot it. It is just so, I think, when we commit a fault, however small, each day, and do not cure ourselves of it. If it has been rooted in us only for a day, or for ten days, and we then tear it out, it is easy. We must ask the Lord in prayer for grace to do this, for of ourselves we can do little: we add to our faults, rather than get rid of them. Remember, in that terrible judgment at the hour of death, this will be of no little moment to us, especially to those of us whom the Judge has taken to be His brides in this life.

Oh, what a great honour is this! Surely it should inspire us[1] to seek diligently to please this our Lord and King! Yet how ill is His friendship requited by those who so soon become His mortal enemies again! Of a truth, the mercy of God is great: what friend shall we find who is so longsuffering? If once such a cleavage takes place between two earthly friends, it is never erased from the memory and their friendship can never again become as close as before. Yet how often has our friendship for Our Lord failed in this way and for how many years does He await our return to Him! Blessed be Thou, my Lord God, Who bearest so compassionately with us that Thou seemest to forget Thy greatness and dost not punish such treacherous treason as this, as would be only right. This seems to me a perilous condition to be in, for though, as we know, God is merciful, we often see souls dying thus without confession. May His Majesty, for His own sake, deliver us, daughters, from a condition of such peril!

There is another and a better sort of friendship than this—namely, that of persons who keep themselves from mortally offending the Lord; as the world goes, those who have arrived thus far have done a great deal. Such persons, though they carefully abstain from mortal sin, do not, I think, avoid occasional falls, for they attribute no importance to venial sins, though they

---

[1] [*Lit.*, with characteristic word-play: "Oh, great worthiness, worthy of awakening us to seek, etc."]

commit many such every day, and thus they come very near to committing mortal sins. "Do you think that matters?" they ask. "There is holy water for that", I have heard many people say, "and the remedies of our Mother the Church". This is really very distressing. For the love of God, take the greatest care about it, and never be neglectful about a venial sin, however small, just because you have remembered this remedy, for it is not right that good should be an occasion of our doing evil. It is another matter, of course, if you remember the remedy after you have committed the fault and at once repair to it.

It is a very important thing that you should always have so pure a conscience that there will be nothing to hinder you from asking Our Lord for the perfect friendship sought by the Bride. What has been described is certainly not this friendship and for many reasons[1] it should cause us serious misgivings; it leads to spiritual self-indulgence and inclines us to be lukewarm and incapable of distinguishing venial sins from mortal. God preserve you from such friendship as that! For those who have it think they have not committed such grave sins as they see in others and it is not a state of perfect humility to consider others to be very wicked. They may even be far better than ourselves, because they weep for their sins and really repent of them, and perhaps have a firmer purpose than we to amend, so that they will try never again to offend God either in small things or in great. Whereas we ourselves, thinking we never do such things, allow ourselves much more freedom in our pleasures; many of us may not, as a rule, even say our vocal prayers well, not troubling about what we think to be such trifling matters.

There is another kind of friendship and peace which Our Lord begins to give to certain persons who would be sorry really to offend Him in any way although they do not flee as often as they might from occasions of falling. They have their set times for prayer; Our Lord grants them tender feelings and tears, and they like to lead good and well-ordered lives. But they would be sorry to give up the pleasures of this world, for they think that these help to make their earthly lives happy. This life brings many changes with it; it will be hard for such persons to continue in virtue, for if they do not abandon the pleasures and consolations of the world they will soon falter on the Lord's path, where there are powerful enemies to bar our way. This, daughters, is not the friendship desired by the Bride, and you must not desire it. Always flee from every occasion of sin, however small it be, if you want your soul to grow and to live in security.

[1] Thus the Baeza MS. Alba has "for many persons", but this may be a slip of the copyist's.

I do not know why I am telling you all this except to show you the dangers which result from our not resolutely turning aside from all worldly things, by doing which we should spare ourselves many sins and many trials. So numerous are the ways in which Our Lord begins to establish friendship with souls that I believe if I began to tell all that I know of I should never finish—and I am only a woman. What, then, could not confessors tell, and those who make the subject their particular study? Some souls bewilder me, for there seems nothing to prevent their becoming the friends of God. In particular I will tell you about one person with whom, a short time ago, I was very intimate. She was fond of communicating very often;[1] she never spoke ill of anyone; she was greatly moved when at prayer; and she enjoyed continual solitude, for she lived in her house alone. So gentle was her disposition that nothing that was said to her ever vexed her, which argued a high degree of perfection, nor did she ever utter a wrong word. She had never married, and was no longer of an age to do so. She had had to bear many annoying experiences, yet she had kept her peace. When I observed all this in her, it seemed to me to point to a soul in a most advanced state, and proficient in prayer, and at first I greatly esteemed her, as I never saw her offend God and I gathered she was careful not to do so.

But, when I came to know her, I began to realize that her placidity lasted only for so long as there was no threat to her self-interest. Once that was involved, her conscience was by no means so strict—in fact it was quite lax. I found that, although she would put up with all kinds of things that were said to her, she was very touchy about her reputation,[2] and it would not be her fault if she lost a jot or a tittle of either her reputation or her worldly esteem. So absorbed was she in her miserable self-regard, so fond was she of getting to know this and learning all about that, that I marvelled she was able to remain alone for a single hour. She was also very fond of her own comfort. Besides all this she would gild over everything she did so as to make it seem blameless. When I listened to the arguments that she put forward about certain matters I thought I should myself have been to blame if I had judged her, though in others she was very obviously in the wrong—perhaps because she misunderstood her own motives. She bewildered me, yet almost everyone else regarded her as a saint. Then I began to see that she must herself have been to blame for some of the persecutions which she used to talk about and I no longer envied her way of life or her

---

[1] [The Spanish is most emphatic: *muy a menudo mucho*—"very, very often."]
[2] [*Honra.* Cf. Vol. I, p. 14, n. 2, above.]

sanctity. In fact, she and two other souls whom I have known in this life (they have just come to my mind) were saints in their own opinion, but, when I got to know them, they frightened me more than all the sinners I have ever met. Let us beseech the Lord to enlighten us.

Give Him great praise, daughters, for having brought you to a convent where, however busy the devil is, he cannot deceive you as much as he can those who live in their own homes. For there are some souls who seem to have nothing that prevents them from flying right away to Heaven; they follow after perfection in everything and there is no one who can see through them; but in convents I have never known any such persons who were not found out, for there, instead of doing what they like, they have to do as they are told. In the world, even though they would really like to learn to know themselves in order to please the Lord, they cannot do so, because they do everything just as they want to, and, although they sometimes meet with reverses, they do not get the same practice in mortification. We may make an exception here of a few people to whom for many years Our Lord has given light, and who seek out someone who will understand them and to whom they may submit their wills even though they be more learned than he, for great humility is not accompanied by self-confidence.

There are others who for the Lord's sake have left everything. They have no houses or property; and they do not care for self-indulgence, but in fact lead lives of penance; nor do they care for any worldly things, because the Lord has given them light to see how miserable these are. Yet they attach a great importance to their reputation.[1] They would do nothing that was not as acceptable to men as to the Lord: they are very discreet and prudent. These two ideals are always very difficult to reconcile; and the worst of it is that, without their realizing how imperfect they are, the world's side always gets much more out of such people than does God's. These souls are generally very much distressed if anything is said against them. They do not embrace the Cross, but drag it after them, and so it distresses and wearies them and wears them to pieces. For it is when we love our cross that it is light to bear; that is certain.

No: this, again, is not the friendship for which the Bride asks; therefore, my daughters, as you have done what I described at the beginning of this book,[2] be very careful not to fail or falter in what comes next. All these things are merely wearisome to

---

[1] [*Honra*.]
[2] [I take the reference to be to the adoption of the Primitive Rule: cf. Prologue, pp. 357–8, above.]

you: if you have already given up most of them, if you are giving up the world and its delights, its pleasures and its riches, which, false as they are, still attract us, what have you to be afraid of? You see, you do not understand the matter. To avoid the displeasure which someone's words may cause you, you burden yourselves with a thousand anxieties and obligations. We have to bear so many of these, if we try to please the world, that it would be impracticable to recount them, so long would it take—in any case, I could never recount them all.

There are other souls—and with this I conclude—whom you will observe, if you watch them, to be beginning in many respects to make progress, yet they stop on the way. I mean those who care little about what men say of them, or about their reputation,[1] but are not practised in mortification or in the denial of their own wills, and thus seem not to have lost the fear of hurting their bodies. They are ready to suffer and they seem already to be quite perfect, yet in grave matters, which concern the Lord's honour, their own honour[2] begins to trouble them again. And this without their realizing it; for they think they are not fearing the world at all, but only God. They imagine dangers, and all kinds of things that may happen, with the result that one virtuous action causes great harm, and the devil himself appears to be teaching them this. On occasions they even prophesy what may happen in a thousand years.

These are not the souls to do what Saint Peter did when he cast himself into the sea,[3] or to imitate many other of the saints. They will bring other souls to the Lord if they can do so peacefully but not if it means running into dangers; and faith does very little to make them more resolute. I have noticed one thing, that we find very few people in the world (apart from those living the religious life) who trust in God for their maintenance; I know only two such persons altogether. In the religious life, of course, they know they will want for nothing, although no one, I think, who enters it for God's sake alone will so much as think of this. Yet how many there must be, daughters, who but for the certainty of this would not leave all they possess! However, though I should never grow tired of talking about these pusillanimous souls, I will say no more of them now, as I have spoken of them in other places where I have given you counsel,[4] and also of the harm they do themselves and of the great advantage of having lofty desires even though our actions may not be

---

[1] [*Honra.*]
[2] [Both times the Spanish has *honra.*]
[3] [St. John xxi, 7.]
[4] E.g., *Way of perfection*, Chaps. II, IV, XXXIV, XXXVIII.

commensurate with them. Since the Lord brings them to so high a state, let them serve Him in it and not be absorbed in themselves; for, if religious (and especially nuns) cannot give direct help to their neighbours, their prayers will have power, provided their determination is sincere and their souls' desires are keen, and it may even perhaps please the Lord to make them of service to others, either in life or in death, as the holy Fray Diego still is. This saint was a lay-brother and performed only menial services; and yet, after he has been dead for so many years, the Lord is reviving his memory so that he may be an example to us.[1] Let us give His Majesty praise.

So, then, my daughters, as the Lord has brought you to this state, you will need little more before obtaining the friendship and peace asked for by the Bride. Do not cease to beg for this with constant desires and tears. Do what you can yourselves so that He may give it you, for you must know that the religious life is not in itself the peace and friendship asked for by the Bride, although the Lord is granting a great favour to those who attain it. This peace will come only as the result of long practice in frequent prayer, penance, humility and many other virtues. May the Lord, Who gives all things, be for ever praised. Amen.

CHAPTER III

Treats of the true peace which God grants to the soul, of His union with it and of the examples of heroic charity given by certain of God's servants.

Let him kiss me with the kiss of his mouth.

O holy Bride! Let us now come to the kiss which you ask for—namely, that holy peace which spurs on the soul to make war with the whole world, while itself remaining at peace and in perfect safety. Oh, what a great happiness it will be to attain this favour! For it consists in a union with God's will of such a kind that no dissension arises between the wills of God and the soul, but they are both one—not in words or in desires alone but in actions. So ardent are the Bride's love and desire to please her Spouse that, when she finds that by doing something she can serve Him the better, she listens to no objections raised by her

---

[1] San Diego was born in Andalusia and entered the Order of St. Francis as a lay brother. He died in 1463 and was canonized in 1588. [He was thus not a saint when this was written, but, though the word *santo* in Spanish means both "saint" and "holy (man)", I have translated it as "saint" here, as his cause was so far advanced.]

mind, nor to any fears that it may set before her, but allows faith to act, and considers neither her own profit nor her own tranquillity, for she has come at last to understand that her profit consists entirely in this.

You will think that this is not right, daughters, and say that it is always a praiseworthy thing to act with discretion. But the point you have to consider is whether (as far as you can tell, I mean—one cannot know for certain) the Lord has heard your petition, that He will "kiss you with a kiss of His mouth". For if you know, by the effects, that He has, you need stop at nothing: you can forget yourselves altogether in order to please your gentlest Spouse. There are many signs by which His Majesty makes Himself known to those who enjoy this favour. One is that they despise all earthly things, holding them to be worthless, as indeed they are, caring not for their own good, since they have learned the vanity of this, and rejoicing only with those who love their Lord. Life wearies them and wealth they esteem at its true value: and there are other things like these which God teaches to those whom He has brought to this state.

The soul that has arrived thus far has no more to fear, save that she may not deserve that God should be pleased to make use of her by giving her trials and opportunities of serving Him at however great cost to herself. Here, then, as I have said, love and faith work together, and the soul has no desire to profit by what the understanding teaches her. For this union which takes place between the Spouse and the Bride has taught her other things which are beyond the grasp of the understanding so that she holds the understanding beneath her feet.[1] Let us think of a comparison which will make this clear to you. A man is held captive in the country of the Moors. He has a poor father or a great friend; and, if one of these does not ransom him, nothing more can be done. But the entire possessions of the father or the friend are not sufficient to ransom him and all that that person can do is to go and take his place. The great love which he has for him prompts him to desire the other's freedom rather than his own. But then comes discretion with all kinds of arguments: it tells him that his first obligation is to himself, or that perhaps he is not so strong as the other, or that he might be led into denying his Faith, or that it is not a good thing to run into danger; and many other things like these.

O strong love of God! I really think nothing seems impossible to one who loves. O happy soul that has obtained this peace from its God! For it has become mistress over all the trials and perils of the world; if only it can serve this its good Spouse and

[1] [I.e., keeps it subject to her.]

Lord it fears none of them—and it is just as right in this as the relative or friend we have spoken of. You must have read, daughters, of a Saint[1] who, not for the sake of a son or a friend, but because he must have attained the great happiness of being granted this peace by God and in order to please His Majesty and to imitate in some degree all that He did for us, went into the country of the Moors and exchanged places with the son of a widow, who had come to him in great trouble: and you will have read how well this turned out and what a great reward came to him.[2]

[I should imagine that his mind would not fail to present to him many more arguments than I have given, for he was a Bishop and had to leave his flock and might very well have had severe misgivings. Think of something which occurs to me now and which is applicable to those who are naturally pusillanimous and have little courage—for the most part these will be women. Although in actual fact their soul has attained this state, the weakness of their nature makes them afraid. We must be on the watch or this natural weakness will deprive us of a great crown. When you find yourselves as pusillanimous as this, have recourse to faith and humility and do not fail to go forward with faith, for God is all-powerful and has thus been able to give many holy maidens courage to endure cruel tortures which they had resolved to suffer for His sake.]

[It is of this resolution and this free-will that the soul wishes to make Him Master, though He has no need of our efforts. Indeed, His Majesty is pleased that His works should shine forth in those who are weak, since in these there is more scope for His power and for the fulfilment of His desire to grant us favours. For this reason you must profit by the virtues that God has given you, so that you may act resolutely and pay no heed to the arguments adduced by your mind and your own weakness: this weakness will only grow if you begin to imagine what will and what will not happen and to wonder if you are too sinful for God to give you the courage He has given to others. This is no time to think about your sins: leave them alone; humility is out of place now—it comes at the wrong time.]

[It is when someone wishes to do you great honour, or when the devil incites you to live an indulgent life or tempts you in some other way, that you must fear that your sins will prevent you from acceding to him and at the same time living uprightly.

[1] St. Paulinus of Nola (353-431). The heroic act recorded here took place during the invasion of Spain by the Vandals. By "the Moors", St. Teresa, who was not too careful about such details as these, means the Vandals.

[2] The three following paragraphs, which are enclosed in square brackets, are not found in the Alba and Baeza codices, but only in those of Consuegra and Las Nieves.

But when it is a question of suffering something for Our Lord, or for your neighbour, you need have no fear because of your sins. You may be able to perform an action of this kind with so much charity that all your sins will be forgiven you and as this is what the devil fears he takes good care to remind you of them. Be sure that the Lord will never forsake those who love Him when they run risks solely for His sake. But let them consider if they are actuated in any way by self-interest, for I am speaking only of those who try to please the Lord with the greatest possible perfection.]

Even in our own time I have known a person—you saw him when he came to see me—whom the Lord inspired with such great charity that it caused him the greatest distress when he was not allowed to exchange places with a captive. He told me about this (he belonged to the Discalced Reform of Fray Peter of Alcántara). After a great deal of importunity, he obtained leave from his General; but, about four leagues from Algiers, when he was about to carry out his good purpose, the Lord took him to Himself.[1] How sure we may be that he received a rich reward! But how many prudent people must have told him he was acting foolishly! And those of us who love the Lord less than he did would agree with them. Yet is it not much more foolish for this dream-life of ours to end in such a spirit of prudence? God grant we may be worthy to enter Heaven, and still more that we may be among those who are so far advanced in their love for God!

I know, of course, that we need a great deal of help from God in such matters, and for this reason, daughters, I advise you to join the Bride in begging Him for this delectable peace, which conquers all petty worldly fears by making war on them with all its quietness and tranquillity. Is it not clear that any soul to whom God grants so great a favour as to unite it with Himself in such a friendship will be left very rich in His blessings? For these things certainly cannot proceed from ourselves. What we can do is to desire and pray Him to grant us this favour, and even this we can only do with His aid: as for the rest, what power has a worm whose sins make it so cowardly and miserable that we imagine all virtues must be measured by our base human nature? So what can we do, daughters? We can make the Bride's prayer[2] our own. If a little peasant girl were to marry a king, and had children of him, would they not be of royal blood? Then if Our

---

[1] This was Alonso de Cordobilla, who took his name from the village of Cordobilla, in the province of Mérida, where he was born. He embarked at Cádiz for Algiers, but was taken ill with a fever on the voyage, and, his ship being driven back by a storm to Spain, he died (October 28, 1566) without ever having landed in Africa.

[2] "Let the Lord kiss me," interpolates the *editio princeps* here.

Lord grants such a favour to a human soul as to unite it indivisibly with Himself, what desires, what fruits, what heroic acts may not be born of the union, except it be through some fault of the soul?[1]

[For this reason I repeat that, if the Lord grants you the favour of an opportunity of doing such things for His sake, you should not allow the fact that you have been sinners to impede you. Here faith must override our misery; and you must not be alarmed if, when you first make this resolution, and even later, you feel weak and fearful: pay no heed to that unless it encourages you to let the flesh do as it pleases. Think of what the good Jesus said in His prayer in the Garden: "The flesh is weak";[2] and remember His most wondrous and pitiful sweat. If His Majesty said that that Divine and sinless flesh of His was weak, how can we expect ours to be so strong that it will not feel the persecution and the trials that may assail it? In the very midst of them, the flesh will become, as it were, subject to the spirit. When once the will is united with that of God, it will complain no more.]

[It occurs to me here that, though our good Jesus revealed the weakness of His human nature before His sufferings, yet when He was plunged into the abyss of suffering He showed such great fortitude that not only did He not complain, but He gave not a sign from which it might appear that He was feeling any weakness. As He was going into the Garden, He said: "My soul is sorrowful even unto death";[3] but, when He was on the Cross, and suffering the pains of death, He made no complaint. After His prayer in the Garden, He went to awaken His Apostles; yet He would have had more reason to complain to Our Lady His Mother when she was at the foot of the Cross, for she was not asleep and her most holy soul was suffering and enduring a most bitter death; and it is always the greatest comfort to us to complain to those who we know feel for our troubles and love us most dearly[4].]

[Let us not, then, lament our fears, or be discouraged at the weakness of our human nature and at our lack of strength; let us try rather to fortify ourselves with humility and understand clearly how little we can do by our own efforts. We must realize that if God does not give us this favour we are nothing, so we

---

[1] The next three paragraphs, which are bracketed, occur only in the codices of Consuegra and Las Nieves.
[2] St. Mark xiv, 38.
[3] St. Mark xiv, 34.
[4] St. Teresa's meaning is that, when suffering in the Garden, Our Lord complained to His disciples that they could not watch with Him one hour; and yet, during His greater sufferings on the Cross, He said nothing to His Mother, though she could have given Him ineffable consolation.

must have no confidence whatever in our own strength, but trust in His mercy—and until we do this all is weakness. It was not without good reason that Our Lord showed us this. He, of course, had no weakness, for He was fortitude itself; He did it for our comfort and in order that we might learn how we must translate our desires into actions, and realize that, when a soul begins to mortify itself, it finds everything painful. It is painful to start giving up comforts; it is a torment to have to forgo honour;[1] even to endure a hard word may become intolerable: in short, the soul will never cease to be sorrowful, even unto death. But when it is fully resolved to die to the world, it will find itself free of these pains; there will be no fear of its complaining—quite the contrary—once it has attained the peace begged by the Bride.]

I am quite sure that, if we could but once approach the Most Holy Sacrament with great faith and love, it would suffice to make us rich. How much more so as we approach it so often! It would seem as if we did this only in order to pay the Lord a conventional visit, and that that is why we gain so little light. O miserable world, which thus blindest the eyes of those who live in thee so that they cannot see the treasures by means of which they could gain everlasting wealth!

O Lord of Heaven and earth! Is it possible, while we are still in this mortal life, for us to enjoy Thee with such special friendship? Clearly as the Holy Spirit asserts that it is in these words, can it be that we do not wish to know what are the joys which Thou bestowest on souls, as we learn from these *Canticles*? What endearments, what sweet words are these, one word of which would suffice to unite us in Thee! Blessed be Thou, Lord, for so far as Thou art concerned we shall lose nothing! By how many paths, in how many manners, through how many means dost Thou reveal Thy love to us! By trials, by bitter death, by tortures, by affronts suffered daily, by Thy forgiveness—and not by these alone but by words which pierce the soul that loves Thee, and which in these *Canticles* Thou dost utter and teach it to utter too. I know not how it will endure them if Thou grant it not Thy help so that it may do so, not for its own merits but because of our weakness.

So, my Lord, I ask Thee for nothing else in this life but that Thou shouldst "kiss me with a kiss of Thy mouth"; and let this be in such a way, Lord of my life, that, even if I should desire to withdraw from this friendship and union, my will may ever be so subject to Thine that I shall be unable to leave Thee. May nothing hinder me from being able to say, O my God and my glory, that "Thy breasts are better and more delectable than wine"!

[1] [*Honra*].

CHAPTER IV

Speaks of the Prayer of Quiet and of Union and of the sweetness and the consolations which these bring to the spirit, by comparison with which the delights of earth are nothing.

> Thy breasts are better[1] than wine, for they give off fragrance of sweet odours.[2]

Oh, my daughters, what tremendous secrets there are in these words! May Our Lord grant us to experience them, for it is with extreme difficulty that they can be described. When in His mercy His Majesty is pleased to fulfil this petition of the Bride, the friendship which He begins to establish with the soul is one which, as I say, only those of you who may experience it will understand. I have written fully about this in two books[3] (which, if it please the Lord, you will see after I am dead), at great length and in great detail, for I realize that you will need to know about it, and so I will do no more than touch upon it here. I do not know if I shall be able to describe them now in the same words as those in which the Lord was pleased to explain them then.

The soul feels within itself such great sweetness that it is well aware of Our Lord's nearness to it. But this is not only a devoutness which causes us satisfaction by moving us to many tears either for the Passion of the Lord or for our own sins. In this prayer of which I am speaking, and which I call the Prayer of Quiet because of the tranquillity which it brings to all the faculties, the soul experiences a great happiness. Yet sometimes, when it is not so much absorbed in this sweetness, the experience comes in another way. Both the inward and the outward man seem to receive comfort, just as if into the marrow of the bones had been poured the sweetest of ointments, resembling a fragrant perfume, or as if we had suddenly entered a room where there was a perfume coming not from one place, but from many, so that we cannot tell what or where the perfume is—we only know that it pervades our whole being.

---

[1] [*Más valen*: cf. p. 359, n. 2, above. Everywhere else in this chapter the phrase used for this quotation is "mejores son."]

[2] [*Lit.*: "of very good odours". The text of Canticles i, 2 has: "Smelling sweet of the best ointments."] As St. Teresa did not divide her text into chapters, she had no need to repeat the verse which she had just quoted. The epigraph, however, was supplied by Gracián, from whose edition it is translated.

[3] *Life*, Chaps. XIV, XV, XVIII, XIX; *Way of perfection*, Chap. XXXI.

Just so does it seem to be with this sweet love of our God. It enters the soul with great sweetness, and brings it such joy and satisfaction that it cannot understand how or in what way this blessing is entering it. So anxious is it not to lose this love that it would fain stay still without moving and neither speak nor even look anywhere lest it should vanish. Elsewhere, in speaking of it, I have described what the soul must do in order to benefit by it, which I am only referring to here so that you may know something of what I am describing. I will therefore say no more than that, in the friendship which the Lord now reveals to the soul, He desires to have such intimacy with it that nothing can separate them. Great truths are communicated to it; for this light, which dazzles it because it cannot understand what it is, shows it the vanity of the world. It does not see the good Master teaching it, although it knows He is at its side. But it receives such good instruction and is so much strengthened in the virtues that it does not know itself, nor can it do anything or say anything but give praises to the Lord. When experiencing this joy, it is so deeply inebriated and absorbed that it seems to be beside itself and in a kind of Divine intoxication, knowing not what it is desiring or saying or asking for. In fact, it is unconscious of itself, yet not so much so that it cannot understand something of what is passing.

But when this most wealthy Spouse desires to enrich and comfort the Bride still more, He draws her so closely to Him[1] that she is like one who swoons from excess of pleasure and joy and seems to be suspended in those Divine arms and drawn near to that sacred side and to those Divine breasts. Sustained by that Divine milk with which her Spouse continually nourishes her and growing in grace so that she may be enabled to receive His comforts, she can do nothing but rejoice. Awakening from that sleep and heavenly inebriation, she is like one amazed and stupefied; well, I think, may her sacred folly wring these words from her: "Thy breasts are better[2] than wine". For, when first in that state of inebriation, she felt it impossible to rise higher; but now that she finds herself in a loftier state, and wholly absorbed in God's indescribable greatness, she realizes how she has been nourished and makes this subtle comparison, saying: "Thy breasts are better than wine." For, just as a child has no idea how it grows, or how it takes its nourishment (since often, without any act or movement of its own, the milk is put into its mouth), so here the soul of itself knows nothing, and does nothing, and neither knows nor is capable of understanding how or whence

---

[1] [The Spanish is stronger: *conviértela tanto en Sí.*]
[2] [*Mejores son*—both here and in the next quotation.]

this exceeding great blessing has come to it. But it knows that it is the greatest blessing that can be enjoyed in life, even if all the delights and pleasures of the world should be put together and compared with it. It finds that it has been nourished and benefited, yet cannot understand how it can have deserved this. It has been instructed in great truths without having seen the Master Who teaches it. It has been strengthened in the virtues and comforted by Him Who so well knows how to comfort it and has also the power to do so. With what to compare this it knows not, save to the caress of a mother who so dearly loves her child and feeds and caresses it.[1]

[This comparison is appropriate, because the soul is raised on high and is unable to make use of the understanding; in some respects it is like a child receiving and delighting in this caress without having the intelligence to understand whence it comes. For in the preceding state of slumber produced by this inebriation the soul has not been so completely precluded from acting as to be unable to understand and work at all. It realizes that it is near God and thus with truth it exclaims: "Thy breasts are better than wine."]

[Great is this favour, my Spouse, and this delectable feast, and this precious wine that Thou givest me, one drop of which makes me forget all created things, and withdraw from the creatures and from myself and no longer desire the satisfactions and joys which until now my senses have longed for. Great is all this and unmerited by me. Now that His Majesty has increased it and drawn me still closer to Him, truly do I exclaim: "Thy breasts are better than wine". Great were Thy past favours, my God, but much greater is this, for I have less part in it, and so in every way it is better. Great is the rejoicing and delight of the soul when it is brought hither.]

Oh, my daughters, may Our Lord grant you to understand—or, rather, to taste, for in no other way can it be understood—how the soul rejoices when this happens to it. Let worldlings come with all their possessions, their riches, their delights, their honours and their feasts: even if all these could be enjoyed without the trials that they bring in their train, which is impossible, they could not in a thousand years cause the happiness enjoyed in a single moment by a soul brought hither by the Lord. "All the trials of the world", says Saint Paul, "are not worthy to be compared with the glory for which we hope."[2]

---

[1] The two bracketed paragraphs which follow are found only in the Consuegra and Las Nieves MSS. [The words translated "comfort" and "caress" in this and the next paragraph are all, in Spanish, *regalo* or *regalar*.]

[2] Romans viii, 18.

I would say that not only are they not worthy to be compared with them, but that they cannot earn a single hour of the satisfaction, joy and delight which God here gives the soul. There is no possible comparison, I think, nor can the base things of the world ever earn from Our Lord so loving a caress,[1] or a union so complete, or a love so expressively shown and so blissfully experienced. Fine things are the trials of the world by comparison with this! Unless borne for God, they are worthless; and even when so borne they are apportioned to us by His Majesty according to our strength, so greatly do our weak and miserable natures make us fear them.

O Christians! O my daughters! For the love of the Lord, let us awake out of this sleep and remember that He does not keep us waiting until the next life before rewarding us for our love of Him. Our recompense begins in this life. O my Jesus! If one could but describe how great a gain it is to cast ourselves into the arms of this Lord of ours and make an agreement with His Majesty that I should look to my Beloved and He towards me,[2] that He would take care of my affairs and I of His![3] Let us not be so fond of ourselves that we blind ourselves, for, as the saying goes, love is blind.[4] Again, my God, I speak to Thee, and beg Thee, by the blood of Thy Son, to grant me this favour: "Let Him kiss me with a kiss of His mouth". For what am I, Lord, without Thee? And what am I worth if I am not near Thee? If once I stray from Thy Majesty, be it ever so little, where shall I find myself?

O my Lord, my Mercy and my Good! What more do I want in this life than to be so near Thee that there is no division between Thee and me? In such company, what can become difficult? What can one not undertake for Thy sake with Thyself so near? What thanks are due to me, Lord? Rather must I blame myself exceedingly for not having served Thee. And so, with Saint Augustine, I beg Thee, most resolutely, to "give me what Thou dost ordain and to ordain in me what Thou wilt".[5] Never, with Thy help and favour, will I turn my back on Thee.[6]

[Now do I see, my Spouse, that Thou art mine; I cannot deny it. For my sake didst Thou come to the world; for my sake

---

[1] [A strong expression: *un regalo tan regalado*. See p. 385, n. 1, above.]
[2] [Canticles ii, 16; vii, 10.]
[3] [An apparent reference to the incident mentioned in *Interior Castle*, VII, ii. (p. 334, above).]
[4] [*Lit.*: "that we put out our own eyes, as the saying goes." I do not know any such "saying" in modern Spanish, so I have expanded the phrase and substituted what I believe to be an English equivalent.]
[5] *Confessions*, Book V, Chap. XXIX.
[6] The remainder of the chapter is found only in the codices of Consuegra and Las Nieves.

didst Thou suffer these great trials; for my sake didst Thou endure these scourgings; for my sake hast Thou remained with us in the Most Holy Sacrament; and now Thou dost bestow on me these exceeding great marks of Thy love.[1] Then, holy Bride that I am (for, as I said, Thou didst call me so), what can I do for my Spouse?]

[Truly, sisters, I know not how to resolve this difficulty. How can I be Thine, my God? What can a person do for Thee who has contrived such evil things as I? I can only lose the favours Thou hast granted me. From such a one what services could be hoped for? And even if, by Thy favour, I should accomplish something, consider how little a miserable worm can do. How can a powerful God have need of it? O love, in how many places would I fain repeat these words, for it is He alone Who dares to say, with the Bride: "I have loved my Beloved." He allows us to think that He needs us—He, this true Lover, my Spouse and my Good.]

[Then, daughters, since He allows us to think this, let us exclaim once more: "My Beloved to me and I to my Beloved!"[2] Thou to me, Lord! If Thou comest to me, how can I doubt that I can render Thee great services? Henceforth, then, Lord, I would forget myself and look solely at the ways in which I can serve Thee and have no will save Thine own. But my will is powerless, my God; it is Thou that art powerful. All I can do is to resolve to serve Thee, and this resolve I make and will henceforth carry into action.]

CHAPTER V

Continues to describe the Prayer of Union and speaks of the riches which the soul acquires therein through the mediation of the Holy Spirit and of its determination to suffer trials for the Beloved.

> I sat down under the shadow of him whom I desired and his fruit is sweet to my palate.[3]

Let us now question the Bride. Let us learn from this blessed soul, which has drawn near to this Divine mouth and been nourished from these heavenly breasts, so that, if the Lord grants us some day to attain to so great a favour, we may know how to behave and what to say. Her words are: "I sat down under

---

[1] [*Regalos.* See p. 385, n. 1, above.]
[2] [Canticles ii, 16; vii, 10.]
[3] Canticles ii, 3.

the shadow of Him Whom I had desired, and His fruit is sweet to my palate. The King brought me into the cellar of wine and set in order charity in me."[1] She says: "I sat down under the shadow of Him Whom I had desired."

Dear God, how this soul is drawn into the very Sun and enkindled by Him! She says that she sat down under the shadow of Him Whom she had desired. Here she likens Him to nothing less than an apple-tree and says that His fruit is sweet to her palate.[2] O souls that practise prayer, savour all these words! In how many ways can we think of our God! To how many different kinds of food can we compare Him! For He is manna, the taste of which is to each of us as we wish it to be. Oh, what heavenly shadow is this! Oh, that one could express all that the Lord signifies by it! I remember how the angel said to the most holy Virgin, Our Lady: "The power of the Most High shall overshadow thee."[3] How well protected is the soul when the Lord sets it in so wondrous a place! Well indeed may it sit down and feel secure!

Observe now that, as a general rule, and almost invariably except in the case of anyone to whom Our Lord addresses a special call, as when He at once raised Saint Paul to the summit of contemplation and appeared to him and spoke to him in such a way as to raise him immediately to great heights,[4] He gives these sublime consolations, and grants these great favours, to persons who have laboured greatly in His service and desired His love and tried to live so that all their actions may be pleasing to His Majesty. Such souls have fatigued themselves by long years of meditation and by long seeking of their Spouse; they are quite weary of worldly things; they "sit down" in the truth; they seek neither comfort nor peace nor rest in any other place save where they know that they can truly find it; and, putting themselves beneath the protection of the Lord, they desire none other. And how well they do to trust His Majesty, for thus they obtain the fulfilment of all they have desired! And how fortunate is the soul that has merited to dwell under this shadow, even as regards the things of earth![5] Much more so, as I have often understood, in things which the soul alone is capable of understanding!

While the soul is enjoying the delight which has been described, it seems to be wholly engulfed and protected by a shadow, and,

---

[1] Canticles ii, 3–4.
[2] The Baeza copy and the *editio princeps* have "her"; the other copies, "my".
[3] St. Luke i, 35.
[4] Acts ix, 3–11.
[5] [There seems here to be a reminiscence of Psalm xc (A.V., xci), 1–4, as well as of Canticles ii, 3.]

as it were, a cloud of the Godhead, whence come to it certain influences and a dew so delectable as to free it immediately, and with good reason, from the weariness caused it by the things of the world. The kind of rest which comes to the soul here is such that it is fatigued even by having to breathe; and the faculties are so quiet and stilled that the will would prefer not to admit any thought—even a good thought—nor will it admit any in the sense of searching for it or striving after it. A person in this state has no need, for any purpose, to move her hand, or to rise (I mean by this to practise meditation), for the Lord is giving her the fruit from the apple-tree with which she compares her Beloved:[1] He picks it and cooks it and almost eats it for her. And so she says: "His fruit is sweet to my palate."[2] For here all is enjoyment, without any labour of the faculties, and in this shadow of the Godhead (well termed "shadow", for we cannot see it clearly on earth but only beneath this cloud) dwells that resplendent Sun, Who sends out to the soul a message of love, communicating His Majesty's nearness to it—a nearness which is ineffable. I am sure that anyone who has experienced it will know how applicable this meaning is to these words spoken here by the Bride.

Personally, I think the Holy Spirit must be the intermediary between the soul and God, moving the soul with such ardent desires that it becomes enkindled by that sovereign Fire, Who is so near it. O Lord, what mercies are these that Thou dost bestow upon the soul! Blessed be Thou and praised for ever, that art so good a Lover! O my God and my Creator! Is it possible that there is any soul who loves Thee not? Unhappy that I am, since for so long a time I myself loved Thee not! Why did I not deserve to know Thee? How this Divine apple-tree bows its branches so that the soul may sometimes pluck them by meditating upon the wonders of God and the multitude of the mercies that He has shown it, and may see and enjoy the fruit produced by Our Lord Jesus Christ in His Passion, when, with such marvellous love, He watered this tree with His precious blood![3] Already the soul has said that she is enjoying the sustenance of His Divine breasts; for, when she was still inexperienced in receiving these favours, the Spouse nourished her. Now that she is more mature, He gradually prepares her to receive more. He stays her up with apples,[4] for He desires her to understand more and more how bound she is to serve and to suffer. Nor is

---

[1] Canticles ii, 3.
[2] *Ibid.*
[3] In the *editio princeps*, followed by all later editions until that of Rivadeneyra Chapter V ends here. We prefer, and have followed, the Rivadeneyra re-grouping
[4] [Canticles ii, 5: the quotation, it will be observed, is not exact.]

He content with this. It is a marvellous thing, upon which we should often meditate, that, when the Lord knows that a soul is all His own, His without other interests and inspired by no other motives save that He is its God and that He loves it, He never ceases to commune with it, in many ways and manners, as One Who is Wisdom Itself.

After God had first bestowed peace upon the soul it seemed as if there were no more for Him to give, yet this which I have said is a much more sublime favour. I have not described it well—indeed, I have only touched upon it. In the book I have referred to, daughters, you will find it described very clearly,[1] if the Lord is pleased that the book should be published. What can we desire further than the things that I have now described? O Lord God, how powerless are our desires to attain Thy wonders! How miserable should we still be, were Thy giving proportionate to our asking! Let us now see what next the Bride says about this.

CHAPTER VI

Describes how the benefits of this loving union surpass all the Bride's desires. Speaks of the suspension of the faculties and describes how some souls rise in a very short time to this sublime degree of prayer.

> The King brought me into the cellar of wine and set in order charity in me.[2]

Now that the Bride is at last resting under the shadow which she has so greatly, and so rightly, desired, what more remains to be desired by a soul which has arrived thus far, save that she may never more lose this blessing? To her it seems that there is no more to desire; but our most holy King has much more to give: He would rejoice to do nothing but give could He find souls capable of receiving. And as I have often said, daughters, you must never forget that the Lord is not content with giving us according to the small measure of our desires: I have noticed that myself. When a person begins to make a few requests of the Lord, He gives him according to his merits and shows him something of what he may suffer for His sake, for his own intentions go no farther than what he thinks to be his capacity, though His Majesty can always increase this. Then, as a recompense for the little that he has resolved to do for Him, He gives him so many

---

[1] *Life*, Chaps. XVII, ff.   [2] Canticles ii, 4.

trials and persecutions and infirmities that the poor man does not know what he is doing.

This happened to me myself when I was very young. I used sometimes to say: "O Lord, I would rather not have as much as that." But His Majesty would give me such strength and patience that even now I marvel that I was able to suffer so much and I would not exchange those trials for all the treasures in the world. The Bride says: "The King brought me." How wonderfully, Almighty King, does that name of Thine enlarge the heart! For there is none greater than He nor will His eternal reign come to an end. The soul in this state will certainly not fail to learn much of the greatness of this King, though it is impossible, in this mortal life, that it should learn to know the whole.

"He brought me," she says, "into the cellar of wine; He set in order charity in me". From this I realize the immensity of this favour. For one may be given a larger or a smaller draught, either of a good or of a superior wine, and be to a greater or a lesser degree intoxicated and inebriated. And so it is with the Lord's favours. To one He gives but little of the wine of devotion; to another, more; while to another He gives such increase of devotion that He begins to take him out of himself—that is, out of his sensuality—and to lead him away from all earthly things. To others He gives great fervour in His service; to others, good impulses; to others, great charity towards their neighbours; and thus they are so inebriated as not to feel the great trials through which they pass. These words of the Bride, therefore, "He brought me into the cellar", can bear a great many meanings at once, and she may come out from that cellar with immeasurable riches. It would seem that the King desires that there shall be nothing left for Him to give: His will is that she shall drink, and become inebriated with all the wines that are in the storehouse of God. Let her rejoice in those joys; let her marvel at His wonders; let her not fear to lose her life through drinking beyond the capacity of her weak nature; let her die in this paradise of delights. Blessed is the death that brings with it such a life! And this is indeed what it does; for so great are the marvellous things learned by the soul, without its knowing how, that it is beside itself, as the soul itself says in the words: "He set in order charity in me."

O words never to be forgotten by the soul to which Our Lord gives such favours! O sovereign favour! Never could we merit thee did not the Lord give us the wherewithal for that purpose in abundance! The soul is not even sufficiently awake to love, but blessed is the sleep, and happy the inebriation, wherein the Spouse supplies what the soul cannot and bestows on it so marvellous an "order" that, though all the faculties are dead or asleep, love remains alive. The Lord ordains[1] that it shall work, without knowing how, and that so marvellously that, in complete purity, the soul becomes one with the very Lord of love, Who is God. For there is none to disturb it—no senses or faculties, by which I mean the understanding and the memory; nor has the will any part in this.

I was wondering just now if there is any kind of difference between will and love. I do not know if this is nonsense, but it seems to me that there is. Love, I think, is an arrow shot by the will, and flying with all the force of which the will is capable, freed from all earthly things and directed towards God alone, so that it must actually strike His Majesty. Once it has pierced God Himself, Who is love, it rebounds, after having won immense benefits, as I shall explain. This really happens, according to information which I have had from certain persons whom Our Lord has given such great favours in prayer that, by means of suspension, He brings them to a state of holy inebriation and even by outward signs it can be seen that they are not in possession of their faculties. When they are asked what it is they are experiencing, they cannot say; for they have never known, or been in the least able to understand, how love works in them.

The immense benefits gained by the soul in this state may be understood by the effects, the virtues and the living faith which it derives from them and by its contempt for the world. But nothing can be understood of how these blessings come to the soul, or of what the soul enjoys in this state, except at the beginning, when its experiences are of a marvellous sweetness. It is clear, then, that what the Bride says is true—that the wisdom of God supplies what the soul lacks and it is He Who ordains that the soul at this time shall receive such immense favours. For once it has been carried out of itself, and is so completely absorbed that its faculties are incapable of action, how can it itself gain any merit? Yet can it be supposed that God is granting it such a great favour in order that it may waste its time and gain nothing from Him? The thing is incredible.

O secrets of God! We can only surrender our understanding and realize that of itself it can do nothing to fathom the greatness of God. It is well that we should remember here how Our Lady the Virgin, with her great wisdom, submitted in this way, and how, when she asked the angel: "How shall this be done?" he answered: "The Holy Ghost shall come upon thee;

---

[1] ["Order" and "ordain" are in the Spanish *orden* and *ordenar*. "Sets it in order so that it may work" is the idea beneath St. Teresa's phrase, *ordenar* being the verb translated "set in order" in the epigraph.]

the power of the Most High shall overshadow thee."[1] Thereupon she was no longer concerned to argue about it; having great faith and wisdom, she at once recognized that, in view of this twofold intervention, there was neither any necessity for further knowledge on her part nor any room for doubt. She was not like certain learned men, who, not having been led in this way of prayer by the Lord and not having the beginnings of spirituality, try so hard to reduce everything to reason and to measure everything by their own understanding that it looks as if all their learning is going to enable them to succeed in comprehending all the wonders of God. If only they would learn something of the humility of the most holy Virgin!

O my Lady, how perfectly can we learn from thy example what passes between God and the Bride, according to the words of the *Canticles*! You can see, daughters, how many quotations from this book there are in the antiphons and the lessons of the Office of Our Lady which we recite weekly. As for other souls, each will be enabled to understand these words according to the degree in which God wishes her to do so; and she will be able to tell quite clearly if she has been granted any of these favours in the way of which the Bride speaks when she says: "He set in order charity in me." Such souls do not know where they have been, nor how, during a time of such great joy, they have pleased the Lord, nor what has been wrought in them, for they have given Him no thanks for it.

O soul beloved of God! Trouble not yourself; for, when His Majesty brings you here and speaks to you as delectably as He speaks to the Bride in the *Canticles*,—using many such phrases (as I have said) as "Thou art all fair, O my love,"[2] to show the pleasure which He takes in her—it is to be supposed that at such a time He will not allow you to displease Him; rather He will give you what you cannot yourself provide so that He may take the greater pleasure in you. He sees that the Bride is lost to herself and enraptured for love of Him, and that the very strength of love has taken from her the power of understanding, so that she may love Him the more. Yes, it is impossible that He should allow this, and His Majesty is neither accustomed, nor able, to fail to give Himself to one who gives herself to Him wholly.

For my own part I think His Majesty is here enamelling gold which He has already prepared for this process by His gifts and has tested, by a thousand ways and means which the soul that has

---

[1] St. Luke i, 34-5. The Alba codex has: "shall be a shadow," but the Baeza, Consuegra and Las Nieves MSS., together with the *editio princeps*, all read as in the text.
[2] Canticles iv, 7.

reached this state can describe, so as to discover how strong is the love which it bears Him. This soul, which is the gold in question, remains all the time as motionless and as inert as if it were really gold; and the Divine Wisdom, well pleased to see it so, since so few love Him with such strength, continues to set in the gold many precious stones and much elaborately worked enamel.

And meanwhile, what is the soul doing? This it is impossible to say: we know nothing more than the words of the Bride: "He set in order charity in me." Certainly, if she is loving, she neither knows how, nor understands what, she is loving; the exceeding great love borne her by the King Who has brought her to this high state must have united her love to Himself in a way that the understanding is not worthy to comprehend. These two loves, then, become one: the love of the soul has been brought into genuine union with that of God. How could the intellect ever grasp this? During the whole of that time, which never lasts long but is quickly over, the intellect loses sight of the love of the soul.[1] Meanwhile God sets love in order in the soul so that it may well know how to please Him, both then and also later, the intellect, as has been said, being unaware of it. But it becomes well aware of it later on, when it sees the soul so wonderfully enamelled and decorated with precious stones and pearls, which are the virtues, that it is amazed and can only say: "Who is she that has been like the sun?"[2] O true King, how rightly did the Bride give Thee this name! For in a moment Thou canst bestow riches, and so endow a soul with them that it will enjoy them for ever. How well is love set in order in such a soul!

I could give some good examples of this, for I have seen several. I remember one such case, in which in three days the Lord granted a soul blessings that would have seemed to me impossible if I had not later found by experience that they lasted[3] for some years and that she kept growing in grace. In another person—both were quite young—the same result was produced in three months. I have known others to whom God granted this favour only after a long period. I have spoken of these two, and I could speak of several others; for, if I have said here that souls are rarely granted these favours by Our Lord without having spent many years in suffering trials, I want you to understand that there are a few such.[4] We cannot set limits to a Lord Who is so great and Who longs so much to

---

[1] [*Lit.*: "of it," and, in the next sentence, "sets it in order." As the latter reference is clearly to love, the former would seem to be so too.]
[2] Canticles vi, 9.
[3] "That she practised them," reads the *editio princeps*.
[4] Cf. *Life*, Chap. XXXIX.

bestow these graces. I will tell you what happens almost invariably when the Lord approaches a soul to grant it these favours—I mean if they are favours from God, and not illusions, or the results of melancholia, or the workings of nature itself, for when they are false time reveals the fact, as also when they are true, in which latter case the virtues are so active and love is so fervent that they cannot remain concealed and the soul always brings profit to others even without so intending.

"The King set in order charity in me"—and He sets it in order in such a way that the soul loses the love which it had for the world, and that which it had for itself turns into indifference;[1] while love of kinsfolk is felt only for God's sake. The soul's love for its neighbours and for its enemies would be thought incredible if it were not proved by experience. It has grown greatly; while its love for God so far exceeds all limits that weak nature is oppressed beyond endurance, and, seeing that it is fainting and at the point of death, cries: "Stay me up with flowers and compass me about with apples: because I languish with love."[2]

CHAPTER VII

Describes the great desires felt by the Bride to suffer much for God's sake and her neighbour's, and the abundant fruits borne in the Church by these souls that are favoured by Divine union and detached from self-interest. Quotes the Samaritan woman as an example of love for one's neighbour. Ends by recalling the aim proposed for this book.

> Stay me up with flowers and compass me about with apples: because I languish with love.[3]

Oh, what Divine language is this in which to express my meaning! What, holy Bride! Is this sweetness killing you? For sometimes, as I have been told, it seems so excessive that it consumes the soul till there appears not to be enough of it left to live. And you ask for flowers! What flowers can you mean? For flowers are no remedy unless you are asking for them so that you may end your life—and, in fact, when the soul reaches this state, that is all it desires. But this cannot be the meaning, for the Bride says: "Stay me up with flowers." To ask to be

---

[1] [*Desamor*: "non-love", a word with no exact correspondence in English, sometimes equivalent to a positive hatred, but more commonly to a failure to show, or to return, affection.]
[2] Canticles ii, 5.
[3] [Cf. note to epigraph of Chap. IV: p. 383, above.]

"stayed up" is not, I think, to ask for death, but rather to remain alive in order to be able in some measure to serve Him to Whom you know you owe so much.

Do not think, daughters, that it is an exaggeration to say that the Bride is dying. It is not: as I have said, it is a literal fact. For love sometimes works with such power that it overmasters the subject's natural strength. I know of a person who, while in this state of prayer, heard a beautiful voice singing; and she assures me that, if the song had not ceased, she believes her soul would have left her body, so great was the delight and sweetness which Our Lord allowed her to enjoy. His Majesty provided for her need by stopping the singer; otherwise the person whose faculties were thus suspended might well have died, yet she herself was not able to bid the singer stop. She had no power whatever to do anything in the way of making a bodily movement or to stir from where she was, though she was quite well aware of her danger. She was like one who is fast asleep and dreaming hard and would like to escape from the dream, but, much as she wants to do so, cannot utter a word.[1]

The soul in this state would be glad never to emerge from it; this would not be in the least grievous to her, but a great satisfaction, for it is what she desires. And how blessed would be the death that she would meet at the hands of this love! Were it not that His Majesty sometimes gives her light by which she can see that it is good for her to live, her weak nature, she knows, could not endure this favour if it were of long duration. So, in order to be able to escape from this immense blessing, she asks Him for another, and thus she says: "Stay me up with flowers". These flowers have a different perfume from any that we know on earth. I understand the Bride to mean that she is asking to be enabled to accomplish great things in the service of Our Lord and her neighbour, and for the sake of this she rejoices to lose her delight and pleasure; for, although it belongs rather to the active life than to the contemplative, and she will apparently be the loser if this petition is granted, yet, when the soul is in this state, Martha and Mary never fail, as it were, to work together. The interior part of the soul works in the active life, and in things which seem to be exterior; but, when active works proceed from this source, they are like wondrous and sweetly scented flowers. For the tree from which they come is love of God for His own sake alone, without self-interest; and the perfume of these flowers is wafted abroad, to the profit of many—it is a perfume which does not vanish quickly, but endures, and works great blessings.

---

[1] This seems to be a reference to the incident recorded in *Interior Castle*, VI, xi (p. 327, above).

In order that you may understand this I want to explain myself further. A preacher delivers a sermon with the intention of profiting his hearers, but he is not so completely detached from human regard for his own profit as not to try to please them by his eloquent preaching, or to gain reputation or credit, or possibly to obtain a canonry. It is just so with other things which people do for the benefit of their neighbours; they do a great deal for them, and their intentions are quite good, but they are careful not to lose by their actions and not to give offence. They are afraid of persecution; they like to keep on good terms with kings and lords and with people in general; and they proceed with that discretion to which the world does so much honour. But what they term discretion really conceals numerous imperfections—may the Lord grant that it really is discretion!

These persons serve His Majesty and progress greatly in virtue; yet I do not think the flowers for which the Bride asks are the good deeds they do, but rather a concern in all things for the honour and glory of God alone. For really, as I have heard from various people, those whom the Lord brings to this state think no more of themselves, and of their own possible loss or gain, than if they did not exist: they think only of serving and pleasing the Lord. And, as they know what love He has for His servants, they like to put aside their own pleasure and profit in order to please Him by serving others, proclaiming the truth to them, and thus doing good to their souls. They do this as well as they can, and, as I say, they never consider if they will lose by it; they have their neighbours' good in mind and nothing further. In order to give God greater pleasure they forget themselves for the sake of their neighbour; and if need be they will even give up their lives, as did many martyrs. Their words are clothed in this sublime love for God, and in their inebriation with that heavenly wine they remember nothing; or if they do remember they care nothing if they displease men. Such persons do great good.

I have just remembered some thoughts which I have often had about that holy woman of Samaria, who must have been affected in this way.[1] So well had she understood the words of the Lord in her heart that she left the Lord Himself so that she might profit and benefit the people of her village. This is an excellent example of what I am saying. As a reward for this great charity of hers she earned the credence of her neighbours and was able

---

[1] [*Lit.*: "must have been wounded by this plant" (or "herb"). No plant has been mentioned: presumably the reference is to the kind of herb to which legends attribute magical properties, such as enamouring those who partake of them, or causing forgetfulness. Possibly there is an implied connection with the idea of inebriation.]

to witness the great good which Our Lord did in that village.[1] This, I think, must be one of the greatest comforts on earth—I mean, to see good coming to souls through one's own agency. It is then, I think, that one eats the most delicious fruit of these flowers. Happy are they to whom the Lord grants these favours and strictly are they bound to serve Him. This woman, in her Divine inebriation, went crying aloud through the streets. To me the astonishing thing is that they should have believed a woman—and she cannot have been a woman of much consequence, as she was going to fetch water. Great humility she certainly had; for, when the Lord told her of her sins, she was not annoyed (as people are nowadays—they find it difficult to stand home truths) but told Him that He must be a prophet. In the end, her word was believed; and, merely on account of what she had said, great crowds flocked from the city to the Lord.

I hold, then, that great good is done by people who, after being for years on speaking terms with[2] His Majesty, are receiving consolations and favours from Him, yet do not fail to serve Him in ways which cost them a great deal even though their favours and joys are interrupted by their so doing. I mean that these flowers are good works which spring from, and are produced by, the tree of fervent love, and their perfume lasts much longer, and one of these souls does more good by its words and deeds than many whose intentions are soiled with the dust of our sensuality and with some measure of self-interest.

It is these flowers that produce fruit;[3] these are the apple-trees[4] of which the Bride speaks when she says: "Compass me about with apples." "Give me trials, Lord," she cries; "give me persecutions;" and she really desires them and emerges from them greatly benefited. For, as she no longer considers her own pleasure but only the giving of pleasure to God, she delights in imitating in some degree, the most toilsome life led by Christ. I understand the apple-tree to signify the tree of the Cross, for as we read in another part of the *Songs*: "Under the apple-tree I raised thee up."[5] To a soul that is surrounded by crosses—that is, by trials and persecutions—it is a great help not to be habitually enjoying the delight of contemplation. It derives a great delight from suffering, and its power is not consumed and wasted, as must happen when the faculties are habitually suspended, as they are in contemplation. The Bride is quite right to make this request,

---

[1] St. John iv.
[2] [*Lit.*: "after having for years been speaking with."]
[3] [*Lit.*: "From these produces (?=is produced) fruit."] Gracián took "produces" to be a slip for "proceeds" and emends the passage accordingly.
[4] Baeza MS. and *editio princeps* have: "the apples."
[5] Canticles viii, 5.

for she cannot always be having enjoyment without service or suffering. I particularly notice in certain persons (there are not many of them, on account of our sins) that the farther they advance in this prayer and the more favours they receive from Our Lord, the more attentive they are to the needs of their neighbours, especially to those of the soul; as I said at the beginning, they would give their lives again and again to save one person from mortal sin.

Who will ever instil this truth into people to whom Our Lord is only beginning to grant favours? Perhaps they think that these others make little progress in their lives and that the important thing is that they should stay in their own little corner and enjoy themselves. I think it is by the Lord's providence that such people do not realize how high these other souls have risen; for, if they did, the fervour which beginners always have would make them want to go rushing after them, and that would not be good for them, for they are not yet weaned and for some time yet need to be fed with the milk of which I first spoke. Let them remain near those Divine breasts; and, when they have sufficient strength, the Lord will take care to lead them on farther. If they advanced now, they would not do themselves as much good as they think, but would only harm themselves. As you will see many times, in the book of which I spoke to you,[1] when the soul ought to wish to go out and be of use to others and what danger it incurs by trying to do so too soon, I will not repeat it now or write of it at greater length; my intention, when I began it, was to explain to you how to appreciate some of the texts in the *Canticles* when you hear them, and think of the great mysteries they contain, even if you find them obscure. For me to write further of this would be presumption.

May it please the Lord that what I have already said has not been presumptuous, although I have only written in obedience to those who have commanded me. May it all redound to the service of His Majesty. If there is anything good in this, you may be quite sure it is not mine, for my sisters who are with me know how hurriedly I have written it on account of my many occupations. Beseech His Majesty that I may learn all this by experience. If any of you thinks she already has some experience of it, let her praise Our Lord and make Him this request which I have just mentioned, so that the gain may not be hers alone. May it please Our Lord to hold us by His hand, and teach us ever to carry out His will. Amen.[2]

[1] *Life*, Chap. XIII.
[2] To this paragraph P. Báñez has appended a note saying that he has read this work "and found no doctrine in it that is bad, but rather doctrine that is good and profitable." The note is dated: "College of St. Gregory, Valladolid, June 10, 1575." See p. 353, above.

EXCLAMATIONS OF THE SOUL TO GOD

INTRODUCTION

Little need be said of these white-hot embers from the fire of the Saint's love, which, despite the centuries that have passed since they were first written in the sacred moments after her Communions, can still enkindle the hearts of those who read them. Many who now come to them for the first time will be amazed at the freshness of their ardour and cold indeed will be those whom they leave wholly unmoved.

The theme of them all is the same—a glowing love for Jesus and a vehement desire for the closest possible union with Him that the soul can achieve. Fervent as it is, St. Teresa's language is wholly devoid both of monotony and of pointless hyperbole. Its spontaneity and naturalness, indeed, are its most precious qualities: there is little more attractive post-Communion literature in existence.

P. Gracián's sister, María de San José, stated, at the time of the Canonization process, that she had seen, "in the handwriting of the same Mother Teresa, the *Book of the Foundations* and the *Way of perfection* and some *Exclamations* which are at the end of her works"—the last reference being to the early editions of St. Teresa's collected works, in which the opuscule now under consideration follows the *Interior Castle*. It must have been at a very early date, however, that the original of the *Exclamations* was lost, and, so far as we know, not a single fragment of this work is in existence. Of the early copies, some of which have been mistaken for autographs, two deserve particular mention—those of Salamanca and Granada.

The text of the Salamancan manuscript, which forms part of the copy of the *Interior Castle* (p. 197, above) to be found in the University of Salamanca, is, apart from the orthography, almost exactly identical with that published by Luis de León, and Ribera makes no corrections in it, as he does in the *Interior Castle*, no doubt because he had not access to the autograph. The copy preserved by the Discalced Carmelite nuns of Granada is faithfully transcribed but unfortunately in a fragmentary condition. [P. Silverio gives the text of both these copies in his appendices.]

Fray Luis de León was the first to publish the *Exclamations*, which in his edition of 1588 follows the *Interior Castle* and bears the title: "Exclamations, or meditations, of the soul to its God, written by Mother Teresa of Jesus, on different days, according to the spirit communicated to her by Our Lord after she had made her Communion, in the year 1569." The editor gives no reasons in support of his date; but presumably so serious a scholar would not have put it in so prominent a place if he were not sure of it, especially as he was not in the habit of dating the works which he published. It does not seem at all an improbable date, though the Bollandists altered it to 1579[1] and the Paris Carmelites, chiefly on internal evidence, made it 1559.[2] An error involving only one figure is, of course, likely enough, but one needs more solid evidence for assuming this than has been adduced as yet.

Were the Granada copy complete it would probably have formed the most suitable basis for a modern text, but the Salamanca copyist, as this work on the *Interior Castle* makes clear, merits no more confidence than Fray Luis de León. Accordingly the text here used is that of the *editio princeps*.

[1] *Acta S. Teresiae a Jesu*, p. 347.
[2] *Oeuvres complètes*, etc., Vol. V, p. 317.

EXCLAMATIONS OF THE SOUL TO GOD[1]

I

O life, life, where canst thou find thy sustenance when thou art absent from thy Life? In such great loneliness, how dost thou occupy thyself? What dost thou do, since all thy actions are faulty and imperfect? Wherein dost thou find comfort, O my soul, in this stormy sea? I grieve for myself, but still more do I grieve for the time when I lived without grief. O Lord, how smooth are Thy paths! Yet who will walk in them without fear? I fear to live without serving Thee, yet when I set out to serve Thee I find no way of doing so that satisfies me or can pay any part of what I owe. I feel that I would gladly spend myself wholly in Thy service, and yet, when I consider my wretchedness, I realize that I can do nothing good unless Thou give it me.

O my God and my Mercy! What shall I do, so as not to destroy the effect of the wonders which Thou workest in me? Thy works are holy, just, of inestimable worth and of great wisdom: and Wisdom itself, Lord, art Thou. But if my mind busies itself with this, my will complains, for it would have nothing hinder it from loving Thee. And in themes of such surpassing greatness the mind cannot attain to a comprehension of the nature of its God; it desires to enjoy Him, yet knows not how, while confined within this grievous prison of mortality. Everything impedes it, though at first it was aided by meditation on Thy wonders, wherein it can the better see the baseness of numberless deeds of its own.

Why have I said this, my God? To whom do I complain? Who will hear me if not Thou, my Creator and Father? But what need have I to speak that Thou mayest understand my grief, since I see so clearly that Thou art within me? This is folly on my part. But ah, my God, how shall I be sure that I am not separated from Thee? O my life, that must be lived in such uncertainty about a matter of such importance! Who would desire thee, since the gain to be derived or hoped for from thee—namely, to please God in all things—is so unsure and fraught with such peril?

[1] On this title, see Introduction, p. 401, above.

II

Often, my Lord, do I think that if life lived apart from Thee can find sustenance it will be in solitude, for there the soul rests with Him Who is its Rest indeed. True, as this cannot be enjoyed with full freedom, the soul's torment is often doubled; yet, by comparison with that of having to deal with creatures and being unable to commune alone with its Creator, it becomes a joy. But how is it, my God, that rest itself is wearisome to the soul which strives after nothing but pleasing Thee? O powerful love of God, how different are thy fruits from those produced by love of the world! For love of the world desires no companions, thinking that they may take from it what it possesses. But love for my God increases more and more as it learns that more and more souls love Him, just as its joys are damped when it sees that all are not enjoying that same blessing. O my Good! Even during the greatest joys and delights which I experience in Thy company, I suffer at the thought of the many who do not desire these joys, and of those who will lose them for ever. And thus the soul seeks means of finding companionship and is glad to abandon its own enjoyment, thinking that this may help others in some degree to strive to attain it.

But, my heavenly Father, would it not be better for the soul to defer these desires until it is enjoying fewer favours from Thee and to spend itself wholly in rejoicing in Thee? O my Jesus, how great is the love that Thou hast for the children of men! The greatest service that we can render Thee is to leave Thee for love of them and for their advantage. By doing this we possess Thee the more completely; for, although the will has less satisfaction in the enjoyment of Thee, the soul is glad that Thou art pleased and sees that, while we live in this mortal life, earthly joys are unsure, even though they seem to be bestowed by Thee, unless they are accompanied by the love of our neighbour. He who loves not his neighbour loves not Thee, my Lord, for in all the blood Thou didst shed we see the exceeding great love which Thou bearest for the children of Adam.

III

When I meditate, my God, upon the glory which Thou hast prepared for those who persevere in doing Thy will, and think how many trials and pains it cost Thy Son to gain it for us, and how little we had deserved it, and how bound we are not to be ungrateful for this wondrous love which has taught us love at such a cost to itself, my soul becomes greatly afflicted. How is it possible, Lord, that all this should be forgotten, and that, when they offend Thee, mortal men should be so forgetful of Thee? O my Redeemer, how forgetful are men! They are forgetful even of themselves. And how great is Thy goodness that Thou shouldst remember us when we have fallen and struck Thee a mortal blow, and shouldst forget what we have done and give us Thy hand again and awaken us from our incurable madness so that we seek and beg Thee for salvation? Blessed be such a Lord, blessed be such great mercy and praised be He for ever for His merciful pity!

O my soul, do thou for ever bless so great a God! How can a soul turn against Him? Oh, how the very greatness of His favour condemns those who are ungrateful! Do Thou come to the help of such, my God. O children of men, how long will you be hard of heart[1] and fight against this most gentle Jesus? What is this? Is it possible that our wickedness will prevail against Him? No, for human life is cut short like the flower of the grass and the Son of the Virgin shall come and pass that terrible sentence. O powerful God of mine! Since Thou shalt judge us, whether we will it or no, why do we not consider how important it is to please Thee against that hour? Yet who, who would not wish to have so just a Judge? Blessed are they who at that dread moment shall rejoice with Thee, O my Lord and my God! When Thou hast raised up a soul and it has understood how miserably it has ruined itself to gain some brief pleasure and is resolved ever to please Thee and Thou dost help it with Thy favour (for Thou, my beloved Good, never forsakest those who love Thee nor failest to answer those who call upon Thee), what help is there, Lord, for such a soul, to enable it to live, instead of dying with the remembrance of having lost all the good that it would have were it in the state of baptismal innocence? The best life that that soul can live is a life which sorrow for its sins turns into death. Yet how can the soul that dearly loves Thee endure this?

But what foolish things I am asking Thee, my Lord! I seem to have forgotten Thy wonders and Thy mercies, and how Thou camest into the world for sinners, and didst purchase us at so great a price, and didst pay for our false pleasures by suffering such cruel tortures and scourgings. Thou didst cure my blindness by allowing men to blindfold Thy Divine eyes, and my vanity by wearing so cruel a crown of thorns. O Lord, Lord, all this causes the greater grief to one who loves Thee; my sole consolation is that, when my wickedness is known,

[1] Psalm iv, 3. [A.V. iv, 2.]

Thy mercy will be praised for ever; and yet I know not if my distress will ever be ended until all the miseries of this mortal life are ended and I see Thee face to face.

IV

My soul seems to find rest, my Lord, in meditating upon the joy which it will have if by Thy mercy it be granted to enjoy Thee. But first of all it would wish to serve Thee, since it is to enjoy what Thou didst gain for it by service. What shall I do, my Lord? What shall I do, my God? Oh, how late have my desires become enkindled, and how early, Lord, didst Thou go in search of me, calling me to spend myself wholly in Thy service! Didst Thou perchance, Lord, forsake the wretched or turn from the poor beggar who sought to approach Thee? Can it be, Lord, that there is any limit to Thy wonders or to Thy mighty works? O my God and my Mercy! Now wilt Thou be able to show Thy mercies in Thy handmaiden! Powerful art Thou, great God. Now will it become clear, Lord, if my soul, looking upon the time it has lost, is right in its belief that Thou, in a moment, canst turn its loss to gain. I seem to be talking foolishly, for it is usual to say that time lost can never be recovered. Blessed be my God!

O Lord, I acknowledge Thy great power. If Thou art mighty, as indeed Thou art, what is impossible to Him Who can do all things? Do Thou will it, my Lord, do Thou will it; for, miserable though I am, I firmly believe that Thou canst do what Thou willest; and, the greater are the marvels of Thine that I hear spoken of, the more do I reflect that Thou canst work others yet greater, the stronger grows my faith and the greater is the resolution with which I believe that Thou wilt perform them. And how can I wonder at what is done by the Almighty? Well knowest Thou, my God, that in the midst of all my miseries I have never ceased to recognize Thy great power and mercy. May it prove of avail to me that I have not offended Thee in this. Restore the time I have lost, my God, by granting me Thy grace both in the present and in the future, that I may appear before Thee with wedding garments,[1] for Thou canst do this if Thou so willest.

V

O my Lord! How can one ask Thee for favours who has served Thee so ill and has hardly been able to keep what Thou

[1] St. Matthew xxii, 11-12.

hast already given? How canst Thou have any confidence in one who has so often betrayed Thee? What, then, shall I do, Comfort of the comfortless, and Help of all who seek help from Thee? Can it be better to keep silence about my necessities, hoping that Thou wilt relieve them? No, indeed; for Thou, my Lord and my Joy, knowing how many they must be and how it will alleviate them if we speak to Thee of them, dost bid us pray to Thee and say that Thou wilt not fail to give.[1]

I sometimes remember the complaint of that holy woman, Martha;[2] her complaint was not merely of her sister—I feel sure that the chief cause of her sorrow was the thought that Thou, Lord, hadst no compassion on her for the labour that she was enduring nor caredst whether or no she was with Thee. Perhaps she thought that Thou hadst less love for her than for her sister, and this would have troubled her more than serving One Whom she loved so dearly, for love turns labour into rest. And so she said nothing to her sister, but made her complaint to Thee, Lord, alone, for love made her bold enough to ask why Thou hadst no care for her. Thine answer, which seems to imply that the source of her complaint was as I have been saying, was that it is love alone which gives value to all things and that the most needful thing is that it should be so great that nothing can hinder its operation. But how can we have this love, my God, in the degree merited by the Beloved, if the love which Thou hast for us is not united with it? Shall I complain with this holy woman? Ah, I have no reason to do so, for I have ever found in my God far greater and stronger proofs of love than I have known how to ask or to desire. I have nothing to complain of save that Thy loving-kindness has borne with me too long. What, then, can one ask of Thee so wretched as I? That Thou wilt give to me, my God (as Saint Augustine said),[3] so that I may give to Thee, to repay Thee some part of all that I owe Thee; that Thou wilt remember that I am Thy handiwork; and that I may know Who my Creator is, and so may love Him.

VI

O my Joy, Lord of all things created and my God! How long must I wait before I shall see Thy Presence? What help canst Thou give to one who has so little on earth wherein she can find repose apart from Thee? O long life! O grievous life! O life which is no life at all! Oh, what utter, what helpless loneliness! When shall it end, then, Lord, when shall it end? How

---

[1] St. John xvi, 24.   [2] St. Luke x, 40.   [3] *Confessions*, Bk. XI, Chap. II.

long shall it endure? What shall I do, my Good, what shall I do? Shall I perchance desire not to desire Thee? O my God and my Creator, Who dost wound and apply no remedy, dost strike so that no wound is seen, dost slay yet leave the slain with more life than before—Who, in short, my Lord, doest what Thou wilt as befits One full of power! Is it Thy will, then, my God, that so despicable a worm should suffer these conflicting distresses? Let it be so, my God, since Thou willest it so, for my only will is to love Thee.

But alas, alas, my Creator, great anguish makes me utter complaints and speak of that for which there is no remedy until Thou be pleased to send one. My imprisoned soul desires its freedom yet desires also not to swerve in the smallest degree from Thy will. Be pleased, my Glory, either to increase its affliction or to heal it altogether. O death, death, I know not why anyone fears thee, since life is in thee!. And yet who that has spent part of his life without loving God would not fear thee? And as I am such a one, what do I ask and what do I desire? Perchance the punishment which my faults have so richly merited. Permit not this, my Good, for my ransoming cost Thee dearly.

O my soul, let the will of thy God be done. It is well for thee that this should be so; serve Him and hope in His mercy, which will relieve thy affliction, when penitence for thy faults has won thee forgiveness for them: seek not fruition without having first suffered. O my true Lord and King, I am not fit even for this if I am not aided by Thy sovereign guidance and greatness, but with these I can do all things.

VII

O my Hope and my Father and my Creator and my true Lord and Brother! When I remember how Thou sayest that Thy delights are to be with the children of men,[1] my soul rejoices greatly. What words are these, O Lord of Heaven and earth, to prevent any sinner from losing trust in Thee! Canst Thou lack souls in whom to delight, Lord, that Thou seekest so unsavoury a worm as I? At the time of Thy Son's Baptism, that voice which was heard said that Thou didst delight in Him.[2] Can it be, then, Lord, that Thou dost delight in us all equally? Oh, what exceeding mercy and what favour far beyond our deserving! And shall we mortals forget all this? Remember our great misery, my God, and look upon our weakness, since Thou knowest all things.

[1] Proverbs viii, 31.   [2] St. Matthew iii, 17.

O my soul, reflect upon the great delight and the great love which the Father has in knowing His Son and the Son in knowing His Father and the ardour with which the Holy Spirit unites with Them, and how none of These can cease from this love and knowledge since They are One and the same. These Sovereign Persons know each other, love each other and delight in each other. What need, then, have They of my love? Why dost Thou seek it, my God, or what dost Thou gain by it? Oh, blessed be Thou! Oh, blessed be Thou, my God, for ever! Let all things praise Thee, Lord, without end, for there can be no end in Thee.

Rejoice, my soul, that there is One Who loves thy God as He merits. Rejoice that there is One Who knows His goodness and worth. Give Him thanks for having given us on earth One Who knows Him—His only Son. Beneath this protection thou wilt be able to approach His Majesty and beseech Him that, since He delights in thee, all things on earth may not suffice to make thee cease delighting in Him, and rejoicing in the greatness of thy God and in the way wherein He merits love and praise. Thou canst beseech Him, too, to aid thee to bear some small part in the blessing of His name so that thou mayest say with truth: "My soul doth magnify and praise the Lord."[1]

VIII

O Lord, my God, Thou hast indeed the words of life,[2] wherein, if we will seek it, we mortals shall all find what we desire. But what wonder is it, my God, that we should forget Thy words when our evil deeds have made us so infirm and foolish? O my God! God, God the Maker of all things created! And yet what are all things created, Lord, if Thou shouldst be pleased to create more? Thou art almighty; Thy works are incomprehensible.[3] Grant, then, Lord, that Thy words may never be absent from my thoughts.

Thou sayest: "Come to Me, all you that labour and are burdened: and I will comfort you."[4] What more do we want, Lord? What do we ask for? What do we seek? Why are worldly people lost if not because they are seeking repose? O God! O God! What is this, Lord? How sad a pity! How blind of us to seek repose where it cannot possibly be found! Have mercy,

---

[1] St. Luke i, 46.
[2] [St. John vi, 69].
[3] Job ix, 10.
[4] St. Matthew xi, 28 [D.V. has "refresh," but the Spanish is *consolar*].

Creator, on these Thy creatures. Reflect that we do not understand ourselves, or know what we desire, nor are we able to ask as we should. Give us light, Lord. Behold, we need it more than the man who was blind from his birth,[1] for he wished to see the light and could not, whereas nowadays, Lord, no one wishes to see it. Oh, what a hopeless ill is this! Here, my God, must be manifested Thy power and Thy mercy.

Ah, how hard a thing am I asking of Thee, my true God! I ask Thee to love one who loves Thee not, to open to one who has not called upon Thee,[2] to give health to one who prefers to be sick and who even goes about in search of sickness. Thou sayest, my Lord, that Thou comest to seek sinners; these, Lord, are the true sinners. Look not upon our blindness, my God, but upon all the blood that was shed for us by Thy Son. Let Thy mercy shine out amid such tremendous wickedness. Behold, Lord, we are the works of Thy hands[3]. Help us by Thy goodness and mercy.

IX

O compassionate and loving Lord of my soul! Thou also sayest: "Come unto Me, all ye that thirst and I will give you to drink."[4] How can anyone fail to have a great thirst who is consumed by living flames of covetousness for these miserable earthly things? They have the greatest need of water, for without it they will be wholly consumed. Well do I know, my Lord, that of Thy goodness Thou wilt give it them; Thou Thyself sayest so and Thy words cannot fail. But if they have grown accustomed to living amid these flames, and are so inured to them that they cannot feel them, or ever realize the greatness of their need, what remedy is there for them, my God? Thou didst come to the world to remedy great ills like these: begin, then, Lord, for it is the hardest things which best manifest Thy compassion. See, my God, how much Thine enemies are gaining. Have compassion upon those who have none upon themselves; since their unhappy state prevents them from desiring to come to Thee, do Thou come to them, my God. I ask this of Thee in their name, and I know that when once again they return to their senses and realize their errors and begin to taste of Thee, they will rise again from the dead.

---

[1] St. John ix, 1.
[2] [*A quien no os llama. Llamar*, to call, has also, without the personal object, the meaning "knock". There is probably, therefore, a reference here to St. Matthew vii, 7.]
[3] Isaias lxiv, 8.
[4] St. John vii, 37.

O Life, Who givest life to all! Deny me not this most precious water which Thou dost promise to those that desire it. I desire it, Lord, and I ask for it and I come to Thee: hide not Thyself from me, Lord, for Thou knowest my need and how this water is true medicine for the soul wounded by Thee. O Lord, how many kinds of fire there are in this life! Oh, how right we are to live in fear! Some of these fires consume the soul, while others purify it so that it may live and enjoy Thee for ever. O living streams, issuing from the wounds of my God! How abundantly do you ever flow for our succour and how safely will one pass through the perils of this miserable life who can draw sustenance from this Divine water!

X

O God of my soul, how quick we are to offend Thee! Yet how much quicker art Thou to forgive us! What reason is there, Lord, for such foolish presumption on our part? Is it that, having learned the greatness of Thy mercy, we forget how righteous is Thy justice? "The sorrows of death compassed me."[1] Alas, alas, alas! How grave a thing is sin, which sufficed to slay God Himself and to cause Him such anguish! And even now, my God, Thou art beset by this same anguish. Whither canst Thou go where they will not torment Thee? Everywhere mortals are wounding Thee.

O Christians, it is time to defend your King and to stand by Him in His great loneliness. For very few of His liegemen have remained faithful to Him, whereas following Lucifer there is a great multitude. And what is worse, they declare themselves His friends in public, yet secretly betray Him: there is scarcely one whom He can trust. O true Friend, how ill art Thou recompensed by him who betrays Thee! O true Christians! Stand by your God as He weeps,[2] for those tears of compassion were not shed for Lazarus only but for others who would never rise from the dead, even though His Majesty were to cry to them in a loud voice.[3] O my Good, all the faults I have committed against Thee were then before Thine eyes. May there be no more of them, Lord, may there be no more either of them or of the faults of others. Raise up these dead souls; and may Thy voice, Lord, be so powerful as to give them life even though they ask it not of Thee, and then, my God, they will come forth, even from the depths of their pleasures.

---

[1] Psalm cxiv (A.V. cxvi), 3.
[2] [*Lit.*: "help your God to weep."] St. John xi, 35.
[3] St. John xi, 43.

Lazarus did not ask Thee to raise him from the dead. Thou didst it for a woman who was a sinner. Behold her here, my God, behold a far greater sinner; let Thy mercy shine forth upon her. Miserable creature though I am, I pray to Thee on behalf of those who will not pray to Thee themselves. Well knowest Thou, my King, how tormented I am to see them so forgetful of the great and endless torments which they will have to suffer if they turn not to Thee. Oh, you who are accustomed to delights and pleasures and comforts and to following your own will, take pity upon yourselves! Remember that, for ever and for ever, you will be subject to the unending furies of hell. Behold, behold, the Judge Who will pass sentence upon you is now entreating you. Not for a single moment are you sure of life: why, then, have you no desire to live for ever? O hardness of human hearts! May Thy boundless compassion soften them, my God.

XI

God help me! God help me! How sorely am I tormented when I think what the feelings will be of the soul of one who on earth was always thought well of, loved, served, highly esteemed and indulged, which after death finds itself eternally lost and knows perfectly well that its punishment will be endless! It will be useless then for such a soul to try, as it did on earth, not to think of the truths of the Faith and it will find itself parted from all the things that it thought it was only beginning to enjoy. And rightly so; for all that ends with life is like a breath of wind. Such a soul will now find itself surrounded by that hideous and ungodly company with which it is to suffer for ever, and plunged into that fetid lake, full of serpents, each one snapping at it more vehemently than the last. In that miserable darkness nothing can be seen save what brings torment and affliction and there is no light save that of a darkly-burning flame.

Oh, how weak is this description by contrast with the reality! Oh, Lord, who has put clay on the eyes of this soul so that it sees nothing of this till it finds itself in that place? Who has stopped its ears, O Lord, and thus prevented it from hearing those things which it has so often been told, and from learning of the endlessness of these torments? O life that will never end! O endless torment! O endless torment! How can it be that there are those who fear thee not, and yet fear to sleep on a hard bed lest it should hurt their bodies?

O Lord, my God! I weep for the time when I knew not this. Thou knowest, my God, how grieved I am to see how very many will not learn it. Let there be just one, Lord, I pray Thee, just one who will ask Thee for light and who in turn will give light to many. And this not for my sake, Lord, for I do not merit it, but for the merits of Thy Son. Look upon His wounds, Lord, and, as He forgave those who inflicted them upon Him, so do Thou pardon us.

XII

O my God and my true Strength! How is it, Lord, that we are cowards in everything save in opposing Thee? To this the children of Adam devote all their energies. Were not reason so blind, the combined energies of all men put together would not suffice to make them bold enough to take up arms against their Creator, and maintain a continual warfare against One Who in a moment can plunge them into the depths. But because reason is blind they act like madmen courting death, for they imagine that this death will bring them new life: they act, in short, like people bereft of reason. What can we do, my God, for those who are in the grip of this infirmity of madness? People say that madness of itself lends men increased strength. So it is with those who depart from my God; they are like sick men and all their fury is spent upon Thee, their greatest Benefactor.

O incomprehensible Wisdom! In truth Thou needest all the love which Thou hast for Thy creatures to enable Thee to endure such folly and to await our recovery and to seek to bring it about by a thousand kinds of means and remedies. It amazes me when I consider how we lack the effort to take in hand a very small thing and how we really persuade ourselves that, even if we so desire, we cannot flee from some occasion of sin and avoid something which imperils our soul, and yet that we have effort and courage enough to attack so great a Sovereign as art Thou. How is this, my Good? How is this? Who gives us this strength? Was not the leader whom men follow in this battle against Thee once Thy servant and didst Thou not consign him to eternal fire? How, then, can he rise against Thee? How can one who is vanquished inspire courage? Why do men follow one who is so poor and has been deprived of the riches of Heaven? What can one give who himself owns nothing but exceeding great misery? What is this, my God? What is this, my Creator? Whence comes it that we have such strength to fight against Thee, yet so much cowardice in fighting against the devil? Even if Thou, my Prince, didst not help Thine own, even if we owed anything to this prince of darkness, there would be no excuse for our exchanging what Thou hast laid up for us eternally for his false and treacherous joys and promises. How will he be true to us, when he was false to Thee?

Oh, my God, what great blindness! Oh, what great ingratitude, my King! Oh, what incurable madness, my God, that we should use what Thou givest us for serving the devil! That we should requite the great love which Thou hast toward us by loving one who hates Thee so and will hate Thee for ever! Despite the blood which Thou didst shed for us and the scourgings and grievous pains which Thou didst suffer and the cruel torments which Thou didst endure, we, instead of avenging Thine Eternal Father (though Thou desirest not vengeance and didst pardon all the sacrilege and violence committed against Thy Son), take those who treated Him in this way as our companions and friends. Since we follow their infernal leader, we shall clearly all become one with him and live for ever in his company unless Thy mercy heals us by restoring us to our right minds and forgiving us the past.

Return, O mortals, return to your right minds! Look upon your King: you will still find Him meek. Let all your evil deeds come to an end; turn your fury and your strength against him who is waging war upon you and would rob you of your birthright. Return, return to your right minds, open your eyes and with loud cries and tears beg light from Him Who gave light to the world. For the love of God, realize that He Whom you are about to exert all your strength to slay is He Who lost His life in giving life to you. Behold, it is He Who is defending you from your enemies. And if all this is not enough, let it suffice you to know that against His power you can do nothing, and that, sooner or later, you will have to atone for your sacrilegious presumption in eternal flames. Will you slay His Majesty because you see Him tied and bound with the love which He bears us? What did those who put Him to death do but give Him blows and wounds after they had bound Him?

O my God, how dost Thou suffer for one who grieves so little for Thy sorrows! The time will come, Lord, when Thy justice will be made clear to all and it will be seen to be equal to Thy mercy. See, Christians, let us consider this well, for we shall never be able to understand the full extent of what we owe to our Lord God, and the exceeding greatness of His mercies. But alas, alas! If His Justice is equally great, what will happen to those who have merited its execution and manifestation in themselves?

XIII

O souls that now rejoice without fear of losing your joy and are for ever absorbed in the praises of my God! Happy has been your lot! How right is it that you should employ yourselves ceaselessly in these praises and how my soul envies you, free as you now are from the affliction caused by the grievous offences which in these unhappy times are committed against my God! No longer do you behold all the ingratitude of men and their blindness to the multitude of souls being carried away by Satan. O blessed, celestial souls! Help us in our misery and intercede for us with the Divine Mercy, so that we may be granted some part of your joy and that you may share with us some of that clear knowledge which is now yours.

Grant us, my God, to understand what it is that Thou givest to those who fight manfully through the dream of this miserable life. Help us, oh lover-souls, to understand what joy it gives you to behold the eternity of your bliss and what delight to possess the certain knowledge that it will never end. Oh, unhappy are we, my Lord, for well do we know and believe these truths, yet our inveterate habit of not reflecting upon them makes them so strange to our souls that they neither know them nor seek to know them! Oh, how selfish and how covetous of their own pleasures and joys are those who, unwilling to wait but a short time—to wait a year, a day, an hour, or perhaps no more than a moment—in order to enjoy them so abundantly, lose everything for the sake of enjoying some miserable thing that they see before them!

Oh, oh, oh! How little do we trust Thee, Lord! How much greater were the riches and the treasures that Thou didst entrust to us! For our sakes—and all those years before we were born—Thou didst give Thy Son three and thirty years of grievous trials, followed by so unbearable and shameful a death. And, though knowing that we could not repay Thee, Thou didst not scruple to trust us with that inestimable treasure, in order on Thy side, merciful Father, to do everything to enable us to obtain from Thee what we win through Him.

O blessed souls, who knew so well how to profit by this gift and to purchase with this precious ransom so delectable and enduring a heritage! Tell us how you won through Him such an eternal blessing. Assist us, since you are so near the Fountain-head. Draw water for those of us on earth who are perishing with thirst.

XIV

O my Lord and true God! He who knows Thee not loves Thee not. Oh, what a great truth is this! But alas, alas, Lord, for those who seek not to know Thee! Terrible is the hour of death. But ah, ah, my Creator! How fearful will be the day of the execution of Thy justice! Often do I think, my Christ, how delectably and happily Thine eyes rest on those who love Thee, when Thou, my Good, art pleased to look upon them with love. I think that even one such gentle glance bestowed upon souls whom Thou countest as Thine own is sufficient reward for many years of service. God help me! How hard it is to explain this save to those who have already found how sweet the Lord is![1]

O Christians, Christians! Think of the brotherhood which you share with this great God. Learn to know Him, and despise Him not; for, if His gaze is pleasant to those who love Him, it is terrible and awful in its fury to those who persecute Him. Oh, why can we not realize that sin is a pitched battle fought against God with all our senses and the faculties of the soul; the stronger the soul is, the more ways it invents to betray its King. Thou knowest, my Lord, that often I was more terrified at thinking I might see Thy Divine face turned from me in wrath on that fearful day of the Last Judgment than of all the pains and furies of hell that I could imagine, and that I begged Thee, by Thy mercy, to save me from a thing so grievous. And this I still beg of Thee, Lord. What could happen to me on earth comparable to this? I will accept it all, my God, but deliver me from so great an affliction; may I never forsake my God or lose the peaceful fruition of such great beauty. Thy Father has given Thee to us, my Lord; may I not lose so precious a Jewel. I confess, Eternal Father, that I have kept it but ill; yet there is a remedy, Lord, there is still a remedy while we live in this land of exile.

O brethren, O brethren, children of this God! Let us brace ourselves, let us brace ourselves anew, for you know how His Majesty says that, if we repent at having offended Him, He will not remember our faults and our evil deeds. O boundless compassion! What more can we desire? Can there be anyone who is not ashamed to ask for so much? Now is the time to take what this our pitiful Lord and God gives us. Since He seeks friends, who will refuse them to One Who refused not to pour out His blood and give His life for us? Behold, this that He asks is nothing, and it will be to our own advantage to give it Him.

[1] Psalm xxxiii, 9 [A.V., xxxiv, 8].

Oh, God help me! O Lord, what hardness of heart! Oh, what folly and blindness! We are distressed if we lose anything: the merest trifle—a sparrow-hawk which is useless save to give a passing delight to our eyes as we see it cleave the air.[1] Then why are we not distressed at losing that mighty eagle which is the Majesty of God, and a kingdom in which our fruition of Him will be endless? Why is this? Why is this? I cannot understand it. Do Thou, my God, cure such great folly and blindness.

XV

Alas, alas, Lord! How long is this exile, and how, as I endure it, do I suffer, out of desire for my God! What can a soul do, Lord, when it is cast into this prison? O Jesus, how long man's life is, though we speak of it as short! Short it is, my God, for gaining life that cannot end, but very long for the soul that desires to see itself in the presence of its God. What cure canst Thou provide for this suffering? There is none, save to suffer for Thee.

Oh, my sweet rest pertaining to the lovers of my God! Fail not those that love thee, for thou dost increase, and yet solace, the torment which the Beloved causes the soul that desires Him.[2] O Lord, I desire to please Thee, and well do I know that my pleasure can be found in no mortal being: since this is so, Thou wilt not blame my desire. Behold me here, Lord; if it is needful for me to live in order to do Thee some service, then, in the words of Thy lover Saint Martin,[3] I refuse none of the trials that may come to me on earth.

But alas, woe is me, my Lord! For he had works to give Thee, whereas I have only words, and am unable to give Thee more. May my desires, my God, be availing in the sight of Thy Divine Presence: consider not my slight deserving. Let us all deserve to love Thee, Lord; since we have to live, let us live for Thee, and let our desires and interests disappear. What greater thing can

---

[1] [For "the merest trifle" the Spanish has *una aguja*, "a needle", which may be meant literally, but probably is not. The contrast between the vulgar sparrow-hawk and the royal eagle (*águila*) is sufficiently obvious. It has been suggested to me that the word *aguja* put *águila* into the Saint's mind, but it is quite unnecessary to assume this, for the royal eagle is a common figure with the Golden Age mystics. Cf., for example, *S.S.M.*, II, 51-2, 205, 212, 228.]

[2] [I believe the "rest" (*descanso*) here apostrophized to refer to the suffering spoken of in the last phrase of the preceding paragraph. Such a paradox is a commonplace with the mystics: cf. *Poems*, xxvi ("Mi descanso en trabajar," where the verb can denote trials as well as labours). P. Silverio writes "thee", and then "Thou", which may either indicate uncertainty as to what the pronoun stands for or, more probably, be a slip.]

[3] For this reference, see *Interior Castle*, VI, vi (p. 299, above).

we gain than to please Thee? Oh, my Pleasure and my God! What shall I do to please Thee? My services, however many I render to my God, are miserable. Then why must I remain in this wretched misery? In order that the will of the Lord may be done. What greater gain is there than that, my soul? Wait, wait, for thou knowest not when the day or the hour will come. Watch carefully, for all passes quickly, although thy desire makes what is certain seem doubtful, and time, which is short, seem long. Reflect that, the longer the battle, the better canst thou prove the love which thou hast to thy God, and the more shalt thou rejoice with thy Beloved with joy and delight which can have no end.

XVI

O true God and my Lord! Greatly does it comfort the soul which is wearied by the loneliness of absence from Thee to see that Thou art present everywhere; but when the ardour of love and the strength and vehemence of this affliction increase, what does it avail, my God, if the understanding is disturbed and if knowledge of this truth is hidden from the reason so that it can have neither knowledge nor understanding? It only knows that it is separated from Thee and for that it can find no remedy. For the heart that loves deeply can receive no counsel or comfort save from Him Who wounded it, and from Him it awaits the remedy for its distress. When it is Thy will, Lord, Thou dost quickly heal the wound Thou hast inflicted; till then there is no hope of health or rejoicing save that which is found in suffering so well employed.

O true Lover! How pitifully, how gently, with what joy, with what comfort and with what exceeding great signs of love dost Thou heal these wounds that Thou hast inflicted with the arrows of love itself! O my God, and my Rest for all distress, how foolish I am! How could there be any human means of curing those stricken by the Divine fire? Who can tell how deeply this wound has entered, or whence it came, or what mitigation there is for so grievous and so delectable a torture? It would be unreasonable if so precious an ill could be soothed by anything so base as the methods used by mortals. How true are the words of the Bride in the *Songs*: "My Beloved to me and I to my Beloved and my Beloved to me;"[1] for no such love could possibly have its source in anything so base as mine.

Yet if it be base, my Spouse, how is it that it will rest in no created thing, but only when it has reached its Creator? O my

[1] [*Sic*.]. Canticles ii, 16.

God! Why "I to my Beloved"? Thou, my true Lover, didst begin this war of love, which seems to be nothing but disquietude in the soul and its abandonment by all the faculties and senses, which go through the squares and suburbs,[1] exhorting the daughters of Jerusalem to tell them of their God. Then, Lord, when this battle has begun, against whom have they to fight save against Him Who has made Himself Master of this fortress where they dwelt, which is the higher part of the soul? From this He has cast them out, so that they can return to vanquish their conqueror. And now, weary of finding themselves without Him, they quickly acknowledge their defeat, and, having lost their whole strength, fight on and fight the better; and in acknowledging their own defeat they defeat their victor.

O my soul! How marvellous a battle hast thou fought during this affliction and how exactly has this been thy case! Since "my Beloved is to me and I am to my Beloved", who is he that will undertake to separate and extinguish two such ardent fires? To do so would be to labour in vain, for both have already become one.

XVII

O my God and my infinite Wisdom, without measure and without bounds, high above the understanding both of angels and of men! O Love, Who lovest me more than I can love myself or conceive of love! Why, Lord, have I the will to desire more than it is Thy will to give me? Why do I wish to weary myself by begging Thee for things fashioned by my desire, since Thou already knowest what are the ends of all that my understanding can conceive and my will desire, while I myself know not what is best for me? The very thing in which my soul thinks to find profit will perchance bring about my ruin. For, if I beg Thee to deliver me from a trial, the object of which is my mortification, what is it that I am begging of Thee, my God? If I beseech Thee to give it me, perchance it may not be proportionate to my patience, which is still weak and cannot bear so great a blow; and if I suffer it with patience and am not strong in humility, I may think that I have achieved something, whereas it is Thou that art achieving it all, my God. If I wish to endure greater sufferings, I have no wish to lose my credit in matters where it seems that to do so would not be for Thy service, although as far as I myself am concerned I have no interest in my own reputation,[2] and it may be that the

---

[1] The *per vicos et plateas* ("in the streets and the broad ways") of Canticles iii, 2.
[2] [*Honra.* Cf. Vol. I, p. 14, n. 2, above.]

very thing which I think would ruin my credit might lead me farther toward the accomplishment of my great aim, which is to serve Thee.

I could say far more about this, Lord, to make myself understand how little I understand myself; but I know that Thou knowest it all, so why do I speak of it? In order that when I awaken again, my God, to a sense of my misery, and when my reason is blinded, I may look for it and find it here in what I have written with my own hand. How often, my God, do I look at myself, so miserable, weak and feeble in spirit, and think of her who became Thy servant and thought she had received favours from Thee with which to fight against the storms of this world. But no, my God, no, no more trust in anything which I can desire for myself: do Thou desire for me that which Thou art pleased to desire; for that is my desire, since all my good consists in pleasing Thee. And if Thou, my God, shouldst be pleased to please me, by fulfilling all that my desire asks of Thee, I know that I should be lost.

How miserable is the wisdom of mortal man! How uncertain is his foresight![1] Do Thou, Who foreseest all, provide the necessary means whereby my soul may serve Thee according to Thy will and not to its own. Punish me not by giving me what I wish or desire, if Thy love (and may it ever live in me!) desire not this. May this self of mine die, and may Another, greater than myself and better for me than myself, live in me, so that I may serve Him. May He live and give me life; may He reign and may I be His captive, for my soul desires no other freedom. How can one be free who is separated from the Most High? What harder or more miserable captivity is there than for the soul to have escaped from the hand of its Creator? Happy are they who find themselves laden with the strong fetters and chains of the gifts of God's mercy, so that they are unable to gain the power to set themselves free. Strong as death is love and hard as hell.[2] Oh that one might die at the hands of love and be cast into this Divine hell, whence there is no hope of escape, or rather, no fear of finding oneself cast forth from it! But alas, Lord, for as long as this mortal life endures our eternal life is all the time in danger.

O life, that art the enemy of my welfare, would that one were permitted to end thee! I endure thee because God endures thee; I sustain thee because thou art His. Betray me not, be not ungrateful to me! And yet, Lord, alas, my exile is long; and time itself is short in exchange for Thine eternity; a single day, even an hour, is very long for one who knows not if he is offending

---

[1] Wisdom ix, 14.   [2] Canticles viii, 6.

Thee and fears lest he may do so. O free-will, thou art the slave of thine own freedom, unless thou be pierced through[1] with fear and love for Him Who created thee! Oh, when will come that happy day in which thou shalt find thyself engulfed in that infinite ocean of supreme truth, wherein thou shalt not be free to sin, nor wish to be so, since thou shalt be secure from all misery, and made of one nature with the life of thy God!

God is happy, since He knows and loves and rejoices in Himself without the possibility of doing otherwise. He is not, nor can He be, free to forget Himself and to cease to love Himself, nor would it be perfection in Him were He to be so. Thou wilt not enter into thy rest, my soul, until thou becomest inwardly one with this Highest Good, knowing what He knows, loving what He loves and enjoying what He enjoys. Then shalt thou see the end of the mutability of thy will; then, then shall there be an end of mutability. For the grace of God will have wrought so much in thee that it will have made thee a partaker of His Divine nature,[2] with such perfection that thou wilt neither desire nor be able to forget the Highest Good, nor cease to rejoice in Him and in His love.

Blessed are those whose names are written in the book of that life. But if thou art among them, my soul, why art thou sad and why dost thou trouble me?[3] Hope in God, for even now I will confess to Him my sins and His mercies and of them all I will make a song of praise and will breathe perpetual sighs to my Saviour and my God. It may be that a day will come when my glory shall sing to Him[4] and my conscience shall be no more afflicted, when at last all sighs and fears shall cease. But meanwhile, in silence and in hope shall my strength be.[5] Rather would I live and die in the expectation and hope of eternal life than possess all created things and all the blessings which belong to them, since these must pass away. Forsake me not, Lord; since I hope in Thee, may my hope not be confounded;[6] may I ever serve Thee; do with me what Thou wilt.

---

[1] [*enclavado*. A very strong word, perhaps suggested to the writer by *esclavo*; its literal sense is "nailed down"—i.e., and thus kept in subjection.]
[2] [2 St. Peter i, 4.]
[3] Psalm xli, 6, 12 [A.V., xlii, 5, 11].
[4] Psalm xxix, 13 [A.V., xxx, 12].
[5] Isaias, xxx, 15.
[6] Psalm xxx, 2 [A.V., xxxi, 1].